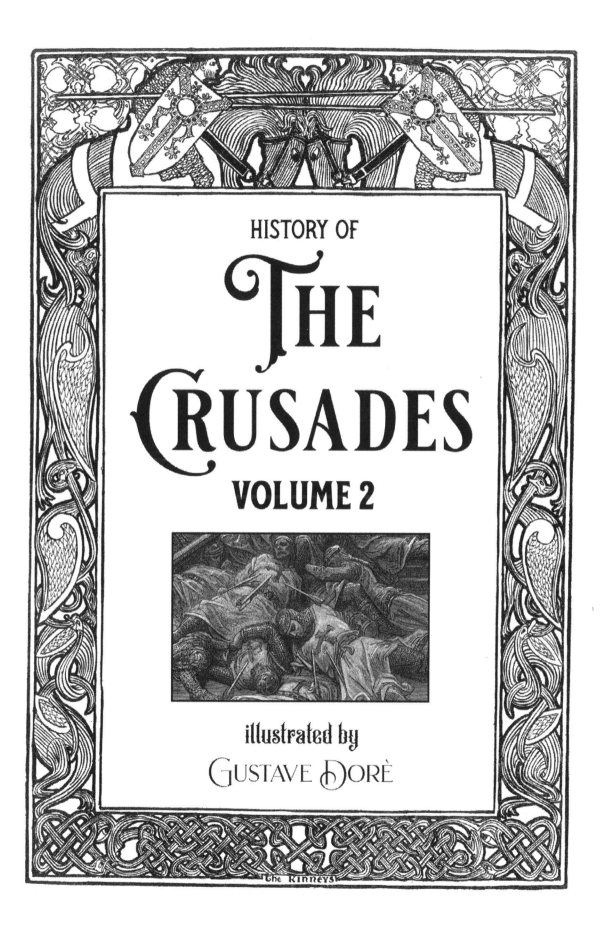

**History of the Crusades Volume 2:
Gustave Doré Restored Special Edition**

By Michaud
Illustrations by Gustave Doré
Translated by William Robson
Cover design by Mark Bussler

Copyright © 2021 Inecom, LLC.
All Rights Reserved

No parts of this book may be reproduced or broadcast in any
way without written permission from Inecom, LLC.

www.CGRpublishing.com

HISTORY

OF THE

CRUSADES

By MICHAUD
Member of the Academy of France

ILLUSTRATED WITH ONE HUNDRED GRAND COMPOSITIONS

BY

GUSTAVE DORÉ

ENGRAVED BY

BELLENGER, DOMS, GUSMAN, JONNARD, PANNEMAKER, PISAN, QUESNEL

VOLUME II

PHILADELPHIA
GEORGE BARRIE PUBLISHER

THE HOLY SEPULCHRE.

BOOK XII

The Sixth Crusade

A. D. 1200 TO 1215

HISTORY OF THE CRUSADES.

BOOK XII.
THE SIXTH CRUSADE.
A.D. 1200—1215.

Famine in Egypt, and its frightful consequences—Saadi, the Persian poet—Death of Bohémond III.—John of Brienne accepts the young queen of Jerusalem in marriage—Malek-Adel renews hostilities against the Christians—John of Brienne takes possession of Ptolemaïs—First dawnings of the Reformation—Philip Augustus king of France, and John king of England, engage in the crusade—Battle of Bouvines—The pope assembles the council of Lateran, and stimulates all Europe to the holy war—His death and character—Censius Savelli chosen pope, under the title of Honorius III.—He urges the crusade—Andrew II., king of Hungary, engages in it—Paganism of Prussia in the thirteenth century—Political state of Hungary—Her king returns from Palestine—The tower of Damietta captured by the Crusaders—Death and character of Malek-Adel—Cardinal Pelagius instigates the prosecution of the crusade, and proceeds to Egypt—Conspiracy to dethrone the sultan of Cairo—Battle before the walls of Damietta—The Mohammedans propose conditions of peace—Damietta captured, and the inhabitants destroyed by famine—The Mohammedans burn the fleet of the Crusaders on the Nile, and compel them to capitulate—Melik-Kamel enters into a treaty of peace, by which Damietta is surrendered to the Mussulmans—The Georgians—Invasions of the Tartars—Marriage of Frederick II., emperor of Germany, with the heiress of the king of Jerusalem—Acknowledged to be king—Persecutions of the Albigeois—The Guelphs and Ghibellines—Frederick of Germany engages in the holy war, sets sail, and returns to Otranto—Gregory IX. succeeds Pope Honorius—His rage against Frederick of Germany—Death of Conraddin, sultan of Damascus—Frederick acknowledged king of Jerusalem—He quits Palestine for Europe—Excommunicated by Gregory IX.—The pope determines on renewing the holy war—Thibault V., king of Navarre, and Pierre de Dreux, engage in it—Council of Tours for promoting the cause of the Crusaders—Decline of the Latin empire in Constantinople—John of Brienne called to the throne—His death—Baldwin, his son-in-law, driven from the throne—Battle of Gaza—Death of Gregory IX.—Richard, duke of Cornwall, joins the Crusaders at Ptolemaïs—Pope Celestine IV.—Pilgrims buy off their vows—Songs of the Troubadours—Leprosy in the West—The sanguinary wars in the name of religion.

IN the preceding books, the imposing spectacle has passed before our eyes of the fall of an old empire, and of the rise and rapid decline of a new one. The imagination of man loves to dwell upon ruins, and the most sanguinary catastrophes even offer him highly attractive pictures. We have reason to fear that our narration will create less interest, awaken less curiosity, when, after the great revolutions we have described, it will be our duty to turn our attention to the petty states the Christians founded in Syria, for the safety of which the nations of the West were constantly called upon to furnish warlike assistance.

At the present day we have great difficulty in comprehending that enthusiasm which animated all classes for the deliverance of the holy places, or that powerful interest that directed the thoughts of all to countries almost forgotten by modern Europe. During the height of the fervour for the crusades, the taking of a city or town of Judea caused more joy than the taking of Byzantium; and Jerusalem was more dear to the Christians of the West than their own country. This enthusiasm, of which our indifference can scarcely form an idea, renders the task of the historian difficult, and makes him often hesitate in the choice of the events that history has to record: when opinions have changed, everything has changed with them: glory itself has lost its splendour, and that which appeared great in the eyes of men, seems only fantastical or vulgar; the historical epochs of our annals have become the objects of our most sover-

CRUSADE AGAINST THE MOORS OF GRENADA.

Innocent promised the warriors who would repair to Spain, the usual indulgences of the holy wars; and a solemn procession was made at Rome, to implore of God the destruction of the Moors and Saracens. The archbishops of Narbonne and Bordeaux, the bishop of Nantes, and a great number of French nobles, crossed the Pyrenees, followed by two thousand knights with their squires and serjeants-at-arms. The Christian army met the Moors in the plains of Las Navas de Tolosa, and fought a battle, in which over two hundred thousand infidels lost either their lives or their liberty.

[BOOK XII.

eign contempt; and when, without due reference to the ages of the holy wars, we wish to submit these extraordinary enterprises to the calculations of reason, we resemble those modern travellers who have only found a dribbling rivulet in the place of that famous Scamander, of which the imagination of the ancients, and still more, the muse of Homer, had made a majestic river.

But if we have no longer the task of describing the revolutions and falls of empires, the epoch of which we are about to trace the picture, will still present to us but too many of those great calamities with which human life supplies history: whilst Greece was a prey to all the ravages of war, the most cruel scourges desolated both Egypt and Syria.

The Nile suspended its accustomed course, and failed to inundate its banks or render the harvests abundant. The last year of this century (1200) announced itself, says an Arabian author, like a monster whose fury threatened to devour everything. When the famine began to be felt, the people were compelled to support themselves upon the grass of the fields and the ordure of animals, the poor routed up cemeteries, and disputed with the worms the spoils of coffins. When this awful scourge became more general, the population of the cities and country, as if pursued by a pitiless enemy, fled away from their homes in despair, and wandered about at hazard from city to city, from village to village, meeting everywhere with the evil they wished to avoid; in no inhabited place could they step a foot without being struck by the appearance of a putrefying carcass, or some unhappy wretch on the point of expiring.

The most frightful effect of this universal calamity was, that the want of food gave birth to the greatest crimes, and rendered every man the enemy of his fellows. At the commencement of the famine much horror was expressed at some being reduced to feed upon human flesh, but examples of so great a scandal increased with such rapidity, that it was soon spoken of with indifference. Men contending with famine, which spared the rich no more than the poor, were no longer sensible to pity, shame, or remorse, and were restrained neither by respect for the laws, nor by the fear of punishment. They came at last to devour each other like wild beasts. At Cairo, thirty women, in one day, perished at the stake, convicted of having killed and eaten their own children. The historian Abdallatif relates a crowd of barbarous and monstrous incidents which make the blood run cold with horror, and to which we will not give a place in our history, for fear of being accused of calumniating human nature.

The plague soon added its ravages to those of famine. God alone, says contemporary history, knows the number of those that died with famine and disease. The capital of Egypt, in the space of a few months, witnessed a hundred and eleven thousand funerals. At length it was found impossible to bury the dead, and the terrified survivors were obliged to be satisfied with casting them over the ramparts. The same mortality was experienced at Damietta, Kous, and Alexandria. It was at the period of seed-time that the plague was at its height; they who sowed the seed were not the same that had ploughed the ground, and they who sowed lived not to reap the harvest. The villages were deserted, and reminded travellers of those expressions of the Koran: "*We have mown them all down and exterminated them; one cry was heard, and all have perished.*" The dead bodies that floated on the Nile were as numerous as the bulbous plants which, at certain seasons, cover the waters of that river. One fisherman counted more than four hundred that passed before his eyes in a single day; piles of human bones were met with everywhere; the roads, to borrow the expression of Arabian writers, "*were like a field sown with dead bodies,* and the most populous provinces *were as a banqueting-hall for the birds of prey.*"

Egypt lost more than a million of its inhabitants; both famine and plague were felt as far as Syria, and the Christian cities suffered equally with those of the Mussulmans. From the shores of the Red Sea to the banks of the Euphrates and the Orontes, the whole country presented one picture of desolation and mourning. As if the anger of Heaven was not satisfied, it was not long before a third calamity, not less terrible, followed in the train of the others. A violent earthquake laid waste the cities and provinces that famine and plague had spared; the shocks resembled the motion of a sieve, or that which a bird makes when he raises and lowers his wings. The rising of the sea, and the agitation of the waves presented a horrible appearance; ships were, on a sudden, carried far on to the land, and multitudes of fish covered the shore; the heights of Libanus opened and sunk in many places. The people of Syria and Egypt believed it to be the earthquake that is to precede the day of judgment. Many inhabited places totally disappeared; a vast number of men perished; the fortresses of Hamath, Barin, and Balbec were thrown down; the only part of the city of Naplouse that was left standing was the street of the Samaritans; in Damascus, all the most superb edifices were destroyed; in the city of Tyre only a few houses escaped, and the ramparts of Ptolemaïs and Tripoli were nothing but heaps of ruins. The shocks were felt with less violence in the territory of Jerusalem, and, in the general calamity, both Christians and Mussulmans returned thanks to Heaven for having spared in its anger the city of prophets and miracles.

Such awful disasters ought to have caused the treaties made between the barons and the infidels to be respected. In the fifth crusade, the sovereign pontiff urged the Christians to take advantage of these calamitous days to invade the Mussulman provinces of Syria and Egypt: but if the advice of the pope had been followed, if the Christian army, on leaving Venice, had directed its march towards the countries devastated by pestilence and famine, it is most probable that the conquerors and the conquered would have perished together. At that period, death, like a formidable sentinel, guarded all the frontiers of the Christians and Mussulmans. All the scourges of nature became the terrible guardians of provinces, and defended the approaches and entrances of cities better than the greatest armies could have done.

The Christian colonies, however, began, not to repair their losses, but to forget the evils they had suffered. Amaury, king of Jerusalem, set his barons an example of wisdom and pious resignation. The three military orders, that had exhausted their treasures to support their knights and soldiers during the famine, made a strong appeal, by messengers and letters, to the charity of the faithful of the West. The Christian cities that had been destroyed by the earthquake were rebuilt, and the sums amassed by Foulque of Neuilly, the preacher of the last crusade, were employed in restoring the walls of Ptolemaïs. As the Christians wanted labourers, they set the Mussulman prisoners to work. Among the prisoners condemned to this service, history must not pass by the celebrated Persian poet, Saadi, who had fallen into the hands of the Franks, whilst on a pilgrimage to Jerusalem. The author of "The Garden of Roses," and several other works, destined at a future day to obtain the admiration of the East and the West, was loaded with irons, led to Tripoli, and confounded with the crowd of captives employed in rebuilding the fortifications of that city.

The truce which had been concluded with the infidels still subsisted; but either pretensions or quarrels daily arose that were frequently followed by hostilities. The Christians were continually kept under arms, and peace was sometimes as abundant in troubles and dangers as an open war would have been. There likewise prevailed at this time, great confusion among the Christian colonies, and even among the Mussulman powers. The sultan of Damascus was at peace with the king of Jerusalem, whilst the count of Tripoli, the prince of Antioch, with the Templars and Hospitallers, were at war with the princes of Hamath, Edessa or some emirs of Syria. Every one, according to his humour, took up or laid down his arms, without any power being sufficiently strong to enforce respect for treaties.

No great battles were fought, but constant incursions upon the territories of enemies were made; cities were surprised, countries were ravaged, and great booty obtained. Amidst these disorders, which were called *Days of Truce*, the Christians of Palestine had to lament the death of their king. Amaury, according to the custom of the faithful, went to Caïfa, during holy week, to gather palm; but fell sick on his pilgrimage, and returned to Ptolemaïs to die. Thus the sceptre of the kingdom of Jerusalem again remained in the hands of Isabella, who had neither the power, nor the ability necessary to govern the Christian states. At the same time, one of the sons of Bohémond, prince of Antioch, fell under the daggers of assassins sent by the Old Man of the Mountains. Bohémond the Third, at a very advanced age, was unable to avenge this murder; and, in addition, before he died, had the mortification of seeing war break out between his second son, Raymond, count of Tripoli, and Livon, prince of Armenia. The order of the Templars, as well as that of the Hospitallers, interested themselves in this quarrel, and were opposed to each other. The sultan of Aleppo and the Turks from Asia Minor mixed themselves with the dissensions of the Christians, and took advantage of their divisions to ravage the territory of Antioch. The Christian states of Syria received no more succours from the West. The remembrance of the evils that had ravaged the countries beyond the seas had damped the zeal and the ardour of pilgrims; the warriors of Europe, accustomed to face with coolness all the perils of war, had not sufficient courage to brave pestilence and famine. A great number of the barons and knights of Palestine, themselves abandoned a land too long laid desolate, some to repair to Constantinople, and others to the kingdoms of the West.

Innocent, who had up to this time made vain efforts for the deliverance of the holy places, and who could not overcome his regret at having seen great Christian armies fruitlessly dissipated in the conquest of Greece, still did not give up his vast designs; from the beginning of his reign, the sovereign pontiff had pointed out the Holy Land to the Christian nations, as the road and the way of salvation. After the example of his predecessors, he not only called piety and virtue in to the defence of the Christian colonies, but remorse and repentance. All who came to him to confess great sins, were allowed but one means of expiating their crimes,—crossing the sea to fight against the infidels.

Among the sinners condemned to this sort of punishment history quotes the names of the murderers of Conrad, bishop of Wurtzburg and chancellor of the empire.* The guilty having presented themselves before the pope, barefooted, in drawers, and with halters round their necks, swore in the presence of the cardinals, to pass their lives in the practice of the most austere mortifications, and to carry arms during four years against the Saracens. A knight, named Robert, scandalized the whole court of Rome by confessing in a loud voice, that, being a prisoner in Egypt during the famine, he had killed his wife and daughter, to feed upon their flesh. The pope imposed the most rigorous penances upon Robert, and ordered him, to complete the expiation of so great a crime, to pass three years in visiting the holy places.

Innocent endeavoured by such means to keep up the devotion of pilgrimages, which had given birth to the crusades, and might again revive the zeal and ardour for holy wars. According to the opinion which the sovereign pontiff sought to spread among the faithful, and by which he himself appeared penetrated, this corrupt world had no crimes for which God would not open the treasures of his mercy, provided the perpetrators would take the voyage to the East. The people however

---

* This penitence and that which follows are mentioned by Fleury, in the sixteenth volume of his History; the guilty were condemned, in addition to the pilgrimage, to wear neither vair, grey squirrel fur, ermine, nor coloured stuffs; they were never to be present at public games; after becoming widowers, were never to marry again; to walk barefooted and be clothed in woollen, and to fast on bread and water on Wednesdays, Fridays, Ember-week, and Vigils; to perform three Lent fasts in the course of the year, to recite the Pater Noster a hundred times, and make a hundred genuflexions every day. When they came to a city, they were to go to the principal church barefooted, in drawers, with halters round their necks and rods in their hands, and there receive from the canons discipline, &c., &c.

were persuaded that the sins and errors of a perverse generation had irritated the God of the Christians, and that the glory of conquering the Holy Land was reserved for another and a better age, to a generation more worthy of attracting the eyes and the blessings of Heaven.

This opinion of the nations of the West was very little in favour of the Christians of Syria, who were daily making rapid strides towards their fall. Isabella, who only reigned over depopulated cities, died soon after her husband. A son that she had had by Amaury preceded her to the tomb; and the kingdom of Jerusalem became the heritage of a young princess, a daughter of Isabella and Conrad, marquis of Tyre. The barons and knights that remained in Syria were more sensible than ever of the necessity of having at their head a prince able to govern them, and immediately set about choosing a husband for the young queen of Jerusalem.

Their choice might have fallen upon one of themselves; but they feared that jealousy would give birth to fresh discords, and that the spirit of rivalry and faction would weaken the authority of him that should be called upon to govern the kingdom. The assembly resolved to seek a king in the West, and to address themselves to the country of Godfrey and the Baldwins,—to that nation that had furnished so many heroes to the crusades, so many illustrious defenders of the Holy Land.

This resolution of the barons of Palestine had not only the advantage of preserving peace in the kingdom of Jerusalem, but also that of arousing the spirit of chivalry in Europe, and of interesting it in the cause of the Christians of the East. Aimar, lord of Cæsarea, and the bishop of Ptolemaïs, crossed the sea, and went, in the name of the Christians of the Holy Land, to solicit Philip Augustus to send them a knight or a baron who might save the little that remained of the unfortunate kingdom of Jerusalem. The hand of a young queen, a crown, and the blessings of Heaven were the rewards held out to the bravery and devotedness of him who was willing to fight for the heritage of the Son of God. The deputies were received with great honours at the court of the king of France. Although the crown they offered was nothing but a vain title, it not the less dazzled the imagination of the French knights; their valorous ambition was seduced by the hope of acquiring great renown, and restoring the throne that had been founded by the bravery of Godfrey of Bouillon.

Among the knights of his court, Philip greatly distinguished John of Brienne, brother of Gauthier, who died in Apulia with the reputation of a hero and the title of king. In his youth, John of Brienne had been destined for the ecclesiastical state; but, brought up in a family of warriors, and less sensible to the charms of piety than to those of glory, he refused to obey the will of his parents; and as his father was inclined to employ force to constrain him, he sought a refuge against paternal anger in the monastery of Citeaux. John of Brienne was mixed with the crowd of cenobites, and gave himself up, as they did, to fasting and mortification. The austerities of the cloister, however, did not at all assimilate with his growing passion for the noble occupation of arms; and often, amidst prayers and religious ceremonies, the images of tournaments and battles would distract his thoughts and disturb his mind. One of his uncles having found him at the door of the monastery in a state very little suited to a gentleman, had pity on his tears, took him away with him, and encouraged his natural inclinations. From that time the glory of combats entirely occupied his thoughts; and he who had been destined to the silence of cloisters and the peace of altars, was not long in creating for himself by his bravery and exploits a great and widely spread renown.

At the period of the last crusade, John of Brienne accompanied his brother in his attempt to obtain the kingdom of Naples, and saw him perish whilst fighting for a throne that was to be the reward of the victor. He had the same fortune to guide his hopes, and the same dangers to encounter, if he espoused the heir of the kingdom of Jerusalem. He accepted with joy the hand of a young queen, for the possession of whose states he must contend with the Saracens; he charged the ambassadors to return and announce his speedy arrival in Palestine, and, full of confidence in the cause he was about to defend, promised to follow them at the head of an army.

When Aymar of Cæsarea and the bishop of Ptolemaïs returned to the Holy Land, the promises of John of Brienne raised the depressed courage of the Christians, and, as it often happens in seasons of misfortune, they passed from despair to the most extravagant hopes.

It was given out in Palestine that a crusade was in preparation, commanded by the most powerful monarchs of the West; and the report of such an extraordinary armament produced a momentary terror among the infidels. Malek-Adel, who, since the death of Al-Aziz, reigned over Syria and Egypt, dreaded the enterprises of the Christians; and as the truce made with the Franks was on the point of expiring, he proposed to renew it, offering to deliver up ten castles or fortresses as a pledge of his good faith and his desire for a continuation of peace. This proposal ought to have been welcomed by the Christians of Palestine; but the hopes of assistance from the West had banished all moderation and foresight from the councils of the barons and knights. The wiser part of the Christian warriors, among whom was the grand master of the order of St. John, were of opinion that the truce should be prolonged. They reminded their companions that they had often been promised succour from the West, without this succour ever having reached the Holy Land; and that in the very last crusade, a formidable army, confidently expected in Palestine, had directed its march towards Constantinople. They added, that it was not prudent to risk the chances of war upon the faith of a vain promise; and that they ought to wait the event, before they formed a determination upon which might depend the safety or the ruin of the Christians of the East. These discourses were full of wisdom and good sense, but as the Hospitallers spoke in favour of the truce, the Templars, with great warmth, declared for war; such was, likewise, the spirit of the Christian warriors, that prudence, moderation, or, indeed, any of the virtues of peace inspired them with a sort of disdain; for them reason was always on the side of perils, and only to speak of flying to arms was quite sufficient to win all their suffrages. The assembly of barons and knights refused to prolong the truce made with the Saracens.

This determination became so much the more fatal, from the situation of France and Europe, which could scarcely allow John of Brienne to entertain the hope of accomplishing his promise of raising an army for the Holy Land.

Germany was still agitated by the rival pretensions of Otho and Philip of Swabia: John of England laboured under the curse of an excommunication, which interdict extended to his kingdom. Philip Augustus was busily employed in taking advantage of all the troubles that were in full action around him; on one side by endeavouring to extend his influence in Germany, and on the other by constant efforts to weaken the power of the English, who were masters of several provinces of his kingdom. John of Brienne arrived at Ptolemaïs with the train of a king, but he only brought with him three hundred knights to defend his kingdom; his new subjects, however, still full of hopes, looked upon him no less as a liberator. His marriage was celebrated in the presence of the barons, the princes, and the bishops of Ptolemaïs. As the truce was about to expire, the Saracens resumed their arms, and disturbed the festivities of the coronation. Malek-Adel entered Palestine at the head of an army, and the infidels not only laid siege to Tripoli, but threatened Ptolemaïs.

The new king, at the head of a small number of faithful warriors, created great admiration for his valour in the field of battle; but he was not able to deliver the Christian provinces from the presence of a formidable enemy. When the defenders of Palestine compared their scanty ranks with the multitude of their enemies, they sank at once into a state of despondency; and even those who so lately scorned the thoughts of peace with the infidels, could not muster either strength or courage to oppose to their attacks. Most of the French knights that had accompanied the new king, quitted the kingdom they had come to succour, and returned into Europe. The dominions of John of Brienne consisted of the city of Ptolemaïs alone, and he had no army to defend even that; he then began to perceive he had undertaken a perilous and difficult task, and that he should not be able to contend for any length of time against the united forces of the Saracens. Ambassadors were sent to Rome to inform the pope of the pressing dangers of the Christian states in Asia, and once more to implore the support of the princes of Europe, and, above all, of the French knights.

These fresh cries of alarm were scarcely heard by the nations of the West. The troubles which agitated Europe at the period of the departure of John of Brienne for Palestine were far from being allayed, and prevented France especially from lending any assistance to the Christian colonies. Languedoc and most of the southern provinces of the kingdom were then desolated by religious wars, which fully employed the bravery of the French knights and nobles.

A spirit of inquiry and indocility, which had arisen among the faithful, and with which St. Bernard had reproached his age, was making alarming progress every day. The most holy doctors had already many times expressed their grief at the abasement of the holy word, of which every one constituted himself judge and arbiter, and which was treated, said Stephen of Tournay in his letters to the pope, with as little discernment as *holy things given to dogs, or pearls cast at the feet of swine.* This spirit of independence and pride, joined to the love of paradox and novelty; to the decline of sound studies, and the relaxation of ecclesiastical discipline; had given birth to heresies which rent the bosom of the Church.

The most dangerous of all the new sects was that of the Albigeois, which took its name from the city of Albi, in which its first assemblies had been held. These new sectarians being unable to explain the existence of evil under a just and good God, as the Manicheans had done, adopted two principles. According to their belief, God had first created Lucifer and his angels; Lucifer, having revolted from God, was banished from heaven, and produced the visible world, over which he reigned. God, to re-establish order, created his second son, Jesus Christ, to be the genius of good, as Lucifer had been the genius of evil. Several contemporary writers represent the Albigeois in the most odious colours, and describe them as given up to all kinds of error; but this opinion must not be adopted in all its rigour by impartial history. For the honour of human nature we feel bound to say, that never did a religious sect dare to endeavour to win the approbation of mankind whilst presenting an example of depravity of morals; and that in no age, among no people, has a false doctrine ever been able to lead astray any number of men, without being supported by at least an appearance of virtue.

The wisest and most earnest Christians were at that period desirous of a reform in the clergy. "But there were," says Bossuet, "vain and proud minds, full of bitterness, which, struck by the disorders that reigned in the Church, and more particularly among its ministers, did not believe that the promises of its eternal duration could possibly subsist amongst these abuses. These, become proud, and thence weak, yielded to the temptation which leads to a hatred of the Church from a hatred of those who preside in it; and as if the malice of man could annihilate the work of God, the aversion they had conceived for the teachers, made them hate at the same time both the doctrine they taught and the authority they had received from God."

This disposition of men's minds gave the apostles of error a most deplorable ascendancy, and multiplied the number of their disciples. Among the new sectarians, the most remarkable were the *Vaudois*, or *Poor of Lyons*, who devoted themselves to a state of idle poverty, and despised the clergy, whom they accused of living in luxury and voluptuousness: the *Apostoliques*, who boasted of being the only mystical body of Jesus Christ; the *Popelicains*, who abhorred the eucharist, marriages, and the other sacraments; the *Aymeristes*, whose teachers announced to the world the future establishment of a purely spiritual worship, and denied the existence of a hell or a paradise, persuaded that sin finds in itself its own punishment, and virtue its own reward.

As the greater part of these heretics exhibited a sovereign contempt for the authority of the Church, which was then the first of all authorities, all those who wished to shake off the yoke of divine laws, and those even to whom their passions rendered the restraint of human laws intolerable, came at length to range themselves under the banners of these innovators, and were welcomed by a sect anxious to increase and strengthen itself, and always disposed to consider as its partisans and defenders, men whom society cast from its bosom, who dreaded justice, and could not endure established order. Thus the pretended reformers of the thirteenth century, whilst themselves affecting austerity of manners, and proclaiming the triumph of virtue and truth, admitted into their bosom both corruption and licentiousness, destroyed every regulation of authority, abandoned everything to the caprice of the passions, and left no bond to society, no power to morals, no check upon the multitude.

The new heresies had been condemned in several councils; but as violence was sometimes employed in executing the decisions of the Church, persecution only tended to sour men's minds, instead of bringing them back to truth. Missionaries and papal legates were sent into Languedoc, to convert the misled wanderers from the flock; but their preaching produced no fruit, and the voice of falsehood prevailed over the word of God. The preachers of the faith, whom the heretics reproached with their luxury, their ignorance, and the depravity of their manners, had neither sufficient resignation nor sufficient humility to support such outrages, or offer them as a sacrifice to Jesus Christ, whose apostles they were. Exposed to the scoffs of the sectarians, and gathering nothing from the labours of their missions but humiliation and contempt, they accustomed themselves to view the people they were sent to convert as personal enemies; and a spirit of vengeance and pride, which certainly came not from heaven, made them believe it was their duty to bring into the right road, by force of arms, all who had denied their power or resisted their eloquence. The sovereign pontiff, whose mind was constantly bent upon the Asiatic war, hesitated at ordering a crusade to be preached against the Albigeois; but he was led away by the opinions of the clergy, perhaps also by that of his age, and at last promised to all Christians who would take up arms against the Albigeois the same privileges as those granted to the Crusaders against the Saracens.* Simon de Montfort, the duke of Burgundy, and the duke of Nevers obeyed the orders of the Holy See: the hatred which this new sect inspired, but still more the facility of gaining indulgences from the sovereign pontiff without quitting Europe, drew a great number of warriors to the standards of this crusade. The Inquisition owes its birth to this war; an institution at once fatal to humanity, religion, and patriotism. Piles and stakes appeared on all sides, cities were taken by storm, and their inhabitants put to the sword. The violences and cruelties which accompanied this unfortunate war have been described by those even who took a most active part in them; their recitals, which we have great difficulty in believing, frequently resemble the language of falsehood and exaggeration. In periods of vertigo and fury, when violent passions come in to mislead both opinions and consciences, it is not rare to meet with men who exaggerate the excesses to which they have given themselves up, and boast of more evil than they have committed.

---

* Notwithstanding the partiality I naturally feel for an author whose work I am translating, and to which task I was led by my admiration of it, I cannot allow such opinions of the war against the Albigeois to pass unnoticed. A very sensible French historian says:—"The inhabitants of these provinces were industrious, intellectual, and addicted to commerce, the arts, and poetry; their numerous cities flourished, governed by consuls with forms approaching to republican; all at once this beautiful region was abandoned to the furies of fanaticism, its cities were ruined, its arts and its commerce destroyed, and its language cast back into barbarism."—TRANS.

For ourselves, the disastrous war against the Albigeois does not enter into the plan of this history, and if we have spoken of it here, it was only the better to describe the situation of France at this period, and the obstacles which then opposed themselves to all enterprises beyond sea. Amidst these constantly increasing obstacles, Innocent III. was deeply afflicted at not being able to send succours to the Christians of Palestine, his regret being the greater from the circumstance that at the very time the Albigeois and the count of Thoulouse were subjected to this frightful crusade, the Saracens were becoming more formidable in Spain. The king of Castile, threatened by an innumerable army, had just called upon all Frenchmen able to bear arms to come to his assistance. The pope himself had written to all the bishops of France, recommending them to exhort the faithful of their dioceses to assist in a great battle which was to be fought between the Spaniards and the Moors, about the octave of Pentecost (1212). Innocent promised the warriors who would repair to Spain, the usual indulgences of holy wars; and a solemn procession was made at Rome, to implore of God the destruction of the Moors and Saracens. The archbishops of Narbonne and Bordeaux, the bishop of Nantes, and a great number of French nobles, crossed the Pyrenees, followed by two thousand knights with their squires and serjeants-at-arms. The Christian army met the Moors in the plains of Las Navas de Tolosa, and fought a battle, in which more than two hundred thousand infidels lost either their lives or their liberty. The conquerors, loaded with spoils and surrounded by the dead, sang the *Te Deum* on the field of battle: the standard of the leader of the Almoades was sent to Rome as a trophy of the victory granted to the prayers of the Christian Church.

On learning the issue of the battle of Tolosa, the sovereign pontiff, amidst the assembled inhabitants of Rome, offered up thanks to God for having scattered the enemies of his people; and at the same time prayed that Heaven in its mercy would, in the end, deliver the Christians of Syria as it had just delivered the Christians of Spain.

The head of the Church renewed his exhortations to the faithful for the defence of the kingdom of Jesus Christ; but amidst the troubles and civil wars that he himself had excited, he could gain no attention to the complaints of Jerusalem, and shed tears of despair at the indifference of the nations of the West. About this period such a circumstance was beheld as had never occurred even in times so abounding in prodigies and extraordinary events. Fifty thousand children, in France and Germany, braving paternal authority, gathered together and pervaded both cities and countries, singing these words :—"Lord Jesus, restore to us your holy cross!" When they were asked whither they were going, or what they intended to do, they replied, "We are going to Jerusalem, to deliver the sepulchre of our Saviour." Some ecclesiastics, blinded by false zeal, had preached this crusade; most of the faithful saw nothing in it but the inspiration of Heaven, and thought that Jesus Christ, to show his divine power, and to confound the pride of the greatest captains, and of the wise and powerful of the earth, had placed his cause in the hands of simple and timid infancy.

Many women of bad character, and dishonest men insinuated themselves amongst the crowd of these new soldiers of the cross, to seduce and plunder them. A great portion of this juvenile militia crossed the Alps, to embark at the Italian ports; whilst those who came from the provinces of France, directed their course to Marseilles. On the faith of a miraculous revelation, they had been made to believe that this year (1213) the drought would be so great that the sun would dissipate all the waters of the sea, and thus an easy road for pilgrims would be opened across the bed of the Mediterranean to the coasts of Syria. Many of these young Crusaders lost themselves in forests, then so abundant and large, and wandering about at hazard, perished with heat, hunger, thirst, and fatigue; others returned to their homes, ashamed of their imprudence, saying, *they really did not know why they had gone.* Among those that embarked, some were shipwrecked, or given up to the Saracens, against

THE CRUSADE OF CHILDREN.

About this period such a circumstance was beheld as had never occurred even in these times so abundant in prodigies and extraordinary events. Fifty thousand children, in France and Germany, braving paternal authority, gathered together and pervaded both cities and countries, singing these words:—"Lord Jesus, restore to us your holy cross!" A great portion of this juvenile militia crossed the Alps, to embark at the Italian ports; whilst those who came from the provinces of France, directed their course to Marseilles. On the faith of a miraculous revelation, they had been made to believe that this year (1213) the drought would be so great that the sun would dissipate all the waters of the sea, and thus an easy road for the pilgrims would be opened across the bed of the Mediterranean to the coasts of Syria. Many of these young Crusaders lost themselves in forests, then so abundant and large, and wandering about at hazard, perished with heat, hunger, thirst, and fatigue; others returned to their homes, ashamed of their imprudence, saying, THEY REALLY DID NOT KNOW WHY THEY HAD GONE. *Among those that embarked, some were shipwrecked, or given up to the Saracens, against whom they had set out to fight; many, say the old chronicles, gathered the palms of martyrdom, and offered the infidels the edifying spectacle of the firmness and courage the Christian religion is capable of inspiring at the most tender age as well as at the most mature.*—BOOK XII.

whom they had set out to fight; many, say the old chronicles, gathered the palms of martyrdom, and offered the infidels the edifying spectacle of the firmness and courage the Christian religion is capable of inspiring at the most tender age as well as at the more mature.

Such of these children as reached Ptolemaïs must have created terror as well as astonishment, by making the Christians of the East believe that Europe had no longer any government or laws, no longer any wise or prudent men, either in the councils of princes or those of the Church. Nothing more completely demonstrates the spirit of these times than the indifference with which such disorders were witnessed. No authority interfered, either to stop or prevent the madness; and when it was announced to the pope that death had swept away the flower of the youth of France and Germany, he contented himself with saying,—"These children reproach us with having fallen asleep, whilst they were flying to the assistance of the Holy Land."

The sovereign pontiff, in order to accomplish his designs, and rekindle the enthusiasm of the faithful, found it necessary to strike the imagination of the nations vividly, and to present a grand spectacle to the Christian world. Innocent resolved to assemble a general council at Rome, to deliberate upon the state of the Church and the fate of the Christians of the East. "The necessity for succouring the Holy Land," said he in his letters of convocation, "and the hope of conquering the Saracens, are greater than ever; we renew our cries and our prayers to you, to excite you to this noble enterprise. No one can imagine," added Innocent, "that God has need of your arms to deliver Jerusalem; but he offers you an opportunity of showing your penitence, and proving your love for him. Oh, my brethren, how many advantages has not the Christian Church already derived from the scourges that have desolated her, and desolate her still! How many crimes have been expiated by repentance! How many virtues revive at the fire of charity! How many conversions are made among sinners by the complaining voice of Jerusalem! Bless, then, the ingenious mercy, the generous artifice of Jesus Christ, who seeks to touch your hearts, to seduce your piety, and is willing to owe to his misled disciples a victory which he holds in his all-powerful hand."

The pope afterwards compares Jesus Christ banished from his heritage, to one of the kings of the earth who might be driven from his dominions. "Where are the vassals," added he, "who will not risk their fortunes and their lives to restore their sovereign to his kingdom? Such of the subjects and servants of the monarch as shall have done nothing for his cause, ought they not to be ranked with the rebels, and be subjected to the punishment due to revolt and treason? It is thus that Jesus Christ will treat those who remain indifferent to the insults heaped upon him, and refuse to take up arms to fight against his enemies."

To raise the hopes and the courage of the Christians, the holy father terminated his exhortation to the faithful, by saying that "the power of Mahomet drew towards its end; for that power was nothing but the beast of the Apocalypse, which was not to extend beyond the number of six hundred years, and already six centuries were accomplished." These last words of the pope were sustained by the popular predictions which were spread throughout the West, and created a belief that the destruction of the Saracens was at hand.

As in preceding crusades, the sovereign pontiff promised all who should take arms against the infidels, the remission of their sins and the especial protection of the Church. Upon so important an occasion, the head of the Christians laid open the treasures of divine mercy to all the faithful, in proportion to their zeal and their gifts. All prelates and ecclesiastics, as well as the inhabitants of cities and countries, were invited to raise a certain number of warriors, and support them for three years, according to their means. The pope exhorted princes and nobles who would not take the cross, to second the zeal of the Crusaders in every way in their power; the head of the Church demanded of all the faithful, prayers; of the rich, alms and tributes; of knights, an example of courage; of maritime cities, vessels; he himself engaging to make the greatest sacrifices. Processions were to be made every month in all parishes, in order to obtain the benedictions of Heaven; all the efforts, all the vows, all the thoughts of Christians were to be directed towards the object of the holy war. That nothing might divert the faithful from the expedition against the Saracens, the Holy See revoked the indulgences granted to those who abandoned their homes to go and fight against the Albigeois in Languedoc, or the Moors on the other side of the Pyrenees.

It is plain that the sovereign pontiff neglected nothing that could render the success of the holy enterprise more certain. A modern historian justly remarks, that he employed every means, even such as were not likely to succeed; for he wrote to the sultan of Damascus and Cairo, inviting him to replace the holy city in the hands of the servants of the true God. Innocent said in his letter, that God had chosen the infidels as his instruments of vengeance; that he had permitted Saladin to get possession of Jerusalem, in order to punish the sins of the Christians; but that the day of deliverance was come, and that the Lord, disarmed by the prayers of his people, was about to restore the heritage of Jesus Christ. The sovereign pontiff counselled the sultan to avoid the effusion of blood, and prevent the desolation of his empire.

This was not the first time that the head of the Church had addressed prayers and warnings to the Mussulman powers. Two years before he had written to the sultan of Aleppo, in the hope of bringing him back to the way of evangelical truth, and making him a faithful auxiliary of the Christians. All these attempts, which ended in nothing, clearly prove that the pope was perfectly unacquainted with the spirit and character of the Mussulmans. The sovereign pontiff was not more fortunate when, in his letters, he desired the patriarch of Jerusalem to use his utmost endeavours to arrest the progress of corruption and licentiousness among the Christians of Palestine. The Christians of Syria made no change in their morals, and all the passions maintained their reign amongst them; whilst the Mussulmans fortified the holy city that was demanded of them, and employed themselves in arming against the attacks of the enemies of Islamism.

Nothing could exceed the ardour and activity of the sovereign pontiff. History can scarcely follow him, whilst seeking in every direction enemies against the Mussulmans; appealing, by turns, to the patriarchs of Alexandria and Antioch, and to all the princes of Armenia and Syria. His eye took in at one view both East and West. His letters and ambassadors passed unceasingly throughout Europe. He sent the convocation for the council and the bull of the crusade into all the provinces of Christendom; and his apostolic exhortations resounded from the shores of the Danube and the Vistula to the banks of the Tigris and the Thames.

Commissaries were chosen to make the decisions of the Holy See known to all Christians: their mission was to preach the holy war, and reform manners; to invoke at the same time the knowledge of the learned and the courage of warriors. In many provinces, the mission of preaching the crusade was confided to the bishops; Cardinal Peter Robert de Courçon, who was then in France, as legate of the pope, received great powers from the Holy See; and travelled through the kingdom, exhorting Christians to take up the cross and arms.

The cardinal de Courçon had been in his youth the disciple of Foulke of Neuilly, and had gained great celebrity by his eloquence. The multitude flocked from all parts to hear so distinguished a preacher of the Word, clothed in all the splendour of Romish power. "The legate," says Fleury, "had the power of regulating everything that was connected with tournaments; and, which will appear more singular, the faculty of granting a certain indulgence to those who were present at the sermons in which he preached the crusade." Faithful to the spirit of the religion of Jesus Christ, the cardinal de Courçon gave the cross to all Christians who asked for it, without reflecting that women, children, old men, the deaf, the blind, the lame, could not make war against the Saracens; or that an army could not be formed as the Gospel composed the feast of the father of the family. Thus this liberty of entering into the holy bands, accorded without distinction or choice, only disgusted the barons and knights, and cooled the ardour of the common soldiers.

Among the orators whom the pope associated with the cardinal de Courçon, one of the most remarkable was James of Vitri, whom the Church had already placed in the rank of its celebrated doctors. Whilst he preached the crusade in the different provinces of France, the fame of his virtues and talents extended even to the East. The canons of Ptolemaïs demanded him of the pope as their pastor and bishop; and the wishes of the Christians of Palestine were immediately granted. James of Vitri, after having excited the warriors of the West to take arms, became afterwards a witness of their labours, and related them in a history which has come down to our times.

The preaching of the holy war awakened everywhere the charity of the faithful. Philip Augustus gave up the fortieth part of his territorial revenues towards the expenses of the crusade, and a great number of nobles and prelates followed his example. As boxes had been placed in all churches to receive the alms of the charitable, these alms brought considerable sums into the hands of the cardinal de Courçon, who was accused of having appropriated to himself the gifts offered to Jesus Christ. These accusations were the more eagerly received, from the legate having taken upon him to exercise, in the name of the Holy See, an authority which was displeasing to both the monarch and his people. The cardinal, without the approbation of the king, levied taxes, enrolled warriors, forgave debts, lavished both rewards and punishments, and, in a word, usurped all the prerogatives of sovereignty. The exercise of such an unbounded power was the cause of trouble to all the provinces.* To prevent disorders, Philip Augustus thought it necessary to lay down regulations which should specify to the general council, the individual position of the Crusaders, and the exemptions and privileges they were to enjoy.

Whilst the cardinal de Courçon continued to preach the crusade throughout the provinces of France, the archbishop of Canterbury was earnestly engaged in inciting the people of England to take up arms against the infidels. During a length of time, the kingdom of England had been troubled by the violent contentions of the commons, the barons, and even the clergy, who had taken advantage of the excommunications† launched by the pope against King John, to obtain a confirmation of their liberties. The English monarch, when subscribing the conditions that had been dictated to him, had yielded much more to necessity and force, than to his own inclinations; he wished earnestly to retract what he had granted, and in order to place his crown under the protection of the Church, he took the cross, and swore to go and fight against the Saracens. The sovereign pontiff placed faith in the submission and promises of the king of England; and after having preached a crusade against this prince, whom he accused of being an enemy of the Church, he employed the whole authority of the Holy See, and all the thunders of religion in his defence.

King John had no other motive in taking the cross but to deceive the pope, and obtain the protection of the Church; the sign of the Crusaders was assumed by him only as a means of preserving

---

* In the royal regulations of Philip Augustus, there is an order relative to the debts contracted by the Crusaders as members of a commune. We think our readers will not be displeased by the particulars of this order. "As to the Crusaders, members of certain communes, we order," says the king, "that if the commune itself be charged with any levy, whether for foot or horse soldiers (l'ost et la chevauchée), the inclosure of the city, the defence of the city in the event of a siege, or for any debt that is due, and contracted before they took the cross, they shall be held subject to the payment of their proportion, equally with the other inhabitants who have not taken the cross; but as to the debts contracted after the period at which they shall have taken the cross, the Crusaders shall remain exempt, not only until their approaching departure, but until their return."—See the *Recueil des Ordonnances*, *Dachery*, and the sixth vol. of the *Notices des Manuscrits, dissertation de M. du Theil sur Robert de Courçon*.

† In the charter granted by King John, that monarch expressly says that he grants this charter by the advice of the Archbishop of Canterbury, of seven bishops, and the pope's nuncio.

his power; a false and deceitful policy, which was soon unmasked, and, without doubt, assisted much in diminishing the public enthusiasm for the holy war. The barons of England, in their turn excommunicated by the pope, employed themselves in defending their liberties, and paid no attention to the holy orators who called upon them to embark for Asia.

The empire of Germany was not less disturbed than the kingdom of England. Otho of Saxony, after having been, during ten years, the object of all the predilections of the Holy See, drew upon himself all at once the implacable hatred of Innocent, by putting forth some claims to certain domains of the Church, and to the kingdom of Naples and Sicily. Not only was he himself excommunicated, but the cities even that remained faithful to him were placed under an interdict. The sovereign pontiff opposed Frederick II., son of Henry VI., to Otho, in the same manner as he had opposed Otho to Philip of Swabia. Germany and Italy were immediately in a state of agitation and trouble. Frederick, who was crowned king of the Romans at Aix la Chapelle, took the cross, from a sentiment of gratitude, and with the hope of securing the support of the Holy See in ascending the imperial throne.

Otho meanwhile neglected no means of preserving the empire, and resisting the views and undertakings of the court of Rome. He made war against the pope, and allied himself with all the enemies of Philip Augustus, who had declared for Frederick. A formidable league, composed of the king of England and the counts of Flanders, Holland, and Boulogne, threatened France with an invasion. The capital and provinces of that kingdom were already shared among the leaders of this league, when Philip gained the celebrated battle of Bouvines. This memorable victory secured the independence and honour of the French monarchy, and restored peace to Europe. Otho, conquered, lost his allies, and sunk beneath the thunders of the Church.

The period was now arrived at which the council summoned by the pope was to meet. From all parts of Europe, ecclesiastics, nobles, princes, and the ambassadors of princes, repaired to the capital of the Christian world. The deputies from Antioch and Alexandria, with the patriarchs of Constantinople and Jerusalem, came to Rome to implore the support of the nations of Christendom; the ambassadors of Frederick, Philip Augustus, and the kings of England and Hungary, in the names of their sovereigns, came to take their places in the council. This assembly, which represented the universal Church, and in which were nearly five hundred bishops and archbishops, and more than a hundred abbots and prelates from all the provinces of the East and West, took place in the church of the Lateran, and was presided over by the sovereign pontiff. Innocent opened the council by a sermon, in which he deplored the errors of his age and the misfortunes of the Church. After having exhorted the clergy and the faithful, to sanctify by their morals, the measures he was about to take against heretics and the Saracens, he represented Jerusalem as clothed in mourning, exhibiting the chains of her captivity, and calling upon all the prophets to lend their voices to reach the hearts of the Christians.

"Oh! ye," said Jerusalem by the mouth of the pontiff, "who pass along the public roads, behold and see if ye have ever witnessed grief like mine. Hasten then all, O ye that love me, to deliver me from the depth of my miseries! I, who was the queen of all nations, am now subjected to a tribute; I, who was formerly filled with people, am now left desolate and almost alone! The roads of Sion mourn, because no one comes to my solemnities. My enemies have crushed down my head; all my sacred places are profaned; the Holy Sepulchre, once so splendid, is covered with disgrace; there, where of late the Son of God was adored, worship is now offered up to the son of perdition and hell. The children of the stranger load me with outrages, and, pointing to the cross of Jesus, say to me, *Thou hast placed thy trust in vile wood; we shall see whether this wood can save thee in the hour of danger.*"

Innocent, after having thus made the mourning Jerusalem eloquent, conjured the faithful to take pity on her misfortunes, and arm for her deliverance. He terminated his exhortation by these words, which breathe both his grief and his ardent zeal:—" My beloved brethren, I give myself up entirely to you; if you think it best, I promise to go in person with the kings, princes, and nations; you shall see if, by my cries and my prayers, I shall be able to excite them to fight for the Lord, to avenge the insults of the crucified, whom our sins have banished from the land wetted with his blood, and sanctified with the mystery of our redemption."

The discourse of the pontiff was listened to in religious silence; but as Innocent spoke of several objects at the same time, and as his oratory was full of allegories, he did not at all succeed in awakening the enthusiasm of the assembly. The fathers of the council appeared to be not less affected by the abuses introduced into the Church, than by the reverses of the Christians of the East; in the first place the assmbly employed itself in endeavouring to find means to reform ecclesiastical discipline, and check the progress of heresy.

In a declaration of faith, the council explained the doctrine of Christians, and recalled to their minds the symbol of evangelical belief. They opposed truth to error, persuasion to violence, and the virtues of the Gospel to the passions of sectarians and innovators: happy would it then have been for the Christian church, if the pope had followed this example of moderation; and if, whilst defending the rights of religion, he had not forgotten the rights of sovereigns and humanity. By an apostolic decree, proclaimed amidst the council, Innocent deposed the count of Thoulouse, who was considered the protector of heresy, and gave his states to Simon de Montfort, who had fought against, or rather slaughtered the Albigeois.

Innocent could not pardon the count of Thoulouse for having provoked a war which had agitated Christendom, and suspended the execution of his designs for the Eastern crusade. The violent policy of the sovereign pontiff aimed at striking terror into all heretics, and encouraging Christians to arm for the cause of Jesus Christ and that of his vicar upon earth.

After having condemned the new errors, and pronounced the anathemas of the Church against all who strayed from the way of the faith, the pontiff and the fathers of the council gave their attention to the Christians of the East, and the means of promptly succouring the Holy Land. All the dispositions expressed in the bull of convocation were confirmed; it was decreed that all ecclesiastics should pay the twentieth of their revenues towards the expenses of the crusade; that the pope and the cardinals should pay the tenth of theirs, and that there should be a truce of four years among all Christian princes. The council launched the thunders of excommunication against all princes that should molest the march of pilgrims, and against all that should furnish infidels with provisions or arms: the sovereign pontiff promised to direct the preparations for the war, to contribute three thousand silver marks, and to supply, at his own expense, several vessels for the transport of the Crusaders.

The decisions of the council and the speeches of the pope made a profound impression upon the minds of the western Christians. All the preachers of the holy war were formally directed to recall the faithful to a sense of penitence, and to prohibit dances, tournaments, and public sports; to reform morals and to revive in all hearts the love of religion and virtue. They were commanded, after the example of the sovereign pontiff, to make the complaints of Jerusalem resound in the palaces of princes; and to earnestly solicit monarchs and nobles to assume the cross, so that the people might be induced to do so likewise.

The decrees concerning the holy wars were published in all the churches of the West; in several provinces, particularly in the north of Europe, the prodigies and miraculous apparitions that had excited enthusiasm at the period of the first crusades, again became common; luminous crosses appeared in the heavens, and made the inhabitants of Cologne and the cities in the vicinity of the Rhine believe that God favoured the holy enterprise, and that the divine power promised the defeat and ruin of the infidels to the arms of the Crusaders.

The orators redoubled their ardour and zeal to engage the faithful to take a part in the holy war. From the pulpits imprecations were poured forth against the Saracens, always accompanied by a repetition of the words of Christ: "I am come to establish war." The eloquence of prelates, bishops, and pastors had no other aim than summoning all Christian warriors to arms. The voices of preachers were not the only trumpet-calls; poetry herself, who had but recently revived in the southern provinces of France, chose the holy expeditions as the themes of her songs; and the profane muse of the troubadours mingled their notes with the animated words of the sacred orators. The Pierres d'Auvergne, the Ponces de Capdeuil, the Folquets de Romano, ceased to sing the love of ladies and the courtesy of knights, to celebrate in their verses, the sufferings of Christ and the captivity of Jerusalem. "The times are come," said they, "in which it will be seen who are the men worthy of serving the Eternal. God now calls upon the valiant and chivalrous; they shall be his soldiers for ever, who, knowing how to suffer for their faith, and fight for God, shall prove themselves frank, generous, loyal, and brave; let the base lovers of life or seekers for gold remain behind; God now only calls upon the good and brave. It is his will that his faithful servants should secure salvation by noble feats of arms; and that glory obtained in fight should open to them the gates of heaven."

One of the minstrels of the holy war celebrates in his verses the zeal, the prudence, and courage of the head of the Church; and to induce the faithful to assume the cross, sings: "*We have a sure and valorous guide, the sovereign pontiff Innocent.*"

It then began to be hoped that the father of the Christians would himself lead the Crusaders, and sanctify the Asiatic expedition by his presence. The pope, in the council of the Lateran, had expressed a desire to assume the cross and to go in person to take possession of the heritage of Christ; but the state of Europe, the progress of heresy, and, doubtless, also, the advice of the bishops and cardinals, prevented the accomplishment of his design.

As germs of dissension still subsisted between several European states, these discords might be prejudicial to the success of the holy war; and the pope sent forth emissaries to act as angels of peace; he himself repairing to Tuscany, to appease the quarrels that had broken out between the Pisans and Genoese. His words soothed down all angry passions; at his voice the most implacable enemies swore to forget their disputes, and unite to combat against the Saracens. His most ardent wishes appeared about to be fulfilled, and the whole West, obedient to his sovereign will, was ready to precipitate itself upon Asia, when he fell suddenly ill and died, leaving to his successors the care and honour of finishing so great an enterprise.

Like all men who have exercised great power amidst political tempests, Innocent, after his death, was, by turns, praised and blamed with all the exaggeration of love and hatred. Some said he had been summoned to the heavenly Jerusalem, as God wished to reward his zeal for the deliverance of the holy places; whilst others had recourse to miraculous apparitions, and made saints speak in condemnation of his memory; sometimes he was seen pursued by a dragon, whose purpose was to inflict justice upon him; and at others he appeared surrounded by the flames of purgatory. Europe had been in a constant state of trouble during his pontificate; there was scarcely a kingdom upon which the wrath of the pontiff had not been poured out; and so many excesses, so many misfortunes had embittered men's minds, that it was natural they should take a pleasure in believing that the vicar of Christ upon earth was expiating in another life the crimes of this. Innocent, nevertheless was irreproachable in his manners; at first he had evinced some degree of moderation; he loved truth and justice; but the unhappy condition of the Church, the obstacles of all kinds which he met with in his spiritual government, irritated his character, and drove him to the excesses of a violent policy; at length, preserving no propriety or self-command, he burst forth with the ever-memorable and reprehensible words: "*Sword, sword, spring from the scabbard, and sharpen thyself to kill.*" As he had undertaken far too much, he left serious embarrassments to those who might assume the reins of power after him; and such was the situation in which his policy had placed the Holy See, that his successors were obliged to follow up his maxims, and complete both the good and the evil he had begun. From this period, the history of the crusades will be incessantly interrupted by the quarrels of popes and princes, and we shall follow the pilgrims to the Holy Land amidst the clashing of the thunders launched by the various heads of the Church.

Censius Savelli, cardinal of St. Lucia, was chosen by the conclave to succeed Innocent, and governed the Church under the name of Honorius III. On the day after his coronation, the new pope wrote to the king of Jerusalem, to announce his elevation, and to revive the hopes of the Christians of Syria. "Let not the death of Innocent," said he, "depress your courage; although I am far from being his equal in merit, I will show the same zeal for the deliverance of the Holy Land; and when the season shall arrive, will do everything in my power to assist you." A pontifical letter, addressed to all bishops, exhorted them to continue to preach the crusade.

In order to secure success to the Oriental expedition, Innocent had first endeavoured to re-establish peace in Europe; and certainly the necessity in which the popes found themselves at such times, to promote concord among nations, was one of the greatest benefits of the holy wars. Honorius followed the example of his predecessor, and was desirous of calming all discords, even such as owed their origin to the pretensions of the Romish see. Louis VIII., son of Philip Augustus, at the solicitation of the pontiff, had taken arms against England, and was not willing to renounce the project of invading a kingdom so long subjected to the anger of the Church. The pope even stooped to supplications to disarm the redoubtable enemy of the king of England. He hoped that England and France, after having suspended their hostilities, would unite their efforts for the deliverance of the holy places; but these hopes were never accomplished. Henry III. ascended the throne of England after the death of John, and took the cross to secure the favour of the sovereign pontiff; but he had no idea of quitting his kingdom. The king of France, constantly occupied with the war against the Albigeois, and perhaps also with the secret designs of his ambition, satisfied himself with expressing the greatest respect for the authority of the Holy See, but took no part in the crusade.

Most of the bishops and prelates of the kingdom, whom the sovereign pontiff had entreated to present an example of devotedness, exhibited much greater eagerness and zeal on this occasion than the barons and knights; many of them took the cross, and prepared to set out for the East. Frederick, who owed the imperial crown to the protection of the Church, renewed, in two solemn assemblies, his oath to make war against the Saracens. The example and promises of the emperor, whatever doubt might be entertained of their sincerity, had a powerful effect over the princes and people of Germany. The inhabitants of the banks of the Rhine, those of Friesland, Bavaria, Saxony, and Norway; the dukes of Austria, Moravia, Brabant, and Lemburg; the counts of Juliers, Holland, De Wit, and Loo; with the archbishop of Mayence and the bishops of Bamberg, Passau, Strasburg, Munster, and Utrecht, emulatively ranged themselves under the banners of the cross, and prepared to quit the West.

Among the princes who took the oath to fight against the Mussulmans, was Andrew II., king of

Hungary. Bela, the father of the Hungarian monarch, had made a vow to go to the Holy Land; but not having been able to undertake the pilgrimage, he had, on his death-bed, required his son to accomplish his oath. Andrew, after having taken the cross, was for a long time detained in his states by the troubles to which his ambition had given birth, and which he had great difficulty in suppressing. Gertrude, whom he had married before the fifth crusade, made enemies of the whole court and nobility by her pride and her intrigues. This imperious princess* committed such extraordinary insults against the magnates of the kingdom, and inspired them with so violent a hatred, that they formed conspiracies against her life, and introduced murderers even into her palace. Disorders and misfortunes without number followed these crimes, the greatest of which, doubtless, was the impunity of the guilty.

In such circumstances policy would certainly have pointed it out to the king of Hungary, as his duty, to remain in his own states; but the spectacle of so many unpunished crimes, without doubt, alarmed his weakness, and strengthened his desire of getting at a distance from a court filled with his enemies. Like his mother, the widow of Bela, he expected to find in the places consecrated by the sufferings of Christ, an asylum against the griefs which beset his life; the Hungarian monarch might likewise think that the holy pilgrimage would make him more respected by his subjects, and that the Church, ever armed in favour of royal Crusaders, would defend the rights of his crown better than he himself could. He resolved at length to perform the vow he had made before his dying father, and earnestly set about preparations for his departure for Syria.

Andrew then reigned over a vast kingdom,—Hungary, Dalmatia, Croatia, Bosnia, Galicia, and the province of Lodomira obeyed his laws, and paid him tribute; and throughout all these provinces, so lately enemies to the Christians, the crusades were preached. Hordes wandering amidst forests, listened to the complaints of Sion, and swore to fight against the infidels. Among the nations of Hungary, who, a century before, had been the terror of the pilgrim companions of Peter the Hermit, a crowd of warriors eagerly took the cross, and promised to follow their monarch to the Holy Land.

Vessels and fleets for the transport of the Crusaders were equipped in all the ports of the Baltic, the ocean, and the Mediterranean; and yet, at the very same time, a crusade was being preached against the inhabitants of Prussia, who still remained in the darkness of idolatry. Poland, Saxony, Norway, and Livonia armed their warriors to overthrow the idols of paganism on the banks of the Oder and the Vistula, whilst the other nations of the West were preparing to make war against the Saracens in the plains of Judæa and Syria.

The still savage people of Prussia, separated by their religion and their customs from the other inhabitants of Europe, presented in the centre of Christendom, in the thirteenth century, a living picture of ancient paganism, and of the superstitions of the old nations of the North. Their character and their manners are worthy of fixing the attention of both the historian and his readers, fatigued, perhaps, by the constant repetition of the preaching of holy wars, and the distant expeditions of the Crusaders.

Much discussion has taken place concerning the origin of the ancient inhabitants of Prussia, and we have nothing on this head but conjectures and systems. The Prussians were, in person, like the Germans; blue eyes, a spirited and lively look, ruddy cheeks, a lofty stature, a robust form, and light hair: this resemblance to the Germans was produced by climate, and not by the mixture of the nations; the inhabitants of Prussia had more affinity with the Lithuanians, whose language they

---

* Bonfinius, the historian of Hungary, says that Gertrude gave up the wife of Banc, the chancellor of the kingdom, to the criminal desires of her brother. He adds that Banc killed the queen to avenge this injury; but this assertion is contradicted by all historians. The same author says that the wife of Andrew was assassinated during his voyage to the Holy Land; but this assertion is as false as the first. Gertrude was assassinated on the 18th of September, 1213.—See Palma, *Notitia Rer. Hung.* t. i.

A FRIENDLY TOURNAMENT.

spoke, and whom they imitated in their dress. They lived by the chase, fishing, and the flesh of their flocks; agriculture was not unknown to them; their mares furnished them with milk, their sheep with wool, their bees with honey; in commercial transactions they had very little to do with money: to prepare flax and leather, to split stones, to sharpen their arms, and to fashion yellow amber, constituted the whole of their industry. They marked time by knots tied in thongs, and the hours by the words *twilight, light, dawn, sunrise, evening, the first sleep,* &c. The appearance of the Pleïades directed them in their labours

The months of the year bore the names of the productions of the earth, and of the objects presented to their eyes by each season; they knew the month of crows, the month of pigeons, that of cuckoos, of the green birch-trees, of the linden-trees, of corn, of the departure of the birds, of the fall of leaves, etc. Wars, the conflagrations of great forests, hurricanes, and inundations, formed the principal epochs of their history.

The people dwelt in huts built of earth, the rich in houses constructed of oak timber; there was not a city in Prussia. Some strong castles appeared upon the hills. This nation, though savage, recognised princes and nobles; he who had conquered enemies, and he who excelled in taming horses, attained nobility. The lords held the right of life and death over their vassals; the Prussians made no wars for the purpose of conquering an enemy's country, but solely to defend their homes and their gods. Their arms consisted of the lance and the javelin, which they handled with much skill. The warriors named their chief, who was blessed by the high priest; before going to battle, the Prussians selected one of their prisoners of war, fastened him to a tree, and transfixed him with arrows.* They believed in omens; the eagle, the white pigeon, the crow, the stork, the bustard, promised victory; the stag, the wolf, the lynx, the mouse, the sight of a sick person, or even of an old woman, announced defeats or reverses; when presenting their hand, they offered peace; when swearing to treaties, they placed one hand upon their breast and the other upon the sacred oak. When victorious, they tried their prisoners of war, and the most distinguished among them expired at the stake,—a sacrifice to the gods of the country.

Amidst all their barbarous customs, the Prussians had the reputation of respecting the laws of hospitality. The stranger and the shipwrecked mariner were sure to find an asylum and succour among them; intrepid in war, simple and mild in peace, grateful but vindictive, respecting misfortune, they had more virtues than vices, and were only corrupted by the excess of their superstitions.

The Prussians believed in another life; they called hell, *Peckla;* chains, thick darkness, and fetid waters constituted the punishment of the wicked. In the Elysian fields, which they called *Rogus,* beautiful women, banquets, delicious drink, dances, soft couches, and fine clothes were the rewards of virtue.

In a place called *Remové*, arose a flourishing oak, which had witnessed the passage of a hundred generations, whose colossal trunk contained three images of their principal gods; the foliage daily dripped with the blood of immolated victims; there the high priest had established his abode, and there administered justice. The priests alone ventured to approach this holy place; the guilty slunk from it trembling. *Perkunas*, the god of thunder and fire, was the first among the deities of the Prussians; he had the countenance of an angry man, his beard was curled, and his head was surrounded with flames. The people called claps of thunder, the march or steps of Perkunas. Near the grove of Remové, on the banks of a sulphureous spring, an eternal fire burned in honour of the god of thunder.

---

* A letter from Pope Honorius to the archbishop of Maïence, says that there is in Prussia a nation of barbarians, of whom it is said that they kill all the girls but one born of each mother; that they prostitute their daughters and wives, immolate captives to their gods, and bathe their swords and lances in the blood of these victims, to bring them success in battle.

Near Perkunas, *Potrimpus* appeared, in the form of a young man, wearing a crown of wheat-ears; he was adored as the god of waters and rivers; he preserved mankind from the scourge of war, and presided over the pleasures of peace. By a strange contradiction, they offered up to this pacific divinity, the blood of animals, and that of the captives slaughtered at the foot of the oak; sometimes children were sacrificed to him; the priests consecrated the serpent to him, as symbolical of fortune.

Beneath the shade of the sacred tree, was still another idol, called *Pycollos*, the god of the dead; he bore the form of an old man, with grey hair, hollow eyes, and a pale countenance, his head enfolded in a shroud; his altars were heaps of human bones; the infernal deities were obedient to his laws; he inspired both grief and terror.

A fourth divinity, *Curko*, whose image ornamented the branches of the oak of Remové, furnished mankind with the necessaries of life. Every year, at autumnal seed-time, his image was renewed; it consisted of a goat-skin, elevated upon a pole eight feet high, crowned with blades of corn; the priest sacrificed upon a stone, honey, milk, and the fruits of the earth, whilst the youth of both sexes formed a circle round the idol.

The Prussians celebrated several other festivals during spring and summer, in honour of the same god; at the spring festival, which took place on the 22nd of March, they addressed Curko in these words: "It is thou who hast chased away winter, and brought fair and fine days back to us; by thee the gardens and the fields rebloom; by thee the forests and the woods resume their verdure." The inhabitants of Prussia had a crowd of other gods, whom they invoked for their flocks, their bees, the forests, the waters, harvest, commerce, the peace of families, and conjugal happiness; a divinity with a hundred eyes watched over the threshold of houses; one god guarded the yard, another the stable; the hunter heard the spirit of the forest howl amidst the tree-tops; the mariner recommended himself to the god of the sea. *Laimelé* was invoked by women in labour, and spun the lives of mankind. Tutelary divinities arrested the progress of conflagrations, caused the sap of the birch-trees to flow, guarded roads, and awakened workmen and labourers before the dawn of day. The air, the earth, the waters were peopled by gnomes or little gods, and with ghosts and goblins, which they called *arvans*. It was believed by all that the oak was a tree dear to the gods, and that its shade offered an asylum against the violence of men or the assaults of destiny. In addition to the oak of Remové, the Prussians had several other trees of the same kind, which they considered the sanctuaries of their divinities. They consecrated also linden-trees, firs, maples, and even whole forests; they held in reverence fountains, lakes, and mountains; they adored serpents, owls, storks, and other animals: in short, in the countries inhabited by the Prussians, all nature was filled with divinities, and, up to the fourteenth century, it might be said of a European nation, as Bossuet said of ancient paganism, "*Everything there was god, except God himself.*"

A long time before the crusades, St. Adalbert had left his native country, Bohemia, to penetrate into the forests of Prussia, and endeavour to convert the Prussians to Christianity; but his eloquence, his moderation, or his charity, could not disarm the fury of the priests of Perkunas. Adalbert died, pierced with arrows, and received the palm of martyrdom; other missionaries shared the same fate; their blood arose against their murderers, and a report of their death, together with an account of the cruelties of a barbarous people, everywhere cried aloud upon the Christians of the North for vengeance. The neighbouring nations were constantly entertaining the resolution to take arms against the idolaters of Prussia. An abbot of the monastery of Oliva, more able, and still further, more fortunate than his predecessors, undertook the conversion of the pagans of the Oder and the Vistula, and succeeded, with the assistance of the Holy See, in getting up a crusade against the worshippers of false gods; a great number of Christians took the cross, at the summons of the pope, who promised them eternal life if they fell in fight, and lands and treasures if they triumphed over the enemies of Christ. The knights of Christ and the knights of the sword, instituted to subdue the pagans of Livonia, with the Teutonic knights, who in Palestine rivaled in power and glory the two other orders of the Temple and the Hospital, at the first signal flocked to the standards of the army assembled to invade Prussia, and convert its inhabitants: this war lasted more than two centuries. In this sanguinary struggle, if the Christian religion sometimes inspired its combatants with its virtues, the leaders of this long crusade were much more frequently influenced by vengeance, ambition, and avarice. The knights of the Teutonic order, whose bravery almost always amounted to heroism, remained masters of the country conquered by their arms. These victorious monks never edified the people they subdued, either by their moderation or their charity; and were often accused before the tribunal of the head of the Church, of having converted the Prussians, not to make them servants of Christ, but to increase the number of their own subjects and slaves.

We have only spoken of the people of Prussia, and of the wars made against them, to exhibit to our readers a nation and customs almost unknown to modern scholars even; and to show how far ambition and a thirst of conquest was able to abuse the spirit of the crusades: we hasten to return to the expedition that was being prepared against the Saracens.

Germany considered Frederick II. as the leader of the war about to be made in Asia; but the new emperor, seated on a throne for a long time shaken by civil wars, dreading the enterprises of the Italian republics, and perhaps those of the popes their protectors, thought it prudent to defer his departure for Palestine.

The zeal of the Crusaders, however, did not abate, and in their impatience they turned their eyes towards the king of Hungary to take the command in the holy war. Andrew, accompanied by the duke of Bavaria, the duke of Austria, and the German nobles who had taken the cross, set out for the East, at the head of a numerous army, and repaired to Spalatro, where vessels from Venice, Zara, Ancona, and other cities of the Adriatic, awaited the Crusaders, to transport them into Palestine.

In all the countries through which he marched, the king of Hungary was followed by the benedictions of the people. When he approached the city of Spalatro, the inhabitants and the clergy came out in procession to meet him, and conducted him to their principal church, where all the faithful were assembled to call down the mercy of Heaven upon the Christian warriors. A few days after, the fleet of the Crusaders left the port of Spalatro, and set sail for the island of Cyprus, at which place were met the deputies of the king and the patriarch of Jerusalem, of the orders of the Temple and St. John, and of the Teutonic knights.

A crowd of Crusaders, who had embarked at Brindisi, at Genoa, and at Marseilles, preceded the king of Hungary and his army. Lusignan, king of Cyprus, and the greater part of his barons, influenced by the example of so many illustrious princes, took the cross, and promised to follow them into the Holy Land. All the Crusaders embarked together at the port of Lemisso, and landed in triumph at Ptolemaïs.

An Arabian historian says, that since the time of Saladin the Christians had never had so numerous an army in Syria. Thanks to Heaven were offered up in all the churches, for the powerful aid it had sent to the Holy Land; but the joy of the Christians of Palestine was quickly troubled by the serious difficulty in which they found themselves to procure provisions for such a multitude of pilgrims.

This year (1217) had been barren throughout the richest countries of Syria;* and the vessels

---

* A letter from the master of the soldiers of the Temple, addressed to Honorius III., enters into several details respecting the situation of the Holy Land at this period. This letter speaks of the scarcity experienced in Syria; the master of the Templars adds, that they could procure no horses. "For this reason," said he to the pope, "exhort all who have taken the cross, or intend to take it, to furnish themselves with such things as they cannot procure here."

from the West had only been laden with machines of war, arms, and baggage. Deficiency of food was soon felt among the Crusaders, and led the soldiers to license and robbery; the Bavarians committed the greatest disorders; pillaging houses and monasteries, and devastating the neighbouring country; the leaders had no other means of reëstablishing order and peace in the army, but by giving the signal for war against the Saracens; and, to save the lands and dwellings of the Christians, they proposed to their soldiers to ravage the cities and territories of the infidels.

The whole army, commanded by the kings of Jerusalem, Cyprus, and Hungary, encamped on the banks of the torrent of Cison. The patriarch of the holy city, in order to strike the imagination of the Crusaders, and prevent their forgetting the object of their enterprise, repaired to the camp, bringing with him a portion of the wood of the true cross, which he pretended to have been saved at the battle of Tiberias. The kings and princes came out, barefooted, to meet him, and received with respect the sign of redemption. This ceremony rekindled the zeal and enthusiasm of the Crusaders, whose ardent desire now was to fight for Christ. The army crossed the torrent and advanced towards the valley of Jesraël, between Mount Hermon and Mount Gelboé, without meeting an enemy. The leaders and soldiers bathed in the Jordan, and passed over the plain of Jericho, and along the shores of the great lake of Genesareth. The Christian army marched singing spiritual songs; religion and its remembrances had restored discipline and peace among them. Every object and place they beheld around them filled them with a pious veneration for the Holy Land. In this campaign, which was a true pilgrimage, they made a great number of prisoners without fighting a battle, and returned to Ptolemaïs loaded with booty.

At the period of this crusade, Malek-Adel no longer reigned over either Syria or Egypt. After having mounted the throne of Saladin by injustice and violence, he had descended from it voluntarily; the conqueror of all obstacles, and having no longer a wish to form, he became sensible of the emptiness of human grandeur, and gave up the reins of an empire that nobody had the power to dispute with him. Melik Kamel, the eldest of his sons, was sultan of Cairo; and Corradin was sultan of Damascus. His other sons had received, as their shares of the empire, the principalities of Bosra, Baalbec, Mesopotamia, &c. Malek-Adel, relieved from the cares of government, visited his children by turns, and preserved peace among them. All he had reserved of his past power was the ascendancy of a great renown, and of a glory acquired by numberless heroic exploits; but this ascendancy held princes, people, and army in subjection. In moments of peril, his counsels became laws: the soldiers still considered him as their leader; his sons as their sovereign arbiter; and all Mussulmans as their defender and support.

The new crusade had spread terror among the infidels, but Malek-Adel calmed their fears by assuring them that the Christians would soon be divided amongst themselves, and by telling them that this formidable expedition resembled the storms which howl over Mount Libanus, and which disperse of themselves: neither the armies of Egypt nor the armies of Syria, made their appearance in Judæa; and the Crusaders assembled at Ptolemaïs were astonished at meeting no enemy to contend with. The leaders of the Christian army had resolved to direct their march towards the banks of the Nile; but winter, which was about to commence, would not permit them to undertake so distant an enterprise. To employ the soldiers, whom idleness always seduced into license, it was determined to make an attack upon Mount Tabor, where the Mussulmans had fortified themselves.

Mount Tabor, so celebrated in the Old and New Testament, arises like a superb dome amidst the vast plain of Galilee. The declivity of the mountain is covered with flowers and odoriferous plants; from the summit of Tabor, which forms a level of a league in extent, may be seen, travellers say, all the banks of the Jordan, the Lake of Tiberias, the Sea of Syria, and most of the places in which Christ performed his miracles.

A church, the erection of which was due to the piety of St. Helena, stood on the very spot where the transfiguration of Christ took place in presence of his disciples, and for a length of time attracted crowds of pilgrims. Two monasteries, built at the summit of Tabor, recalled for centuries the memory of Moses and Elias, whose names they bore; but, from the reign of Saladin, the standard of Mahomet had floated over this holy mountain; the church of St. Helena and the monasteries of Moses and Elias had been demolished, and upon their ruins was raised a fortress, from which the Mussulmans constantly threatened the territories of Ptolemaïs.

It was impossible to ascend Mount Tabor without encountering a thousand dangers; but nothing intimidated the Christian warriors: the patriarch of Jerusalem, who marched at their head, showed them the true cross, and animated them by his example and his eloquent words. Enormous stones rolled from the heights occupied by the infidels, who poured down an endless shower of javelins and arrows upon all the roads which led to the top of the mountain. The valour of the soldiers of the cross braved all the efforts of the Saracens; the king of Jerusalem distinguished himself by prodigies of bravery, and killed two emirs with his own hand. The summit of the mountain being attained, the Crusaders dispersed the Mussulmans, and pursued them to the gates of their fortress: nothing could resist their arms. But all at once several of the leaders began to entertain suspicions regarding the intentions of the Sultan of Damascus; and the fear of a surprise acted the more strongly on their minds from no one having foreseen it. Whilst the Mussulmans retired filled with terror behind their ramparts, a sudden panic seized the conquerors: the Crusaders renounced the attack of the fortress, and the whole Christian army retreated without effecting anything; as if it had only ascended Mount Tabor to contemplate the spot rendered sacred by the transfiguration of the Saviour.

We could scarcely yield faith to the account of this precipitate flight, without the evidence of contemporary historians; the ancient chronicles, according to their custom, do not fail to attribute to treachery an event they cannot comprehend; it appears to us, however, much more natural to suppose that the retreat of the Crusaders was produced by the discord and want of foresight which prevailed in all their undertakings.

This retreat had most fatal results; whilst the leaders reproached each other with the disgrace of the army and the egregious error they had committed, the knights and soldiers sank into a state of discouragement. The patriarch of Jerusalem refused from that time to bear the wood of the true cross in the van of the Crusaders, as he found the sight of it could neither revive their piety nor reanimate their courage. The kings and princes who directed the crusade, wishing to retrieve so shameful a reverse before they returned to Palestine, led the army towards Phœnicia. In this new campaign no exploit signalized their arms; being winter, a great number of the soldiers, overcome by cold, remained abandoned on the roads, whilst others fell into the hands of the Bedouin Arabs. On Christmas eve, the Crusaders, who were encamped between Tyre and Sarphat, were surprised by a violent tempest; wind, rain, hail, whirlwinds, incessant peals of thunder killed their horses, carried away their tents, and scattered their baggage. This disaster completed their despondency, and created a belief that Heaven refused them its support.

As they were in serious want of provisions, and the whole army could not subsist in one place, they resolved to divide themselves into four different bodies till the end of winter. This separation, which was made amidst mutual complaints, appeared to be the work of discord much more than of necessity. The king of Jerusalem, the duke of Austria, and the grand master of St. John encamped in the plains of Cæsarea; the king of Hungary, the king of Cyprus, and Raymond, son of the prince of Antioch, retired to Tripoli; the grand masters of the Templars and the Teutonic knights, and Andrew d'Avesnes, with the Flemish Crusaders, went to fortify a castle built at the foot of Mount Carmel; the other Crusaders retired to Ptolemaïs with the intention of going back to Europe.

The king of Cyprus fell ill and died just as he was upon the point of embarking for his own kingdom. The king of Hungary was discouraged, and began to despair of the success of a war so unfortunately commenced. This prince, after a sojourn of three months in Palestine, thought his vow accomplished, and resolved, all at once, to return to his dominions.

The West had doubtless been surprised to see Andrew abandon his kingdom, torn by factions, to repair to Syria; and the Eastern Christians were not less astonished at seeing this prince leave Palestine without having done anything for the deliverance of the holy places. The patriarch of Jerusalem reproached him with inconstancy, and employed his utmost efforts to retain him beneath the banners of the cross; but finding Andrew would not yield to his prayers, he had recourse to threats, and displayed the formidable train of the weapons of the Church. Nothing, however, could shake the resolution of the king of Hungary, who satisfied himself with not appearing to desert the cause of Christ by leaving half his troops under the command of the king of Jerusalem.

After having quitted Palestine, Andrew remained for a long time in Armenia, appearing to forget his own enemies, as he had forgotten those of Christ. He came back into Europe through Asia Minor, and beheld, whilst passing Constantinople, the wreck of the Latin empire, which ought to have roused him from his pious indolence, and have reminded him of his own dangers. The Hungarian monarch, who had left his army in Syria, took back with him a number of relics; such as the head of St. Peter, the right hand of the apostle Thomas, and one of the seven vases in which Christ changed water into wine at the marriage in Cana: his confidence in these revered objects made him negligent of the means of human prudence; and, if we may believe a contemporary chronicle, when he returned into Hungary, the relics which he brought from the Holy Land sufficed for the suppression of all the troubles of his states, and caused peace, the laws, and justice, to flourish throughout his provinces. The greater part of the Hungarian historians, however, hold quite another language, and reproach their monarch with having dissipated his treasures and his armies in an imprudent and an unfortunate expedition; the nobility and people took advantage of his long absence to impose laws upon him, and obtain liberties and privileges which weakened the royal power, and scattered the germs of a rapid decay in the kingdom of Hungary.

After the departure of the king of Hungary, a great number of Crusaders arrived from the ports of Holland, France, and Italy. The Crusaders from Friesland, Cologne, and the banks of the Rhine had stopped on the coast of Portugal, where they had conquered the Moors in several great battles, killed two Saracen princes, and mounted the banners of the cross upon the walls of Alcazar. They described the miracles by which Heaven had seconded their valour, and the apparition of angels, clothed in resplendent armour, who had fought on the banks of the Tagus, in the ranks of the soldiers of Christ. The arrival of these warriors, with the account of their victories, revived the courage of the Crusaders who had remained in Palestine under the command of Leopold, duke of Austria; with such a powerful reinforcement, nothing was talked of but renewing the war against the Mussulmans.

The project of conquering the banks of the Nile often occupied the thoughts of the Christians; since the idea of a war in Egypt had been put forth by the pope himself amidst the council of the Lateran, it had been considered as an inspiration from Heaven; they only thought of the advantages of a rich conquest, and the perils of so difficult an enterprise appeared of no importance in the eyes of the soldiers of the cross.

The Christian army, commanded by the king of Jerusalem, the duke of Austria, and William, count of Holland, embarked at the port of Ptolemaïs, and landed within sight of Damietta, on the northern bank of the second mouth of the Nile. The city of Damietta, situated at the distance of a mile from the sea, had a double rampart on the river side, and a triple wall on the land side; a tower arose in the middle of the Nile, and an iron chain, which reached from the city to the tower, prevented the passage of vessels. The city contained a numerous garrison, with provisions and munitions of war for a long siege. Damietta had already several times resisted formidable attacks of the Christians. Roger, king of Sicily, had made himself master of it in the preceding century, but he was not able to retain and defend it, against the united forces of the Mussulmans.

The Crusaders arrived before Damietta early in April; having pitched their tents in a vast plain, they had behind them lakes and pools abounding in fish of all kinds; before them the Nile, covered with their vessels; a thousand canals, crowned with evergreen papyrus and reeds, intersected the lands, and spread freshness and fertility around them. In the fields which had so lately been the theatre of sanguinary contests, no traces of war were to be seen; harvests of rice covered the plains in which Christian armies had perished by famine; groves of oranges and citrons loaded with flowers and fruit; woods of palms and sycamores, thickets of jasmines and odoriferous shrubs, with a crowd of plants and wonders, unknown to the pilgrims, created the image of an earthly paradise, and made them fancy that Damietta must have been the first dwelling of man in his state of innocence. The aspect of a beautiful sky and a rich climate intoxicated them with joy, kept hope alive in their hearts, and held out to them the accomplishment of all the divine promises. In their religious and warlike enthusiasm, they believed they saw Providence prodigal of its miracles for the success of their arms; scarcely had they established their camp on the bank of the Nile, when an eclipse of the moon covered the horizon with darkness; and even this phenomenon inflamed their courage, as it appeared to them a presage of the greatest victories.

The first attacks were directed against the tower built in the middle of the Nile; vessels, in which were placed towers, ladders, and drawbridges, approached the walls. The soldiers who manned them, braving the arrows and murderous machines of the Mussulmans, made several assaults; but prodigies of strength, courage, and skill were useless. The most intrepid of the Crusaders, victims of their own rash bravery and devotedness, perished, swallowed up by the waves, without being able to be succoured or avenged by their companions. In all the attacks, nothing could equal the impetuous valour of the Western warriors; but this valour was not seconded by either the prudence of the commanders or the discipline of the soldiers; each nation had its leader, its machines of war, its days for fighting; no order governed either attack or retreat; the soldiers on board the vessels wished to manœuvre them, the sailors would fight.

The frequent checks they experienced, at length, however, taught them prudence: the lightest of their vessels ascended the Nile, and returning to cast anchor above the tower built in the middle of the river, attacked and broke asunder the bridge of boats which united the tower with the city. Industry likewise lent its assistance to the bravery of the Crusaders; machines of war were invented, of which no models had previously existed. An enormous wooden castle, built upon two vessels, joined together by beams and joists, was admired as a miraculous invention, and considered as a certain pledge of victory. Upon this floating castle was a drawbridge, which could be lowered upon the tower of the Saracens, and galleries destined to receive the soldiers who were to attack the walls. A poor priest of the church of Cologne, who had preached the crusade on the banks of the Rhine, and followed the Christian army into Egypt, was charged with the superintendence of the erection of this formidable edifice. As the popes in their letters always advised the Crusaders to take with them to the East men skilled in the mechanical arts, the Christian army was in no want of workmen to perform the most difficult labours; the liberality of the leaders and soldiers supplied all the necessary expenses.

The whole army looked with impatience for the moment at which the enormous fortress should be brought near to the tower on the Nile; prayers were offered up in the camp for the protection of Heaven; the patriarch and the king of Jerusalem, the clergy and the soldiers, during several days, submitted to all the austerities of penitence,—all marched in procession barefooted to the seashore. The leaders had fixed upon the festival of the apostle St. Bartholomew as the day for the assault, and the Crusaders were filled with hope and ardour. They vied with each other in eagerness to be of the assaulting party, for which the best soldiers of each nation were selected, and Leopold, duke of Austria, the model of Christian knights, obtained the honour of commanding an expedition with which the first success of the crusade was connected.

On the appointed day, the two vessels surmounted by the wooden tower received the signal for moving. They carried three hundred warriors fully armed; and an innumerable multitude of Mussulmans assembled on the walls contemplated the spectacle with surprise mingled with dread. The two vessels pursued their silent course up the middle of the river, whilst all the Crusaders, either drawn up in battle-array on the left bank of the Nile, or dispersed over the neighbouring hills, saluted with loudest acclamations the moving fortress which bore the fortunes and the hopes of the Christian army. On drawing near to the walls the two vessels cast anchor, and the soldiers prepared for the assault. Whilst the Christians hurled their javelins and got ready their lances and swords, the Saracens poured upon them torrents of Greek fire, and employed every effort to make the wooden castle on which their enemies fought a prey to the flames. The one party was encouraged by the shouts and applauses of the Christian army, the other by the thousand times repeated acclamations of the inhabitants of Damietta. Amidst the fight, the machine of the Crusaders all at once appeared on fire; the drawbridge lowered on to the walls of the tower wavered and was unsteady; the flagstaff of the duke of Austria fell into the Nile, and the banner of the Christians remained in the hands of the Mussulmans. At this sight the Saracens uttered the most extravagant cries of joy, whilst groans and sounds of grief were heard along the shore on which the Crusaders were encamped; the patriarch of Jerusalem, the clergy, the whole army, fell on their knees, and raised their supplicating hands towards heaven.

But soon, as if God had been favourable to their prayers, the flames were extinguished, the machine was repaired, the drawbridge was replaced, and the companions of Leopold renewed the attack with more ardour than ever. From the top of their fortress they commanded the walls of the tower, and dealt mighty blows with sabre, spear, battle-axe, and iron mace. Two soldiers sprang upon the platform upon which the Saracens defended themselves; they carried terror among the besieged, who descended tumultuously to the first stage of the tower; the latter set fire to the floor, and endeavoured to oppose a rampart of flames between themselves and the enemies who rushed down in pursuit of them; but these last efforts of despair and bravery presented but a vain resistance to the Christian soldiers. The Mussulmans were attacked in all parts of the tower; and their walls, shaken by the machines, appeared to be sinking around them, and about to bury them beneath the ruins: in this hopeless condition they laid down their arms, and sued to their conquerors for life.

After this memorable victory, the Christians, masters of the tower of the Nile, broke the chain which impeded the passage of vessels, and their fleet was able to approach close to the ramparts of the city.

About the same time (September, 1217) Malek-Adel, who had rendered himself so formidable to the Christians, died in the capital of Egypt. He heard before his death of the victory which the

FOR THE DEFENCE OF CHRIST.

Christians had gained at Damietta; and the Crusaders did not fail to say that he had sunk under the effects of despair, and that he carried with him to the tomb the power and glory of the Mussulmans.

The Christians, in their histories, have represented Malek-Adel as an ambitious, cruel, and stern prince; Oriental writers celebrate his piety and mildness. An Arabian historian boasts of his love of justice and truth, and paints, by a single trait, the moderation of the absolute monarch of Asia, when he says, "that the brother of Saladin listened without anger to that which displeased him."

Historians unite in praising the bravery of the Mussulman prince, and the ability he displayed in the execution of all his designs. No prince knew better how to make himself obeyed, or to give to supreme power that brilliant exterior which strikes the imagination of nations, and disposes them to submission. In his court, he always appeared surrounded with the pomp of the East: his palace was as a sanctuary which no one durst approach: he rarely appeared in public; when he did, it was in a manner to inspire fear: as he was fortunate in all his undertakings, the Mussulmans had no difficulty in believing that the favourite of fortune was the favourite of Heaven: the caliph of Bagdad sent ambassadors to salute him *king of kings*. Malek-Adel was pleased to be styled in camps Seïf Eddin (the sword of religion), and this glorious name, which he had merited by his contests with the Christians, drew upon him the love and confidence of the soldiers of Islamism. He astonished the East by his abdication, as much as he had astonished it by his victories; the surprise he excited only added to his glory as well as to his power; and, that his destiny might in everything be extraordinary, fortune decreed that when he had descended from the throne, he should still remain master. His fifteen sons, of whom several were sovereigns, still trembled before him; nations prostrated themselves on his passage; up to the very hour in which he closed his eyes, his presence, his name only, maintained peace in his family and the provinces, and order and discipline in the armies.

At his death the face of everything began to change; the empire of the Ayoubites, which he had sustained by his exploits, gave tokens of decline; the ambition of the emirs, for a long time restrained, broke out into conspiracies against the supreme authority; a spirit of license began to be apparent in the Mussulman armies, and particularly among the troops that defended Egypt.

The Crusaders ought to have profited by the death of Malek-Adel, and the consequences it was sure to produce, by attacking the discouraged Mussulmans without intermission. But instead of following up their success, after they had obtained possession of the Tower of the Nile, they all at once neglected the labours of the siege, and appeared to have fallen asleep over their first victories. A great number of them, persuaded that they had done enough for the cause of Christ, only thought of embarking to return into Europe. Every vessel that left the port recalled to the pilgrims remembrances of home; and the beautiful sky of Damietta, which had inflamed their imaginations at the commencement of the siege, was not sufficient to retain them in a country which they began to consider as a place of exile.

The clergy, however, warmly censured the retreat and desertion of the Crusaders, and implored Heaven to punish the base soldiers who thus abandoned the standards of the cross. Six thousand pilgrims from Brittany, who were returning to Europe, were shipwrecked on the coast of Italy, and almost all perished; and the ecclesiastics, with the most ardent of the Crusaders, did not fail to see, in so great a disaster, a manifestation of divine anger. When the Crusaders of Friesland, after having deserted the banners of the Holy Land, had returned into the West, the ocean all at once broke through the dykes, and overflowed its customary boundaries; the richest provinces of Holland were submerged, and a hundred thousand inhabitants, with whole cities, disappeared beneath the waters. Many Christians attributed this calamity to the culpable retreat of the Frieson and Dutch Crusaders.

The pope beheld with pain the return of the pilgrim deserters from the cause of Christ. Honorius neglected nothing to secure the success of a war he had preached; and he every day, both by prayers and threats, pressed the departure of those who, after having taken the cross, delayed the accomplishment of their vow.

According to the usual custom of navigators, two periods of the year were fixed upon at which it was best to cross the sea. The pilgrims almost always embarked in the month of March and in the month of September, whether to repair to the East or to return to Europe; which caused them to be compared to those birds of passage that change their climate at the approach of a new season, and towards the end of fine weather. At each passage, the Mediterranean was covered with vessels which transported Crusaders, some returning to their homes, others going to fight the infidels. At the very moment the Christians were deploring the loss of the Frieson and Dutch warriors, their spirits were restored by seeing Crusaders from Germany, Pisa, Genoa, Venice, and several provinces of France, arrive in the camp at Damietta.

Among the French warriors, history names Hervé, count of Nevers; Hugh, count de la Marche; Miles de Bar-sur-Seine; the lords John of Artois and Ponce de Crancey; Ithier de Thacy, and Savary de Mauléon; they were accompanied by the archbishop of Bordeaux, the bishops of Angers, Autun, Beauvais, Paris, Meaux, Noyon, &c. England also sent the bravest of her knights into Egypt. Henry III. had taken the cross after the council of the Lateran; but as he could not quit his dominions, at that time a prey to civil wars and torn by discord, the earls of Harcourt, Chester, and Arundel, with Prince Oliver, were honoured with the charge of acquitting, in his name, the vow he had taken to fight in the East for the cause of Christ.

At the head of the pilgrims who arrived at that time in Egypt were two cardinals, whom the pope had sent to the Christian army. Robert de Courçon, one of the preachers of the crusade, was charged with the mission of inculcating the moral precepts of Christ in the camp of the Crusaders, and animating the zeal and devotion of the soldiers by his eloquence. Cardinal Pelagius, bishop of Albano, was invested with the entire confidence of the Holy See; he brought with him the treasures that were to defray the expenses of the war; the Crusaders from Rome and several other cities of Italy marched under his orders, and recognised him as their military leader.

Cardinal Pelagius, by his position, was endowed with great authority in the Christian army, and his naturally imperious character led him to assume even more power than he had received from the Holy See. In whatever affair he was employed, he acknowledged no equal, and would not endure a superior. He had been known to oppose the sovereign pontiff in the bosom of the conclave; he would have resisted the most powerful monarchs, even in their own councils. Cardinal Pelagius, persuaded that Providence meant to make use of him to accomplish great designs, believed himself fit for all works, and appointed to all kinds of glory; when he had formed a determination, he maintained it with invincible obstinacy, and was influenced by neither obstacles nor perils, nor even by the lessons of experience. If Pelagius originated any advice in council, he supported it with all the menaces of the court of Rome, and often gave cause for a belief that the thunders of the Church had only been confided to his hands, that he might secure the triumph of his own opinions.

Pelagius had scarcely arrived in Egypt, when, as legate of the pope, he disputed the command of the army with John of Brienne. To support his pretensions, he asserted that the Crusaders had taken up arms at the desire of the sovereign pontiff; that they were the soldiers of the Church, and ought to recognise no other head than the legate of the Holy See: these assumptions gave great offence to the barons and principal leaders. From that time it was easy to foresee that discord would be introduced by him whose mission it was to establish peace; and that the envoy of the pope, charged to preach humility among Christians, was about to ruin everything by his mad presumption. Cardinal de Courçon died shortly after his arrival.

The continuator of William of Tyre, whilst deploring the death of this legate, who had been remarkable for his moderation, characterizes, by a single word, the conduct of Pelagius, and the consequences that might be expected from it, by saying: "Then died Cardinal Peter, and Pelagius lived, which was a great pity."

In the mean time, the approach of danger had reunited the Mussulman princes. The caliph of Bagdad, whom James of Vitri styles *the pope of the infidels*, exhorted the nations to take up arms against the Christians. All the sons of Malek-Adel, who reigned over the provinces of Syria and of Yemen, prepared to march to the assistance of Egypt. The sultan of Damascus, after having made several incursions into the territories of Ptolemaïs, gathered together his whole army, and resolved to go and defend Damietta. As he had reason to fear the Christians might take advantage of his absence to seize Jerusalem and fortify themselves in it, he caused the ramparts of the holy city to be demolished. He also ordered the fortress of Tabor, and all those that the Mussulmans held along the coasts of Palestine, to be destroyed; a vigorous measure that afflicted the infidels, but was calculated to afflict the Christians still more; as it proved to them that they had to contend with enemies animated by despair and disposed to sacrifice everything to secure their own safety.

The sultan of Cairo encamped in the vicinity of Damietta, where he awaited the princes of his family. The garrison of the city received every day provisions and reinforcements, and was in a condition to resist the Christian army for a length of time. The preparations and the approach of the Mussulmans at length roused the Crusaders from their state of inaction. Animated by their leaders, but more by the appearance of danger and the presence of a formidable enemy; still led by the king of Jerusalem, who had resisted the pretensions of Pelagius, the Christian soldiers resumed the labours of the siege, and made several assaults upon the city on the river side. The winter, which had just set in, did not at all prevent their attacks; nothing could equal the heroic constancy with which they braved, during several months, cold, rain, hunger, all the fatigues of war, and all the rigours of the season. A contagious malady committed great ravages in the Christian army: a frightful storm, which lasted three days, carried away the tents and the baggage of both leaders and soldiers; but nothing diminished the fury of the contests, which were incessantly renewed.

At length the Christians, having become masters of all the western bank of the Nile, determined to cross the river, and attack the city on the land side. The passage was difficult and dangerous; the sultan of Cairo had fixed his camp on the opposite shore; the plain on which the Crusaders wished to pitch their tents was covered with Mussulman soldiers; an unexpected event removed all obstacles.

We have spoken of the seditious spirit of the emirs, who, since the death of Malek-Adel, had openly shown their ambitious designs and sought to introduce divisions into the Mussulman armies. The most remarkable among these emirs, was the leader of a troop of Curds, named Emad-eddin, who had taken a part in all the revolutions of Egypt and Syria. Associated with the destinies of the sons of Ayoub, this emir had witnessed the rise and fall of several Mussulman dynasties, and held in contempt the powers of which he knew both the source and the origin. An intrepid soldier, a faithless subject, always ready to serve his sovereigns in fight or betray them in a conspiracy, Emad-eddin could not endure a prince who reigned by the laws of peace, or recognise a power which was not the fruit of his intrigues or of a revolution. As fortune had always favoured his audacity, and as all his treacheries had been well rewarded, every fresh revolt augmented his credit and his renown; an enemy to all acknowledged authority, the hope of all who aspired to empire, he was almost as redoubtable as the Old Man of the Mountain, whose menaces made the most powerful monarchs tremble. Emad-eddin resolved to change the government of Egypt, and conceived the project of dethroning the sultan of Cairo, and replacing him by another of the sons of Malek-Adel.

Several emirs were drawn into this conspiracy. On the day appointed, they were to enter the tent of Melic-Kamel, and compel him, by violence, to renounce the supreme authority. The sultan was warned of the plot prepared against him, and on the eve of the day on which it was to be carried into effect, he left his camp in the middle of the night. The next day, at dawn, the conspirators were made aware that their designs had been discovered; they endeavoured in vain to draw the soldiers into a revolt; the greatest confusion prevailed throughout the camp; among the emirs, some gathered around Emad-eddin, and swore to follow his fortunes; others, doubtful of the success of his enterprise, remained silent; many took an oath to defend Melic-Kamel. Amidst these debates, the Mussulman army, conscious that they were without a leader, feared they might be surprised by the Christians. A panic terror all at once seized upon the soldiers, who abandoned their tents and their baggage, and rushed in the greatest disorder in the traces of their fugitive sultan.

This retreat, of which the Christians could not imagine the cause, and which their historians explain by a miracle from heaven,* opened to them the passage of the Nile. The army hastened to cross the river, took possession of the Mussulman camp, made an immense booty, and drew near to the walls of Damietta.

The panic, however, which had put the Mussulman troops to flight, had not at all communicated itself to the garrison of the city: this intrepid garrison offered the most vigorous resistance, and gave the army of Melic-Kamel time to recover from its fright. The sultan of Damascus soon joined his brother the sultan of Cairo. Emad-eddin and the other leaders of the conspiracy were arrested and loaded with chains. Order and discipline were reëstablished among the Saracens, and the Christian army had to contend with all the united forces of the infidels, impatient to repair their check, and recover the advantages they had lost.

The burning days of summer were approaching: the Nile, increased by the rains of the tropics, began to issue from its bed. The Christian army was encamped under the walls of Damietta, having the lake Menzaleh in its rear. The Saracens came and pitched their tents at a short distance from the camp of the Christians, who, oppressed by the consuming heat of the season and the climate, were subject every day to the spirited attacks of the infidels. In one of these conflicts, the Mussulmans got possession of a bridge which the Crusaders had thrown over the Nile; the banks of the river were covered with dead, and the Christian army only owed its safety to the heroic bravery of the duke of Austria, the king of Jerusalem, and the grand masters of St. John and the Temple. Soon after, another battle was fought still more bloody than the first. In this fight, as it is described by James of Vitri, an ocular witness, not a person among the Christians was idle: the clergy were at prayers or attending the wounded; whilst the women and children carried water, wine, food, stones, and javelins, to the combatants. Whirlwinds of scorching dust arose in the air, and enveloped the two armies. The cries of the wounded and the dying, the sound of the trumpets, and the clashing of arms resounded from the neighbouring hills and from both shores of the Nile. Sometimes the Saracens were put to flight, and whole battalions, says James of Vitri, disappeared submerged in the Nile, as formerly the armies of Pharaoh perished in the Red Sea. Sometimes the Christians were repulsed in their turn, and left a great number of their warriors on the field of battle: the carnage lasted during the whole day, without either side being able to claim the victory. Whilst the two

---

* All the Christian historians of the middle ages, and Maimbourg after them, appear persuaded that Providence, by a miracle of its will, put the Saracens to flight.

ST. FRANCIS OF ASSISE ENDEAVOURS TO CONVERT SULTAN MELIC-KAMEL.

At this period a holy person, named Francis of Assise, made his appearance in the Christian army, whose reputation for piety was spread throughout the Christian world, and had preceded him into the East. Francis was led into Egypt by the fame of the crusade, and by the hope of there effecting some great conversion. The day preceding the last battle, he had a miraculous presentiment of the defeat of the Christians, and imparted his prediction to the leaders of the army, who heard him with indifference. Dissatisfied with the Crusaders, and devoured by the zeal of a mission from God, he then conceived the project of securing the triumph of the faith by his eloquence and the arms of the Gospel alone. He directed his course towards the enemy's camp, put himself in the way of being taken prisoner by the Saracen soldiers, and was conducted into the presence of the sultan. Then Francis addressed Melic-Kamel, and said to him, "It is God who sends me towards you, to point out to you the road to salvation." After these words the missionary exhorted the sultan to embrace the Gospel; he challenged in his presence all the doctors of the law, and to confound imposture and prove the truth of the Christian religion, offered to cast himself into the midst of a burning funeral-pile. The sultan, astonished, ordered the zealous preacher from his presence, who obtained neither of the objects of his wishes, for he did not convert the sultan, nor did he gather the palm of martyrdom.—BOOK XII.

armies were contending with such fury on the banks, the Genoese and the Pisans, on board their vessels, made an attack upon the ramparts of the city. Several of their ships were consumed by the Greek fire, and the bravest of their soldiers were crushed beneath the beams and stones hurled from the top of the walls. At the approach of night the Crusaders returned to their tents despairing of ever being able to subdue the Saracens, and reproaching each other with want of courage in this unfortunate day.

On the morrow fresh disputes arose between the horse and foot soldiers,* each of which bodies accused the other with having been the cause of the losses the army had experienced. These debates became so warm that at length the foot and the horse both demanded, with loud cries, to be led again to battle, and rushed tumultuously out of the camp, to give convincing proofs of their bravery; the leaders could neither restrain nor direct the ardour and impetuosity of their soldiers, who fought in disorder, and were repulsed by the Saracens after a horrible carnage.

At this period a holy person, named Francis of Assise, made his appearance in the Christian army, whose reputation for piety was spread throughout the Christian world, and had preceded him into the East. From his earliest youth, Francis had left the paternal roof to lead a life of edification. One day, whilst present at mass in a church in Italy, he was struck with the passage of the Gospel in which our Saviour says, "Take with you neither gold nor silver, nor other moneys; neither scrips for the journey, nor sandals, nor staff." From that period Francis had held in contempt all the riches of this world, and had devoted himself to the poverty of the apostles; he travelled through countries and cities, exhorting all people to penitence. The disciples who followed him braved the contempt of the multitude, and glorified themselves with it before God: when asked whence they came, they were accustomed to answer, "We are poor penitents from Assise."

Francis was led into Egypt by the fame of the crusade, and by the hope of there effecting some great conversion. The day preceding the last battle, he had a miraculous presentiment of the defeat of the Christians, and imparted his prediction to the leaders of the army, who heard him with indifference. Dissatisfied with the Crusaders, and devoured by the zeal of a mission from God, he then conceived the project of securing the triumph of the faith by his eloquence and the arms of the Gospel alone. He directed his course towards the enemy's camp, put himself in the way of being taken prisoner by the Saracen soldiers, and was conducted into the presence of the sultan. Then Francis addressed Melic-Kamel,† and said to him, "It is God who sends me towards you, to point out to you the road to salvation." After these words, the missionary exhorted the sultan‡ to embrace the Gospel; he challenged in his presence all the doctors of the law, and to confound imposture and prove the truth of the Christian religion, offered to cast himself into the midst of a burning funeral-pile. The sultan, astonished, ordered the zealous preacher from his presence, who obtained neither of the objects of his wishes, for he did not convert the sultan, nor did he gather the palm of martyrdom.

After this adventure, St. Francis returned to Europe, where he founded the religious order of the Cordeliers, who at first, possessing neither churches, monasteries, lands, nor flocks, spread themselves throughout the West, labouring for the conversion of penitents. The disciples of St. Francis

---

* The infantry must have rendered, during the siege, greater services than the cavalry, in defending the intrenchments, mounting to the assault, or fighting on board the ships. This dispute alone proves that the infantry had made great progress; for till that time they would not have dared to compare themselves with the cavalry.

† The continuator of William of Tyre speaks at length of the interview between St. Francis and his companion and the sultan of Cairo. St. Francis at first proposed to the sultan to renounce Mahomet, under pain of eternal damnation.

‡ The sultan said he had archbishops and bishops of the law, and without them he could not listen to what they had to say. The clerks, St. Francis and his companion, answered him, "Send for them here"—and they came to him in his tent. He then related to them what the clerks had said, and they answered: "Sire, thou art the sword of the law. We command you, by Mahomet, to order their heads to be cut off." They then made their obeisance and went away. The sultan and the said clerks remained. Then the sultan came towards them and said, "Seignors, they have commanded me, by Mahomet, to order your heads to be cut off; but I shall act contrary to the commandment," &c., &c.

sometimes carried the word of God among savage nations; some went into Africa and Asia, seeking, as their master had done, errors to confute and evils to endure; they frequently planted the cross of Christ upon the lands of the infidels, and in their harmless pilgrimages, constantly repeated the scriptural words, *Peace be with you;* they were only armed with their prayers, and aspired to no glory but that of dying for the faith.

The Crusaders had been encamped seventeen months before the walls of Damietta, and not a single day had passed without a murderous conflict. The Mussulmans, although they had obtained some advantages, began to lose all hope of triumphing over an enemy proof against the evils of war and an unhealthy climate. Report proclaimed the approaching arrival of the emperor of Germany, who had taken the cross, and this news, whilst it sustained the courage of the Christians, made the Mussulmans tremble at the idea of having to contend with the most powerful of the monarchs of the West. The sultan of Damascus, in the name of all the princes of his family, sent ambassadors to the camp of the Crusaders to ask for peace. He offered to abandon to the Franks the city and kingdom of Jerusalem, and only to reserve to themselves the places of Krak and Montréal, for which they proposed to pay a tribute. As the ramparts and towers of the holy city had been recently destroyed, the Mussulmans engaged to pay two hundred thousand dinars to re-establish them; they further agreed to give up all Christians made prisoners since the death of Saladin.

The principal leaders of the Christian army were called together to deliberate upon the proposals of the Mussulmans. The king of Jerusalem, the French barons, the English, Dutch, and Germans, were of opinion that the terms should be acceded to, and the peace accepted: the king of Jerusalem would regain his kingdom, and the barons of the West would see the happy end of a war that had detained them so long from their homes.

"By accepting the peace they attained the object of the crusade,—the deliverance of the holy places. The Christian warriors had besieged Damietta during seventeen months, and the siege might be still prolonged. Many Crusaders daily returned to Europe; whilst crowds of Mussulman warriors as constantly joined the standards of the sultans of Cairo and Damascus. If they should take Damietta, they would be but too happy to exchange it for Jerusalem. The Mussulmans offered to give, before victory, quite as much as they could demand after having subdued them. It was not wise to refuse that which fortune offered to bestow upon them without conflicts or perils. The effusion of blood should be avoided, and they ought to reflect that victories purchased by the death of the soldiers of the cross, were such as were most acceptable to the God of the Christians."

The king of Jerusalem and most of the barons spoke thus, and endeavoured to bring to their opinion the Italian nobles and the body of the prelates, whom Cardinal Pelagius led in an opposite direction. The legate of the pope regarded himself as the head of this war, and he wished it to continue, in order to prolong his power and to procure for him additional renown. "He could see nothing in the proposals of the enemy but a new artifice to delay the capture of Damietta, and gain time. The Saracens offered nothing but desert countries and demolished cities, which would fall again into their power. Their only object was to disarm the Christians, and furnish them with a pretext for returning into the West. Things had gone too far to allow them to retreat without dishonour. It was disgraceful for Christians to renounce the conquest of a city they had besieged seventeen months, and which could hold out no longer. They must take possession of it first, and then they should know what was best to be done—once masters of Damietta, the Crusaders might conclude a glorious peace, and reap all the advantages of victory."

The motives alleged by Cardinal Pelagius were not unreasonable, but the spirit of party and faction reigned in the council of the leaders of the crusade. As it always happens in similar circumstances, every one formed his opinion not upon that which he believed to be useful and just, but upon that which appeared most favourable to the party he had embraced; some advised that the siege should be prosecuted, because the king of Jerusalem had offered a contrary opinion; others wished the proposed capitulation should be accepted, because this capitulation was rejected by the legate of the pope. The Christian army exhibited a strange spectacle. On one side, John of Brienne and the most renowned warriors were advocates for peace; on the other, the legate and most of the ecclesiastics demanded with great warmth the continuation of the war: they deliberated during several days without a chance of bringing the two parties to an agreement; and whilst the discussions became more intemperate, hostilities were renewed: then all the Crusaders united to prosecute the siege of Damietta.

The sultan of Cairo employed every means to throw succours into the city, and keep up the courage of the garrison and the inhabitants. Some Mussulman soldiers, taking advantage of the darkness of night, attempted to effect an entrance into the place; a few were able to gain and pass through the gates, but by far the greater number were surprised and massacred by the Crusaders, who kept constant and close watch around the walls.

The news which the sultan, Melic-Kamel, received from Damietta, became every day more alarming; the Mussulman army, not daring to succour the besieged, remained inactive, and confined themselves to the defence of their own intrenchments. Communication was soon entirely cut off between the place and the camp of the infidels; some divers crossed the Nile through the Christian fleet, attained Damietta, and returned to inform the sultan that pestilence, famine, and despair reigned throughout the city. The Mussulmans had recourse to all sorts of stratagems to convey food to the garrison; sometimes they filled leather sacks with provisions, which, being abandoned to the stream of the Nile, floated under the ramparts of the city; at others, they concealed loaves in the sheets that enveloped dead bodies, which, being borne on by the waters, were stopped in their course by the besieged. It was not long before these stratagems were discovered by the Christians, and then famine began to make horrible ravages; the soldiers, overcome by fatigue and weakened by hunger, had not the strength to fight or guard the towers and ramparts. The inhabitants, given up to despair, abandoned their houses, and fled from a city that presented nothing but images of death: many came to implore the pity of the Crusaders. The commander of Damietta, whose name history has not perserved, in vain endeavoured to keep up the courage of the people and the soldiers. To prevent desertion, he caused the gates of the city to be walled up; and from that period neither the sultan of Cairo nor the Crusaders were able to know what was passing in the besieged place, in which a dismal silence reigned, and which, according to the expression of an Arabian author, *was no longer anything but a closed sepulchre.*

The Christians had placed their machines at the foot of a tower, and as they saw no one defending it, the legate, at the head of the Italian Crusaders, took advantage of a dark and stormy night to penetrate within the first inclosure of the walls. The king of Jerusalem and the other leaders resolved at the same time to make an assault and enter the city, sword in hand. As soon as day appeared, the boldest ascended into the tower, which they found deserted, and called aloud upon their companions to join them. The Christian army applauded their success, and answered by shouts of joy; the soldiers flew to arms, and instantly put the rams in motion. The walls were scaled, the gates were beaten to pieces, and a passage opened; the eager Crusaders rushed forward with naked swords and ready lances to encounter the enemy; but when they penetrated into the streets, a pestilential odour enveloped them, and a frightful spectacle made them recoil with horror! The public places, the mosques, the houses, the whole city, were strewed with dead! Old age, infancy, ripened manhood, maiden beauty, matronly grace—all had perished in the horrors of the siege! At the arrival of the Crusaders, Damietta contained seventy thousand inhabitants; of these only three thousand of the most robust remained, who, ready to expire, glided like pale, fading shadows among tombs and ruins.

This horrible spectacle touched the hearts of the Crusaders, and mingled a feeling of sadness with the joy their victory created. The conquerors found in Damietta immense stores of spices, diamonds, and precious stuffs. When they had pillaged the city, it might have been believed, says an historian, that the warriors of the West had conquered Persia, Arabia, and the Indies. The ecclesiastics launched the thunders of excommunication against all who secreted any part of the booty; but these menaces had no effect upon the cupidity of the soldiers: all the wealth brought to the public stock only produced two hundred thousand crowns, which were distributed among the troops of the victorious army.

Damietta boasted a celebrated mosque, ornamented by six vast galleries and a hundred and fifty columns of marble, surmounted by a superb dome, which towered above all the other edifices of the city. This mosque, in which, on the preceding evening, Mussulmans had lifted their imploring, tearful eyes to their prophet, was consecrated to the virgin mother of Christ, and the whole Christian army came thither to offer up thanks to Heaven for the triumph granted to their arms. On the following day the barons and prelates assembled in the same place, to deliberate upon their conquest; and, by a unanimous resolution, the city of Damietta was assigned to the king of Jerusalem. They then turned their attention to the fate of the unfortunate inhabitants who had escaped pestilence and famine. James of Vitri, when describing the miseries of Damietta, and speaking of the horrible famine which swept away so many families during the siege, sheds tears over the little children who in vain asked their dead parents for bread. The fate of such of those as remained alive inspired the virtuous bishop of Ptolemaïs with pity, and he purchased many of them, in order to have them baptised and brought up in the Christian religion. The pious charity of the prelate, however, could only procure them eternal life, for they almost all died after having been baptised. All the Mussulmans who had sufficient strength to work received liberty and bread, and were employed in cleansing and purifying the city. Whilst the leaders were thus watching over a mourning city, and gave their anxious attentions to prevent new calamities, the spectacle that Damietta presented, and the empoisoned air they breathed within its walls, obliged the Christian army to return to their camp, and wait for the time at which the conquered city might be inhabited without danger.

When the news of the taking of Damietta was spread through Syria and Upper Egypt, the Mussulman nations, seized with terror, flew to their mosques to implore the intervention of their prophet against the enemies of Islamism. The sultans of Cairo and Damascus sent ambassadors to the caliph of Bagdad, conjuring him to exhort all true believers to take arms to defend the religion of Mahomet. The caliph contemplated with grief the calamities about to fall upon the princes of the family of Saladin; but other dangers threatened him more nearly. Tartar hordes had issued from their mountains, invaded several provinces of Persia, and were advancing towards the Euphrates. The caliph, far from being able to assist the Mussulmans of Syria and Egypt by his prayers and exhortations, invoked their succour to defend his capital, and turn aside the storm ready to burst over the whole East. When the Mussulman ambassadors returned to Damascus and Cairo, their accounts added new alarms to those which the conquests of the Christians had already inspired.

The Ayoubite princes, however, did not delay endeavouring to unite all their efforts against the Crusaders, postponing, to a more favorable moment, the defence of the head of Islamism. The Mussulman nations had a much greater dread of the invasion of the Christians than of the irruptions of the hordes of Tartary. The conquerors whom nations fear the most, are those that desire to change the laws and religion of the conquered country. The Tartars, whose habits and manners were not formed, easily complied with those of the people they subdued; the Christians, on the contrary, only made war to destroy all and enslave all. Already rich cities, great provinces, were in their power: everything had changed its form under their domination. Thus the Mussulman princes and people, from the Euphrates to the Red Sea, forgot or neglected the storm which growled over Persia and was advancing slowly towards Syria, and resolved to take arms against the Crusaders, who were masters of the Nile.

After the taking of Damietta, the Mussulman soldiers who defended Egypt were struck with such excessive fear, that, during several days, not one of them durst face a Christian soldier. The Egyptian warriors who guarded the fortress of Tannis, built beyond the lake Menzaleh, abandoned their ramparts at the approach of a few Crusaders, and thus one of the firmest bulwarks of the Mussulman empire fell without defence into the hands of the Franks. From that time, the Christians had reason to believe they had no more enemies on the banks of the Nile; and, during the rigours of winter, many of the pilgrims returned to Europe. Half the army took advantage of the March passage to quit Egypt; such as remained under the banners of the crusade forgot the labours and perils of war, and gave themselves up to indulgence and voluptuousness, to all the pleasure which the approach of spring, and the fine climate and beautiful sky of Damietta inspired.

During the leisure of peace, the divisions which had so often interrupted the course of the war, soon revived; the taking of Damietta had inflamed the pride of Cardinal Pelagius, who, in the Christian army, spoke as a conqueror and commanded as a master. The king of Jerusalem was so dissatisfied, that he abandoned a city that had been given to him, and quitted an army of which he was the head, to retire to Ptolemaïs.

New Crusaders, however, eager to signalize their valour against the Mussulmans, arrived daily. The duke of Bavaria, with four hundred German knights and barons, sent by Frederick II., landed on the banks of the Nile. A short time afterwards, the Christian army received into its ranks Crusaders from Milan, Pisa, and Genoa, and prelates and archbishops conducted a crowd of defenders of the cross, who came from the various provinces of Germany, and from France and Italy. The sovereign pontiff had neglected nothing to secure the success of the holy war; he sent to Cardinal Pelagius provisions for the army, and a considerable sum of money, partly from his own treasury, and partly from the charity of the faithful of the West. The legate was desirous of profiting by the succours he had just received, and proposed to follow up the war, and march directly against the capital of Egypt. The clergy adopted the advice of Pelagius, but such of the Crusaders as saw with disgust a prelate at the head of warriors, refused to take up arms. The duke of Bavaria and the barons and knights would acknowledge no leader but the king of Jerusalem; the legate Pelagius was obliged to send deputies to John of Brienne, who, pressed by the pope himself, was at length prevailed upon, and consented, after an absence of several months, to come back and take the command of the army.

Whilst the Crusaders remained thus in inaction, all the Mussulmans were flying to arms: the sultans of Damascus and Aleppo, the princes of Hamah, Balbec, and of Arabia, assembled fresh armies. After the taking of Damietta, the sultan of Cairo had retired, with his troops, to the spot where the two eastern branches of the Nile separate: there he daily beheld troops of Mussulman warriors join his standard, and, awaiting a favourable opportunity, he constructed a palace in the centre of his camp, surrounded by walls.

The Mussulmans there built houses, baths, and bazaars, and the camp of the sultan became a city, called Mansourah, which was destined to be celebrated in history by the defeat and ruin of the Christian armies.

As soon as the king of Jerusalem returned to Damietta, the leaders of the Crusaders assembled in council, to deliberate upon what they had to do: the legate of the pope was the first to offer his opinion, and proposed to march against the capital of Egypt. "We must attack the evil at its source, and, in order to conquer the Saracens, destroy the foundation of their power. Egypt supplies them with soldiers, provisions, and arms. By taking possession of Egypt, we should cut off all their resources. At no period were the soldiers of the cross animated by more zeal; never were the infidels more depressed. To lose such an opportunity was to betray the common cause. When a great empire was attacked, prudence commanded the assailants not to lay down their arms till they had subdued it; by stopping after the first victory, they exhibited more weakness than moderation. The eyes of the whole Christian world were upon the army of the Crusaders; it was not only the deliverance of the holy places that was looked for from their valour, but the death of all the enemies of Christ, the destruction of every nation that had imposed a sacrilegious yoke upon the city of God."

The bishops, the prelates and most of the ecclesiastics were loud in their applause of the speech of the legate; but John of Brienne, who did not at all partake of their opinion, arose, and protesting his devotion to the cause of Christ, began by appealing to the assembly, if any one could be more interested in the conquests of the Christians in the East, than the man who had the honour to be king of Jerusalem. He then pointed out how imprudent it would be to go up the Nile at the very moment at which that river was beginning to overflow, and would most likely inundate the roads which led to Cairo. "Mark," said he, "all the perils of the expedition proposed to you. We are to march into an unknown land, through the midst of an enemy's country: if conquered, there can be no place of asylum for us; if conquerors, our victories will only weaken our army. However easy it may be for us to conquer provinces, it will be almost impossible for us to defend them. The Crusaders, always eager to return to Europe, are incalculably more serviceable in gaining battles than in securing the possession of conquered countries. Nobody can suppose, that with the brave bands that surround us, we entertain any fear of the Mussulman armies which are gathering together from all parts; but in order to secure our safety, we must not only subdue our enemies, we must destroy them—we have not to deal with an army, but with an entire nation animated by despair. The whole Mussulman race are about to become so many intrepid soldiers, impatient to shed their blood in the field of battle. But what do I say? we shall have much less to dread from their courage than from their timid prudence. They will not fail to shun the fight, and will wait until diseases, want, fatigue, discord, the inconstancy of men's minds, the overflowing of the Nile, and the heat of the climate shall have triumphed over our efforts and secured the failure of all our enterprises."

John of Brienne strengthened his opinion by other motives, with which his knowledge of the art of war supplied him, and terminated his speech by saying, "That Damietta and Tannis were powerful enough to restrain the people of Egypt; that it was necessary to recapture the cities they had lost, before they thought of conquering countries that had never been in their possession; and that, in short, they had not assembled under the banners of the cross to besiege Thebes, Babylon, or Memphis, but to deliver Jerusalem, which opened its gates to the Christians, and which they could fortify against all the attacks of the infidels."

This moderate and pacific language would well have become the mouth of an envoy of the pope; but Pelagius listened to the king of Jerusalem with the most evident impatience: he answered, that weakness and timidity screened themselves behind the veil of moderation and prudence; that Christ did not summon to his defence such wise and far-sighted soldiers, but warriors who sought for battle rather than for reasons, and who could see the glory of an enterprise, and be blind to its dangers.

The legate added several more reasons to those he had already advanced, and expressed them with great bitterness; at length, led away by the heat of the discussion, he threatened all those who did not partake of his opinions with excommunication. Most of the leaders, and the king of Jerusalem himself, fearing to be excommunicated, but dreading much more to see the least suspicion cast upon their bravery, at length yielded to the obstinate will of Pelagius: the council of the barons and the bishops decided that the Christian army should leave Damietta, and march against the capital of Egypt.

This army, composed of more than seventy thousand men advanced up the banks of the Nile. A numerous fleet, laden with provisions, arms, and machines of war, ascended the river at the same time. The Christian army passed through Farescour and several other villages, that had been abandoned by their inhabitants; all fled away at the approach of the Crusaders, who began to believe they should meet with no obstacle to their victories, and celebrated, beforehand, the conquest of Memphis and Cairo. The legate of the pope exulted in the resolution he had dictated to the Christian army; and, full of confidence in the prediction that had been made concerning him in his youth, the presumptuous cardinal flattered himself that he was about to overthrow the worship of Mahomet; and indulged in the most insulting railleries against those who had been opposed to the war. Without fighting a single battle, the Christians gained the extremity of the Delta, at the angle formed by the arm of the river which descends towards Damietta and the canal of Almon, whose waters flow into the sea on the eastern side. The Saracens were encamped in the plain of Mansourah, on the opposite bank of the river: the Crusaders halted on the hither shore, and their fleet cast anchor as near to them as possible.

The sultan of Damascus, and the princes of Aleppo, Balbec, Hamah, and Bosra, had united their troops with those of the sultan of Cairo. The Nile, whose bank was covered with intrenchments, presented a barrier very difficult to be overcome. But Melic-Kamel did not dare to match himself with the Crusaders; dreading their rash bravery, so accustomed to sport with perils and triumph over all obstacles. Reports of the arrival of Frederick, and of the approach of the Tartars, kept the Mussulmans in a continual state of alarm, and made them anxious to terminate a war which exhausted their resources, consumed their strength, and did not promise them, even in victory, a compensation for so many efforts and so many sacrifices.

Ambassadors were sent to propose peace to the leaders of the Christian army: the Mussulmans offered their enemies, if they would consent to an entire cessation of hostilities, to give up to them Damietta and its territories, and to restore Jerusalem, with all the places of Palestine that had been conquered by Saladin.

These conditions assured to the Christians all the advantages of both war and peace. The king of Jerusalem, and most of the barons, who saw the difficulties and perils of the expedition they had entered upon, listened with as much surprise as joy to the proposals of the infidels, and did not hesitate to accept them; but they had absolutely no power in the army. The legate, who exercised an arbitrary authority, and who was constantly dreaming of conquests, persisted in thinking that these pacific proposals were only the effects of fear, and that the enemy who sued for peace was the one with whom war should be prosecuted with most spirit.

The ambassadors returned to the camp of the Mussulmans, to announce that the Christians refused the peace: their account excited indignation, and indignation roused courage. When the Ayoubite princes proposed peace, they were in possession of ample means to carry on the war with advantage; they every day received reinforcements, and their camp rapidly assumed a more formidable aspect; but soon a terrible auxiliary, against whose attacks Pelagius had no defence, came to the assistance of the Mussulmans, and procured them a complete triumph without either battles or danger.

The Christian warriors, who flattered themselves they had now only to deal with a conquered enemy, were satisfied with surrounding their camp with a ditch and a wall; the army remained for several days in this position, without making an effort either to attack the Saracens or pass the Nile. Pelagius, who was constantly promising victory to his soldiers, remained, nevertheless, in a state of inactivity in his tent. During this period, many of the Crusaders grew weary of a war in which no battles were fought; some fancied that the cause no longer stood in need of their assistance; whilst others, with more foresight, feared coming reverses: more than ten thousand Crusaders abandoned the camp and returned to Damietta.

The Christian army had been for more than a month in face of the enemy, always in expectation of the victories that had been promised to them. At length, the overflowing of the Nile, in a most alarming manner, disturbed their imagined security. The Saracens opened the sluices, and filled all the canals of Lower Egypt. The Mussulman fleet, which had not been able to ascend the Nile by Damietta, took advantage of the canals, and came up with the Christian ships. In a single engagement, the vessels of the Crusaders were almost all dispersed and consumed by the Greek fire: from that moment terror seized upon the Christians, for they were in want of provisions, and had neither means nor hopes of obtaining any. The Saracens, after having crossed the Nile on bridges, occupied all the circumjacent hills. The Christian soldiers wandered about the fields at hazard, pursued by the waves of the rising river, and by the Mussulmans, whose bravery they had so lately held in contempt. The whole army was on the point of being submerged or perishing with hunger, and had no hope but in the clemency of an enemy with whom they had recently refused to make peace.

In this extremity, the king of Jerusalem and the principal leaders of the Christians sent several of their knights to offer the Saracens battle; but the latter were neither sufficiently imprudent, nor sufficiently generous to accept a proposal dictated by despair. The Crusaders were exhausted with hunger and fatigue; the cavalry sunk into, and encumbered by mud and slime, could neither advance nor retreat; the foot-soldiers cast away their arms; the baggage of the army floated away upon the waters, and nothing was heard but groans and lamentations. "When the Christian warriors," says an Arabian historian, "saw nothing before them but death, their minds sank into a state of despondency, and their backs bent beneath the rod of God, *to whom be all praise!*"

Pelagius must then have been sensible of the full extent of his error: his project of marching to Cairo had, doubtless, something great in it, if it could have been executed; but the presumptuous legate disdained all counsels, all lessons of experience, and foresaw none of the obstacles he was certain to meet with on his route; he conducted an army filled with discontent; the soldiers had neither that confidence nor that enthusiasm that leads men to brave dangers or cheerfully encounter fatigue. The king of Jerusalem, the duke of Bavaria, and a great number of the barons were his personal enemies, and took very little interest in the success of an enterprise of which they had disapproved.

Amidst the cries and lamentations of an army to which he had promised victory, Pelagius was obliged to negotiate for peace, and his pride humbled itself so far as to implore the clemency of the Saracens. Christian ambassadors, among whom was the bishop of Ptolemaïs, went to propose a capitulation to the conquerors; they offered to give up the city of Damietta, and only asked for the Christian army liberty to return to Ptolemaïs.

The Mussulman princes assembled in council to deliberate upon the proposals of the Crusaders. Some were of opinion they should be accepted; others declared that all the Christians ought to be made prisoners of war. Among those who proposed the harshest measures, the sultan of Damascus,

THE BAPTISM OF INFIDELS.

an implacable enemy of the Franks, was conspicuous. "No treaty can be made," said he, "with warriors without humanity and without faith. We should remember their barbarities in war and their treachery in peace. They armed themselves to ravage provinces, to destroy cities, and overthrow the worship of Mahomet. Since fortune has placed these most cruel enemies of Islamism, these devastators of the East, in the hands of *the true believers*, we ought to immolate them to the safety of the Mussulman nations, and take an advantage of our victory that will create a terror among the people of the West for ever."

Most of the princes and emirs, animated by fanaticism and vengeance, applauded this violent speech. The sultan of Cairo, more moderate, and, doubtless, more prescient than the other leaders, dreading likewise the arrival of Frederick and the invasion of the Tartars, combated the opinion of the sultan of Damascus, and advised that the capitulation of the Franks should be accepted. "All the Franks were not comprised in this army now in their power; other Crusaders guarded Damietta, and might be able to defend it; the Mussulmans had sustained a siege of eight months, the Christians might hold out as long. It was more advantageous for the princes of the family of Saladin to return to their cities than to retain a few of their enemies in chains. If they destroyed one Christian army, the West, to avenge the defeat of its warriors, was able to send numberless legions into the East. They ought not to forget that the Mussulman armies had lost a portion of that spirit of obedience and discipline that was the sole guarantee of victory; that they were worn out with fatigue, and sighed for repose. Other enemies than the now disarmed Christians, other perils than those they had just escaped, might soon hang over both Syria and Egypt. It was wise to make peace at this moment, in order to prepare for fresh contests, for new wars, perhaps much more cruel than that which they had now an opportunity of terminating with so much glory to the Mussulman arms."

The speech of Melik-Kamel brought back the princes of his family to sentiments of moderation. The capitulation was accepted; the sultan of Cairo sent his own son to the camp of the Christians as a pledge for his word. The king of Jerusalem, the duke of Bavaria, the legate of the pope, and the principal leaders repaired to the camp of the Saracens, and remained as hostages till the accomplishment of the treaty.

When the deputies of the imprisoned army came to Damietta and announced the disasters and captivity of the Christians, their account drew tears from the crowd of Crusaders who at that time arrived from the West. When these same deputies informed them that the city must be given up to the infidels, the most intrepid of the Franks could not restrain their indignation, and refused to recognise a treaty so disgraceful to the soldiers of the cross. The greatest tumult prevailed throughout the city. Some, filled with despair, determined to return to Europe, and prepared to desert the banners of the cross; others ran towards the ramparts, and getting possession of the towers, swore to defend them.

A few days after, fresh deputies arrived to declare that the king of Jerusalem and the other leaders of the army would be obliged to give up Ptolemaïs to the Mussulmans if they refused to surrender Damietta. In order to overcome the obstinate resistance of those who wished to defend the city, and who reproached the imprisoned army with disgracing the Christians, they added, that this army, though defeated, had obtained a prize worthy of their former exploits, for the Saracens had engaged to restore to them the true cross of the Saviour, which had fallen into the hands of Saladin at the battle of Tiberias. The fear of losing Ptolemaïs, the hope of regaining the cross of Christ, together with the speeches of the deputies, brought back the spirit of peace and resignation to the minds of the most ardent of the Crusaders, and disposed them to the performance of the conditions of the treaty.

In the mean time, the Christian army having lost their tents and their baggage, passed many days and many nights in a plain covered with the waters of the Nile. Hunger, disease, and inundation threatened their entire destruction. The king of Jerusalem, then in the camp of the Saracens, upon being informed of the horrible distress of the Christians, went to conjure Melik-Kamel to have pity on his disarmed enemies. The continuator of William of Tyre, who is our guide in this part of our history, reports, in his old, quaint language, the touching interview between John of Brienne and the sultan of Egypt. "The king sat down before the sultan, and began to weep; the sultan, on seeing the king weep, said, 'Sire, why do you weep?' 'Sire, I have good cause,' replied the king, 'for I behold the people whom God has confided to me perishing amidst the waters, and dying with hunger.' The sultan felt great pity at seeing the king weep, and he wept also; then he sent thirty thousand loaves to the poor as well as the rich; and sent the same quantity daily during four days."

Melik-Kamel caused the sluices to be closed, and the waters rapidly retired from the plain; as soon as Damietta was surrendered to the Mussulmans, the Christian army began its retreat. The Crusaders, who owed their liberty and lives to the mercy of the Saracens, passed through the city which had cost them so many conflicts and so much labour; and, weeping, quitted the banks of the Nile, where so short a time before they had sworn to make the cause of Christ triumphant. They bore away in sadness the wood of the true cross, the identity of which they had reason to suspect, since it no longer performed miracles, and was not for them now the signal of victory. The sultan of Egypt caused them to be accompanied by his son, who had orders to provide for all their wants on their route. The Saracen leaders were impatient to get rid of an army that had threatened their empire; they could scarcely give credit to their own triumph, and some little apprehension was, no doubt, mingled with the pity with which their conquered enemies inspired them.

Great rejoicings had been made at Ptolemaïs for the victories obtained by the Christians on the banks of the Nile; they believed that they already saw the holy places delivered, and the empire of the Saracens destroyed. Consternation took place of their joy on seeing the army return. As in all the other reverses which their arms had met with, the Christians mutually reproached each other with their defeat; they accused the leaders of ambition, and the king of Jerusalem of weakness; the Templars and Hospitallers, who had on all occasions set an example of courage and the most generous devotedness, were obliged to make a public apology for their conduct. When it became known in the West that Damietta had fallen again into the hands of the Saracens, all the faithful were affected by the deepest grief, and sought, by their prayers, to mitigate the anger of Heaven. Violent murmurs arose against the legate Pelagius, and represented him to the sovereign pontiff as the author of all the disasters of the crusade; but Honorius was not willing to condemn his minister, and reproached Frederick, who had three times renewed his vow to fight against the infidels, with having remained an idle spectator of an unfortunate war, and with having neglected to succour his brethren of the East.

Frederick, who had sent vessels, provisions, and soldiers to the holy war, thought that he had fully performed his part in the crusade, and was at first much astonished at the reproaches of the Holy See. When the pope threatened him with the anger of Heaven and the thunders of Rome, he could not restrain his indignation; in his letters the emperor complains bitterly of the tyranny of both Innocent and Honorius, and talks of opposing war to war, and vengeance to injustice. After this, Honorius, who acted less from the dictates of his own mind than after the policy of his predecessors, changed his tone, attempted to justify both Innocent and himself, and, employing prayers instead of menaces, conjured Frederick to have pity on the Church of the East.

This paternal language appeased Frederick; in an interview which he had with the pope at

Veroli, the emperor of Germany repeated his vow to repair to Palestine at the head of an army. In another assembly, which was held some time afterwards at Verona, the Pope endeavoured to engage Frederick, on account of his own interests; he proposed to him to espouse Yolande, daughter of John of Brienne, and heir to the kingdom of Jerusalem. The grand masters of the Templars, the Hospitallers, and the Teutonic order, with the patriarch and the king of Jerusalem, all summoned to Italy to deliberate on the affairs of the crusade, approved of a union which would secure them the assistance of a powerful monarch. Frederick accepted a kingdom which he promised to defend, and consented to undergo excommunication if he failed in his promises.

After the conference of Verona, King John of Brienne visited the principal states of Europe, for the purpose of soliciting aid for the Holy Land. At the time of John's arrival in France, the French were mourning the death of Philip Augustus. The king of Jerusalem assisted at the funeral ceremonies of his master and benefactor, who, at his death, had bequeathed three thousand silver marks to the defenders of Palestine. After having paid the last duties to Philip, John went first to England, and afterwards to Germany, in both of which countries his presence and his discourses strongly moved Christians with the misfortunes of the Holy Land.

The emperor Frederick, on his part, made all the requisite preparations for an expedition which he was to lead in person; he ordered vessels to be constructed in all the ports of Sicily for transporting the Crusaders. "Heaven and earth," wrote he to the pope, "are witnesses that I desire the success of the Christian arms with my whole soul, and that I will neglect nothing that can assist in securing the success of the holy enterprise." In all his letters Frederick exhorted the sovereign pontiff to employ every means to augment the numbers of the soldiers of Christ. Become, all at once, more zealous for the crusade than the pope himself, he reproached the court of Rome with being sparing in indulgences, and with confiding the preaching of the crusade to vulgar orators; he advised the pope to redouble his efforts to appease the quarrels of Christian princes, and to compel the kings of France and England to sign a peace, in order that the nobles and people of these two kingdoms might take part in the crusade. Frederick not being able to go into Germany, sent thither the grand master of the Teutonic order, with directions to exhort the landgrave of Thuringia, the duke of Austria, the king of Hungary, and the other princes of the empire, to take the oath to fight against the infidels. He undertook to furnish the Crusaders with vessels, provisions, arms, and everything necessary for the expedition beyond the sea; in short, he displayed so much activity, and showed so much ardour and zeal, that all the attention of the Christians was directed towards him, and he was considered as the soul, the moving principle, and the head of the holy enterprise.

The Christians of Palestine placed all their hopes in him; the patriarch of Alexandria, in a letter to the pope, said that they looked for the emperor of Germany on the banks of the Nile and the Jordan, *as formerly the saints had looked for the coming of the Messiah or Saviour of the world.* The patriarch spoke with grief of the oppression and servitude that had been inflicted upon the Christians established in Egypt since the last invasion of the Crusaders. The unfortunate disciples of Christ were not allowed to keep in their dwellings either arms or horses, nor even to bear a crucifix at the funeral processions of their relations; a hundred and fifteen of their churches had been destroyed since the conquest of Damietta. Oppressed by tributes, condemned to disgraceful labours, banished from their homes, wandering around their temples and their altars, they invoked the mercy of Heaven and the valour of the warriors of the West for their deliverance.

The report of Frederick's preparations was spread even to the remote nations of Georgia; and the queen of that country wrote to the head of the Church of Rome, that the constable of her kingdom and a great number of warriors only waited for the arrival of the emperor of Germany, to fly to the assistance of Palestine. The Georgians had the reputation of being a warlike people, and were dreaded by the Mussulmans; their pilgrims enjoyed the privilege of entering Jerusalem without paying the tribute imposed upon other Christians. When the sultan of Damascus caused the ramparts of the holy city to be destroyed, the warriors of Georgia swore to avenge the outrage committed on the city of God; but an invasion of the Tartars prevented them from leaving their own territories. Since that period, the hordes of Tartary having directed their ravages towards other countries, the Crusaders of Caucasus and the shores of the Caspian Sea promised to unite themselves in the plains of Syria and Egypt, with the Crusaders from the banks of the Rhine and the Danube.

Frederick, however, was not yet in a position to perform his so often repeated promises; the kingdom of Sicily and Naples contained germs of discord and rebellion; the republics of Lombardy were openly opposed to the emperor of Germany; and the Holy See, which observed with anxiety the ambitious projects of Frederick upon Italy, encouraged all the enemies of a power of which it dreaded the too close neighbourhood. Thus, the policy of the court of Rome, the revolts of Sicily, and the enterprises of the Italian republics, would not allow the emperor to lead his armies into Asia. Frederick demanded of the pope the indulgence of a delay of two years for the performance of his vow; founding his request upon the length of time required for assembling his armies, and declared that he was not willing to begin the war before the expiration of the truce made with the Mussulmans; thus showing much more respect for treaties with infidels, than had till that time been common among Christians, indeed, more respect than he had himself shown. The pope, although much dissatisfied, could not refuse the delay the emperor demanded; he, however, dissembled his anger, and contented himself with requiring fresh promises, which were made, as all the rest had been, with the greatest solemnity.

The new vows of Frederick were strengthened by his marriage with the heir of the king of Jerusalem. The marriage was celebrated at Rome, amidst the benedictions of the clergy and the acclamations of the people; all the Christians of the West heard of it with joy, and this union appeared to them to be the most certain pledge of the victories the Crusaders would gain over the infidels. John of Brienne, who assisted at the ceremony, congratulated himself upon having obtained an emperor for a son-in-law and a supporter; but his joy was not of long duration. Frederick, after his marriage, only saw in him the brother of that Gauthier de Brienne, who had borne the title of king of Naples and Sicily; he considered him as an enemy to his power, a dangerous rival, and he disputed the possession of the kingdom of Jerusalem with him. The pope was secretly pleased at this claim or pretension, as he hoped it would promote the interests of the crusade. Honorius was delighted to see the ambition of the emperor mix itself up with the great designs for the execution of which he was so anxious. Frederick was therefore acknowledged king of Jerusalem. Thus John of Brienne, who had always proved himself the most ardent apostle of the holy war, deprived of his crown, and from that time a stranger to the affairs of Palestine, was obliged to wait in retirement and silence for a favourable opportunity to avenge himself on his son-in-law, and recover his kingdom.

Frederick carried on his preparations for the holy war, and appeared more than ever disposed to set out for the East. The crusade was preached in the name of the head of the Church, in all the kingdoms of Europe; the sovereign pontiff wrote to the princes to exhort them to suspend their divisions and occupy themselves solely with the war beyond the sea.

As hostilities had just been renewed between England and France, Honorius ordered Louis VIII. to lay down his arms, and threatened him with excommunication, if he did not immediately make peace. The king of France, before he obeyed the orders of the pope, was desirous of completing the conquest of Poitou; and whilst the thunders of Rome were growling over his head, the people and clergy were returning Heaven thanks for his victories, in every church in his kingdom.

The war against the English was not the only obstacle to the departure of the French Crusaders for the Holy Land; the exterminating crusade against the Albigeois was still going on, and Louis VIII. took a more active interest in it than his father Philip had done. When Louis VIII. had concluded a truce with England, he at length resolved to take the cross, and made a vow, not to go and fight against the Saracens in Asia, but against the heretics in Languedoc. In this crusade the king of France had the double advantage of scarcely going out of his own territories, and of making conquests that might some day enlarge his kingdom. The lords and barons followed Louis into the southern provinces, and thought no more about the deliverance of Jerusalem.

At the same time the envoys of the pope and the emperor were busy in exhorting the nations of Germany to succour the Christians of Palestine. Their orations, which at first had great success, ended by diminishing both confidence and enthusiasm. As the pope had recommended the preachers to be prodigal of the indulgences of the Church, the people beheld with astonishment the greatest criminals take the cross, and swear to expiate their sins by the holy pilgrimage. They remembered that St. Bernard had called thieves and murderers to the defence of Christ; but opinions and morals began to change, and that which had succeeded in the preceding century was now only a source of reproach. The monk of Upsberg, a contemporary author, informs us that the facility granted to the most vicious of mankind to redeem their crimes by taking up arms and the cross, only served to increase great offences, and cool the zeal of the true defenders of Christ.

The orators who preached the crusade in England gathered more fruit from their labours, but owed great part of their success to celestial phenomena, which came very opportunely to second their eloquence. A luminous crucifix, with the marks of the five wounds of the Saviour, appeared suddenly in the heavens. This miraculous spectacle greatly inflamed the enthusiasm of the people; and, if we may believe Matthew Paris, more than sixty thousand English took the oath to arm themselves for the deliverance of the tomb of Christ.

Spain was constantly the seat of a sanguinary war between the Moors and the Christians; the one party supported by warriors from Africa, the other by knights and soldiers from the provinces of France, fought battles every day without destroying their means of either attack or defence: amidst such wars, in which, by turns, Mahomet and Christ were invoked, Spain was not likely to hear or attend to the complaints and appeals of Jerusalem.

Another enthusiasm than that of the crusades,—an ardent desire for liberty,—then agitated the finest countries of Italy. The greater part of the cities, acted upon by jealousy and the other passions of republics, were all at war among themselves; fighting sometimes for territory, and sometimes for independence. In all these small states, parties attacked and pursued each other with fury, and disputed the exercise of power, sword in hand. Some of the cities, principalities, and baronies invoked the authority of the pope, others that of the emperor of Germany; the factions of the Guelphs and the Ghibellines troubled every city, and created divisions in most families. These discords and civil wars naturally turned the attention of Christian nations from the crusades.

The cities of Lombardy had formed a powerful confederacy, which gave Frederick continual cause of inquietude, and detained him in the West; Honorius employed every means in his power to re-establish peace, and direct men's minds towards his darling object; and at last succeeded in getting the Lombard republics to join the emperor of Germany for the deliverance of the holy places.

Although the people had lost some portion of their enthusiasm for the holy war, it was still possible to form a redoubtable army, by gathering together all the warriors that had taken the cross in the various countries of Europe; and the new Crusaders were ordered to meet at the port of Brindisi, where vessels were being prepared to transport them to the East. On their arrival in the kingdom of Naples, the emperor of Germany supplied them with provisions and arms; everything was ready, and the pope was about, at length, to see his wishes accomplished, and receive the reward of all his labours and preachings, when inexorable death deprived Christendom of its head.

Gregory IX., who succeeded him, had all the abilities, the virtues, and the ambition of Innocent III. In the execution of his designs, he feared neither difficulties nor perils; the most violent measures had no terrors for his obstinacy or audacity, when the triumph of his will was in question. Gregory had scarcely ascended the pontifical throne, when the preparations for the holy war engrossed all his thoughts, and became the principal object of his active solicitude.

The Crusaders assembled in Apulia had much to suffer from the influences of the climate and the season; the sovereign pontiff neglected nothing to alleviate their distresses and hasten their departure. He exhorted the emperor to embark, by saying to him, "The Lord has placed you in this world as a cherubim with a flaming sword, to direct those who stray from the way of the tree of life." Frederick at length yielded to the prayers of the pope, and sailed from the port of Brindisi with his fleet and army. Prayers were being put up for the prosperity of his voyage and the success of his expedition, in all the provinces of his empire, when, at the end of three days, being attacked by the malady that had made such ravages in the Christian army, he retraced his course, and landed in the port of Otranto.

Gregory had celebrated the departure of Frederick as a triumph of the Church; he considered his return as an absolute revolt against the Holy See. The little city of Agnani, to which the pope had retired, witnessed the rage of the pontiff, and beheld the birth of that formidable storm which so long disturbed the Christian world. Accompanied by the cardinals and several bishops, Gregory repaired to the principal church, and having mounted the pulpit, before the assembled people, he pronounced a sermon which had for its text, "It is necessary that scandals should arise." After having called upon the prophets, and spoken of the triumph of St. Michael over the dragon, he launched against Frederick all the anathemas of the Church.

The emperor at first sent messengers to the pope to explain and justify his conduct; but the inexorable Gregory refused to listen to them, and complained to all the sovereigns in Europe, representing Frederick as a faithless and perjured prince. He accused him of having consigned his wife Yolande to close imprisonment, in which she died of grief; of having left the Crusaders to perish with hunger, thirst, and heat in the plains of Apulia; and of having, at last, under the frivolous pretext of sickness, violated his oath and deserted the banners of Christ, *in order to return to the customary enjoyments of his kingdom.* He made him many other reproaches; and in his anger called down upon him the maledictions of all Christians.

Frederick, exceedingly irritated, replied to the accusations of Gregory with much bitterness. In his apology, which he sent to all the princes of Christendom, he complained strongly of the usurpations of the Holy See, and exposed, in the most odious colours, the policy and ambitious designs of the court of Rome. "The Church of Rome," said he, "sends legates everywhere, *with power to punish, to suspend, and excommunicate, not with the designs of spreading the word of God, but to heap up money, and reap that which they have not sown.*" The emperor reminded the princes, in his letters, of the violences which the pope had exercised against the count of Thoulouse and the king of England; he said that the domains of the clergy did not now satisfy the ambition of the Holy See, and that the sovereign pontiffs wished to lay their hands upon every kingdom. From that moment open war was declared between the pope and the emperor; neither of them possessed a pacific character or a love of quiet; both were animated by boundless ambition, jealous to excess of their power, implacable in their revenge, and always ready to employ the arms which the Church or fortune placed in their hands. Gregory displayed an indefatigable activity, leaving his enemies no repose, but pursuing them at the same time with the thunders of religion and war. In addition to the arms of eloquence, the pontiff did not disdain to employ satire; the manifestoes which he published against his adversaries constantly recalled the spirit of the denunciations made by the prophets. These denunciations, mixed with obscure allegories, gave to his words a dark and mysterious tone, which caused him to be considered as the interpreter of angry Heaven. Frederick was neither a less able prince nor a less redoubtable enemy: the art of war contained no stratagems or secrets with which he was unacquainted; policy dictated no means that he scrupled to employ. Endowed with all the gifts of mind, and with a keen spirit of raillery, he was as competent to confound his enemies in a discussion, as to conquer them in the field of battle. Descended, on the female side, from those famous Normans who had conquered Sicily and the kingdom of Naples, he united, as they had done, courage with subtlety, and audacity with dissimulation: to please the court of Rome, he had made barbarous laws against heretics; and, now become the enemy of the popes, he did not fear to arm heretics or Saracens against the court of Rome. When the kingdom of Jerusalem was offered to him, he set no great value upon the acquisition; but he accepted it with joy, in order to increase his popularity in the Christian world, and to arm himself, one day, against the sovereign pontiff with a title, which was then held in universal veneration.

A war between such enemies must necessarily prove terrible, and spread desolation and confusion throughout Christendom. Gregory, on his return to Rome, repeated his excommunications in the church of St. Peter; Frederick, in order to revenge himself, seduced into his party most of the Roman nobles, who took up arms, insulted the sovereign pontiff at the very foot of the altar, and compelled him to abandon the capital of the Christian world. The pope, driven from his states, pursued his enemy with more fury than ever; and, availing himself of the formidable authority of the Church, he released the subjects of Frederick from their oath of fidelity, by reminding them that they could owe no obedience to those who *opposed themselves to God and his saints.* On his side, Frederick drove the Templars and Hospitallers from the kingdom of Naples, plundered the churches, and ill-treated all ecclesiastics whom he suspected of being attached to the party of the Holy See. He sent troops to ravage the patrimony of St. Peter, and enlisted the Saracens established in Sicily, under the banners of a Christian prince, to combat the head of the Christian church. The Roman states were ravaged, and given up to the horrors of war. The eyes of all Europe were fixed upon these deplorable scenes, and every one seemed to have forgotten the holy war.

The Christians of Palestine, however, never ceased to implore aid from the West. A letter to the pope from the patriarch of Jerusalem, the bishops of Cæsarea and Bethlehem, and the grand masters of the three military orders, painted in strong colours the despair into which the Christians of the East had fallen, when they learnt that Frederick had deferred his departure. The pope received their complaints with expressions of sorrow and kindness, and communicated them to the faithful with greater zeal, from their furnishing him with a fresh opportunity of accusing the emperor of Germany. But the nations of the West, occupied with their own dangers, and terrified at the sight of the violent storms that had recently burst forth, were not in the least moved by either the lamentations from Palestine or the pressing exhortations of Gregory. In this unfortunate position of European affairs, the Christian colonies, abandoned to themselves and their own feeble resources, and a prey to the greatest disorders, must have been invaded and entirely destroyed, if Providence had not stirred up fresh discords among their enemies.

During the siege of Damietta, the common danger had united the children of Malek-Adel; after victory, ambition resumed the place of fear; and the Ayoubite princes quarreled for the provinces which their union had wrested from the power, or saved from the invasion of the Christians. Conraddin, sultan of Damascus, dreading the views of Melik-Kamel, called Gelaleddin, prince of the vast empire of Carismia, to his aid. The sultan of Cairo, in great apprehension of the consequences of this alliance, turned his eyes towards the princes of the West. During several years, the report alone of the preparations of Frederick had been a source of terror to the Mussulman powers. The emperor of Germany was considered, in the East, as the head of all the nations of Europe. The sultan of Egypt attached the greatest importance to the disarming of a formidable enemy; and as the complaints of the pope, and the report of the discords that had broken out among the Christians, had reached his ears, he conceived a hope of finding in Frederick a sincere ally and a powerful auxiliary.

Melik-Kamel sent presents and ambassadors to the emperor of Germany; he invited Frederick to come into the East, and promised to deliver Jerusalem up to him. This proposition gave the emperor as much surprise as joy; and he, in reply, sent an ambassador into Egypt, to ascertain the exact intentions of the sultan of Cairo, and offer him his friendship. The envoy of Frederick was received at the court of the sultan with the greatest honours, and returned to announce to his master that Melik-Kamel was ready to favour his expedition to Palestine.

This negotiation, with which the pope and the Christians of the West were perfectly unacquainted, made Frederick determine to follow up the project of the crusade: he had, besides, several other motives for not renouncing the Eastern enterprise. He knew that John of Brienne was on the point of returning to Palestine, and resuming possession of the kingdom of Jerusalem. The pope continued to represent him as the enemy of Christ, and the scourge of Christians. To secure the failure of the plan of John of Brienne, and at the same time, reply to the sovereign pontiff in a victorious manner, Frederick resolved to embark for the Holy Land. He was desirous of proclaiming his intention with the greatest pomp; and caused a magnificent throne to be erected in the plain of Barletta, which he ascended in the presence of an immense crowd of spectators. In all the splendour of imperial magnificence, he presented himself invested with the pilgrim's cross, and announced to the assembled people that he was about to set out for Syria. In order to give more solemnity to this pompous ceremony, and affect the hearts of the multitude, the emperor caused his will to be read with a loud voice; and the barons and nobles swore at the foot of the throne, to see that his last commands should be executed, if he should chance to lose his life, either in the perils of the sea or the wars of the East.

When the pope learnt this determination of Frederick's, he sent ecclesiastics to forbid him to embark. The sovereign pontiff reproached the emperor with presenting to the Christian world the scandal of a crusade directed by a prince reproved of God: as the fleet of Frederick consisted of only twenty galleys, and as he took with him only six hundred knights, Gregory reproached him with not having fulfilled his promises, and compared his imprudent attempts to the expedition of a captain of pirates. The emperor did not condescend to make any reply to the messengers of the pope; the more opposition the head of the Church gave to his departure, the more impatient Frederick appeared to set out and accomplish his design: in his indignation, he congratulated himself at having to brave the anger of the Church and the arms of the Saracens at the same time. He left the greater part of his army in Sicily; charging his lieutenant, the duke of Spoleto, to negotiate for peace with the pope, but at the same time to carry on the war commenced against the Roman states with unabated vigour.

When he heard of the departure of the emperor, Gregory was in the little city of Assisi, occupied in the canonization of St. Francis. During several days, he had sung nothing but hymns of hope and joy: "Francis," said he, "had appeared like the star of morning, like the orb of day, like the moon in its splendour." This language of peace, this festive pomp, were all at once interrupted by the maledictions that the pope pronounced against Frederick: the sovereign pontiff repaired to the foot of the altar, and there implored Heaven to confound the pride of impious monarchs, and frustrate all their sacrilegious enterprises.

The emperor, notwithstanding, arrived safely on the coast of Syria, and was received at Ptolemaïs by the patriarch, the clergy, and the grand masters of the military orders. For some days, the Christians of the East viewed him as the liberator and the king of Jerusalem; but a change speedily took place. Two disciples of St. Francis, sent by the pope, came to announce to the faithful that they had received a prince rebellious to the will of the Church. From that moment, contempt, hatred, and mistrust took place of respect and submission. They began by perceiving that Frederick was followed by only a small number of warriors, and that he had not troops enough to render him formidable to either the Saracens or the Christians. Nothing was talked of in Ptolemaïs but the excommunication of the pope, and the means of withdrawing themselves from obedience to a heretic prince: never had the deliverance of Jerusalem been less thought of.

At the moment in which Frederick arrived in Syria, Conraddin, sultan of Damascus, died; and the death of this prince gave birth to more discords among the Mussulman powers. The principality of Damascus was governed by a young inexperienced prince; and the spirit of license and insubordination, which had, in the last wars, been already observed among the troops of Syria and Egypt, made, every day, greater progress, and put all the Mussulman thrones in peril.

The sultan of Cairo, when informed of the arrival of Frederick, came into Palestine, at the head of an army. Some asserted that he came to defend Jerusalem, and to fight with the Christians; but his true design was to take advantage of the chances of war, and of the discords which everywhere prevailed, to get possession of Damascus, and defeat the plans of the enemies that jealousy and ambition had raised up against him among the Mussulmans and princes of his family.

The emperor of Germany marched out of Ptolemaïs, at the head of his small army, and directed his course towards the mountains of Naplouse. He had sent Count Thomas de Celano to Melik-Kamel, to remind him of his promises, and to tell him, that, being master of the most vast provinces of the West, he was not come into Asia for the purpose of making conquests; that he had no other design but that of visiting the holy places, and taking possession of the kingdom of Jerusalem, which belonged to him. The sultan received the ambassador of Frederick with due respect; but whether he was ashamed to make peace before he had begun the war, or whether he feared to draw upon himself the hatred of the Mussulmans, by showing too much deference for a Christian prince, he at first made no reply to the propositions that were made to him.

Nevertheless the two princes sent fresh ambassadors, charged on both sides to express a desire for peace; both were placed in embarrassing circumstances, being surrounded by enemies who blamed their proceedings, and did not allow them to publish all their sentiments freely. The Mussulman army from Damascus, encamped in the neighbourhood of Jerusalem, watched all the movements of the sultan of Egypt, and seemed much more disposed to fight with him than to repulse the Christians. The emperor of Germany found himself in the presence of two hostile armies, and that which he himself commanded inspired him with no more confidence than he inspired in it. The Hospitallers and Templars had left him, and followed him at a distance; in the camp of the Christians no one durst pronounce the name of the prince who commanded the army. Frederick had been obliged to withdraw the standard of the empire, and his orders were only issued to the soldiers of the cross in the name of God and of the Christian republic.

In this difficult situation, Frederick and Melik-Kamel were equally sensible of the necessity for peace, and of the danger of commencing war; they therefore gave more employment to their ambassadors than to their soldiers; this crusade was nothing but a long negotiation, disapproved of by both Christians and infidels. As the two sovereigns covered their policy with a veil of profound mystery, it was easy for hatred to spread and procure countenance for sinister reports. Criminal intentions were discovered in the simplest actions. In the Christian army it was conceived that Frederick had committed a crime by sending his sword and cuirass to the sultan of Cairo, as a pledge of his wish for peace. Among the Mussulmans, Melik-Kamel was reproached with seeking an alliance with the enemies of Islamism, by sending to the leader of the Franks an elephant, some camels, and the rarest productions of Arabia, India, and Egypt. The scandal reached its height when the emperor received as a present from the sultan of Cairo, a troop of girls, brought up, according to the custom of the Orientals, to sing and dance in the banqueting-hall.

At length prejudices were carried so far on both sides, that Frederick was judged more favorably of by his enemies than by his own army; and Melik-Kamel would sooner have found grace among the Christians than among his own troops. The infidels regarded the emperor of Germany as a prince full of wisdom and moderation; Abulfeda, and all the Arabian authors, have celebrated the qualities and virtues of the monarch of the Franks, whilst the continuator of William of Tyre only speaks of this prince with bitterness, and reports in his history, that all the apostles and other Christians had great doubt and great suspicion that he was far gone in infidelity, and warm in his belief in the law of Mahomet.

Hatred soon broke out in acts of treachery and the most odious plots. As the emperor had expressed an intention of going to bathe in the waters of the Jordan, the Templars addressed a letter to Melik-Kamel, pointing out the means of surprising the head of the Christian army in his pilgrimage: the sultan of Cairo despised such treachery, and sent the letter he had received to Frederick. At the same time Melik-Kamel learnt that the sultan of Damascus had declared war against him, and would be joined by several other Mussulman princes. The sultan of Cairo and the emperor of Germany had carried on their negotiations for peace during several months, but now, pressed on all sides by enemies, and surrounded by dangers, even in their own camp, they at length resolved to end the matter, and conclude a treaty, which would permit them to dispose of their forces for their security or for their personal ambition. They agreed between themselves, that they would make a truce of ten years, and that Jerusalem, Nazareth, Bethlehem, and Thoron should be given up to Frederick or his lieutenants. According to the conditions of the treaty, the Mussulmans were to retain in the holy city, the mosque of Omar and the free exercise of their worship: the principality of Antioch and the county of Tripoli were not comprised in the treaty. The emperor of Germany undertook to divert the Franks from every kind of hostility against the subjects or lands of the sultan of Egypt.

When the articles of the treaty became known in the two camps, the peace was considered by both as impious and sacrilegious. The imauns and cadis, invoking the name of the caliph of Bagdad, loudly condemned a truce which conveyed away from the Mussulmans the holy city, which they called *the house of God, the city of the prophet*. The prelates and bishops, speaking in the name of the pontiff of Rome, declaimed vehemently against a treaty which left mosques standing by the side of the Holy Sepulchre, and in some sort confounded the worship of Mahomet with that of Christ. When the envoy of the emperor of Germany went to Damascus, to procure the ratification of the treaty which had been concluded, the sultan and his vizier refused to hear him. The peace made with the Christians was a subject of affliction and scandal for all true believers. One of the most celebrated orators of Islamism pronounced the panegyric of Jerusalem in the great mosque; and, when recalling in pathetic terms the loss the Mussulmans had experienced, he drew tears from all the assembled people.

The patriarch of Jerusalem put an interdict upon the recovered holy places, and refused pilgrims permission to visit the sepulchre of Christ. Jerusalem was no longer, in the eyes of Christians, the holy city and the heritage of the Son of God; when the emperor made his public entrance, the faithful preserved a sullen and melancholy silence as he passed along. Accompanied by the German barons and the Teutonic knights, he repaired to the church of the Holy Sepulchre, which was hung with mourning, and appeared as if guarded by the angel of reprobation; all the ecclesiastics had deserted the sanctuary, and everything wore the air of abomination and desolation. Frederick himself took the crown, and placing it upon his head, he was proclaimed king of Jerusalem without any religious ceremony; the images of the apostles were veiled; nothing was seen around the altars but swords and lances; and the sacred vaults gave back no sounds but the noisy acclamations of warriors.

After his coronation, Frederick wrote to the pope and to all the princes of the West, that he had reconquered Jerusalem without the effusion of blood; in his account he endeavoured to enhance the splendour and merit of this victory, which must fulfil all the hopes of the Christian world. At the same time, the patriarch wrote to Gregory, and all the faithful of Christendom, to show them the impiety and the disgrace of the treaty Frederick had just concluded. When he heard of the success of the emperor, the sovereign pontiff deplored the conquest of Jerusalem as he would have deplored its loss, and compared the new king of Judæa to those impious monarchs whom the anger of God placed upon the throne of David.

Frederick was not able to remain long in the holy city, which resounded with imprecations against him. He returned to Ptolemaïs, where he found only revolted subjects and Christians scandalized at his successes. The patriarch and the clergy placed an interdict upon the city during the time the emperor should remain in it; all religious worship was suspended; the altars were deprived of their ornaments, and the crosses, relics, and images of the saints were cast upon the ground; no more bells, no more religious hymns were to be heard; a melancholy silence prevailed in the sanctuary, where mass was celebrated in a low voice, and with closed doors. The dead were buried in the fields, without funeral ceremonies or monumental stones; everything, in short, denoted a season of great calamities, and a dread of the vengeance of Heaven: it was thus that the liberator of Jerusalem was welcomed at Ptolemaïs.

It was Passion-week, and this religious period gave additional influence to the clergy and more solemnity to the maledictions of the Church. Frederick found himself obliged to negotiate for peace with the Christians, as he had done with the infidels, and being unable to regain their good will, he still further exasperated them by his violence. He caused the gates of the city to be closed, and prohibited the bringing in of provisions; he planted archers and arbalatiers in every place where they could insult the Templars and pilgrims; and by his orders, mendicant preaching monks were dragged from the foot of the altar, and beaten with rods in the public places of the city.

Hatred and vengeance were carried, on both sides, to the greatest excess. It was impossible for the emperor, surrounded as he was by enemies, to remain long at Ptolemaïs, in addition to which motive, he daily received letters from Europe urging his return. Two formidable armies, under the banners of the Holy See, had entered the kingdom of Naples, pillaged the cities, ravaged the country, mutilated prisoners, and committed all kinds of enormities. These armies were under the command of John of Brienne, impatient to revenge his own injuries, and two Sicilian counts, whom the emperor of Germany had driven from the kingdom of Naples.

Frederick at length quitted Palestine and returned to his own dominions. As he left Ptolemaïs, the inhabitants chanted hymns of deliverance and joy. He accused the Templars of having endeavoured to deliver him up to the Saracens; the Templars, on their part, accused him of having wished to surrender all the Christian cities to the sultan of Cairo: these accusations, and a thousand others, dictated by hatred, ought to inspire the historian with great and just suspicions. The Christians might have urged against Frederick a much more reasonable reproach; he had taken no means to secure his conquest, and they were warranted in believing that he had only made his triumphal entry into Jerusalem with the view of annoying the Holy See, and dating a reply to the inculpations of Gregory from the holy places: having attained his object, he had deceived the faithful, by inviting them to a city that he was disposed neither to defend nor fortify. In addition to this, Frederick himself felt very little pride in the advantages of which he made such a pompous display throughout Europe; and the crusade in which he had taken a part was frequently the object of his pleasantries and sarcasms.

On his return to Italy, he found a much more serious war than that he had carried on in Asia. The pope had not only levied troops to ravage his states, he had induced the Lombard republics to take up arms against him. John of Brienne, deprived of his title of king of Jerusalem, determined to endeavour to be acknowledged emperor, and his pretensions were supported by all that was then held most sacred, the authority of the Church and the right of victory. The presence of Frederick restored courage to his subjects, whose fidelity was still unshaken; he met his enemies in several engagements, in which he always gained the advantage. The army of John of Brienne was dispersed, and the pontifical troops quitted all the cities and provinces they had conquered, in the greatest disorder.

The pope, learning that fortune had deserted his banners, again had recourse to the thunders of religion, and employed the most terrible of its denunciations against Frederick. He declared that all were excommunicated who should hold any kind of commerce with the emperor, all who should sit at his table, be present at his councils, celebrate divine service before him, or offer him any mark of attachment or respect. Frederick was terrified at this sentence, which was published with great solemnity in all parts of Europe, particularly in his own dominions; and sent ambassadors to the pope, who, in spite of the thunders with which he was armed, dreaded the consequences of war, and showed himself disposed to receive the submission of an enemy he dreaded.

After a negotiation of several days, a treaty was made, in which the conquered pope dictated laws to his conqueror, and appeared, whilst receiving peace, to accord a pardon. But in spite of this treaty of peace, the effects of discord still subsisted, and were felt even in the East, where debates, raised in the name of the Church, had divided men's minds, and depressed the general courage; and where the Christian states, for which Europe had taken up arms, remained without support and without defence. As Frederick had abandoned Jerusalem without fortifying it, the Christians were in constant dread of the invasion of the Mussulman peasants, whom the hopes of pillage attracted from the mountains of Naplouse. The great bell of the church of the Holy Sepulchre often gave warning of the approach of an enemy eager for carnage; and most of the inhabitants retired with their terrified families, some to the fortress of St. David, which was still standing among the ruins, and others into desert places.

The patriarch of Jerusalem, the prelates, barons, and people of Palestine, who had no longer either a leader or a king, in vain implored the assistance of the warriors and princes of the West: prayers and complaints so frequently repeated, had no power to awaken in the hearts of the faithful either the sentiments of pity or the enthusiasm which had so often caused them to take up arms and

THE DEPARTURE OF THIBAULT, KING OF NAVARRE.

Thibault, count of Champagne, and King of Navarre, son of Thibault, who died before the fifth Crusade, undertook to discharge the vow his father had made to the Church and to Christ. The king of Navarre was celebrated among knights and among troubadours; his muse, which had sung profane loves, now gave voice to the complaints of Jerusalem, and awakened, by Christian songs, the ardour of the soldiers of the cross. "Learn," said he, "that Heaven is closed to all those who will not cross the seas to visit and defend the tomb of God. Yes, all the brave, all who love God and glory, will not hesitate to take up the cross and arms. Those who prefer repose to honour, those who dread perils, will remain alone in their homes. Jesus Christ, in the day of judgment, will say to the one party: 'You, who helped me to bear my cross, go to the place in which dwell the angels and my mother Mary;' he will say to the others: 'You, who have not succoured me, descend to the abode of the wicked!'" The example and the exhortations of Thibault attracted princes, barons and knights, from all the provinces of France.—BOOK XII.

the cross. They could have no faith in perils that followed so closely upon victory; and they despaired of ever being able to assure the deliverance of a country which required to be delivered so often.

The pope, however, had not abandoned the project of the crusade, and still entertained the hope of reviving the ardour and zeal of the Christian warriors by his exhortations. He convoked an assembly at Spoleto, at which Frederick, with the patriarchs of Constantinople, Antioch, and Jerusalem assisted. It was resolved in this assembly, to renew the war in Palestine, notwithstanding the truce concluded with the sultan of Cairo.

Gregory was impatient to accomplish his designs, and proclaim the laws of the Church in the rich countries of the East; and, to employ the time till warriors could be gathered together, he sent several missionaries across the sea, armed with the sword and the word, to endeavour to convert the infidels of Syria and Egypt. The sovereign pontiff was so persuaded of the success of this pacific crusade, that he wrote to the caliph of Bagdad, the sultan of Damascus, and the principal Mussulman chiefs, to exhort them to embrace Christianity. History does not say what the fate was of these mendicant preachers in the East; but the caliph of Bagdad and the Mussulman princes did not cease to be inveterate enemies to the Christians. Gregory IX. was better inspired and more fortunate when he sent sacred orators into several of the provinces of the West, to appease the troubles and civil wars that were so injurious to the cause of religion, and diverted the minds of the people from the great enterprise of the holy wars.

The disciples of St. Dominick and St. Francis of Assisi, charged with a mission worthy of the Gospel, pervaded cities and countries, preaching peace and concord. Among the preachers thus sent to pacify states, Brother John of Vicentia made himself conspicuous by the miracles effected by his eloquence. In all the countries he visited, the nobles, the peasants, the citizens, and the warriors flocked to listen to him, and swore to pardon all injuries and terminate all quarrels. After having re-established peace in several cities troubled by the spirit of jealousy, and animated by the stormy passions of undefined, ill-understood liberty, he announced that he should preach in the plain of Peschiera, on the banks of the Adige. All the inhabitants of the neighbouring cities, headed by their clergy and their magistrates, repaired to the place appointed, to listen to the *Angel of Concord* and the orator of public peace. In the presence of more than four hundred thousand auditors, Brother John mounted a pulpit elevated in the centre of the plain of Peschiera; a profound silence prevailed throughout the assembly; every eye was fixed upon the holy preacher; his words seemed to descend from heaven. He took for his text these words of the scripture: "I give you my peace, I leave you my peace." After having drawn a frightful picture of the evils of war and the effects of discord, he ordered the Lombard cities to renounce their enmities, and dictated to them, in the name of the Church, a treaty of universal pacification. At no period had the middle ages presented a more sublime and touching spectacle; the historian of that time, who has nothing but troubles and wars to describe, ought to be delighted at an opportunity to tell of such an imposing and solemn scene, wherein religion recalled assembled nations to a sense of all that her maxims contain that is most consoling and salutary. The discourse of Brother John filled his auditory with a holy love of peace, and the cities then at war swore, before him, to forget for ever the subjects of their long divisions and eternal rivalries.

These evangelical discourses restored to Italy a few days of peace, and gave the Holy See an opportunity of preaching a new crusade with success. Gregory addressed pastoral instructions to all the bishops and prelates of Christendom. In his letters to the French bishops, he applied these words of Christ to the holy war: "If any one would come with me, let him renounce himself, let him take up my cross and follow me." The sovereign pontiff declared all who would not employ their utmost efforts to conquer the heritage of Christ, guilty of treason. The circulars of the pope ordered all the faithful, of both sexes, to pay a denier per week towards the expenses of the crusade. The head of the Church compared these alms to those which St. Paul solicited for the poor of Jerusalem, and did not fear to assert, beforehand, that they would suffice for the maintenance of the army of Crusaders for ten years.

The preaching of this crusade was confided to the fraternities of St. Dominick and St. Francis, which had, in Asia, missionaries for the conversion of infidels, and in the West, preachers to re-establish peace among Christians; the new apostles of the holy war received from the pope the power, not only to give the cross, but to commute the vow of pilgrimage to a pecuniary alms, a practice that had never been seen since the beginning of the crusades; they had likewise the faculty of granting indulgences for several days to all who came to listen to their sermons. According to the spirit of their institutions, the disciples of St. Francis and St. Dominick lived amidst austerities and penance; they devoted themselves to poverty, and were bound to furnish a constant example of Christian humility; but, in this instance, the pope desired they should be received into monasteries and cities with pomp and ceremony; and that the clergy should come out to meet them, with the banners and most splendid ornaments of their churches. Whether this magnificence changed the simplicity of their manners, or that the people did not like to behold men whom they had lately seen devoted to evangelical poverty, treated with ceremonial pomp, the preachers of the crusade inspired their auditors with neither esteem nor respect, and the crowd diminished every day. As they received abundant alms, of which no one could see the employment, neither the solemnity of their mission nor the sanctity of their characters could screen them from the suspicions and accusations of the multitude: the murmurs and complaints which arose on all sides, at length weakened the authority of their words, and assisted in cooling the zeal and devotion of the Christians for the holy war.

The enthusiasm of the people, which Christian eloquence could not revive, stood in need of the example of the most illustrious princes and warriors. France was then at peace; the war against the Albigeois was drawing towards its end: most of the knights and barons, reared amidst battles, could not endure rest, and sighed for an opportunity of signalizing their warlike temperament. They took the oath to go into Asia and fight against the Saracens.

Thibault V., count of Champagne, and king of Navarre, son of Thibault, who died before the fifth crusade, undertook to discharge the vow his father had made to the Church and to Christ. The king of Navarre was celebrated among knights and among troubadours; his muse, which had sung profane loves, now gave voice to the complaints of Jerusalem, and awakened by Christian songs, the ardour of the soldiers of the cross. "Learn," said he, "that heaven is closed to all those who will not cross the seas to visit and defend the tomb of God. Yes, all the brave, all who love God and glory, will not hesitate to take up the cross and arms. Those who prefer repose to honour, those who dread perils, will remain alone in their homes. Jesus Christ, in the day of judgment, will say to the one party: 'You, who helped me to bear my cross, go to the place in which dwell the angels and my mother Mary;' he will say to the others: 'You, who have not succoured me, descend to the abode of the wicked.'" The example and the exhortations of Thibault attracted princes, barons, and knights from all the provinces of France.

Pierre de Dreux, duke of Brittany, whom the clergy surnamed Mauclerc, because, in his youth, he had abandoned the ecclesiastical state, wished to expiate his numerous felonies, his unjust wars, his tyranny towards his subjects, his perfidies towards his allies, by the holy pilgrimage. Hugh IV., duke of Burgundy, the counts of Bar, Ferez, Mâcon, Joigny, Sancoure, and Nevers; Simon de

Montfort, Andrew de Vitri, Amoury fils, Geoffrey d'Ancenes, and a crowd of barons and knights took the cross, and engaged to follow the duke of Brittany and the king of Navarre into Palestine.

As the preaching of the crusade had been accompanied by several abuses that might prove injurious to the success of the holy expedition, a council assembled at Tours, employed itself in remedying and stopping the evil at its source. We have seen, on preceding occasions, that preachers of the crusades, by receiving criminals under the banners of the cross, had scandalized Christian knights; and crusades, as was seen in the twelfth century, were not considered as a means of salvation for the faithful, and as the way of the Lord, in which all the world might enter. Great criminals no longer found a place in the ranks of the pious defenders of Christ. The council of Tours decided that Crusaders, arrested by justice, should be transferred to the hands of an ecclesiastical judge, who would pay no respect to their privileges, and should even take the cross from them, if he found them guilty of homicide or any other great crime committed against divine and human laws.

As in other crusades, the people were led into violent excesses against the Jews, whom they accused of having immolated the God for whom they were going to fight, and who retained immense treasures in their hands, whilst the Crusaders were obliged to pledge their property to perform the voyage to Palestine. In order to stop the course of these popular violences, the council forbade any ill-treatment of the Jews, either by plundering them of their wealth or by doing them personal injury, under pain of heavy ecclesiastical censures.

Another abuse, not less prejudicial to the Crusaders than all the others, had been likewise observed. The preachers of the holy wars and many other theologians had permitted Crusaders to buy off their vow by paying a sum of money equal to that which they would have expended in their pilgrimage: this abuse caused great scandal among the faithful, but the Holy See, which derived considerable sums from it, paid no attention to the complaints made on account of it in England and many other states of Europe.

The Crusaders were preparing for their departure, when, all at once, a fresh cry of alarm resounded through the West. The empire of the Latins, at Constantinople, was reduced to the lowest extremity. After the reigns of Baldwin of Flanders, and his son Henry, the family of Courtenay, called to the throne, derived nothing from their exaltation but the griefs and reverses inseparable from the government of an empire which is hastening to decay. Peter of Courtenay, count of Auxerre, when on his way to take possession of the throne of Baldwin, was surprised and massacred in Macedonia, by the orders of Theodore Comnenus, prince of Epirus. A short time afterwards, the empress, who had arrived at Constantinople by sea, died of grief, on learning the tragical end of her husband. Robert of Courtenay, second son of Peter, only ascended the throne to experience the rapid decline of the empire; conquered in a great battle by Vataces, the successor of Lascaris, he lost all the provinces situated beyond the Bosphorus and the Hellespont; whilst, on the other side, the prince of Epirus took possession of Thessaly and a great part of Thrace. Constantinople, threatened by formidable enemies, beheld from its towers the standards of the Greeks of Nice and of the barbarians of Mount Hemus, floating near its walls and insulting its majesty. Amidst these various disasters, Robert died, leaving, as his only successor, his brother Baldwin, still in his childhood. John of Brienne, whom fortune had made, for a short period, king of Jerusalem, was called to the tottering throne of Constantinople, at the moment that the Greeks and Bulgarians, animated by the ardour of pillage, were at the gates of the capital. Their fleets penetrated to the port, their numerous battalions were preparing to scale the ramparts; but the new emperor fought several battles with them, obtained possession of their ships, and dispersed their armies. The miraculous victories of John of Brienne added greatly to his renown, but only served to diminish his forces: after having defeated his enemies, he found himself without an army; and whilst the poets were comparing him to Hector, Roland, and Judas Machabæus, he was obliged to wait in his capital for succours that had been promised him, and which never arrived. More than eighty years of age, he terminated his active career in contesting with the barbarians the remains of a power which had been founded by arms, and the miserable wreck of which could only be preserved by prodigies of valour.

The ruins which surrounded him in his last moments must have made him sensible of the nothingness of human grandeur, and produced sentiments of Christian humility. He had passed the early days of his life amidst the austerities of the cloister. On his deathbed he laid aside the imperial purple, and was desirous of breathing his last sigh in the habit of a Cordelier. A simple French knight, seated for some few days upon two thrones, both ready to pass away, son-in-law of two kings, father-in-law of two emperors, John of Brienne only left, when dying, the remembrance of his extraordinary exploits, and the example of a wonderful destiny. Young Baldwin, who had married his daughter, and who was to have succeeded him, was unable to obtain his inheritance; and departing as a fugitive from his capital, he wandered through Europe as a suppliant, braving and enduring the contempt of princes and nations. Spectacle worthy of pity! the successor of the Cæsars, clothed in the purple, was beheld imploring the charity of the faithful, begging for the assistance granted to the lowest indigence, and frequently not obtaining that for which he sued.

Whilst the emperor of the East was thus travelling through Italy, France, and England, Constantinople was left without an army, and sacrificed for the defence of the state, even to its relics, the objects of the veneration of the people, and the last treasures of the empire. The sovereign pontiff was touched with the misery and degradation of Baldwin, and, at the same time, could not hear without pity the complaints of the Latin church of Byzantium: he published a new crusade for the defence of the empire of the East.

The Crusaders, who were about to set out for the Holy Land, were invited to lend their assistance to their brethren of Constantinople; but the prayers and exhortations of the Holy See produced but very feeble effects; opinions were divided; some wished to defend the empire of the Latins, others, the kingdom of Jerusalem.

The French princes and nobles, however, persisted in their resolution of going to fight against the Saracens in Asia. The barons and knights either pawned or sold their lands to purchase horses and arms, quitted their donjons and their castles, and tore themselves from the embraces of their wives. Thibault, their leader and interpreter, bade adieu to France in verses which are still extant, and which express, at the same time, the devotion of a Christian and the spirit of chivalry. His muse, at once pious and profane, deplores the torments of love, the griefs of absence, and celebrates the glory of the soldiers of Christ; to console himself for having left the lady of his thoughts, the king of Navarre invokes the Virgin Mary, *the lady of the heavens*, and finishes his complaints, by this verse, which so admirably paints the manners of the time:

> Quand dame perds, Dame me soit aidant,
> "My lady lost, holy lady be my aid."

Other troubadours, after the example of the king of Navarre, sang the departure of the pilgrims; they promised, in their verses, the indulgences of the crusade to the warriors that would set out for Syria, advising the dames and demoiselles not to listen to those that should be left in Europe; for, said they, there will remain none but cowards: all the brave are going to seek glory in the battles of the East. Whilst France was repeating the songs of the troubadours, and prayers were offered up to Heaven in the churches for the success of the expeditions, the Crusaders from all the provinces of the kingdom commenced their march, directing their course towards the port of Marseilles, where vessels waited, to transport them into Asia; all were animated by the most ardent zeal for the deliverance of the holy places; but the pope, at whose voice they had taken up arms, no longer applauded their enthusiasm. Gregory, who had made himself a great many formidable enemies in the West, appeared to have forgotten a war he had so warmly promoted, and was entirely engrossed by his own dangers.

Most of the leaders of the crusade were assembled at Lyons to deliberate upon the best means of carrying on their enterprise, when they received a nuncio from the sovereign pontiff, who commanded them to return to their homes. This unexpected order from Gregory IX. gave great offence to the princes and barons, who told the envoy of the court of Rome, that the pope might change his policy, and disapprove of that which he himself had set on foot; but that the defenders of the cross, they who had devoted themselves to the service of Christ, would remain steadfast in their intentions. "We have made," added they, "all our preparations; we have pledged or sold our lands, our houses, and our goods; we have quitted our friends and our families, giving out our departure for Palestine: religion and honour forbid us to retrace our steps."

As the pope's nuncio wished to speak and uphold the authority of the Church, and as he accused the barons of betraying the cause they were going to defend, the Christian warriors could not restrain their indignation; the soldiers and leaders were so exasperated, that they even ill-treated the ambassador of the pontiff; and, but for the intercession and prayers of the prelates and bishops, would have immolated him to their anger.

Scarcely had the Crusaders dismissed the pope's nuncio with contempt, than deputies arrived from the emperor of Germany, equally supplicating them to suspend their march, and wait till he had collected his troops, in order to place himself at their head. The knights and barons, animated by a sincere zeal for the objects of their expedition, could not comprehend the meaning of the delays thus attempted to be thrown in the way of it, and sighed over the blindness of the powers that wished to turn them aside from the road to salvation. The king of Navarre, the dukes of Brittany and Burgundy, with most of the nobles that had taken the cross, persisted in the design of accomplishing their vow, and embarked for Syria at the port of Marseilles.

A new misunderstanding had broken out between the pope and Frederick, who were disputing the sovereignty of Sardinia; all the passions were soon engaged in this quarrel, and armed themselves, by turns, with the vengeance of Heaven and the furies of war. Gregory, after having excommunicated Frederick afresh, was determined to attack his reputation, and degrade him in the opinion of his contemporaries. Monitories and briefs from the pope were read in all the churches of Europe, in which the emperor was represented as an impious man, an accomplice of heretics and Saracens, an oppressor of religion and humanity. Frederick replied to the accusations of the sovereign pontiff by the most violent invectives; he addressed himself to the Romans, to excite them against the Holy See, and called upon all the princes of Europe to defend his cause as their own. "Kings and princes of the earth," said he, "look upon the injury done to us as your own, *bring water to extinguish the fire that has been kindled in our neighbourhood;* a similar danger threatens you." The irritated pope hurled all the thunders of the Church against his adversary; and even went so far as to preach a crusade against the emperor, saying, "There was more merit in combating a prince who was rebellious to the successors of St. Peter, than in delivering Jerusalem." Throughout this scandalous contest, the Church was allowed to possess nothing that was sacred, the authority of princes nothing that was legitimate; on one side, the sovereign pontiff considered all who remained faithful subjects to the emperor as the ministers and accomplices of the demon; on the other, the emperor would not acknowledge the pope as the vicar of Christ. At last, Gregory promised the imperial crown to any

Christian prince who would take up arms against the emperor, and drag him from his throne: Louis IX., more wise than the Church itself, refused the empire which was offered to him for his brother Robert, and employed earnest but vain endeavours to restore peace to Europe, disturbed by the pretensions and menaces of the pope.

They soon came to hostilities; and Frederick after having gained a great victory over the Milanese, and carried terror amongst all the republics of Lombardy, marched towards Rome at the head of an army. Gregory, who had no troops at all, went through the streets of his capital at the head of a procession; he exhibited to the Romans the relics of the apostles, and, melting into tears, told them he had no means of defending this sacred deposit without their assistance. The nobility and people, touched by the prayers of the pope, swore to die in defence of the Holy See. They set about preparations for war, they fortified the city with the greatest expedition; and when the emperor drew near to the gates, he saw those same Romans, who, a short time before, had embraced his cause against the pope, drawn up in battle array on the ramparts, determined to die in the cause of the head of the Church. Frederick besieged the city, without being able to get possession of it; in his anger, he accused the Romans of perfidy, and revenged himself by exercising horrible cruelties on his prisoners. The hatred enkindled between the pope and the emperor soon passed into the minds of the people, and the furies of civil war devastated the whole of Italy.

Amidst such general disorder and agitation, the cries and prayers of the Christians of Palestine were scarcely audible. At the expiration of the truce concluded with Frederick, the sultan of Damascus re-entered Jerusalem, and destroyed the tower of David and the weak ramparts erected by the Christians: this conquest, which revived the courage of the Mussulmans, necessarily produced more than proportionate despair among the unfortunate inhabitants of the Holy Land. Instead of receiving within its walls the innumerable armies that fame had announced, Ptolemaïs only had to welcome the arrival of a few unarmed pilgrims, who had nothing to relate but the deplorable quarrels of Christian monarchs and princes. Most of the communications with the East were closed; all the maritime powers of Italy were contending for the empire of the sea; sometimes in league with the sovereign pontiff, sometimes with the emperor. Several of the Crusaders who had sworn to go to Constantinople or Ptolemaïs, took part in the crusade that had been preached against Frederick; others resolved to proceed to Syria by land, and almost all perished in the mountains and deserts of Asia Minor; the French lords and princes, who, in spite of the orders of the pope, set out for Asia from the ports of Provence, were able to bring with them into Palestine but a very small number of warriors.

At the period of the arrival of these Crusaders, the East was not less troubled than the West. Melik-Kamel, the sultan of Cairo, had recently died, and his death became the signal for many sanguinary wars among the princes of his family, who disputed by turns the kingdom of Egypt, and the principalities of Damascus, Aleppo, and Hamah. Amidst these divisions, the emirs and the Mamelukes, whose dangerous support was constantly sought for, were accustomed to dispose of power, and proved themselves more formidable to their sovereigns than to the enemies of Islamism. Supreme authority seemed to be the reward of victory or of skill in treachery; the Mussulman thrones were environed by so many perils, that a sultan of Damascus was seen abandoning his sceptre, and seeking retirement, saying, "a hawk and a hound afforded him more pleasure than empire." The princes, divided among themselves, called for the succour of the Carismians and other barbarous nations, who burnt their cities, pillaged their provinces, completed the destruction of the powers they came to defend, and perfected all the evils that were born of discord.

The Crusaders might have taken advantage of all these troubles, but they never united their forces against the enemy they had sworn to contend with; the kingdom of Jerusalem had no government capable of directing the forces of the crusade; the crowd of pilgrims had no tie, no common point of interest which could hold them together for any length of time under the same standards: scattered troops of soldiers were to be seen, but there was nowhere an army; each of the leaders and princes followed a plan of his own, declared war or proclaimed peace in his own name, and appeared to fight entirely for his own ambition or renown.

The duke of Brittany, followed by his knights, made an incursion into the lands of Damascus, and returned to Ptolemaïs with a rich booty; the other Crusaders, jealous of the success of this expedition, were desirous of distinguishing themselves by exploits, and formed the project of attacking the city of Gaza. As they marched without order or precaution, they were surprised and cut to pieces by the Saracens. The duke of Burgundy, who was at the head of this expedition, escaped the pursuit of the conquerors almost alone, and came back to Ptolemaïs, to deplore the loss of his knights and barons, who had all met with slavery or death on the field of battle. This reverse, instead of uniting the Christians more closely, only increased their discords; in the impossibility of effecting any triumph for their arms, they treated separately with the infidels, and made peace, as they had made war. The Templars and some leaders of the army agreed for a truce with the sultan of Damascus, and obtained the restitution of the holy places; on their side, the Hospitallers, with the count of Champagne, and the dukes of Burgundy and Brittany, concluded a treaty with the sultan of Egypt, and undertook to defend him against the Saracens who had just given up Jerusalem to the Christians.

After having disturbed Palestine by their disorders, the Crusaders abandoned it to return to Europe, and were replaced at Ptolemaïs by some English, who arrived under Richard of Cornwall, brother to Henry III. Richard, who possessed the tin and lead mines of the county of Cornwall, was one of the richest princes of the West: if old chronicles are to be believed, Gregory had forbidden him to go to the East, hoping that he would consent to remain in Europe, and would impart a portion of his treasures to the Holy See, to procure the indulgences of the crusade. When Richard arrived before Ptolemaïs, he was received by the people and the clergy, who went out to meet him, singing, "Blessed be he who comes in the name of the Lord." This prince was the grandson of Richard Cœur de Lion,[*] whose courage and exploits had rendered him so famous in the East. The name alone of Richard spread terror among the Saracens; the prince of Cornwall equalled his ancestor in bravery; he was full of zeal and ardour, and his army shared his enthusiasm for religion and glory. He prepared to open the campaign, and everything seemed to promise success; but, after a march of some days, and a few advantages obtained over the enemy, finding himself very ill-seconded by the Christians of Palestine, he was obliged to renew the truce made with the sultan of Egypt. As the whole fruit of his expedition, he could only obtain an exchange of prisoners, and permission to pay the honours of sepulture to the Christians killed at the battle of Gaza.

Without having seen either the walls of Jerusalem or the banks of the Jordan, Richard embarked for Italy, where he found the pope still engaged in the war against Frederick. All Europe was in a blaze; a council convoked for the peace of the Church had not been able to assemble; the emperor still besieged the city of Rome, and threatened the head of Christendom. Amidst this general disorder, Gregory died, cursing his implacable adversary, and was succeeded by Celestine IV., who only wore the tiara sixteen days. The war was continued with renewed fury, the Church remained without a head, and Christ without a vicar upon earth; the cardinals wandered about dispersed; Frederick

---

[*] This is a mistake; Richard had no legitimate children. Richard, duke of Cornwall, who was likewise king of the Romans, was the son of John, Richard's brother. In the same manner Gibbon calls Edward I. Richard's *nephew*;—he was his *great-nephew*.—TRANS.

holding several of them in chains. "The court of Rome," says Fleury, "was desolate, and fallen into great contempt." This deplorable anarchy lasted nearly two years; all Christendom was loud in complaints, and demanded of Heaven a pope able to repair the evils of Europe and the Church.

The conclave met at length, but the election of Innocent IV., made amidst trouble and discord, put an end to neither the public scandal nor the furies of the war, which grieved all true Christians. The new pontiff followed the example of Innocent III. and Gregory IX., and soon surpassed all their excesses. Under his pontificate, disorder continued increasing, until it had reached its height. The Christians of Greece and Palestine were quite forgotten. Missionaries in vain perambulated the kingdoms of the West, to exhort the faithful to make peace among themselves, and turn their arms against the Saracens; many of these angels of peace were proscribed by Frederick, who was, at once, at war with the sovereign pontiff, the emperor of the East, and all those who, in taking the cross, had sworn to defend Rome, or to deliver Constantinople or Jerusalem. We will not attempt to describe the violent scenes of which the West, but particularly Italy, was the theatre. Attention becomes fatigued by dwelling long upon the same pictures; the wars and revolutions which lend so much life to history finish by presenting only a wearisome, twice-told tale; and thus, likewise, may the reader perceive that the passions have their uniformity and tempests their monotony.

Each of the preceding crusades had a distinct object, a march which could be easily followed, and was only remarkable for great exploits or great reverses. That which we have just described, which embraces a period of thirty years, is mingled with so many different events, with so many clashing interests, so many passions foreign to the holy wars, that it at first appears to present only a confused picture; and the historian, constantly occupied in relating the revolutions of the East and of the West, may with reason be accused of having, as a European Christian, forgotten Jerusalem and the cause of Christ.

When we have read the twelfth book of this history, we perceive that we are already far from the age that gave birth to the crusades, and witnessed their brilliant progress. When comparing this war with those that preceded it, it is easy to see that it has a different character, not only in the manner in which it was conducted, but in the means employed to inflame the zeal of the Christians, and induce them to take up arms.

When we observe the incredible efforts of the popes to arm the nations of the West, we are at first astonished at the small quantity of success obtained by their exhortations, their menaces, and their prayers. We have but to compare the Council of Clermont, held by Urban, with the Council of the Lateran, presided over by Gregory. In the first, the complaints of Jerusalem excite the tears and sobs of the auditory; in the second, a thousand different objects intrude, to occupy the attention of the fathers of the Church, who express themselves upon the misfortunes of the Holy Land, without emotion and without pain. At the voice of Urban, knights, barons, and ecclesiastics all swore together to go and fight against the infidels; the council became, in a moment, an assembled host of intrepid warriors: it was not so at the Council of the Lateran, in which no one took the cross, or burst forth into an expression of that high enthusiasm which the pope desired to awaken in all hearts.

We have drawn attention, in the course of our recital, to the circumstance of pilgrims being permitted by the preachers of the holy war to buy off their vow by paying a sum of money; this mode of expiating sins appeared to be a scandalous innovation: and the indulgence of the missionaries of the holy war, who thus released the faithful from the pilgrimage, made them lose a considerable portion of their ascendancy. They were not, as formerly, the messengers of Heaven; the multitude no

THE CRUSADERS' WAR-MACHINERY.

longer endowed them with the power of working miracles; they were even sometimes obliged to employ the menaces and promises of the Church to draw hearers to their sermons; in short, at length the people ceased to consider them as the interpreters of the gospel, and saw in them only the collectors of the dues of the Holy See. This sale of the privileges of the crusade, purchased at an extravagant price, necessarily checked the effects of all generous passions, and, in the minds of Christians, confounded that which belonged to Heaven with that which belonged to earth.

Preceding ages were unacquainted with any other motive but religion and its promises. The companions of Peter the Hermit and Godfrey, the warriors who followed Louis the Young, Philip Augustus, Richard Cœur de Lion, Boniface, and Baldwin of Flanders, could not have possibly believed that gold could be made a substitute for the merit and glory of the holy war.

We find another remarkable difference in the preaching of this crusade,—the refusal to admit great criminals under the banners of the cross. The astonishment which the enrolment of a crowd of obscure persons in the holy militia caused among the Christian knights, suffices to denote a great change in the manners and opinions of the Crusaders. The sentiment of honour, which is allied with a love of glory, and has a tendency to establish distinctions among men, appears to have prevailed over the purely religious feeling which inspires humility, acknowledges the equal rights of all Christians, and confounds repentance with virtue. The crusade, into which none were admitted but men of acknowledged bravery and good conduct, ceased, in some sort, to be a simply religious war, and began to resemble other wars, in which leaders have the power of selecting the soldiers they have to command.

The enthusiasm for the holy wars only revived at intervals, like a fire upon the point of going out of itself: the people required some great event, some extraordinary circumstance, some striking example of princes or warriors, to induce them to take arms against the infidels; the subtleties of theologians, who insisted upon everything being subservient to their discussions, contributed to cool the remains of that pious and warlike ardour, which, till that time, it had been found necessary to moderate and restrain within just limits. Disputes were started in the schools upon such questions as these: In what case was a Christian exempt from the accomplishment of his vow? What sum was sufficient to redeem a promise made to Christ? If certain pious exercises could be substituted for pilgrimage? If an heir was bound to fulfil the oath of a testator? Whether the pilgrim who died on his way to the Holy Land, had more merit in the eyes of God than one who died on his return? Whether a wife could take the cross without the consent of her husband, or the husband without the consent of the wife? &c. From the moment in which all these questions were solemnly discussed, and, upon several points, the opinions of theologians differed, enthusiasm, which never reasons, was rendered languid by the cold arguments of the doctors; and pilgrims appeared to yield less to the transports of a generous feeling, than to the necessity of performing a duty or of following an established rule.

This sixth crusade was more abundant in intrigues and scandalous quarrels than in military exploits; the Christians never united all their efforts against the infidels; no spirit of order presided over their enterprises; the Crusaders, who only held their mission of their zeal, set out at the time their will or their fancy selected; some returned to Europe without having faced a Saracen in fight; others abandoned the colours of the cross, after a victory or a defeat; and fresh Crusaders were constantly summoned to defend the conquests or repair the faults of those that had preceded them. Although the West had counted in this crusade more than five hundred thousand of her warriors departing for Palestine or Egypt, great armies were rarely assembled on the banks of the Nile or the Jordan. As the Crusaders were never gathered together in great bodies, they were not subjected to famine, or the other scourges that had so fearfully thinned the ranks of the early defenders of the cross; but if they experienced fewer reverses, if they were better disciplined, we may say that they showed none of that ardour, or of those lively passions which men communicate to each other, and which acquire a new degree of force and activity amidst a multitude assembled for the same cause and under the same banners.

By transferring the theatre of the war to Egypt, the Christians no longer had before their eyes, as in Palestine, the revered places and monuments, which could recall to them the religion and the God they were about to fight for; they had no longer before them and around them the river Jordan, Libanus, Thabor, or Mount Sion, the aspect of which had so vividly affected the imagination of the first Crusaders.

When the people of Europe heard the head of the Church exhort the faithful to the conquest of Jerusalem, and at the same time curse Frederick, the liberator of the holy city, the object of the crusade lost its sacred character in the eyes of Christians. The emperor of Germany, after his return from his expedition, sometimes said, "If God had been acquainted with the kingdom of Naples, he never could have preferred the barren rocks of Jerusalem to it." These sacrilegious words of Frederick must have been a great subject of offence to pilgrims; but, indeed, this prince only sent to the Holy Land such of his subjects as he was dissatisfied with, or wished to punish. The popes also condemned to pilgrimage the great criminals whom society rejected from its bosom, which was very repugnant to the manners and opinions of the nobles and knights of Europe. As a crowning misfortune, the reverses or exploits of the Crusaders beyond the seas frequently created divisions among the princes of the West. From that time, Palestine was no longer, in the eyes of the faithful, a land of blessedness, flowing with milk and honey, but a place of exile. From that time Jerusalem was less considered the city of God and the heritage of Christ, than a subject of discord, or the place in which were born all the storms that disturbed Christendom.

In the other crusades, the popes had been satisfied with awakening the enthusiasm of pilgrims, and addressing prayers to Heaven for the success of the Crusaders; but in this war, the heads of the Church insisted upon directing all the expeditions, and commanding, by their legates, the operations of the Christian armies. The invasion of Egypt was decided upon in the Council of the Lateran, without a thought of asking the advice or opinions of any of the skilful captains of the age. When hostilities began, the envoys of the pope presided over all the events of the war; weakening the ardour of the soldiers of the cross, by their ambitious pretensions, as well as by their ignorance. They let all the fruits of victory slip through their hands, and gave birth to an injurious rivalry between the spiritual and the temporal powers. This rivalry, this reciprocal mistrust, were carried so far, that the sovereign pontiff and the emperor of Germany, by turns, arrested the march of the pilgrims; the first fearing that the Crusaders, on embarking for Palestine, would become the soldiers of Frederick; the second, that these same soldiers might become the defenders of the temporal power of the popes.

At the period of which we have just retraced the history, so many crusades were preached at once, that the eyes of the faithful were necessarily diverted from the first object of these holy expeditions. Called upon to defend so many causes, no one could distinguish which was the cause of God and Jesus Christ; so many interests presented themselves at the same time to the attention of Christians, and were recommended to the bravery of warriors, that they gave birth to hesitation and reflection; and these produced indifference. Europe, for a length of time in a state of fermentation, was undergoing the vague uncertainty of a change; states began to think more of their independence, people of their liberty. The passions which politics bring forth, took the place of passions of which religion is the motive.

The sanguinary quarrels of the emperor and the popes contributed greatly to the revolution which was brought about in men's minds: the motive which animated the heads of the Church was not always a religious one; the emperor of Germany and the pontiffs of Rome had pretensions to the domination of Italy, and had been, for a long time, engaged in a rivalry of ambition. Gregory could not see Frederick master of the kingdom of Naples without great pain; and when he pressed him to go into Asia, to make war upon the Saracens, he might have been compared to that personage of ancient fable, who, in order to get rid of his rival, sent him to combat the Chimera.

Four popes, although of a different character, finding themselves in the same circumstances, pursued the same policy. Frederick, by his cruelties, injustice, and extravagant ambition, often justified the violences of the Holy See, of which he was, by turns, the ward, the protector, and the enemy; like his predecessors, he made no secret of his project of restoring the empire of the Cæsars; and, had it not been for the popes, it is not improbable that Europe would have been brought under the yoke of the emperors of Germany.

The policy of the sovereign pontiffs, whilst weakening the imperial power, favoured, in Germany, the liberty of cities, and the growth and duration of small states; we do not hesitate to add, that the thunders of the Church preserved the independence of Italy, and perhaps that of France, which was less ill treated by the court of Rome than neighbouring nations. The French monarchy took advantage of the troubles that existed on the other side of the Rhine, and of the interdict set upon England, to repel the invasions of the English and Germans; and, at the same time, availed itself of the absence of the king of Navarre, the dukes of Brittany and Burgundy, with several other great vassals, whom the crusade attracted beyond the seas, to increase the prerogatives of the royal authority, and extend the limits of the kingdom.

England herself owes something to the authority of the popes, who, by overwhelming John Lackland with excommunications, rendered him powerless in his attempts to enslave the English people, or to resist the demands of the barons and the commons. This is a truth which impartial history cannot deny or doubt, and which disposes us not to approve, but to blame with less bitterness, excesses and abuses of power of which all the effects have not been deplorable. The populace of London, who burn every year the effigy of the pope, would be much astonished if, amidst a fanatical delirium, they were told that the army which once fought for the independence of Great Britain was called *the army of God and of the Holy Church;* if they were reminded that the great charter of the Forest, the first monument of British liberty, was the fortunate fruit of the menaces and thunders of the Church of Rome, and that this charter would never have been granted by John, without the redoubtable influence and the imperious counsels of the sovereign pontiff.

Without wishing to justify the domination of the popes, we may say that they were led to grasp at supreme power by the circumstances in which Europe was placed in the eleventh and twelfth centuries. European society, without experience or laws, and plunged in ignorance and anarchy, cast itself into the arms of the popes, and believed that it placed itself under the protection of Heaven.

As nations had no other ideas of civilization than such as they received from the Christian religion, the sovereign pontiffs naturally became the supreme arbiters between rival or neighbouring countries; amidst the darkness which the light of the Gospel had a continued and never-ending tendency to diminish, their authority must naturally have been the first established and the first recognised; temporal power stood in need of their sanction; people and kings implored their support and consulted their wisdom: they believed themselves authorized to exercise a sovereign dictatorship.

This dictatorship was often exercised to the advantage of public morality and social order; it often protected the weak against the strong; it arrested the execution of criminal plots; it re-established peace between states; and it preserved a young society from the excesses of ambition, licentiousness, and barbarism. When we cast our eyes over the annals of the middle ages, we cannot help being struck by one of the most beautiful spectacles that human society has ever presented,—it is that of Christian Europe recognising but one religion, having but one law, forming as it were but one empire, governed by a single head, who spoke in the name of God, and whose mission was to make the Gospel reign upon earth.

In the general reflections by which we shall terminate this work, we will enter into much greater developments upon this head; we will compare modern Europe with the Europe of the middle ages, and we will make it clear that, if we have acquired some wisdom in the art of civilization, we are still far from having turned it to the advantage of public liberty: nations are at the present day led away by the spirit of the French revolution, as they were in the middle ages by the spirit of the court of Rome and enthusiasm for the crusades. The French revolution began by liberal ideas, it was continued by victories. The military spirit allied itself with the fanaticism of new ideas, as it formerly allied itself with religious enthusiasm. On casting a glance over our Europe, we are astonished at seeing two contradictory things, which should naturally exclude each other; we see almost everywhere a tendency to favour the propagation of liberal ideas, and at the same time an inclination to increase the mass of armies; it is difficult to explain a policy which tends, on the one side, to multiply the apostles of liberty, on the other to multiply soldiers; which, by turns, proclaims a principle, and raises a regiment; which speaks, at the same time, of recruiting, and of a constitution; which appears never to have laws enough, and yet is insatiable of cannons and bayonets. It is easy to foresee the near and distant results of such a monstrous amalgamation. Everything leads us to believe that these results, like those of the crusades and the influence of the pope in the middle ages, will not turn out *entirely* for the advantage of civilization.

But without dwelling longer on these distressing reflections, we will return to our subject, from which, perhaps, we have strayed too long. In the eleventh and twelfth centuries, the nations of Europe, subject to the authority of St. Peter, were united together by a tie more strong than that of liberty. This motive, this tie, which was that of the universal Church, for a length of time kept up and favoured the enthusiasm for and the progress of holy wars. Whatever may have been the origin of the crusades, it is certain they never would have been undertaken without that unity of religious feelings which doubled the strength of the Christian republic. The Christian nations, by the agreement of their sentiments and their passions, showed the world all that can be done by enthusiasm, which increases by communication, and that lively faith, which, spread among men, is a miraculous power, since the Gospel accords it the faculty of *moving mountains*. In proportion as people, united by one same spirit, separated, and ceased to make one common cause, it became more difficult to collect together the forces of the West, and pursue those gigantic enterprises of which our age can scarcely perceive the possibility.

It may have been observed, that the pontifical authority and the enthusiasm for the crusades experienced the same vicissitudes; the opinions and the exaltation of the religious spirit which caused men to take up arms, necessarily, at the same time, increased the influence of the sovereign pontiffs. But springs so active and so powerful could not possibly last long; they broke by the violence with which they were employed.

The popes, invested with authority without limit, exercised that authority without moderation; and as the abuse of power brings on, sooner or later, its own ruin, the empire of the sovereign pontiffs finished by declining as other empires have done. Their fall commenced with their long contests with Frederick; all Europe was called upon to judge their cause; their power, founded upon opinion, the origin of which was entirely religious, lost much of its prestige by being given over to the discussions of men of the world.

At the same time that the sovereign pontiffs abused their power, the spirit and enthusiasm that had produced the holy wars were likewise abused. Many Christian princes took the cross, sometimes to obtain the protection of the popes; sometimes as a pretext for assembling armies, and enjoying the temporal advantages accorded to the soldiers of Christ. The leaders of Christendom, without having originated the wars of the East, were eager to profit by them; in the first place, to extend their dominions, and in the next to gratify violent passions. From that moment society sought other supports than that of the Holy See, and warriors another glory than that of the crusades.

Thibault, king of Navarre, who, in his verses, had preached the war beyond the seas, was disgusted at the troubles excited in Europe by the heads of the Church, and deplored with bitterness *a time full of felony, envy, and treachery*. He accused the princes and barons of being without *courtoisie*, and reproached the popes with excommunicating those who were most in the right (*ceux qui avaient le plus raison*). If a few troubadours still raised their voices to exhort Christians to take up the cross and arms, the greater part did not partake of their enthusiasm for the holy wars; and beheld nothing in these pilgrimages beyond the seas, but the griefs of a long absence, and the rigours of a pious exile.

In a Tenson which has come down to us, Folquet de Romans asks Blaccas, the model of troubadours and of knights, whether he will go to the Holy Land? After having answered that he loves and is beloved, and that he will remain at home with his ladye-love, (she was countess of Provence), Blaccas thus ends his simple song:—

> "Je ferai ma pénitence,
> Entre mer et Durance,
> Auprès de son manoir."

> "I will perform my penitence
> Between the sea and swift Durance
> Near to my lady's bower."

These sentiments belonged to the manners of troubadours and knights; but at the time of the first crusades, religious ideas were much more mixed up with ideas of gallantry; a poet, invited to take the cross, would not have dared to speak of his ladye-love, without likewise speaking of the mercy of God and the captivity of Jerusalem.

During the other crusades, the religion and morality of the Gospel resumed their empire, and spread their benefits everywhere; at the voice of the holy orators, Christians became penitent and reformed their morals; all political tempests were laid by the simple name of Jerusalem, and the West remained in profound peace. It was not so at the period we have just described; Europe was perhaps never more agitated, or, perhaps, more corrupted than during the thirty years which this crusade lasted.

In the relations between the Christians and Mussulmans, little respect had, to this time, certainly, been paid to treaties; but in this crusade, contempt for sworn faith and forgetfulness for the laws of nations was carried to an extreme: signing a truce was a preparation for war;—the Christian armies owed their safety to a treaty of peace; and the sovereign pontiff, far from respecting the conditions of it, preached a new crusade against the infidels. It must be allowed, also, that the most solemn treaties were often violated by the Mussulmans. The duration of peace depended solely upon the want of power in both parties to resume hostilities with advantage. The least hope of success was sufficient to induce them to fly to arms; the slightest circumstance was an excuse for rekindling all the flames of war. The continuator of William of Tyre says, with great ingenuousness, when speaking of the death of a sultan of Damascus: " When the sultan died, all the truces died with him." These words alone are sufficient to give an idea of the state of the East during the sixth crusade, and of the small degree of respect then entertained for the laws of peace and war.

If, in the preceding crusade, the expedition of the soldiers of the cross against Greece did not produce great advantages to the West, it at least illustrated the arms of the Venetians and the French. In the war we have just described, the knights and barons who took the cross, added nothing to their glory or their renown. The Crusaders who were fortunate enough to revisit their homes, brought back with them nothing but the remembrance of most shameful disorders. A great number of them had nothing to show their compatriots but the chains of their captivity; nothing to communicate but the contagious disorders of the East.

The historians we have followed are silent as to the ravages of the leprosy among the nations of the West; but the testament of Louis VIII., an historical monument of that period, attests the existence of two thousand *léproseries* (hospitals for lepers) in the kingdom of France alone. This horrible sight must have been a subject of terror to the most fervent Christians; and was sufficient to disenchant, in their eyes, those regions of the East, where, till that time, their imaginations had seen nothing but prodigies and marvels.

Among the abuses then made of the spirit of the crusades, and the misfortunes they brought in their train, we must not forget the civil and religious wars of which France and several other countries of Europe were the theatre. In their expeditions into the East, Christians had become familiarized with the idea of employing force and violence to change men's hearts and opinions. As they had long made war against infidels, they were willing to make it, in the same manner, against heretics; they first took up arms against the Albigeois, then against the pagans of Prussia; for the same reason, and in the same manner, that they had armed themselves against the Mussulmans.

Modern writers have declaimed with great vehemence and eloquence against these disastrous wars; but long before the age in which we live, the Church had condemned the excesses of blind fanaticism. Saint Augustine, St. Ambrose, the fathers of councils, had long taught the Christian world that error is not destroyed by the sword, and that the truths of the Gospel ought not to be preached to mankind amidst threats and violences.

The crusade against the Prussians shows us all that ambition, avarice, and tyranny can exhibit that is most cruel and barbarous; the tribunal of history cannot judge with too much severity the leaders of this war, the ravages and furies of which were prolonged during more than a century; but, whilst condemning the excesses of the conquerors of Prussia, we must admit the advantages Europe gained by their victories and exploits. A nation that had been separated from all other nations by its manners and customs, ceased to be a foreigner in the Christian republic. Industry, laws, religion, which marched in the train of the conquerors, to moderate and remove the evils of war, spread their blessings among hordes of savages. Many flourishing cities arose from amidst the ashes of forests, and the oak of Remové, beneath the shade of which human victims had been immolated, was replaced by churches, in which the virtues and charity of the Gospel were inculcated. The conquests of the Romans were sometimes more unjust, their wars more barbarous; they procured less advantages to the civilized world, and yet they have never ceased to be objects of the admiration and eulogy of posterity.

The war against the Albigeois was more cruel and more unfortunate than the crusade directed against the nations of Prussia. Missionaries and warriors outraged, by their conduct, all the laws of justice and of the religion whose triumph they pretended to aim at. The heretics, naturally, sometimes employed reprisals against their enemies; both sides armed with the steel and axe of murderers and executioners, humanity had to deplore the most guilty excesses.

When casting a retrospective glance over the annals of the middle ages, we are particularly grieved to see sanguinary wars undertaken and carried on in the name of a religion of peace, whilst we can scarcely find an example of a religious war among the ancients and under the laws of paganism.* We must believe that modern nations and those of antiquity have, and had the same passions; but, amongst the ancients, religion entered less deeply into the heart of man or into the spirit of social institutions. The worship of false gods had no positive dogma; it added nothing to morality; it prescribed no duties to the citizen; it was not bound up with the maxims of legislation, and existed, in some sort, only upon the surface of society. When paganism was attacked, or when a change was effected in the worship of false gods, the affections, morals, and interests of pagan society were not deeply wounded. It was not thus with Christianity, which, particularly in the middle ages, mixed itself up with all civil laws, recalled man to all the duties due to his country, and united itself with all the principles of social order. Amidst the growing civilization of Europe, the Christian religion was blended with all the interests of nations; it was, in a manner, the foundation of all society; it was society itself: we cannot wonder, then, that men were passionate in its defence. Then all who separated themselves from the Christian religion, separated themselves from society; and all who rejected the laws of the Church, ceased to acknowledge the laws of their country. We must consider the wars against the Albigeois and the Prussians in this light; they were rather social wars than religious wars.

---

* We may name, among the Greeks, the sacred war undertaken for the lands which belonged to the temple of Delphos; but on reading closely the history of this war, it is easy to see that they did not fight for a dogma or a religious opinion, as in the wars which, among the moderns, have had religion for a motive or a pretence.

BOOK XIII

THE SEVENTH CRUSADE

1242 TO 1245

GAINING CONVERTS.

BOOK XIII.

THE SEVENTH CRUSADE.

A.D. 1242–1245.

The Tartars of the middle ages—Their history and conquests—Gengiskhan, the Tartar Chief—Temugin—Prester John—Khan of the Karaites—Conquest of China, Carismia, and other extensive countries in Asia and Europe, by Gengiskhan—His death—Victorious career of Octaï, khan of the Tartars—Hungary conquered—The warriors of Carismia join the sultan of Cairo, and capture Jerusalem—The Mohammedans of Syria defeated by the Carismians, and Damascus captured—The Carismians rebel against the sultan of Cairo—They are defeated and dispersed—Barbarous hordes of the Comans—Distress of the Christians—Valeran, bishop of Berytus—Innocent IV., at the council of Lyons, determines on the seventh crusade, and excommunicates Frederick, emperor of Germany—Cardinals first clothed in scarlet—Louis IX., king of France, recovers from a dangerous malady, and determines on prosecuting the seventh crusade against the infidels—The illustrious names engaged in it—Blanche, the queen-mother—Agitated state of Germany and Italy—Frederick of Germany deposed by the pope—Civil contests thence arising—The nobles of France form a league to resist the exactions of the pope—Louis makes extensive preparations for the holy war—The earl of Salisbury, and Haco king of Norway, engage in it—Ameliorated state of society resulting from the crusades—Louis embarks and arrives at Cyprus—Pope Innocent IV. takes charge of his kingdom—Marguerite, wife of Louis—Archambault de Bourbons—Sieur de Joinville—Antioch ravaged by the Turcomans—Louis receives an embassy from the Tartar prince, Ecalthai—Political discord among the Mohammedans—Family of the Ayoubites—Malek-Salek Negmeddin, sultan of Egypt—Military and political state of Egypt at the time of the crusade—Louis IX. and the Christian forces arrive before Damietta—His address to the Crusaders—He besieges Damietta—Fakreddin, the Egyptian leader—Louis attacks and defeats the infidel troops—Damietta captured—Negotiations with Negmeddin—Livre Tournois—Bravery of the Bedouin Arabs—Sidon captured by the Mohammedans.

HEN I began this work, I was far from being aware of the task I was imposing upon myself; animated by the interest of my subject, full of a too great confidence in my own powers, like those villagers who, when they set out for the first crusade, fancied every city they saw to be Jerusalem, I constantly believed I was approaching the end of my labours. As I advanced in my career, the horizon expanded before me, difficulties multiplied at every step, so that to sustain my courage, I have often been obliged to recall to my mind the kindness with which the early volumes of this history have been received by the public.

The difficulty did not consist in placing a narrative of the holy wars before our readers; it became necessary to present exact ideas of the manners and characters of the nations which, in any way, took part in them. We have endeavoured to make all the peoples known who have in turn passed across the scene; the Franks, with their soldier-like roughness, their love of glory, and their generous passions; the Turks and Saracens, with their military religion and their barbarous valour; the Greeks, with their corrupted manners, their character at once superstitious and frivolous, and their vanity, which with them supplied the place of patriotism: a new nation is now about to offer itself to the pencil of history, and mingle with the events of which we are attempting to give the picture. We are about to say a few words upon the manners and conquests of the Tartars in the middle ages.

The hordes of this nation, at the period of the sixth crusade, had invaded several countries of Asia, and the progress of their arms had a great influence over the policy of the Mussulman powers of Syria and Egypt, which were then at war with the Christians. At the time of which we are speaking, the fame of their victories filled the East, and spread terror even to the most remote countries of Europe.

The Tartars inhabited the vast regions which lie between ancient Emaüs, Siberia, China, and the Sea of Kamschatka; they were divided into several nations, which all boasted of having the same origin; each of these nations, governed by a khan, or supreme leader, was composed of a great number of tribes, each tribe commanded by a particular chief, called Myrza. The produce of the chase, the milk of their mares, and the flesh of their flocks, satisfied the simple wants of the Tartars; they lived under tents with their families; and moveable dwellings, drawn by oxen, transported from one place to another their wives, their children, and all they possessed. In summer, the whole tribe drew towards the northern countries, and encamped upon the banks of a river or a lake; in winter, they directed their course southward, and sought the shelter of mountains that could protect them from the icy winds of the north.

The Tartar hordes assembled every year, in either autumn or spring. In these assemblies, which they called *Couraltaï*, they deliberated on horseback, upon the march of the tribes, the distribution of the pasturages, and peace and war. It was from the bosom of this tumultuous assembly that issued the legislation of the people of Tartary; a simple and laconic legislation, like those of all barbarous nations, whose only objects are to maintain the power of the leaders, and keep up discipline and emulation among the warriors.

The nations of Tartary acknowledged one God, the sovereign of heaven, to whom they offered up neither incense nor prayers. Their worship was reserved for a crowd of genii, whom they believed to be spread through the air, upon the earth, and amidst the waters; a great number of idols, the rough work of their own hands, filled their dwellings, followed them in their courses, and watched over their flocks, their slaves, and their families. Their priests, brought up in the practices of magic, studied the course of the stars, predicted future events, and employed themselves in abusing the minds of the people by sorcery. Their religious worship, which inculcated no morality, had neither softened their rude manners nor ameliorated their character, which was as boisterous and unkindly as their climate. No monument raised under the auspices of religion, no book inspired by it, reminded them of deeds of glory, or laid before them precepts and examples of virtue. In the course of their wandering life, the dead, whom they sometimes dragged with them in their waggons, appeared to them an annoying burden, and they buried them in haste in retired places; where, covering them with the sands of the desert, they were satisfied with concealing them from the eyes or the outrages of the living.

Everything that might fix them to one spot rather than another, or lead them to change their manner of living, excited the animadversion and disdain of these races. Of all the tribes that inhabited Mogul Tartary, one alone was acquainted with writing, and cultivated letters; all the rest despised commerce, arts, and learning; which constitute the true splendour of polished societies. The Tartars disdained the idea of building; in the twelfth century their vast country contained but one city,* the extent of which, according to the monk Rubruquis, did not equal that of the little town of Saint Denis. Confining themselves to the care of their flocks, they regarded agriculture as a degrading occupation, only fit to employ the industry of slaves or conquered people. Their immense plains had never become yellow with harvests sown by the hand of man; no fruit had there ripened

---

* Karakoroum, the residence of the principal branch of the successors of Gengiskhan. It is only lately that the true situation of this city has been fixed by M. Abel-Remusat; it was on the left bank of the Orgon, not far from the junction of that river with the Selinga to the south of the Lake of Baïkal, by the 49° of latitude and the 102° of longitude. The same country has since been the residence of the Grand Lama.

which he had planted. The spectacle most agreeable to a Tartar was the desert, upon which grass grew without cultivation, or the field of battle covered with ruin and carnage.

As the limits of their pastures were under no regulation, frequent quarrels necessarily arose among the Tartars; the spirit of jealousy constantly agitated the wandering hordes; the ambitious leaders could endure neither neighbours nor rivals. Thence civil wars; and from the bosom of civil wars issued a fully-armed despotism, to support which the people flocked with cheerfulness, because it promised them conquests. The entire population was military, to whom fighting appeared to be the only true glory, and the most noble occupation of man. The encampments of the Tartars, their marches, their hunting-parties, resembled military exhibitions. Habit imparted so much ease and firmness to their seat on horseback, that they took their food, and even indulged in sleep, without dismounting. Their bow, of an enormous size, announced their strength and skill; their sharp steel-headed arrows flew to an immense distance, and struck down the bird amidst its rapid career, or pierced through and through the bear or tiger of the desert; they surpassed their enemies in the rapidity of their evolutions; they excelled them in the perfidious art of fighting whilst flying; and retreat was often, for them, the signal of victory. All the stratagems of war appeared familiar to them; and as if a fatal instinct had taught them all that could assist in the destruction of the human race, the Tartars, who built no cities, knew how to construct the most formidable machines of war, and were not unacquainted with any means that could spread terror and desolation among their enemies. In their expeditions, their march was never impeded by the inclemency of seasons, the depth of rivers, the steepness of precipices, or the height of mountains. A little hardened milk, diluted with water, sufficed for the food of a horseman during several days; the skin of a sheep or a bear, a few strips of coarse felt, formed his garments. The warriors showed the most blind obedience to their leaders, and, at the least signal, were ready to encounter death in any shape. They were divided into tens, hundreds, thousands, and tens of thousands; their armies were composed of all that could handle the bow or lance; and what must have caused their enemies as much surprise as terror, was the order and discipline that prevailed in a multitude that chance seemed to have gathered together. According to their military legislation, the Tartars were never allowed to make peace but with a conquered enemy; he who fled from battle, or abandoned his companions in danger, was punished with death; they shed the blood of men with the same indifference as that of wild animals, and their ferocity added greatly to the terror which they inspired in their enterprises.

The Tartars, in their pride, despised all other nations, and believed that the whole world ought to be subject to them. According to certain opinions, transmitted from age to age, the Mogul hordes abandoned the north to the dead they left behind them in the deserts, and kept their faces constantly directed towards the south, which was promised to their valour. The territories and the riches of other nations excited their ambition; and, possessing neither territories nor riches themselves, they had almost nothing to fear from conquerors. Not only their warlike education, but their prejudices, their customs, the inconstancy of their character, everything with them seemed to favour distant expeditions and warlike invasions. They carried with them neither regrets nor endearing remembrances from the countries they abandoned; and if it be true, when we say that country is not within the walls of a city, or the limits of a province, but in the affections and ties of family, in the laws, manners, and customs of a nation, the Tartars, when changing their climate, had always their country with them. The presence of their wives, of their children; the sight of their flocks and their idols, everywhere inflamed their patriotism, or love of their nation, and sustained their courage. Accustomed to consult their own inclinations, and take them for their sole rule of conduct, they were never restrained by the laws of morality or by feelings of humanity; as they had a profound indifference for all the religions of the earth, this indifference even, which aroused no hatred in other nations, facilitated their conquests, by leaving them the liberty of readily receiving or embracing the opinions and creeds of the people they conquered, and whom they thus completely subjected to their laws.

In very remote antiquity, the hordes of Tartary had several times invaded the vast regions of India, China, and Persia, and had extended their ravages even into the West: the ambition or the caprice of a skilful leader, excess of population, want of pasturage, the predictions of a wizard, were quite sufficient to inflame this tumultuous race, and precipitate them in a mass upon distant regions. Woe to the people whom the Tartars encountered in their passage! At their approach, empires fell with a horrible crash; nations were driven back upon one another, like the waves of the sea; the world was shaken and covered with ruins. History has preserved the remembrance of several of their invasions; the most remote posterity will never pronounce without a species of terror the names of the Avari, the Huns, the Heruli, of all those wandering nations who, some flowing from the depths of Tartary, and others dragged in the wake of the conquerors or driven before them, poured down upon the tottering empire of the Romans, and divided the spoils of the civilized world amongst them: in the middle ages, the wars of the Tartars were compared to tempests, inundations, or the bursting forth of volcanoes; and the resigned nations believed that the justice of God held these innumerable swarms of barbarians in reserve in the north, to pour out his anger upon the rest of the earth, and chastise corrupted nations by their hands.

The Tartars never proved themselves more redoubtable than under the reign of Gengiskhan. Temugin, which was the first name of the heroic barbarian, was born of a prince who reigned over some hordes of ancient Mogulistan. Traditions relate that the seventh of his ancestors was engendered in the womb of his mother by the miraculous influence of the rays of the sun. At the birth of Temugin, his family remarked with joy some coagulated blood in the hands of the infant, a sinister presage for the human race, in which flattery or superstition saw the future glory of a conqueror. Some historians informs us that nothing was neglected in the education of Temugin; others, more worthy of faith, affirm that he could not read; but all agree in saying that he was born for war, and to command a warlike people. Endowed with great penetration of mind, and with a sort of eloquence, knowing how to dissemble in season, skilful in working upon the passions, uniting bravery to a boundless ambition, that was never checked by any scruple, he had all the qualities and all the vices which lead to empire among barbarians, and sometimes even among polished nations. His natural propensities developed themselves in adversity, which hardened his character, and taught him to brave everything in order to carry out his designs. From the age of fourteen, despoiled of his paternal heritage, and a fugitive with the khan of the Karaïtes, he sacrificed without pain the most holy duties of hospitality to his future grandeur. The khan of the Karaïtes was known by the name of Prester John among the Christians of the middle ages, who celebrated his conversion to Christianity, and considered him as one of the most fervent apostles of the Gospel, which, doubtless, he never had known. He confided the care of his states to young Temugin, who insinuated himself into the favour of the army, and dethroned his benefactor. As he had outraged all the laws of morality to usurp empire, he violated all the laws of humanity to maintain himself in it. Seventy of his enemies plunged into seventy caldrons of boiling water, and the skull of the chief of the Karaïtes enchased in a golden box, announced very plainly what the master was whom fortune was about to place over the nations of Asia.

Victory was to achieve what treachery, violence, and ingratitude had begun; the arms of Temugin and his lieutenants subdued successively all the hordes whose camps arose between the wall of China and the Volga. Temugin was the all-powerful leader of many millions of shepherds and warriors, impatient to quit their own climate and invade the regions of the south. In order to attach the companions of his victories to his fortunes, he was desirous of reigning by their suffrages, and called together a couraltaï or general diet, in which he was proclaimed sovereign of the Moguls. The ambition of Temugin did not neglect the influence of superstition; he took the title of Gengis, *king of kings*, or *master of the world*, and fame gave out that he had received this pompous title from a prophet who descended from heaven upon a white horse.

Eastern historians have praised Gengiskhan for having given laws to nations he had conquered. These laws, the aim of which was to maintain the peace of families, and to direct the minds of the people towards war, for a length of time retained the obedience and the respect of the Moguls. As Gengiskhan, in his legislation, acknowledged one God, the sovereign of the earth and heaven, and, at the same time, permitted all kinds of creeds, some modern writers have taken occasion to boast of his religious tolerance. But what could be the tolerance of a savage conqueror, who caused himself to be styled the son of the sun, the son of God; who himself followed no worship, and to whom all religions were equally indifferent, provided they crossed neither his ambition nor his pride?

The lieutenants and warriors of Gengiskhan had recognised him with the greater joy, as universal conqueror and master of the earth, from the hopes they entertained of enriching themselves with the spoils of all the nations subdued by his arms. His first enterprises were directed against China, of which empire he had been the vassal. Neither the barrier of the great wall, nor the ascendancy of knowledge and arts, nor the use of gunpowder, said to be then known among the Chinese, was able to defend a flourishing empire against the attacks of a multitude, whom the thirst for booty and a warlike instinct, urged forward to face perils, and rendered invincible.

The wars we have seen in our days, and of which we deplore the calamities, give nothing but a feeble idea of these gigantic invasions, in which many millions of men perished by sword and famine. China experienced twice all the evils inseparable from a war which appeared to be directed by the genius of destruction; and, in the space of a few years, the most ancient and the most powerful kingdom of Asia, covered with blood and ruins, and deprived of half its population, became one of the provinces of the new empire founded by the shepherds of Mogulistan.

The conquest of Carismia soon followed that of China; Carismia was close to the frontiers of the Mogul empire, and, on one side extended to the Gulf of Persia, and on the other, to the limits of India and Turkistan. Gengis learnt that a Tartar caravan and three of his ambassadors had been massacred in one of the cities of the Carismians. It is easy to imagine the effect that this news would produce upon the emperor of the Moguls, who himself compared the anger of kings to the fire of conflagrations, which the lightest wind may light up. After having fasted and prayed, during three days and three nights, upon a mountain, where a hermit announced to him, the second time, the conquest of the whole world, the terrible Gengiskhan commenced his march, at the head of seven hundred thousand Tartars. This army met that of the Carismians on the banks of the Jaxartes; Mahomet, sultan of Carismia, who had several times carried his victorious arms into Turkistan and Persia, commanded the host of the Carismians. The plain in which this battle was fought was covered by twelve hundred thousand combatants; the shock was terrific, the carnage horrible; victory was adverse to Mahomet, who, from that day, together with his family and the whole of his nation, sunk into the lowest abyss of misfortune.

The cities of Otrar, Bochara, Samarcand, Candahar, and Carismia, besieged by an innumerable multitude, fell in turn into the power of the conqueror, and witnessed the extirpation of their garrisons and inhabitants. We cannot suppress a feeling of pity when history presents to us, on one side, an entire population flying from their devastated homes, to seek an asylum in deserts and mountains; and on the other, the family of a powerful monarch dragged into slavery or groaning in exile; and this monarch himself, whose prosperity all Asia had boasted or envied, abandoned by his subjects, and dying with misery and despair in an island of the Caspian Sea.

The army of Gengiskhan returned to Tartary, loaded with the spoils of Carismia: the sovereign of the Moguls appeared to form the desire of governing his conquests in peace; but the world, agitated by his victories, and always eager to throw off his yoke, together with the warlike spirit of his nation, to whom he had afforded a glimpse of the riches of other people, would not permit him again to enjoy repose; he was on the point of undertaking a third expedition against China, which seemed disposed to rebel, when death put an end to his career. Some historians assert that he was struck dead by thunder, as if Heaven had determined itself to crush the instrument of its wrath; others, much more worthy of belief, inform us that the Tartar hero died in his bed, surrounded by his children, to whom he recommended to preserve union among themselves, that they might achieve the conquest of the world. Octaï, the eldest of his sons, succeeded him in the empire, and, according to the custom of the Moguls, the great men assembled and said to him, "We wish, we pray, we command you to accept of entire power over us." The new emperor answered by this formula, which contains the whole spirit of the despotic governments of the East: "If you desire that I should be your khan, are you resolved to obey me in everything; to come when I shall call you, to go where I shall send you, and to put to death all those I shall command you to kill?" After they had answered "Yes," he said to them, "Henceforth my simple word shall serve me as a sword." Such was the government of the Tartars. Octaï was about to reign over an empire composed of several great empires; his brothers and nephews commanded the innumerable armies that had conquered China and Carismia; they governed in his name in the north, in the south, and the east, kingdoms of which the extent was scarcely known; each of his lieutenants was more powerful than the greatest kings of the earth, and all obeyed him as his slaves. For the first time, perhaps, concord was preserved among conquerors; and this monstrous union effected the ruin of all the nations of Asia: Turkistan, Persia, India, the southern provinces of China, which had escaped the ravages of the first invasion, all that remained of the empire of the Abassides and of that of the Seljoucides—all fell before the arms of the redoubtable posterity of Gengiskhan. Many of the sovereigns whom, in these days of disorder and calamity the chance of war hurled from their thrones, had invoked the succour of the Moguls, and favoured the enterprises of that warlike people against neighbouring or rival powers. Fortune enveloped them all in the same ruin, and oriental history compares them to the three dervises whose indiscreet wishes and prayers reanimated, in the desert, the bones of a lion, who sprang up from the bosom of the sand and devoured them.

The conquest of the richest countries of Asia had inflamed the enthusiasm of the Tartars to such a degree, that it would have been impossible for their leaders to confine them within the limits of their own territories, or bring them back to the peaceful labours of pastoral life. Octaï, whether desirous of obeying the paternal instructions, or whether he felt the necessity of employing the restlest and turbulent activity of the Moguls, resolved to turn his arms towards the West. Fifteen hundred thousand shepherds or warriors inscribed their names upon the military register; five hundred thousand of the most robust were selected for the great expedition; the others were to remain in Asia, to maintain the submission of the vanquished nations, and complete the conquests commenced by Gengiskhan. Rejoicings, which lasted forty days, preceded the departure of the Mogul army, and were as a signal of the desolation they were about to spread among the countries of Europe.

In their rapid course, the Tartars crossed the Volga, and penetrated, almost without obstacle, into Muscovy, then a prey to the fury of civil war. The devastation of their country, the conflagrations of Kiow and Moscow, and the disgraceful yoke that so long oppressed these northern regions, were the punishments due to the feeble resistance of the Muscovites. After the conquest of Russia, the multitude of Moguls, led by Batou, son of Tuli, directed their victorious course towards Poland and the frontiers of Germany, and repeated, wherever they went, the horrors of Attila and his Huns. The cities of Lublin and Warsaw disappeared on their passage, and they laid waste both shores of the Baltic. In vain the duke of Silesia, the Polish palatines, and the grand master of the Teutonic order, united their forces to arrest the progress of this new scourge of God; the generous defenders of Europe succumbed upon the plains of Lignitz, and nine sacks, filled with human ears, were the trophy of the victory of the barbarians. The Carpathian mountains presented but a feeble barrier to these invincible hordes; and the Tartars soon burst like a fearful tempest over the territories of those Hungarians who, two centuries before, had, like them, quitted the deserts of Scythia, and conquered the fertile banks of the Danube. Bela, king of Hungary, had recently attracted forty thousand families of Comans into his dominions, who betrayed him; the palatines and magnates of the kingdom were divided among themselves, and not even the aspect of danger could induce them to unite or submit themselves to the laws of the monarch. Disobedience, treachery, and discord, delivered the whole kingdom up to the furies of a pitiless enemy; the flocks, the harvests, the entire wealth of the country, became the prey of the Moguls; half the population was exterminated. Of all the cities of Hungary, only three offered an earnest and true resistance, and thus preserved themselves from scenes of carnage and destruction. The shepherds of Scythia, who could not read, have left to the vanquished the task of describing their conquests, and we have great difficulty in crediting the accounts of the old Hungarian chronicles, when they describe the unheard-of cruelties by which the Moguls disgraced their victories; but several provinces entirely depopulated and changed into deserts, the ruins of two thousand churches, fifty destroyed cities, the traditions of these great disasters transmitted from age to age, and the terror that pervaded Europe, are evidences so worthy of faith, that we cannot reject them.

In the general consternation, it is surprising that the Moguls did not direct their arms against the Latin empire of Constantinople, then menaced by the Greeks, and little better than a ruin; but the shepherds of the desert did not employ themselves in inquiries concerning the interior revolutions of states or of the signs of their decay; they preserved, as did all the nations of Asia, a vague and confused idea of the power of the armies of ancient Byzantium, but took little heed whether the moment were come to attack it and conquer it. The great advantages which the imperial city derived from its position between Europe and Asia, did not at all strike the Tartars, who were ignorant of both navigation and commerce, and infinitely preferred rich pastures to the sumptuous edifices of great capitals. Thus we may equally believe, either that the city of Constantine was protected on this occasion by the memories of its past greatness, or that it owed its safety to the contempt and indifference of the barbarians.

The Franks established in Syria enjoyed the same good fortune as the Greeks of Byzantium. The armies of the Moguls had not yet crossed the Euphrates.

Whilst the tumult of war and the fall of empires resounded from the Yellow River to the Danube, the Christians of Palestine, protected by the discords of the Saracens, resumed possession of Jerusalem: they were beginning to repair the walls of the holy city, and rebuild the churches; and thanked Heaven in peace, for having preserved them from the scourges that were devastating the rest of the world. The Tartars were scarcely aware of the existence or the name of a country for which so much blood had been spilt, and were not likely to be attracted to the revered but barren banks of the Jordan, by either the hopes of booty or by the remembrances which excited the warlike enthusiasm of the nations of the West. Happy would it have been for the Christian colonies, if a people, conquered by the Moguls, driven from their own territories, and seeking an asylum everywhere, had not come to disturb their transient security, and plunge the city of Christ into fresh calamities.

After the death of Mahomet, sultan of Carismia, his son Gelaleddin gathered together an army. The valour which he displayed in several battles astonished his enemies, and, for a moment, brought back to his standard the sad remains of his empire; fortune favoured his expeditions into Georgia and India; but at last he forgot the lessons of adversity amidst the intoxication of pleasures; he lost all his conquests, and perished miserably among the Curds, where he had sought refuge. The Carismian warriors, incessantly pursued by the Tartars, abandoned a country they could no longer defend, and, under the command of one of their leaders named Barbakan, spread themselves through Asia Minor and Syria.

These hordes, banished from their own country, marched, sword and torch in hand, and, in their despair, seemed to wish to avenge upon other nations the evils they had suffered from the Tartars. History describes these furious bands, wandering along the banks of the Orontes and the Euphrates, dragging in their train a multitude of men and women that had fallen into their hands; a great number of waggons conveyed the spoils of the ravaged provinces they passed through. The most brave of them ornamented their lances with the hair of those they had immolated in fight. Clothed in the produce of pillage, their army presented a spectacle at once terrific and ridiculous. The Carismian warriors had no resource but in victory, and all the harangues of their leaders consisted of these words: *You will conquer, or you will die.* They gave no quarter to their enemies on the field of battle; when conquered themselves, they submitted to death without a complaint. Their fury spared neither Christians nor Mussulmans; all they met on their passage were their enemies; their approach spread terror everywhere, put the distracted peoples to flight, and changed cities and towns into deserts.

The Mussulman powers of Syria several times united in a league against the Carismians, and drove them back to the other side of the Euphrates. But the spirit of rivalry which at all times divided the princes of the family of Saladin, soon recalled an enemy always redoubtable, notwithstanding defeats. At the period of which we are speaking, the princes of Damascus, Carac, and Emessa had just formed an alliance with the Christians of Palestine; they not only restored Jerusalem, Tiberias, and the principality of Galilee to them, but they promised to join them in the conquest of Egypt, a conquest for which the whole of Syria was making preparations. The sultan of Cairo, to avenge himself upon the Christians who had broken the treaties concluded with him, to punish their new allies, and protect himself from their invasion, determined to apply for succour to the hordes of Carismia; and sent deputies to the leaders of these barbarians, promising to abandon Palestine to them, if they subdued it.

This proposition was accepted with joy, and twenty thousand horsemen, animated by a thirst for booty and slaughter, hastened from the further parts of Mesopotamia, disposed to be subservient to the vengeance or anger of the Egyptian monarch. On their march they ravaged the territory of Tripoli and the principality of Galilee, and the flames which everywhere accompanied their steps, announced their arrival to the inhabitants of Jerusalem.

Fortifications scarcely commenced, and the small number of warriors in the holy city, left not the least hope of being able to repel the unexpected attacks of such a formidable enemy. The whole population of Jerusalem resolved to fly, under the guidance of the knights of the Hospital and the Temple. There only remained in the city the sick and a few inhabitants who could not make their minds up to abandon their homes and their infirm kindred. The Carismians soon arrived, and having destroyed a few intrenchments that had been made in their route, they entered Jerusalem sword in hand, massacred all they met, and as, amidst a deserted city the conquerors found no victims to glut their vengeance with, they had recourse to a most odious stratagem to lure back the inhabitants who had taken flight. They raised the standards of the cross upon every tower, and set all the bells ringing. The crowd of Christians who were retiring towards Jaffa, marched on in silence, and advanced but slowly, constantly hoping that Heaven would be touched by their misery, and, by some miracle, lead them back to the homes they had quitted: from time to time, their eyes involuntarily turned towards the holy city. All at once they saw the banners of the cross unfurled, and the sound of the sacred brass, which every day called them to prayers, resounded in their ears. The news soon spread that either the barbarians had marched their army in another direction, or that they had been repulsed by the Christians who were left in the city. They became soon persuaded that God had taken pity on his people, and would not permit the city of Christ to be defiled by the presence of a sacrilegious horde. Seven thousand fugitives, deceived by this hope, returned to Jerusalem and gave themselves up to the fury of the Carismians, who put them all to the sword. Torrents of blood flowed through the streets and along the roads. A troop of nuns, children, and aged people, who had sought refuge in the church of the Holy Sepulchre, were massacred at the foot of the altars. The Carismians finding nothing among the living to satisfy their fury, burst open the sepulchres, and gave the coffins and remains of the dead up to the flames; the tomb of Christ, that of Godfrey of Bouillon, the sacred relics of the martyrs and heroes of the faith, nothing was respected, and Jerusalem then witnessed within its walls such cruelties and profanations as had never taken place in the most barbarous wars, or in days marked by the anger of God.

In the mean time, the grand masters of the Templars and the Hospitallers, assembled with the patriarch of Jerusalem and the nobles of the kingdom, in Ptolemaïs, endeavoured to devise means by which the Carismians might be repulsed and Palestine saved. All the inhabitants of Tyre, Sidon, Ptolemaïs, and other Christian cities, able to bear arms, repaired to their standards. The princes of Damascus, Carac, and Emessa, whose assistance the Christians implored, united their forces, and assembled an army to stop the progress of the general devastation. This Mussulman army soon arrived in Palestine. Its appearance before the walls of Ptolemaïs raised the courage of the Franks, who, in so pressing a danger, appeared to have no repugnance to fight in company with the infidels. Almansor, prince of Emessa, who commanded the Mussulman warriors, had recently signalized his valour against the hordes of Carismia. The Christians took pleasure in relating his victories in the plains of Aleppo, and on the banks of the Euphrates. He was received in Palestine as a liberator, and carpets bordered with gold and silk were spread upon his passage. "The people," says Joinville, " considered him as one of *the best barons of paganism.*"

The preparations of the Christians, the zeal and ardour of the military orders, the barons, and prelates; the union that subsisted between the Franks and their new allies, altogether seemed to form a presage of success in a war undertaken in the names of religion, humanity, and patriotism. The Christian and Mussulman armies, united under the same banners, set out from Ptolemaïs, and encamped upon the plains of Ascalon. The army of the Carismians advanced towards Gaza, where they were to receive provisions and reinforcements sent by the sultan of Egypt. The Franks became impatient to meet their enemies, and to avenge the deaths of their companions and brethren massacred at Jerusalem. A council was called, to deliberate upon the best mode of proceeding. The prince of Emessa and the more wise among the barons thought it not prudent to expose the safety of the Christians and their allies to the risk of a battle. It appeared to them most advisable to occupy

THE TRUE CROSS.

an advantageous position, and wait, without giving battle, till the natural inconstancy of the Carismians, want of provisions, or discord, might assist in dispersing this vagabond multitude, or lead them into other countries.

Most of the other chiefs, among whom was the patriarch of Jerusalem, did not agree with this opinion, and could see nothing in the Carismians but an undisciplined horde that it would be very easy to conquer and put to flight: any delay in attacking them would only raise their pride and redouble their audacity. Every day the evils of war were increasing; humanity and the safety of the Christian colonies required that they should promptly put an end to so many devastations, and that they should make haste to chastise the brigands, whose presence was at once an opprobrium and a calamity for the Christians, and all the allies of the Christians.

This opinion, too congenial with the impatient valour of the Franks, prevailed in the council. It was resolved to march, and offer the enemy battle.

The two armies met in the country of the ancient Philistines. Some years before, the duke of Burgundy and the king of Navarre, surprised in the sandy plains of Gaza, had lost the best of their knights and soldiers. Neither the sight of places where the Crusaders had been defeated, nor the remembrance of their recent disaster, diminished the imprudent ardour of the Christian warriors; as soon as they perceived the enemy, they were eager for the signal for battle. The Christian army was divided into three bodies; the left wing, in which were the knights of St. John, was commanded by Gauthier de Brienne, count of Jaffa, nephew to king John, and son of that Gauthier who died at the conquest of Naples. The Mussulman troops, under the orders of the prince of Emessa, formed the right wing. The patriarch of Jerusalem, surrounded by his clergy, with the wood of the true cross borne before him, the grand master of the Templars with his knights, and the barons of Palestine with their vassals, occupied the centre of the army.

The Carismians formed their line of battle slowly, and some degree of disorder was observable in their ranks. Gauthier de Brienne was anxious to profit by this circumstance and attack them with advantage; but the patriarch restrained his valour by a severity not less contrary to the interests of the Christians than to the spirit of the Gospel.

The count of Jaffa, having been excommunicated for detaining in his hands a castle to which the prelate laid claim, asked, before he commenced the encounter in which he might lose his life, to be relieved from his excommunication. The patriarch twice rejected his prayer, and refused to absolve him. The army, which had received the benedictions of the priests and bishops, arising from their knees, awaited in silence the signal for battle. The Carismians had formed their line and advanced, uttering loud cries and discharging a cloud of arrows. Then the bishop of Rama, in complete armour, impatient to signalize his bravery against the enemies of the Christians, approached the count of Jaffa, exclaiming, "Let us march,—the patriarch is wrong: I absolve you, in the name of the Father, of the Son, and of the Holy Ghost." After having pronounced these words, the intrepid bishop of Rama and Gauthier de Brienne, followed by his companions in arms, rushed amidst the ranks of the enemy, burning to obtain victory or the crown of martyrdom.

The two armies were soon generally engaged, and mingled on the field of battle. The ardour to conquer was equal on both sides; neither the Christians nor their enemies could be ignorant that a single defeat must cause their ruin, and that their only safety was in victory. On this account, the annals of war present no example of a more murderous and obstinate contest; the battle began with the dawn, and only ended at sunset. On the following morning fighting was renewed with the same fury; the prince of Emessa, after having lost two thousand of his horsemen, abandoned the field of battle, and fled towards Damascus. This retreat of the Mussulmans decided the victory in favour of the Carismians; the Christians for a long time sustained the repeated shocks of the enemy; but at length, exhausted by fatigue and overwhelmed by a multitude, almost all were either killed or taken prisoners. This sanguinary battle cost life or liberty to more than thirty thousand Christian and Mussulman warriors; the prince of Tyre, the patriarch of Jerusalem, and some of the prelates, with great difficulty escaped the slaughter, and retired to Ptolemaïs. Among the warriors who regained the Christian cities, there were only thirty-three knights of the Temple, twenty-six Hospitallers, and three Teutonic knights.

When the news of this victory reached Egypt, it created a universal joy; it was announced to the people by sound of drums and trumpets; the sultan ordered public rejoicings throughout the provinces, and all the public edifices of the capital were illumined during three nights. In a short time the prisoners arrived at Cairo, mounted on camels, and pursued by the insulting clamours of the multitude. Before their arrival, the heads of their companions and brethren killed at the battle of Gaza were exhibited on the walls. This horrible monument of their defeat foreboded all they had to fear for themselves from the barbarity of the conquerors. They were cast into dungeons, where they were abandoned to the mercies of cruel gaolers, and where they had the melancholy satisfaction of embracing the barons and knights made prisoners in the last crusade.

Whilst all Egypt was celebrating the victory of Gaza, the inhabitants of Palestine deplored the death and captivity of their bravest warriors. As long as any hope existed of conquering the Carismians with the assistance of the Mussulmans of Syria, their alliance had created neither mistrust nor scruple; but reverses quickly revived prejudices; the last disaster was attributed to divine justice, irritated by having seen the banners of Christ mingled with those of Mahomet. On the other hand, the Mussulmans believed they had betrayed the cause of Islamism by allying themselves with the Christians; the aspect of the cross on the field of battle awakened their fanaticism and diminished their zeal for a cause which appeared to be that of their enemies. At the moment of beginning the fight, the prince of Emessa was heard to pronounce these words: "I am armed for battle, and yet God tells me, in the depths of my heart, that we shall not be victorious, because we have sought the friendship of the Franks."

The victory of the Carismians delivered up the greater part of Palestine to the most redoubtable enemies of the Christian colonies. The Egyptians took possession of Jerusalem, Tiberias, and the cities ceded to the Franks by the prince of Damascus. The hordes of Carismia ravaged all the banks of the Jordan, with the territories of Ascalon and Ptolemaïs, and laid siege to Jaffa. They dragged the unfortunate Gauthier de Brienne in their train, hoping that he would cause a city that belonged to him to open its gates to them: this model of Christian heroes was fastened to a cross before the walls. Whilst thus exposed to the eyes of his faithful vassals, the Carismians loaded him with insults, and threatened him with instant death if the city of Jaffa offered the least resistance. Gauthier, braving death, exhorted the inhabitants and the garrison, with a loud voice, to defend themselves to the last extremity. "Your duty," cried he, "is to defend a Christian city; mine is to die for you and Jesus Christ." The city of Jaffa did not fall into the hands of the Carismians, and Gauthier soon received the reward of his generous devotedness. Sent to the sultan of Cairo, he perished beneath the brutal blows of a furious mob, and thus obtained the palm of martyrdom for which he had wished.

In the mean time, fortune, or rather the inconstancy of the barbarians, came to the assistance of the Franks, and delivered Palestine from the presence of an enemy nothing could resist. The sultan of Cairo sent robes of honour and magnificent presents to the leaders of the victorious hordes, proposing to them to crown their exploits by directing their arms against the city of Damascus. The

Carismians immediately laid siege to the capital of Syria. Damascus, which had been hastily fortified, was able to oppose but a very slight resistance to their impetuous attacks. Having no hope of succour, they opened their gates, and acknowledged the domination of the sultan of Egypt. It was then that the Carismians, inflated by their victory, demanded, in a menacing tone, that the lands that had been promised to them in Palestine should immediately be given up to them. The sultan of Cairo, who dreaded such neighbours, attempted to defer the fulfilment of his promise. In the fury which his refusal created, the barbarians offered their services to the prince whom they had just despoiled of his states, and laid fresh siege to Damascus, in order to deprive the Egyptians of it. The garrison and the inhabitants defended themselves with obstinacy; the fear of falling into the hands of a pitiless enemy supplying the place of courage. All the evils that war brings in her train, even famine itself, appeared to them a less terrible scourge than the hordes assembled under their ramparts.

The sultan of Egypt sent an army to assist the city, which was augmented by the troops of Aleppo and of several of the principalities of Syria. The Carismians were conquered in two battles. After this double defeat, Oriental history scarcely mentions their name, or furnishes us with means of following their track. The greater part of those that escaped the sword perished with hunger and misery in the countries they had devastated; the most brave and the best disciplined went to seek an asylum in the states of the sultan of Iconium: and if faith can be given to the conjectures of some historians, they were the obscure origin of the powerful dynasty of the Ottomans.

The Christians of Palestine must have been grateful to Heaven for the destruction of the Carismians; but the loss of Jerusalem and the defeat of Gaza could not permit them to indulge in many joyful sensations. They had lost their allies, and could reckon upon nothing but enemies among the Mussulmans. The sultan of Egypt, whose alliance they had rejected, was extending his dominions in Syria, and his power became every day more formidable. The cities which the Christians still retained on the coasts of the sea were almost all without defenders. The orders of St. John and the Temple had offered the sultan of Cairo a considerable sum for the ransom of his prisoners; but the sultan refused to listen to their ambassadors, and threatened them with all the terrors of his wrath: these two bodies, formerly so much dreaded by the Mussulmans, were no longer able to serve the cause of the Christians with any advantage, and were compelled to wait, in a state of inaction, till the warlike nobility of Europe should come to replace the knights held in captivity by the infidels, or swept away on the field of battle. The emperor of Germany made not the least effort to save the wreck of his feeble kingdom; he had sent several warriors to protect his rights in Ptolemaïs; but as these rights were not recognised, the presence of the imperial troops only added to the other scourges that desolated the Holy Land, that of discord and civil war.

Palestine, threatened every day with a fresh invasion, could not entertain the smallest hope of being succoured by the other Christian states of the East. The Comans, a barbarous people from the confines of Tartary, and who surpassed the hordes of Carismia in ferocity, ravaged the banks of the Orontes, and submitted everything in the principality of Antioch to fire and sword; the king of Armenia was in dread, at the same time, of the ravages of the Tartars, and of the aggressions of the Turks in Asia Minor; the kingdom of Cyprus, a prey to factions, had recently been the theatre of a civil war, and had reason to fear the incursions of the Mussulman nations of Syria and Egypt. In this deplorable situation, it might be believed that the kingdom of Godfrey was on the eve of perishing entirely, and that all that remained of the Christians in the Holy Land would soon share the fate of the Carismians. But, on turning their eyes towards the West, the Franks of Palestine again felt their hopes and their courage revive; more than once the Christian states of Syria had owed their safety, and even a few days of prosperity and glory, to the excess of their abasement and misery. Their groans and complaints were seldom heard in vain by the warlike nations of Europe, and their extreme distress became almost always the signal for a new crusade, the very report of which was enough to make the Saracens tremble.

Valeran, bishop of Berytus, had been sent into the West to solicit the protection of the pope and the assistance of princes and warriors. The pope received the envoy of the Christians with kindness, and promised his succour to the Holy Land. But the West was at that period agitated by troubles: the quarrel that had broken out between the Holy See and the emperor of Germany was carried on with an animosity that disgraced both religion and humanity. Frederick II. exercised all sorts of violences against the court of Rome and the partisans of the sovereign pontiff; the pope, every day more irritated, invoked the arms of the Christians against his enemy, and promised the indulgences of the crusade to all who would minister to his anger.

On another side, the Latins established at Constantinople were environed by the greatest perils. The emperor Baldwin II., after having conducted a feeble reinforcement to his capital, had returned into the West, and was, the second time, soliciting the alms and the succours of the faithful to sustain the deplorable remains of his empire, exposed, almost without defence, to the attacks of the Greeks and Bulgarians. At the same time, the Tartars continued to ravage the banks of the Danube and threaten Germany; their barbarous exploits had carried terror to the very extremities of Europe; everywhere the excited imagination of nations represented these terrible conquerors as monsters vomited up by hell, clothed in hideous forms, and endowed with strength against which no man was able to contend. The deficiency of communication, which did not allow of exact information as to their march, gave birth to the most frightful rumours. Fame declared at one time they were invading Italy, and immediately afterwards, that they were ravaging the banks of the Rhine; every nation dreaded their prompt arrival, every city believed they were at its gates.

It was amidst this general disorder and consternation, that Innocent IV., a refugee at Lyons, resolved to convoke an œcumenic council in that city, to remedy the evils that desolated Christendom in both the East and the West. The sovereign pontiff, in his letters addressed to the faithful, exposed the deplorable situation of the Romish Church, and conjured the bishops to come around him, and enlighten him with their counsels. The patriarchs of Constantinople, Antioch, and Aquilæa, a great number of prelates and doctors, with several secular princes, responded to the invitation of the head of the Church. Among the crowd of bishops, one alone seemed to attract general attention: this was the bishop of Berytus; his presence, and the grief impressed upon his brow, reminded the assembly of all the misfortunes of the Holy Land. Baldwin II., emperor of Byzantium, created very little less notice; and his suppliant attitude but too plainly showed what the empire founded by the sixth crusade had become.

Most of the Western monarchs had sent their ambassadors to this assembly, in which the safety and the great interests of the Christian world were about to be discussed. Frederick in particular, who had so long been the object of the anger of the sovereign pontiff, neglected nothing to turn aside the thunders suspended over his head, and ministers invested with his confidence were commissioned to defend him before the fathers of the council. Among the deputies of the emperor of Germany, history names Pierre Desvignes, who had written, in the name of Frederick, eloquent letters to all the sovereigns of Europe, to complain of the tyranny exercised by the Holy See; and Thadæus of Suesse, who was not prevented by the profession of arms from employing the arts of eloquence, or fathoming the depths of the study of laws. The latter had often served his master with glory amidst the perils of war, but he had never had an opportunity of showing so much firmness, courage, and devotion as in this assembly, in which the court of Rome was about to put forth all its power and realize all its threats.

Before the opening of the council, the pope held a congregation in the monastery of St. Just, where he had chosen to fix his residence. The patriarch of Constantinople exposed the deplorable state of his church: heresy had resumed its empire in a great part of Greece, and the enemies of the Latin church were advancing to the very gates of Constantinople; the bishop of Berytus read a letter, in which the patriarch of Jerusalem and the barons and prelates of Palestine described the ravages of the Carismians, and showed that the heritage of Christ was upon the point of becoming the prey of the barbarians, if the West did not take arms for its defence. The dangers and misfortunes of the Christians of the East affected the fathers of the council deeply. Thadæus, taking advantage of their emotion, announced that the emperor, his master, fully partook of their profound grief, and that he was ready to employ all his powers for the defence of Christendom. Frederick promised to arrest the progress of the irruption of the Tartars, to re-establish the domination of the Latins in Greece, to go in person to the Holy Land, and to deliver the kingdom of Jerusalem; he still further promised, in order to put an end to all divisions, to restore to the Holy See all he had taken from it, and to repair all wrongs offered to the sovereign pontiff. Such lofty promises, made by the most powerful monarch of Christendom, created as much joy as surprise in the greater part of the bishops; the whole assembly appeared impatient to know what would be the reply of Innocent. The pope proved inflexible, and rejected with scorn propositions, as he said, already made several times, and which had no other guarantee but the too suspicious loyalty of Frederick. He was determined to view the new protestations of the emperor as nothing but a fresh artifice to deceive the Church, and turn aside the course of its justice. "*The axe*," added he, "*is already lifted, and ready to cut the roots of the tree;*" words very ill assorted with the charity of the Gospel, and which plainly show that Innocent had prepared the solemn pomp of a council with less purpose to oppose the foes of Christendom than to prepare the fall, and consummate the ruin of his personal enemy.

The pope held this preparatory sitting in order to make a trial of his strength, and to become acquainted with the dispositions of the bishops. A few days afterwards, the council was opened with great solemnity in the metropolitan church of St. John; the sovereign pontiff, wearing the tiara, and clothed in pontifical robes, was placed upon an elevated seat, having on his right hand the emperor of Constantinople, and on his left the count of Provence and the count of Thoulouse. After having given out the *Veni Creator*, and invoked enlightenment from the Holy Ghost, he pronounced a discourse, for the subject of which he took the five griefs with which he was afflicted, and compared them to the five wounds of the Saviour of the world upon the cross. The first was the irruption of the Tartars; the second, the schism of the Greeks; the third, the invasion of the Holy Land by the Carismians; the fourth, the relaxation of ecclesiastical discipline and the progress of heresy; and the fifth, the persecution he endured from Frederick.

Whilst describing the misfortunes of Christendom, the pontiff could not restrain his tears. His voice, if we may believe a contemporary historian, was often stifled by sobs; he conveyed to all hearts the sentiments by which he was affected; but he soon abandoned the language of compassion and despair, and assumed that of anger and menace. The Tartars, the Carismians, and the Mussulmans, inspired him with less hatred than the emperor of Germany, and it was for this prince he reserved all the thunders of his eloquence. He reproached him, in the most vehement expressions, with all the crimes that could draw upon his head the maledictions of his age, the hatred of his contemporaries, and the contempt of posterity. When the pope had pronounced his discourse, a profound silence reigned throughout the assembly; it appeared to the greater part of the terrified bishops that the voice of Heaven had made itself heard for the purpose of condemning Frederick : all eyes were turned upon the deputies of the emperor, and no one could believe that either of them would dare to reply to the interpreter of the anger of Heaven. All at once Thadæus of Suesse arose, and addressed the council, calling upon God, who searches all hearts, to witness that the emperor was faithful to all his promises, and had never ceased to endeavour to serve the cause of the Christians. He combated all the accusations of the sovereign pontiff, and in his reply did not hesitate to allege numerous complaints against the court of Rome. The angry pope replied from his lofty throne; he again accused the emperor, and evinced but too great a desire to find him guilty : the first sitting of the council, entirely occupied with these violent debates, exhibited the unedifying spectacle of a contest between the head of the faithful, who accused a Christian prince of perjury, felony, heresy, and sacrilege ; and the minister of an emperor, who reproached the court of Rome with having exercised an odious despotism, and committed revolting iniquities.

This contest, the results of which were likely to prove equally injurious to the head of the Church and the head of the Empire, was prolonged during several days; it doubtless scandalized all those that the pope had not associated with him in his resentments, and most of the bishops must have been afflicted at being thus diverted from the principal object of the convocation.

At length, however, the calamities of the Eastern Christians, the captivity of Jerusalem, and the dangers of Byzantium engaged the attention of the fathers of the council. The pope and the assembly of prelates decided that a new crusade should be preached for the deliverance of the Holy Land and the Latin empire of Constantinople. They renewed all the privileges granted to Crusaders by preceding popes and councils, as well as all the penalties directed against such as should favour either pirates or Saracens : during three years all who should take the cross would be exempted from every kind of tax or public office; but if after taking the vow they did not perform it, they incurred excommunication. The council recommended to the barons and knights to reform the luxury of their tables and the splendour of their dress; they advised all the faithful, and particularly ecclesiastics, to practise works of charity, and to arm themselves with all the austerities of penitence against the enemies of God. In order to obtain the protection of Heaven by the intercession of the Holy Virgin, the pope and the fathers of the council ordered that the octave of the Nativity should be celebrated in the church. In several councils Christian knights had been forbidden to take part in the profane solemnities of tournaments; the council of Lyon renewed the prohibition, persuaded that these military festivals might turn aside the minds of the warriors from the pious thoughts of the crusades, and that the expenses they occasioned would render it impossible for the bravest of the lords and barons to make the necessary preparations for the pilgrimage beyond the seas. The council ordered that the clergy should pay the twentieth part of their revenue, and the sovereign pontiff and cardinals the tenth of theirs, to provide for the expenses of the holy war. Half of the revenues of all non-resident benefices were specially reserved for the assistance of the empire of Constantinople. The decrees of the council ordered all whose mission it was to preach the word of God, to urge princes, counts, barons, and the corporations of cities, to contribute to the extent of their power to the success of the holy war; the same statutes recommended the clergy to show to the faithful that sacrifices offered to the crusade were the surest means of redeeming their sins; but above all they recommended the clergy to excite the faithful, in the tribunal of penitence, to multiply their offerings, or at least to bequeath in their testaments something for the assistance of the Christians of the East.

It was thus the council declared war against nations opposed to the Christians, and prepared means for assuring the triumphs of the soldiers of Christ. We are nevertheless surprised that the pope said nothing about preaching a crusade against the Tartars, whose invasion he had compared to one of the wounds of the Saviour on the cross. In the state of desolation in which Hungary was then placed, none of the bishops of that unfortunate kingdom had been able to appear at the council, and no friendly voice was raised to direct attention to, or implore favour for the Hungarian nation. The Tartars, it is true, repulsed by the duke of Neustadt, had fallen back from the banks of the Danube; but there was great reason to dread their return: to prevent fresh invasions, the council contented itself with advising the Germans to dig ditches and build walls on the roads the Tartarian hordes were likely to take. These measures, which even then must have been known to be insufficient, assist us at the present day in forming an opinion of the spirit of improvidence and blindness which then presided over political councils. Who can fail to be surprised at seeing, in an assembly so grave as a council, Europe pressed to lavish its treasures and sacrifice its armies for the deliverance of Constantinople and Jerusalem, whilst the most redoubtable of the barbarians were at their doors, and threatening to invade their own territories?

We may, however, remark, that Frederick himself had solicited the powers of Europe to assist him in repelling the Tartars; and the pope took much less interest in succouring the empire than he did in endeavouring to wrest it from Frederick. Innocent seemed very little disposed to set an example of that spirit of concord and charity which the council had just recommended to Christian princes; history can but deplore the zeal and ardour he evinced in carrying out his projects of vengeance against the emperor of Germany, at the risk of arousing evil passions, of perpetuating discord, and thus giving up the West to the invasion of the barbarians. In the second sitting of the council he was preparing to crush his enemy and completely overwhelm him with the weight of ecclesiastical power when Thadæus of Suesse demanded a delay of a few days, to allow the emperor to come in person to justify his conduct and demonstrate his loyalty. The defender of Frederick hoped that the presence of a powerful monarch, by awakening in the minds of the assembly the respect due to the majesty of kings, would bring about the triumph of justice. The pope consented, though very unwillingly, to defer the accomplishment of his menaces; but the emperor could not condescend to appear as a suppliant before an assembly convoked by the most implacable of his enemies: he did not come to the council, and when the required period of delay had expired, the sovereign pontiff took advantage of his absence to reproach him afresh with his bad faith, and his resistance to the laws of the Church.

At the moment in which the assembly of the bishops tremblingly awaited the terrible sentence, the English ambassadors arose to complain of the agents of the court of Rome, whose ambition and avarice were ruining the kingdom of England; they at the same time protested against the feudal supremacy which the pope, in consequence of a cession made by King John, pretended to exercise over the English monarchy and nation. These claims could not restrain the ever-boiling anger of the sovereign pontiff. In vain Thadæus again rose to urge that a great number of bishops were absent—that several princes had not sent their ambassadors to the council; in vain he declared that he should appeal from this to a more numerous and more solemn council; nothing could turn aside the storm or retard the hour of vengeance. Innocent at first replied with moderation to the deputies of England, and even to those of Frederick; but soon assuming the tone of a judge and a master, "I am," said he, "the vicar of Jesus Christ; all that which I shall bind on earth shall be bound in heaven, according to the promises of the Son of God made to the prince of the apostles; and therefore, after having deliberated upon it with our brethren the cardinals, and with the council, I declare Frederick attainted and convicted of sacrilege and heresy, to be excommunicated and degraded from the empire; I absolve from their oaths, for ever, all who have sworn fidelity to him; I forbid any, under pain of excommunication incurred by that single fault, to henceforth yield him obedience; to conclude, I command the electors to elect another emperor, and I reserve to myself the right of disposing of the kingdom of Sicily."

During the reading of this sentence, the pope and the prelates held lighted wax tapers in their hands, and bent towards the earth in sign of malediction and anathema. The envoys of Frederick retired filled with confusion and despair; Thadæus of Suesse was heard to pronounce these words of the Scripture: "*O terrible day! O day of anger and calamity!*" A deep and melancholy silence prevailed throughout this assembly, into the bosom of which it appeared as if the bolts of heaven had just fallen amidst awful peals. The pope alone appeared collected, and his countenance was radiant with joy; he gave out the *Te Deum*, as if he had obtained a victory over the infidels, and declared that the council had terminated its labours.

Such was the council of Lyons, too celebrated in the annals of the middle ages, which has frequently supplied the enemies of religion with a pretext for attacking the judgments of the Church. The pope in his opening discourse had deplored the progress of heresy; but always more eager to combat the enemies of his power than those of religion, he did not propose a single measure to arrest the progress of the new errors. In this council, which had no tendency to the enlightenment of the faithful, the majesty of kings was violently outraged; all the maxims of the rights of nations, and all the precepts of scriptural charity were in it trampled under foot. When Innocent announced the intention of deposing the emperor, not a single bishop raised his voice to divert the sovereign pontiff from this revolting use of his power. The real wrongs that Frederick had committed against the Church; the remembrance of the persecutions he had exercised towards several bishops; the intention which they believed he entertained of plundering the clergy; the threatening language and tone of the pope; that invincible influence under which all feel themselves in a numerous assembly—all assisted in preventing any of the bishops from pleading the cause of reason or recalling the maxims of the Gospel to the mind of the enraged pontiff. Nevertheless the fathers of the council, whatever might be their prejudices or their resentments, did not take part in all the fury of Innocent, and did not actively assist in carrying out his acts of injustice and violence.

The pope did not appeal to their wisdom, and seemed afraid to ask their opinions. Without repeating here that which has frequently been said in schools of theology, impartial history must disapprove of the silent neutrality of the council; but it must at the same time assert that the odious decree against Frederick was not an act of the Church; that the bishops and prelates did not give their formal approbation to it; and that the shame of this great iniquity falls entirely upon the memory of Innocent.

It was at this deplorable period that the cardinals, by order of the pope, clothed themselves for the first time in the scarlet robe, a symbol of persecution, and a sad presage of the blood that was about to flow. Frederick was at Turin when he heard of his condemnation; at this news he called for his imperial crown, and placing it upon his head, exclaimed in a loud and angry voice, "There it is, and before it shall be wrested from me, my enemies shall well know the terror of my arms; let this pontiff tremble, who has broken every tie that bound me to him; he at length permits me henceforth to listen to nothing but the dictates of my just anger." These threatening words announced a formidable contest, and every friend of peace must have been seized with terror: the fury which animated the emperor and the pope quickly passed into the minds of the people; in the provinces of Germany and Italy all flew to arms. Amidst the agitation in which the West was then plunged, it is probable that Jerusalem and the Holy Land would have been quite forgotten, if a powerful and highly-revered monarch had not placed himself at the head of the crusade which had been proclaimed in the council of Lyons.

BENEDICTION.

The preceding year, at the very moment the nations of the West heard of the last misfortunes of Palestine, Louis IX. of France fell dangerously ill. The most earnest prayers were offered up by the people of his kingdom for the preservation of the virtuous monarch. The malady, the attacks of which became every day more violent, at length created serious alarm. Louis sunk into a mortal lethargy, and the intelligence soon circulated that he was dead. The court, the capital, the provinces were struck with the deepest grief; nevertheless, the king of France, as if Heaven had not been able to resist the prayers and tears of a whole nation, recovered, even when apparently at the portals of the tomb. The first use he made of speech, after again beholding the light, was to ask for the cross and express his determination of going to the Holy Land.

Those who surrounded him considered his return to life as a miracle effected by the crown of thorns of Christ, and by the protection of the apostles of France; they cast themselves on their knees to return thanks to Heaven, and in the joy they experienced, scarcely paid attention to the vow Louis had made of quitting his kingdom and going to fight against the infidels in the East. When the king began to recover his strength, he repeated his vow, and again asked for the cross of the Crusaders.* The queen Blanche, his mother, the princes of his family, and Pierre d'Auvergne, bishop of Paris, then endeavoured to divert him from his purpose, and conjured him, with tears in their eyes, to wait till he was perfectly restored to health before he directed his thoughts to so perilous an enterprise; but Louis thought he was only obeying the will of Heaven. His imagination had been forcibly affected by the calamities of the Holy Land; Jerusalem given up to pillage, the tomb of Christ profaned, were constantly present to his mind. Amidst the height of a burning fever, he had fancied he heard a voice which came from the East, and addressed these words to him: *"King of France, thou seest the outrages offered to the city of Christ; it is thou whom Heaven hath appointed to avenge them."* This celestial voice resounded still in his ears, and would not allow him to listen to the prayers of friendship or the counsels of human wisdom. Steadfast in his resolution, he received the cross from the hands of Pierre d'Auvergne, and caused it to be announced to the Christians of Palestine—sending them at the same time succours of both men and money—that he would cross the seas as soon as he could assemble an army, and had reëstablished peace in his dominions.

This information, which conveyed such joy to the Christian colonies, spread grief and consternation through all the provinces of France. The sieur de Joinville expresses warmly the regret of the royal family, particularly the despair of the queen-mother,† by saying that when the princess saw her son wearing the cross, *she was struck as fearfully as if she had looked upon him dead.* The late disasters of Jerusalem had drawn tears from most Christians in the West, but without inspiring them, as in the preceding age, with any earnest desire of going to fight the infidels. It was impossible to see, in these distant expeditions, anything but great perils and inevitable reverses; and the project of recovering the city of God awakened more alarm than enthusiasm.

The sovereign pontiff, however, sent ecclesiastics into all the Christian states with a charge to preach the holy war. Cardinal Eudes, of Chateauroux, arrived in France with the express commission of publishing and causing to be executed the decrees of the council of Lyons respecting the

---

* This great incident in the life of Louis IX. is differently, and indeed more strikingly, related by most French historians. "When he felt himself better, to the great astonishment of all, he ordered the red cross to be affixed to his bed and his vestments, and made a vow to go and fight for the tomb of Christ. His mother, and the priests themselves, implored him to renounce his fatal design. It was all in vain; and scarcely was he convalescent than he called his mother and the bishop of Paris to his bedside, and said to them, 'Since you believe that I was not perfectly myself when I pronounced my vows, there is my red cross, which I tear from my shoulders; I return it to you: but now, when you must perceive that I am in the full enjoyment of all my faculties, restore to me my cross; for He who is acquainted with all things, knows also that no kind of food shall enter into my mouth until I have again been marked with His holy sign.' 'It is the hand of Heaven,' cried all who were present; 'its will be done.'" (*Bonnechose*).—TRANS.

† English readers should acknowledge a familiar acquaintance in this excellent mother and good queen: she is the *Lady Blanche* of Shakespear's *King John.*—TRANS.

crusade. The holy expedition was preached in all the churches of the kingdom. Contemporary history scarcely mentions the effect of these preachings, and everything leads us to believe that those who then took the oath to fight against the Saracens were induced to do so more by the example of the king than by the eloquence of the holy orators.

In order to give more solemnity to the publication of the crusade, and to excite the ardour of the warriors for the deliverance of the holy places, Louis IX. convoked a parliament in his capital, in which were assembled the prelates and magnates of the kingdom. The cardinal legate there repeated the exhortations addressed by the head of the Church to the faithful. Louis IX. spoke after the cardinal of Chateauroux, and retraced the picture of the disasters of Palestine. "According to the expression of David, an impious nation has entered into the temple of the Lord; blood has flowed like water around Jerusalem; the servants of God have been massacred in the sanctuary; and their remains, deprived of sepulture, are abandoned to the birds of heaven." After having deplored the miseries of Sion, Louis IX. reminded his barons and knights of the example of Louis the Young and of Philip Augustus; he exhorted every generous soldier who heard him to take arms, to go across the seas, fight against the infidels, and defend the glory of God and of the French name in the East. Louis, invoking by turns the charity and the warlike virtues of his auditory, endeavoured to awaken in all hearts both inspirations of piety and sentiments of chivalry. There is no necessity for repeating what was the effect of the exhortations and prayers of a king of France who addressed himself to the honour, and appealed to the bravery of his subjects. He had scarcely ceased speaking, when his three brothers, Robert, count d'Artois, Alphonse, duke of Poictiers, and Charles, duke of Anjou, took the oath to go and defend the heritage of Christ and the French colonies in Asia. Queen Marguerite, the countess d'Artois, and the duchess of Poictiers, likewise took the cross and resolved to accompany their husbands. Most of the bishops and prelates who were present at this assembly, influenced by the discourse of the king and the example of the cardinal-legate, did not hesitate to enrol themselves in a war for which, it is true, less enthusiasm was shown than had appeared in a former age, but which was still termed *the war of God*. Among the great vassals of the crown who swore to quit France for the purpose of fighting the Saracens in Asia, the friends of the French monarchy must have numbered, with much joy, Pierre de Dreux, duke of Brittany, Hugh, count de la Marche, and several other lords whose jealous ambition had so long disturbed the kingdom. Quickly after them were seen the duke of Burgundy, Hugh de Chatillon, the count de St. Pol, the counts of Dreux, Bar, Soissons, Blois, Rhotel, Montfort, and Vendôme; the seigneur de Beaujeu, constable of France, and John de Beaumont, great admiral and great chamberlain; Philip of Courtenay, Guy of Flanders, Archambaud de Bourbon, young Raoul de Coucy, John of Barres, Gilles de Mailly, Robert de Bethune, and Oliver de Thermes. There was not an illustrious family in the kingdom that did not supply one hero for the crusade. In the crowd of these noble Crusaders, history is gratified in observing the celebrated Boilève, who was afterwards provost of the traders of Paris, and the sieur de Joinville, whose name will for ever appear in the history of France by the side of that of Louis IX.

In the assembly of prelates and barons several measures were adopted for the maintenance of public peace and the preparations for the holy war. An immense number of processes at that period disturbed the peace of families, and those processes, of which many were decided by the sword, often amounted to actual wars. The tribunals were enjoined to terminate all affairs brought before them, and in cases in which they could not oblige the parties to acquiesce in a definite judgment, the judges were directed to make them swear to a truce of five years. In agreement with the authority of the pope, and the decrees of the council of Lyons, it was ordered that ecclesiastics should pay to the king the tenth of their revenues, which created a dissatisfaction in the clergy that Louis had great trouble in dispelling. A postscript, issued by royal authority, in concert with the will of the pope, decreed that Crusaders should be protected during three years from the pursuits of their creditors, reckoning from the day of their departure for the Holy Land; this postscript, which likewise excited much murmuring, had great effect in determining many barons and knights to leave the West.

Louis IX. occupied himself constantly in carrying his design into execution, and neglected no means of winning to his purpose all the nobility of his kingdom; his piety did not disdain to employ, for what he considered a sacred cause, all the empire that kings generally possess over their courtiers; he sometimes even lowered himself to seduction and trick, persuaded that the sanctity of the crusade would excuse everything. After an ancient custom, the kings of France, at great solemnities, gave such of their subjects as were at court certain capes or furred mantles, with which the latter immediately clothed themselves before leaving the court. In the ancient *comptes* (a sort of audits) these capes were called *livrées* (whence, no doubt, our word livery), because the monarch gave them (*les livrait*) himself. Louis ordered a vast number of these to be prepared against Christmas Eve, upon which crosses were embroidered in gold and silk. The moment being come, every one covered himself with the mantle that had been given to him, and followed the monarch to the chapel. What was their astonishment when, by the light of the wax tapers, they at once perceived upon all before them, and then upon themselves, the sign of an engagement they had never contracted. Such was, however, the character of the French knights, that they believed themselves obliged to respond to this appeal to their bravery; all the courtiers, as soon as divine service was ended, joined in the laugh with *the skilful fisher of men*, and took the oath to accompany him into Asia.

Notwithstanding all these efforts, the publication of the holy war created in the nation much more sorrow than warlike ardour, and the approaching departure of the monarch afflicted all France. Queen Blanche, and the most prudent of the ministers, who had at first endeavoured to divert Louis IX. from the crusade, repeated their attempts several times: resolved to make a last effort, they went to the king in a body. The bishop of Paris was at their head, and spoke for all; this virtuous prelate represented to Louis, that a vow made in the height of a disease ought not to bind him in an irrevocable manner, particularly if the interests of his kingdom imposed upon him the obligation of dispensing with it. "Everything demanded the presence of the monarch in his dominions; the Poitevins were threatening to take up arms again; the war of the Albigeois was ready to be rekindled; the animosity of England was always to be dreaded, as it paid little heed to treaties; the wars occasioned by the pretensions of the pope and the emperor inflamed all the states adjoining to France, and the conflagration was not unlikely to extend to that kingdom." Many of the nobles to whom Louis had confided the most important functions of the state, spoke after the bishop of Paris, and represented to the monarch that all the institutions founded by his wisdom would perish in his absence; that France would lose by his departure the fruits of the victories of Saintes and Taillebourg, with all the hopes that the virtues of a great prince made her entertain. Queen Blanche spoke the last. "My son," said she, "if Providence has made use of me to watch over your infancy and preserve your crown, I have perhaps the right to remind you of the duties of a monarch, and of the obligations which the safety of the kingdom over which God has placed you imposes upon you; but I prefer speaking to you with the tenderness of a mother. You know, my son, that I can have but few days to live, and your departure leaves me only the thought of an eternal separation: happy still if I die before fame may have borne into Europe the intelligence of some great disasters. Up to this day, you have disdained both my counsels and my prayers; but if you will not take pity on my sorrows, think at least of your children, whom you abandon in the cradle; they stand in need of your lessons and your assistance; what will become of them in your absence? are they not as dear to you as the Christians of the East? If you were now in Asia, and were informed that your deserted family was the sport and prey of factions, you would not fail to hasten to us. Well! all these evils that my tenderness makes me dread, your departure is most likely to give birth to. Remain then in Europe, where you will have so many opportunities of displaying the virtues of a great king, of a king the father of his subjects, the model and support of the princes of his house. If Christ requires his heritage to be delivered, send your treasures and your armies into the East; God will bless a war undertaken in his name. But this God, who hears me, believe me, never commands the accomplishment of a vow which is contrary to the great designs of his providence. No; that God of mercy who would not permit Abraham to complete his sacrifice, does not permit you to complete yours, and expose a life upon which so entirely depend both the fate of your family and the welfare of your kingdom."

On finishing these words, Queen Blanche could not restrain her tears; Louis himself was deeply moved, and threw himself into the arms of his mother; but soon resuming a calm and serene countenance, he said: "My dear friends, you know that all Christendom is acquainted with my resolution; during several months the preparations for the crusade have been carried on under my orders. I have written to all the princes of Europe that I was about to leave my dominions and to repair to Asia; I have announced to the Christians of Palestine that I would succour them in person; I have myself preached the crusade in my kingdoms; a host of barons and knights have obeyed my voice, followed my example, and sworn to accompany me into the East. What do you now propose to me? to change my projects publicly proclaimed, to do nothing that I have promised to do, or that Europe expects of me, and to deceive at once the hopes of the Church, of the Christians of Palestine, and of my faithful nobility.

"Nevertheless, as you think that I was not in possession of my reason when I took the cross; well, I give it back to you; there is that cross which gives you so much alarm, and which I only took, you say, in a fit of delirium. But now that I am in the full enjoyment of my reason I ask it of you again, and I solemnly declare that no food shall enter my mouth until you have returned it to me. Your reproaches and your complaints affect me with the deepest sorrow; but learn to be better acquainted with my duties and your own; aid me in seeking for true glory; second me in the powerful cause in which I am engaged, and do not alarm yourselves on account of my destiny or that of my family and people. The God who made me victorious at Taillebourg will watch over the designs and plots of our enemies; yes, the God who sends me into Asia to deliver his heritage, will defend that of my children, and pour his blessings upon France. Have we not still her who was the support of my childhood and the guide of my youth, her whose wisdom saved the state in so many perils, and who, in my absence, will want neither courage nor ability to crush factions? Allow me, then, to keep all the promises I have made before God and before men; and do not forget that there are obligations which are sacred for me, and ought to be sacred for you—I mean the oath of a Christian and the word of a king!"

Thus spoke Louis IX.: Queen Blanche, the bishop of Paris, and the other counsellors of the king preserved a religious silence, and from that time only thought of seconding the endeavours the monarch was making to forward the execution of an undertaking which appeared to emanate from God.

The crusade was preached at this time in all the countries of Europe; but as most states were filled with agitation and discord, the voices of the sacred orators were lost amidst the din of factions and the tumult of arms. When the bishop of Berytus went into England, to entreat the English monarch to succour the Christians of the East, Henry III. was fully employed in repelling the aggressions of the king of Scotland, and in appeasing the troubles of the country of Wales. The barons menaced his authority, and did not permit him to engage in a distant war. This prince not only refused to take the cross, but forbade the preaching of a crusade in his kingdom.

All Germany was in a blaze in consequence of the quarrel between the Church and the Empire. After having deposed the emperor at the council of Lyons, Innocent IV. offered the imperial crown to any one who would take up arms against the excommunicated prince, and bring about the triumph of the Holy See. Henry, landgrave of Thuringia, allowed himself to be seduced by the promises of the sovereign pontiff, and was crowned emperor by the archbishops of Mayence and Cologne, and a few other ecclesiastical electors. From that event civil war broke out in all parts; Germany was filled with missionaries from the pope, with the power of the evangelical word against Frederick, whom they styled the most redoubtable of infidels. The treasures collected for the equipments of the holy war were employed in corrupting fidelity, laying plots, fomenting treasons, and keeping up troubles and discords; so that it may well be supposed the cause of Christ and the deliverance of Jerusalem were entirely forgotten.

Italy was not less agitated than Germany; the thunders of Rome, so often hurled at Frederick, had redoubled the fury of the Guelphs and the Ghibellines. All the republics of Lombardy were leagued in opposition to the party of the emperor; the threats and the manifestoes of the pope would not allow a single city to remain neuter, or leave peace an asylum in the countries situated between the Alps and Sicily. The missionaries of Innocent employed, by turns, the arms of religion and of policy; after having declared the emperor to be a heretic and an enemy to the Church, they represented him as a bad prince and a tyrant, and dazzled the eyes of the people with the charms of liberty, always so powerful a motive upon the minds of nations. The sovereign pontiff sent two legates into the kingdom of Sicily, with letters for the clergy, the nobility, and the people of the cities and country. "We have not been able to see without some surprise," wrote Innocent, "that, burdened as you are, living under the opprobrium of servitude, and oppressed in your persons and your property, you have hitherto neglected the means of securing yourselves the sweets of liberty. Many other nations have presented you with an example; but the Holy See, far from accusing you, is satisfied with pitying you, and finds your excuse in the fear that must hold possession of your hearts under the yoke of a new Nero." On terminating his letter to the Sicilians, the pope endeavoured to make them understand that God had not placed them in a fertile region and beneath a smiling sky to wear disgraceful chains; and that by shaking off the yoke of the emperor of Germany, they would only second the views of Providence.

Frederick, who had at first defied the thunders of Rome, was terrified at the new war declared against him by the pope. The interdict placed upon his states, the terrible array of the maledictions of the Church, strongly affected the minds of the multitude, and might at length shake the fidelity of his subjects; he himself felt his courage forsake him; his party in Italy grew weaker every day; his armies had experienced some checks in Germany; many conspiracies had been formed against his life, and amongst the conspirators, he had the grief to find some of his servants whom he had loaded with kindnesses. This haughty monarch became convinced that he had no course but to seek a reconciliation with the Church, and addressed himself to Louis IX., whose wisdom and piety rendered him the arbiter of sovereigns and nations. Frederick, in his letters, promised to abide by the decision of the king of France and his barons, and engaged, beforehand, to go in person to the conquest of the Holy Land or to send his son, the king of the Romans. In order to interest Louis in his cause, the emperor offered to supply him with provisions, vessels, and everything he should stand in need of in the expedition to the East.

Louis eagerly embraced this opportunity for reëstablishing peace in Europe and assuring the success of the holy war. Several ambassadors were sent to the pope at Lyons, conjuring the father of the faithful to listen to the voice of mercy rather than to that of anger. The king of France had two long conferences with Innocent in the monastery of Cluni, and supplicated him afresh to appease by his clemency the troubles of the Christian world; but enmity had been carried too far to leave any hopes of peace; it was not possible for Innocent and Frederick to pardon each other sincerely the outrages they had mutually committed. The emperor had spared neither threats nor violences against the popes; he did not hate them more for the injuries he had received from them than for those he had done them. On the other side, it had for a length of time been determined, in the councils of Rome, to effect the overthrow of the house of Swabia, which was suspected, and with reason, of entertaining the project of invading Italy and establishing the seat of imperial domination in the city of St. Peter. This policy, embraced with ardour, had assumed all the character of a personal vengeance in the mind of Innocent. The triumph, even, of the pontiff, whilst flattering his pride and ambition, appeared to double his hatred, and the hope of completing the ruin of his enemy rendered him implacable.

In vain the emperor of Germany, overcome by fear rather than won by the love of peace, promised to descend from his throne, and pass the remainder of his days in Palestine, on condition that he should receive the benediction of the pope, and that his son Conrad should be raised to the empire. This entire abnegation of power, this strange abasement of royal majesty, produced no effect upon Innocent, who did not believe, or feigned not to believe, the promises of Frederick; in vain Louis IX., whose mind was incapable of suspecting imposture, represented to the pope the advantages that Europe, Christendom, and the court of Rome itself might derive from the repentance and offers of the emperor; in vain he spoke to him of the vows and the safety of pilgrims, of the glory and peace of the Church; the discourses of the holy king were scarcely listened to, and his pious mind could not view, without being moved with disgust, this inflexible rigour in the father of the Christian world.

Whilst the report of these discords, upon gaining the East, spread joy among the infidels, the unhappy inhabitants of Palestine gave themselves up to despair on learning that so many untoward events retarded the preparations for the crusade. Several messages from the Christians beyond the seas were sent to the sovereign pontiff to intercede for a prince from whom they hoped for such powerful assistance. The patriarch of Armenia wrote to the Court of Rome to demand favour for Frederick; he demanded it in the name of the threatened Christian colonies; in the name of the city of God, fallen into ruins; in the name of the sepulchre of Christ, profaned by barbarians. The pope made no reply whatever to the patriarch of the Armenians, and appeared to have forgotten Jerusalem, the holy sepulchre, and the Christians of Syria; he had, indeed, but one thought,—that of carrying on the war against Frederick. Innocent pursued his redoubtable enemy even to the East, and endeavoured to induce the sultan of Cairo to break his engagements with the emperor of Germany. The sultan of Cairo received, with as great joy as surprise, a message which informed him so authentically of the divisions that existed among the Christian princes; he answered the pope with a severity full of contempt; and the more he was pressed to be unfaithful to the treaties made with Frederick, the more he affected to display a fidelity from which he hoped to obtain an advantage over the Christian Church.

It was at this period that the emperor of Germany, urged on to despair, in some sort justified the most violent proceedings of the court of Rome by his conduct. He could not pardon Louis IX. for having remained neuter in a quarrel that interested all Christendom, and if the Arabian historian Yafey may be believed, he sent an ambassador secretly into Asia to warn the Mussulman powers of the expedition projected by the king of France. Throwing off at once the tone of submission to the pope, he resolved to repel force by force, and violence by violence. Some successes which he obtained in Germany raised his courage, and completely dissipated all his scruples. He laid siege to the city of Parma, at the head of a formidable army. Horrible cruelties signalized his first triumphs; the bishop of Arezzo, who fell into his hands, with many other prisoners of war, were loaded with irons, and handed over to the executioner without even the ceremony of a trial.

In the intoxication of success, Frederick threatened to cross the Alps, and attack Innocent within the walls of Lyons. Heaven, however, would not permit the execution of a project formed by hatred and revenge. The Guelphs beat and dispersed the imperial army. Fortune changed, and the irresolute character of Frederick changed as suddenly with it. Victory had inflamed his pride and redoubled his fury; a single defeat cast him into despondency, and rendered him again accessible to fear. From that time he resumed the part of a suppliant to the pope; from that time protestations and prayers seemed to cost his terrified mind no effort.

As the extent of his empire gave umbrage to the court of Rome, Frederick promised to divide his dominions, and give Sicily to his son Henry, and Germany to his son Conrad. He submitted his religious belief to the examination of several bishops, and sent their decision to the pope. He went at last even so far as to promise to come in person to solicit the clemency of Innocent. The sovereign pontiff had just caused the count of Holland to be nominated emperor, in the place of the landgrave of Thuringia, who had died on the field of battle. In this state of things he dreaded less the hostilities and angry threats of Frederick, than he did his protestations of submission and repentance. The supplications of princes and nations, who demanded favour for a power he wished to destroy, annoyed Innocent; they seemed to accuse him, in the eyes of Christendom, of obstinacy in his refusal, and without inducing him to renounce his policy, only embarrassed him in the execution of his designs.

The pope remained constantly inflexible; but astonished Europe began to ask what powerful interest it was that commanded all these rigours. Frederick, pursued with so much inveteracy, found at length the number and zeal of his friends and partisans increase. Germany, Cologne, and several other cities, rejected the decrees of the Holy See, and proceeded to violent excesses. The angry pope launched all his thunders against the guilty, and by an injustice which characterizes these times of discord and vengeance, many of the penalties he pronounced extended to the fourth generation. This senseless rage completed the alienation of men's minds, and the fanaticism of heresy was added to the furies of civil war.

As the court of Rome, under the imposing pretext of the crusade, levied tributes in all the states of Europe to keep up the fire of sedition and revolt, so many violences, and so much injustice infused dissatisfaction everywhere, and gave birth to a spirit of opposition among nations even, that had been exempt from the consequences of the terrible quarrel. The commissaries of the Holy See ruined the provinces of France; they pervaded the cities and countries, compelling the curates and chaplains of the nobles to sell all their little property; they required from all, church dues; and from religious communities, now the twentieth for the crusade against Constantinople, then the tenth for that of Palestine, and at last a contribution towards carrying on the war against the emperor. The French nobility, stimulated by a feeling of patriotism, by the spirit of chivalry which led all the *preux* of that time to enter the lists against iniquity of any kind, and perhaps also by the fear of being oppressed in their turn, spoke loudly in favour of Frederick, and expressed their anger at seeing the kingdom of France a prey to the agents of the pope. Just remonstrances were at first made;

but in a short time no measures were observed, and they proceeded so far as to agitate the question, whether they ought to acknowledge a pontiff, whose conduct appeared so contrary to the spirit of the Gospel, as the vicar of Jesus Christ. The principal French nobles at length formed a confederacy against the proceedings of the pope and the clergy. Throughout this new struggle, Louis IX., equally removed from that sacrilegious impiety which pretends to brave everything, and from that superstitious pusillanimity which believes itself obliged to suffer everything, managed to restrain the excesses of both parties, and maintain peace; the league which was then formed, without embittering men's minds, succeeded in enlightening them; it served, during the absence of the king, to repress the enterprises of the Holy See, and many writers trace to this period the origin of those Gallican liberties which have constituted the glory of the French clergy up to modern times.

Nevertheless, Louis IX. was constantly employed in preparations for his departure. As no other route to the East was available but that by sea, and as the kingdom of France had no port in the Mediterranean, Louis made the acquisition of the territory of Aigues-Mortes, in Provence; the port, choked with sand, was cleansed, and a city large enough to receive the crowd of pilgrims was built on the shore. Louis at the same time busied himself in provisioning his army, and preparing magazines in the isle of Cyprus, where he meant to land. Thibault, count de Bar, and the sieur de Beaujeu, sent into Italy, found everything necessary for the provisioning and transport of an army, either in the republic of Venice, or in the rich provinces of Apulia and Sicily, whither the directions of the emperor Frederick had preceded them.

The fame of these preparations soon reached Syria, and the authors of the times describe the Mussulman powers as struck with terror, and as immediately and earnestly employed in fortifying their cities and their frontiers against the approaching invasion of the Franks. Such popular rumours as were then in circulation that history has deigned to preserve, accuse the Saracens of having employed perfidious means and odious stratagems to avenge themselves upon the Christian nations, and ruin their enterprise. It was asserted that the life of Louis IX. was in danger from the emissaries of the Old Man of the Mountain; it was reported in cities, and the multitude did not fail to give credit to it, that the pepper which came from the East was empoisoned; and Matthew Paris, a grave historian, does not hesitate to affirm that a great number of persons died of it before this horrible artifice was discovered. We may well believe that the policy of the time itself invented these gross fables, to render the enemies they were about to combat more odious, and that indignation might increase and animate the courage of the warriors. It is natural also to suppose, that such rumours had their origin in popular ignorance, and that they gained credit from the opinion that was then entertained of the manners and characters of infidel nations.

Three years had passed away since the king of France assumed the cross. He convoked a new parliament at Paris, in which he at length fixed the departure of the holy expedition for the month of June of the following year (1248). The barons and prelates renewed with him the promises of fighting against the infidels, and engaged to set out at the period assigned, under the penalty of incurring ecclesiastical censures. Louis took advantage of the moment that the magnates of his kingdom were assembled in the name of religion, to require that they should take the oath of fealty and homage to his children and to make them swear (these are the expressions of Joinville) "that they should be loyal to his family, if any misadventure should befall his person in the holy voyage beyond the seas."

It was then that the pope addressed a letter to the nobility and people of France, in which he celebrated in solemn terms the bravery and other warlike virtues of the French nation and its pious monarch. The sovereign pontiff gave his benediction to the French Crusaders, and threatened with

DISPERSION OF THE SYRIAN ARMY BY A SAND TEMPEST.

the thunders of the Church all who, having made the vow of pilgrimage, deferred their departure. Louis IX., who had no doubt requested this warning from the pope, saw with joy all the nobility of his kingdom hasten to join his standard; many nobles, whose ambition he had repressed, were the first to set the example, for fear of awakening old mistrusts or incurring fresh disgraces; others, seduced by the habitual spirit of courts, declared themselves with ardour champions of the cross, in the hope of obtaining, not the rewards of Heaven, but those of the earth. The character of Louis IX. inspired the greatest confidence in all the Christian warriors. "If, till this time," said they, "God has permitted the crusades to be nothing but a long course of reverses and calamities, it is because the imprudence of the leaders has compromised the safety of the Christian armies; it is because discord and licentiousness of manners have reigned too long among the defenders of the cross: but what evils have we to dread under a prince whom Heaven appears to have inspired with its own wisdom,—under a prince who, by his firmness, has succeeded in suppressing every division in his own country, and is about to exhibit to the East an example of all the virtues?"

Many English nobles, among whom were the earls of Salisbury and Leicester, resolved to accompany the king of France, and share with him the perils of the crusade. The earl of Salisbury, grandson of "Fair Rosamond," who had gained by his exploits the surname of "Long Sword," had just been stripped of all his possessions by Henry III. In order to place himself in a condition to make preparations for the war, he addressed himself to the pope, and said to him, "Beggar as I am, I have made a vow to perform the pilgrimage to the Holy Land. If Prince Richard, brother to the king of England, has been able to obtain, without taking the cross, the privilege of levying a tax upon those who have just laid it down, I have thought that I might obtain a similar favour;—I, who have no resource but in the charity of the faithful." This discourse, which informs us of a very curious fact, made the sovereign pontiff smile: the earl of Salisbury obtained the favour he asked, and deemed it his duty to set out for the East.

The preachings for the holy war, which had produced but little effect in Italy and Germany, had nevertheless been successful in the provinces of Friesland and Holland, and in some of the northern kingdoms. Haco, king of Norway, celebrated for his bravery and exploits, took the oath to fight against the infidels; and the Norwegians, who had several times distinguished themselves in the holy wars, followed the example of their monarch. Haco, after completing his preparations, wrote to Louis IX. to announce his approaching departure. He asked his permission to land upon the coast of France, and to furnish himself there with the supplies necessary for his army. Louis made a most cordial reply, and proposed to the Norwegian prince to share with him the command of the crusade. Matthew Paris, who was charged with the message from Louis IX., informs us in his History that the king of Norway declined the generous offer of the French king, persuaded, he said, that harmony could not long subsist between the Norwegians and the French,—the first, of an impetuous, restless, and jealous character, the others, full of pride and haughtiness.

Haco, after having made this reply, thought no more of embarking, and remained quietly in his kingdom, history being perfectly unable to discover the motives which produced this sudden change. It may be believed, that in accordance with the example of several other Christian monarchs, this prince had made use of the crusade as a cloak for his political designs. By levying a tax of a third upon the revenues of the clergy, he had amassed treasures which he might employ in strengthening his power. The army he had raised in the name of Christ might minister to his ambition much more effectually in Europe than in the plains of Asia. The pope, from whom he had received the title of king, at first exhorted him to assume the sign of the Crusaders; but everything leads us to believe that he afterwards advised him to remain in the West, where he hoped to raise in him one more enemy against the emperor of Germany. Thus the king of Norway had promised to go into the East in the hope of obtaining the favour and protection of the court of Rome; and to preserve this favour and this support, he had but one thing to do, and that was to forget his promises.

However this may be, it is certain that the pope, at that time, took but very little interest in the success of the eastern crusade. We may judge of this by the facility with which he liberated so many from their vows of fighting against the infidels: he went even so far as to forbid the Crusaders from Friesland and Holland to embark for Palestine. In vain Louis IX. made some serious remonstrances on this head; Innocent would not listen to him. Engrossed by one passion, he found it much more advantageous to grant dispensations for the voyage to Syria; for, on one part, those dispensations which were bought with solid money, contributed to fill his treasury, and on the other, they left soldiers in Europe that he might arm against his personal enemies.

Thus France was the only country in which the crusade was really an object of interest; the piety and zeal of Louis IX. brought back all those whom the indifference of the pope had cooled; and the love of the French for their king, replacing religious enthusiasm, sufficed for the removal of all obstacles. The cities whose liberties the monarch had protected, voluntarily sent him considerable sums. The farmers of the royal domains, which were then very extensive, advanced the revenues of a year. The rich taxed themselves, and poured their hoards into the coffers of the king; poverty dropped its mite into the poor-boxes of churches; and we may add, that at that period there was scarcely a will made in the kingdom which did not contain some legacy towards the expenses of the holy war. The clergy were not content with addressing prayers to Heaven for the crusade, they paid the tenth of their revenues for the support of the soldiers of the cross.

The barons, nobles, and princes, who equipped themselves at their own expense, imposed taxes on their vassals, and found, after the example of the king of France, the money necessary for the voyage in the revenues of their domains and in the pious generosity of the towns and cities. Many, as in other crusades, pledged their lands, sold their property, and ruined themselves, to provide means to support their soldiers and knights. They forgot their families, they forgot themselves in the sad preparations for departure, and appeared never to look forward to the period of return. Many prepared themselves for the voyage as they would have prepared for exile or death; the most pious of the Crusaders, as if they only went to the East to find a tomb, were particularly anxious to appear before God in a state of grace; they expiated their sins by penitence; they pardoned offences repaired the ill they had done, disposed of their goods, gave them to the poor, or divided them amongst their natural heirs.

This disposition of men's minds was greatly to the advantage of humanity and justice; it imparted generous sentiments to people of property; whilst, in the wicked, it awakened a remorse that was nearly allied to virtue. Amidst civil wars and feudal anarchy, a crowd of men had enriched themselves by strife, rapine, and brigandage; religion inspired them with a salutary repentance, and this time of penitence was marked by a great number of restitutions, which for a moment made the triumphs of iniquity to be forgotten. The famous count de la Marche set the example; his conspiracies, his revolts, his unjust enterprises had often troubled the peace of the kingdom, and ruined a great number of families; he became desirous of expiating his faults; and to mitigate the just anger of God, he, by his will, ordered a complete restitution to be made of all the property he had acquired by injustice and violence.* The sieur de Joinville tells us, with great simplicity, in his History, that his conscience did not reproach him with anything serious, but that, nevertheless, he assembled

---

* We do not observe that this worthy penitent opened his hand and relaxed his grasp whilst living; death-bed repentances and posthumous restitutions are very suspicious affairs.—TRANS.

his vassals and neighbours to offer them reparation for the wrongs he might have done them without knowing it.

In those days of repentance monasteries were founded and treasures lavished on churches: "The most sure means," said Louis IX., "to avoid perishing like the impious, is to love and enrich the place in which dwells the glory of the Lord." The piety of the Crusaders was not forgetful of the poor and infirm; their numerous offerings endowed cloisters as asylums for want; hospices, or small convents, for the reception of pilgrims; and particularly leper hospitals, which were established in all the provinces, the melancholy abodes of victims of the holy wars.

Louis IX. distinguished himself by his liberality towards churches and monasteries; but that which must particularly have drawn upon him the blessings of his people, was the care he took to repair all injustice committed in the administration of government. The holy monarch knew, that if kings are the images of God upon earth, they are never so truly so as when justice is seated beside them on the throne. Restitution-offices, established by his orders in the royal domains, were charged with the repairing of all wrongs that might have been committed by the agents or farmers of the king. In most of the great cities it was the duty of two commissaries, one an ecclesiastic, the other a layman, to hear and decide upon complaints made against his ministers and officers: a noble exercise of the supreme authority, which rather employs itself in seeking out the unfortunate to assist them, than the guilty to punish them! which watches for the murmurs of the poor, encourages the weak, and submits itself to the tribunal of the laws! It was not sufficient for Louis to have established regulations for the administration of justice,—their execution excited his most anxious solicitude. Preachers announced the intentions of the king in all the churches, and as if he thought himself responsible to God for all judgments pronounced in his name, the monarch secretly sent holy ecclesiastics and good monks to make fresh observations, and learn from faithful reporters, if the judges whom he believed to be worthy men, were not themselves corrupt. The historian pauses complacently over this touching picture; so noble an example presented to the kings of the earth, appeared likely to bring down the blessings of Heaven upon Saint Louis; and when we reflect upon the deplorable results of this crusade, with the chroniclers of his own time, we feel astonished that so many calamities should have been the reward of such exalted virtue.

The preparations were now carried on with redoubled zeal and activity; all the provinces of France appeared to be in arms; the people of cities and country had but one thought, and that was the crusade. The great vassals assembled their knights and troops; the nobles and barons visited each other, or exchanged messengers, in order to settle the day of their departure. Relations and friends engaged to unite their banners, and place everything in common—money, glory, and perils. Devotional practices were mingled with military preparations. Warriors were seen laying aside the cuirass and sword, and walking, barefooted and in their shirts, to visit monasteries and churches, to which the relics of saints attracted the concourse of the faithful. Processions were formed in every parish; all the Crusaders appeared at the foot of the altars, and received the symbols of pilgrimage from the hands of the clergy. Prayers were put up in all churches for the success of the expedition. In families, abundance of tears were shed at the moment of departure; and most of the pilgrims, on receiving these last endearments of their friends, seemed to feel, more than ever, the value of all they were leaving behind them. The historian of Saint Louis tells us, that after visiting Blanchicourt and Saint-Urbain, where holy relics were deposited, he would not once turn his eyes towards Joinville, for his heart was softened at the idea of the beautiful castle he was leaving, and of his two children. The leaders of the crusade took with them all the warlike youth, and left in many countries nothing but a weak and unarmed population; many abandoned castles and fortresses must, naturally, fall to ruins; much flourishing land must be changed into a desert, and a vast many families must be left without support. The people, no doubt, had cause to regret the nobles whose authority was supported by kindnesses, and who, after the example of Saint Louis, loved truth and justice, and protected the weak and the innocent; but there were some whose departure was witnessed with gladness; and more than one town, more than one village, rejoiced at seeing the donjon, from which they had been accustomed to experience all the miseries of servitude, empty and abandoned.

It was an affecting spectacle to see the families of artisans and poor villagers lead their children to the barons and knights, and say to them: "You will be their fathers; you will watch over them amidst the perils of war and of the sea." The barons and knights promised to bring back their soldiers to the West, or to perish with them in fight; and the opinion of the people, the nobility, and the clergy, devoted, beforehand, all who should fail in this sacred promise, to the anger of God and the contempt of men.

Amidst these preparations, the most profound calm prevailed throughout the kingdom. In all preceding crusades, the multitude had exercised great violence against the Jews; but by the firmness and wisdom of Saint Louis, the Jews, though depositaries of immense wealth, and always skilful in taking advantage of circumstances to enrich themselves, were respected among a nation they had plundered, and which was now completing its own ruin by the holy war. Adventurers and vagabonds were not admitted beneath the banners of the cross; and, upon the demand of Saint Louis, the pope forbade all who had committed great crimes to take up arms in the cause of Christ. These precautions, which had never been observed in former crusades, were highly calculated to insure the maintenance of order and discipline in the Christian army. Among the crowd that presented themselves to go into Asia, artisans and labourers met with the best reception,—which is a remarkable circumstance, and clearly proves that views of a wise policy were mingled with sentiments of devotion, and that, though the ostensible object was the deliverance of Jerusalem, hopes were entertained of founding useful colonies in the East.

At the appointed time Louis IX., accompanied by his brothers, the duke of Anjou and the count d'Artois, repaired to the abbey of St. Denis. After having implored the support of the apostles of France, he received from the hands of the legate the pilgrim's staff and scrip, and that oriflamme which his predecessors had already twice unfurled before the nations of the East. Louis then returned to Paris, where he heard mass in the church of Notre Dame. The same day he quitted his capital, not again to enter it before his return from the Holy Land. The people and clergy were softened to tears, and accompanied him to the abbey of St. Antoine, singing psalms by the way. There he mounted on horseback to go to Corbeil, at which place the Queen Blanche and Queen Marguerite were to meet him.

The king gave two more days to the affairs of his kingdom, and confided the regency to his mother, whose firmness and wisdom had defended and preserved the crown during the troubles of his minority. If anything could excuse Louis IX., and justify his pious obstinacy, it was his leaving his country in profound peace. He had renewed the truce with the king of England; and Germany and Italy were so occupied with their own internal discords, that they could not give France the least subject for alarm. Louis, after having employed every precaution against the spirit of disaffection, took with him into the Holy Land almost all the powerful nobles that had disturbed the kingdom. The county of Mâcon, sold at the end of the preceding crusade, had recently reverted to the crown; Normandy had escaped from the yoke of the English; the counties of Thoulouse and Provence, by the marriage of the counts of Anjou and Poictiers, were about to become apanages of the princes of the royal family. Louis IX., after he took the cross, never ceased in his endeavours to preserve the recent conquests of France, to appease the murmurs of the people, and remove every pretext for revolt. The spirit of justice, which was observable in all his institutions; the remembrance of his virtues, which appeared more estimable amidst the general grief caused by his departure; the religion which he had caused to flourish by his example, were quite sufficient to maintain order and peace during his absence.

As soon as Louis had placed the administration of his kingdom in other hands, he gave himself up to the exercises of piety, and appeared to be no more than the most meek of Christians. The dress and attributes of a pilgrim became the only adornments of a powerful monarch. He wore no more splendid stuffs, no more valuable furs; his arms even, and the harness of his horses, glittered with nothing but the polish of steel and iron. His example had so much influence, says Joinville, that on the voyage not a single instance of an embroidered coat was seen, either upon the king or any one else. When endeavouring to reform splendour in equipages or dress, Louis caused the money he had been accustomed to spend in these to be distributed to the poor. Thus royal magnificence was in him nothing but the luxury of charity.

Queen Blanche accompanied him as far as Cluny. This princess was persuaded she should never see her son again until they met in heaven, and took leave of him in the most affectionate manner; the tears of mother and son bearing witness to the truth of their grief at parting. On his way, he saw the pope at Lyons, and conjured him, for the last time, to be merciful to Frederick, whom reverses had humiliated, and who implored pardon. After having represented the great interests of the crusade, after having spoken in the name of the numerous pilgrims who were abandoning everything for the cause of Christ, the pious mind of the king was astonished to find the pontiff still inexorable. The king then directed all his attention to the prosecution of his journey. Innocent promised to protect the kingdom of France against the heretic Frederick and the king of England; the latter of whom he always styled his vassal: he witnessed without regret the departure of a prince venerated for his love of justice, whose presence in Europe might be an obstacle to his policy. The sovereign pontiff had not much trouble in keeping his promise of defending the independence and peace of France; for the discords he excited in other states preserved that kingdom from all foreign annoyance during the time of the crusade.

The fleet, which awaited Louis at Aigues-Mortes, was composed of twenty-eight vessels, without reckoning those that were to transport the horses and the provisions. The king embarked, followed by his two brothers, Charles duke of Anjou, and Robert count d'Artois, and the queen Marguerite, who did not dread less the idea of remaining with her mother-in-law than that of living away from her husband. Alphonse, count of Poictiers, deferred his departure till the following year, and returned to Paris to assist the queen regent with his counsels and authority. When the whole army of the Crusaders was embarked, the signal was given, the priests, according to the custom in maritime expeditions, sang the *Veni Creator*, and the fleet set sail.

France had then no marine, the sailors and pilots were almost all Spaniards or Italians. Two Genoese performed the functions of commanders or admirals. A great part of the barons and knights had never before seen the sea, and everything they saw filled them with surprise and dread; they invoked all the saints of Paradise, and recommended their souls to God. The good Joinville does not at all dissemble his fright, and cannot help saying: "A great fool is he who, having any sin on his soul, places himself in such a danger; for if he goes to sleep at night, he cannot be certain he shall not find himself at the bottom of the sea in the morning."

Louis IX. embarked at Aigues-Mortes, the 25th of August, and arrived at Cyprus on the 21st of

September.* Henry, grandson of Guy of Lusignan, who obtained the kingdom of Cyprus in the third crusade, received the king of France at Limisso, and conducted him to his capital of Nicosia, amidst the acclamations of the people, nobility, and clergy.

A short time after the arrival of the Crusaders, it was decided in a council, that the arms of the Christians should, in the first place, be directed against Egypt. The reverses that had been met with on the banks of the Nile, in preceding wars, did not at all alarm the king of France and his barons; it is even more than probable that Louis, before he left his kingdom, had formed the design of carrying the war into the country from which the Mussulmans drew their wealth and their strength. The king of Cyprus, who had recently received the title of king of Jerusalem from the pope, the more strongly applauded this determination, from its giving him reason to hope to be delivered from the most formidable of his neighbours, and the most cruel enemy of the Christian colonies in Syria. This prince also caused a crusade to be preached in his kingdom, for the sake of being placed in a condition to accompany the French Crusaders, and associate himself usefully in their conquests. He proposed to the king of France and his barons to wait till he had concluded his preparations. "The lords and prelates of Cyprus," says William of Nangis, "all took the cross, appeared before Louis, and told him they would go with him wherever it should please him to lead them, if he would stay till the winter had passed away." As Louis and the principal French nobles appeared but little disposed to delay their march, the Cypriots spared neither protestations of friendship, caresses, nor prayers to detain them. Every day was devoted to rejoicings and feastings, in which the nobility and wealthy men of the kingdom exhibited the splendour of eastern courts. The enchanting aspect of the isle, a country rich in all the delicious productions of nature, particularly that Cyprus wine which Solomon himself has not disdained to celebrate, seconded in a powerful manner the entreaties and seductions of the court of Nicosia. It was decided that the Christian army should not depart before the following spring.

It was not long before they became fully aware of the error they had committed. Amidst the excessive abundance that reigned in their camp, the Crusaders gave themselves up to intemperance; in a country in which pagan fables placed the altars of voluptuousness, the virtue of the pilgrims was every day exposed to fresh trials; a protracted idleness relaxed the discipline of the army, and, to crown these evils, a pestilential disease exercised great ravages among the defenders of the cross. The pilgrims had to lament the death of more than two hundred and fifty knights from this calamity. Contemporary chronicles mention among the lords and prelates that were victims to it, the counts of Dreux and Vendôme, Robert, bishop of Beauvais, and the brave William des Barres; the army had likewise to regret the loss of the last of the race of the Archambault de Bourbons, whose county became afterwards the heritage of the children of Saint Louis, and gave to the royal family of France a name that it has rendered for ever illustrious in the annals of that country.

A great number of barons and knights were in want of money to maintain their troops, and Louis freely opened his treasury to them. The sieur de Joinville, who had no more than one hundred and twenty livres tournois left, received from the monarch eight hundred livres; a considerable sum in those days.

Many of the nobles complained of having sold their lands and ruined themselves to follow the king to the crusade. The liberality of Louis could not possibly supply all these complainants. A

---

* Michaud has omitted to mention the cause of Louis' unfortunate choice of a route,—the residence in Cyprus proving so injurious to the army. The most regular and advisable route would have been by Sicily; but after Louis had in vain tried every means of subduing the anger of the pope, his superstitious reverence for the head of the Church prevailed over even his good sense and his prudence, and he declined stopping in Sicily, because that island was part of the dominions of an excommunicated prince.—TRANS.

great number of knights, after being ruined by the abode in the isle of Cyprus, could not endure the idleness they were condemned to, but were anxious to set out for Syria or Egypt, hoping to make the Saracens pay the expenses of the war. Louis had a great deal of trouble to restrain them; historians agree in saying that he was *only half obeyed;* therefore, he had much more frequent occasion to exercise his patience and evangelical mildness than his authority; and if he succeeded in appeasing all discords and suppressing all murmurs, it was less by the ascendancy of his power than by that of his virtue.

Differences arose between the Greek clergy and the Latin clergy of the isle of Cyprus. Louis succeeded in putting an end to them. The Templars and Hospitallers appealed to him as judge in their constantly reviving quarrels; he made them swear to be reconciled, and to have no other enemies than those of Christ. The Genoese and Pisans resident at Ptolemaïs, had long and serious disputes, both parties having recourse to arms, and nothing appeared able to check the fury and scandal of a civil war in a Christian city. The wise mediation of Louis reëstablished peace. Aitho, king of Armenia, and Bohemond, prince of Antioch and Tripoli, implacable enemies, both sent ambassadors to the king of France: he induced them to conclude a truce: thus Louis IX. appeared among the nations of the East as an angel of peace and concord.

At this period the territory of Antioch was ravaged by vagabond bands of Turcomans; Louis sent Bohemond five hundred cross-bowmen. Aitho had just formed an alliance with the Tartars, and was preparing to invade the states of the sultan of Iconium in Asia Minor. As the Armenian prince enjoyed a great reputation in the East for skill and bravery, many French knights, impatient to display their valour, left Cyprus for the purpose of joining his standard, and sharing the fruits of his victories. Joinville, after having spoken of their departure, says nothing of their exploits, and only informs us of their unhappy destiny by these words: "not one of them ever came back."

Fame had announced the arrival of Louis throughout all the countries of the East, and the news produced a great sensation among both Mussulmans and Christians. A prediction, that was credited in the most distant regions, and which missionaries found spread even through Persia, announced that a king of the Franks was destined speedily to disperse all infidels and deliver Asia from the sacrilegious worship and laws of Mahomet. It was believed that the time was now come for the accomplishment of this prediction. A crowd of Christians hastened from Syria, Egypt, and all the countries of the East, to salute him whom God had sent to fulfil his divine promises.

It was at this period that Louis received an embassy that excited the curiosity and attention of the Crusaders in the highest degree; the marvellous account of it occupies a conspicuous place in the chronicles of the middle ages. This embassy came from a Tartar prince, named Ecalthaï, who professed himself to be converted to the Christian faith, and displayed the most ardent zeal for the triumph of the Gospel. The head of this deputation, named David, remitted to the king a letter filled with sentiments expressed with so much exaggeration as ought to have rendered it doubtful; he said that the great khan had received baptism three years before, and that he was prepared to assist the expedition of the French Crusaders with all his power. The news of this embassy soon spread through the army, and from that time nothing was talked of but the promised succour of the great khan or emperor of the Tartars; the leaders and soldiers flocked to the residence of Louis to see the ambassador of the prince Ecalthai, whom they considered *as one of the first barons of Tartary.*

The king of France interrogated the deputies several times respecting their journey, their country, and the character and disposition of their sovereign; and as all he heard flattered his most cherished thoughts, he conceived no mistrust, and discovered no signs of imposture in their replies. The Tartar ambassadors were received at his court, and admitted to his table; he himself conducted them to the celebration of divine service in the metropolitan church of Nicosia, where all the people were edified by their devotion.

At their departure, the king of France and the legate of the pope charged them with several letters for the prince Ecalthaï and the great khan of the Tartars. To these letters were added magnificent presents; among which was a scarlet tent, upon which Louis had caused to be worked "The Annunciation of the Virgin Mary, the Mother of God, and all the other points of faith." The king wrote to Queen Blanche, as did the legate to the sovereign pontiff, to announce the extraordinary embassy that had arrived from the most distant regions of the East. The propitious news of an alliance with the Tartars, who were then looked upon as the most formidable of all nations, spread joy among the people of the West, and increased their hopes of the success of the crusade.

Missionaries that were sent into Tartary by Louis were very soon satisfied that the conversion of the great khan was nothing but a fable. The Mogul ambassadors had advanced many other impostures in their accounts, which has induced some learned moderns to think that this great embassy was nothing but a trick, the contrivance of which may be attributed to some Armenian monks. However it may be, there can be no doubt that the Moguls, who were at war with the Mussulmans, might have some interest in conciliating the Christians, and might be led, from that time, to consider the Franks as useful auxiliaries.

Winter, in the mean time, was drawing towards an end, and the period fixed upon for the departure of the French Crusaders was approaching. The king of France ordered a great number of flat-bottomed boats to be constructed, to facilitate the descent of the Christian army upon the coast of Egypt. As the Genoese fleet, in which the French had embarked at Aigues-Mortes, had left the port of Lemisso, it required considerable trouble to get together, from all parts, vessels sufficient to transport the army and the numerous magazines formed in the isle of Cyprus. Louis IX. applied to the Genoese and Venetians established on the coast of Syria, who, to the great scandal of the knights and barons, showed, in this instance, more cupidity than devotion, and placed an exorbitant price upon services demanded of them in the name of Christ.

At this time Louis received a communication from the emperor of Germany, still pursued by the thunders of Rome. This prince sent provisions to the Crusaders, and expressed great grief, in his letters, at being unable to share the perils of the holy war. The king of France thanked Frederick, and sighed at the obstinacy of the pope, which deprived the defenders of the cross of such a powerful auxiliary.

Preparations were continued with the greatest activity; every day fresh Crusaders arrived, who came from the ports of the West, or had passed the winter in the isles of the Archipelago, or on the coasts of Greece. All the nobility of Cyprus had taken the cross, and were preparing for their conflict with the infidels. The greatest harmony prevailed between the two nations; in the Greek as well as the Latin churches, prayers were offered up to Heaven for the success of the Christian arms; and throughout the host nothing was talked of but the wonders of the East, and the riches of Egypt, which they were about to conquer.

Whilst enthusiasm and joy were thus exuberant among the Christian warriors, the grand masters of St. John and the Temple wrote to Louis IX., to consult him upon the possibility of opening a negotiation with the sultan of Cairo. The leaders of these two orders anxiously desired to break the chains of their knights who were detained in captivity since the defeat of Gaza; they did not otherwise partake with the Crusaders their blind confidence in victory; experience of other crusades had taught them that the warriors of the West, at first very redoubtable, almost always began their wars with splendour, but that afterwards, weakened by discord, exhausted by the fatigues of a distant

ST. LOUIS BEFORE DAMIETTA.

As soon as they were within bow shot, a shower of stones, arrows, and javelins was poured at the same instant from the shore and from the line of the Crusaders. The ranks of the Christians appeared for a moment shaken. The king commanded the rowers to redouble their efforts to gain the shore. He himself set the first example; in spite of the legate, who endeavoured to restrain him, he plunged into the waves, in full armour, his buckler over his breast, and his sword in his hand; the water being up to his shoulders: the whole Christian army, after the example of the king, cast themselves into the sea, crying, "MONT JOIE! ST. DENIS!" This multitude of men and horses, endeavouring to gain the shore, elevated the waves which broke at the feet of the Saracens; the warriors pressed on, clashing against each other in their progress—nothing was heard but the noise of the waves and the oars, the cries of the soldiers and the sailors, and the tumultuous shock of the barks and vessels, which advanced in disorder. . . . Already the oriflamme was planted on the shore; Louis had landed. Without giving the least reflection to the danger, he immediately fell on his knees to offer up his thanks to Heaven; and springing up again, filled with fresh ardour, called his bravest knights around him.—BOOK XIII.

expedition, and sometimes led away by their natural inconstancy, they only thought of returning into Europe, abandoning the Christian colonies to all the furies of an enemy irritated by former defeats. According to these considerations, the two grand masters would have wished to take advantage of the powerful succours from the West, to conclude a useful and durable peace. The mode of negotiation presented them much greater future advantages than a war, whose chances were doubtful, and whose perils might, in the end, all recoil upon them.

Their pacific message arrived at the moment when nothing was spoken of in the Christian army but the conquests they were about to make; when all minds were heated by the enthusiasm of glory, and the hope of a rich booty. The proposition alone of peace with the infidels was a true subject of scandal for these warriors, who believed themselves called upon to destroy, throughout the East, the domination and the power of all the enemies of Christ. The general surprise and indignation gave credence to the blackest calumnies against the grand master of the Temple, who was loudly accused of keeping up a secret intelligence with the sultan of Cairo, and of having joined in barbarous ceremonies to bind this impious union. Louis IX., who did not come into the East to sign a treaty of peace and to deliver only a few prisoners, shared the indignation of his companions in arms, and forbade the grand masters of the Temple and St. John to reiterate propositions insulting to the Christian warriors, insulting to him.

The Crusaders, intoxicated with their future success, were not aware of half the obstacles they were about to encounter; they thought more about the wealth than the strength of their enemies; acquainted with neither the climate nor the country to which their wishes were directed, their ignorance redoubled their security, and fed hopes that were doomed soon to fade away.

The leaders of the crusade were particularly sanguine with respect to the divisions of the Mussulman princes, who were quarrelling for the provinces of Syria and Egypt: in fact, since the death of Saladin, discord had rarely ceased to trouble the family of the Ayoubites. But as their dissensions broke out in civil wars, and as civil wars rendered the population more warlike, their empire, which grew weaker every day inwardly, often, consequently, became the stronger outwardly; when common danger united the Mussulman powers, or that one of those powers mastered the rest, everything was to be dreaded from an empire always tottering in peace, but which seemed to derive fresh strength from the animosities and perils of a war against the Christians.

Malek Selah Negmeddin, who then reigned in Egypt, was the son of the sultan Camel, celebrated by the victory gained at Mansourah over the army of John of Brienne and the legate Pelagius. Driven from the throne by a conspiracy, he endeavoured to recover it by arms; conquered, he fell into the chains of his rival, and profited by the lessons of adversity. Very soon, the esteem in which his abilities were held; the hatred which the prince who reigned in his place inspired; the want of change, and perhaps a certain partiality for revolt and treason, recalled him to empire. The new sovereign showed himself much more skilful and more fortunate than his predecessors; he knew how to preserve obedience in the provinces; to maintain discipline in his army; and to keep fear alive among his enemies. He had taken advantage of the arms of the Carismians to get possession of Damascus, and to crush both the Christians and their allies. From this period Negmeddin extended his conquests upon the banks of the Euphrates, and at length gathered under his laws the greater part of the empire of Saladin.

At the moment Louis IX. landed in the isle of Cyprus, the sultan of Cairo was in Syria, where he was making war against the prince of Aleppo, and held the city of Emessa in siege. He was acquainted with all the projects of the Christians, and gave orders for the defence of all the avenues of Egypt. When he learnt that the Christian army was about to embark, he immediately abandoned the siege of Emessa, and concluded a truce with enemies of whom he entertained very little dread, to return to his states that were threatened with invasion.

The Orientals considered the French as the bravest people of the race of the Franks, and the king of France as the most redoubtable monarch of the West. The preparations of Negmeddin were commensurate with the dread these new enemies naturally inspired. He neglected nothing in fortifying the coasts or in provisioning Damietta, which was most likely to be the object of the first hostilities. A numerous fleet was equipped, descended the Nile, and was placed at the mouth of the river; an army, commanded by Fakreddin, the most skilful of the emirs, encamped on the coast, to the west of the mouth of the river, at the very same point where, thirty-three years before, the army of John of Brienne had landed.

All these preparations would, no doubt, have been sufficient to meet the first attacks of the Crusaders, if the sultan of Cairo had been able to direct them himself, and command his troops in person; but he was attacked by a disease which his physicians pronounced to be mortal. In a state of things in which everything depended upon the presence and life of the prince, the certainty of his approaching end necessarily weakened confidence and zeal, cooled the general courage, and was injurious to the execution of all the measures taken for the defence of the country.

Such was the military and political situation of Egypt at the time Louis embarked from the ports of the isle of Cyprus. Many historians say, that before his departure, according to the custom of chivalry, he sent a herald-at-arms to the sultan Negmeddin, to declare war against him. In the early crusades, many Christian princes had in this manner addressed chivalric messages to the Mussulman powers they were about to attack: it was quite possible that Louis might imitate this example; but the letter attributed to him bears no character of truth about it. The same historians add, that the sultan of Cairo could not refrain from tears on reading the letter of St. Louis. His reply, quoted in Makrisy, is at least conformable to his known character, and to the spirit of the Mussulman princes. He affected to brave the unexpected threats and attacks of the disciples of Christ: he referred with pride to the victories of the Mussulmans over the Christians; and whilst reproaching the king of France with the injustice of his aggressions, he quoted in his letter this passage from the Koran:—"They who fight unjustly shall perish."

This message contained predictions that were but too fully realized in the end. There is nothing, however, to lead us to believe that any correspondence was then established between Louis and the sultan of Cairo. Prudence, at least, required the king of France to send messengers and emissaries into Egypt, to reconnoitre the state, strength, and resources of the country. It is more than probable, that in preceding crusades it was not only in obedience to the spirit of chivalry, but to ascertain the position of their enemies, that ambassadors were sent; we must confess, however, that we cannot find in any chronicle of the times evidence of their having taken any precaution of this kind. A foresight which might bear the slightest association with timidity, stratagem, or even policy, was not the least in accordance with the character of Louis and his knights. History has no hesitation in affirming that the Crusaders, ready at this period to embark for Egypt, knew nothing of the countries into which they were about to carry their arms, but that which they had learnt from the uncertain accounts of common report.

The signal of departure was given on the Friday before Pentecost; and a numerous fleet, in which embarked the French army and the warriors of the isle of Cyprus, sailed gallantly out from the port of Limisso. "This was a thing most beautiful to behold," says Joinville; "for it appeared as if the sea, as far as the eye could reach, was covered with the sails of vessels, which were to the number of eight hundred, as well large as small." All at once a wind blowing full from the coast of

Egypt gave rise to a violent storm, which dispersed all the fleet; and Louis IX., who was forced to put back to port, found, with great grief, that at least the half of his vessels had been carried by the wind on to the coasts of Syria. At this moment of disappointment, however, unexpected reinforcements arrived, which restored the hopes of Louis and his captains. These consisted of the duke of Burgundy, who had passed the winter in the Morea; William of Salisbury, at the head of two hundred English knights; and William of Villehardouin, prince of Achaia, who forgot the dangers of the Latin empire of Constantinople to go and fight the infidels on the banks of the Nile and the Jordan. Without waiting for the vessels which the tempest had dispersed, they again set sail, and the fleet, with a favourable wind, directed its course towards Egypt. On the fourth day at sunrise, the watch on deck cried, "Land! land!" A sailor, who served as pilot, ascended to the round top of the leading vessel, and such was the sentiment which the sight of the land inhabited by the infidels inspired in the Christians, that this man cried out, "We have nothing to do but to recommend ourselves to God; for here we are before Damietta." These words flew from rank to rank, and the whole fleet drew as near as they could to the vessel of Louis IX. The principal leaders endeavoured to get on board of it; the king awaited them in a warlike attitude, and exhorted them to offer thanks to God for having brought them face to face with the enemies of Jesus Christ. As the greater part of the leaders seemed to fear his life would be too much exposed in the course of a war which must be terrible: "Follow my example," said he to them; "leave me to brave all perils, and in the midst of the hottest fight never once think that the safety of the state and the Church resides in my person; you yourselves are the state and the Church, and you ought to see in me nothing but a man whose life, like that of any other, may be dissipated like a shadow, when it shall please the God for whom we combat." Thus Louis forgot himself and his state, and before the infidels, the king of France was but a simple soldier of Jesus Christ.

This discourse animated the courage of the barons and knights; orders were given for the whole fleet to prepare for action. In every vessel the warriors embraced each other with joy at the approach of peril; such as quarrels had alienated, swore to forget all divisions and injuries, and to conquer or to die together. Joinville says he forced two knights, who had been irreconcilable enemies, to make peace, by persuading them that their discord might draw down the maledictions of Heaven, and that union among the Christian soldiers could alone open to them the road to Egypt.

Whilst the Crusaders were thus preparing, the Mussulmans neglected nothing for their defence; their sentinels had perceived the Christian fleet, from the walls of Damietta, and the news was soon spread through the city; a bell, which had remained in the great mosque since the conquest of John of Brienne, gave the signal of danger, and was heard on both sides of the river. Four Mussulman galleys advanced to reconnoitre the strength of the Crusaders; three of them were sunk, and the fourth, getting back with great difficulty to the Nile, announced to the infidels what enemies they had to contend with.

In the mean time the Christian fleet advanced in order of battle, and cast anchor within a quarter of a league of the coast, at the moment at which the sun had performed half his daily course. The shore and sea presented the most imposing spectacle; the coast of Egypt was *lined with all the powers of the soldan, who were people goodly to look upon.* The sea appeared to be covered with ships, over which floated the banners of the cross. The Mussulman fleet, laden with soldiers and machines of war, defended the entrance of the Nile. Fakreddin, the leader of the infidel army, appeared amidst their ranks in a panoply so splendid, that Joinville, in his surprise, compares him to the sun. The heavens and the earth resounded with the noise of the bended horns and the naccaires, a kind of enormous kettle-drum, a thing very frightful to hear, and very strange to the French.

All the leaders assembled in council in the king's vessel; some proposed to defer the descent till the vessels which had been dispersed by the tempest should rejoin them: "To attack the infidels without having all their forces, would be to give them an advantage that might greatly elevate their pride; and even if success were certain, it appeared but just to wait, that all the Crusaders might have their share of the glory they came so far to seek." Some went still further, and spoke of the embarrassments and perils of a descent in an unknown country; of the disorders which must accompany a first attack; and of the difficulty of rallying the army and fleet, if the obstacles they met with should prove invincible. Louis IX. did not at all agree with this opinion: "We have not come thus far," he said, "to listen coolly to the menaces and insults of our enemies, or to remain, during several days, motionless spectators of their preparations. To temporize is to raise their courage, and weaken the ardour of the French warriors. We have neither road nor port, in which we can shelter ourselves from the winds, or from the unexpected attacks of the Saracens; a second tempest may again disperse what remains of our fleet, and deprive us of all means of beginning the war with a chance of success. To-day God offers us victory; later he will punish us for having neglected the opportunity to conquer."

The majority of the leaders were of the opinion of Louis IX., and it was resolved that the descent should be made on the morrow. A strict watch was preserved during the night; a vast number of flambeaux were kept burning, and vessels were placed near the mouth of the Nile, to observe the motions of the Saracens.

At daybreak the whole fleet weighed anchor, and the Mussulmans at the same time got under arms. Their infantry and cavalry occupied the entire shore of the point at which they expected the Crusaders to land.

When the vessels drew near the shore, the Christian warriors got into the barks that accompanied the fleet, and ranged themselves in two lines. Louis IX., accompanied by the two princes his brothers, and his chosen knights, placed himself at the right point. The cardinal legate, bearing the cross of the Saviour, was on his right hand, and in a bark in front of him floated the oriflamme of France.

The count of Jaffa, of the illustrious family of Brienne, was at the left point towards the mouth of the Nile; he appeared at the head of the knights from the isle of Cyprus and the barons of Palestine. He was on board the lightest bark of the fleet. This boat bore the arms of the counts of Jaffa, painted on its poop and prow. Around his standard floated banderoles of a thousand colours, and three hundred rowers impelled the vessel through the waves like the flight of the swallow over the stream. Erard of Brienne, surrounded by a chosen troop, occupied the centre of the line, with Baldwin of Rheims, who commanded a thousand warriors. The knights and barons stood erect in their boats, looking earnestly at the shore, lance in hand, with their horses beside them. In the front and on the wings of the army, a crowd of crossbow-men were placed to keep off the enemy.

As soon as they were within bowshot, a shower of stones, arrows, and javelins was poured at the same instant from the shore and from the line of the Crusaders. The ranks of the Christians appeared for a moment shaken. The king commanded the rowers to redouble their efforts to gain the shore. He himself set the first example; in spite of the legate, who endeavoured to restrain him, he plunged into the waves in full armour, his buckler over his breast, and his sword in hand; the water being up to his shoulders; the whole Christian army, after the example of the king, cast themselves into the sea, crying, "*Montjoie! St. Denis!*" This multitude of men and horses, endeavouring to gain the shore, elevated the waves which broke at the feet of the Saracens; the warriors pressed on, clashing against each other in their progress—nothing was heard but the noise of the waves and the oars, the cries of the soldiers and the sailors, and the tumultuous shock of the barks and vessels, which advanced in disorder.

The Mussulman battalions assembled on the shore could not stop the French warriors. Joinville and Baldwin of Rheims landed the first; after them came the count of Jaffa. They were drawing up in order of battle, when the cavalry of the Saracens came pouring down upon them; the Crusaders closed in their ranks, covered themselves with their bucklers, and presenting the points of their lances, checked the impetuosity of the enemy. All their companions who had reached the shore, immediately formed in rear of this battalion.

Already the oriflamme was planted on the shore; Louis had landed. Without giving the least reflection to the danger, he immediately fell on his knees to offer up his thanks to Heaven; and springing up again, filled with fresh ardour, called his bravest knights around him. An Arab historian relates that the king of the Franks then caused his tent to be pitched, which was of a bright scarlet, and attracted all eyes. At length, all the army being landed, a sanguinary contest began on every part of the coast; the Saracens and Franks, seeking and attacking each other, formed one conflicting mass. Nobody remained inactive; the two fleets quickly became engaged at the mouth of the Nile. Whilst the shore and the sea resounded thus with the shock of arms, Queen Marguerite and the duchess of Anjou, who remained on board a vessel at a distance, awaited in terrible anxiety the issue of the double battle; they offered up fervent prayers, and pious ecclesiastics assembled around them, and joined in holy psalms to obtain the protection of the God of armies.

The fleet of the Saracens was soon dispersed; many of the vessels were sunk, the remainder escaped up the river. In the mean time, the troops of Fakreddin, broken in all directions, retired in the greatest confusion; the French pursuing them up to their intrenchments. After a last desperate struggle, the Mussulmans abandoned their camp and the western bank of the Nile, leaving several of their emirs on the field of battle: nothing could resist the French, animated by the presence and the example of their king.

In the course of the battle several messenger pigeons had been sent to the sultan of Cairo, whose malady confined him in a small town situated between Damietta and Mansourah: as no answer was received, a report of his death began to prevail, and completed the discouragement of the Egyptian troops. Many of the emirs were impatient to know, and at the same time were doubtful of the fate that awaited them under a new reign. Several deserted their standards, and by that means augmented the disorder: towards evening the whole army dispersed, and the soldiers, abandoned by their leaders, thought of nothing but seeking safety in flight. The Crusaders remained masters of the coast and of both banks of the Nile; and this glorious victory had cost but little Christian blood, for only two or three knights were killed: of the French nobles the army had only to deplore the count de la Marche, who appeared to seek death, and, dying thus by the side of his king, expiated, say our historians, his numerous treasons and crimes.

Towards the end of the day, the tents were pitched on the field of battle; the clergy chanted the *Te Deum*, and the night was passed in rejoicings. Whilst the victorious army was thus giving itself up to exultation, the greatest confusion reigned in Damietta; the fugitives had passed through the city, spreading, as they went, the contagion of the fear that pursued them. Fakreddin himself gave no orders for the security of the place: the inhabitants expected every instant to see the French enter; some dreaded a surprise, others feared a siege; there was no one to reassure them, and the darkness of night came on to complete their terror and confusion. Fear rendered them barbarous; they pitilessly massacred all the Christians that were in the city; the troops, on retiring, pillaged the houses and set fire to the public edifices; whole families abandoned their homes, carrying with them their furniture and movable wealth. The garrison was composed of the bravest of the Arab tribe of the Benou-Kenaneh; but fear gained dominion over them as well as the rest; they abandoned the towers and the ramparts intrusted to their guardianship, and fled away with the army of Fakreddin. Before the dawn of day, the city was without defenders, and almost without inhabitants.

The columns of flame that arose from the bosom of the city were soon observed in the Christian camp; the whole horizon was on fire. On the morrow, at daybreak, the soldiers advanced towards the city, all the gates of which they found open. They met with nothing in the streets but the carcasses of the victims immolated by the despair and fanaticism of the infidels, and a few living Christians, who, having contrived to conceal themselves from the murderers and executioners, had, in their turn, massacred all the Mussulmans whom age and infirmities prevented from flying with their compatriots. The soldiers returned to announce what they had seen, and could scarcely gain credit from their companions. The army advanced cautiously in order of battle. When they were assured that the city was deserted, the Crusaders took possession of it. They employed themselves, in the first place, to stop the progress of the flames; then the soldiers spread themselves throughout the city, for the purpose of pillaging it, and all that escaped the conflagration became the reward of victory.

In the mean time, the king of France, the pope's legate, and the patriarch of Jerusalem, followed by a crowd of prelates and ecclesiastics, entered Damietta in procession, and repaired to the great mosque, which was once more converted into a church, and consecrated to the Holy Virgin, the mother of Jesus Christ. The French monarch, the clergy, and all the leaders of the army, marched with heads uncovered and barefooted, singing psalms of thanksgiving, and attributing to God all the glory of this miraculous conquest.

The news of this victory was soon spread through all the Egyptian provinces. The continuator of Tabary, who was then at Cairo, informs us in his History, that this event was considered as one of the greatest calamities. All Mussulmans were sunk in despondency and fear; the most brave even despaired of being able to save Egypt.

Negmeddin was still ill, and unable to mount on horseback; the defeat of his army, and the victory of the Christians, were announced to him by the soldiers and inhabitants that had fled from Damietta. He broke into a violent rage against the garrison, and pronounced a sentence of instant death upon fifty-four of the most guilty: in vain they alleged the retreat of the emir Fakreddin as an excuse; the sultan said they merited death for having feared the arms of their enemies more than the anger of their master. One of these, condemned to suffer with his son, a young man of singular beauty, implored the sultan to allow him to die first; the sultan refused even this grace, and the unhappy father underwent the agony of seeing his son killed before his eyes, ere he himself was handed over to the executioner. When we reflect upon the barbarity of these executions, we are astonished that a prince without an army should find instruments to execute his wrath, or even that he should dare to display it in this frightful manner upon deserters and cowards; but this public and awful exhibition of punishment, which kept up the belief in the power of the master, acted strongly upon the minds of the multitude, and assisted in bringing back the vulgar crowd of the Mussulman soldiery to discipline and order. But it was not thus with the principal emirs; already but little disposed to tremble before a sovereign whom they regarded as their own work, and who stood in such need of their support. The sultan would willingly have punished Fakreddin, but the circumstances, says an Arabian historian, dictated patience. He contented himself with addressing a few reproaches to him. "The presence of these Franks," said he to him, "must have something very terrible in it, since men like you cannot support it during one whole day." These words created more indignation than fear among the emirs that were present, and some of them looked at Fakreddin, as if to tell him they were ready to sacrifice the sultan; but the print of the cold hand of death was on the brow of the sultan, and the sight of a dying man took away the wish to commit a useless crime :—deplorable situation of a prince who had within a few leagues of him a formidable enemy, that he was not able to contend with ; near him traitors, that he did not dare to punish ; and who, whilst seeing his authority every day diminish, and feeling himself hourly dying, appeared to have no salvation to expect for either himself or his empire.

During this time the Crusaders established themselves in Damietta without obstacle ; Queen Marguerite and the other princesses, with the legate and the clergy, occupied the palaces and principal houses ; the rest of the city was abandoned to the pilgrims who did not bear arms : the towers and ramparts were guarded by five hundred knights, and the Christian army was encamped upon the plain on the banks of the Nile. In this situation the Crusaders only thought of enjoying the fruits of their victory in peace, and appeared to have forgotten that they had still enemies to contend with.

The sultan of Cairo had caused himself to be transported to Mansourah, where he endeavoured to rally his army, and re-establish discipline among the troops. Whether he had recovered from his terror, or that he was willing to conceal his alarm and the progress of his malady, he sent several messages to Louis IX. In one of these letters, Negmeddin, joining menaces to irony, congratulated the king of France upon his arrival in Egypt, and asked him at what period it would please him to depart again. The Mussulman prince added, among other things, that the quantity of provisions and agricultural instruments with which the Crusaders had burdened their vessels, appeared to him to be a useless precaution ; and to perform the duties of hospitality towards the Franks, in a manner worthy of himself and them, he engaged to supply them with corn during their sojourn in his states. Negmeddin, in another message, offered the king of France a general battle on the 25th day of June, in a place that should be determined upon. Louis IX. answered the first letter of the sultan by saying that he had landed in Egypt on the day he had appointed, and as to the day of his departure, he should think about it at leisure. With regard to the proposed battle, the king contented himself with replying, that he would neither accept the day nor choose the place, because all days and all places were equally fit for fighting with infidels. The French monarch added, that he would attack the sultan wherever he should meet with him ; that he would pursue him at all times and without intermission ; and would treat him as an enemy till God had touched his heart, and Christians might consider him as a brother.

Fortune presented King Louis with an opportunity and the means of accomplishing his threats. The Crusaders, whom the tempest had separated from the fleet, continued to arrive every day, and the knights of the Temple and of St. John, who had been accused of being anxious for peace, joined the banners of the army, and breathed nothing but war. They were acquainted with the country, and with the best manner of combating the infidels ; and with this useful reinforcement, the king was able to undertake an expedition against Alexandria, or, by obtaining possession of Mansourah, render himself master of the route to Cairo. After the taking of Damietta, several of the leaders had proposed to pursue the Mussulmans, and take advantage of the terror that the first victory of the Christians had inspired. But the period was approaching at which the waters of the Nile began to rise, and the remembrance of the overthrow of Pelagius and John of Brienne, dispelled the idea of marching against the capital of Egypt. Before he pursued his conquests, Louis wished to wait the arrival of his brother, the count of Poictiers, who was to embark with the *arrière ban* of the kingdom of France. Most historians view in this delay the cause of all the evils that afterwards befell the Crusaders. We have nothing like sufficient positive documents to test the truth of their opinion ; but we may say with certainty, that the inaction of the Christian army became, from that time, a source of most fatal disorders.

These disorders began to break out when the division took place of the booty made at the taking of Damietta. To animate the courage of the Crusaders, the treasures of this city, the entrepôt of the merchandises of the East, had often been boasted of; but as the richest quarters had been destroyed by the conflagration, and as the inhabitants had, when they fled, taken their most valuable effects with them, the spoils were very far from answering the hopes of the victorious army. In spite of the threats of the legate, several of the Crusaders had not brought all that fell into their hands to the common stock. The whole of the booty obtained in the city only produced the sum of six thousand *livres tournois*, to be divided among the Crusaders, whose surprise and indignation found vent in violent murmurs.

As it had been determined that no division should be made of the provisions, but that they should be preserved in the royal magazines, for the support of the army, this resolution, so contrary to ancient usages, gave birth to loud complaints. Joinville informs us that the *prud'homme* John of Valery, whose stern probity and bravery were the admiration of the whole army, addressed some warm representations to the king on this subject. John of Valery alleged the laws of the Holy Land, and the custom pursued till that time in the crusades; he mentioned the example of John of Brienne, who, at the first conquest of Damietta, had only retained one-third of the riches and provisions found in the city, abandoning the rest to the general army. This custom was even less consecrated by the holy wars than by the feudal laws, according to which every lord carried on the war at his own expense, and by right had a share in all the plunder obtained from the enemy. But it might be objected, that Louis IX. furnished most of the leaders of the army with money, and by that the counts and barons had renounced the conditions of the feudal compact. This law of the division of provisions, which had, in fact, been observed in preceding crusades, sufficiently accounts for the scarcity that had so often desolated the Christian armies. The pious monarch was anxious to avoid evils that were the fruit of want of prudence and foresight, and refused to listen to the complaints of most of the French nobles. Thus, says Joinville, scarcity continued, and made the people very much dissatisfied.

This spirit of dissatisfaction was quickly joined by other disorders, the consequences of which were still more deplorable. The knights forgot, in their fatal inactivity, both their warlike virtues and the object of the holy war. The riches of Egypt and the East being promised to them, the lords and barons made haste to consume, in festivities and pleasures, the money which they had obtained from the liberality of the king, or by the sale of their lands and castles. The passion for gaming had got entire possession of both leaders and soldiers; after losing their fortune, they risked even their horses and arms. Even beneath the shadow of the standards of Christ, the Crusaders gave themselves up to all the excesses of debauchery; the contagion of the most odious vices pervaded all ranks, and places of prostitution were found even in the close vicinity of the pavilion inhabited by the pious monarch of the French.

To satisfy the boundless taste for luxury and pleasure, recourse was had to all sorts of violent means. The leaders of the army pillaged the traders that provisioned the camp and the city; they imposed enormous tributes upon them, and this assisted greatly in bringing on scarcity. The most ardent made distant excursions, surprised caravans, devastated towns and plains, and bore away Mussulman women, whom they brought in triumph to Damietta. The sharing even of this sort of booty often gave rise to angry quarrels, and the whole camp resounded with complaints, threats, and confusion.

One of the most afflicting phases of this picture was, that the authority of the king became less respected daily; as corruption increased, the habits of obedience declined; the laws were without power, and virtue had no longer any empire. Louis IX. met with opposition to his wishes, even

TE DEUM AFTER VICTORY.

In the mean time, the king of France, the pope's legate, and the patriarch of Jerusalem, followed by a crowd of prelates and ecclesiastics, entered Damietta in procession, and repaired to the great mosque, which was once more converted into a church, and consecrated to the Holy Virgin, the mother of Jesus Christ.

The French monarch, the clergy, and all the leaders of the army marched with heads uncovered and bare-footed, singing psalms of thanksgiving, and attributing to God all the glory of this miraculous conquest.—BOOK XIII.

from the princes of his own family. The count d'Artois, a young, ardent, and presumptuous prince, unable to endure either rivalry or contradiction, proud of his military renown, and jealous to excess of that of others, was in the habit of constantly provoking the other leaders, and of heaping upon them, without motive, the most outrageous affronts. The earl of Salisbury, to whom he had behaved very ill, complained of him to Louis, and being unable to obtain the satisfaction he demanded, in his anger pronounced those memorable words: *"You are then not a king, if you are unable to administer justice."* This indocility of the princes, and the licentiousness of the great, completed the disorder; every day relaxation of discipline was observed to increase; the guarding of the camp, which extended far over the plains and along the banks of the Nile, was scarcely attended to; the advanced posts of the Christian army were constantly exposed to the attacks of the enemy, without being able to oppose any other means of resistance than imprudent and rash bravery, which only increased the danger.

Among the Mussulman soldiers sent to harass the Crusaders, the most successful in their mission were the Bedouin Arabs; intrepid warriors, indefatigable horsemen, having no other country but the desert, no other property but their horses and arms, the hopes of plunder supported them through all toils, and taught them to brave all dangers. With the Arabs of the desert were joined some Carismian horsemen, who had escaped from the ruin of their warlike nation. Accustomed to live by brigandage, both these watched night and day, to dog the Christian soldiers, and appeared to possess the instinct and activity of those wild animals that prowl constantly around the dwellings of man in search of their prey. The sultan of Cairo promised a golden byzant for every Christian head that should be brought into his camp; sometimes the Arabs and Carismians surprised the Crusaders who wandered from the army, and often took advantage of the darkness of night to get access to the camp; sentinels asleep on their post, knights in bed in their tents, were struck by invisible hands, and when day appeared to lighten the scene of carnage, the barbarians fled along the banks of the Nile, to demand their wages of the sultan of Egypt.

These surprises and nocturnal attacks had a considerable effect in reanimating the courage of the Mussulmans. To raise the confidence of the multitude and the army, great care was taken to exhibit the heads of the Christians; all captives were paraded about in triumph, and the least advantage obtained over the Franks was celebrated throughout Egypt. Contemporary historians, led away by common exaggeration, talk of the most trifling combats as memorable victories; and we are astonished, at the present day, to read in the history of a period so abounding in great military events, that in the month of Ramadan thirty-seven Christians were brought in chains to Cairo, that they were followed, some days afterwards, by thirty-eight other captives, among whom were distinguished five knights. The activity of Negmeddin appeared to increase as his end approached. He employed the greatest exertions to get together all his troops; was indefatigably attentive in watching the movements of the Crusaders, and seldom failed to take advantage of their errors. Men were employed night and day in repairing the towers and fortifications of Mansourah; the Mussulman fleet, which had ascended the Nile, cast anchor immediately in front of the city. Whilst these preparations were going on, news arrived that the garrison of Damascus had taken possession of the city of Sidon, belonging to the Franks, and that the important place of Carac had just declared in favour of Negmeddin. This unexpected intelligence, the sight of the prisoners, but above all, the inactivity of the Christian army, which was attributed to fear, completed the dissipation of the terror of the Mussulmans. Whilst new reinforcements were every day arriving in the camp of the sultan, the people flocked in crowds to the mosques of Cairo and the other cities of Egypt, to invoke the protection of Heaven, and return thanks to the God of Mahomet, for having prevented the Christians from taking advantage of their victories.

BOOK XIV

Damietta and Louis IX

A. D. 1248 TO 1255

BOOK XIV.

DAMIETTA AND LOUIS IX.

A. D. 1248-1255.

Alphonse count of Poictiers, and Hugh Lebrun count of Angoulême, engage in the holy war—Opposition of Henry III. of England to his barons and the pope—Raymond, count of Thoulouse—Count d'Artois—Death of Negmeddin—Beauty and genius of Chegger-Eddour, sultana of Egypt—Scharmesah captured by the Crusaders—Fakreddin takes the command of the Egyptian forces—Treachery of the Mamelukes—Military operations on the canal of Aschmoum—Terrific effects of the Greek fire—Fakreddin slain and the Saracens defeated—Rashness of Count d'Artois, and his death—Battle of Mansourah—The Crusaders defeated by the Mamelukes—The earl of Salisbury, Robert de Vair, and other illustrious warriors slain—Continued contests with the Egyptians, and severe losses of the Crusaders—Instances of devoted heroism and individual bravery—The Crusaders exposed to famine and pestilence, and the Saracens victorious—The canal of Mehallah fatal to the Crusaders—Sufferings and losses of the Christian army—Guy du Chatel, Gaucher de Chatillon, and other distinguished Crusaders slain—Louis attempts to regain Damietta—Is defeated, and surrenders as a prisoner of war—His entire army annihilated by the Saracens—Sieur de Joinville taken prisoner—Agonizing situation of Marguerite, queen of Louis—30,000 Crusaders massacred, or taken into slavery—Religious resignation of Louis—He enters into an abject treaty for his ransom—Revolt of the Mamelukes—Death of Almoadan—Octaï, chief of the Mamelukes—The emirs of Egypt—Chegger-Eddour elected sultana of Egypt, and Ezz-Eddin Aybek the governor—Extinction of the Ayoubite dynasty—Damietta delivered up to the Mussulmans—Ransom paid for Louis—Consternation in France on hearing of his capture—He arrives at Ptolemaïs—Deliberates with his knights as to their future operations—The Syrians refuse to acknowledge the authority of the Mamelukes—Civil commotions in Egypt—Chegger-Eddour marries Ezz-Eddin, and yields her regal authority—Death of Frederick II. of Germany—Conrad, his successor, excommunicated—Jacob of Hungary—"Pastors"—Pope Innocent IV. urges the preaching of a fresh crusade—Singular message of the "Old Man of the Mountain" to Louis—A visit to his court—Cities of Palestine fortified by Louis—War between the sultans of Cairo and Damascus—Treaty between them, and hostilities resumed against the Christians—The Turcomans surprise Sidon, and slaughter the inhabitants—Belinas pillaged by the Crusaders—Pious devotedness of Louis—He fortifies Sidon—Death of Blanche, queen-regent of France—Louis quits Palestine, and arrives at Paris—Excellence of Joinville's history—On the character and misfortunes of Louis—Damietta destroyed by the Mussulmans, and the mouth of the Nile filled with stones—Rise and fall of the Mamelukes—Hospital of Quinze Vingts—The Tartars and Moguls—"Assizes of Jerusalem"—Characters of Frederick II. of Germany and Pope Innocent IV.—Papal crusade against Eccelino de Romano.

WHILST the Christian army was forgetting in its sojourn at Damietta both the laws of discipline and the object of the holy war, Alphonse, count of Poictiers, prepared to set out for the East. All the churches of France still resounded with pathetic exhortations addressed to the Christian warriors; the bishops, in the name of the sovereign pontiff, conjured the faithful to second, by means of charity, the enterprise against the Saracens; an apostolic brief, granted to the brother of the king not only the tribute imposed upon the Crusaders who repurchased their vow, but all the sums destined by testament to acts of piety, the object of which was not distinctly signified. These sums must have been considerable, but could scarcely suffice for the expenses of an expedition which bore the appearance of another crusade. The knights and barons who had not been affected by the example of Louis IX., showed but very little enthusiasm, or else wanted money for so long a voyage. Piety and the love of glory were not powerful enough to seduce them to join the banners of the holy war. History has preserved an agreement, by which Hugh Lebrun, count of Angoulême, consented to set out for the crusade with twelve knights, but on the express condition that the count of Poictiers should feed them at his own table during the expedition; that he would advance the seigneur Hugh Lebrun the sum of four thousand libres; and should pay him, in perpetuity, a pension of six hundred livres tournois. This agreement and several other similar ones were innovations in the military usages of feudalism, and even in the usages consecrated by the holy wars.

The English nobles, however, were impatient to follow the example set them by Louis IX. We read in Matthew Paris, that the English lords and knights had already sold or empawned their lands, and placed themselves entirely at the mercy of the Jews; which appeared to be the preliminary of a departure for the Holy Land. It is not out of place to add here, that this impatience to set out for the East, arose less from a religious motive than from the spirit of opposition that animated the barons against their monarch, Henry III., who was accused of being desirous of taking advantage of the absence of Louis IX., and did all in his power to retain the barons and lords of his kingdom; and as the latter resisted his solicitations with contempt, he resolved to employ the influence of the Church; "so that," says Matthew Paris, "like a young child who, having been ill-used, goes to its mother to complain, the king of England carried his complaints to the sovereign pontiff, adding that he proposed to go himself, and lead his barons shortly to the Holy Land." The pope, in his replies, forbade Henry III. to undertake anything against the kingdom of France; but, at the same time, he threatened with the thunders of the Church, all the knights and barons that should leave the kingdom against the will of the king. Henry, supported by the authority of the pope, ordered the commanders at Dover and the other ports to take measures that no Crusader should embark. Thus the court of Rome on one side preached the crusade, and on the other prevented the departure of the soldiers of the cross; which must have tended to dissipate all the illusions and annihilate the spirit of the holy war.

Raymond, count of Thoulouse, had likewise taken the oath to combat the infidels; but the inconstancy of his character, and the policy of the pope, soon led him into other enterprises. His age had seen him, by turns, full of zeal for the Church, ardent to persecute it; the apostle of heresy, and the terror of heretics; sometimes abandoned to the furies of revolt, sometimes submissive to servitude; braving the thunders of the court of Rome, afterwards seeking the favour of the pontiffs; pursued by unjust wars, and himself declaring war without a motive. At the epoch of which we are speaking, the count of Thoulouse had given up all idea of fighting against the infidels, and was preparing to minister to the personal vengeance of Innocent IV., by turning his arms against Thomas of Savoy, who had recently married a daughter of the emperor Frederick, in opposition to the commands of the pope. He had already received the money necessary for his preparations from the pope, and had taken leave of his daughter the countess of Poictiers, about to depart for the East, when he fell sick at Milan. From that time all the projects of his ambition faded away, and, to borrow the expression of a modern historian, *he went into another world to learn the result of the incomprehensible varieties of his life.*

With him the illustrious house of Thoulouse became extinct, a house of which several of the princes had been heroes of the holy wars, others deplorable victims of crusades. The county of Thoulouse thus became a property of the family of the king of France, and whilst Louis IX. was dissipating his armies and his treasures in vain endeavours to make conquests in the East, conquests less brilliant, but also less expensive, more useful and more durable, were increasing the power of the monarchy and extending the limits of the kingdom.

Germany, Holland, and Italy, filled with troubles, at that time occupied all the attention of Frederick II., and did not allow him to turn his thoughts towards the East. He sent the count of Poictiers fifty horses and a quantity of provisions, delighted, as he said, to seize an opportunity of acquitting some of the obligations he had received from France; he put up prayers for the success of the crusade, and deeply regretted his inability to take a part in it. Frederick had lived as the count of Thoulouse had done, and like him, he was soon, in another world, to behold the end of his ambition, of the inconstancy of his designs, and of the vicissitudes of fortune.

Although the count of Poictiers was little favoured by circumstances, he finished his preparations and got together an army. The new Crusaders embarked at Aigues-Mortes, at the moment the news of the taking of Damietta arrived in the West. The Christian army expected them in Egypt with greater anxiety, from the circumstance of the Sea of Damietta having been, for more than a month, agitated, unceasingly, by a furious tempest. Three weeks before their arrival, all the pilgrims had put up prayers on their account; on the Saturday of each week they went in procession to the seashore, to implore the protection of Heaven in favour of the warriors about to join the Christian army. At length, after a passage of two months, the count of Poictiers disembarked before Damietta. His arrival not only diffused joy and hope among the Crusaders, but permitted them to leave their long and fatal state of inactivity.

Louis IX. assembled the council of the princes and barons, to consult them on the line of march most advisable to be taken, and upon measures for perfecting the conquest of Egypt. Several of the leaders proposed to lay siege to Alexandria: they represented that that city had a commodious port; that the Christian fleet would there find certain shelter; and that they could there procure munitions and provisions with great facility: this was the opinion of all that had experience in war. The headstrong youth of the army, persuaded that they had sacrificed sufficiently to prudence by remaining several months in idleness, maintained that they ought to proceed immediately against Cairo; they thought nothing of the dangers the Christian army must encounter in an unknown country, where they must expect to meet with enemies irritated by fanaticism and despair. The count d'Artois put himself particularly forward among those who wished them to attack the capital of Egypt. "When you wish to kill the serpent," cried he, "you ought always first to endeavour to crush his head." This opinion, expressed with warmth, prevailed in the council; Louis himself partook of the ardour and hopes of short-sighted youth, and the order was given for marching towards Cairo.

The army of the Crusaders consisted of sixty thousand fighting men, more than twenty thousand of whom were horse. A numerous fleet ascended the Nile, laden with provisions, baggage, and machines of war. Queen Marguerite, with the countesses of Artois, Anjou, and Poictiers, remained at Damietta, where the king had left a garrison under the command of Olivier de Thermes.

The Crusaders encamped at Pharescour the 7th of December; terror had preceded their triumphant march, and everything seemed to favour their enterprise. One circumstance, of which they were ignorant, would have increased the security and joy of the Christian knights if they had known of it; Negmeddin, after having struggled for a long time against a cruel malady, was at length dead. This death might have produced serious trouble in both the Egyptian nation and army, if it had not been carefully concealed for several days. After the sultan had breathed his last, the Mamelukes guarded the gates of his palace as if he had been still living; prayers were put up, and orders were issued in his name: with the Mussulmans, nothing interrupted the preparations for defence or attention to the war against the Christians. All these precautions were the work of a woman—a woman who had been purchased as a slave, and had become the favourite wife of Negmeddin. The Arabian historians are eloquent in the praise of the courage and talents of Chegger-Eddour, and agree in saying, that no woman surpassed her in beauty, and no man excelled her in genius.

After the death of Negmeddin, the sultana assembled the principal emirs; in this council the command of Egypt was given to Fakreddin, and they acknowledged as sultan Almoadam Touranschah, whom his father had banished to Mesopotamia: some authors assert that in this council it was resolved to send ambassadors to the king of the Franks, to propose peace in the name of the prince of whose death he was still ignorant. The ambassadors, in order to obtain a truce, were to offer the Christians Damietta with its territories, and Jerusalem with several other cities of Palestine. It was

THE CRUSADERS ON THE NILE.

The Crusaders had soon to contend with calamities more destructive to them than even the power or the arms of the Mussulmans; a contagious disease made its appearance in the Christian army. They had neglected to bury the dead after the last two battles; the bodies cast confusedly and heedlessly into the Aschmonur, and floating on its waters stopped before the bridge of boats constructed by the Crusaders, and covered the surface of the canal from one shore to the other. Pestilential exhalations quickly arose from this heap of carcasses. Louis IX. ordered the bodies of the Christians to be buried in the ditches dug by the Saracens on the bank; but these spoils of death, moved and transported without precaution, only assisted the progress of the epidemic. The spectacle which was then presented to the eyes of the Crusaders spread the deepest grief throughout the camp, and awakened a more perfect consciousness of their losses. Christian soldiers were seen searching among bodies which wounds, the hues of death, and the action of the sun and air had disfigured, for the deplorable remains of their friends or companions. Many of those upon whom friendship imposed this pious task, fell sick and died almost instantly.—BOOK XIV.

not probable that this negotiation should succeed; the Christians had advanced too far, and had too much confidence in their arms, to listen to any proposition.

The Christian army pursued its march along the banks of the Nile, and entered the town of Scharmesah, without meeting any other enemy than five hundred Mussulman horsemen. These horsemen at first evinced nothing but pacific intentions, and, from the smallness of their numbers, they inspired no dread. Louis IX., whose protection they seemed to implore, forbade the Crusaders to attack them; but the Mamelukes, abusing the confidence that was placed in them, and taking advantage of a favourable opportunity, fell all at once upon the Templars, and killed a knight of that order. A cry to arms immediately rung through the French army, and the Mussulman battalion was assailed on all sides: such as did not fall beneath the swords of the Crusaders, were drowned in the Nile. In proportion with the approach of the Christians to Mansourah, the anxiety and terror of the Egyptians increased; the emir Fakreddin exposed the dangers of the country in a letter that was read at the hour of prayer in the great mosque of the capital. After the formula, *"In the name of God and of Mahomet his prophet,"* the letter of Fakreddin began by these words of the Koran: *"Hasten, great and small, the cause of God has need of your arms and of your wealth."* "The Franks," added the emir, "the Franks (Heaven curse them) are arrived in our country with their standards and their swords; they wish to obtain possession of our cities and ravage our provinces: what Mussulman can refuse to march against them, and avenge the glory of Islamism?"

Upon hearing this letter read, all the people were melted to tears; the greatest agitation prevailed throughout the city of Cairo; the death of the sultan, which began to be known, added greatly to the general consternation; orders were sent to raise troops in all the Egyptian provinces; war was preached in all the mosques, and the imauns endeavoured by every means to awaken fanaticism, in order to combat the depression of despair.

The Christian army arrived before the canal Aschmoum Theriah on the 19th of December. The Mussulman army was encamped on the opposite shore, having the Nile on its left, and behind it the city of Mansourah; close to them, in the direction of Cairo, the Saracens had a numerous fleet upon the river. That of the Christians had advanced to the head of the canal. Everything seemed to announce that the fate of the war would be decided on this spot. The Crusaders marked out their camp in the place in which the army of John of Brienne had encamped thirty years before. The remembrance of a great disaster ought to have served them as a lesson, and, at least, have tempered the excessive confidence that the too easy conquest of Damietta had given them.

The canal of Aschmoum was of the width of the Seine, its bed was deep, and its banks steep. In order to cross it, it was necessary that a dike should be constructed: the work was begun, but as fast as they heaped up the sand and stones, the Saracens dug away the earth in front of the dike, and thus removed further back the opposite bank of the canal; in vain the causeway advanced, the Crusaders had always the same distance to fill up, and each of the trenches dug by the enemy tended to make their labours useless. In addition to which, they were night and day interrupted in their works, and were constantly exposed to the arrows and javelins of the Saracens.

Although the Mussulman general had fled without fighting at the first appearance of the Franks, the chronicles of the times speak very highly of his bravery and military talents. They add that he had been made a knight by Frederick II., and that he bore the arms of the emperor of Germany with those of the sultans of Cairo and Damascus upon his escutcheon. These distinctions might draw the attention of the multitude; but that which was for Fakreddin a true title of glory is, that he was able, by his speeches and his example, to reanimate the courage and confidence of a conquered army.

Scarcely had the Crusaders seated themselves down in their camp, and begun the works necessary for the passage of the Aschmoum, than Fakreddin sent a party of troops to Scharmesah, to attack the rear of the Christian army. The Saracens, by this unexpected assault, spread disorder and terror through the camp of their enemies. The first advantage redoubled their audacity, and soon after an assault was made upon the Christians, along the whole line of their camp, extending from the canal to the Nile. The Mussulmans several times passed the intrenchments of the Crusaders; the duke of Anjou, Guy count of Forest, the sieur de Joinville, and several other knights, were compelled to exert all their bravery to repulse from their camp an enemy whom every fresh combat taught that the French were not invincible, and that it was at least possible to stop them on their march.

Conflicts took place every day in the plain and upon the river. Several vessels belonging to the Christians fell into the hands of the Mussulmans; the Arabs, constantly prowling round the camp, bore away into captivity every man that ventured to stray from his colours. As the emir Fakreddin could only learn from the reports of prisoners the state and disposition of the Christian army, he promised a recompense for every captive that should be brought into his tents; all the means that audacity and cunning could suggest were employed to surprise the Crusaders. It is related that a Mussulman soldier having buried his head in a melon that had been hollowed out, threw himself into the Nile, and swam down the stream. The melon, which appeared to float upon the water, attracted the eyes of a Christian warrior, who sprang into the river, and as he stretched out his hand to seize the floating melon, he himself was seized and dragged away to the camp of the Mussulmans. This anecdote, more whimsical than instructive, is related by several Arabian historians, who scarcely say anything of the preceding combats. Such are the spirit and character of the greater part of oriental histories, in which the most frivolous details often take the place of useful truths and important events.

Whilst the armies were thus in face of each other, the Crusaders pursued the work they had begun upon the Aschmoum. Towers of wood and machines were constructed, to protect the workmen employed in making the dike upon which the Christians were to cross the canal. On their side, the Mussulmans redoubled their efforts to prevent their enemies from completing their work. The dike advanced but very slowly, and the wooden towers that had been constructed in front of the causeway, could not defend either the workmen or the soldiers against the arrows, stones, and fiery darts that were being constantly launched from the camp of the Egyptians. Nothing could equal the surprise and terror that the sight alone of the Greek fire caused the Christian army. According to the relation of ocular witnesses, this redoubtable fire, cast sometimes through a brass tube, and sometimes by an instrument that was called the *perrière*, was of the size of a tun or large cask; the flaming tail, which it drew after it, was many feet in length; the Crusaders imagined they beheld a fiery dragon flying through the air; the noise of its explosion resembled that of thunder, which rolls in repeated peals. When it was launched during the night, it cast a lurid splendour over the whole camp. At the first sight of this terrible fire, the knights set to guard the towers, ran here and there, like men bewildered; some called their companions to their aid, whilst others threw themselves on the ground, or fell on their knees, invoking the celestial powers. Joinville could not conceal his fright, and thanked Heaven with all his heart when the Greek fire fell at a distance from him. Louis IX. was not less terrified than his barons and knights, and when he heard the detonation of the fire, he burst into tears, exclaiming: "Great God! Jesus Christ, protect me and all my people!"

"The good prayers and orisons of the king," says his historian, "were of great service to us;" nevertheless, they were not able to save the towers and wooden works constructed by the Crusaders: all were consumed by the flames in sight of the Christian army, without their having any power to arrest their devastation. This misfortune was a lesson by which they ought to have profited; the Christians ought to have perceived that they had undertaken an impossible enterprise, and that they ought to seek for some means, more easy and more certain, of crossing the canal. But, unhappily, the leaders persisted in causing other erections to be made, which shared the fate of the first. They thus lost much time, and the futility of their attempts assisted in raising the pride and confidence of the Saracens.

The Mamelukes at this time learned that their new sovereign had arrived in Damascus, and that he was hourly expected in his capital. This arrival gave them fresh hopes, and rendered them more confident of victory. To redouble the ardour of his soldiers, Fakreddin often repeated, with a tone of assurance, that he should soon go and sleep in the tent of the king of the Franks.

The Christians had been a month before Aschmoum, exhausting themselves in useless efforts. Their leaders never took the trouble to examine if it were possible to ford the canal, or cross it by swimming, as the Egyptian cavalry had done. They were beginning to despair, when chance revealed to them a means of extricating themselves from their embarrassment, a means they might have known much sooner, if they had had less obstinacy and more foresight. A Bedouin Arab came to propose to Imbert de Beaujeu, constable of France, to show him, at a distance of half a league from the camp, a ford, by which the Crusaders might cross without danger or obstacles, to the opposite bank of the Aschmoum. After having ascertained that the Arab told the truth, they paid him the sum of five hundred golden byzants, which he had demanded, and the Christian army prepared to profit by this happy but late discovery.

The king and the princes his brothers, with all the cavalry, began their march in the middle of the night; the duke of Burgundy remained in the camp with the infantry, to observe the enemy, and guard the machines and the baggage. At daybreak, all the squadrons that were to cross the canal, awaited the signal on the bank. The count d'Artois was ambitious of crossing first; the king, who knew the impetuous character of his brother, at first wished to restrain him; but Robert insisted warmly, and swore upon the Gospel, that when he arrived on the opposite shore, he would wait till the Christian army had passed. Louis imprudently placed faith in the promise of a young, fiery, and haughty knight, to master his warlike transports, and resist all the temptations of glory on the field of battle. The count d'Artois placed himself at the head of the van, in which were the Hospitallers, the Templars, and the English. This van crossed the Aschmoum, and put to flight three hundred Saracen horsemen. At the sight of the flying Mussulmans, young Robert was on fire to pursue them. In vain the two grand masters represented to him that the flight of the enemy was perhaps nothing but a stratagem, and that he ought to wait for the army, and follow the orders of the king. Robert feared to lose an opportunity of triumphing over the infidels, and would listen to nothing but his ardour for conquest. He rushed on to the plain, sword in hand, drawing the whole van after him, and pursuing the Saracens to their camp, into which he entered with them.

Fakreddin, the leader of the Mussulman army, was at the moment in the bath, and, after the custom of the Orientals, was having his beard coloured. He sprang on horseback, almost naked, rallied his troops, and resisted for some time; but soon, left almost alone on the field of battle, he was surrounded, and died, covered with a thousand wounds.

The whole Mussulman army fled away towards Mansourah. How was it possible to resist the inclination to pursue them? What was to be feared from enemies that abandoned their camp? Might it not be believed that the Saracens fled as they had done at Damietta, and that terror would prevent their rallying? All these thoughts arose in the mind of the count d'Artois, and would not permit him to wait for the rest of the army to complete his victory. The grand-master of the Temple in vain renewed his representations; the young prince replied with great heat to the counsels of experience. In his passion he accused the Templars and Hospitallers of maintaining an intelligence with the infidels, and with wishing to perpetuate a war that was advantageous to their ambition. "Thus, then," replied the two grand masters, "it would appear that we and our knights have abandoned our families and our country, and would desire to pass our days in a foreign land, amidst the fatigues and perils of war, in order to betray the cause of the Christian Church!" On finishing these words, the master of the Templars sternly bade the standard-bearer of his order to unfurl the banner of battle. The earl of Salisbury, who commanded the English, ventured to speak of the danger to which the army would be exposed, thus separated from its van; but the count d'Artois interrupted him by saying sharply, "Timid counsels do not suit us!" Then the quarrels that had so often disturbed the discipline of the army were renewed, and the heat of debate completely stifled the voice of prudence. Whilst they were thus inflaming each other, the ancient governor of the count d'Artois, who was deaf, and who believed they were preparing for battle, never ceased crying, "Ores à eux, ores à eux!" (Hurrah! on them! hurrah! on them!) These words became a fatal signal for warriors, urged on at once by anger and impatience for victory. The Templars, the English, the French, all set forward together, all flew towards Mansourah, and penetrated into the city abandoned by the enemy; some stopped to pillage, whilst the others pursued the Saracens along the road to Cairo.

If all the Christian troops had crossed the canal at the moment that the count d'Artois entered Mansourah, the defeat of the enemy could have been complete. But the passage was made with much difficulty and confusion; and when the French army had crossed the Aschmoum, a space of two leagues separated it from its van.

The Mussulmans, who had been driven from their camp, at first believed they had fought with all the forces of the Crusaders, commanded by the king of France; but they soon became aware of the small number of their enemies, and were astonished at having been put to flight. From the very bosom of peril and disorder, a skilful leader arose among them, whose presence of mind all at once revived their courage. Bibars Bondocdar, whom the Mamelukes had recently placed at their head, having perceived the imprudence of the Christians, rallied the Mussulmans, led a part of his army between the canal and Mansourah, got possession of the gates of the city, and, with a chosen part of his troops, poured down upon the Crusaders, who were pillaging the palace of the sultan. "*The Mamelukes, lions of fights,*" says an Arabian historian, "*rushed upon the Franks, like a furious tempest; their terrible maces dealing deaths and wounds in all directions.*" The Christians, dispersed about in the city, had scarcely time to rally; pressed together in narrow streets, they could neither fight on horseback nor make use of their swords. From the roofs of the houses and from the windows, the Mussulmans hurled stones and other missives, or poured down upon them heated sand and boiling water. The gates of the city were closed, a multitude of Mussulmans occupied all the roads, and there remained not a single hope of salvation for warriors who had so recently put to flight a whole army.

This first disaster brought on several others; and soon the Christian army, which had just crossed the canal, found itself in the greatest danger. As fast as the Crusaders arrived on the other bank of the Aschmoum, some learned that the count d'Artois was pursuing the enemy, others that he was shut up in Mansourah, and most of the barons and knights, who burned, according to what they heard, to share his glory or aid him in his danger, without waiting for those who followed them, flew first towards the camp of the Saracens, and then towards the city.

The count of Brittany was one of the first who moved forward, and he was quickly followed by

Guy of Malvoisin, the sieur de Joinville, and the bravest knights of the Christian army. They advanced in great haste, and without the least precaution, through a country covered with enemies; they were not long in being separated from each other, when some retraced their steps, but the greater part were surrounded by the Mussulmans. A thousand combats were fought at once upon the plain; here the Christians were conquerors, further on they were conquered; in every direction they, by turns, attacked their enemies or defended themselves, at one moment putting the Saracens to flight, and the next flying before them.

All at once a cloud of dust arose from the bank of the Aschmoum, and the sound of trumpets and clarions arose, mingled with the neighing of horses and the shouts of warriors; it was the main body of the Christian army advancing. Saint Louis, marching at the head of the cavalry, halted on the summit of an acclivity, where all eyes were turned towards him. The knights scattered about at the foot of the hill, no longer able to resist the Saracens, believed they saw the angel of battles come to their assistance; Joinville, in particular, who, though pressed hard by the enemy, was, nevertheless, struck by the majestic aspect of the monarch. Louis wore a golden helmet, and held in his hand a German sword; his armour was resplendent, and his noble bearing animated all his warriors; "in short," says the ingenuous seneschal, in whom, perhaps, the feeling of danger increased that of admiration, "I declare that a more noble armed man was never seen."

Many of the knights who accompanied the French king, seeing the Christian warriors engaged with the Saracens in all directions, broke from their ranks and rushed down to the *mêlée*. Then the confusion proceeded fast to its climax; every one hastened forward without knowing where the enemy's army was, and they very soon became equally ignorant where that of the Christians was, or the king that commanded it; there was no one to issue an order, and no signal was given, except that of peril. In this horrible tumult, prudence and caution were useless, strength and skill in arms alone were triumphant; the mace and the battle-axe dashed polished casques and proudly-deviced shields to fragments; some knights sink covered with wounds, others are trampled to death beneath the feet of the horses, the cry of the French, "Montjoie, St. Denis!" and that of the Mussulmans, "Islam! Islam!" are confounded together, and mingle with the plaintive voices of the dying, and the menacing clamours of the triumphant, with the clash of cuirasses, lances, and swords. From the canal to Mansourah, and from the Nile to the shore whereon the Crusaders had just landed, the country presented but one vast field of battle, where fury and despair by turns animated the combatants, where torrents of blood were shed on both sides, without allowing either Christians or Mussulmans to claim the victory.

The Crusaders had the advantage in almost all the combats, or more properly duels, as the fights were generally man to man; but their army was in a great measure dispersed. At this moment, Bibars, having left in Mansourah a sufficient number of troops to triumph over the resistance of the count d'Artois and his knights, set forward with all his forces, directing his course towards the canal, for the purpose of sustaining the Mussulmans, who were beginning to fly, or to bring on a decisive battle. Louis and the leaders that surrounded him at once perceived the movement and the plans of the enemy. It was immediately decided that the Christian army should draw near to the canal, in order to prevent its being surrounded, and, at the same time, to preserve some communication with the duke of Burgundy, who remained on the opposite bank. The oriflamme, at the head of the battalions, already pointed out the direction the army was to take, when the counts of Poictiers and Flanders, who had advanced into the plain, sent word to the king that they must succumb unless speedily succoured; at the same moment, Imbert de Beaujeu came to announce that Robert of Artois was perishing in Mansourah. Struck by the conflicting demands, Louis hesitated for a moment, and in that moment a crowd of impetuous warriors, unable to wait for his orders, galloped off, some to the succour of the Poitevins and the Flemings, others to the aid of the count d'Artois; the Saracens completely covered the country, and the French warriors, who had thus separated themselves from the king, were totally unable to contend with such a multitude of enemies, and, falling back upon the Christian army, produced disorder and created terror.

Amidst the general confusion, a report was spread that the Mussulmans were everywhere victorious, and that the king had given orders for retreat. Several squadrons disbanded and rushed towards the canal. In an instant the waters appeared covered with drowning men and horses. In this extreme peril, Louis in vain endeavoured to rally his troops. His voice was scarcely heard, no one executed the orders he endeavoured to give. He then precipitated himself into the thickest of the fight, and so impetuously was he carried forward by his ardour, that his squires had great difficulty in keeping up with him; at last he remained alone, surrounded on all sides by Saracens. Thus situated, he had to defend himself against six Mussulman horsemen, who were determined to take him prisoner. Louis defeated all their endeavours, and succeeded in disengaging himself, and putting them to flight. This brilliant act of bravery reanimated the flying Crusaders that witnessed it; they crowded after their gallant king, recommenced the fight, and once more dispersed the Mussulman battalions.

Whilst the whole Christian army was thus fighting to repair the faults and save the life of the count d'Artois, this unfortunate prince was defending himself with heroic bravery; but all his efforts, without the walls and within the walls of Mansourah, could not free him from the host of Saracens his imprudence had drawn upon him. Robert, with his knights, the Templars, and the English, forgetting all their fatal quarrels, resolved to die together as knights and Christian soldiers. The combat had lasted from ten o'clock in the morning till three in the afternoon; the Crusaders, covered with wounds and stained with blood and dust, fought on bravely, though only sustained by the flickering strength of exhausted life. They fell almost all at the same time; Salisbury was killed at the head of the warriors he commanded; Robert de Vair, who bore the English banner, folded it round him before he died; Raoul de Coucy expired on a heap of dead; the count d'Artois, intrenched within a house, defended himself for a long time, but at length sank amidst carnage and ruins. The Christian warriors had entered Mansourah to the number of fifteen hundred, and almost all met with death there. The grand master of the Hospitallers, left alone upon the field of battle, was taken prisoner. The master of the Templars escaped by a miracle, and came back in the evening to the Christian camp, wounded in the face, his vestments torn to rags, and his cuirass pierced in several places. He had beheld two hundred and eighty of his knights fall around him.

Most of those who advanced towards Mansourah to succour the count d'Artois, fell victims to their intrepid zeal. The brave Guy de Malvoisin succeeded in reaching the walls, but not in gaining entrance to the city. The duke of Brittany made incredible efforts to gain the place of combat; he heard the threats, cries, and tumult with which the city resounded, without being able to force the gates or scale the ramparts. He returned towards nightfall; he vomited blood in streams; his horse, stuck all over with arrows, had lost its bridle and part of its furniture; and every warrior that followed him was wounded. Even in this state he proved himself terrible to the enemy, killing or driving away, with powerful thrusts of his lance, all who dared to pursue or oppose him, and jeering at their abortive attempts.

When night separated the combatants, the prior of the hospital of Rosnay came towards the king, and kissing his hand, asked him if he had received any tidings of the count d'Artois. "All that I know," replied the pious monarch, "is that he is now in Paradise." The good knight, to remove such sad thoughts, was about to expatiate upon the advantages they had gained; but then Louis, raising his eyes towards heaven, burst into tears. The prior of Rosnay became silent; the barons and lords assembled round the king were unable to offer a word of consolation, but were all oppressed with pain, compassion, and pity at seeing him weep.

The Christian army, although it had to reproach the count d'Artois for all the misfortunes of this day's conflict, sympathized with the sorrows of Louis. Such was the ascendancy of bravery among the French warriors, that the greatest faults appeared to them to be expiated by a glorious death. It was likewise acknowledged in all the crusades, that they who died with arms in their hands were placed in the rank of martyrs. The Christian warriors only considered the count d'Artois as a soldier of Christ, whom God had recalled to his bosom: it was thus that piety accorded with glory, and that men honoured as saints the same persons they admired as heroes. Matthew Paris asserts in his History that the mother of Salisbury saw her son ascending into heaven on the day of the battle of Mansourah. The same opinion was established among the Saracens; all who fell in the field of battle, in the wars against the Christians, passed for martyrs of Islamism. "The Franks," says the continuator of Tabary, "sent Fakreddin to the banks of the celestial river, and his end was a glorious end."

History has not preserved the names of all the warriors who signalized their valour at the battle of Mansourah. The seneschal of Champagne was not one of those who were backward in seeking danger, or in evincing want of courage; one of six, he defended a bridge against a host of Saracens. He was twice unhorsed. In such great distress, the pious knight did not forget his patron saint, and exclaimed to him: "My lord, great sire, St. James, I supplicate thee, aid me and succour me in this my need." Joinville continued fighting during the whole day; his horse received fifteen wounds, and he himself was pierced by five arrows.

The seneschal informs us that during the battle of this memorable day, he saw several men of high distinction running disgracefully away, in general confusion: he does not name them, because at the time he wrote they were dead, and it does not appear becoming to him to speak ill of the departed. The reserve with which the historian here expresses himself, shows plainly enough what was the general spirit of the French army, in which it was considered as an ineffaceable shame, and as the greatest of misfortunes, to have ever experienced a single moment of fear.

The greater part of the French warriors, when in the presence of danger, were never abandoned by that sentiment of honour that constituted the spirit and character of chivalry. Erard de Severy, whilst fighting bravely with a small number of knights, received a sabre-cut in the face; his blood flowed fast, and it appeared not at all likely that he would survive the wound; when, addressing the knights that fought near him, he said, "If you will assure me that I and my children shall be free from all blame, I will go and demand help for you, of the duke of Anjou, whom I see yonder on the plain." All praised this determination highly, and he immediately mounted on horseback, pierced through the enemy's squadrons, reached the duke of Anjou, and returned with him to rescue his companions, who were near perishing. Erard de Severy expired shortly after this heroic achievement; he died, bearing away with him, not the sentiments of a vain glory, but the consoling certainty that no blame, as he had desired, should stain his name or that of his children.

That which at the same time astonishes and charms us in the relations of the old chroniclers who have spoken of this battle of Mansourah is, to find, amidst scenes of carnage, traces of French gaiety, of that gaiety which despises death and laughs at peril. We have spoken of six knights who defended the passage of a bridge against a great number of Saracens; whilst these *preux chevaliers*, surrounded by enemies, maintained such a perilous post, the count de Soissons, addressing Joinville, exclaimed: "Seneschal, let us leave this rascally *canaille* to cry and bray as they please, you and I will yet talk of this day, and in ladies' bowers too."

The Mussulmans having retired, the Christian army occupied their camp, which the van had taken possession of in the morning, and which the Arabs had plundered during the battle. The camp of the enemy, and the machines of war they had left in it, were the only fruit of the exploits of this day. The Crusaders had shown what valour could effect, and their triumph would have been complete if they had been able to rally and fight together. Their leaders had not sufficient ability or ascendancy to repair the error of the count d'Artois; the Mussulman leaders, who proved themselves to be more skilful, were also better seconded by the discipline and obedience of the Mamelukes.

When they became fully aware of the losses they had experienced, the Christians gave up all idea of celebrating their victory. To appreciate the result of so many bloody conflicts, it was quite sufficient to contemplate the contrast between the sentiments that animated the two armies. A melancholy sadness prevailed among the conquerors; whilst the Saracens, on the contrary, although driven from their camp, and obliged to fall back upon Mansourah, considered it a triumph to have stopped the march of their enemies; and, reassured as to the issue of the war, they abandoned themselves to the greater joy, from having, before the battle, entertained the most depressing fears.

In fact, nothing can paint the consternation which the first attack of the count d'Artois had created among the infidels. At the beginning of the day, a pigeon that was sent to Cairo, conveyed a message expressed in these words: "At the moment this bird is dispatched, the enemy is attacking Mansourah; a terrible battle has been fought between the Christians and the Mussulmans." At this news the people of Cairo were seized with the greatest terror; and sinister reports soon added to the alarm. The gates of the city were left open all night, to receive such as might have fled; and all of these exaggerated the danger to excuse their desertion. It was believed that the days of Islamism were numbered, and many were already abandoning the capital, to seek an asylum in Upper Egypt, when, on the morrow, another pigeon arrived, bearing news calculated to raise the spirits of the Mussulmans. The fresh message announced that the God of Mahomet had declared himself to be against the Christians; then all fears were dispersed, and the issue of the battle of Mansourah, says an Arabian author, *was the note of joy for all true believers.*

During the very night that followed the battle, the Mussulmans made several attempts to recover their camp and the machines of war that remained in the hands of the Franks. The Christian warriors, oppressed by fatigue, were repeatedly aroused by cries to arms; the continual attacks of the enemy would not allow them to repair their strength by sleep; many among them were so weakened by their wounds, they could scarcely put on their cuirasses; nevertheless, they defended themselves with their accustomed bravery.

The day after the battle was Ash-Wednesday, and the priests performed the ceremonies ordered by religion for the opening of Lent. The Christian army passed a part of the day in prayer, the rest of it in preparations for defence. Whilst the soldiers of the cross prostrated themselves at the foot of their altars, or prepared to repulse the infidels, images of mourning were mingled in their hearts with sentiments of piety and bravery. Whilst remembering their past victories, they could not forbear dreading the future; and the symbol of human fragilities, that the Church offers to each of her children on that solemn day, must have kept up their sad presentiments.

On the same day they employed themselves in throwing a bridge over the Aschmoum, in order to form a junction with the camp of the duke of Burgundy. The leaders and soldiers all lent a hand to the work, which was finished in the space of a few hours. The infantry, which had been left on the other side of the canal came to reinforce the army, which was fated to be soon engaged in fresh contests.

A MESSAGE FROM THE EAST.

Bibars, who had the command of the Mamelukes, hastened to take advantage of his first successes. When the body of the count d'Artois was found, the Mamelukes exhibited his cuirass, sown over with *fleurs de lis*, and declared it was the spoil of the king of France. They carried about the heads of several knights in triumph, and heralds-at-arms repeated in a loud voice: "The Christian army is nothing but a trunk without life, like the heads you behold on the points of these lances."

This spectacle completely inflamed the ardour of the Mussulmans. The leaders and soldiers, with great cries, demanded to be led against the Christians. The Mussulman army had orders to hold themselves in readiness for battle on the morrow, the first Friday in Lent.

Louis IX. was warned of the intention of the Saracens; he gave orders to the leaders to fortify the camp, and prepare their troops for the conflict. On the Friday, by daybreak, the Christians were all under arms; and at the same time the leader of the Mussulmans appeared in the plain, ranging his men in battle-array. He placed his cavalry in the front, behind them the infantry, and still further back, the reserve. He extended or strengthened his lines according to the positions he saw his enemies take. His army covered the plain from the canal to the river. At midday he unfurled the banners and sounded the charge.

The duke of Anjou was at the head of the camp on the side towards the Nile; he was the first attacked. The infantry of the Saracens commenced by launching the Greek fire. This fire seized the clothes of the soldiers and the caparisons of the horses. The soldiers, enveloped in flames they could not extinguish, ran about uttering the most frightful cries; the horses broke away, and created confusion in the ranks. By means of this disorder, the enemy's cavalry opened themselves a passage, dispersed such as were still fighting, and penetrated within the intrenchments. The duke of Anjou was unable to resist the multiplied attacks of the Saracens; his horse having been killed under him, he fought on foot, and, nearly overwhelmed by the number of his enemies, he at length sent to Louis IX. for aid.

The king, himself engaged with the Mussulmans, redoubles his ardour and his efforts, drives the enemy back on to the plain, and then flies where other dangers call him. The knights who follow him precipitate themselves upon the Mussulman battalions which were attacking the quarter of the duke of Anjou. Louis is not stopped, either by the numberless arrows shot at him, or by the Greek fire, which covers his arms and the caparison of his horse. In the account of this battle, Joinville is astonished that the king of France escaped being killed, and can in no other way explain this species of miracle than by attributing it to the power of God: "Then it may well be believed" (we let the seneschal of Champagne speak) "that the holy king had his God in remembrance and wish: for, in truth, our Lord was then a great friend to him in his need, and aided him so effectually, that he delivered his brother, the duke of Anjou, and drove away the Turks."

On the left of the duke of Anjou, the Crusaders from the isle of Cyprus and Palestine were encamped, under the command of Guy d'Ibelin and his brother Baldwin. These Crusaders had not been engaged in the last battle, and had lost neither their horses nor their arms. Near them fought the brave Gauthier de Chatillon, at the head of a chosen troop. These intrepid warriors were proof against all attacks, and remaining firm at the post confided to them, contributed greatly to the saving of both the camp and the army.

The Templars, having lost the greater part of their knights in Mansourah, formed an intrenchment or barricade in front of them, of the wood of the machines taken from the Saracens; but this feeble defence was of little avail against the Greek fire. The enemy rushed into the camp through the flames; the Templars formed an impenetrable rampart of their bodies, and resisted the violent attacks of the assailants during several hours. The conflict was so severe at this point, that the earth could scarcely be seen behind the spot occupied by the Templars, so completely was it covered with arrows and javelins. The grand master of the Templars lost his life in the *mêlée*, and a great number of knights died in defending or avenging him. The prodigies of their bravery at last succeeded in arresting the progress of the enemy, and the last who fell in this hardly-contested battle had the consolation, when dying, to see the Saracens fly.

Guy de Malvoisin was placed near to the post which the knights of the Temple defended so bravely; the battalion he commanded was composed almost entirely of his relations, and in battle presented the spectacle of a family of warriors, ever united and ever invincible. Guy incurred the greatest peril; he was wounded several times, but never dreamt of retiring from the contest. His example and the sight of his wounds redoubled the courage of his companions, who, at length, repulsed the Mussulmans. Not far from Guy de Malvoisin, descending towards the canal, the Flemish Crusaders were posted. William, their count, was at their head; they sustained the furious shock of the Mussulmans without giving way in the least: Joinville, with some other knights, fought on their left, and on this occasion owed his safety to the warriors of Flanders, to whom he accords the warmest praises. The Flemings, united with the Champenois, put the Mussulman cavalry and infantry to flight, pursued them out of the camp, and returned loaded with the bucklers and cuirasses they had taken from their enemies.

The count of Poictiers occupied the left wing of the army; but as this prince had only infantry under his command, he was unable to resist the cavalry of the Saracens. Such were the warriors of these remote times, that when they were not on horseback, they seemed to be disarmed, and could not fight even for the defence of intrenchments. The quarter confided to the Poitevins was attacked by the Mussulmans at an early period of the fight; the Mamelukes plundered the tents of the Christians; the brother of the king was dragged out of the camp by some Saracen horsemen, and was being carried away a prisoner. In this extreme peril the count of Poictiers could not look to Louis IX. for any assistance, as he had gone to the succour of the count of Anjou; nor to the other leaders of the Christian army, all so closely pressed by the enemy themselves. This prince was adored by the people for his goodness; and on this occasion received the reward of his virtues, by owing his deliverance to the love with which he inspired all the Crusaders. When the workmen, sutlers, and women that followed the army saw him made a prisoner, they assembled in the greatest fury, and arming themselves with axes, clubs, sticks, or anything that fell in their way, flew after the Mussulmans, delivered the count of Poictiers, and brought him back in triumph.

At the extremity of the camp, close to the quarters of the Poitevins, fought Josserant de Brançon, with his son and his knights. The companions in arms of Josserant had all left Europe well mounted and magnificently equipped: now they all fought on foot, and had nothing left but lance and sword. Their leader alone was on horseback, and rode from rank to rank, exciting the soldiers, and flying to every point where the danger seemed most pressing. This weak troop would entirely have perished, if Henry of Brienne, who remained in the camp of the duke of Burgundy, had not caused his cross-bowmen to shoot across the arm of the river, every time the Saracens renewed their attacks. Of twenty knights that accompanied Josserant, twelve were left upon the field of battle. This old warrior had been present in thirty-six battles, in all of which he had borne away the prize of valour. Joinville, when relating the exploits of this day, remembers that he had formerly seen Josserant de Brançon come out victorious from a combat against some Germans who were pillaging the church of Mâcon; he had seen him prostrate himself at the foot of the altar, and pray with ardour for the favour of dying in fight against the enemies of Christ. And Josserant obtained the blessing he had asked of God; for a few days after the battle he died of his wounds.

Such was the contest of which Louis IX., in the account which he sent to France, speaks with such admirable simplicity. "On the first Friday in Lent, the camp being attacked, God favoured the French, and the infidels were repulsed with much loss."

In this battle, as in the last, the Christians had had all the glory, the Saracens all the advantage. The Christian army lost a great number of its warriors, and almost all its horses: the enemy was reinforced every day; the Crusaders could not attempt to march upon Cairo, and prudence seemed to suggest that they should retrace their steps to Damietta. Retreat, still easy, offered a means of preserving the army for a more favourable season: but this plan could only be counselled by despair, and despair has great difficulty in mastering the hearts of the brave. Nothing could appear more disgraceful to the French than flying, or appearing to fly, before a conquered enemy: they resolved to remain.

Towards the end of February, Almoadam, whom Chigger-Eddour and the principal leaders of the Mamelukes had called to the throne of his father, arrived in Egypt, and was received with loud acclamations by the people, always desirous of change, and always delighted with a new reign. The emirs and magnates likewise displayed great joy, but their demonstrations were less sincere; they looked for the coming of the successor of Negmeddin with more anxiety than impatience; placing a very high value upon that which they had done for him, they, beforehand, expected his ingratitude. On the other side, the young prince was jealous of his authority; and the power of the emirs, the nature even of their services, gave him alarms that he had not the prudence to dissemble. It was not long before a mutual mistrust and a reciprocal estrangement arose between Almoadam and the leaders of the Mussulman army; the latter repented of having raised to empire a prince who showed a disposition to rule alone, and the former was determined to defend his power, even against those who had bestowed it upon him. This state of things and the disposition of men's minds, appeared ominous of new revolutions in Egypt; unhappily these revolutions broke out too late to allow the Christians to derive any advantage from them.

The Crusaders likewise had soon to contend with calamities more destructive to them than even the power or the arms of the Mussulmans; a contagious disease made its appearance in the Christian army. They had neglected to bury the dead after the last two battles; the bodies cast confusedly and heedlessly into the Aschmoum, and floating on its waters, stopped before the bridge of boats constructed by the Crusaders, and covered the surface of the canal from one shore to the other. Pestilential exhalations quickly arose from this heap of carcases. Louis IX. ordered the bodies of the Christians to be buried in the ditches dug by the Saracens on the bank; but these spoils of death, moved and transported without precaution, only assisted the progress of the epidemic. The spectacle which was then presented to the eyes of the Crusaders spread the deepest grief throughout the camp, and awakened a more perfect consciousness of their losses. Christian soldiers were seen searching among bodies which wounds, the hues of death, and the action of the sun and air had disfigured, for the deplorable remains of their friends or companions. Many of those upon whom friendship imposed this pious task, fell sick and died almost instantly. The devotedness and grief of one of the knights of Robert count d'Artois, were conspicuous among these affecting instances. This inconsolable knight passed whole nights and days on the banks of the canal, with his eyes intensely fixed upon the waters, braving contagion and death, in the hope of recovering and burying the young prince, whose loss was so deeply deplored by the French army.

The fatigues of war did not at all prevent the pious warriors from observing the abstinence of Lent; and the privations and austerities of penitence completed the exhaustion of their strength.

The contagion attacked the most robust as well as the most weak;* their flesh withered away, their skin became livid, and was covered with black spots; their gums were inflamed and swollen so as to prevent the passage of food; the flowing of the blood from the nose was the sign of approaching death. Most of the diseased viewed the grim monarch without fear, and considered his dominions as the wished-for end of all their sufferings.

Dysentery and dangerous fevers were soon added to the above malady; nothing was heard in the Christian camp but prayers for the dying or the dead; nothing was seen but the pale and haggard countenances of unhappy beings who accompanied their companions to the tomb, and whom death must soon sweep away in their turn. The soldiers capable of bearing arms did not suffice for the guarding of the avenues of the camp. A thing unheard of in Christian armies, the grooms of knights were seen clothed in the armour of their masters, and taking their places in the post of danger. The clergy, who attended the sick and buried the dead, suffered greatly from the epidemic; very quickly there were not ecclesiastics enough to minister at the altars and perform the Christian ceremonies. One day, the sieur de Joinville, himself sick, and listening to the mass in his bed, was obliged to rise and support his almoner, ready to faint upon the steps of the altar. "*Thus supported,*" adds the kindly historian, "*he finished his sacrament, chanted the mass quite through—but never chanted more.*"

We have seen in former holy wars, multitudes of Crusaders a prey to the most cruel scourges; the bravest of the warriors often despaired of the cause of the pilgrims, and deserted the banners of the cross; and many times the excess of their misery drew from them imprecations and blasphemies. We must here remark that the soldiers and companions of Louis IX. supported their evils with more patience and resignation. Not one knight thought of deserting the banners of the crusade, and not a seditious or sacrilegious complaint was heard in the army; the example of the pious monarch doubtless strengthened the courage of the Crusaders, and preserved them from the excesses of despair. Louis IX., deeply affected by the evils that desolated his army, employed every effort to mitigate and end them. If anything could have consoled the Crusaders in the miserable condition in which they were placed, it must have been seeing a king of France himself attending the sick, lavishing upon them every kind of assistance, and preparing them for death. In vain he was conjured not to expose himself to dangers still greater than those of the field of battle; nothing could shake his courage or check the ardour of his charity; he considered it his duty (it is thus he expressed himself) to expose his life for those who every day exposed theirs for him. One of his servants, a worthy man, being at the point of death, and exhorted by a priest to meet his fate like a Christian, replied, "*I will not die till I have seen the king.*" The king complied with his desire, and the man died in peace, consoled by the presence and words of his kind master. But at length he who consoled all others fell sick himself. The king was not able to leave his tent; the desolation became more profound and more general; they who suffered began now to lose all hope; it seemed as if Providence had abandoned them, and that heaven no longer protected the soldiers of the cross.

The Saracens remained motionless in their camp, leaving their awful auxiliaries, diseases, to perform their mission undisturbed; only Almoadam, in order to add famine to the other evils his ene-

---

* This disease was the scurvy; "it was such," says Joinville, "that the flesh of our legs dried away to the bone, and our skins became of a black or earth colour, like an old saddle which has been a long time laid aside: and besides this, we who were afflicted by this disease were soon subjected to another persecution, in a complaint of the mouth, which arose from our having eaten of those fish; it putrified the flesh of the gums, so that it rendered the breath horribly stinking." Joinville here speaks of the *burbotte*, a fish of the Nile, which is a voracious fish, and feeds upon dead bodies. The seneschal adds, in another passage of his memoirs, "that the malady having seized upon the army, it became necessary for the barbers to cut out the swollen flesh of the gums of all who were afflicted with this disease, so that they could not eat. Great pity was it to hear all from whom this dead flesh had been cut, going about in the army crying and moaning. They appeared to me like poor women who are in labour with their children when they come upon earth: nobody can tell how pitiable that sight was."

mies experienced, resolved to interrupt all communication between the Christians and Damietta, whence they received provisions by way of the Nile. Having got together a great number of boats, the sultan caused them to be taken to pieces, and afterwards transported over land to the mouth of the canal of Mehallah. A French flotilla came up the river without suspicion, bearing provisions for the camp, and fell directly into an ambuscade of galleys, placed behind a small island. All at once the enemies appear, surprise the Christians, attack them with fury, kill a thousand soldiers, and obtain possession of fifty vessels laden with provisions. A few days afterwards, other vessels coming up the river towards Mansourah experienced the same fate. No one arrived at the camp; no news came from Damietta, and the Christians were abandoning themselves to the most melancholy presentiments, when a vessel belonging to the count of Flanders, which had escaped the enemy by a miracle, came to announce to them that all the vessels of the Crusaders had been taken, and that the Mussulman flag dominated along the whole course of the river.

Famine soon made frightful ravages in the army; and such as had been spared by disease, were threatened with death from misery and hunger. Both leaders and soldiers were seized with the deepest despondency; and the king at length judged it best to attempt to enter into a truce with the Mussulmans. Philip de Montfort was employed in the embassy to the sultan of Egypt; commissioners were named on both sides to conclude a treaty. Those of the king of France proposed to surrender Damietta to the sultan, on condition that Jerusalem and all the other places in Palestine, that had fallen into the hands of the Mussulmans in the late wars, should be given up to the Christians. The sultan, who dreaded the bravery and the despair of the Crusaders, who, besides, had reason to fear that his enemies might receive reinforcements, and that Damietta might hold out for a considerable time, accepted the proposed conditions. When the question of hostages came to be discussed, the king offered his two brothers; but whether the sultan placed no faith in the loyalty of his enemies, or whether he was wanting in it himself, he required that the king of France should remain in his hands, as a guarantee of the treaty. Sergines, one of the commissioners, could not listen to this proposal without anger. "You ought to know Frenchmen better," cried he, "than to suppose they would ever allow their king to remain a prisoner with Mussulmans." A council was held on this subject in the Christian army. The king consented to everything, but the lords and barons exclaimed with vehemence against the giving up of their sovereign. On one side, the monarch was willing to purchase the safety of his people by his own personal danger; on the other, a crowd of warriors all warmly declared they could not suffer such a disgrace, and that *they would rather die than place their king in pledge*. The more Louis was beloved by his warriors, the less he was master in this circumstance; and every one thinking it to his honour, and almost consistent with his duty, to disobey him, the negotiation was abandoned.

To paint the frightful scarcity that desolated the Christian camp, contemporary chronicles relate, as an extraordinary thing, that a sheep was sold for as much as ten crowns, an ox for eighty livres, and an egg for twelve deniers. Such high prices exceeded the means of most of the pilgrims; some were obliged to live upon the fish caught in the Nile, others upon herbs and roots.

Louis IX., preserving his courage and tranquillity of mind amidst the general mourning and depression, as a means of endeavouring to save the miserable remains of his army, resolved to repass to the other side of the Aschmoum. Whilst the Christians were crossing the wooden bridge thrown over the canal, they were warmly attacked by the Mussulmans. Gaucher de Chatillon, who commanded the rear, at first repulsed them; but as the Saracens returned several times to the charge, and as they had greatly the advantage in numbers, victory was upon the point of being adverse to the Crusaders. The brilliant valour of the count of Anjou checked the impetuosity of the Mussulmans. Erard and John de Valeri performed prodigies of bravery. Jeffroi de Hassemburgh likewise distinguished himself by heroic actions, and merited the palm of valour in that day's fight. Thus glory was always mingled with the misfortunes of the French Crusaders: but victory procured them no advantages, and always left them still exposed to the same perils, still a prey to the same calamities. They were not more fortunate on one side of the Aschmoum than on the other; and after remaining some days in their old camp, they were obliged at length to form the disheartening resolution of returning to Damietta.

As soon as Almoadam was informed of these last dispositions of the Christians, he himself harangued his troops, distributed provisions and money to them, and reinforced them with a great number of Arabs, attracted to his standards by the hopes of booty. By his orders, boats loaded with soldiers descended the Nile, and joined the Mussulman fleet that had intercepted the convoys of the Crusaders. Bodies of light cavalry were distributed along the whole course of the roads which the French army would take in its retreat.

On the fifth day of April, the Tuesday after the octave of Easter, Louis IX. ordered everything to be prepared for the departure of his army: the women, the children, and the sick were embarked upon the Nile; they waited till night-fall, to conceal these sad preparations from the enemy. The bank of the Nile presented the most heart-breaking spectacle; nothing was to be seen but Crusaders overcome by their sufferings, parting, with tears in their eyes, from friends they were doomed never to see again. Amidst these painful scenes, the Arabs, taking advantage of the darkness of the night, penetrated into the camp, plundered the baggage, and slaughtered every living creature they met with. A terrified crowd fled on all sides, and cries of alarm resounded along the whole bank of the river. The mariners perceiving, by the light of the fires in the boats, this frightful disorder, and that the Christians were being massacred, became terrified on their own account, and prepared to depart. The king, who, in spite of his weakness, was present everywhere, and watched over everything, drove the infidels from the camp, reassured the Christian multitude, and commanded the vessels which had left the shore, to put back and take the rest of the sick on board.

The pope's legate and several French nobles got on board a large vessel. The king was pressed to follow this example, but he could not make up his mind to abandon his army. In vain his anxious and loving friends represented to him that his state of weakness would not permit him to fight, and exposed him to the risk of falling into the hands of the Saracens; in vain they added, that by thus hazarding his life he compromised the safety of the army. These and many other remonstrances, dictated by a sincere attachment for his person, were not able to make him change his resolution. He replied, that no danger should separate him from his faithful warriors; that he had brought them with him; that he would return with them; or, if it proved necessary, die in the midst of them. This heroic determination, the inevitable consequences of which were foreseen, plunged all his knights into consternation and grief. The soldiers, partaking the feelings of the knights, ran along the bank of the Nile, crying with all their strength to those that were going down the river, "Wait for the king! wait for the king!"* Arrows and javelins were falling thick upon the vessels which continued to go down the river. Many stopped; but Louis insisted upon their pursuing their course.

Most of the French warriors were borne down by disease and weakened by hunger. The fatigues

---

* This generous trait of St. Louis, who refused to quit his army, is attested by both French and Oriental historians. Joinville expresses himself thus:— "Seeing the king had the same disease as the army, and great weakness, as others had, we thought he would be much safer on board one of the great galleys; but he said 'he would rather die than leave his people.'" Geoffrey of Beaulieu, equally an eye-witness, attests this fact. To the evidence of these two historians we may add that of the Arabian historian Aboul Mahassem. "The king of France," says he, "might have escaped from the Egyptians, either on horseback, or in a boat; but this generous prince would never consent to abandon his troops."

and new perils they were about to undergo did not at all diminish their courage; but they could not endure the thoughts of abandoning places rendered dear to them by the remembrance of their victories. The duke of Burgundy set out on his march at nightfall; and, a short time after, the rest of the troops quitted the camp, taking away their tents and baggage. Louis, who was determined to go with the rear-guard, only kept with him the brave Sargines and a few other knights and barons who were still fortunate enough to have horses. The king, scarcely able to support himself in his saddle, appeared in the midst of them mounted on an Arabian horse; he wore neither helmet nor cuirass, and had no other weapon but his sword. The warriors who had surrounded his person followed him in silence; and in the deplorable state to which they were reduced, evinced still some joy at having been chosen to defend their king and die by his side.

The retreat of the Christian army was already known to the Saracens. The king had ordered the bridge of Aschmoum to be broken; but this order had not been executed, and it furnished the Mussulmans with an easy means of crossing the canal. In a moment the whole plain which extended on the Damietta side was covered with enemies. The rear-guard of the Christians was stopped at every step of its route, sometimes by the crossing of a rivulet, but more frequently by a charge of Mussulman cavalry. Amidst the darkness of the night, the Crusaders could not see which way to direct their blows, and when they did obtain some trifling advantage, they did not dare to pursue their enemy; they advanced fighting, and in disorder; fearing to lose themselves, such as were at any distance from their companions, called upon them by name; such as adhered closely to the standard, ran against and impeded each other in their march: over the whole plain nothing was heard but the neighing of horses, the clash of arms, and the cries of rage and despair; but the most deplorable spectacle in this defeat was that of the wounded lying stretched along the roads, holding up their hands to their comrades, and conjuring them, with tears, not to leave them exposed to the fury of the Saracens. They looked for day with the most anxious impatience; but the daylight, by discovering the small number of the Christians, redoubled the confidence of the Mussulmans: it filled the former with proportionate dread, as it showed them the multitude of their enemies.

Menaced and pursued on all sides, the knights who had taken the route by land, envied those who had embarked upon the Nile; but these latter were in no less danger than their unfortunate companions. A short time after their departure, a high wind arose, and drove back the vessels towards Mansourah: some of them were run aground, others were dashed violently against accompanying boats, and were near being sunk. Towards dawn their flotilla arrived near Mehallah, a place fatal to the Christians. The Mussulman fleet awaited them there. The archers charged to proceed along the shore and protect them, had fled, and in their place appeared a multitude of Mussulman horsemen, launching such a number of arrows armed with the Greek fire, that it might have been believed, says Joinville, "*that all the stars of heaven were falling.*"

The wind disconcerted all the manœuvres of the mariners. The Crusaders, crowded closely in their vessels, could scarcely stand upright, and were most of them without arms. Turning their eyes sometimes towards the shore, where they perceived clouds of dust at a distance, and sometimes towards heaven, whose mercy they implored, they still hoped that some unexpected event might deliver them, or else that the army advancing towards Damietta would come to their succour; thus placing their last hopes in the miracles of Providence and in those of bravery. Deceitful illusions! one division of the Christian troops had been dispersed; the rear-guard, encouraged by the presence of the king, made incredible but useless efforts to repulse the crowd of Saracens, which increased from moment to moment. The despair of the French warriors gave birth to a thousand glorious actions; but so much heroism was only able to procure them the palm of martyrdom. Guy du Châtel, bishop of Soissons, giving up all hopes of gaining Damietta or revisiting France, resolved to seek death, and rushed, followed by several knights, into the thickest of the ranks of the Saracens, who, according to the expression of Joinville, *killed them, and sent them into the company of God.* Gaucher de Chatillon and Sergines still fought on, in the hope of saving the life of the king of France. Sergines, adhering close to the side of the king, drove away the enemies with mighty blows of the sword; danger seemed to have doubled his strength. Contemporary history, which describes him to us driving away the Saracens that surrounded Louis, compares him to the vigilant servant who carefully drives away the flies from his master's cup.

In the mean time the hope of victory inflamed the enthusiasm and the fanaticism of the Mussulmans; they were persuaded they were fighting for the cause of their prophet: their dervises and imauns, who had preached the war against the Christians, followed them on the field of battle, pervaded the ranks of the army, and excited the soldiers to carnage. An Arabian historian, mixing the marvellous with his account, relates that the scheikh Ezzedin, seeing that victory for a moment inclined towards the Christians, because a whirlwind of dust covered the Mussulmans and prevented them from fighting, addresses these words to the wind: *"Oh wind, direct thy breath against our enemies!"* The tempest, adds the same historian, obeyed the voice of this holy person, and victory was the reward of the soldiers of Islamism. We only report this circumstance here, to show the spirit that animated the Mussulmans in their wars against the Christians. The Saracens did not require a miracle to triumph over a dispersed army reduced to so small a number of combatants. The rear-guard of the Christians, always pursued and unceasingly attacked, arrived with much difficulty before the little town of Minieh. The king, escorted by a few knights, preceded the troops into the city, where he alighted as weak "as a child in its mother's lap," says Joinville. Fatigue, sickness, and the grief which such disasters caused him, had so overcome him, that all believed (we still quote the same author) he was about to die.

The intrepid Gaucher de Chatillon watched over his safety; alone, he for a length of time defended the entrance of a narrow street, which led to the house in which his faithful servants were endeavouring to recall the exhausted monarch to life. At one moment he rushed like lightning upon the infidels, dispersed them, cut them down; then, after turning to pull from his cuirass, and even his body, the arrows and darts with which he was stuck all over, he flew again upon the enemy, rising from time to time in his stirrups, and shouting with all his force, "Chatillon, knights! Chatillon, to the rescue! Where are ye, my gallant men?" The remainder of the rear-guard were still at some distance; nobody appeared, but the Saracens, on the contrary, came up in crowds; at length, overwhelmed by numbers, bristling with arrows, and covered with wounds, he fell; none of the Crusaders could succour him, not one could witness his heroic end! His horse, one sheet of blood and foam, became the prey of the infidels, and his last exploits were narrated by a Mussulman warrior, who exhibited his sword, and boasted of having killed the bravest of the Christians.

The rear-guard drew up upon a neighbouring hill, and still defended themselves with some advantage. Philip de Montfort, who commanded them, came to inform the king that he had just seen the emir with whom they had treated for a suspension of hostilities at the camp of Mansourah; and if it were his good pleasure, he would go and speak to him about it again. The monarch consented, promising to submit to the conditions the sultan had first required. However miserable the situation of the Crusaders, they still inspired considerable dread in their enemies. Five hundred knights remained under arms, and many of those who had gone past Minieh, retraced their steps to dispute the victory with the Saracens. The emir accepted the proposition for a truce. Montfort, as a pledge of his word, gave him a ring which he wore on his finger. Their hands already touched, when a

ST. LOUIS A PRISONER IN EGYPT

During this time Louis IX. was more calm at Mausoural than they were at Damietta. He had no covering at night but a coarse cassock, which he owed to the charity of another prisoner. In this state, he never addressed one petition to his enemies, nor did the tone of his language announce either fear or submission. Thus religious sentiments and remembrances sustained the courage of Louis even in fetters; and the pious monarch, surrounded every day by fresh perils, amidst a Mussulman army that he had irritated by his victories, might still cry out with the prophet-king: "Supported by the living God, who is my buckler and my glory, I will not fear the crowd of enemies encamped around me."

The sultan of Cairo, appearing inclined to soften his rigorous policy, sent Louis fifty magnificent dresses for himself and the lords of his train. Louis refused to clothe himself in them, saying that he was the sovereign of a greater kingdom than Egypt, and that he would never wear the livery of a foreign prince. Almoadam ordered a great feast to be prepared, to which he invited the king. But Louis would not accept of this invitation, as he was persuaded it was only meant to exhibit him as a spectacle to the Mussulman army.—BOOK XIV

traitor, a rascal doorkeeper, named Marcel, cried aloud: "Seigneurs, noble French knights, surrender yourselves all, the king commands you by me; do not cause him to be killed!" At these last words, the consternation became general; they believed that the life of the monarch was in great danger, and the leaders, officers, and soldiers, all laid down their arms.

The emir, who had begun to treat for peace, perceived this sudden change, and he broke off the negotiation by saying: "It is not customary to treat with conquered enemies." Soon after, one of the principal emirs, Djemal-eddin, entered Minieh. Finding the king surrounded by his weeping servants, he took possession of his person, and without any regard for royal majesty, without any respect for the greatest misfortunes, ordered chains to be placed upon his hands and feet; from that moment there was no safety for the Crusaders. Both the brothers of the king fell into the hands of the infidels; all those that had reached Pharescour were seized, and lost either their lives or their liberty. Many of them might have gained Damietta; but when they learnt the captivity of the king, they lost all strength or spirit to continue their route or to defend themselves. These knights, but lately so intrepid, remained motionless on the high roads, and allowed themselves to be slaughtered or manacled, without offering the least complaint or making the slightest resistance. The oriflamme, the other standards, and the baggage, all became the prey of the Saracens. Amidst scenes of carnage, the Mussulman warriors uttered the most horrible imprecations against Jesus Christ and his defenders: they trampled under-foot, they profaned by insults, crosses and sacred images—a crowning cause for scandal and despair for Christians, who, having seen their king loaded with chains, beheld their God given up to the outrages of the conqueror!

The Crusaders who had embarked upon the Nile had no better destiny; all the vessels of the Christians, except that of the legate, were sunk by the tempest, consumed by the Greek fire, or taken by the Mussulmans. The crowd of Saracens, assembled on the shore or on board the barks, immolated all that came within reach of their arms. They spared neither the women nor the sick. Avarice, rather than humanity, saved such as could expect to be ransomed. The sieur de Joinville, still suffering from his wounds and the disease that had prevailed in the camp of Mansourah, had embarked with the only two knights he had left and some of his serving-men. Four Mussulman galleys came up to his vessel, which had just cast anchor in the middle of the river, and the soldiers threatened them with instant death if they did not at once surrender. The seneschal deliberated with the persons of his suite upon what was best to be done in such an imminent danger: all agreed that it would be most prudent to surrender, except one of his ecclesiastics, who said it would be best to be killed, that they might go at once to Paradise; but this the others were not willing to comply with. Joinville then took a little coffer, and emptying it of the jewels and relics it contained, he threw them into the water, and surrendered at discretion. In spite of the laws of war, the seneschal would have been killed, if a renegade, who knew him, had not covered him with his body, crying: "It is the king's cousin!" Joinville, scarcely able to support himself, was dragged into a Mussulman galley, and from that transported to a house close to the shore. As they had deprived him of his coat of mail, and he remained almost without covering, the Saracens, whose prisoner he was, gave him a little cap, which he placed upon his head, and threw over his shoulders a scarlet cloak of his own, furred with minever, which his mother had given him: he was trembling all over, as well from his disease as the great fear that possessed him. Being unable to swallow a glass of water that was given to him, he believed himself to be dying, and called his servants around him, who all began to weep. Among those who wept the most bitterly, was a young boy, a natural son of the seigneur Montfaucon. This child, upon seeing the persons perish who had charge of him, had thrown himself into the arms and under the protection of Joinville. The sight of abandoned infancy and the despair of the worthy seneschal, excited the compassion of some of the emirs that were present, and one of them, whom Joinville at one time calls the *good Saracen*, and at another the *poor Saracen*, took pity on the boy, and when he left the seneschal, he said to him, "Be sure to hold this little child constantly by the hand, or I am certain the Saracens will kill him."

The carnage was prolonged for a considerable time after the battle; it lasted during many days. All the captives that had escaped the first fury of the Mussulman soldiers, were landed; and woe to such as sickness had weakened or as exhibited marks of poverty! the more worthy the victims were of pity, the more they roused the barbarity of the conquerors. Soldiers armed with swords and maces, charged to execute the terrible sentence of victory, awaited the prisoners on the shore. John of Vaissy, the priest, and some other servants belonging to Joinville, crawled from the ships in a dying state: the Saracens completed the work before the eyes of their master, saying that these poor wretches were good for nothing, and could pay for neither their liberty nor their lives.

In these days of disasters and calamities, more than thirty thousand Christians lost their lives, killed on the field of battle, drowned in the Nile, or massacred after the fight. The news of this victory obtained by the Mussulmans was soon spread throughout Egypt. The sultan of Cairo wrote to the governor of Damascus, to inform him of the last triumphs of Islamism. "Let thanks be rendered," said he in his letter, "to the All Powerful, who has changed our sadness into joy; it is to him alone we owe the glory of our arms; the blessings with which he has deigned to favour us are numberless, and the last is the most precious of all. You will announce to the people of Damascus, or rather to all Mussulmans, that God has enabled us to gain a complete victory over the Christians, at the moment they were conspiring to effect our ruin."

The day after that on which the Christian army had laid down their arms, the king of France was taken to Mansourah on board a war-boat, escorted by a great number of Egyptian vessels. The trumpets and kettle-drums carried the notes of triumph to a vast distance. The Egyptian army, in order of battle, marched along the eastern bank of the Nile as the fleet advanced. All the prisoners whom the fury of the enemy had spared, followed the Mussulman troops, with their hands tied behind them. The Arabs were in arms on the western bank, and the multitude flocked from all parts to witness this strange spectacle. On his arrival at Mansourah, Louis IX. was confined in the house of Fakreddin ben Lokman, secretary of the sultan, and placed under the guard of the eunuch Sabyh. A vast inclosure, surrounded by walls of earth, and guarded by the fiercest of the Mussulman warriors, received the other prisoners of war.

The news of these disasters carried consternation and despair to the city of Damietta, over the walls of which the standard of the French still floated. Confused reports at first were circulated; but soon a few Crusaders, who had escaped from the carnage, announced that the whole Christian army had perished. Queen Marguerite was on the point of being confined: her terrified imagination, at one moment, represented to her her husband falling beneath the swords of the enemy, and at the next, the Saracens at the gates of the city. Her emotions became so violent, that her servants believed her to be expiring. A knight of more than eighty years of age served her as esquire, and never left her either night or day. This unhappy princess, after having, for a moment, sobbed herself to sleep, started up in the greatest terror, imagining that her chamber was filled with Saracens about to kill her. The old knight, who had held her hand while she slept, pressed it, and said: "Be not afraid, madam, I am with you." An instant after she had reclosed her eyes, she awoke again, and uttered loud and fearful cries, and the grave esquire reassured her again. At length, to free herself from these cruel alarms, the queen ordered every one to leave her chamber except her knight, and then throwing herself upon her knees before him, with tearful eyes, she exclaimed: "Sir knight, promise that you will grant the favour I am about to ask of you." He promised upon his oath. Marguerite then continued: "I require you, on the faith you have pledged to me, that if the Saracens should take this city, you will cut off my head rather than allow me to become their captive." "Certainly, I will do it," replied the old knight; "I meant to do so, if the thing should so happen!"

On the morrow the queen was brought to bed of a son, who was named Jean Tristan, on account of the melancholy circumstances amidst which he was born. The same day her attendants informed her that the Pisans, and many Crusaders from the maritime cities of Europe, were desirous of abandoning Damietta and returning to their homes. Marguerite caused the leaders of them to be brought before her bed, and said to them: "Seigneurs, for the love of God, do not quit this city; its loss would bring on that of the king and of the whole Christian army. Be moved by my tears, have pity on the poor child that you behold lying beside me!" The merchants of Genoa and Pisa were at first but very little affected by these words. Joinville reproaches them with bitterness for their want of feeling for the cause of Christ, or for that of humanity. As they answered the queen that they had no provisions left, this princess gave orders that all the provisions in Damietta should be immediately bought up, and caused it to be announced to the Genoese and Pisans, that from that time they should be supported at the expense of the king. By this means, the city of Damietta preserved a garrison and defenders, whose presence, more than their valour, produced an effect upon the Saracens. It is even asserted that the Mussulmans, after the victory of Minieh, being desirous of surprising Damietta, presented themselves before the walls, clothed in the arms and bearing the standards of the conquered Christians; but they were betrayed by their language, their long beards, and their bronzed countenances. As the Christians showed themselves in great numbers upon the ramparts, the enemy drew off in haste from a city which they believed was disposed to defend itself, but in which, really, nothing but despondency and fear prevailed.

During this time Louis IX. was more calm at Mansourah than they were at Damietta. That which misery and misfortune have of the most bitter for the exalted of this world, only served to develop in him the virtue of a Christian hero and the character of a great king. He had no covering at night but a coarse cassock, which he owed to the charity of another prisoner. In this state, he never addressed one petition to his enemies, nor did the tone of his language announce either fear or submission. One of his almoners afterwards attested upon oath, that Louis never suffered a word of despair or a movement of impatience to escape from him. The Mussulmans were astonished at this resignation, and said among themselves, that if ever their prophet should leave them a prey to such great adversities, they would abandon his faith and his worship. Of all his riches, Louis had only saved his book of psalms, too sterile a spoil to be worth the attention of the Saracens; and when all the world seemed to have abandoned him, this book alone consoled him in his misfortunes. He every day recited those hymns of the prophets in which God himself speaks of his justice and his mercy, reassures virtue which suffers in his name, and threatens with his anger those whom prosperity intoxicates, and who abuse their triumph.

Thus religious sentiments and remembrances sustained the courage of Louis even in fetters; and the pious monarch, surrounded every day by fresh perils, amidst a Mussulman army that he had irritated by his victories, might still cry out with the prophet-king: "Supported by the living God, who is my buckler and my glory, I will not fear the crowd of enemies encamped around me."

The sultan of Cairo, appearing inclined to soften his rigorous policy, sent Louis fifty magnificent dresses for himself and the lords of his train. Louis refused to clothe himself in them, saying that he was the sovereign of a greater kingdom than Egypt, and that he would never wear the livery of a foreign prince. Almoadam ordered a great feast to be prepared, to which he invited the king.

But Louis would not accept of this invitation, as he was persuaded it was only meant to exhibit him as a spectacle to the Mussulman army. At length the sultan sent his most skilful physicians to him, and did all he could to preserve a prince whom he destined to adorn his triumph, and by whose means he hoped to obtain the advantages attached to his last victory. Before long he proposed to the king to break his chains upon condition of his giving up Damietta and the cities of Palestine that were still under the power of the Franks. Louis replied, that the Christian cities of Palestine did not belong to him; that God had recently replaced Damietta in the hands of the Christians, and that no human power had the right to dispose of it. The sultan, irritated by this refusal, resolved to employ violence. At one time he threatened Louis to send him to the caliph of Bagdad, who would closely imprison him till death; at another, he announced the project of leading his illustrious captive throughout the East, and of exhibiting to all Asia a king of the Christians reduced to slavery. At length he went so far as to threaten to have him placed in the *bernicles*, a frightful punishment reserved for the greatest criminals. Louis still showed himself firm, and, as the only reply to all these menaces, said, "I am the sultan's prisoner, he can do with me what he pleases."

The king of France suffered, though he did not complain; he feared nothing on his own account, but when he thought of his faithful army, and of the fate of the other captives, his heart was a prey to the deepest sorrow. The Christian prisoners were crowded into one open court, some sick, others wounded, the greater part naked, and all exposed to hunger, the injuries of the elements, and the ill-treatment of their pitiless guards. A Mussulman was commanded to write the names of all these wretched captives, whose number amounted to more than ten thousand. They led all such as could purchase their liberty into a vast tent; the others remained in the place into which they had been driven like a flock of animals, destined to perish miserably. Every day an emir, by the sultan's orders, entered this abode of despair, and caused two or three hundred prisoners to be dragged out of the enclosure. They were asked if they would abjure the religion of Christ; and those whom the fear of death induced to desert their faith, received their liberty; the others were put to the sword, and their bodies were cast into the Nile. They were slaughtered during the night; silence and darkness adding to the horrors of the execution. During several days the steel of the executioner thus decimated the unhappy prisoners. None were ever seen to return who went out of the inclosure. Their sad companions, on bidding them farewell, wept beforehand over their tragical end, and lived in certain expectation of a similar fate. At length the lassitude of slaughter caused those that remained to be spared. They were led away to Cairo; and the capital of Egypt, into which they had flattered themselves they should enter in triumph, beheld them arrive covered with rags and loaded with chains. They were thrown into dungeons, where many died of hunger and grief; the others, condemned to slavery in a foreign land, deprived of all assistance and of all communication with their leaders, without knowing what was become of their king, were hopeless of ever recovering their liberty, or of revisiting the West.

The Oriental historians relate the scenes we have just described with indifference; many even seemed to consider the massacre of prisoners of war as a second victory; and, as if the misfortune and murder of a disarmed enemy could heighten the glory of a conqueror, they exaggerate in their accounts the misery of the vanquished, and particularly the number of the victims immolated to Islamism.

The barons and knights that were shut up in the pavilion, were not ignorant of the fate of their companions in arms; they passed their days and nights in continual terrors. The sultan wished to obtain from them that which he had not been able to obtain from Louis IX. He sent an emir to inform them that he would set them at liberty if Damietta and the Christian cities of Palestine were restored to the Mussulmans. The count of Brittany replied in the name of all the prisoners, that that which was asked of them was not in their power, and that French warriors had no other will than that of their king. "It is plainly to be perceived," said the messenger of Almoadam, "that you care very little for liberty or life. *You shall see some men accustomed to sword playing.*" The emir retired, leaving the prisoners in the expectation of an early death. The apparatus of punishment was exhibited before them. The sword remained several days suspended over their heads; but Almoadam could make no impression upon their firmness. Thus, neither the captivity of an entire army, nor the death of so many warriors, had been able to deprive the Christians of a single one of their conquests, and one of the bulwarks of Egypt was still in their hands. The conquerors prayed and threatened by turns; the conquered resisted all their endeavours, and always appeared masters.

In the mean time several French nobles offered to pay their own ransom. Louis was informed of this; and as he feared that many, not having the means to redeem themselves, would remain in chains, he forbade any particular treaty. The barons and knights, but lately so intractable, did not persist in opposing the will of an unfortunate king, and instantly gave up all idea of a separate negotiation. The king said he would pay for everybody, and that he would never think about his own liberty till after he had assured that of all others.

Whilst the sultan of Cairo was thus making useless attempts to overcome the pride and lower the courage of Louis and his knights, the favourites he had brought with him from Mesopotamia pressed their master to conclude the peace quickly. "You have," said they to him, "enemies much more dangerous than the Christians; they are the emirs, who wish to reign in your place, and who never cease to boast of their victories, as if you had not yourself conquered the Franks, as if the God of Mahomet had not sent pestilence and famine to aid you in triumphing over the defenders of Christ: hasten, then, to terminate the war, in order that you may strengthen your power within, and begin to reign." These speeches, which flattered the pride of Almoadam, induced him to make rather more reasonable proposals to his enemies. The sultan limited his demand to a ransom of a million of golden byzants, and the restitution of Damietta. Louis, aware that the city of Damietta could not resist, consented to the proposals that were made to him, *if the queen approved of them.* As the Mussulmans expressed some surprise at this, the king added, "*The queen is my lady, I can do nothing without her consent.*" The ministers of the sultan returned a second time, and told the French monarch, that if the queen would pay the sum agreed upon, he should be free. "A king of France," answered he, "is not to be redeemed by money; the city of Damietta shall be given up for my deliverance, and a million of golden byzants paid for that of my army." The sultan agreed to all; and whether he was pleased at having terminated the negotiations, or whether he was touched by the noble character the captive monarch had displayed, he reduced the sum fixed upon as the ransom of the Christian army a fifth.

The knights and barons were daily encouraged by the priests to maintain their religion and their courage; they were still ignorant of the conclusion of the treaty, and were revolving in their minds their customary melancholy reflections, when they saw an old Saracen enter their pavilion. His venerable figure and the gravity of his carriage inspired respect. His train, composed of men-at-arms, inspired fear. The old man, without any preliminary discourse, asked the prisoners, by means of an interpreter. if it was true that they believed in a God, born of a woman, crucified for the salvation of the human race, and resuscitated the third day? All having answered at once that that was their belief: "In that case," added he, "congratulate yourselves at suffering for your God; you are yet far from having suffered as much for him as he suffered for you. Place your hopes in him, and if he has been able to recall himself to life, he will not want power to put an end to the evils that afflict you now."

On finishing these words, the old Mussulman retired, leaving the Crusaders divided between surprise, fear, and hope. On the next day it was announced to them that the king had concluded a truce, and wished to take counsel of his barons. John of Vallery, Philip de Montfort, and Guy and Baldwin d'Ibelin were deputed to wait upon the king. It was not long before the Crusaders learnt that their captivity was about to end, and that the king had paid the ransom of the poor as well as the rich. When these brave knights turned their thoughts towards their victories, they never could conceive how it was possible for them to have fallen into the hands of the infidels; and when they reflected on their late misfortunes, their deliverance appeared equally miraculous to them. All raised their voices in praises to God and benedictions to the king of France.

All the cities of Palestine that had belonged to the Christians at the arrival of the Crusaders in the East, were comprised in the treaty. On both sides, the prisoners of war made since the truce concluded between the emperor Frederick and Melik-Kamel, were to be given up. It was agreed, also, that the munitions and machines of war belonging to the Christian army should remain provisionally at Damietta, under the safeguard of the sultan of Egypt.

It next became the object to perform the conditions of the treaty of peace. Four large galleys were prepared to transport the principal prisoners to the mouth of the Nile. The sultan left Mansourah, and repaired to Pharescour by land.

After the battle of Minieh, a vast palace, built of fir timber, of which the chronicles of the times have left pompous descriptions, had been erected in that city. It was in this palace Almoadam received the felicitations of the Mussulmans, upon the happy issue of a war against the enemies of Islamism. All the cities, all the principalities of Syria, sent ambassadors to salute the conqueror of the Christians. The governor of Damascus, to whom he had sent a helmet, found on the field of battle, that had belonged to the king of France, replied to him thus: "There is no doubt that God destines for you the conquest of the universe, or that you will proceed from victory to victory; who can doubt of this when we already see your slaves clothed in the spoils of conquered kings?" Thus the young sultan imbibed intoxicating draughts of praise, and passed his time in the festivities and pleasures of peace, forgetting the cares of his empire, and foreseeing none of the dangers which threatened him amidst his triumphs.

Almoadam had disgraced, and deprived of their places, many of the ministers of his father; most of the emirs were in fear of a similar fall, and this fear even led them to brave everything for the preservation of their fortunes and their lives. Among these malcontents, the Mamelukes and their leader were most conspicuous. This military body owed their origin to Saladin, and they had enjoyed the greatest privileges under the preceding reign. They reproached the sultan with preferring young favourites to old warriors, the support of the throne and the saviours of Egypt. They reproached him with having concluded a peace, without consulting those who had supported the burden of the war; and with having bestowed the spoils of the vanquished upon courtiers, who had only deserved them by coming from the banks of the Euphrates to the shores of the Nile. In order to justify beforehand all they might attempt against the prince, they attributed to him projects of the most sinister nature; and nascent rebellion inflamed itself by the recital of future persecutions. The emirs who were to die were designated; the instruments of death were named, the day was fixed, everything was appointed, everything was ready. It was asserted that the sultan, in the course of one of his nocturnal orgies, had cut off the tops of the flambeaux in his apartment, crying, "Thus shall fly the heads of all the Mamelukes." A woman animated the minds of the warriors by her discourse: this was Chegger-Eddour, who, having disposed of the empire, could not endure the neglect of the new sultan. From complaints they soon passed to open revolt; for it was less perilous to attack the prince sword in hand, than to declaim for any length of time against him. A conspiracy was formed, in which the Mamelukes and all the emirs who had outrages to avenge or to fear were concerned. The conspirators were impatient to execute their project, and fearing that the sultan, if once arrived at Damietta, might escape them, they resolved to proceed to the consummation at Pharescour.

The galleys which transported the Christian prisoners arrived before that city. The king landed, with the princes, his brothers, and was received in a pavilion, where he had an interview with the sultan. History says nothing of this conference between two princes, who equally commanded attention, and whose position was so different; the one intoxicated by his victories, blinded by his prosperities; the other, the conqueror of ill-fortune, coming out much greater from the ordeal of adversity.

The two sovereigns had appointed Saturday, the eve of the Ascension, for the giving up of Damietta. According to this convention, the Crusaders, who had been detained more than a month in chains, had only to endure the pains of captivity three days longer; but new misfortunes awaited them, and their courage and resignation were doomed to further trials. The day after their arrival before Pharescour, the sultan of Cairo, in celebration of the peace, determined to give a banquet to the principal officers of the Mussulman army. The conspirators took advantage of this opportunity, and, towards the end of the repast, all rushed upon him, sword in hand. Bendocdar struck the first blow. Almoadam, being only wounded in the hand, arises in a state of terrified amazement, escapes through his motionless guards, takes refuge in a tower, shuts the door of it, and appears at a window, sometimes imploring succour, and sometimes demanding of the conspirators what they required of him. The envoy of the caliph of Bagdad was at Pharescour. He mounted on horseback, but the Mamelukes threatened him with instant death if he did not return to his tent. At the same moment some drums were heard, giving the signal for assembling the troops; but the leaders of the conspiracy told the soldiers that Damietta was taken, and immediately the whole army precipitated themselves upon the road to that city, leaving the sultan at the mercy of men who thirsted for his blood. The Mamelukes accuse and threaten him. He endeavours to justify himself; but his words are drowned in the tumult. A thousand voices cry out to him to descend; he hesitates; he groans; he weeps; arrows fly against the tower in showers; the Greek fire, hurled from every direction, gives birth to a conflagration. Almoadam, nearly surrounded by the flames, precipitates himself from the window; a nail catches his mantle, and he remains for a moment suspended. At length he falls to the earth; sabres and naked swords wave over him on all sides; he casts himself on his knees, at the feet of Octaï, one of the principal officers of his guard, who repulses him with contempt. The unhappy prince arises, holding forth his imploring hands to all the assembly, saying, that he was willing to abandon the throne of Egypt, and would return into Mesopotamia. These supplications, unworthy of a prince, inspire more contempt than pity; nevertheless, the crowd of conspirators hesitate; but the leaders know too well there can be no safety for them but in completing the crime they have begun. Bendocdar, who had inflicted the first blow, strikes him a second time with his sabre; Almoadam, streaming with blood, throws himself into the Nile, and endeavours to gain some vessels that appear to be drawing near to the shore to receive him; nine Mamelukes follow him into the water, and pour upon him a thousand blows, within sight of the galley which Joinville was on board of!

Such was the end of Almoadam, who neither knew how to reign nor how to die. Arabian authors point it out as a remarkable circumstance, that he perished at once by the sword, fire, and water. The same authors agree in saying, that he himself provoked his ruin by his imprudence and his injustice. But oriental history, accustomed to laud success and blame all who succumb, repeats the complaints of the Mamelukes without examining them; and, passing lightly over this revolution, contents itself with saying, *"When God wills an event, he prepares the causes beforehand."*

The Nile and its shore presented, at that moment, two very different spectacles: on one side was a prince, whilst revelling in all the pomps of grandeur, in all the triumphs of victory, massacred by his own guards; on the other, an unfortunate king, surrounded by his knights, as unfortunate as himself, inspiring them with more respect in his adversity than when he was encompassed with all the splendour of prosperity and power. The French knights and barons, although they had been victims of the barbarity of the sultan, felt more astonishment than joy at the sight of his tragical death; they could not comprehend the murderous attack of the Mamelukes; and these revolutions of military despotism, at war with itself, filled them with dread.

After this sanguinary scene, thirty Saracen officers, sword in hand and battle-axes on their shoulders, entered the galley in which were the counts of Brittany and de Montfort, Baldwin and Guy d'Ibelin, and the sieur de Joinville. These furious men vomited imprecations, and threatening the prisoners with both voice and gesture, made them believe that their last hour was come. The Christian warriors prepared themselves for death, and throwing themselves on their knees before a monk of the Trinity, asked him for absolution of their sins; but as the priest could not hear them all at once, they confessed to each other. Guy d'Ibelin, constable of Cyprus, confessed to Joinville, who gave him "such absolution as God had given him the power to give." It was thus, in after-times, history represents the Chevalier Bayard, wounded to death, and ready to expire, confessing himself at the foot of an oak to one of his faithful companions in arms.

But these menaces and violences of the emirs might have a politic aim. At the conclusion of a conspiracy that had divided men's minds, in order to awaken fresh passions, it was necessary for the leaders to excite the fanaticism of the multitude, and direct the general fury against the Christians. It was important for them to make others believe, and they might have believed it themselves, that Almoadam had endeavoured to find an asylum amongst the enemies of Islamism.

The lords and barons did not meet with the fate they expected; but as if their understanding with Almoadam had been really dreaded, they were thrust into the hold of the vessel, where they passed the night with the terrible images of death constantly before their eyes.

Louis, shut up in his tent with his brothers, had heard the tumult. In ignorance of what was passing, he concluded that either they were massacring the French prisoners, or else that Damietta was taken. He was a prey to a thousand terrors, when he saw Octaï, the chief of the Mamelukes, enter his tent. This emir ordered the guards to retire, and pointing to his bloody sword, exclaimed: "Almoadam is no more; what will you give me for having delivered you from an enemy who meditated your destruction as well as ours?" Louis made no reply. Then the furious emir, presenting the point of his sword, cried, "Dost thou not know that I am master of thy person? Make me a knight, or thou art a dead man." "Make thyself a Christian," replied the monarch, "and I will make thee a knight."* Without insisting further, Octaï retired, and in a very short time the tent of the king was filled with Saracen warriors, armed with sabres and swords. Their demeanour, their cries, the fury painted on their countenances, announced sufficiently that they had just committed a great crime, and that they were ready to commit others; but by a species of miracle, changing, all at once, both countenance and language at the sight of the king, they approached him with respect; then, as if they felt in the presence of Louis the necessity for justifying themselves, they told him that they

---

* This is really one of those tales that require "seven justices' names" to vouch for their authenticity. How such a man, at such a time, could be ambitious of the honour of knighthood, it is very difficult to imagine. But when we recollect that the evidence of sixty-five miracles performed by him was produced to procure his canonization, we must not be sceptical in what regards Louis IX.—TRANS.

ARRIVAL AT CAIRO OF PRISONERS OF MINICH.

Every day an emir, by the sultan's orders, entered this abode of despair, and caused two or three hundred prisoners to be dragged out of the enclosure. They were asked if they would abjure the religion of Christ, and those whom the fear of death induced to desert their faith, received their liberty; the others were put to the sword, and their bodies were cast into the Nile. They were slaughtered during the night; silence and darkness adding to the horrors of the execution. At length the lassitude of slaughter caused those that remained to be spared. They were led away to Cairo; and the capital of Egypt, into which they had flattered themselves they should enter in triumph, beheld them arrive covered with rags and loaded with chains.—BOOK XIV.

had been forced to kill a tyrant, who aimed at their destruction as well as that of the Christians; now, they added, they had only to forget the past; all they required for the future was the faithful execution of the treaty concluded with Almoadam. Then lifting their hands to their turbans, and bending their brows to the ground, they retired in silence, and left the monarch in a state of astonishment at seeing them thus pass, all at once, from transports of rage to sentiments apparently the most respectful.

This singular scene has made some historians say that the Mamelukes offered the throne of Egypt to St. Louis. This opinion has rather gained ground in our days, so easy is it for us to give faith to everything that appears favourable to the glory of the French name. The sieur de Joinville, who is quoted in support of this assertion, only relates a conversation he had held with Louis. The king asked him what he thought he ought to have done, in case the emirs had offered him the supreme authority. The good seneschal conceived it was not possible to accept a crown from the hands of those seditious emirs, who had killed their sovereign. Louis was not of this opinion, and said that, truly, if they had proposed to him to become the successor of the sultan, he would not in the least have refused to be so (*il ne l'eût mie refusé*). These words alone prove sufficiently that they had proposed nothing to the captive monarch. Joinville, it is true, adds to this recital, that according to reports that were circulated in the Christian army, the emirs had caused the trumpets to be sounded and the drums to be beaten before the tent of the king of France, and that at the same time they deliberated among themselves, whether it would not be best to break the chains of their prisoner, and make him their sovereign. The sieur de Joinville relates this fact, without affirming it; and as oriental history preserves the most profound silence upon it, an historian of the present day cannot adopt it without compromising his veracity. It is, without doubt, possible that the emirs might have expressed the desire of having a prince amongst them possessed of the firmness, bravery, and virtues of Louis IX.; but how can it be believed that Mussulmans, animated by the double fanaticism of religion and war, could have, for a moment, entertained a thought of choosing an absolute master among the Christians, whom they had just treated with unexampled barbarity; and thus place their property, their liberty, their lives in the hands of the most implacable enemies of their country, their laws, and their faith?

The supreme power, of which the emirs had shown themselves to be so jealous, and which they had wrested with so much violence from the hands of Almoadam, appeared at first to terrify their ambition, when they had it in their power to dispose of it. In a council called to nominate a sultan, the wisest declined to rule over a country filled with troubles, or command an army given up to the spirit of sedition. Upon their refusal, the crown was given to Chegger-Eddour, who had had so great a share, first in the elevation, and then in the fall of Almoadam. As governor with her, in the quality of Atabec, they chose Ezz-Eddin Aybek, who had been brought a slave into Egypt, and whose barbarous origin procured him the surname of the *Turcoman*.

The new sultana soon arrived at Pharescour, and was proclaimed under the name of Mostassemieh Salehieh, queen of the Mussulmans, mother of Malek-Almansor Khalil. Almansor Khalil, a young prince, the son of Negmeddin, had preceded his father to the tomb. Thus finished the powerful dynasty of the Ayoubites, a dynasty founded by victory, and overturned by an army which the pride of victory had rendered seditious. Whilst they were thus forming a new government, the body of Almoadam was abandoned on the banks of the Nile, where it remained two days without sepulture. The ambassador from the caliph of Bagdad at length obtained permission to bury it, and deposited in an obscure place the sad remains of the last successor of Saladin.

The elevation of Chegger-Eddour astonished the Mussulmans; the name of a woman or of a slave had never till that time been seen engraved upon the coins, or pronounced in public prayers. The caliph of Bagdad protested against the scandal of this innovation; and when he afterwards wrote to the emirs, he asked them if they had not been able to find a single man in all Egypt to govern them. The supreme authority, placed in the hands of a woman, could neither restrain the passions which troubled the empire, nor cause treaties to be respected; which became very fatal to the Christians, condemned to suffer by turns from the revolt and the submission from the union and the discord of their enemies.

Among the emirs, some wished that the treaty concluded with the sultan should be executed; whilst others were desirous that a fresh one should be made: many were indignant that the Christians should be treated with at all. After long debates, they returned to that which had been done at first, adding to it the condition that the king of France should give up Damietta before he was set at liberty, and that he should pay half of the sum agreed upon for the ransom of himself and his army, before he left the banks of the Nile. These last conditions announced the mistrust of the emirs, and might give the Christian prisoners reason to fear that the day of their deliverance was not yet arrived.

When the observance of the treaty was to be sworn to, the forms of the oaths caused some discussion. The emirs swore that if they failed in their promises, "they consented to be jeered at like the pilgrim who makes the journey to Mecca bareheaded; or else to be as much despised as he who takes back his women after having left them." The Mussulmans, according to their manners and customs, had no more solemn expression with which to guarantee their sworn faith. They proposed to Louis the following formula: "If I keep not my oath, I shall be like to him who denies his God, who spits upon the cross, and tramples it under-foot." This formula of the oath which they wished the king to take, appeared to him to be an insult to God and himself. He refused to pronounce it. In vain the emirs showed their anger and their passion; he braved all their menaces. This resistance of St. Louis, celebrated by his contemporaries, will not perhaps obtain the same eulogies in the age we now live in; nevertheless it must be considered that the king was not only restrained on this occasion by the scruples of an exaggerated devotion, but by a feeling of royal dignity. It may be remembered, that in the third crusade, Richard and Saladin had judged it unworthy of the majesty of kings to degrade their word to the formula of an oath; and had been satisfied with a touch of the hand, to cement the peace. Seditious emirs, still stained with the blood of their master, might undervalue the dignity of the supreme rank; but, on important occasions, Louis never forgot he was a great king; and the supposition of a perjury, the thought even of a blasphemy, could not ally itself in his mind with the character of a Christian prince and of a king of France.

The Mussulmans, irritated at seeing a king in fetters dictate laws to them, and resist all their demands, began to talk of putting him to death accompanied by tortures. "You are masters of my body," he replied, "but you have no power over my will." The princes, his brothers, implored him to pronounce the required formula; but he was as firm against the entreaties of friendship and affection, as he had been against the threats of his enemies. Even the exhortations of the prelates had no more effect. At length the Mamelukes, attributing such an obstinate resistance to the patriarch of Jerusalem, seized this prelate, who was more than eighty years of age, fastened him to a post, and tied his hands behind him so tightly, that the blood sprang from beneath the nails. The patriarch, overcome by the pain, cried, "Sire! Sire! swear; I will take the sin upon myself." But Louis, who was throughout persuaded that they insulted his good faith, and that they demanded of him a thing unjust and dishonourable, remained immovable. The emirs, at length subdued by so much firmness, consented to accept the simple word of the king, and retired, saying that "this Frank prince was the most haughty Christian that had ever been seen in the East."

All now gave their attention to the execution of the treaty. The galleys, on board of which were the prisoners, heaved their anchors, and descended towards the mouth of the Nile; the Mussulman army accompanying them by land. The Christians were to deliver up Damietta the next morning at daybreak. It is impossible to describe the trouble, consternation, and despair that reigned in the city throughout the night. The unfortunate inhabitants ran about the streets, asking each other questions, and communicating their fears with breathless anxiety. The most sinister reports prevailed; it was said that the whole of the Christian army had been massacred by the Mussulmans, and that the king of France was poisoned. When they received orders to evacuate the place, most of the warriors declared aloud that they would not obey, and that they preferred dying on the ramparts to being slaughtered as prisoners of war.

At the same time excitement began to prevail in the Mussulman army. It was whispered that the king of France refused to execute the treaty, and that he had ordered the garrison of Damietta to defend themselves. The soldiers and their leaders repented of having made a truce with the Franks, and appeared determined to take advantage of the least pretext for breaking it.

The commissioners of Louis IX., however, at length persuaded the Christians of Damietta to evacuate the city. Queen Marguerite, scarcely recovered from her confinement, went on board a Genoese vessel. She was accompanied by the duchess of Anjou, the countess of Poictiers, and the unhappy widow of the count d'Artois, who, amidst present calamities, still wept over the first misfortune of the war. Towards the end of the night, Olivier de Thermes, who commanded the garrison, the duke of Burgundy, the pope's legate, and all the Franks, except the sick that remained in the city, embarked on the Nile.

Geoffrey de Sergines having entered Damietta, brought the keys to the emirs; and when day broke, the Mussulman standards were seen floating over the towers and ramparts. At sight of this, the whole Egyptian army rushed tumultuously into the city. The reports that had been circulated during the night, had excited the fury of the soldiers, and they entered Damietta as if the opening of the gates had been the result of a sanguinary contest; they massacred the sick wherever they found them, they pillaged the houses, and gave to the flames the machines of war, the arms, and all the munitions that belonged to the Christians.

This early violation of the treaty, the intoxication of carnage, and the impunity of license, only served to inflame still further the minds of the Mussulmans, and to lead them to greater excesses. The emirs, partaking of the fury of the soldiers, formed the idea of putting all the Christian prisoners to death. The galleys in which the French barons and knights were crowded, immediately received orders to re-ascend the river towards Pharescour, "which caused great grief amongst us," says Joinville, "and many tears issued from our eyes; for we all believed they were about to kill us."

Whilst the galleys re-ascended the Nile, the Mussulman leaders deliberated in council upon the fate of the king of France and the French warriors. "Now we are masters of Damietta," said one of the emirs, "and a powerful monarch of the Franks, with the bravest of his warriors, may receive from our hands death or liberty. Fortune offers us an opportunity of securing peace to Egypt for ever, and with it the triumph of Islamism. We have shed the blood of Mussulman princes without scruple; why should we then respect that of Christian princes, who have come into the East to set fire to our cities and to reduce our provinces to slavery?" This opinion was that of the people and the army; and most of the emirs, actuated by the general spirit, held similar language. An emir of Mauritania, whose name Joinville has not preserved, opposed, almost alone, this violation of the laws of war and peace. "You have," said he, "put to death your prince, whom the Koran commands you *to cherish as the apple of your eye.* This death might, doubtless, be necessary for your own safety;

but what can you expect from the action that is proposed to you, except the anger of God and the maledictions of men?" This speech was interrupted by murmurs; the language of reason only added heat to hatred and fanaticism. As violent passions are never at a loss for motives of self-justification, or for excuses for their excesses, the Crusaders were accused of perfidy, treachery, and all the crimes that they themselves contemplated against them. There was no imputation that did not appear probable, consequently no violence that did not appear just. "If the Koran ordered Mussulmans to watch over the lives of their princes, it likewise commanded them to watch over the preservation of the Mussulman faith: death ought to be the reward of those who came to bring death, and their bones ought to whiten upon the same plains that they had laid waste. The safety of Egypt and the laws of the prophet required that it should be so."

After a very stormy deliberation, the terrible sentence of the captives was about to be pronounced; but cupidity came to the aid of justice and humanity; the emir who had spoken in favors of the Christian prisoners, had, in his speech, more than once repeated the words, *Dead men pay no ransom;* and they at length acknowledged that the sword, by immolating the Crusaders, would only rob victory of its dues, and deprive the conquerors of the fruit of their labours. This observation at length calmed the minds of the assembly, and brought about a change of opinions. The fear of losing eight hundred thousand golden byzants caused the treaty to be respected, and saved the lives of the king of France and his companions in misfortune.

The emirs issued orders for the galleys to be brought back towards Damietta. The Mamelukes appeared, all at once, to be governed by the most pacific sentiments; and, as it is natural for the multitude to pass from one extreme to another, they treated with all the attentions of hospitality the very men whom, a few hours before, they had wished to put to death. On their arrival before the city, the prisoners were treated with fritters cooked in the sun, and with hard eggs, "which," says Joinville, "in honour of our persons, were painted of various colours."

The knights and barons at length had permission to leave the ships that had been their prisons, to go and join the king, whom many of them had not seen since the disaster of Minieh. As they left their vessels, Louis was marching towards the mouth of the Nile, escorted by Mussulman warriors; an innumerable multitude followed him, and contemplated, in silence, the features, the bearing, and the arms of the Christian monarch. A Genoese galley awaited him; as soon as he was on board, eighty archers, with their cross-bows strung, appeared suddenly upon the deck of the vessel: the crowd of Egyptians immediately dispersed, and the ship glided away from the shore. Louis had with him the count of Anjou, the count de Soissons, Geoffrey de Sergines, Philip de Nemours, and the seneschal de Joinville. The count of Poictiers remained as a hostage in Damietta, until the payment of four hundred thousand golden byzants, which the king ought to have paid to the emirs before he put to sea, should be completed. Louis had not enough by thirty thousand livres; this sum was requested of the Templars, who, to the great scandal of the lords and barons, at first refused it. They were threatened with being forced to furnish it; and then complied. The amount stipulated in the treaty was paid to the Saracens. The count of Poictiers had left Damietta, and everything was ready for the departure of the Crusaders, when Philip de Montfort, who had been directed to make the payment, returned to give an account of his mission, and told the king that he had contrived to cheat the emirs out of ten thousand livres. Louis expressed himself much dissatisfied with such a proceeding, and sent Philip de Montfort back to Damietta, to make restitution of the money he had kept back—a lesson of justice which he wished to give to both his enemies and his servants. This last mission is spoken of by an Arabian author, who attributes it to a very whimsical and singular motive. He says that Philip de Montfort was sent to the emirs to tell them that they were deficient in religion and good sense; in religion, because they had murdered their sovereign; in good sense, because, for a moderate sum, they had released a powerful prince, who would have given half of his kingdom to recover his liberty. This explanation, however improbable it may be, at least serves to inform us of the opinion then common in the East, that the Egyptian emirs were reproached with having destroyed their sultan, and allowed their enemy to escape.

Louis IX., with the miserable wreck of his army, soon passed out at the mouth of the Nile, and in a few days arrived at Ptolemaïs, where the people and the clergy were still putting up prayers for his deliverance.

The Egyptians celebrated the restitution of Damietta with public rejoicings; the Mussulman army broke up their camp, and returned towards the capital. The sultana, Chegger-Eddour, caused vests of gold and silver to be distributed to the leaders, and her liberality even extended to the soldiers. An Arabian poet composed some verses upon this occasion, which history has preserved, and which contain the remarkable passage that follows:—

"When thou shalt see this Frenchman (the king of France), tell him these words from the mouth of a sincere friend:

"Thou camest into Egypt, thou covetedest its riches; thou believedst that its powers would fade away as smoke.

"Behold now thine army! see how thy imprudent conduct has precipitated it into the bosom of the tomb!

"Fifty thousand men! and not one that is not either killed, a prisoner, or covered with wounds!

"And if he should be ever tempted to come to avenge his defeat; if any motive should bring him back to these places;

"Tell him, that the house of the son of Lokman is reserved for him; that he will still find there both his chains and the eunuch Sabyh."

Whilst Louis IX. was landing at Ptolemaïs, general consternation prevailed in the West; as it always happens in distant wars, fame had spread the most extraordinary reports relative to the expedition of the Crusaders. At first it was believed that the Christian standards were floating from the walls of Cairo and Alexandria; but to these news other rumours soon succeeded, announcing great disasters. The most marvellous accounts had found plenty of credulous minds in France to receive them; they refused to believe in reverses, and the first who spoke of them were given up to the hands of justice, as enemies of religion and of the kingdom. The sinister reports, however, were not long in being confirmed; the people passed from the excess of joy to the excess of grief; there was not a family in the kingdom that had not to deplore a loss in the disasters of which they acquired the painful certainty. But for the French, that which rendered so many misfortunes irreparable, and for which no one could find consolation, was the captivity of the king! Dances, festivals, spectacles, everything that bore the air of joy or pleasure, was forbidden: the kingdom, plunged in sorrow and abasement, appeared, all at once, to be like one of those cities of which the Scripture speaks,—threatened with the wrath of God, they gave themselves up to grief, and covered themselves with the mourning garb of penitence.

The whole Church deplored so great a misfortune with torrents of tears; the father of the faithful was nearly in despair for the safety of Christendom. He addressed letters filled with affliction to all the prelates of the West. He ordered the clergy to put up public prayers; he exhorted the faithful to take up arms. Innocent wrote to Blanche to console her, and to Louis to sustain him in his adversity. When addressing the king of France, he is astonished at finding one man oppressed by so many calamities, and endowed with so many virtues; and demands of God what justice had been able to find in the most Christian of kings, which deserved to be expiated by misfortunes so great.

England was likewise much afflicted by the captivity of the French monarch; the barons and knights were indignant towards their king for having prevented them from going into the East to share the perils of the Crusaders. The king of Castile, then at war with the Moors, was sensible only of the evils of the Christians beyond the seas, and swore to go and fight with the victorious infidels on the banks of the Nile or the Jordan. No monarch of the West expressed more grief than Frederick II., emperor of Germany; in his letters he spoke of the king of France as his best friend, and deplored the disasters of the crusade with bitterness. Frederick, still at variance with the pope, did not neglect this opportunity of accusing Innocent, whom he reproached with the ruin of the Christians. Frederick repaired to Sicily, for the purpose of arming a fleet that might convey prompt assistance to the Crusaders; and whilst the vessels were getting ready, he sent an embassy into the East, to solicit of the sultan of Egypt the deliverance of the king of France and his army.

Amidst the universal desolation, a single Christian city gave demonstrations of joy: Florence, according to Villani, celebrated the reverses of the French Crusaders with festivities. Some pirates from Genoa, Pisa, and Venice took advantage of the disasters of Louis IX. to put to sea, and pillage the Crusaders that were returning into Europe. The joy of the Florentines, and the brigandages of the Italian pirates, were subjects of great scandal for all Christendom.

Louis IX., on his arrival at Ptolemaïs, had only been able to retain a small number of faithful knights; many of the French nobles, the companions of his captivity, instead of following him to Palestine, returned into the West. Among those who had quitted the banner of the crusade, were the duke of Burgundy and the brave count of Brittany: the latter, worn out with sickness and covered with wounds, died on his passage: his mortal remains, preserved by his knights, were transported to the abbey of Villeneuve, near Nantes, where, many ages afterwards, his tomb was still to be seen.

The appearance of the sad remains of the Christian army must have excited the compassion of the inhabitants of Ptolemaïs. Both knights and soldiers were almost naked; the seneschal of Champagne, in order to appear at the king's table, was forced to make himself a vestment of the shreds of a bed-quilt. An epidemic disease, the fruit of lengthened misery and all sorts of privations, broke out among the Crusaders, and soon extended its ravages to the city. Joinville, who was lodged in the house of the curé of Ptolemaïs, informs us that he saw daily twenty convoys pass beneath his windows; and that every time he heard the funeral words, "*Libera me, Domine*," he burst into tears, and addressed himself to God crying, *Mercy!*

In the mean time the king of France was engaged in endeavouring to deliver the captives that still remained in Egypt. These captives amounted to twelve thousand, and most of them might be able to resume their arms and serve under the banner of the crusade. Louis sent his ambassadors to pay the four hundred thousand francs that he still owed to the Saracens, and to press the execution of the last treaties. These ambassadors found Egypt filled with troubles; the emirs were divided into several factions, all disputing for power: fanaticism animated these divisions; they reciprocally accused each other of having favoured or spared the Christians. Amidst these debates, many captives had been massacred, and some forced to abjure the faith of Christ. The messengers of Louis IX. could scarcely obtain a hearing; in answer to their demands, they were told that the king of France might esteem himself fortunate in having regained his liberty, and that the Mamelukes would soon go and besiege him in Ptolemaïs. At length the Christian ambassadors were obliged to quit Egypt without having obtained anything; and only brought back to Palestine four hundred prisoners, the greater part of whom had paid their own ransom.

On their return, Louis IX. was plunged in the deepest distress; he had just received a letter from Queen Blanche, who exhorted him to leave the East. He, thereupon, was desirous of returning to France; but how could he make up his mind to abandon twelve thousand Christians in slavery, or to quit the Holy Land when it was threatened with invasion? The three military orders, the barons, and the nobles of Palestine, conjured Louis not to abandon them; repeating with accents of despair, that if they were deprived of his support, the Christians of Syria would have no other resource than to follow him into the West.

Louis was touched by their prayers, but before he would form a resolution, he was desirous of consulting his two brothers and the principal nobles that had remained with him. He exhibited to them the reasons he had for returning to France, and those that would lead him to remain in Palestine: on the one side, his kingdom threatened by the king of England, and the impossibility of his undertaking anything against the infidels, ought to induce him to quit the East; on the other side, the want of good faith in the emirs, who had failed in executing the first conditions of the treaty; the perils to which the Holy Land would be exposed by his departure; the hope, in short, of receiving succours, and profiting by them, to break the chains of the Christian prisoners and deliver Jerusalem, in some sort, imposed upon him the obligation to defer his return.

After having thus described the state of things, without saying a word that might reveal his own opinion, he requested his knights and barons to reflect seriously upon the line of action it would be best for them to pursue. On the following Sunday he again convoked them, and demanded their opinion. The first that spoke was Guy de Malvoisin, whose bravery in fight and wisdom in council were admired and respected by all the Crusaders. "Sire," said he, addressing Louis, "when I consider the honour of your person and the glory of your reign, I do not think you ought to remain in this country. Remember that flourishing army with which you left the ports of Cyprus, and then turn your eyes upon the warriors you have with you; on that day we reckoned two thousand eight hundred knights with banners in the Christian army; now, one hundred knights constitute your whole force; most of them are sick; they have neither arms nor horses, nor the means of procuring any; they have not the power of serving you with either honour or advantage. You do not possess a single city of war in the East; that in which you now are belongs to several different nations; by remaining here, you inspire no fear in the infidels, and you allow the audacity of your enemies in Europe to increase; you expose yourself to the risk of losing both the kingdom of France, where your absence may embolden ambitious neighbours, and the kingdom of Jesus Christ, upon which your presence will draw the attacks of the Mussulmans. We are all persuaded that the pride of the Saracens should be punished; but it is not in a country far distant from home that the preparations for a decisive and glorious war can be carried on. Thus, then, we advise you to return into the West, where you will watch in safety over the welfare of your states; where you will obtain, amidst a peace which is your own work, the necessary means for avenging our defeats, and, some day, repairing the reverses we have undergone."

The duke of Anjou, the duke of Poictiers, and most of the French nobles, who spoke after Guy de Malvoisin, expressed the same opinion. When they came to the count of Jaffa, he refused to speak, saying, "that he possessed several castles in Palestine, and might be accused of defending his own personal interests." Upon being pressed by the king to give his opinion as the others had done, he contented himself with saying, "that the glory of the Christian arms, that the safety of the land of Jesus Christ, required that the Crusaders should not at that time return to Europe." When it came to Joinville's turn, the good seneschal remembered the advice that his cousin, the seigneur de Bollaincourt, had given him on the eve of his departure for the crusade. "You are going beyond the seas,"—it was thus the good seigneur Bollaincourt expressed himself,—"but take care how you return; no knight, either poor or rich, can come back without shame, if he leaves any of the common people in whose company he quits France in the hands of the Saracens." Joinville, full of the remembrance of these words, declared that they could not abandon the great numbers of Christian prisoners without shame. "These unhappy captives," added he, "were in the service of the king as well as in the service of God; and never will they escape from their captivity if the king should go away." There was not one of the lords and knights who had not either relations or friends among the prisoners; therefore, many of them could not restrain their tears whilst listening to Joinville; but this kindly feeling was not sufficiently strong to stifle in their hearts their desire to revisit their own country. In vain the seneschal added that the king had still a portion of his treasure left; that he could raise troops in the Morea and other countries; and that with the succours which would come from Europe, they should soon be in a condition to renew the war. These reasons, with many others, made no impression upon the greater part of the assembly; they could only view the crusade as a long and painful exile. The sieur de Chastenai, and Beaumont marshal of France, were all that agreed with the opinion of Joinville. "What shall we reply," said they, "to those who shall ask us on our return what we have done with the heritage and the soldiers of Jesus Christ? Listen to the unfortunate inhabitants of Palestine: they accuse us of having brought war to them, and reproach us with preparing their entire ruin by our departure. If we do not receive succours, it will be then time enough to go; but why anticipate days of despair? The Crusaders, it is true, are not in great numbers; but can we forget that their leader, even when in chains, made himself respected by the Saracens? Report, likewise, tells us, that discord prevails among our enemies, and that the sultan of Damascus has declared war against the Mamelukes of Egypt." These two knights spoke amidst the murmurs of their companions; and the more reasonable the opinions they advanced appeared, the greater was the impatience with which they were listened to. The seigneur de Beaumont was about to continue; but he was interrupted with great warmth by his uncle, John de Beaumont, who loaded him with the most bitter reproaches. In vain the king urged the right that every one had to express his opinion; authority of blood prevailed over the authority of the king; the stern old man continued to raise his voice, and reduced his nephew to silence. When he had received the opinions of the assembly, the king dismissed them, and convoked them again for the following Sunday. Upon leaving the council, Joinville found himself exposed to the railleries and insults of the knights, for having expressed an opinion contrary to that of the general meeting. To complete his chagrin, he thought he had incurred the displeasure of the king; and in his despair, he formed the resolution of joining the prince of Antioch, his relation. As he was revolving these gloomy thoughts in his mind, the king took him aside, and opening his heart to him, declared that it was his intention to remain some time longer in Palestine. Then Joinville forgot all the scoffs of the barons and knights; he was so joyous with what the king had told him, that all his griefs were at an end. On the following Sunday the barons assembled for the third time. The king of France invoked the inspiration of the Holy Ghost by a sign of the cross, and pronounced the following words:—Seigneurs, I thank equally those who have advised me to remain in Asia, and those who have advised me to return to the West. Both, I am convinced, had no other view but the interest of my kingdom and the glory of Jesus Christ. After the most serious and lengthened reflection, I think I may, without injury or peril to my states, prolong my sojourn in this country. The queen, my mother, has defended the honour of my crown in troublesome times; she will now exhibit the same firmness, and will meet with fewer obstacles. No, my kingdom will not suffer by my absence; but if I quit this land, for which Europe has made so many sacrifices, who will protect it against its enemies? Is it to be wished, that, having come here to defend the kingdom of Jerusalem, I shall be hereafter reproached with its ruin? I remain then to save that which is left, to deliver our prisoners, and if possible, to take advantage of the discords of the Saracens. I am not willing, however, to impose restraint upon anybody; such as are desirous of quitting the East are free to depart; as to those who shall determine to remain beneath the banners of the cross, I promise that they shall want for nothing, and that I will ever share with them both good and ill fortune."

After these words, says Joinville, most were astonished, and many began to shed hot tears

CHRISTIAN CAVALIERS CAPTIVE AT CAIRO.

The knights and barons were still ignorant of the conclusion of the treaty, and, daily encouraged by the priests to maintain their religion and their courage, they were revolving in their minds their customary melancholy reflections, when they saw an old Saracen enter their pavilion. His venerable figure and the gravity of his carriage inspired respect. His train, composed of men-at-arms, inspired fear. The old man, without any preliminary discourse, asked the prisoners, by means of an interpreter, if it was true that they believed in a God, born of a woman, crucified for the salvation of the human race, resuscitated the third day? All having answered at once that that was their belief: "In that case," added he, "congratulate yourselves at suffering for your God; you are yet far from having suffered as much for him as he suffered for you. Place your hopes in him, and if he has been able to recall himself to life, he will not want power to put an end to the evils that afflict you now."—BOOK XIV.

From that time, the dukes of Anjou and Poictiers, with a great number of the leaders, made preparations for their departure. Louis charged them with a letter addressed to the clergy, the nobility, and people of his kingdom. In this letter, Louis described, with a noble simplicity, the victories, defeats, and captivity of the Christian knights, and conjured his subjects of all classes to take up arms for the assistance of the Holy Land.

As soon as the two brothers of the king were gone, a levy of soldiers was commenced, and Palestine was placed in a state of defence. But that which most materially favoured the Crusaders, and gave a chance of security to the Christian colonies, was the discord that then prevailed among the Saracens. After the murder of Almoadam, the Mussulmans of Syria refused to recognise the authority of the Mamelukes. The principality and city of Damascus had recently been given up to Nasser, who was preparing to march against Cairo, at the head of a formidable army; the greatest agitation reigned amongst the Mamelukes of Egypt, in whom remorse seemed to be accompanied by fear. The sultana, Chegger-Eddour, was forced to descend from the throne, and to yield the supreme authority to the Turcoman Ezz-Eddin, whose wife she had become. This change allayed agitation for a time; but in such a state of things, one revolution seemed immediately to bring on another. The turbulent, restless soldiery, that had overthrown the empire of the Ayoubites, could neither endure that which was ancient, nor that which was new. To suppress sedition, the leaders at one time exhibited to the multitude a child of that family which they had proscribed, and decorated him with the vain title of sultan. They afterwards declared that Egypt belonged to the caliph of Bagdad, and that they governed it in his name.

It was at this period that the sultan of Aleppo and Damascus sent ambassadors to Louis IX. to invite the French monarch to unite with him to chastise the pride and the revolt of the soldiery of Cairo. He promised the Christians to share with them the spoils of the conquered, and to restore to them the kingdom of Jerusalem. These brilliant promises were likely to produce an effect upon the king of France, and at least merited all his attention. The emirs of Egypt equally solicited the alliance of the Christians, and proposed very advantageous conditions. In the choice before him, there were powerful motives to incline the king to the party of the sultan of Damascus. He had, on one side, to treat with emirs whose good-will was very uncertain, whose fortune might be transitory, and whose authority was menaced and tottering. On the other, he had to deal with a powerful prince, whose authority being much better established, offered a more sure guarantee to his allies. Another motive, which could not be indifferent in the eyes of the virtuous monarch, was, that the only aim of the policy of the Mamelukes was to secure impunity for a great crime, and that the sovereign of Damascus was aiming to avenge the cause of princes. All these considerations were, no doubt, presented in the council of Louis, and must have left the monarch great difficulty in deciding which side it would be best for him to take. But he could not forget that he had signed a treaty with the emirs, and that nothing could liberate him from his oath; but above all, he could not forget that the Mamelukes still held in their hands the destiny of twelve thousand Christian prisoners, and that by breaking with them, he should renounce the hope of delivering the unhappy companions of his captivity. Louis answered the Syrian ambassadors, that he would willingly join his arms to those of the sultan of Damascus, if the Mamelukes did not perform their treaties. At the same time, he sent John de Valence to Cairo, with directions to offer the emirs peace or war. The latter promised at length to fulfil all the conditions of the treaty, if Louis should consent to become their ally and auxiliary: more than two hundred knights were immediately set at liberty.

These unfortunate victims of the crusade arrived at Ptolemaïs about the month of October (1251): the people flocked in crowds to see them land; they exhibited too evident signs of their late captivity, and the remembrance of what they had undergone, together with their present wretchedness, drew tears of compassion from all the spectators. These prisoners, whose chains Louis had succeeded in breaking, brought with them, in a kind of triumph, a coffin, containing the bones of Gauthier de Brienne, who fell into the hands of the infidels at the battle of Gaza, and had been massacred by a furious mob at Cairo. The clergy accompanied the remains of the Christian hero to the church of the Hospitallers; and the companions in arms of Gauthier described his exploits and the glorious death he had undergone for the cause of Christ. Religion displayed all its pomps, and in its holy songs celebrated the glory of a martyr, and the devotion that it alone had inspired. The charity of the faithful relieved and consoled the misery of the captives, and Louis took into his service all whom age or infirmities rendered incapable of bearing arms.

The king learnt with much pain that many Christian prisoners still remained in Egypt. As the Egyptian ambassadors arrived at that time at Ptolemaïs, Louis IX. declared that they must not at all depend upon the alliance they came to solicit, if the emirs did not hasten to liberate all the captives and all the children of Christians brought up in the Mussulman faith, and even send to him the heads of the Crusaders that had been exposed upon the walls of Cairo.

Thus the position of the Christians was ameliorated daily by the divisions among their enemies. The king of France dictated the conditions to the emirs, and if he had had troops, he might have repaired some of the reverses he had experienced in Egypt; but the East furnished him with but a very small number of soldiers, and the West did not seem at all disposed to send him any supplies.

The king of Castile, who had taken the cross, died at the moment he was preparing to set out. In England, Henry III., who had likewise assumed the cross, obtained from the pope and the parliament the power to levy a tenth upon his people and clergy; he at the same time imposed enormous taxes upon the Jews of his kingdom. The preachers of the crusade were directed to announce his approaching departure for the East, and he himself swore upon the Gospel, in the presence of the assembled barons and people, that he would go to the Holy Land, at the head of his army; but after having obtained what he wanted, he forgot all his promises.

Frederick II., at the moment he was about to assist Louis IX., died at Naples; and his death proved to be a fresh source of trouble and agitation for Christendom. Although he had, when dying, bequeathed a hundred thousand ounces of gold for the succour of the Holy Land, and by his testament had restored to the Church all that had belonged to it, Innocent received the news of his death with a joy that he did not seek to conceal. "Let the Heavens rejoice!" wrote he to the clergy and people of Sicily; "let the earth be in gladness!" and he pursued with anathemas the memory of a prince who had borne the title of king of Jerusalem during thirty-eight years. He excommunicated Conrad, whom Frederick had named as his successor to the empire; he sent emissaries into the kingdom of Naples, to corrupt the fidelity of the people; and ecclesiastics in Germany received the mission to preach a crusade against the princes of the house of Swabia.

France was not less agitated than other countries; on the return of the dukes of Anjou and Poictiers, the letter of Louis addressed to his subjects was read in all the churches. This letter revived all the sorrow that had been felt when the account was received of the captivity of the king and his army. The exhortations which Louis addressed to the French to obtain assistance, together with the news that arrived daily from the East, affected all hearts; and as the people have no idea of moderation in either grief or joy, a spirit of sedition, mixed with enthusiasm for the crusade, agitated the cities, pervaded the provinces, and, for a time, placed the kingdom in peril.

Princes and magnates having failed in their enterprise, the multitude was led to believe that Christ rejected the great ones of the earth from his service, and was only willing to have for defenders humble men, shepherds, and labourers. A man appeared, who undertook, with the help of this popular opinion, to inflame the public mind, and to create a general movement. This man, named Jacob, born in Hungary, and far advanced in age, was said to have preached the crusade of children, of which we have spoken in the twelfth book of this work. A long beard, which descended to his girdle, with a pale face and mysterious language, gave him the air of a prophet. He passed from hamlet to hamlet, saying that he was sent by Heaven to deliver the city of God, and avenge the king of France. Shepherds left their flocks, labourers laid down the plough to follow his footsteps. Jacob, who was called the master of Hungary, caused a standard to be borne before him, upon which was painted a lamb, the symbol of the Saviour of the world; provisions were brought to him from all parts, and his disciples asserted that, like Christ, he had the gift of multiplying loaves.

The name of *Pastors* was given to these village Crusaders. Their first meetings, to which little attention was paid, were held in the provinces of Flanders and Picardy; they then directed their course towards Amiens, and afterwards towards the capital; increasing as they went, with a crowd of vagabonds, thieves, and prostitutes. Although they had committed some disorders, Queen Blanche tolerated them, in the hope they might be the means of procuring some assistance for the king. The implied protection of the queen regent inflamed their pride, and impunity increased their license and redoubled their audacity. The impostor Jacob and the other heads of his gang, with whom chance or corruption had associated him, declaimed with vehemence against the wealth and the supremacy of the clergy, which pleased the multitude they drew at their heels; to the great scandal of all pious men, they themselves performed sacerdotal functions, and took the place, in the pulpits, of the sacred orators, employing violence against the ministers of the altars, and seeking to awaken the passions of the people. At length, assembled to the number of more than a hundred thousand, these redoubtable pilgrims left Paris, and divided themselves into several troops, to repair to the coast, whence they were to embark for the East. The city of Orleans, which happened to be in their passage, became the theatre of frightful disorders. The progress of their enormities at length created serious alarm in the government and the magistracy; orders were sent to the provinces to pursue and disperse these turbulent and seditious bands. The most numerous assemblage of the pastors was fixed to take place at Bourges, where the master of Hungary was to perform miracles and communicate the will of Heaven. Their arrival in that city was the signal for murder, fire, and pillage. The irritated people took up arms and marched against these disturbers of the public peace; they overtook them between Mortemer and Villeneuve-sur-le-Cher, where, in spite of their numbers, they were routed, and received the punishment due to their brigandages. Jacob had his head cut off by the blow of an axe; many of his companions and disciples met with death on the field of battle, or were consigned to punishment; the remainder took to flight.

Thus this storm, formed so suddenly, was dispersed in the same manner; another band, which had directed its course towards Bordeaux, was likewise subdued; some of the pastors who succeeded in getting to England, were served in the same way. A report was spread that correspondences with the Saracens had been found upon the persons of their leaders, and they were accused of having formed the project of delivering up Christian people to the swords of the infidels; which accusation, however improbable, completed the hatred the people began to entertain for them. The government, which had not at first strength enough to oppose them, armed the passions of the multitude against them, and tranquillity was soon reëstablished in the kingdom.

In the mean time the crusade to the East was preached in most of the countries of Europe; new indulgences were added to those which had been accorded to the soldiers of Christ; the bishop of Avignon received power to absolve those who had struck clerks, or burnt churches; the same bishop had the faculty of converting all vows, except that of religion, into a vow for the crusade: similar powers were given to the prior of the Jacobins at Paris. These new encouragements might have aroused a momentary ardour in the faithful, if the court of Rome had not been constantly diverted from the cares of a crusade in the East, by the war it had declared against the house of Swabia. The Holy See willingly granted dispensations to Crusaders who took a part in its cause, or who paid it a tribute; which made the good bishop of Lincoln accuse Innocent of exchanging the treasures of heaven for those of earth, and of selling the Crusaders as the heifers and rams of sacrifice were formerly sold in the Temple. At length, no longer concealing either his hatred or his ambition, the sovereign pontiff ordered the Cordeliers to preach a crusade against the heir and successor of Frederick; the indulgence for those who took the cross extended to the father and mother of the Crusaders, a thing that had never taken place in any other crusade. At the moment when Louis IX. was so earnestly requesting succour, the preaching of this impious crusade excited great scandal among the French nobility; the new Crusaders were treated as rebels; Queen Blanche caused their lands to be seized; and the princes and lords followed the example of the queen in their domains. The Cordeliers were severely reprimanded, and thier preaching proved ineffectual.

Whilst the crusade against Conrad was being suppressed, no increased zeal was exhibited for the war in the East. Those who entertained the warmest attachment for Louis IX. might with justice believe, that by sending him assistance they should prolong his absence. Thus, in spite of the reiterated prayers of the king, France, which had shed so many tears over his captivity, could not resolve to take up arms to succour him, and was satisfied with putting up vows for his return.

All that Blanche was able to do for her son was to send him a vessel laden with money, which was lost on the coast of Syria. A small number of those who had taken the cross in the West, determined to cross the sea; the young count of Eu, and Raymond count of Turenne, whom the queen commanded to set out for Palestine, were almost the only nobles of this party. Most of the knights and barons that had remained in Palestine with the king, having spent everything, and being entirely ruined, fixed so high a price upon their services, and, according to the expression of the commissaries of Louis, *made themselves so dear*, that the treasury of the monarch would not suffice to support them. Levies were made in Greece, in Cyprus, and in the Christian cities of Syria; but these levies only brought to the banners of the crusade a few adventurers, very ill calculated to share the labours and dangers of a great enterprise.

Among the warriors whom the love of danger and distant adventures led at this time to the Holy Land, history speaks of Alemar of Selingan. This knight had come from a country of the West, in which the summer, he said, had almost no nights. Selingan and his companions sought every opportunity for signalizing their skill in arms and their romantic bravery. Whilst waiting for the happy moment at which they might fight with the Saracens, they made war upon the lions, which they pursued on horseback into the deserts, and killed with their arrows; which was a subject of great surprise and admiration for the French warriors.

Another very noble knight also arrived, says Joinville, who was called De Toucy. The chevalier de Toucy had been regent of the Latin empire of Constantinople, in the absence of Baldwin, and prided himself upon belonging to the family of the kings of France. In company with nine other knights, he abandoned an empire which was falling rapidly to ruin, in order to endeavour to support the miserable remains of the kingdom of Jerusalem. Toucy related the misfortunes of Baldwin, and the deplorable circumstances that had forced a Christian emperor to ally himself with a chief of the Comans. According to the custom of the barbarians, the prince of the Comans and the emperor of Constantinople had punctured themselves, and mixing the blood in a cup, had both drunk of it, as a sign of alliance and brotherhood. The knights who accompanied the seigneur de Toucy had borrowed this practice of the barbarians: the French warriors at first were disgusted with it; but soon, led away by the strange novelty of the thing, they themselves mingled their blood with that of their companions, and diluting it with floods of wine, they got intoxicated together over the mystical draught, which, as they said, made them brothers.

The manners and customs of the Eastern nations strongly raised the curiosity and fixed the attention of the Crusaders. When the missionaries whom Louis IX. had sent into Tartary returned to Ptolemaïs, the French warriors were never tired of interrogating and listening to them. Andrew de Lonjumeau, who was at the head of the mission, had set out from Antioch, and travelling ten leagues every day, had prosecuted his journey for a year before he arrived at the place at which the great khan of the Tartars resided. The missionaries traversed deserts where they met with enormous heaps of human bones—sad monuments of the victories of a barbarous people: they related marvellous things of the court of the monarch of the Moguls, of the manners and customs of the countries they had travelled through, of the conquests and legislation of Gengiskhan, and of the prodigies which had prepared the power and greatness of the conqueror of Asia. Among the extraordinary and somewhat fabulous circumstances they related, the Christians learned with much joy that the religion of Christ was extending its empire among the most distant nations; the missionaries declared they had seen, in a single horde of Tartars, more than eight hundred chapels, in which the praises of the true God were celebrated. Louis IX. hoped that the Moguls might some day become auxiliaries of the Christians in the great struggle against the infidels; and this hope made him resolve to send fresh missionaries into Tartary.

But if the Crusaders were thus astonished at all they heard concerning the most distant regions of Asia, they had close to them a barbarous colony which must have excited their surprise to a still greater degree. Some months after his arrival, Louis received an embassy from the Old Man of the Mountains, who, as we have already said, reigned over about thirty villages or towns, built on the southern declivity of Mount Libanus. The envoys of the prince of the Assassins, when admitted into the presence of the king of France, asked him if he was acquainted with their master. "I have heard of him," replied the monarch. "Why, then," added one of the ambassadors, "have you not sought after his friendship by sending him presents, as the emperor of Germany, the king of Hungary, the sultan of Cairo, and so many other great princes have done?" The king listened to this strange language without anger, and appointed the ambassadors another audience, at which the grand masters of the Templars and the Hospitallers were present. The name alone of the two military orders, which the poniard of the Assassins did not venture to attack, inspired some degree of terror in the Old Man of the Mountain, who had been constrained to pay them a tribute. In the second audience, the two grand masters sternly reproved the ambassadors, and told them that if the lord of the Mountain did not send presents to the king of France, his insolence would draw upon him a prompt and just chastisement. The envoys repeated these threatening words to their master, who himself experienced some of the fear he wished to inspire, and sent them back to Louis to express much more pacific sentiments. Among the presents which they were charged to offer to the king of the Franks, there were several vases, a chess-board, and an elephant in rock crystal; to these the lord of the Mountain added a shirt and a ring, as symbols of alliance, according to which, said the envoys to the French monarch, "you and our master will remain united as the fingers of the hand are, and as the shirt is to the body."*

---

* The reader may remember a curious ceremony of alliance, wherein the one party passes through the shirt of the other whilst he has it on.—TRANS.

Louis IX. received this new embassy with distinction, and by their hands sent to the prince of the Assassins vases of gold and silver, and stuffs of scarlet and silk; he commanded brother Yves, a man learned in Arabic, to accompany them. Yves, who remained for some time at the court of the Old Man of the Mountain, on his return related many curious particulars, which history has not despised. The prince of the Assassins belonged to the sect of Ali, and professed some admiration for the Gospel. He had, in particular, a veneration for *Monseigneur St. Peter*, who, according to his belief, was still living, and whose soul, he said, had been successively that of Abel, Noah, and Abraham. Brother Yves spoke strongly of the terror with which the Old Man of the Mountain inspired his subjects. A fearful silence reigned around his palace, and when he appeared in public, he was preceded by a herald-at-arms, who cried with a loud voice, "Whoever you may be, dread to appear before him who holds the life and death of kings in his hands."

Whilst these marvellous recitals were amusing the leisure of the Crusaders, war was declared between the sultans of Damascus and Cairo. The Christian warriors, impatient for fight, sighed at being thus condemned to waste their time in listless idleness. But they mustered scarcely seven hundred knights beneath the banners of the cross; and their small number would not permit Louis to think of attempting any important enterprise.

Whilst anxiously looking forward to the perils and hazards of war, the holy monarch never relaxed in his endeavours to ameliorate the destiny and break the chains of the captives who still remained in the hands of the Mussulmans. But the captivity of the Christian warriors was not the only grief with which his heart was afflicted: it added greatly to his sorrow to learn that many of his companions in arms had embraced Islamism. It is a singular circumstance to remark that the Crusaders, whose aim always was to bring about the triumph of Christianity, present us with frequent examples of apostasy, and history does not hesitate to affirm, that during the course of the holy wars more Christians became Mussulmans than Mussulmans became Christians. Joinville informs us in his Memoirs, that most of the mariners who manned the Christian fleet in the retreat from Mansourah, renounced their faith to save their lives: in these disastrous days, many warriors were unable to resist the menaces of the Saracens, and the fear of death made them forget a religion for which they had taken up arms. We have seen what evils the Crusaders had endured in the expeditions to the East; among the crowd of pilgrims there were always some who had not sufficient virtue to pass through the ordeal of great misfortunes: on the arrival of Louis IX. in Egypt, that country already contained many of these perjured and unfaithful Christians, who, in the perils and calamities of preceding wars, had forsaken the God of their fathers. All these renegadoes were despised by the Saracens. Oriental authors quote a saying of Saladin's on this subject, which expresses an opinion generally established, and which was maintained to the very last days of the crusades; he said that *a good Christian was never made of a bad Mussulman, nor a good Mussulman of a bad Christian.* History affords a few details upon the lives of these degenerate Franks, who had renounced their religion and their country; many employed themselves in agriculture and the mechanical arts; a great number were enrolled in the Mussulman armies; some obtained employments, and succeeded in amassing great wealth. We may well, however, believe, that remorse empoisoned every moment of their lives, and would not permit them to enjoy the advantages they had acquired among the infidels: the religion they had quitted still inspired them with respect, and the presence and language of the Franks, who had been their brothers, recalled to them the most saddening remembrances; but, withheld by I know not what false shame, and as if God had struck them with an eternal reprobation, they remained chained to their error by an invincible link, and although sensible of the misery of living in a foreign land, they did not dare to entertain the idea of returning to their own country.

One of these renegadoes, born at Provins, who had fought under the banners of John of Brienne, came to salute Louis IX., and bring him presents, at the moment the monarch was embarking on the Nile, to repair to Palestine. As Joinville told him, that if he persisted in practising the religion of Mahomet, *he would go straight to hell after his death;* he replied, that he believed the religion of Christ to be better than that of the prophet of Mecca; but, he added, that if he returned to the faith of the Christians, he should sink into poverty, and that during the rest of his life he should be loaded with infamous reproaches, and be everywhere hooted as a renegado! a renegado! Thus, the fear of poverty, together with a dread of the judgments of the world, held fast the deserters from the Christian faith, and prevented their return to the belief they had abandoned. Louis IX. neglected no means to bring them back to the right path; his liberality always met half-way such as were disposed to revert to Christianity; and to shield them from the contempt of men, he issued an ordinance that none should reproach them with their apostasy.

The king of France expended considerable sums in placing several of the Christian cities in a state of defence; the towers and walls of Cæsarea, as well as those of Ptolemaïs, were heightened and enlarged; the walls and fortifications of Jaffa and Cäipha, which were almost in ruins, were repaired. Amidst these useful labours, carried on in peace, the warriors remained idle, and not a few of them began to be forgetful of both military discipline and Gospel morality. The precaution that the sieur de Joinville took to place his bed in such a manner as to remove all evil thoughts respecting his familiarity with women, proves that the morals of the Christian knights were not entirely free from suspicion at least. Louis was much more severe against licentiousness of manners than he had been during his abode at Damietta. History mentions several instances of his severity; and such was the strangeness of the penal laws charged with the protection of public decency and morality, that excess of libertinism would at the present day appear less scandalous than the punishments then inflicted on the guilty.

The clergy, however, never relaxed in their endeavours to recall the Crusaders to the principles of the Christian religion; and their efforts were not fruitless. There was no city, no place in Palestine, that did not remind the warriors of the holy traditions of the Scriptures, or of the mercy and justice of God. Many of the French nobles, who had been models of courage, showed an equally bright example of devotion and piety. It was common to see the bravest knights lay down their arms, and assuming the scrip and staff of the pilgrim, repair to the spots consecrated by the miracles and the presence of Christ and the holy personages whose memory is preserved by religion. Louis himself visited Mount Thabor and the village of Cana several times, and went on a pilgrimage to Nazareth. The sultan of Damascus, who sought every opportunity of forming an alliance with him, invited him to come as far as Jerusalem; and this pilgrimage would have crowned the wishes of the pious monarch; but his barons, and more particularly the bishops, represented to him that it was not befitting for him to enter Jerusalem as a simple pilgrim, and that he had come into the East not only to visit, but to deliver the holy tomb. They added, that the Western princes who should take the cross after him, would believe, from his example, that they had fulfilled their duty, and performed their vow, by merely visiting the holy city; and thus the devotion of the Crusaders would no longer have the deliverance of the sepulchre of Christ for its object. Louis IX. yielded to the representations of the prelates, and consented not to visit Jerusalem at that time, as he still cherished the hope of one day entering it sword in hand. But this hope was doomed soon to fade away—God never afterwards permitted the holy city to be wrested from the yoke of the infidels.

The sultans of Cairo and Damascus continued to negotiate with the monarch of the Franks. Each of these two Mussulman princes hoped to have the Christians for allies, and was particularly anxious not to have them for enemies. Every time they entertained a fear of being vanquished, the emirs of Egypt renewed their proposals, and they at length accepted all the conditions that the Christians required. A treaty was concluded, by which the Mamelukes engaged to liberate all the captives that remained in Egypt, the children of Christians brought up in the Mussulman faith, and, which had often been demanded by Louis, the heads of the martyrs of the cross that had been exposed upon the walls of Cairo. Jerusalem and all the cities of Palestine, with the exception of Gaza, Daroum, and two other fortresses, were to be placed in the hands of the Franks. The treaty likewise stipulated that, during fifteen years, the kingdom of Jerusalem should have no war with Egypt; that the two states should combine their forces; and that all conquests should be shared between the Christians and the Mamelukes. Some ecclesiastics expressed their doubts and scruples upon an alliance with the enemies of Christ; but the pious monarch disdained to notice their representations; no treaty had ever offered so many advantages for the Christian cause, if good faith had presided over its execution; but the generous loyalty of Louis rendered him incapable of suspecting fraud or perfidy in his allies, or even in his enemies.

The leaders of the Mussulmans were to repair to Gaza, and from thence to Jaffa, to confirm the alliance they had just contracted, and to arrange with the French king the plan for carrying on the war. When the sultan of Damascus heard of the treaty thus entered into, he sent an army of twenty thousand men to take a position between Gaza and Daroum, so as to prevent the junction of the Egyptians and Franks. Whether the Mamelukes were prevented by their internal divisions, or whether they did not dare to face the troops of Damascus, they did *not* appear at Jaffa at the time agreed upon. They, however, fulfilled all the other conditions of the treaty, and added to the convoy of captives and funereal relics, the present of an elephant, which Louis sent to Henry III. of England. As they often repeated their promise of coming to Jaffa, Louis was constantly in expectation of them, and waited for them an entire year. The French monarch being thus deceived in his hopes, might, without injustice, have renounced a treaty that the other contracting party did not execute; he might again have opened a communication with the sultan of Damascus, who offered the same advantages, with much more probability of his promises being fulfilled. The emirs of Egypt had sought the alliance of the Christians when their own situation appeared desperate, and when they had reason to believe that the king of France would receive succours from the West; seeing, however, that Louis had no army, and that all the forces he could muster did not amount to more than seven hundred knights, they were fearful of entering too deeply into engagements that would expose them to the hatred of the Mussulmans, without offering them any substantial support against their enemies. All these emirs, besides, only fought to secure for themselves impunity for their crime, and to be left in quiet possession of the fruits of their revolt. They were at all times ready to lay down their arms, if they procured pardon for the past, and had Egypt abandoned to them. The caliph of Bagdad was always anxious to establish peace among the Mussulman powers; he prevailed upon the sultan of Damascus and Aleppo to forget his causes of resentment, and upon the emirs of Egypt to express repentance, with a desire for peace. Several battles were fought without any decisive results; in one of these battles a party of Syrian troops were defeated by the Mamelukes, and fled away towards Damascus; whilst other bodies of Mamelukes were beaten by the Syrians, and pursued up to the gates of Cairo. A war in which victory was always uncertain, necessarily weakened the courage and exhausted the patience of both parties; and they appealed to the spiritual father of the Mussulmans to arbitrate between them. The sultans of Syria and Egypt at length concluded a peace, and agreed to unite their arms against the Christians. From that time the hopes of the Crusaders all vanished; the king of France, from having procrastinated so long,

DEATH OF ALMOADAM.

Almoadam, nearly surrounded by the flames, precipitates himself from the window; a nail catches his mantle, and he remains for a moment suspended. At length he falls to the earth; sabres and naked swords wave over him on all sides; he casts himself on his knees, at the feet of Octai, one of the principal officers of his guard, who repulses him with contempt. The unhappy prince arises, holding forth his imploring hands to all the assembly, saying that he was willing to abandon the throne of Egypt, and would return into Mesopotamia. These supplications, unworthy of a prince, inspire more contempt than pity; nevertheless, the crowd of conspirators hesitate; but the leaders know too well there can be no safety for them but in completing the crime they have begun. Bendocdar, who had inflicted the first blow, strikes him a second time with his sabre; Almoadam, streaming with blood, throws himself into the Nile, and endeavours to gain some vessels that appear to be drawing near the shore to receive him; nine Mamelukes follow him into the water, and pour upon him a thousand blows, within sight of the galley which Joinville was on board of!—BOOK XIV.

and at the same time neglected a favourable opportunity, had, all at once, two united enemies to dread. It is necessary to be perfectly acquainted with the situation and policy of the Mussulman powers, to ascertain how far history has reason to blame the indecision and tardiness of Louis IX. Le père Maimbourg does not scruple to blame him with much severity, and declares plainly, *that to be a saint, it appears not necessary to be infallible, particularly in political affairs, and even still less in those of war.*

The treaty concluded between the Mamelukes and Syrians was the signal for war; the sultan of Damascus, at the head of an army, came under the very walls of Ptolemaïs, and threatened to ravage the gardens and fields which supplied the city with provisions, if the inhabitants did not pay him a tribute of fifty thousand golden byzants. The Christians were not in a condition to resist their enemies, if the latter had then had any intention of attacking them in earnest; but the Syrians, exhausted by fatigue, were in want of provisions, and returned to Damascus, whilst the Mamelukes, at the same time, retook the route to Cairo; both of them departing with an intention of returning on the first favourable occasion to invade and desolate Palestine.

The threats of the Mussulmans redoubled the zeal and the efforts of Louis to place the Christian cities in a state of defence; he determined to restore the fortifications of Sidon, which had been demolished by the Saracens of Damascus, at the time that the Crusaders landed in Egypt. He sent a great number of workmen into this city, and the works were rapidly advancing, when they were all at once interrupted by the most deplorable occurrence. The place having a weak garrison, was surprised, and every Christian it contained put to the sword by the Turcomans, a wandering, ferocious race, accustomed to live by murder and plunder. Louis was at Tyre when he learned this disastrous news, and was about to go to Sidon. Some of the few Syrian inhabitants that had escaped the carnage, described to him the unheard-of cruelties of the barbarians; the fury of the Turcomans had spared neither age nor sex, and in their retreat they had slaughtered two thousand prisoners. Louis, deeply afflicted by what he heard, formed at once the determination to go and attack the Turcomans in Belinas, to which place they had retired. At the first signal all the warriors that accompanied him eagerly assumed their armour. The king wished to place himself at their head, but the barons strongly opposed his intention, saying, "that he must not expose a life of so much consequence to the Holy Land, in such an expedition. The Christian warriors set forward on their march. Belinas, or Cæsarea Philippi, was built upon a declivity of Mount Libanus, near the sources of the Jordan: the place was only to be approached by narrow roads and steep ascents; but nothing could stop the Crusaders, impatient to avenge their murdered brethren. Upon their arrival at Belinas, the enemy fled in all directions; the city was taken, and this victory would have been complete, if the Christian warriors had observed the laws of discipline, and followed the orders of their leaders. Whilst the French were taking possession of Belinas, the Teutonic knights went to attack a Mussulman castle, built upon the neighbouring heights, whose towers appeared mingled with the peaks of Libanus. The Saracens, who had rallied at this place, and began to recover their courage, repulsed the assailants, and pursued them across the rocks and precipices. The precipitate retreat of the Teutonic knights threw the other Christian warriors into confusion; these latter being huddled together upon a mountainous piece of ground, where they could neither fight on horseback nor form a line of battle. The sieur de Joinville, who led the king's guards, was more than once upon the point of losing his life, or of falling into the hands of the Turcomans. At length the French, by hard fighting, repaired the error of the Germans; Olivier de Thermes, and the warriors he commanded, succeeded in repulsing the Mussulmans. The Crusaders, after having pillaged Belinas, abandoned it, and returned to Sidon.

Louis IX. arrived there before them: on his approach to the city, what was his sorrow at seeing on his route the ground covered with plundered and bloody carcases! These were the miserable remains of the Christians that had been slain by the Turcomans. They were putrefying fast, and there had been no one to undertake the charge of burying them. Louis stopped at beholding the melancholy spectacle, and turning to the legate, requested him to consecrate a cemetery, and then gave orders for the burial of the dead that covered the roads; but instead of obeying him, every one turned away his eyes and recoiled with disgust. Louis then sprang from his horse, and taking in his hands one of the bodies from which exhaled an infectious odour, exclaimed, "*Come, my friends, come, let us bestow a little earth upon the martyrs of Jesus Christ.*" The example of the king reanimated the courage and the charity of the persons of his suite; all were eager to imitate him, and the Christians, whom the barbarians had slaughtered, thus received the honours of sepulture. This act of pious devotedness of Louis IX. to the memory of his companions in arms, has been celebrated by all historians; it presents a strange contrast to the insensibility of a hero of modern times, who, in a circumstance almost similar, and in the same country, caused all the wounded who were left upon a field of battle to be poisoned.

The king remained several months at Sidon, employed in fortifying the city. In the mean time Queen Blanche was constantly writing to him and entreating him to return to France, as she greatly feared she should never see her son again.

Her presentiments were but too quickly realized. Louis was still at Sidon, when a message arrived in Palestine, announcing that the queen regent was no more. It was the legate of the pope who first received this melancholy news. He went to seek the king, accompanied by the archbishop of Tyre and Geoffrey de Beaulieu, Louis's confessor. As the prelate announced that he had something important to communicate, and at the same time exhibited marks of great grief upon his countenance, the monarch led him into his chapel, which, according to an old author, "*was his arsenal against all the crosses of the world.*" The prelate began by reminding the king that all that man loves upon the earth was perishable; "be thankful to God," added he, "for having given you a mother who has watched over your family and your kingdom with such anxious care, and so much ability." The legate paused for a moment, and then, breathing a profound sigh, continued, "This tender mother, this virtuous princess, is now in heaven." At these words, Louis uttered a piercing cry, and then burst into a torrent of tears. As soon as he had a little recovered himself, he fell on his knees before the altar, and joining and raising his hands, exclaimed, "I thank you, O my God! for having given me so good a mother; it was a gift of your mercy; you take her back to-day as your own; you know that I loved her above all creatures; but since, before all things, your decrees must be accomplished, O Lord! be your name blessed for ever, and for ever!" Louis sent away the two prelates, and, remaining alone with his confessor, he recited the service for the dead. Two days passed away before he would see anybody. He then desired Joinville to be called, and upon seeing him, said, "Ah! seneschal, I have lost my mother." "Sire," replied Joinville, "I am not surprised at that; you knew that she must die at some time; but I marvel at the great and extravagant grief that you feel for it, you who have always been so wise a prince." When Joinville left the king, *Madame Marie de bonnes Vertus* came to beg that he would come to the queen and endeavour to console her. The good seneschal found Marguerite bathed in tears, and could not refrain from expressing his surprise by saying to her, "It is a difficult matter to believe you are a woman by your weeping, for the grief you show is for the loss of a woman that you hated more than any other in the world." Marguerite replied that it was not, in fact, for the death of Blanche she was weeping, "but for the great uneasiness in which I see the king, and also for our daughter, left under the guardianship of men."

Louis IX. was present every day at a funeral service celebrated in memory of his mother. He sent into the West a great number of jewels and precious stones to be distributed among the principal churches of France; at the same time exhorting the clergy to put up prayers for him and for the repose of the queen Blanche. In proportion with his endeavours to procure prayers for his mother his grief yielded to the hope of seeing her again in heaven; and his mind, when calmed by resignation, found its most effectual consolations in that mysterious tie which still unites us with those we have lost, in that religious sentiment which mixes itself with our affections to purify them, and with our regrets to mitigate them.

The death of Queen Blanche seemed to impose an obligation upon Louis IX. to return to his dominions; and the news he received from the West convinced him that his presence was becoming more necessary every day. A war for the succession of Flanders had broken out again; the truce with England had just expired; the people were murmuring: on the other hand, Louis had now nothing he could undertake in Palestine. He therefore gave his serious attention to the subject of his return; but as if, on this occasion, he mistrusted his own understanding, he determined, before he formed a definitive resolution, to consult the will of God. Processions were made, and prayers were put up in all the Christian cities of Palestine, that Heaven might deign to enlighten those who had been charged with the directing of a war undertaken in its name. The clergy and barons of the kingdom of Jerusalem, persuaded that the presence of Louis was no longer necessary, and that his return to the West might rouse the enthusiasm of the French warriors for a new crusade, advised him to embark for Europe; at the same time expressing their fervent gratitude for all the services he had rendered to the cause of Jesus Christ during five years. On preparing for his departure, Louis left a hundred knights in the Holy Land, under the command of Geoffrey de Sergines, who fought against the Saracens for thirty years, and became, in his old age, viceroy of Jerusalem. Louis quitted Sidon, and, with the queen and three children that he had had in the East, repaired to Ptolemaïs, in the spring of 1254. A fleet of fourteen vessels was ready to receive him and all that remained of the warriors of the crusade. The day being arrived (April 24th), the king, walking on foot, followed by the legate, the patriarch of Jerusalem, and all the nobles and knights of Palestine, took the road to the port, amidst an immense crowd collected on his passage. All classes as they saw him depart, recollected the virtues of which he had given so bright an example, particularly his kindness to the inhabitants of Palestine, whom he had treated as his own subjects. Some expressed their gratitude by warm acclamations, others by a melancholy silence; but all proclaimed him *the father of the Christians*, and implored Heaven to shower its blessings upon the virtuous monarch, and upon the kingdom of France. The countenance of Louis plainly indicated that he fully partook of the regrets of the Christians of the Holy Land; he addressed a few consoling words to them, gave them useful counsels, reproached himself with not having done enough for their cause, and expressed an earnest desire that God would some day judge him worthy of finishing the work of their deliverance.

At length the fleet set sail. Louis had obtained permission from the legate to take with him, in his vessel, the Holy Sacrament, for the assistance of the dying and the sick; so, when beholding altars raised on board a ship, priests clothed in their sacerdotal habits, celebrating divine service, and invoking the protection of Heaven at every hour in the day, it was easy to recognise the pious wreck of a crusade, and the last trophies of the war of Jesus Christ. As the fleet approached the isle of Cyprus, the vessel in which the king was struck violently against a sand-bank; all the crew were seized with terror; the queen and her children uttered piercing cries; but Louis prostrated himself at the foot of the altar, and addressed himself to Him who commands the sea. When the vessel was examined, it was found that it had received considerable damage, and the pilots pressed the king to leave it; but seeing that they themselves did not purpose to abandon the ship, he determined to remain in it. "There is no one here," said he, "who does not love his body as dearly as I do mine; if I leave, they will leave also, and, perhaps, will not see their country for a length of time; I prefer placing myself, my queen, and my children in the hands of God, to doing such an injury to so great a number of people as there are here." These words, inspired by an heroic charity, revived the courage of the sailors and the pilgrims, and they resumed their course. When leaving the coasts of Sicily, the fleet very carefully kept clear of the coast of Tunis, as if a secret presentiment warned the French Crusaders of the misfortunes that awaited them upon that shore in a still more disastrous expedition. A tempest placed the fleet in great peril; it was upon this occasion Queen Marguerite made a vow to offer a ship of silver to St. Nicholas of Lorraine, and requested Joinville to become her security with the patron saint of such as are shipwrecked. Whilst everybody else was in despair, Louis found calmness in a philosophy derived from religion; and when the danger was past, he said to his companions: "See if God has not proved to us how vast is his power, when by means of a single one of the four winds, the king of France, the queen, their children, and so many other persons have escaped drowning." The navigation lasted more than two months, during which many marvellous adventures and accidents were encountered by the pilgrims, which history has preserved an account of, and which would not figure unworthily in a Christian Odyssey.

The fleet at length cast anchor at the isles of Hières. Louis crossed Provence, and passing by Auvergne, arrived at Vincennes on the 5th of September, 1254. The people flocked from all parts to greet him on his passage; the more they appeared to forget his reverses, the more strongly was Louis affected by the remembrance of his lost companions; and the melancholy that clouded his countenance formed a painful contrast with the public joy. His first care was to go to St. Denis, to prostrate himself at the feet of the apostle of France; on the following day he made his public entrance into his capital, preceded by the clergy, the nobility, and the people. He continued to wear the cross upon his shoulder, the sight of which, whilst recalling the cause of his long absence, gave his subjects reason to fear that he had not yet abandoned his enterprise of the crusade. The greater number of the barons and knights that had gone with Louis, had found a grave in either Syria or Egypt. Such as had survived so many disasters, reëntered their castles, which they found deserted and falling to ruins. The good seneschal, after having revisited his home, repaired, barefooted, to the church of St. Nicholas of Lorraine, to discharge the vow of Queen Marguerite. He then set earnestly about repairing the evils his absence had caused, and swore never again to quit the castle of Joinville to seek adventures in Asia.

Thus terminated this holy war, the commencement of which had filled the Christian nations with so much delight, and which had, in the end, plunged the whole West into mourning. Throughout the events I have just described, the seneschal de Joinville has been my guide, and I cannot terminate my recital without paying him the just tribute of my gratitude. The unpretending tone of his narration, the simplicity of his style, the gaiety of his character, have afforded me a happy relief amidst a labour always dry and sometimes revolting. I take delight in beholding him intrepid in the field of battle, preserving his cheerfulness amidst the misfortunes of war, resigned in his captivity, and in all his actions recalling to our minds the true spirit of chivalry. Like his compatriot Villehardouin, he often makes his heroes weep, and as often weeps himself. He braves danger, when danger is present; but he thanks God with all his heart when he has no longer anything to fear.

When I read his memoirs, I am transported back to the thirteenth century, and I think I am listening to a knight who is returned from the crusade, and who tells to me all he has seen and all he has done. He has neither method nor rule; he drops the line of his discourse, and takes it up again; and he extends or abridges his narration, as his imagination is more or less struck by that which he relates. When we read the narratives of Joinville, we are not surprised that Louis should have taken so much delight in his conversation; there is not one of his readers who does not feel the same confidence and friendship for him that the virtuous monarch accorded him, and history adopts without hesitation all that he affirms *upon his honour*, persuaded that he who was bold enough to speak the truth in the courts of kings will not deceive posterity.

The crusade of St. Louis was like that which immediately preceded it. The enthusiasm for these distant expeditions was daily losing its vivacity and its energy: the crusade no longer appeared anything to the knights beyond a common war, in which the spirit of chivalry was a more powerful principle than religion. It was only a religious affair to Louis IX.

The manner in which this crusade was preached in Europe, the troubles amidst which the voices of the preachers were raised, and particularly the means that were employed to levy the tributes in the West, were calculated to turn away all minds from the object that would be supposed to be the governing one in a holy expedition.

And yet Louis took precautions that had been neglected in preceding wars. Three years were employed in preparing this great enterprise; the knights who arrived in the isle of Cyprus could not express their astonishment at seeing the casks of wine piled one upon another, so high that *they appeared like houses;* and heaps of wheat, barley, and other grains, so immense, *that they might be believed to be mountains.* There is no doubt that the princes and nobles who accompanied Louis imitated his example: happy had it been for the Crusaders, if their leaders had shown in war the same prudence and sagacity they displayed in preparing for their expedition!

The French warriors upon all occasions evinced their accustomed bravery; but throughout the crusade there was never exhibited one instance of the genius of a great captain; Louis himself, when in danger, afforded no example to his troops beyond courage and firmness. We have related the prodigies of French valour, and we have described the prodigies of pious resignation in reverses; the Crusaders and their leaders merited, even in their disasters and in the depth of their misery, the esteem and admiration of their enemies; and it is here that history presents the most beautiful spectacle she can offer to man: "*Glory, the faithful companion of misfortune.*"

We have had occasion, in the course of our narrative, to remark that French gaiety never abandoned the cross-knights in their distant expeditions. This gaiety often mixed itself with the saddest images, and sometimes even did not respect severe propriety. We beg to be permitted to repeat on this head a singular anecdote related by Joinville. On the eve of the battle of Mansourah, one of the knights of the seneschal of Champagne, named Landricourt, died; and whilst the funeral honours were being paid to him, six of his companions in arms talked so loud that they interrupted the priest who was chanting mass. Joinville reproved them warmly, and they then laughed aloud, saying they were talking about remarrying the wife of Messire Hugh de Landricourt, *who was on the bier there.* The good Joinville was very much scandalized at such discourse, and ordered them to keep silent. When speaking of this indiscreet gaiety of his knights, the seneschal takes care to add that God punished them on the day of battle; for of all the six, he says, there was not one that was not killed and buried, and whose wife did not afterwards find it convenient to marry again.

The manners of the European knights formed a very striking contrast with those of the Mussulmans, who were always grave and serious, even amidst the festivities in which they celebrated the deliverance of their country and the defeat of the Christians.

We have spoken many times of the want of discipline of the Crusaders; the Saracens were very little better in this respect; but in addition to having the advantage of fighting in their own country, with every foot of which they were acquainted, fortune gave them, in their greatest dangers, skilful and experienced leaders, who knew how to take advantage of all the errors of the Christians, and bring back to their banners that victory that appeared to have been driven away by the valour of their enemies.

History describes the whole Egyptian nation as struck with terror at the first appearance of the Crusaders; but the Mussulmans, reassured by their leaders, soon felt as much security and confidence as they had experienced alarm; and as if there was nothing that men forgot so easily as danger, a year after the taking of Damietta, they could not conceive what species of madness had led a king of France to the banks of the Nile. The continuator of Tabary relates a circumstance on this subject, which paints at once the opinion and the character of the Mussulmans. The emir Hossam-Eddin, in the course of a conference with the captive monarch, said to him: "How did it come into the mind of the king, whom I perceive endowed with wisdom and good qualities,—how did it ever enter his thoughts to trust himself to a fragile wooden bark, to brave the rocks of the sea, to venture into a country filled with warriors impatient to fight for the Mussulman faith; how could he possibly believe that he should take possession of Egypt, or that he should land upon these coasts, without exposing both himself and his people to the greatest dangers?" The king of France smiled, but made no reply; and the emir thus continued: "Some of the doctors of our law have decided that he who embarks upon the sea twice consecutively, by thus exposing his life and his fortune, renders himself unfit to have his evidence taken in a court of justice, because such gross imprudence sufficiently proves the weakness of his reason and the unsoundness of his judgment." Louis IX. again smiled, and answered the emir: "He who said so was not deceived; that is a wise decision."

We have transcribed the account of the Arabian historian, without according him more credit than he merits. Christian authors have not been less severe towards St. Louis, and can find no excuse for his expedition beyond the seas. Without seeking to justify this crusade, we will content ourselves with saying here, that the aim of Louis IX. was not only to defend the Christian states of Syria and to fight with the enemies of the faith, but to found a colony which might unite the East and the West by the happy interchange of productions and knowledge. We have produced, in the thirteenth book of this history, a letter from the sultan of Cairo, by which it may be plainly perceived, that the king of France had other views than those of a mere conqueror. The historian Mezerai formally says that the project of the king of France was to establish a colony in Egypt, a project of which the execution has been attempted in modern times. "For this purpose," says Mezerai, "he took with him a great number of labourers and artisans, capable, nevertheless, of bearing arms and fighting in case of need." To support our opinion, we might add to the authority of Mezerai that of Leibnitz, who, in a memoir addressed to Louis XIV., does not hesitate to affirm that the motives which determined Louis IX. to undertake the conquest of Egypt, were inspired by profound wisdom, and merited the attention of the most skilful statesmen, and of the most enlightened political writers.

We must however believe that Louis IX. did not contemplate in their full extent the advantages that might be derived from his expedition, or that have been discovered in our age. All the policy of those distant ages consisted in religious ideas, which insinuated themselves into human affairs, and often directed them towards an end that human intelligence was incapable of perceiving. What we do now for the interests of commerce or civilization, was then done for the interests of Christianity; and the results were often the same. Religion, in those times of barbarism and ignorance, was like a mysterious reason, like a sublime instinct, given to man to assist him in his search for all that was doomed to become good and useful to him. We must not forget that the Christian religion always directed the conduct of Louis IX., and that it was to the religious inspirations of this monarch, that France owed those treaties, at which frankness and good faith presided; those institutions that consecrated the principles of justice; and all those monuments of a wise policy, to which modern philosophers have not been able to refuse their admiration.

The expedition of Louis IX. produced two results for Egypt that were not at all expected. Two years after the deliverance of the king, and whilst he was still in Palestine, the Mamelukes, fearing a fresh invasion of the Franks, in order to prevent their enemies from taking Damietta and fortifying themselves in that city, entirely destroyed it. Some years after, as their fears were not yet removed, and the second crusade of Louis IX. spread fresh alarms throughout the East, the Egyptians caused immense heaps of stones to be cast into the mouth of the Nile, in order that the Christian fleets might not be able to sail up the river. Since that period a new Damietta has been built at a small distance from the site of the former city; but the entrance to the Nile is still, in our days, closed against all vessels, a sad and deplorable testimony of the terror which the arms of the Franks formerly inspired.

History has a deeper lament to make over the second consequence of this crusade. It is certain that it contributed greatly to change the form of the Egyptian government, and to fill that unhappy country with all the scourges that military despotism brings in its train. It was a spectacle worthy of our attention and our pity, to see, after a bloody revolution, a rich and vast country abandoned all at once to slaves purchased in the most barbarous regions of Asia. Despotism, which always suspects everything that approaches it, dreaded the natural defenders of Egypt, and was willing to confide its safety to men without country and without family; to those men who, according to the expression of Tacitus, when speaking of the guards of Artabanus, have not the least idea of virtue, are incapable of remorse, are instruments always ready for crime, and only know the hand that pays them. Most of the dynasties of Syria had already perished victims of their imprudent confidence in foreign soldiers. That of Saladin shared the same fate, and was, like all the others, overthrown by the barbarians whom it had intrusted with its defence. The dynasty of the Baharite Mamelukes, which succeeded that of Ayoub, was not destined to have a long duration; and a body of slaves, purchased in Circassia, in their turn got possession of the power that had armed them. Two centuries after, the Ottoman empire overcame the second dynasty of the Mamelukes; but their military government, amidst the crimes of tyranny and excesses of disorder, for a long time braved the power of the conqueror, and subsisted to the end of the eighteenth century, when the presence of a French army completed its annihilation. Thus, two French expeditions into Egypt were marked, one by the revolt and elevation of the Mamelukes, the other by their destruction.

Philosophy and humanity, however, derived some advantages from the expedition of St. Louis, which history does not dispute. The French monarch heard in Syria that a powerful emir was collecting a great number of books, and forming a library which was to be open to all the learned, and to all desirous of gaining knowledge. He became anxious to imitate this noble example, and gave orders for having all the manuscripts preserved in the monasteries transcribed. This literary treasure, confided to the care of Vincent de Beauvais, was placed in an apartment near the holy chapel, and became the first model of those bibliographical establishments, of those precious depositories of letters and sciences, of which the capital of France is now so justly proud.

It has often been said, that the hospital of the Quinze-Vingts was established by Louis IX. as an asylum for three hundred gentlemen who had returned blind from the holy war. The ordinance by which Louis founded this hospital says nothing to confirm the opinion at first spread by several writers, and which has since become sanctioned as a popular tradition. Joinville speaks of the institution of the Quinze-Vingts; but he says nothing of the motives that induced the pious monarch to found this establishment. Besides, we should add that the origin of the Quinze-Vingts is posterior by several years to his return from the crusade. Mezerai relates in his history, that an hospital for the blind was established at Rouen in the middle of the twelfth century; and this ancient monument of charity might give Louis the idea of founding a similar institution in his capital.

Before this crusade, Tartary was only known by the formidable emigrations of the Moguls. This vast region was in some sort revealed to the West by the missionaries sent thither by the king of France. William de Longjumeau, who set out from the isle of Cyprus, collected a great number of fabulous traditions in the course of his voyage; but he likewise brought back some curious notices and some exact observations. Rubruquis, who started during the king's abode in Palestine, and returned after the departure of the Crusaders, did not succeed in his embassy to the powerful emperor of the Moguls; but, as a traveller, he observed with sagacity the country, the manners, and the laws of the Tartars; and his relation is still a valuable monument, that more recent voyages have not thrown into oblivion.

The chroniclers of the time, even Joinville himself, who never turned their attention to anything but the events of the war, and gave no heed to the progress of civilization, have said nothing of the knowledge Louis might have acquired concerning the legislation of the East. What interest would not the old chronicles possess in our eyes, if they had reported the conversations of the royal legislator with the Oriental Christians versed in the study of the laws and customs that prevailed in the colonies of the Franks! It was during the sojourn of the king in Syria, that the chancellor of the kingdom of Cyprus collected all the laws that formed *the Assizes of Jerusalem*. Should we not be warranted, then, in saying that we owe this precious collection to the counsels, and still more to the encouragement, of Louis IX.? It is certain that the pious monarch neglected nothing that would enable him to acquire a knowledge of the usages and customs of the countries he visited; and that the Assizes of Jerusalem served as a model for the monument of legislation which afterwards constituted the greatest glory of his reign.

One advantage of this crusade, and that, doubtless, the greatest of all, was, that Louis returned much better than he was when he went, and that adversity developed and perfected in him all the qualities to which his subjects looked for their future prosperity. A Protestant historian, when speaking of this subject, makes use of these remarkable words: "The fruit of his voyage and of his affliction was, that he returned a much better man, having increased in zeal, modesty, prudence, and diligence; and that he was more honoured and beloved by his people than he had ever been before his departure; and by the universal earth was held in singular admiration for his good life and constancy amidst dangers, as a miracle among kings."

Far from seeking to forget his misfortunes, Louis was constantly referring to them, as a great example that God had been willing to present to the world. He attributed them principally to his own faults; and the austerities to which he condemned himself during the remainder of his life, were, says Father Daniel, a kind of mourning, which he always wore for the brave men who had perished in the crusade. On his return, he reformed the coinage, and by his order, silver Parisis and Gros Tournois were struck, upon which chains were figured, in order to preserve the memory of his captivity. These remembrances rendered him more dear to his people, and greater in the eyes of all Christians. Happy are princes upon whom the lessons of misfortune are not lost! happy also is the age in which men are not judged according to the favours of fortune, and in which the adversity of the great ones of the earth has in it something respectable and sacred!

THE EMIR'S HEAD SHOWN IN THE SERAGLIO.

The misfortune of the time, as we have already said, had ruined a great number of the most illustrious families of the kingdom. We know that many nobles had sold their lands to provide means for undertaking the crusade; and history has preserved acts passed in the camp, even of Mansourah, by which several gentlemen sold their domains to the crown. Louis was not at all willing that his companions in arms should be condemned to poverty for having followed him into the East, and for having shared with him the labours and perils of the holy war; he therefore ordered a list to be made of the indigent nobility, and found means to assist them out of his own revenue; he relieved, with affecting kindness, the widows and orphans of the brave knights he had seen fall by his side; and his solicitude extended even to the poor labourers who had suffered, either in the war of the Pastors, by his absence, or by the inefficiency of the laws. "Serfs," said he, "belong to Jesus Christ as well as to us, and in a Christian kingdom we ought never to forget that they are our brethren." Since his war with the Mussulmans, he could not endure the idea of the blood of Christians being shed in battle. His ordinances forbade war between individuals in all the domains of the crown; and the authority of his example contributed to maintain order and peace throughout the provinces.

Before his departure, Louis had sent commissaries to repair the iniquities committed in the government of his kingdom. On his return, he was determined to see everything himself, and pervaded his provinces; being convinced that God will not pardon kings who have neglected any opportunity or means of becoming acquainted with the truth. What a touching spectacle it must have been to see a king as anxious to discover all the ills that had been effected in his name, as other men are to trace out any injustice done to themselves! In short, his paternal vigilance succeeded in destroying all abuses, and repairing all faults; "and finally," says the noble confidant of his thoughts, "in lapse of time, the kingdom of France multiplied so greatly by the justice and rectitude that reigned in it, that the domains, feudal fines, rents, and revenues, increased in one year by a half, and vastly improved the kingdom of France."

We cannot finish the account of this crusade without speaking of the emperor Frederick II. and Innocent IV., who had so much influence over the events we have described. It may be said of Frederick, that his glory underwent as many vicissitudes as his fortune. Contemporary chronicles sometimes praise him with exaggeration, and at others blame him without measure. Such is ever the fate of princes who have lived amidst the conflict of parties. The spirit of party, which has judged them in their lifetime, leaves to history nothing but uncertainties, and appears still to exist for them in posterity. No historian has denied the talent or the genius of Frederick; he was one of the most illustrious captains of his times; he is placed among the princes who, by their example and their munificence, encouraged the revival of letters in the middle ages. He displayed great qualities upon the throne, but he did not know how to put himself in harmony with the spirit of his contemporaries; he had neither the defects nor the virtues of his age, and that is the reason that he succumbed in the obstinate struggle with the popes. If this struggle had not troubled and divided Europe, and if Frederick had been animated by the same sentiments as St. Louis, there is no doubt that Christianity would have triumphed over Islamism, and that the Crusaders would have subdued a great portion of the East.

The memory of Innocent IV. has been judged as variously as that of his redoubtable adversary. When looking at his manifestoes, his warlike enterprises, his spiritual and temporal triumphs, we might believe that the most able and ambitious of conquerors was seated in the chair of St. Peter. The events to which he has attached his name, and which he directed by his policy, leave us nothing to say regarding his genius or his character. After the death of Frederick, this pontiff returned to Italy, which country he traversed in triumph; but by a singular contrast, he who had shaken the power of emperors, only entered Rome tremblingly. The Romans had sent envoys to him to express their surprise at seeing him lead a wandering life far from his capital, and from the flock of which he would have to render an account to the sovereign judge.

Although obedient in this respect to the will of the people of Rome, Innocent pursued his projects against the remains of the imperial family, and death surprised him in the kingdom of Naples, of which he was taking possession in the name of the Church; having lost all care for the fate of the Christian colonies of the East. The pontiff who succeeded him, although he had neither his ambition, nor his authority, nor his genius, followed not the less the career that had been marked out for him. He endeavoured to accomplish all the threats of the Holy See, and the thunders of Rome reposed no more in the hands of Alexander VI. than they had done in those of his predecessors.

That which might justify the persevering, obstinate ardour with which the popes pursued the posterity of Frederick, is that by it they liberated Italy from the yoke of the emperors of Germany; and that this rich country remained sixty years without seeing the armies of the Germanic empire. But, on the other side, this advantage was purchased by so much violence, and by so many calamities, that the nations were never able to enjoy or know the value of it. The popes, who were not always sufficiently strong to maintain the work of their policy, were sometimes obliged to call in foreign princes to their aid, who introduced fresh subjects of discord into Italy. War constantly brought on war; conquerors were expelled by other conquerors. This revolution lasted during several centuries, and became fatal, not only to Italy, but to Germany, France, and Spain, to all who wished to partake of the spoils of the house of Swabia.

It is not our task to describe these afflicting scenes: to return to that which more particularly belongs to our subject, we will glance, whilst terminating these general considerations, at the crusade which was then being preached in all the Italian cities against Eccelino de Romano, whom the voice of the people, as well as the voice of the Church, had declared to be the enemy of God and men.

This Italian noble had taken advantage of the disorder of the civil wars, to usurp a tyrannical domination over several cities of Lombardy and Trevisano. All that we are told of the tyrants of fabulous antiquity falls short of the cruelties of Eccelino. Contemporary history compares his barbarous reign to pestilence, inundations, conflagrations, and the most terrible convulsions of nature. The pope at first excommunicated Eccelino, *in whom he could see nothing but a wild beast in a human form;* a short time afterwards he published a crusade against this scourge of God and humanity. John of Vicenza, who had preached public peace twenty years before, was the first preacher of this holy war. The faithful who took up arms against Eccelino, were to receive the same indulgences as those who went to Palestine. This crusade, which was undertaken in the cause of humanity and liberty, was preached in all the republics of Italy: the eloquence of the holy orators easily prevailed over the multitude; but that which most inflamed the zeal and ardour of the people, was the sight of the wretches whom Eccelino had caused to be mutilated amidst tortures, and the groans and lamentations of the families from which the tyrant had chosen his victims. In most of the provinces of Italy, the inhabitants of the cities and country took up arms to defend the cause of religion and their native land; eager to obtain the civic crown, if they triumphed over tyranny, and the crown of martyrdom, if they chanced to fall.

The standard of the cross was displayed at the head of the army; the crowd of Crusaders marched against Eccelino, singing this hymn of the Church,—

"Vexilla regis prodeunt,
Fulget crucis mysterium."

The army of the faithful at first obtained rapid successes; but as the archbishop of Ravenna, who commanded it, wanted skill, and as the Crusaders of each town had no leaders but monks and ecclesiastics, they did not profit by their early advantages. The intrigues of policy and the spirit of rivalry relaxed the ardour of the combatants; victory was sometimes balanced by reverses: four years of labours and perils scarcely sufficed for the suppression of an impious domination, or to avenge humanity by the defeat and death of Eccelino.

I regret that the plan of this work does not permit me to speak in greater detail of this war, in which religion so happily assisted the cause of liberty, and which forms so great a contrast with most contemporary events. At this period such a number of crusades were preached, that history can scarcely follow them, and we feel astonished that the population of the West was not exhausted by so many unfortunate wars. Whilst Louis IX. was returning from the East, where he had left his army, and a holy league was being formed in Italy against the tyrant Eccelino, sixty thousand Crusaders, commanded by a king of Bohemia, marched against the people of Lithuania, still addicted to the worship of idols; and another army of Crusaders was leaving the banks of the Oder and the Vistula to combat the pagans of Prussia, so many times attacked and conquered by the Teutonic knights. History is gratified at being able to remark that in this last expedition the cities of Brunsbad and Konigsberg were founded; but the founding of two flourishing cities cannot obliterate the remembrance of the desolation of many provinces. If any advantages could arise from these sanguinary expeditions, they were certainly the progressive steps of Christianity, which brought together people till that time separated by difference in manners and religious belief; they were the lessons of misfortune and the fruits of experience, which in the end enlightened Europe, and gave to the human mind a new direction more conformable with the laws of justice and reason, more favourable to the interests of humanity. It is thus that Providence, always mixing good with evil, renews human societies, and sows the prolific seeds of civilization in the very heart of disorder and barbarism.

BOOK XV

THE EIGHTH CRUSADE

1255 TO 1270

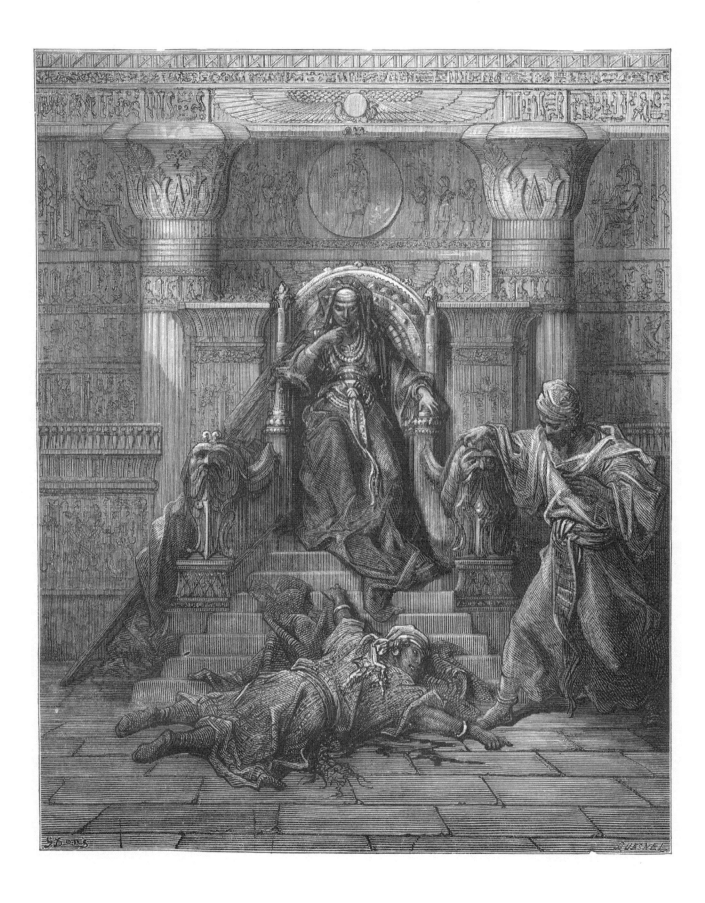

THE SULTANA CHEGGER-EDDOUR AND THE EMIR SAIF-EDDIN.

Chegger-Eddour could not pardon Aibek for having asked the hand of a daughter of the prince of Mossoul, and the faithless husband was assassinated by slaves. The sultana, after having gratified her woman's vengeance, called in the ambition of the emirs and the crimes of policy to her aid. She sent for the emir Saif-Eddin, to ask his advice, and to offer him her hand and empire. Upon being introduced into the palace, Saif-Eddin found the sultana seated, with the bleeding body of her husband at her feet; at this spectacle, the emir was seized with horror, and the calmness which the sultana displayed, together with the sight of the bloody throne, upon which she proposed to him to take his seat with her, added to his fright; Chegger-Eddour summoned two other emirs, who could not endure her presence, but fled away, terrified at what they saw and heard. This scene passed during the night, at break of day, the news of it was spread throughout Cairo, and the indignation of the people and the army was general and active; the mother of Aibek amply revenged the death of her son. Chegger-Eddour, in her turn, perished by the hands of slaves, and her body, which was cast naked into the castle ditch, might teach all the ambitious who were contending for the empire, that all revolutions, likewise, sometimes have their justice.—BOOK XV.

BOOK XV.

EIGHTH CRUSADE.

A.D. 1255–1270.

Christian cities of Palestine fortified by Louis IX.—Quarrels among the Crusaders—Divisions among the Saracens—Aibek, sultan of Egypt, assassinated—Chegger-Adour, the sultana, assassinated—The Moguls, or Tartars, capture Bagdad—Koutouz elected sultan of Egypt—The Moguls capture the principal cities of Syria—The general terror inspired among the Mussulmans and Christians—Apprehensions of Bela IV., king of Hungary—Assassination of Koutouz—The Mamelukes of Egypt—Bibars proclaimed sultan of Egypt—Declares war against the Christians of Palestine—The Mamelukes defeat and expel the Tartars from Palestine—Constantinople recaptured by the Greeks, and the Latins expelled—The Christians defeated by the Mamelukes, and Palestine laid waste—Cæsarea, Arsouf, and Sefed besieged and captured—Slaughter of the Christians—Mohammedanism not a religion of the sword—Charlemagne's career—Capture of Jaffa by the sultan of Egypt—Bohemond forms a treaty with Bibars—Antioch captured and destroyed, and the inhabitants slaughtered—Quarrels of the popes with the sovereigns of Europe—Royal family of Swabia—Charles, count of Anjou, crowned by the pope as king of Sicily—Mainfroy—Conraddin disputes the crown of Sicily—Louis IX. determines upon a fresh crusade to the Holy Land—The illustrious personages who take the cross in his support—Joinville declines to accompany him—Abaga, khan of the Tartars, sends ambassadors to Rome—Pope Clement IV. supports the new crusade—The clergy oppose the levying of contributions—A council held at Northampton for aiding the crusade—James king of Arragon, and Edward prince of England, engage in the crusade—Death of Clement IV.—The Crusaders arrive at Tunis—Historical notice of Tunis—The Mohammedans resist the Crusaders—Sickness and mortality among the Crusaders—Death of the duke de Nevers—Illness and fervent devotion of Louis—His death—Charles of Anjou lands at Tunis, and takes the command of the Crusaders—Returns to France with the bodies of his father, wife, and brother—The virtues and piety of Louis IX.—Prince Edward of England arrives in Palestine—Nazareth captured by the Crusaders—Prince Edward returns to England—Thibault elected pope, under the title of Gregory X.—He convokes the council of Lyons for reviving a new crusade—Curious document issued by Humbert de Romanis—Three pretenders to the throne of Jerusalem—The continued victories of Bibars—His death and character—Death of Gregory X.—Revolt in Sicily—The Sicilian vespers—Kealaoun, the sultan of Egypt, concludes a treaty with the Christians of Ptolemaïs, and enters into treaties with European princes—Fort of Margat captured by the Mussulmans—Sieur Barthélemi becomes a Mohammedan renegade—Tripoli captured and destroyed, and the Christians slaughtered—Description of Ptolemaïs—Chalil elected sultan of Egypt—The Mussulman sect of Chages—Ptolemaïs captured and destroyed by Chalil—Virgins of St. Clair self-mutilated and destroyed—Death of William de Clermont—Devoted heroism of the Templars—Capture and destruction of Tyre, Berytus, Sidon, and all the Christian cities along the coast of Palestine.

LOUIS IX., during his sojourn in Palestine, had not only employed himself in fortifying the Christian cities; he had neglected no means of establishing that union and harmony among the Christians themselves, which he felt would create their only security against the attacks of the Mussulmans: unhappily for this people, whom he would have preserved at the peril of his life, his counsels were not long in being forgotten, and the spirit of discord soon displaced the generous sentiments to which his example and discourses had given a momentary life.

It may have been observed in the course of this history, that several maritime nations had stores, counting-houses, and considerable commercial establishments at Ptolemaïs, which had become the capital of Palestine. Among these nations, Genoa and Venice occupied the first rank: each of these colonies inhabited a separate quarter, and had different laws, besides interests, which kept them at constant variance; the only thing they possessed in common, was the Church of St. Sabbas, in which the Venetians and Genoese assembled together to celebrate the ceremonies of their religion.

This common possession had often been a subject of quarrel between them; a short time after the departure of St. Louis, discord broke out anew, and roused all the passions that the spirit of rivalry and jealousy could give birth to between two nations which had so long contended for the empire of the sea and pre-eminence in commerce. Amidst this struggle, in which the very object of the contest ought to have recalled sentiments of peace and charity to their hearts, the Genoese and Venetians often came to blows in the city of Ptolemaïs, and more than once, the sanctuary, which the two parties had fortified like a place of war, resounded with the din of their sacrilegious battles.

Discord very soon crossed the seas, and carried fresh troubles into the West. Genoa interested the Pisans in her cause, and sought allies and auxiliaries even among the Greeks, at that time impatient to repossess Constantinople. Venice, in order to avenge her injuries, courted the alliance of Manfroi, who had been excommunicated by the head of the Church. Troops were raised, fleets were armed, and the parties attacked each other both by land and sea; and this war, which the sovereign pontiff was unable to quell, lasted more than twenty years, sometimes to the advantage of the Venetians, as frequently to that of the Genoese; but always fatal to the Christian colonies of the East.

This spirit of discord likewise extended its baneful influence to the rival orders of St. John and the Temple; and the blood of these courageous defenders of the Holy Land flowed in torrents in cities of which they had undertaken the defence; the Hospitallers and Templars pursued and attacked each other with a fury that nothing could appease or turn aside, both orders invoking the aid of the knights that remained in the West. Thus the noblest families of Christendom were dragged into these sanguinary quarrels, and it was no longer asked in Europe whether the Franks had conquered the Saracens, but if victory had been favourable to the knights of the Temple or to those of the Hospital.

The brave Sergines, whom Louis IX. had at his departure left at Ptolemaïs, and the wisest of the other defenders of the Holy Land, had neither authority enough to reëstablish tranquillity, nor troops enough to resist the attacks of the Mussulmans. The only hope of safety which appeared to be left to the Christians of Palestine, arose from the divisions which also troubled the empire of the Saracens; every day new revolutions broke out among the Mamelukes; but, by a singular contrast, feuds, that weakened the power of the Franks, often seemed only to increase that of their enemies. If, from the feeble kingdom of Jerusalem, we pass into Egypt, we there behold the strange spectacle of a government founded by revolt, and strengthening itself amidst political tempests. The Christian colonies, since the taking of Jerusalem by Saladin, had no longer a common centre or a common tie; the kings of Jerusalem, in losing their capital, lost an authority which served at least as a war-cry by which to rally ardent spirits around them. Nothing was preserved of royalty but the name, nothing was gained from republicanism but its license. As to the Mamelukes, they were less a nation than an army, in which they at first quarrelled for a leader, and in which they afterwards obeyed him blindly. From the bosom of each of their revolutions sprang a military despotism, armed with all the passions that had given birth to it, and, what must have redoubled the alarm of the Christians, this despotism breathed nothing but war and conquest.

We have said, in the preceding book, that Aibek, after having espoused the sultana Chegger-Eddour, had mounted the throne of Saladin; but it was not long before his reign was disturbed by the rivalries of the emirs. The death of Phares-Eddin Octhaï, one of the leaders opposed to the new sultan, disconcerted the projects of the faction, but the jealousy of a woman did that which neither faction nor license had been able to effect. Chegger-Eddour could not pardon Aibek for having asked the hand of a daughter of the prince of Mossoul, and the faithless husband was assassinated in the bath by slaves. The sultana, after having gratified her woman's vengeance, called in the ambition of the emirs and the crimes of policy to her aid. She sent for the emir Saif-Eddin, to ask his advice, and to offer him her hand and empire. Upon being introduced into the palace, Saif-Eddin found the sultana seated, with the bleeding body of her husband at her feet: at this spectacle, the emir was seized with horror, and the calmness which the sultana displayed, together with the sight of the bloody throne, upon which she proposed to him to take his seat with her, added to his fright; Chegger-Eddour summoned two other emirs, who could not endure her presence, but fled away, terrified at what they saw and heard. This scene passed during the night. At break of day, the news of it was spread throughout Cairo, and the indignation of the people and the army was general and active: the mother of Aibek amply revenged the death of her son. Chegger-Eddour, in her turn, perished by the hands of slaves, and her body, which was cast naked into the castle ditch, might teach all the ambitious who were contending for the empire, that revolutions, likewise, sometimes have their justice.

Amidst the tumult, a son of Aibek, fifteen years of age, was raised to the throne; but the approach of a war soon caused a new revolution to break out, and precipitated the youth from his giddy eminence: great events were ripening in Asia, and a storm was brewing in Persia, which was soon to burst over both Syria and Egypt.*

The Moguls, under the command of Oulagon, had laid siege to Bagdad, at a moment when the city was divided into several sects, all more earnest in their conflicts with each other than in their preparations to repulse a formidable enemy. The caliph, as well as his people, was sunk deep in voluptuous effeminacy, and the pride created by the vain adulation of the Mussulmans, made him neglect true and available means of defence. The Tartars took the city by storm, and gave it up to all the horrors of war. The last and thirty-seventh of the successors of Abbas, dragged away like the vilest captive, lost his life in the midst of such tumult and disorder, that history is unable to say whether he died of despair, or whether he fell beneath the sword of his enemies. Many chronicles say that Oulagon shut the caliph up in the midst of all his treasures, and left him to die of hunger: this circumstance is not at all probable, and has not been acknowledged by M. Deguignes.

This violence, committed upon the head of the Mussulman religion, with the march of the Moguls towards Syria, threw the Mamelukes into the greatest consternation. They then deemed it necessary to displace the son of Aibek, and elect a leader able to guide them amidst the perils that threatened them, and their choice fell upon Koutouz, the bravest and most able of the emirs.

Whilst Egypt was earnestly engaged in preparations to resist the Moguls, the Christians appeared to expect their deliverance from this war against the Mussulmans; the khan of Tartary had promised the king of Armenia to carry his conquests as far as the banks of the Nile; and oriental chronicles relate that the Armenian troops were united with those of the Moguls. The latter, after having crossed the Euphrates, took possession of Aleppo, Damascus, and the principal cities of Syria. On all sides, the Mussulmans fled before the Tartars, and the disciples of Christ were protected by the victorious hordes; from that time the Christians only beheld liberators in these redoubtable conquerors. In the churches, and even upon the tomb of Christ, prayers were put up for the triumph of the Moguls, and in the excess of their joy, the Christians of Palestine abandoned their general practice of imploring aid from the powers of Europe.

In the mean time Europe itself entertained a very different idea of this war; the progress of the Moguls created the greatest terror in all the nations of the West; they not only dreaded the Mogul arms on account of the Christian colonies of the East; they trembled for themselves; for

---

* One of the principal difficulties that an historian of this epoch experiences, is, to preserve the connection in his narrative, from having to speak at the same time of the West and of the East, of the Christians, the Mamelukes, and the Tartars. Here a new people start up upon the stage, there an old empire falls to decay: all the events are hurried and confounded together, and the march of history is embarrassed among so many ruins. We endeavour to be as clear as possible.

whilst the hordes of Oulagon were ravaging Syria, other armies of the same nation were desolating the banks of the Dniester and the Danube. Pope Alexander, addressing the princes, prelates, and all the faithful, exhorted them to unite against the barbarians. Councils were assembled in France, England, Italy, and Germany, to deliberate upon the dangers of Christendom; the head of the Church ordered prayers to be offered up and processions to be made, blasphemies to be punished, and luxury to be suppressed at the table and in dress,—measures which might be conceived proper to mitigate the anger of Heaven, but very insufficient to stop the invasion of the Moguls.

The hordes, however, which ravaged Hungary and Poland were dispersed, and terror again took possession of the Christians of the East, whose hopes had been so sanguine. Oulagon, recalled into Persia by civil wars, left his lieutenant, Ketboga, in Syria, with directions to follow up his conquests. The Christians were still applauding the victories of the Moguls, when a quarrel, provoked by some German crusaders, all at once changed the state of things, and made enemies of those who had been considered as auxiliaries. Some Mussulman villages which paid tribute to the Tartars, having been pillaged, Ketboga sent to demand a reparation of the Christians, which they refused. In the course of the dispute raised on this subject, the nephew of the Mogul commander was killed. From that time the Tartar leader declared open war against the Christians, ravaged the territory of Sidon, and menaced that of Ptolemaïs. At the aspect of their desolated plains, all the hopes of the Christians vanished; they had had no bounds to their hopes and their joy, they had now none to their grief or their fears. The alarm created in them by a barbarous people, made them forget that most of their misfortunes came from Egypt, and as they had given over all idea of succours from the West, many of them now placed all their confidence in the arms of the Mamelukes.

A great portion of Palestine had already been invaded by the Moguls, when the sultan of Cairo set out on his march to meet them at the head of his army; he remained three days in the neighbourhood of Ptolemaïs, where he renewed a truce with the Christians. Soon after, a battle was fought in the plain of Tiberias; Ketboga lost his life in the middle of the conflict, and the army of the Tartars, beaten and scattered, abandoned Syria.

To whichever side victory might have inclined, the Christians had nothing to hope from the conqueror; the Mussulmans could not pardon them for having sought the support of the victorious Moguls, and having taken advantage of the desolation of Syria, to insult the disciples of Mahomet. The churches were demolished at Damascus; the Christians were persecuted in all the Mussulman cities, and these persecutions were the presage of a war in which fanaticism exercised all its furies. On all sides complaints and menaces arose against the Franks of Palestine; the cry of *war with the Christians* resounded through all the provinces in the power of the Mamelukes; the animosity was so great, that the sultan of Cairo, who had just triumphed over the Tartars, was the victim to his fidelity in observing the last truce concluded with the Franks. Bibars, who had killed the last sultan of the family of Saladin, took advantage of this effervescence of the public mind to endeavour to raise a party against Koutouz, by affecting great hatred for the Christians, and by reproaching the sultan with a criminal moderation towards the enemies of Islamism.

When the fermentation had been worked up to the highest point, Bibars, having assembled his accomplices, surprised the sultan whilst hunting, struck him several mortal blows, then, all stained as he was with the blood of his master, he hastened to the Mameluke army, at that time collected at Sallhie; he presented himself to the atabek or lieutenant of the prince, announcing the death of Koutouz. Upon being asked who killed the sultan, "It was I," answered he. "In that case," said the atabek, "reign in his place." Strange words, which characterize at a single stroke the spirit of the Mamelukes, as well as of the government they had founded! The army proclaimed Bibars sultan of Egypt, and the ceremonies prepared at Cairo for the reception of the conqueror of the Tartars, served to celebrate the coronation of his murderer.

This revolution gave the Mussulmans the sovereign most to be dreaded by the Christians. Bibars was named *the pillar of the Mussulman religion and the father of victories;* and he was destined to merit these titles by completing the ruin of the Franks. He had scarcely mounted the throne before he gave the signal for war.

The Christians of Palestine being totally without means of resisting the Mameluke forces, sent deputies to the West to solicit prompt and efficient succour. The sovereign pontiff appeared affected by the account of the perils of the Holy Land, and exhorted the faithful to take the cross; but the tone of his exhortations, and the motives that he named in his circulars, only too plainly evinced his desire to see Europe take up arms against other enemies than the Mussulmans. "The Saracens," said he, "know that it will be impossible for any Christian prince to make a long abode in the East, and that the Holy Land will never have any but transient succour from distant countries."

Alexander IV. was much more sincere and far more eloquent in his manifestoes against the house of Swabia; the interest he took in the contest he was carrying on in the kingdom of Naples could not be diverted by the undertaking of a holy war. Clement IV., who succeeded him, made some few demonstrations of zeal to engage the European nations to take arms against the Mussulmans; but the policy of his predecessors had left too many germs of discord and trouble in Italy, to allow him to give much attention to the East. On one side, Germany, still without an emperor, though with three pretenders to the empire, could spare no warriors for the Holy Land. England was a prey to a civil war, in which the barons wore a white cross as their badge of union against the king, and in which priests exhorted them to the fight, pointing to heaven as the reward of their bravery and their rebellion. This strange crusade precluded all thoughts of one beyond the seas. France was the only kingdom from which the prayers of the Christians of Palestine were not repulsed; some French knights took the cross, and chose Eudes, count of Nevers, son of the duke of Burgundy, as their leader; and these were all the succours Europe could afford to send to the East.

At the same time that the afflicting news arrived from the Holy Land, an event was announced which would have plunged the whole West in mourning, if the conquests of the Crusaders had then excited anything like the interest to which they had given birth in former ages. We have frequently had occasion to deplore the rapid decline of the Latin empire of Constantinople; for a length of time, Baldwin had had no means for supporting the imperial dignity, or paying his scanty troop of soldiers, but the alms of Christendom, and some loans obtained from Venice, for which he was obliged to give his own son as a hostage, or, more properly, a pledge. In pressing moments of want, he sold the relics, he tore the lead from the roofs of the churches, and the timber of public edifices was used for heating the fires of the imperial kitchens. Towers half-demolished, ramparts without defences, palaces smoky and deserted, houses and whole streets abandoned, such was the spectacle presented by the queen of eastern cities.

Baldwin had concluded a truce with Michael Palæologus. The facility with which this truce was made ought to have inspired the Latins with some suspicion; but the deplorable state of the Franks did not prevent them from despising their enemies or dreaming of fresh conquests. In hopes of pillage, and forgetful of the perfidious character of the Greeks, a Venetian fleet bore such as remained of the defenders of Byzantium in an expedition against Daphnusia, situated at the embouchure of the Black Sea. The Greeks of Nice, informed by some peasants from the shores of the Bosphorus, did not hesitate to take advantage of the opportunity fortune thus presented. These

A CELESTIAL LIGHT.

The capitulation of Sefed granted the Christians permission to retire wherever they wished, upon condition that they would take away with them nothing but their clothes. . . . . . On the morrow, two only of those captives were set at liberty; one was a brother Hospitaller, whom Bibars sent to Ptolemaïs to announce to the Christians the taking of Sefed; the other was a Templar, who abandoned the faith of Christ, and attached himself to the fortunes of the Sultan; all the others, to the number of six hundred, fell beneath the sword of the Mamelukes.

It is impossible to describe the despair and consternation of the Christians of Palestine, when they learned the tragical end of the defenders of Sefed. Their superstitious grief invented or blindly received the most marvellous accounts, which the Western chroniclers have not disdained to repeat; it was said that a celestial light shone every night over the bodies of the Christian warriors that remained unburied. It was added that the Sultan, annoyed by this prodigy, which was every day renewed before his eyes, gave orders that the martyrs of the Christian faith should be buried, and that around their place of sepulture high walls should be built, in order that nobody might witness the miracles operated in favour of the victims he had immolated to his vengeance.—BOOK XV.

peasants pointed out to the general of Michael Palæologus, who was about to make war in Epirus, an opening that had been made under the ramparts of Constantinople, close to the Golden Gate, by which more troops might be introduced than would be necessary for the conquest of the city. Baldwin had none with him but children, old men, women, and traders; among the latter of whom were the Genoese newly allied to the Greeks. When the soldiers of Michael had penetrated into the city, they were surprised to find no enemy to contend with; whilst they preserved their ranks, and advanced with precaution, a troop of Comans, whom the Greek emperor had in his pay, traversed the city, sword and fire in hand. The small, terrified crowd of the Latins fled towards the port; whilst the Greek inhabitants hastened to meet the conqueror, shouting, " Long life to Michael Palæologus, emperor of the Romans!" Baldwin, awakened by these cries and the tumult that drew near to his palace, hastened to quit a city that no longer was his. The Venetian fleet, returning from the expedition to Daphnusia, arrived in time to receive the fugitive emperor and all that remained of the empire of the Franks upon the Bosphorus. Thus the Latins were deprived of that city that it had cost them such prodigies of valour to obtain; the Greeks reëntered it without striking a blow, seconded only by the treachery of a few peasants and the darkness of night. Baldwin II., after having reigned in Byzantium during thirty-seven years, resumed the mendicant course he had practised in his youth, and wandered from one court to another, imploring the assistance of Christians. Pope Urban received him with a mixture of compassion and contempt. In a letter addressed to Louis IX., the pontiff deplored the loss of Constantinople, and groaned bitterly over the obscured glory of the Latin Church. Urban expressed a desire that a crusade should be undertaken for the recovery of Byzantium; but he found men's minds but very little disposed to undertake such an enterprise: the clergy of both England and France refused subsidies for an expedition which they pronounced useless. The pope was obliged to content himself with the submission and presents of Michael Palæologus, who, still in dread in the bosom of his new conquest, promised, in order to appease the Holy See, to recognise the Church of Rome, and to succour the holy places.

In the mean time the situation of the Christians of Palestine became every day more alarming, and more worthy of the compassion of the nations and princes of the West. The new sultan of Cairo, after having ravaged the country of the Franks, returned a second time, with a more formidable army than the former. The Franks, alarmed at his progress, sent to him to sue for peace; his only reply was to give up the church of Nazareth to the flames; the Mussulmans ravaged all the country situated between Naïn and Mount Thabor, and then encamped within sight of Ptolemaïs.

The most distinguished of the Christian warriors had attempted an expedition towards Tiberias; but this gallant troop, the last resource of the Franks, had just been defeated and dispersed by the infidels; fifty knights had arrived in Palestine with the duke of Nevers; but what could such a feeble reinforcement do to arrest the progress of a victorious army?

The country was laid waste, and the inhabitants of the cities kept themselves closely shut up behind their ramparts, in the constant apprehension of beholding the enemy under their walls. After threatening Ptolemaïs, Bibars threw himself upon the city of Cæsarea; the Christians, after a spirited resistance, abandoned the place, and retired into the castle, which was surrounded by the waters of the sea. This fortress, which appeared inaccessible, was only able to resist the attacks of the Mussulmans a few days. The city of Arsouf was the next object of the Mussulman leader. The inhabitants defended themselves with almost unexampled bravery; several times the machines of the besiegers and the heaps of wood which they raised to the level of the walls, were consigned to the flames. After having fought at the foot of the ramparts, the besieged and the besiegers dug out the earth beneath the walls of the city, and sought each other, to fight in the mines and subterranean passages; nothing could relax the ardour of the Christians or the impatient activity of Bibars. Religious fanaticism animated the courage of the Mamelukes; the imauns and doctors of the law flocked to the siege of Arsouf, to be present at the triumph of Islamism: at length the sultan planted the standard of the prophet upon the towers of the city, and the Mussulmans were called to prayers in the churches at once converted into mosques. The Mamelukes massacred a great part of the inhabitants; the remainder were condemned to slavery. Bibars distributed the captives among the leaders of his army; he then ordered the destruction of the city, and the Christian prisoners were compelled to demolish their own dwellings. The conquered territory was divided and shared among the principal emirs, according to an order of the sultan, which the Arabian chronicles have preserved as an historical monument. This liberality towards the conquerors of the Christians, appeared to the Mussulmans worthy of the greatest praise, and one of the historians of Bibars exclaims, in his enthusiasm, "That so noble an action was written in the book of God, before being inscribed upon the book of the life of the sultan."

Such encouragement bestowed upon the emirs, announced that Bibars still stood in need of their valour to accomplish other designs. The sultan returned into Egypt, to make fresh preparation and recruit his army. During his sojourn at Cairo, he received ambassadors from several kings of the Franks, from Alphonso, king of Arragon, the king of Armenia, and some other princes of Palestine. All these ambassadors demanded peace for the Christians; but their pressing solicitations only strengthened the sultan in his project of continuing the war; the more earnest their entreaties, the greater reason he had to believe they had nothing else to oppose to him. He answered the envoys of the count of Jaffa: "The time is come in which we will endure no more injuries; when a cottage shall be taken from us, we will take a castle; when you shall seize one of our labourers, we will consign a thousand of your warriors to chains."

Bibars did not delay putting his threats into execution; he returned to Palestine, and made a pilgrimage to Jerusalem, to implore the protection of Mahomet for his arms. His army immediately received the signal for war, and ravaged the territory of Tripoli. If some Oriental chronicles may be believed, the project of Bibars then was to attack Ptolemaïs; and in so great an enterprise, he did not disdain the assistance of treachery. The prince of Tyre, says Ibn-Ferat, united with the Genoese, was to attack Ptolemaïs with a numerous fleet on the sea side, whilst the Mamelukes attacked it by land. Bibars in fact presented himself before Ptolemaïs, but his new auxiliaries no doubt repented of the promises they had made him; and did not second his designs. The sultan retired filled with fury, and threatened to avenge himself upon all the Christians whom war should place in his power.

He first went to discharge his anger upon the fortress of Sefed, which was situated in lower Galilee, fifteen leagues from Ptolemaïs. This fortress had to defend itself against all the forces that the sultan had gathered together for his great enterprise. When the siege had begun, Bibars neglected no means of forcing the garrison to surrender; he was constantly at the head of his troops, and in one conflict, his whole army burst into a loud cry to warn him of a danger that threatened him. To inflame the ardour of the Mamelukes, he caused robes of honour and purses of money to be distributed on the field of battle; the great cadi of Damascus had come to the siege to animate the combatants by his presence; and the promises he addressed, in the name of the prophet, to all the Mussulman soldiers, added greatly to their warlike enthusiasm.

The Christians, however, defended themselves valiantly. This resistance at first astonished their enemies, and soon produced discouragement; in vain the sultan endeavoured to reanimate his soldiers, in vain he ordered that all who fled should be beaten back with clubs, and placed several emirs in chains for deserting their posts; neither the dread of chastisements, nor the hopes of reward, could revive the courage of the Mussulmans. Bibars would have been obliged to raise the siege, if discord had not come to his assistance. He himself took great pains to give birth to it among the Christians; in the frequent messages sent to the garrison, perfidious promises and well-directed threats sowed the seeds of suspicion and mistrust. At length the divisions burst forth; some were anxious that they should surrender, others that they should hold out to death: from that moment the Mussulmans met with a less obstinate resistance, and renewed their own attacks with greater ardour; whilst the Christians accused each other of treacherous proceedings or intentions, the war-machines made the walls totter, and the Mamelukes, after several assaults, were upon the point of opening themselves a road into the place. At length, one Friday (we quote an Arabian chronicle), the cadi of Damascus was praying for the combatants, when the Franks were heard to cry from the top of their half-dismantled towers, "O Mussulmans, spare us, spare us!" The besieged had laid down their arms, and fought no longer—the gates were immediately opened, and the standard of the Mussulmans floated over the walls of Sefed.

A capitulation granted the Christians permission to retire wherever they wished, upon condition that they should take away with them nothing but their clothes. Bibars, when seeing them defile before him, sought for a pretext to detain them in his power. Some were, by his orders, arrested and accused of carrying away treasures and arms; and the command was instantly issued to stop all. They were reproached with having violated the treaty, and were threatened with death if they did not embrace Islamism. They were loaded with chains and crowded together in a mass upon a hill, where they expected nothing but death. A commander of the Temple and two Cordeliers exhorted their companions in misfortune to die like Christian heroes. All those warriors, whom discord had divided, now reunited in one common evil, had only one feeling and one thought;[*] they wept as they embraced each other, they encouraged each other to die becomingly; they passed the night in confessing their sins towards God, and in deploring their errors and their differences. On the morrow, two only of these captives were set at liberty; one was a brother Hospitaller, whom Bibars sent to Ptolemaïs, to announce to the Christians the taking of Sefed; the other was a Templar, who abandoned the faith of Christ, and attached himself to the fortunes of the sultan; all the others, to the number of six hundred, fell beneath the sword of the Mamelukes. This barbarity, committed in the name of the Mussulman religion, appears the more revolting, from the Franks never having given an example for it, and that amidst the furies of war, they were never known to require the conversion of infidels, sword in hand.

It is impossible to describe the despair and consternation of the Christians of Palestine, when they learnt the tragical end of the defenders of Sefed. Their superstitious grief invented or blindly received the most marvellous accounts, which the Western chroniclers have not disdained to repeat; it was said that a celestial light shone every night over the bodies of the Christian warriors that remained unburied. It was added that the sultan, annoyed by this prodigy, which was every day renewed before his eyes, gave orders that the martyrs of the Christian faith should be buried, and that around their place of sepulture high walls should be built, in order that nobody might witness the miracles operated in favour of the victims he had immolated to his vengeance.

After the taking of Sefed, Bibars returned into Egypt, and the Franks hoped for a few days of repose and safety; but the indefatigable sultan never gave his enemies much time to rejoice at his absence. He only remained in Egypt till he had recruited his army with fresh troops, and soon brought back additional desolation to the states of the Christians. In this campaign, Armenia was

---

[*] The Arabian chronicles describe this event in a very obscure and equivocal manner; they scarcely mention the massacre of the prisoners, and say but little of the capitulation; they accuse the Franks of having taken Mussulman prisoners away with them, which is not very probable.

the point to which his anger and the power of his arms were directed; he reproached the Armenian monarch with forbidding Egyptian merchants to enter his dominions, and could not pardon him for preventing his own subjects from obtaining merchandise from Egypt. These differences were quickly settled on the field of battle; one of the sons of the king of Armenia lost his liberty, and the other his life: the army of Bibars returned loaded with booty, and followed by an innumerable multitude of captives.

As, after each of his victories, the sultan presented himself before Ptolemaïs, the capital of the Christian states, he did not fail on his return from this last expedition, to exhibit before the walls of this city the spoils of the people of Armenia, together with his own machines of war; but the moment was not yet arrived in which such a great undertaking as the capture of Ptolemaïs could be attempted. After terrifying the inhabitants by his appearance, he suddenly departed, for the purpose of surprising Jaffa. This city, the fortifications of which had cost Louis IX. a considerable sum,* after a very slight resistance, fell into the hands of Bibars, who caused all the walls to be levelled with the ground. During this excursion, the sultan of Cairo obtained possession of the castle of Carac and several other forts, and then marched towards Tripoli. Bohemond having sent to demand of him what the purpose of his coming was: "I am come," replied he, "to gather in your harvests; in my next campaign I will besiege your capital." Nevertheless, he concluded a truce with Tripoli, in the midst of these hostilities; foreseeing that a treaty of peace would serve as a veil for the project of another war, and that he should soon find an opportunity of violating the truce with advantage.

The author of the life of Bibars, who was sent to Bohemond, count of Tripoli and prince of Antioch, says that the sultan was in the train of the ambassador, in the character of a herald-at-arms. His project was to examine the fortifications and the means of defence of the city of Tripoli. In drawing up the treaty the Mussulman deputies only gave Bohemond the title of count, whilst he claimed that of prince; the discussion becoming warm, the envoys of Bibars naturally turned their eyes towards their master, who made them a sign to yield. On his return to his army, the sultan laughed heartily with his emirs at this adventure, saying, "The time is come in which God will curse the prince and the count."

By this, Bibars alluded to his project of conquering and ruining the principality of Antioch. The Egyptian army received orders to march towards the banks of the Orontes; and but very few days had passed away before this same army was encamped under the walls of Antioch, badly defended by its patriarch, and abandoned by most of its inhabitants. Historians say very little of this siege, in which the Christians made but a feeble resistance, and appeared more frequently as suppliants than as warriors: their submission, their tears, their prayers, however, made no impression upon a conqueror whose sole policy was the destruction of the Christian cities.

As the Mussulmans entered Antioch without a capitulation, they gave themselves up to all the excesses of license and victory. In a letter which Bibars addressed to the count of Tripoli, the barbarous conqueror takes a pleasure in describing the desolation of the subdued city, and all the evils which his fury had caused the Christians to undergo. "Death," says he, "came among the besieged from all sides and by all roads: we killed all that thou hadst appointed to guard the city or defend its approaches. If thou hadst seen thy knights trampled under the feet of the horses, thy provinces given up to pillage, thy riches distributed by measures-full, the wives of thy subjects put to public

---

* "I cannot tell the amount," says Joinville, "of what the king laid out for the fortification of Jaffa, it was so great. He closed the canal between the two seas, he built twenty-four towers, and cleansed the ditches without and within. There were three gates, of which the legate built one, and likewise part of the walls. And in order to show you what the king must have expended, I will tell you what the legate said when I asked him how much that gate and the wall had cost him. I had reckoned that the first cost him five hundred livres, and the latter three hundred livres; but he told me, as God might help him, that the gate and the wall had cost him thirty thousand livres."

THE CRUELTIES OF BIBARS.

As the Mussulmans entered Antioch without a capitulation, they gave themselves up to all the excesses of license and victory. In a letter which Bibars addressed to the count of Tripoli, the barbarous conqueror takes a pleasure in describing the desolation of the subdued city, and all the evils which his fury had caused the Christians to undergo. "Death," says he, "came among the besieged from all sides and by all roads; we killed all that thou hadst appointed to guard the city or defend its approaches. If thou hadst seen thy knights trampled under the feet of the horses, thy provinces given up to pillage, thy riches distributed by measures-full, the wives of thy subjects put to public sale; if thou hadst seen the pulpits and crosses overturned, the leaves of the gospel torn and cast to the winds, and the sepulchres of thy patriarchs profaned; if thou hadst seen thy enemies, the Mussulmans, trampling upon the tabernacle, and immolating in the sanctuary monk, priest, and deacon; in short, if thou hadst seen thy palaces given up to the flames, the dead devoured by the fire of this world, the Church of St. Paul and that of St. Peter completely and entirely destroyed, certes, thou wouldst have cried out: 'Would to Heaven that I were become dust!'"—BOOK XV.

sale; if thou hadst seen the pulpits and crosses overturned, the leaves of the Gospel torn and cast to the winds, and the sepulchres of thy patriarchs profaned; if thou hadst seen thy enemies, the Mussulmans, trampling upon the tabernacle, and immolating in the sanctuary, monk, priest, and deacon; in short, if thou hadst seen thy palaces given up to the flames, the dead devoured by the fire of this world, the Church of St. Paul and that of St. Peter completely and entirely destroyed, certes, thou wouldst have cried out: *Would to Heaven that I were become dust!*"

Bibars distributed the booty among his soldiers, the Mamelukes reserving as their portion, the women, girls, and children. At that time, says an Arabian chronicle, "*there was not the slave of a slave that was not the master of a slave.*" A little boy was worth twelve dirhems, a little girl five dirhems. In a single day the city of Antioch lost all its inhabitants, and a conflagration, lighted by order of Bibars, completed the work of the barbarians. Most historians agree in saying that seventeen thousand Christians were slaughtered, and a hundred thousand dragged away into slavery.

When we recall to our minds the first siege of this city by the Crusaders, and the labours and the exploits of Bohemond, Godfrey, and Tancred, who founded the principality of Antioch, we are afflicted at beholding the end of all that which the glory of conquerors had produced. When, on the other side, we see a numerous population, inclosed within ramparts, making but a feeble defence against an enemy, and allowing themselves to be slaughtered without resistance, we cannot help asking what can have become of the posterity of so many brave warriors as had defended Antioch, during almost two centuries, against all the Mussulman powers.

Complaints were made among the Christians against William, the patriarch, whom they accused of having at least favoured the invasion and conquest of the Mussulmans, by a weak pusillanimity. Without offering an opinion upon the accusation, we content ourselves with saying, that the timid prelate did not long enjoy the fruit of his base conduct; for the Mamelukes, after having permitted him to retire to Cosseïr with all his treasures, dragged him from his retreat by violence; and the faithless pastor, despoiled of his wealth, and plunged in ignominy, underwent at last a much more cruel death than he might have expected amidst his flock, and upon the ramparts of a Christian city.

After the taking of Antioch, the Christians had nothing left to arrest the progress of the Mussulmans, but the cities of Tripoli and Ptolemaïs. Bibars was impatient to attack these last bulwarks of the Franks; but he did not dare to put trust in his fortune, and aim the last fatal blow at that power before which the Mussulman nations so lately trembled. The sultan of Cairo could not forget that the dangers of the Christians had often roused the whole West, and this thought alone was sufficient to keep him in inaction and dread. Thus the sad remains of the Christian colonies of the East were still protected by the warlike reputation of the nations of Europe, and by the remembrance of the wonders of the early crusades.

Fame had not failed to carry the news of so many disasters across the seas. The archbishop of Tyre, the grand-masters of the Temple and the Hospital, passed over into the West, to repeat the groans of the Christian cities of Syria; but on their arrival, Europe seemed but little disposed to give ear to their complaints. In vain a crusade was preached in Germany, Poland, and the more remote countries of the North; the inhabitants of northern Europe evinced nothing but indifference for events that were passing at such a distance from them. The king of Bohemia, the marquis of Brandenburg, and some other lords that had taken the cross, seemed in no hurry to perform their oath. No army set forward on its march; everything was reduced to preachings and vain preparations.

The misfortunes of the Holy Land were deeply deplored in the kingdom of France; in a *sirvente*,[*] composed on this subject, a contemporary troubadour appears to reproach Providence with

---

[*] Sirvente is a kind of poem peculiar to the troubadours.

the defeats of the Christians of Palestine, and in his poetical delirium, abandons himself to an impious despair:—"Sadness and grief," cried he, "have taken possession of my soul to such a degree, that little is wanting to bring me to instant death; for the cross is disgraced,—that cross which we have taken in honour of him who died upon the cross. Neither cross nor faith protects us longer, or guides us against the cruel Turks,—whom God curse! But it appears, as far as man can judge, that it is God's will to support them for our destruction. And never believe that the enemy will stop in his career after such success; on the contrary, he has sworn and publicly announced that not a single man who believes in Jesus Christ shall be left alive in Syria; that the temple even of the holy Mary will be converted into a mosque. Since the son of Mary, whom this affront ought to afflict, wills it to be so, *since this pleases him, does it follow that it should please us likewise?*

"He is then mad who seeks a quarrel with the Saracens, when Jesus Christ opposes them in nothing, as they have obtained victories, and are gaining them still (which grieves me) over the Franks, the Armenians, and the Persians. Every day we are conquered; for he sleeps,—that God that was accustomed to be so watchful: Mahomet acts with all his power, and the fierce Bibars seconds him."

We cannot believe that these exceedingly remarkable words expressed the feelings of the faithful; but at a time when poets ventured to speak in this manner, we may well suppose that men's minds were not favourable to a crusade. The troubadour we have quoted does not advise the making of any war against the Saracens, and inveighs bitterly against the pope, who sold *God and indulgences* to arm the French against the house of Swabia. In fact, the dissensions raised by the disputed succession of the kingdom of Naples and Sicily, then occupied the entire attention of the Holy See, and France was not quite free from party spirit on the occasion.

Not satisfied with launching excommunications and ecclesiastica thunders against Frederick and his family, the sovereign pontiffs wished to add the force of arms to the authority conferred upon them by the Church, and the right of conquest to that which they thought they possessed over a kingdom so near to their own capital. As they had no experience in war, and their lieutenants were equally deficient in capacity and courage, their armies were defeated. The court of Rome, thus conquered in the field of battle, was compelled to acknowledge the ascendancy of victory, and in this profane struggle lost some of that spiritual power which alone rendered it formidable.

With the exception of Mainfroy, a natural son of Frederick, and Conradin, his grandson, the family of Swabia was extinct. Mainfroy, who possessed both the abilities and courage of his father, had recently elevated the German cause in Italy, and braved both the arms and the power of the pontiffs. The court of Rome, upon finding it could not retain the kingdom of Sicily for itself, offered it to any one who would undertake the conquest of it. The crown to which Mainfroy pretended was first offered to Richard of Cornwall, and upon his prudent refusal, to Edmund, younger son of the king of England; but the English parliament would not grant the subsidies necessary for so great an undertaking. It was then offered to Louis IX. for his brother, the count of Anjou; and although the scruples of the pious monarch for a moment checked the projects of Pope Urban, Clement IV., on his accession, used fresh persuasions, and Louis at length suffered himself to be overcome by the prayers of Charles; at the same time entertaining a secret hope that the conquest of Sicily would some day prove instrumental to the defence of the Holy Land.

Charles, after being crowned by the pope in the church of St. John of the Lateran, entered the kingdom of Naples at the head of a considerable force, preceded by the fulminations of the court of Rome. The soldiers of Charles wore a cross, and fought in the name of the Church; priests exhorted the combatants, and promised them the protection of Heaven. Mainfroy succumbed in this, miscalled, holy war, and lost both his life and his crown at the battle of Cosenza.

The pope being delivered from the cares of this political crusade, turned his attention to the holy one beyond the seas; his legates solicited various princes, some to take the cross, others to accomplish their vows. Clement did not neglect to press Michael Palæologus to prove the sincerity of his promises. Charles, who was the acknowledged vassal of the pope, and who owed his kingdom to him, received many messages, representing the dangers of the Holy Land, and reminding him of what he owed to Jesus Christ, who was outraged by the victories of the Mussulmans. The new king of Sicily contented himself with sending an embassy to the sultan of Cairo, and with commending the unfortunate inhabitants of Palestine to the mercy of Bibars. The sultan replied to Charles, that he did not reject his intercessions; but the Christians were destroying themselves with their own hands; that no one among them had the power to enforce the observance of treaties, *and that the most contemptible of them were constantly undoing that which the greatest had done.* Bibars, in his turn, sent ambassadors to Charles, less for the purpose of following up any negotiations, than to obtain information upon the state and views of Christendom.

Young Conradin, who was preparing to dispute the crown of Sicily with Charles of Anjou, in order to avail himself of every means of supporting his claim, sent deputies to the sultan of Cairo, in the character of king of Jerusalem, conjuring him to protect his rights against his rival. Bibars, in his reply, pretended to endeavour to console Conradin, but, doubtless, received with joy these proofs of the divisions that existed among the princes of Europe.

In the state in which Europe then was, one monarch alone took serious interest in the fate of the Christian colonies of Asia. The remembrance of a land in which he had so long dwelt, and the hope of avenging the honour of the French arms in Egypt, once more directed the thoughts of Louis IX. to a new crusade. He however concealed his purpose, and this great project, says one of his historians, was formed, so to say, between God and himself. Louis consulted the pope, who hesitated to answer him, reflecting upon the dangers that his absence might bring upon France, and even upon Europe. The first letter of Clement aimed at diverting the French monarch from so perilous an enterprise; but, upon being consulted again, the sovereign pontiff showed none of the same scruples, and declared it to be his duty to encourage Louis in his design, as he was persuaded, he said, that this design came from God.

The purpose, however, of this negotiation remained still buried in profound mystery. Louis, no doubt, was fearful of prematurely announcing his designs, lest reflection might weaken the enthusiasm of which he must stand in so much need, or that a powerful opposition to the undertaking of a crusade might be formed in both his court and his kingdom; he thought that, by announcing his project unexpectedly, at the moment of its being ripe for execution, he should affect men's minds more forcibly, and induce them more easily to follow his example. An assembly of the barons, nobles, and prelates of the kingdom was solemnly convoked at Paris towards the middle of Lent. The faithful Joinville was not forgotten in this convocation; the seneschal foresaw, he says in his Memoirs, that Louis was about to take the cross, and the cause of his having this presentiment was, that in a dream he had seen the king of France clothed in a chasuble of a bright red colour, made of Rheims serge, which signified the cross. His almoner, when explaining this dream to him, added, that the chasuble being of Rheims serge, denoted that the crusade would be but a trifling or small exploit.

On the twenty-third day of March, the great parliament of the kingdom being assembled in a hall of the Louvre, the king entered, bearing in his hand the crown of thorns of Christ. At sight of this, the whole assembly became aware of the monarch's intentions. Louis, in a speech delivered with great animation, described the misfortunes of the Holy Land, and proclaimed that he was resolved to go and succour it; he then exhorted all who heard him to take the cross. When he ceased to speak, a sad but a profound silence expressed at once the surprise and grief of the barons and prelates, with the respect that all entertained for the will of the holy monarch.

Cardinal de St. Cecilia, the pope's legate, spoke after him, and in a pathetic exhortation, called upon the French warriors to take arms. Louis received the cross from the hands of the cardinal, and his example was followed by three of his sons. Among these princes, the assembly was affected at beholding John, count of Nevers, who was born at Damietta amidst the calamities of the preceding crusade. At the same time the legate received the oath of John, count of Brittany, of Alphonso de Brienne, count of Eu, of Marguerite, the ancient countess of Flanders, and of a great number of prelates, nobles, and knights.

The determination of St. Louis, of which a sad presentiment had been entertained, spread deep regret throughout his kingdom; his people could not behold without sorrow the departure of a prince whose presence alone preserved peace, and maintained order and justice everywhere. The health of the king was very much weakened, and there was great reason to fear that he would not be able to support the dangers and fatigues of a crusade; he took his sons with him; which circumstance added greatly to the public grief. The disasters of the first crusade were still fresh in the memory of his subjects, and whilst they thought of the captivity of the whole of the royal family, they dreaded greater misfortunes in the future. Joinville does not fear to say, "that they who had advised the king to undertake this voyage beyond the seas, had sinned mortally."

Notwithstanding the general regret, there were neither complaints nor murmurs against the king; the spirit of resignation, which was one of the virtues of the monarch, appeared to have passed into the minds of all his subjects, and, to employ the very expressions of the pope's bull, "the French people saw in the devotion of their king nothing but a noble and painful sacrifice to the cause of the Christians, to that cause for which God had not spared his only Son."

The greater that was the affection for the king, the greater was the general grief; but the zeal to partake his perils more than kept pace with these. Joinville, when present at the mass in the chapel, heard two knights conferring; one said, that if the king took the cross, it would be one of the most fatal days ever seen in France; for if we take the cross, we shall ruin the king; and again, if we take the cross, we shall lose God's grace, because we do not take the cross for the sake of him. Louis alone thought of delivering the tomb of Christ and the Christian colonies; the warlike nobility of the kingdom only thought of following their king in an expedition which was already looked upon as unfortunate.

Among those who took the cross after the assembly of the Louvre, history names Thibault, king of Navarre; Henry, count of Champagne, and his brother, the count d'Artois, son of Robert, killed at Mansourah; the counts of Flanders, de la Marche, St. Pol, and Soissons; the seigneurs de Montmorency, de Nemours, de Pienne, &c. The sieur de Joinville was warmly pressed to take the cross, but he resisted all the persuasions that could be made to him, alleging the vast injuries sustained by his vassals during the last expedition. The good seneschal also was not forgetful of the predictions of his almoner; he earnestly wished to accompany the king, whom he loved sincerely; but he was not yet recovered from the terrors he had experienced in Egypt, and no earthly motive could induce him to revisit the land of the Saracens.

The determination of the king of France created a lively sensation throughout Europe, and revived in men's minds the little that remained of the old enthusiasm for the crusades. As he was the chief of the enterprise, most of the warriors were ambitious of fighting under his immediate banners; the confidence entertained for his wisdom and virtues, in some sort fortified minds that

THE CAPTIVES.

After the capture of Antioch, Bibars distributed the booty among his soldiers, the Mamelukes reserving as their portion, the women, girls, and children. "At that time," says an Arabian chronicle, "THERE WAS NOT THE SLAVE OF A SLAVE THAT WAS NOT THE MASTER OF A SLAVE." A little boy was worth twelve dirhems, a little girl, five dirhems. In a single day the city of Antioch lost all its inhabitants, and a conflagration, lighted by order of Bibars, completed the work of the barbarians. Most historians agree in saying that seventeen thousand Christians were slaughtered, and a hundred thousand dragged away into slavery.—BOOK XV.

dreaded distant expeditions, and restored hopes to the Christian nations, that they appeared to have forgotten. The remembrance, even, of the misfortunes of the first voyage added to the security of the future, and created a belief in many that the triumph of the Christian armies would at length be the reward of past labours and calamities, and the fruit of a salutary experience.

Clement IV. wrote to the king of Armenia to console him for the evils he had suffered by the invasion of the Mamelukes, and to announce to him that the Christians of the East were about to receive powerful succours. Abaga, khan of the Tartars, who was then prosecuting a war against the Turks of Asia Minor, sent ambassadors to the court of Rome, and to several princes of the West, proposing to attack the Mamelukes in concert with the Franks, and drive them from Syria and Egypt. The pope received the Mogul ambassadors with great solemnity; he told them that an army, led by a powerful monarch, was about to embark for the East, that the hour fatal to the Mussulmans was come, and that God would bless his nation, and all the allies of his nation.

Louis, constantly occupied by his expedition, fixed the period of his departure for 1270; so that three long years must pass away before the assistance promised by the sovereign pontiff could arrive in the East. Vessels to transport the Crusaders were demanded of the republics of Genoa and Venice: the Venetians at first refused; but upon learning that applications were being made to the Genoese, they sent ambassadors to offer a fleet. After protracted negotiations, in which Venice evinced more jealousy of the Genoese than zeal for the crusade, she again refused to concur in the embarkation of the Christian army, being in less dread of the anger of Louis IX. than of that of the sultan of Cairo, who had it in his power to ruin her mercantile establishments in the East. At length the Genoese engaged to furnish vessels for the expedition.

But the greatest difficulty was to find the money necessary for the preparations of the war. Up to this period, the tenths levied upon the clergy had supplied the expenses of the crusades; and an opinion generally prevailed, that a holy war ought to be paid for by men attached to the Church and devoted to the altars of Jesus Christ. Urban IV., the predecessor of Clement, had already ordered throughout the West, that a levy of a hundredth should be made upon the revenues of the clergy; and, what might be considered a traffic in holy things, the court of Rome permitted the distributing of indulgences, which faculty was granted in proportion with what was given beyond the tribute required. The French clergy had addressed several petitions to the pope upon this subject; but these petitions always remained unnoticed.

When the late determination of Louis IX. became known, the Holy See had recourse to the customary means, and, without the least attention to complaints, which were not without foundation, the order was issued to levy again a tenth during three years. Upon this the clergy redoubled their opposition, and were much more earnest in the defence of their own revenues than in the defence of the Holy Land. They complained to the king, and they sent deputies to Rome, to show the depth of the misery into which the Church of France was plunged by the burdens imposed upon it;* these deputies represented to the sovereign pontiff that the exactions of latter times became every day more intolerable, and that the property of the clergy was no longer sufficient to support the altars and feed the poor of Jesus Christ. They added, that injustice and violence had formerly separated the Greek Church from that of Rome; giving his holiness to understand, that new rigours would not fail to produce new schisms. They further said, that if most crusades, particularly the expedition of Louis IX. into Egypt, had been unfortunate, it no doubt arose from the sanctuary having

---

* All these details upon the tenths are of great importance for the history of the crusades: for this negotiation the following authorities may be consulted: Raynaldi, No. 59; the *Spicilège*, vol. xiii., p. 221; the *Supplement* to Raynaldi, book lxix., No. 42; Fleury's *Ecclesiastical History*, and the *Acts* of Rymer.

been plundered, and the churches ruined for the sake of them; as a last reason, they prognosticated much greater calamities for the future than any that had been experienced.

Such an address necessarily inflamed the anger of the sovereign pontiff. Clement, in his reply, warmly reproached the deputies, and they who had sent them, with their indifference for the cause of all Christians, and for their avarice, which made them deny their superfluous wealth for the prosecution of a war in which so many princes and illustrious warriors perilled their lives. He pointed to the excommunication ready to fall upon their heads, and, what must have much more terrified them, he threatened to deprive them of their property and their benefices. Such was then the power of Rome, that nothing could be possessed without its pleasure: the clergy were obliged to submit, and pay the tenth during four years. The pope further empowered the king to dispose of all the sums bequeathed by will for the assistance of the Holy Land; he equally abandoned to him the money that might be drawn from those who, having taken the cross, were desirous of redeeming their vows; which latter means must have produced a considerable sum, as the clergy gave the cross to everybody, and refused dispensation to nobody.

Louis IX. neglected none of the resources that his position as king of France placed in his hands; at this period no regular impost was known, and, to support the splendour of their thrones, kings had nothing to depend upon but the revenues of their domains. In order to provide for all the expenses he was obliged to incur on this occasion, the king had recourse to the impost called the capitation-tax, which suzerain lords, according to feudal customs, required of each of their vassals in any extraordinary circumstances. Usage authorized him to levy this contribution on account of the crusade, but he had also the right, on the occasion of a ceremony, at that time very important, in which his eldest son Philip was to be received as a knight. Thus, the impost was demanded in the name of chivalry and in the name of religion; it was paid without a murmur, because Louis confided the gathering of it to men of acknowledged integrity.

When Philip received the sword of knighthood, the French, and particularly the Parisians, expressed their love for Louis IX. and his family by public rejoicings; all the nobility hastened from the provinces to be present at the festivities and spectacles that were celebrated in the capital on this occasion. Amidst the tournaments, the exercises of the tilt-yard, and the sports in which the skill and courage of the *preux* and the *paladins* were displayed, the crusade was not forgotten. The pope's legate pronounced a discourse, in the isle of St. Louis, upon the misfortunes of the Holy Land; all the people appeared to be deeply moved by the exhortations of the prelate; a crowd of knights, and warriors of all classes, took the cross; thus Louis IX. found in this circumstance an opportunity of raising money for the support of his army, and of procuring recruits for the holy war.

Whilst all France was engaged in preparing for the expedition beyond the seas, the crusade was preached in the other countries of Europe. A council was held at Northampton, in England, in which Ottobon, the pope's legate, exhorted the faithful to arm themselves to save the little that remained of the kingdom of Jerusalem; and Prince Edward took the cross, to discharge the vow that his father Henry III. had made when the news reached Europe of the captivity of Louis IX. in Egypt. After the example of Edward, his brother Prince Edmund, with the earls of Pembroke and Warwick, and many knights and barons, agreed to take arms against the infidels. The same zeal for the deliverance of the holy places was manifested in Scotland, where John Baliol and several nobles enrolled themselves under the banners of the cross.

Catalonia and Castile furnished a great number of Crusaders: the king of Portugal, and James, king of Arragon, took the cross. Dona Sancha, one of the daughters of the Arragonese prince, had made a pilgrimage to Jerusalem, and had died in the hospital of St. John, after devoting many years to the service of pilgrims and the sick. James had several times conquered the Moors; but neither his exploits against the infidels, nor the remembrance of a daughter who had fallen a martyr to Christian charity, could sustain his piety against the attacks of his earthly passions, and his shameful connection with Berengaria scandalized Christendom.

The pope, to whom he communicated his design of going to the Holy Land, replied that Jesus Christ could not accept the services of a prince *who crucified him every day by his sins*. The king of Arragon, by a strange combination of opposite sentiments, would neither renounce Berengaria nor give up his project of going to fight against the infidels in the East. He renewed his oath in a great assembly at Toledo, at which the ambassadors of the khan of Tartary and of the king of Armenia were present. We read in a Spanish dissertation upon the crusades, that Alphonso the Wise, who was not able to go to the East himself, furnished the king of Arragon with a hundred men and a hundred thousand marvedis in gold; the order of St. James, and other orders of knighthood, who had often accompanied the conqueror of the Moors in his battles, supplied him also with men and money. The city of Barcelona offered him eighty thousand Barcellonese sols, and Majorca fifty thousand silver sols, with two equipped vessels. The fleet, composed of thirty large ships and a great number of smaller craft, in which were embarked eight hundred men-at-arms and two thousand foot-soldiers, set out from Barcelona on the 4th of September, 1268. When they arrived off Majorca, the fleet was dispersed by a tempest; one part of the vessels gained the coasts of Asia, another took shelter in the ports of Sardinia; the vessel the king of Arragon was on board of was cast upon the coast of Languedoc.

The arrival at Ptolemaïs of the Arragonese Crusaders, commanded by a natural son of James, restored some hopes to the Franks of Palestine. An envoy from the king of Arragon, according to the Oriental chronicles, repaired to the khan of the Tartars, to announce to him that the Spanish monarch would soon arrive with his army. But whether he was detained by the charms of Berengaria, or whether the tempest that dispersed his fleet made him believe that Heaven was averse to his pilgrimage, James did not arrive. His departure, in which he appeared to despise the counsels of the Holy See, had been severely censured; and his return, which was attributed to his disgraceful passion, met with an equal share of blame. Murmurs likewise arose against the king of Portugal, who had levied the tenths, but did not leave his kingdom.

All those who in Europe took an interest in the crusade, had, at this time, their eyes directed towards the kingdom of Naples, where Charles of Anjou was making great preparations to accompany his brother into the East; but this kingdom, recently conquered, was doomed again to be the theatre of a war kindled by vengeance and ambition. There fell out in the states of Naples and Sicily, which had so often changed masters, that which almost always takes place after a revolution: deceived hopes were changed into hatreds: the excesses inseparable from a conquest, the presence of an army proud of its victories, with the too violent government of Charles, animated the people against their new king. Clement IV. thought it his duty to give a timely and salutary warning: "Your kingdom," he wrote to him, "at first exhausted by the agents of your authority, is now torn by your enemies; thus the caterpillar destroys what has escaped the grasshopper. The kingdom of Sicily and Naples has not been wanting in men to desolate it; where now are they that will defend it?" This letter of the pope announced storms ready to break forth. Many of those who had called Charles to the throne, regretted the house of Swabia, and directed their new hopes towards Conradin, heir of Frederick and of Conrad. This young prince quitted Germany with an army, and advanced towards Italy, strengthening himself in his march with the party of the Ghibellines, and with all those whom the domination of Charles had irritated. All Italy was in flames, and the pope,

Charles's protector, retired to Viterbo, had no defence to afford him, except the thunders of the Church.

Charles of Anjou, however, assembled his troops, and marched out to meet his rival. The two armies met in the plain of St. Valentine, near Aquila; the army of Conradin was cut to pieces, and the young prince fell into the power of the conqueror. Posterity cannot pardon Charles for having abused his victory even so far as to condemn and decapitate his disarmed and vanquished enemy.* After this execution, Sicily and the country of Naples were given up to all the furies of a jealous, suspicious tyranny; for violence produces violence, and great political crimes never come alone. It was thus that Charles got ready for the crusade; but, on the other hand, Providence was preparing terrible catastrophes for him: "So true it is," says an historian, "that God as often gives kingdoms to punish those he elevates, as to chastise those whom he brings low."

While these bloody scenes were passing in Italy, Louis IX. was following up the establishment of public peace and his darling object, the crusade, at the same time. The holy monarch did not forget that the surest manner of softening the evils of war, as well as of his absence, was to make good laws; he therefore issued several ordinances, and each of these ordinances was a monument of his justice. The most celebrated of all is the Pragmatic Sanction, which Bossuet called the firmest support of Gallican liberties. He also employed himself in elevating that monument of legislation which illustrated his reign, and which became a light for following ages.

The count of Poictiers, who was to accompany his brother, was in the mean time engaged in pacifying his provinces, and established many regulations for maintaining public order. He, above everything, endeavoured to abolish slavery; having for a maxim, "That men are born free, and it is always wise to bring back things to their origin." This good prince drew upon himself the benedictions of his people; and the love of his vassals assured the duration of the laws he made.

We have said that Prince Edward, son of Henry III., had taken the oath to combat the infidels. He had recently displayed a brilliant valour in the civil war that had so long desolated England; and the deliverance of his father and the pacification of the kingdom had been the reward of his exploits. It was his esteem for the character of Louis IX., more than the spirit of devotion, that induced him to set out for the East. The king of France, who himself exhorted him to take the cross, lent him seventy thousand livres tournois for the preparations for his voyage. Edward was to follow Louis as his vassal, and to conduct under his banners the English Crusaders, united with those of Guienne. Gaston de Béarn, to whom the French monarch advanced the sum of twenty-five thousand livres, prepared to follow Prince Edward to the Holy Land.

The period fixed upon for the departure of the expedition was drawing near. By order of the legate, the curés in every parish had taken the names of the Crusaders, in order to oblige them to wear the cross publicly, and all had notice to hold themselves in readiness to embark in the month of May, 1270. Louis confided the administration of his kingdom, during his absence, to Matthew, abbot of St. Denis, and to Simon, sieur de Nesle; he wrote to all the nobles who were to follow him into the Holy Land, to recommend them to assemble their knights and men-at-arms. As religious enthusiasm was not sufficiently strong to make men forget their worldly interests, many nobles who had taken the cross entertained great fears of being ruined by the holy war, and most of them hesitated to set out. Louis undertook to pay all the expenses of their voyage, and to maintain them at his own cost during the war,—a thing that had not been done in the crusades of Louis VII. or

---

* Migeray thus describes the murder of Conradin:—"As Charles had determined to go into Africa with the king, St. Louis, not knowing what to do with Conradin and Frederick, whom it was dangerous to keep, and still more to release, in a kingdom filled with faction and revolt, he ordered them to be brought to trial before the syndics of the cities of the kingdom."

THE DEPARTURE FROM AIGUES-MORTES.

The king of Sicily had taken the cross without having the least inclination to embark for Asia; and when the question was discussed in council, he gave it as his opinion that Tunis should be the object of the first attack. The kingdom of Tunis covered the seas with pirates, who infested all the routes to Palestine; it was, besides, the ally of Egypt, and might, if subdued, be made the readiest road to that country. These were the ostensible reasons put forth; the true ones were, that it was of importance to the king of Sicily that the coasts of Africa should be brought under European subjection, and that he did not wish to go too far from Italy. The true reason with St. Louis, and that which, no doubt, determined him, was, that he believed it possible to convert the king of Tunis, and thus bring a vast kingdom under the Christian banners.

At length the unwilling Crusaders, stimulated by repeated exhortations, and by the example of Louis, set forward on their march from all the provinces, and directed their course towards the ports of Aigues-Mortes and Marseilles.

Before he embarked, the king wrote once more to the regents of the kingdom, to recommend them to watch carefully over public morals, to deliver France from corrupt judges, and to render to everybody, particularly to the poor, prompt and perfect justice, so that He who judges the judgments of men might have nothing to reproach him with.

[BOOK XV.

Philip Augustus, in which the ardour of the Crusaders did not allow them to give a thought to their fortunes, or to exercise so much foresight. We have still a valuable monument of this epoch in a charter, by which the king of France stipulates how much he is to pay to a great number of barons and knights during the time the war beyond the seas should last.

Early in the month of March, Louis repaired to the church of St. Denis, where he received the symbols of pilgrimage, and placed his kingdom under the protection of the apostles of France. Upon the day following this solemn ceremony, a mass for the crusade was celebrated in the church of Notre Dame, at Paris. The monarch appeared there, accompanied by his children and the principal nobles of his court; he walked from the palace barefooted, carrying his scrip and staff. The same day he went to sleep at Vincennes, and beheld, for the last time, the spot on which he had enjoyed so much happiness in administering justice to his people. And it was here too that he took leave of Queen Marguerite, whom he had never before quitted,—a separation rendered so much the more painful by the sorrowful reflection it recalled of past events, and by melancholy presentiments for the future.

Both the people and the court were affected by the deepest regret, and that which added to the public anxiety was the circumstance that every one was ignorant of the point to which the expedition was to be directed: the coast of Africa was only vaguely conjectured. The king of Sicily had taken the cross without having the least inclination to embark for Asia; and when the question was discussed in council, he gave it as his opinion that Tunis should be the object of the first attack. The kingdom of Tunis covered the seas with pirates, who infested all the routes to Palestine; it was, besides, the ally of Egypt, and might, if subdued, be made the readiest road to that country. These were the ostensible reasons put forth; the true ones were, that it was of importance to the king of Sicily that the coasts of Africa should be brought under European subjection, and that he did not wish to go too far from Italy. The true reason with St. Louis, and that which, no doubt, determined him, was, that he believed it possible to convert the king of Tunis, and thus bring a vast kingdom under the Christian banners. The Mussulman prince, whose ambassadors had been several times in France, had himself given birth to this idea, by saying, that he asked nothing better than to embrace the religion of Jesus Christ: thus, that which he had said to turn aside an invasion, was precisely the cause of the war being directed against his territories. Louis IX. often repeated that he would consent to pass the whole of his life in a dungeon, without seeing the sun, if, by such a sacrifice, the conversion of the king of Tunis and his nation could be brought about; an expression of ardent proselytism that has been blamed with much bitterness, but which only showed an extreme desire to see Africa delivered from barbarism, and marching with Europe in the progress of intelligence and civilization, which are the great blessings of Christianity.

As Louis traversed his kingdom on his way to Aigues-Mortes, where the army of the Crusaders was to embark, he was everywhere hailed by the benedictions of his people, and gratified by hearing their ardent prayers for the success of his arms; the clergy and the faithful, assembled in the churches, prayed for the king and his children, and all that should follow him. They prayed also for foreign princes and nobles who had taken the cross, and promised to go into the East; as if they would, by that means, press them to hasten their departure.

Very few, however, responded to this religious appeal. The king of Castile, who had taken the cross, had pretensions to the imperial crown, nor could he forget the death of his brother Frederick, immolated by Charles of Anjou. It was not only that the affairs of the empire detained the German princes and nobles; the death of young Conradin had so shocked and disgusted men's minds in Germany, that no one from that country would have consented to fight under the same banners as the king of Sicily. So black a crime, committed amidst the preparations for a holy war, appeared to presage great calamities. In the height of their grief or indignation, people might fear that Heaven would be angry with the Christians, and that its curse would fall upon the arms of the Crusaders.

When Louis arrived at Aigues-Mortes, he found neither the Genoese fleet nor the principal nobles who were to embark with him; the ambassadors of Palæologus were the only persons who did not cause themselves to be waited for; for a great dread of the crusade was entertained at Constantinople, and this fear was more active than the enthusiasm of the Crusaders. Louis might have asked the Greek emperor why, after having promised to send soldiers, he had only sent ambassadors; but Louis, who attached great importance to the conversion of the Greeks, contented himself with removing the apprehensions of the envoys, and as Clement IV. died at that period, he sent them to the conclave of the cardinals, to terminate the reunion of the two churches.

At length the unwilling Crusaders, stimulated by repeated exhortations, and by the example of Louis, set forward on their march from all the provinces, and directed their course towards the ports of Aigues-Mortes and Marseilles. Louis soon welcomed the arrival of the count of Poictiers, with a great number of his vassals; the principal nobles brought with them the most distinguished of their knights and their most brave and hardy soldiers; many cities likewise contributed their supply of warriors. Each troop had its banner, and formed a separate corps, bearing the name of a city or a province; the battalions of Beaucaire, Carcassonne, Châlons, Perigord, &c., attracted observation in the Christian army. These names, it is true, excited great emulation, but they also gave rise to quarrels, which the wisdom and firmness of Louis had great difficulty in appeasing. Crusaders arrived from Catalonia, Castile, and several other provinces of Spain; five hundred warriors from Friesland likewise ranged themselves with full confidence under the standard of such a leader as Louis, saying, that their nation had always been proud to obey the kings of France.

Before he embarked, the king wrote once more to the regents of the kingdom, to recommend them to watch carefully over public morals, and to deliver France from corrupt judges, and to render to everybody, particularly to the poor, prompt and perfect justice, so that He who judges the judgments of men might have nothing to reproach him with.

Such were the last farewells that Louis took of France. The fleet set sail on the fourth of July, 1270, and in a few days arrived in the road of Cagliari. Here the council of the counts and barons was assembled in the king's vessel, to deliberate upon the plan of the crusade. Those who advocated the conquest of Tunis, said that by that means the passages of the Mediterranean would be opened, and the power of the Mamelukes would be weakened; and that after that conquest the army would go triumphantly into either Egypt or Palestine. Many of the barons were not of this opinion; they said, if the Holy Land stood in need of prompt assistance, they ought to afford it without delay; whilst they were engaged on the coast of Africa, in a country with which they were unacquainted, the Christian cities of Syria might all fall into the hands of the Saracens; the most redoubtable enemy of the Christians was Bibars, the terrible sultan of Cairo; it was him they ought first to attack; it was into his states, into the bosom of his capital, that the war should be carried, and not to a place two hundred leagues from Egypt. They added to this, remembrances of the defeats of the French army on the banks of the Nile,—defeats that ought to be avenged upon the very theatre of so many disasters.

Contemporary history does not say to what extent Louis was struck with the wisdom of these last opinions; but the expedition to Tunis flattered his most cherished hopes. It had been proposed by the king of Sicily, whose concurrence was necessary to the success of the crusade. It was, therefore, decided that the Genoese fleet should direct its course towards Africa; and two days after, on the twentieth of July, it arrived in sight of Tunis and Carthage.

On the western coast of Africa, opposite Sicily, is a peninsula, described by Strabo, whose circumference is three hundred and forty stadii, or forty-two miles. This peninsula advances into the sea between two gulfs, one of which, on the west, offers a commodious port; the other, on the southeast, communicates, by means of a canal, with a lake which extends three leagues into the land, and which modern geographers term the Gullet. It was upon this spot was built the great rival of Rome, whose site extended over the two shores of the sea. Neither the conquests of the Romans, nor the ravages of the Vandals, had been able to entirely destroy this once flourishing city; but in the seventh century, after being invaded and laid waste by the Saracens, it became nothing but a mass of ruins; a moderate-sized village upon the port, called Marsa, a tower on the point of the cape, a pretty strong castle on the hill of Byrsa,—these were all the remains of that city whose power so long dominated over the Mediterranean and the coasts of Africa and Asia.

At five leagues' distance, towards the south-east, a little beyond the gulf and the lake of the Gullet, arose a city, called in ancient times Tynis or Tunissa, of which Scipio made himself master before he attacked Carthage. Tunis had thriven by the fall of other cities, and in the thirteenth century she vied in wealth and population with the most flourishing cities of Africa. It contained ten thousand houses, and had three extensive suburbs; the spoils of nations and the produce of an immense commerce had enriched it; and all that the art of fortification could invent had been employed to defend the access to it.

The coast on which Tunis stood was the theatre of many revolutions, of which ancient history has transmitted accounts to us; but modern history has not, in the same manner, consecrated the revolutions of the Saracens. We can scarcely follow the march of the barbarians who planted the standard of Islamism upon so many ruins. All that we positively know is, that Tunis, for a long time united to the kingdom of Morocco, was separated from it under a warlike prince, whose third successor was reigning in the time of St. Louis.

At the sight of the Christian fleet, the inhabitants of the coast of Africa were seized with terror, and all who were upon the Carthage shore took flight towards the mountains or towards Tunis. Some vessels that were in the port were abandoned by their crews; the king ordered Florent de Varennes, who performed the functions of admiral, to get into a boat and reconnoitre the coast. Varennes found nobody in the port or upon the shore; he sent word to the king that there was no time to be lost, he must take immediate advantage of the consternation of the enemy. But it was remembered that in the preceding expedition the descent upon the coast of Egypt had been too precipitate; in this it was determined to risk nothing. Inexperienced youth had presided over the former war; now it was directed by old age and ripe manhood: it was resolved to wait till the morrow.

The next day, at dawn, the coast appeared covered with Saracens, among whom were many men on horseback. The Crusaders, not the less, commenced their preparations for landing. At the approach of the Christians the multitude of infidels disappeared; which, according to the account of an eye witness, was a blessing from Heaven, for the disorder was so great, that a hundred men would have been sufficient to stop the disembarkation of the whole army.

When the Christian army had landed, it was drawn up in order of battle upon the shore, and, in accordance with the laws of war, Pierre de Condé, almoner to the king, read, with a loud voice, a proclamation, by which the conquerors took possession of the territory. This proclamation, which Louis had drawn up himself, began by these words: "I proclaim, in the name of our Lord Jesus Christ, and of Louis, king of France, his sergeant," &c.

The baggage, provisions, and munitions of war were landed; a vast space was marked out, and the Christian soldiers pitched their tents. Whilst they were digging ditches and raising intrenchments to protect the army from a surprise, they took possession of the tower built on the point of the cape; and on the following day, five hundred sailors planted the standard of the lilies upon the castle of Carthage. The village of Marsa, which was close to the castle, fell likewise into the hands of the Crusaders; the women and the sick were placed here, whilst the army remained beneath their tents.

Louis still hoped for the conversion of the king of Tunis, but this pious illusion was very quickly dissolved. The Mussulman prince sent messengers to the king, to inform him that he would come and meet him at the head of a hundred thousand men, and would require baptism of him on the field of battle; the Moorish king added, that he had caused all the Christians in his dominions to be seized, and that every one of them should be massacred if the Christian army presumed to insult his capital.

The menaces and vain bravadoes of the prince of Tunis effected no change in the plans of the crusade; the Moors, besides, inspired no fear, and they themselves could not conceal the terror which the sight only of the Christians created in them. Not daring to face their enemy, their scattered bands sometimes hovered around the Christian army, seeking to surprise any stragglers from the camp; and at others, uniting together, they poured down towards the advanced posts, launched a few arrows, showed their naked swords, and then depended upon the swiftness of their horses to secure them from the pursuit of the Christians. They not unfrequently had recourse to treachery: three hundred of them came into the camp of the Crusaders, and said they wished to embrace the Christian faith, and a hundred more followed them, announcing the same intention. After being received with open arms, they waited for what they deemed a favourable opportunity, and fell upon a body of the Christians, sword in hand; but being overwhelmed by numbers, most of them were killed, and the rest were allowed to escape. Three of the principals fell on their knees, and implored the compassion of the leaders. The contempt the Franks had for such enemies obtained their pardon, and they were driven out of the camp.

At length the Mussulman army, emboldened by the inaction of the Christians, presented itself several times on the plain. Nothing would have been more easy than to attack and conquer it; but Louis had resolved to act upon the defensive, and to await the arrival of the king of Sicily for beginning the war,—a fatal resolution, which ruined everything: the Sicilian monarch, who had advised this ill-starred expedition, was destined to complete, by his delays, the evil he had begun by his counsels.

The Mussulmans flocked from all parts of Africa to defend the cause of Islamism against the Christians. Preparations were carried on in Egypt to meet the invasion of the Franks, and in the month of August, Bibars announced by messengers, that he was about to march to the assistance of Tunis. The troops which the sultan of Cairo maintained in the province of Barka received orders to set forward. Thus, the Moorish army was about to become formidable; but it was not this host of Saracens that the Crusaders had most to dread. Other dangers, other misfortunes threatened them: the Christian army wanted water; they had none but salted provisions; the soldiers could not endure the climate of Africa; winds constantly prevailed, which, coming from the torrid zone, appeared to the Europeans to be the breath of a devouring fire. The Saracens upon the neighbouring mountains raised the sand with certain instruments made for the purpose, and the dust was carried by the wind in burning clouds down upon the plain upon which the Christians were encamped. At last, dysentery, that fatal malady of warm climates, began to commit frightful ravages among the

THE NIGHT OF AUGUST 25TH, 1270.

We have spoken of the profound grief which prevailed among the Crusaders when Louis fell sick. There was not a leader or a soldier that did not forget his own ills in his anxiety for the king. At every hour of the day and night these faithful warriors crowded round the monarch's tent, and when they beheld the sad and apprehensive air of all who came out of it, they turned away, with their eyes cast to the earth, and their souls filled with the most gloomy thoughts. In the camp, the soldiers scarcely durst ask each other a question, for they heard none but sorrowful tidings. At length, when the event that all had dreaded was announced to the army, the French warriors abandoned themselves to despair; they saw in the death of Louis a signal for all sorts of calamities, and anxiously inquired of each other what leader was to conduct them back to their homes.—BOOK XV.

troops; and the plague, which appears to be born of itself upon this burning, arid sand, spread its dire contagion through the Christian army.

They were obliged to be under arms night and day; not to defend themselves from an enemy that always fled away from them, but to guard against surprise. A vast number of the Crusaders sunk under fatigue, famine, and disease. The French had soon to regret the loss of Bouchard, count de Vendome, the count de la Marche, Gauthier de Nemours, the lords de Montmorency, de Pienne, de Bressac, Guy d'Aspremont, and Raoul, brother of the count de Soissons. It became impossible to bury the dead; the ditches of the camp were filled with carcases, thrown in in heaps, which added to the corruption of the air and to the spectacle of the general desolation.

At length Olivier de Termes, a Languedocian gentleman, coming from Sicily, announced that King Charles was quite ready to embark with his army. This news was received with joy, but had no power to alleviate the evils the Crusaders were then exposed to. The heats became excessive; the want of water, bad food, disease, which continued its ravages, and the grief at being shut up in a camp without the power to fight, completed the despondency that had taken possession of the minds of leaders and soldiers. Louis endeavoured to cheer them both by his words and his example; but he himself fell ill with dysentery. Prince Philip, the duke de Nevers, the king of Navarre, and the legate also felt the effects of the contagion. The duke de Nevers, surnamed Tristan, was born at Damietta during the captivity of the king, and was particularly the object of his father's love. The young prince remained in the royal tent; but as he appeared to be sinking under the effects of the disease, it was judged best to convey him on board one of the vessels. The monarch incessantly demanded news of his son: but all who surrounded him preserved a melancholy silence. At length they were obliged to inform him that the duke de Nevers was dead; the feelings of the father prevailed over the resignation of the Christian, and he wept bitterly. A short time afterwards, the pope's legate died, deeply regretted by the clergy and the soldiers of the cross, who regarded him as their spiritual father.

In spite of his sufferings, in spite of his griefs, Louis IX. was constantly engaged in endeavours to alleviate the situation of his army. He gave orders as long as he had any strength left, dividing his time between the duties of a Christian and those of a monarch. The fever, however, increased; no longer able to attend either to his cares for the army or to exercises of piety, he ordered the cross to be placed before him, and stretching out his hands, he in silence implored Him who had suffered for all men.

The whole army was in a state of mourning; the soldiers walked about in tears, demanding of Heaven the preservation of so good a prince. Amidst the general grief, Louis turned his thoughts towards the accomplishment of the divine laws and the destinies of France. Philip, who was his successor to the throne, was in his tent; he desired him to approach his bed, and in a faltering voice gave him counsels in what manner he should govern the kingdom of his fathers. The instructions he gave him comprise the most noble maxims of religion and loyalty; and that which will render them for ever worthy of the respect of posterity is, that they had the authority of his example, and only recalled the virtues of his own life. After having recommended Philip to respect, and cause to be respected, religion and its ministers, and at all times, and above all things, to fear to offend God: "My dear son," added he, "be charitable and merciful towards the poor and all who suffer. If thou attainest the throne, show thyself worthy, by thy conduct, of receiving the holy unction with which the kings of France are consecrated. When thou shalt be king, show thyself just in all things, and let nothing turn thee aside from the path of truth and rectitude. If the widow and orphan contend before thee with the powerful man, declare thyself of the party of the feeble against the strong, until the truth shall be known to thee. In affairs in which thou thyself shalt be interested, support at first the cause of the other; for if thou dost not act in that sort, thy counsellors will hesitate to speak against thee, which thou oughtest not to desire. My dear son, above all things I recommend thee to avoid war with every Christian nation; if thou art reduced by necessity to make it, at least take care that the poor people, who are not in the wrong, be kept safe from all harm. Give all thy efforts to appease the divisions that may arise in thy kingdom, for nothing is so pleasing to God as the spectacle of concord and peace. Neglect nothing to provide good lieutenants (baillis) and provosts in thy provinces. Give power freely to men who know how to use it, and punish all who abuse it; for if it is thy duty to hate evil in another, much greater reason hast thou to hate it in them who hold their authority of thee. Be just in the levying of thy public taxes, and be wise and moderate in the expenditure of them; beware of foolish expenses, which lead to unjust imposts; correct with prudence all that is defective in the laws of thy kingdom. Maintain with loyalty the rights and franchises that thy predecessors have left, for the happier that thy subjects shall be, the greater thou wilt be; the more irreproachable thy government shall be, the more thy enemies will fear to attack it."

Louis gave Philip several more counsels upon the love he owed to God, his people, and his family; then pouring out his full heart, he uttered nothing but the language of a parent who is about to be separated from a son he loves tenderly. "I bestow upon thee," said he, "all the benedictions that a father can bestow upon a dear son. Aid me by masses and prayers, and let me have a part in all the good actions thou shalt perform. I beseech our Lord Jesus Christ, by his great mercy, to guard thee from all evils, and to keep thee from doing anything contrary to his will; and that after this mortal life we may see Him, love Him, and praise Him together in a life everlasting."

When we reflect that these words were pronounced on the coast of Africa by a dying king of France, we experience a mixture of surprise and emotion, which even the coldest and most indifferent hearts can scarcely fail to partake of. Judge, then, of the effect they must have produced upon the feelings of a desolate son! Philip listened to them with respectful sorrow, and commanded them to be faithfully transcribed, in order that he might have them before his eyes all the days of his life.

Louis then turned to his daughter, the queen of Navarre, who sat, drowned in tears, at the foot of his bed: in a precept which he had prepared for her, he laid before her all the duties of a queen and a wife. Above all, he recommended her to take the greatest care of her husband, who was then sick; and, never forgetful of even the smallest circumstances, he advised the king of Navarre, on his return to Champagne, to pay all his debts before he began to rebuild the convent of the Cordeliers of Provins.

These instructions were the last words that Louis addressed to his children; from that time they never saw him again. The ambassadors of Michael Palæologus arriving in the camp, the king consented to receive them. In the state in which Louis then was, it was impossible for him to see through the false promises of the Greeks, or the alarms and deceitful policy of their emperor; he no longer gave attention to the things of this world. He confined himself to the expression of his earnest wishes that the reunion of the two churches might at length be effected, and promised the ambassadors that his son Philip would do everything in his power to bring it about. These envoys were Meliteniote, archdeacon of the imperial chapel, and the celebrated Vechus, chancellor of the church of Constantinople. They were both so much affected by the words and the virtues of St. Louis, that they afterwards gave their most zealous endeavours to promote the reunion, and both ended by becoming victims to the policy of the Greeks.

After this interview Louis thought of nothing but his God, and remained alone with his confessor. His almoners recited before him the prayers of the Church, to which he responded. He then received the Viaticum and extreme unction. "From Sunday, at the hour of nones," says an ocular witness, "till Monday, at the hour of tierce, his mouth never ceased, either day or night, to praise our Lord, and to pray for the people he had brought to that place." He was heard to pronounce these words of the prophet-king: "Grant, Lord, that we may despise the prosperities of this world, and know how to brave its adversities." He likewise repeated, as loudly as his feeble state would permit, this verse of another psalm: "Oh, God! deign to sanctify thy people, and to watch over them." Sometimes he invoked St. Denis, whom he was accustomed to invoke in battle, and implored him to grant his heavenly support to this army he was about to leave without a leader. In the night between Sunday and Monday he was heard to pronounce the word *Jerusalem* twice, and then he added: "We will go to Jerusalem." His mind was constantly occupied with the idea of the holy war. Perhaps, likewise, he saw nothing then but the heavenly Jerusalem, the last country of the just man.

At nine o'clock in the morning of Monday, the twenty-fifth of August, he lost his speech; but he still looked upon all who were round him kindly (*débonnairement*). His countenance was calm, and it was evident that his mind was, at the same time, divided between the purest of earthly affections and the thoughts of eternity. Feeling that death was approaching fast, he made signs to his attendants to place him, covered by hair-cloth, upon a bed of ashes. Between the hours of tierce and mid-day he appeared to sleep, and lay with his eyes closed for more than half an hour at a time. He then seemed to revive, opened his eyes, and looking towards heaven, exclaimed: "O Lord! I shall enter into thy house, and shall worship thee in thy holy tabernacle!" He died at three o'clock in the afternoon.

We have spoken of the profound grief which prevailed among the Crusaders when Louis fell sick. There was not a leader or a soldier that did not forget his own ills in his anxiety for the king. At every hour of the day and night these faithful warriors crowded round the monarch's tent, and when they beheld the sad and apprehensive air of all who came out of it, they turned away, with their eyes cast to the earth, and their souls filled with the most gloomy thoughts. In the camp, the soldiers scarcely durst ask each other a question, for they heard none but sorrowful tidings. At length, when the event that all had dreaded was announced to the army, the French warriors abandoned themselves to despair; they saw in the death of Louis a signal for all sorts of calamities, and anxiously inquired of each other what leader was to conduct them back to their homes. With the general groans and tears were mingled many bitter reproaches against those who had advised this fatal expedition, particularly the king of Sicily, whom all accused of being the cause of the disasters of the war.

On the very day of the king's death Charles of Anjou and his army landed near Carthage; trumpets and other warlike music resounded along the shore, but a profound and melancholy silence was preserved in the camp of the Crusaders, and not a man went forth to meet the Sicilians, whom they had looked for with so much impatience. Sad forebodings rushed into the mind of Charles; he galloped forward, and flying to the tent of the king, found his royal brother dead, and stretched upon his bed of ashes. The features of Louis were scarcely altered, his death had been so calm. Charles prostrated himself at his feet, watering them with his tears, and calling him sometimes his brother, and sometimes his lord. He remained a long time in this attitude, without seeing any of those who surrounded him, continuing to address Louis as if he had been still living, and reproaching himself, in accents of despair, with not having heard, with not having received, the last words of the most affectionate of brothers and best of kings.

The mortal remains of Louis were deposited in two funeral urns. The entrails of the holy monarch were granted to Charles of Anjou, who sent them to the abbey of Montréal, where these precious relics, for a length of time, attracted the devotion and respect of the faithful. The bones and the heart of Louis remained in the hands of Philip. This young prince was desirous of sending them to France, but the leaders and soldiers would not consent to be separated from all that was left to them of their beloved monarch. The presence of this sacred deposit amongst the Crusaders appeared to them a safeguard against new misfortunes, and the most sure means of drawing down the protection of Heaven upon the Christian army.

Philip was still sick, and his malady created great anxiety. The army considered him the worthy successor of Louis, and the affection that had been felt for the father descended to the son; he received, amidst the public grief, the homage and oaths of the leaders, barons, and nobles. His first care was to confirm the regency, and all that his father had established in France before his departure. Geoffrey de Beaulieu, William de Chartres, and John de Mons, confessors and almoners to the king, were directed to carry these orders of Philip's into the West. Among the letters which these ecclesiastics took with them into France, history has preserved that which was addressed to the clergy *and to all people of worth* in the kingdom. After having described their labours, the perils and the death of Louis IX., the young prince implored God to grant that he might follow the steps of so good a father, might accomplish his sacred commands, and put in practice all his counsels. Philip concluded his letter, which was read aloud in all churches, by supplicating the ecclesiastics and the faithful "to put up to the King of Kings their prayers and their offerings for that prince, with whose zeal for religion, and tender solicitude for the kingdom of France, which he loved as the apple of his eye, they were so well acquainted."

The death of Louis had greatly raised the confidence of the Saracens. The mourning and grief which they observed in the Christian army were, by them, mistaken for discouragement, and they flattered themselves they should obtain a triumph over their enemies; but these hopes were speedily dispelled. The king of Sicily took the command of the Christian army during the sickness of Philip, and resumed the war. The troops he had brought with him were eager for fight, and all the French seemed anxious to seek a distraction from their grief in the field of battle. The disease which had desolated their army appeared to have suspended its ravages, and the soldiers, a long time imprisoned in their camp, felt their strength revive at the sight of the perils of war. Several conflicts took place around the lake of the Gullet, of which the Christians wished to get possession, to facilitate their approach to Tunis. The Moors who, but a few days before, threatened to exterminate or make slaves of all the Crusaders, were not able to sustain the shock of their enemies; the cross-bowmen alone were frequently sufficient to disperse their numberless multitude. Horrible howlings, with the noise of kettle-drums and other instruments, announced their approach; clouds of dust descending from the neighbouring heights announced their retreat, and screened their flight. In two encounters they were overtaken, and left a great many of their host stretched upon the plain. Another time their camp was carried, and given up to pillage. The sovereign of Tunis could not reckon upon his army for the defence of his states, and he himself set them no example of bravery, for he remained constantly shut up in his subterranean grottoes, to avoid at the same time the burning rays of the sun and the perils of fight. Pressed by his fears, he at length could see no hopes of safety but in peace, and he resolved to purchase it, even at the cost of all his treasures. His ambassadors came repeatedly to the Christian army with directions to make proposals, and, above all, to endeavour to seduce the king of Sicily by brilliant promises. We read in the life of Bibars, and in the chronicles of Ibn-Ferat, that the sultan of Cairo was much dissatisfied with the conduct of the king

PRAYERS FOR THE DEAD.

The return from the siege of Tunis. It was not the flag of victory, but a funeral pall that preceded the French warriors in their march. Funeral urns, the wreck of an army but lately so flourishing, a young sick prince, who had only escaped by a miracle the death that had swept away his family—this was all that came back from the crusade! The people came from all parts to meet the melancholy train; they surrounded the young king, they strove to approach the remains of St. Louis, and it was made evident, by their pious propriety and their religious sadness, that the sentiments which led them there were not such as generally precipitate the multitude upon the steps of the masters of the earth.

On the arrival of Philip in his capital, the bones and the heart of St. Louis were conveyed to the church of Notre Dame, where ecclesiastics sang the hymns of the service of the dead during the whole night. On the following day the funeral of the royal martyr was celebrated in the church of St. Denis. In the midst of an immense assemblage of all classes of the people, deeply affected by what they saw, the young monarch advanced, bearing on his shoulders the mortal remains of his father. He stopped several times on his way, and crosses, which were placed at every station, recalled, up to the last century, this beautiful picture of filial piety.—BOOK XV.

of Tunis. The peace which the latter made, left the Crusaders at liberty to carry their arms into Egypt. Bibars would have wished the Christian army to have been detained on the coast of Africa. He threatened to dethrone his ally, and told the ambassadors of the king of Tunis, that such a prince as he was not worthy to reign over Mussulmans.

When the report of these negotiations was spread through the camp of the Crusaders, it gave birth to very different opinions. The soldiers, to whom the plunder of Tunis had been promised, wished to continue the war; some of the leaders, to whom other hopes had been given, did not evince the same ardour as the soldiers. By the death of Louis IX. and the apostolic legate, the crusade had lost both its principal motive and that moral force which had animated everything. The spirit of the Crusaders, which nobody directed, worked upon by a thousand various passions, floated in uncertainty, and this uncertainty was likely, in the end, to keep the army in a state of inaction, and bring about the abandonment of the war. Philip was desirous of returning to France, whither the affairs of his kingdom peremptorily called him. Most of the barons and French nobles began to sigh for their country. At length it was agreed that the pacific proposals of the king of Tunis should be deliberated upon.

In the council, those to whom no promise had been held out, and who were not so impatient as the others to quit the coast of Africa, were of opinion that they ought to prosecute the war. "It was for the conquest of Tunis that Louis IX. had embarked at Carthage, and that the Christian army had undergone so many evils. How could they pay higher honour to the memory of Louis and so many Frenchmen, like him, martyrs to their zeal and their faith, than by carrying on and completing their work? All Christendom knew that the Crusaders threatened Tunis, that the Moors fled at the sight of them, and that the city was ready to open its gates. What would Christendom say on learning that the Crusaders had fled before the vanquished, and robbed themselves of their own victory?"

Those who were of opinion that the peace should be concluded, answered, that the question was not only to enter Tunis, but to conquer the country, which could only be done by exterminating the population. "Besides, a prolonged siege would very much weaken the Christian army. Winter was approaching, in which they could procure no provisions, and in which continual rains would, perhaps, cause more diseases than excessive heat had done. The taking of Tunis was not the principal object of the crusade; it was necessary to make peace on advantageous conditions, to obtain means to carry the war afterwards where circumstances might require. The leaders who spoke thus were themselves the same that had promoted the expedition against Tunis: the king of Sicily was at their head; they no longer urged the necessity for clearing the Mediterranean of pirates who infested the route of pilgrims; they said no more about depriving the sultan of Egypt of his most powerful ally. The reasons they gave for putting an end to the war were precisely the same as they had given for commencing it. Their opinion, however, prevailed; not because others were convinced by what they heard, but, as it often happens in the most important deliberations, the majority decide rather from motives they do not avow, than from those they appear to support.*

On the thirty-first of October a truce of ten years was concluded between the king of Tunis and the leaders of the Christian army. All the prisoners were to be given up on both sides, and Christians who had been previously captives were to be set at liberty. The sovereign of Tunis engaged not to require of the Franks any of the dues imposed in his kingdom upon foreign commerce. The treaty granted all Christians liberty to reside in the states of Tunis, to build churches there,

---

* For the events that followed the death of St. Louis, see Duchesne, and *le Spicilège*, vol. ii.

and even to preach their faith there. The Mussulman prince was bound to pay to the king of Sicily an annual tribute of forty thousand crowns, and two hundred and ten thousand ounces of gold to the leader of the Christian army for the expenses of the war.

It was, doubtless, the last condition that decided the question: the two hundred and ten thousand ounces of gold exceeded the sum that Louis IX. had paid in Egypt for the ransom of his army; but a part of it only was received at first. Who could assure the payment of the rest when the Christian army had quitted the coast of Africa? The king of Sicily alone could derive any advantage from this treaty, so disgraceful to the French arms; he had not only found means of making a Mussulman prince pay the tribute of forty thousand gold crowns, which he owed the Pope as vassal of the Holy See; but the peace which they had concluded, in some sort, placed at his disposal an army capable of undertaking much greater conquests than that of Tunis. Thus, complaints immediately arose reproaching the king of Sicily with having, at his pleasure, changed the aim of the crusade, in order to make the Christian army subservient to his ambition.

A few days after the signing of the truce, Prince Edward arrived off the coast of Carthage, with the English and Scotch Crusaders. Having sailed from Aigues-Mortes, he directed his course towards Palestine, and came to take orders from the king of France. The French and Sicilians were prodigal in their expressions of sincere friendship for the English. Edward was received with great honours, but when he learned they had made peace, he retired into his tent, and refused to be present at any of the councils of the Christian army.

The Crusaders became impatient to quit an arid and murderous land, which recalled to them nothing but misfortunes, without the least mixture of glory. The Christian army embarked on the eighteenth of November for Sicily; and, as if Heaven had decreed that this expedition should be nothing but a series of misfortunes, a frightful tempest assailed the fleet just as it was about to enter the port of Trapani. Eighteen large ships and four thousand Crusaders were submerged, and perished in the waves. Most of the leaders and soldiers lost their arms, equipments, and horses. If one historian is to be believed, the money received from the king of Tunis was lost in this shipwreck.

After so great a misfortune, the king of Sicily neglected no means of succouring the Crusaders. We may believe in the generous sentiments which he expressed upon the occasion; but there is little doubt that, with his feelings a hope was mixed of deriving something favourable to his projects from this deplorable circumstance. When all the leaders were arrived, several councils were held to ascertain what remained to be done. As every one deplored his own losses, Charles proposed a sure means of repairing them, which was the conquest of Greece. This was the plan he had arranged: in the first place, all the Crusaders should pass the winter in Sicily; in the spring, the count of Poictiers should set out for Palestine with a part of the army, the rest was to follow Charles to Epirus, and from thence to Byzantium. This project had something adventurous and chivalric in it, very likely to seduce the French barons and nobles; but letters to the young king arrived from France, in which the regents represented in strong colours the grief and alarms of his people. Philip declared that he could not stay in Sicily, but should immediately return to his own dominions. This determination destroyed all Charles's hopes; the French lords would not abandon their young monarch, and the princes and all the leaders of the Christian army laid aside the cross. An Italian chronicle reports that Charles, in his vexation, confiscated to his own profit all the vessels and all the effects which, after the late shipwreck, were thrown upon the coasts of Sicily. He had profited by the misfortunes of the army before Tunis, and he now enriched himself with the spoils of his companions in arms. This act of injustice and violence completed the dislike that most of the Crusaders had conceived for him; this was particularly the case with the Genoese, to whom the fleet belonged in which the Christian army had embarked.

It was, however, decided that they should resume the crusade four years later. The two kings, the princes, and the most influential leaders, engaged themselves by oath to embark for Syria with their troops in the month of July of the fourth year;—a vain promise, that not one of them was destined to keep, and which they only made then to excuse in their own eyes the inconsistency of their conduct in this war. Edward, who had announced his resolution of passing the winter in Sicily, and setting out for Palestine in the spring, was the only one that did not break his promises.

The French warriors abandoned all thoughts of the crusade; but they were yet far from seeing the closing of that abyss of miseries which it had opened beneath their feet. The king of Navarre died shortly after landing at Trapani, and his wife Isabella was so deeply affected by his death, that she immediately followed him to the tomb. Philip set out on his return to France in the month of January, and the young queen, who had accompanied him, became another victim of the crusade. In crossing Calabria, whilst fording a river near Cosenza, her horse fell, and she being pregnant, this fall caused her death. Thus Philip pursued his journey, bearing with him the bodies of his father, his brother, and his wife. He learnt on his march that the count and countess of Poictiers, returning to Languedoc, had both died in Tuscany from the effects of the contagious malady of the coast of Africa. Passing by Viterbo, Philip witnessed the tragical end of one of the most illustrious of his companions in arms; Henry d'Allemagne was attacked by Simon and Guy de Montfort, the sons of the earl of Leicester, pursued into a church, and massacred at the foot of the altar. Henry was nephew of the king of England. He had entered the church to hear Mass, and suddenly was surprised by a well-known voice crying, "Traitor Henry, thou shalt not escape me." Turning, he saw his two cousins running towards him with swords in their hands. The unfortunate prince threw himself on the altar; two priests interposed, but they were pushed aside. Henry was assassinated, his body mutilated, and then dragged to the door of the church. Thus, great crimes were joined with great calamities, to add to the cruel remembrances that this crusade was destined to leave behind it.

Philip, after crossing Mount Cenis, returned to Paris through Burgundy and Champagne. What days of mourning for France! At the departure of Louis IX. for the East, the whole nation had been impressed by the most melancholy presentiments; and, alas! all these presentiments were but too fully realized!

It was not the flag of victory, but a funeral pall that preceded the French warriors in their march. Funereal urns, the wreck of an army but lately so flourishing, a young sick prince, who had only escaped by a miracle the death that had swept away his family—this was all that came back from the crusade! The people came from all parts to meet the melancholy train; they surrounded the young king, they strove to approach the remains of St. Louis, and it was made evident, by their pious propriety and their religious sadness, that the sentiments which led them there were not such as generally precipitate the multitude upon the steps of the masters of the earth.

On the arrival of Philip in his capital, the bones and the heart of St. Louis were conveyed to the church of Notre Dame, where ecclesiastics sang the hymns of the service of the dead during the whole night. On the following day the funeral of the royal martyr was celebrated in the church of St. Denis. In the midst of an immense assemblage of all classes of the people, deeply affected by what they saw, the young monarch advanced, bearing on his shoulders the mortal remains of his father. He stopped several times on his way, and crosses, which were placed at every station, recalled, up to the last century, this beautiful picture of filial piety.

Louis IX. was deposited near his grandfather Philip Augustus, and his father Louis VIII.

Although he had forbidden his tomb to be ornamented, it was covered with plates of silver, which were afterwards carried away by the English. At a later period a more terrible revolution broke into his tomb and scattered his ashes; but this revolution has not been able to destroy his memory.

No, posterity will never cease to praise that passion for justice which filled the whole life of Louis IX., that ardour in search of truth, so rare even among the greatest kings; that love of peace, to which he sacrificed even the glory he had acquired in arms; that solicitude for the good of all; that tender consideration for poverty; that profound respect for the rights of misfortune and for the lives of men, and virtues which astonished the middle ages.

The ascendancy which his virtue and piety gave him he only employed in defending his people against everything that was unjust. This ascendancy, which he preserved over his age, gave to his laws an empire, which laws, whatever they may be, rarely obtain but with time. A few years after his reign, provinces demanded to be united to the crown, under the sole hope and the sole condition of enjoying *the wise ordinances of the king, who loved justice.* Such were the conquests of St. Louis. It is well known, that after his victories over the English he restored Guienne to them, in spite of the advice of his barons, who considered this act of generosity to be contrary to the interests of the kingdom. Perhaps it only belongs to elevated minds like his to know how much wisdom there is in the counsels of moderation! An illustrious writer of the last age has said, in speaking of Louis IX., *that great moderate men are rare*, and it is doubtless on that account that the world does not understand them.

In the position in which France at that time was placed, a vulgar genius would have fomented divisions; whereas Louis only sought to appease them; and it was this spirit of conciliation which rendered him the arbitrator of kings and nations, and gave him more strength and power than could have been procured by the combinations of the wisest policy. Among the contemporaries of St. Louis persons were not wanting who blamed his moderation, and many who pride themselves upon being skilful politicians blame him even now. Strange skill, which tends to create a belief that morality is foreign to the happiness of nations, and which cannot afford to the leaders of empires the same virtues that God has bestowed upon man for the preservation of society!

The more we admire the reign of Louis IX. the greater is our astonishment at his having twice interrupted the course of its blessings, and quitted a people he rendered happy by his presence. But, whilst beholding the passions which agitate the present generation, who will dare to raise his voice for the purpose of accusing past ages! If at the moment in which I write this history all Europe is moved by the rumour of a general rising against the Mussulmans, now masters of Byzantium;— if the most ardent disciples of the modern school of philosophy are putting up vows for the triumph of the Gospel over the Koran, for the deliverance of the Greeks, and the resurrection of Athens and Lacedæmon, how can we believe that in the middle ages princes and Christian nations would not be affected by the horrible state of slavery of Jerusalem, and all those holy regions from which the light first broke upon Christendom? Consistently with the character which Louis IX. displayed in all the circumstances of his life, how could he remain indifferent to the calamities of the Christian colonies, which were principally peopled by Frenchmen, and which were considered as another France,—the France of the east? We must not forget, likewise, that the great aim of his policy was to unite the nations of the east and west by the ties of Christianity; and that this aim, if he had succeeded in it, would have been greatly to the advantage of humanity. Ambition itself has been sometimes pardoned for projects much more chimerical, and wars much more unfortunate.*

---

* Among the numerous panegyrics of Louis IX. there are few that have stood the test of time. Voltaire has drawn a fine portrait of the good king. M. Dampmartin, in his work upon the kings of France, has spoken of this great prince with ability and truth.

ASSASSINATION OF HENRY OF GERMANY.

Passing by Viterbo, Philip witnessed the tragical end of one of the most illustrious of his companions in arms; Henry d'Allemagne was attacked by Simon and Guy de Montfort, the sons of the earl of Leicester, pursued into a church, and massacred at the foot of the altar. Henry was nephew of the King of England. He had entered the church to hear Mass and suddenly was surprised by a well-known voice crying, "Traitor Henry, thou shalt not escape me." Turning, he saw his two cousins running towards him with swords in their hands. The unfortunate prince threw himself on the altar, two priests interposed, but they were pushed aside. Henry was assassinated, his body mutilated, and then dragged to the door of the church. Thus, great crimes were joined with great calamities, to add to the cruel remembrances that this crusade was destined to leave behind it.—BOOK XV.

However it may be, we can venture to say that the captivity and death of St. Louis in distant regions did not at all lessen the respect in which his name and his virtues were held in Europe. Perhaps even such extraordinary misfortunes, suffered in the name of religion and of all that was then reverenced, added something to the splendour of the monarchy; for the times we have seen were then far distant in which the misfortunes of kings have only served to despoil royalty of that which makes it respected among men. The death of Louis IX. was a great subject of grief for the French; but with the regret which his loss created, there was mingled, for the whole people, the thoughts of the happy future which Louis had prepared, and for pious minds the hope of having a guardian and a support in heaven. Very shortly the death of a king of France was celebrated as a fresh triumph for religion,—as a fresh glory for his country; and the anniversary of the day on which he expired became thereafter one of the solemn festivals of the Christian Church and of the French monarchy.

A beautiful spectacle was that canonical inquiry in which the common father of the faithful interrogated the contemporaries of Louis IX. upon the virtues of his life and the benefits of his reign! Frenchmen of all classes came forward to attest, upon the Gospel, that the monarch whose death they lamented was worthy of all the rewards of heaven. Among them were many of his old companions in arms, who had shared his chains in Egypt, and beheld him dying on his bed of ashes before Tunis. The whole of Europe confirmed their religious testimony, and repeated these words of the head of the Church:—"*House of France, rejoice at having given to the world so great a prince; rejoice, people of France, at having had so good a king!*"

The death of Louis IX., as we have already said, had suddenly suspended all enterprises beyond the seas. Edward only, accompanied by the count of Brittany, his brother Edmund, and three hundred knights, had gone into Syria, at the head of a small army of five hundred Crusaders from Friesland. All these Crusaders together only formed a body of a thousand or twelve hundred combatants; and this was all that reached Asia of those numberless armies that had been raised in the West for the deliverance of the Holy Land. So feeble a reinforcement was not calculated to inspire confidence or restore security to the Christians of Palestine, not yet recovered from their consternation at hearing of the retreat of the Crusaders from before Tunis, and their return into Europe.

Most of the princes and Christian states of Syria, in the fear of being invaded, had concluded treaties with the sultan of Cairo; many must have hesitated at engaging in a war from which the slender succours from Europe could allow them no hopes of great advantages, and in which likewise they had to dread being abandoned by the Crusaders, ever eager to return to the West. Nevertheless, the Templars and the Hospitallers, who never missed an opportunity of fighting with the Saracens, united themselves with Prince Edward, whose fame had preceded him into the East. Bibars, who was then ravaging the territories of Ptolemaïs, drew his forces off from a city which he had filled with alarm, and appeared for a moment to have abandoned the execution of his projects.

The little army of the Christians, composed of from six to seven thousand men, advanced upon the Mussulman territories, directing its course towards Phœnicia, in order to re-establish the communication that had been interrupted between the Christian cities. In this expedition the Crusaders had much to suffer from excessive heat; many died from indulging in fruits and honey, which the country produced in abundance. They marched afterwards towards the city of Nazareth, upon the walls of which they planted the standard of Christ. The soldiers of the cross could not remember without indignation that Bibars had completely destroyed the church of this city, consecrated to the Virgin. Nazareth was given up to pillage, and all the Mussulmans found in the city expiated, by being put to the sword, the burning and destruction of one of the most beautiful monuments raised by the Christians of Syria.

After this victory, for which we cannot praise the Crusaders, the Christian army had to combat the Mussulman troops, who were impatient to avenge the excesses committed at Nazareth. Whether he had learnt to respect the superiority of his enemies, or whether he had cause to complain of the warriors of Palestine, Edward returned within the walls of Ptolemaïs, and sought for no more contests. The frequent excursions of the Saracens could not provoke him to take up arms; but whilst he remained thus safe from the perils of war, he was on the point of perishing by the hand of a Mussulman whom he had taken into his service. The perfidious servant entered his chamber, poignard in hand, and immediately plunged at Edward, who was in bed. The blow was misdirected, only wounding Edward in the arm. Edward, who was endowed with great strength, lifted himself up, overthrew the assassin, wrenched the poignard from his hand, and plunged it into the bosom of the Mussulman. It was thought that the poignard was poisoned, and Eleanor, the wife of the black prince, had the courage to suck the wound in the arm. Every effort was unavailing, and it was thought that Edward would die, when an Arab presented himself and offered to cure Edward if he would send away his wife and his mistress and follow his régime. The advice of this physician was followed and Edward recovered. Some of the chronicles of the time tell us that the emir of Jaffa armed the hand of the assassin; others say that the blow was directed by the sect of the Ismaëlians, who still subsisted, notwithstanding the war declared against them by both the Tartars and the Mamelukes.

After having thus run the danger of losing his life, Edward, cured of his wounds, only thought of concluding a truce with Bibars; and being recalled into England by the prayers of Henry III., whose successor he was, he quitted the East without having done anything important for the cause he had sworn to defend. Thus all the results of this crusade, which had so much alarmed the Mussulmans, were reduced, on one side, to the massacre of the unarmed population of Nazareth, and on the other, to the vain conquest of the ruins of Carthage. Another result of this war, and the only one it had for Europe, was to entirely discourage the Christian warriors, and make them forget the East. After Edward, no prince from the West ever crossed the seas to combat with the infidels in Asia, and the crusade in which he took a part so little glorious, was the last of those which had for object the deliverance or recovery of the Holy Land.

Among the circumstances that produced the failure of this crusade, history must not forget the protracted vacancy of the papal throne, during which no voice was raised to animate the Crusaders, in which there was no authority powerful enough, particularly after the death of St. Louis, to direct their enterprise. After a lapse of two years, however, the conclave chose a successor of St. Peter; and, fortunately for the eastern Christians, the suffrages fell upon Thibault, archdeacon of Liege, who had followed the Frisons into Asia, and whom the intelligence of his elevation found still in Palestine. The Christians of Syria had reason to hope that the new pontiff, for so long a time a witness of their perils and their miseries, would not fail to employ all his power to succour them. Thibault gave them an assurance of it before he quitted Ptolemaïs, and in a discourse which he addressed to the assembled people, he took for his text this verse of the hundred and thirty-seventh Psalm: "If I forget thee, O Jerusalem, may I myself be forgotten among men!"

The patriarch of Jerusalem, and the grand masters of the Temple and the Hospital accompanied Gregory X. into the West. On his return, the pontiff applied himself at once to the re-establishment of peace in Italy and Germany. He engaged the princes, particularly the king of France, to unite their efforts in assisting the Holy Land. Philip contented himself with sending a few troops into the East, and with advancing thirty-six thousand silver marks to the Pope, for which sum he held as security all the possessions of the Templars in his kingdom. Pisa, Genoa, and Marseilles furnished several galleys, and five hundred warriors were embarked for Ptolemaïs, at the expense of the sovereign pontiff.

This assistance was far from answering the hopes or the wants of the Christian colonies. Gregory resolved to interest all Christendom in his project, and for that purpose convoked a council at Lyons, in 1274. This council was much more numerous and more solemn than that which Innocent IV. had assembled thirty years before in the same city. At this were present the patriarchs of Jerusalem and Constantinople, more than a thousand bishops and archbishops, the envoys of the emperors of the East and of the West, those of the kings of France and Cyprus, and of all the princes of Europe and beyond the seas. In this numerous assembly, no person attracted so much attention as the Tartar princes and ambassadors, sent by the powerful head of the Moguls, to form an alliance with the Christians against the Mussulmans; several of these Tartar princes received baptism from the hands of the Pope, and Christians who were witnesses of this ceremony saw in it an assured pledge of the Divine promises.

All admired the power of God who had chosen the instruments of his designs from remote and little known regions; the crowd of the faithful looked upon the supreme head of the hordes of Tartary as another Cyrus, whom Providence had charged with the destruction of Babylon and the deliverance of Jerusalem. At the last sitting, the Council of Lyons decreed that a new crusade should be undertaken, and that during ten years a tenth should be levied upon all ecclesiastical property. Palæologus, who at length submitted to the Latin church, promised to send troops for the deliverance of the heritage of Christ; the Pope recognised Rodolph of Hapsbourg as emperor of the West, upon condition that he would go into Palestine at the head of an army.

But notwithstanding the grand spectacle of such a council, the decisions and the exhortations of the Pope and the prelates could not arouse the enthusiasms of the faithful, which was no longer anything, to borrow an expression from Scripture, "but the smoking remains of a burnt cloth." Gregory X. had succeeded in re-establishing peace among the Italian republics, and in terminating all the discords of Germany relative to the succession to the empire: no war interfered with the crusade; but the minds of both princes and nations had taken a fresh direction. We still possess a written document of this period, which, doubtless, obtained the approbation if not the encouragement of the pope, and which appears to us well calculated to throw a light upon the spirit of the age, and show us what was then the general opinion of expeditions to the East. In this document, which will be considered whimsical, at least in its form, the author, Humbert de Romanis, endeavours to revive the zeal of Christians for the holy war, and, while deploring the indifference of his contemporaries, he points out eight obstacles to the effects of his preaching: 1st. *A sinful habit;* 2nd. *The dread of fatigue;* 3rd. *Repugnance to quit their native country;* 4th. *An excessive love of family;* 5th. *The evil discourses of men;* 6th. *A weakness of mind that creates a belief that everything is impossible;* 7th. *Bad examples;* 8th. *A faith without warmth.* To all these motives for indifference the author might have added other reasons drawn from the policy and the new interests of Europe; but without allowing himself to be stopped by so many obstacles, the intrepid defender of the crusades, proceeding always by enumerations and categories, hastens to denote seven powerful passions, which, according to him, ought to cause the partisans of the holy to triumph; these reasons were: 1st. *Zeal for the glory of God;* 2nd. *Zeal for the Christian faith;* 3rd. *Brotherly charity;* 4th. *Devotional respect for the Holy Land;* 5th. *The war commenced by the Mussulmans;* 6th. *The example of the first Crusaders;* 7th. *The blessings of the Church.* After these enumerations, Humbert de Romanis repeats the objections that were made in his time against undertaking crusades. Some said that wars, of whatever kind they might be, only served to promote the shedding of blood, and that there were quite enough of those that could not be avoided, and of those that people were obliged to make in self-defence; others said that it was tempting God to quit a land in which his will had caused us to be born, and in which his goodness heaped blessings upon us, to go into a country which God had given to other nations, and in which we were constantly abandoned by him to all the miseries of exile. It was further said, that it was not permissible to invade the territories of the Saracens, that there was no more reason for pursuing the Mussulmans than the Jews, that the wars made against them would never effect their conversion, and in short, that this war did not appear to be agreeable to God, since he permitted so many misfortunes to overwhelm the Crusaders.

Humbert de Romanis, in his book, answers all these and many other objections; but these objections themselves were founded upon the spirit of the age, which could not be changed by reasoning. He in vain repeated that the Holy Land originally belonged to the Christians, and that they had the right to endeavour to reconquer it; that the vine of the Lord ought to be defended by the sword against those who wished to root it up; that if they extirpated the brambles from a barren soil, they were much more strongly bound to drive from a holy land a rude and barbarous nation. He in vain repeated what had been so often said before, that the misfortunes of the crusades did not happen because those crusades were displeasing to God, but because it was God's will to punish the Crusaders, and try their constancy and faith. All this display of ecclesiastical erudition and argumentation persuaded nobody; not because people were more enlightened than they had been some years before, but because they entertained other thoughts: similar discourses would have succeeded admirably in the preceding century, when addressed to dominant passions; but they produced no effect when addressed to indifference.

This European indifference was fatal to the Christian colonies of the East; it gave them up without defence to the mercy of an enemy who every day became more powerful, and whose fanaticism was inflamed by victory. On the other hand, fresh symptoms of decay, and new signs of approaching ruin, were observable in the confederation of the Franks of Syria. All those petty principalities, all those cities scattered along the Syrian coasts were shared among them; and all the passions which the spirit of rivalry gives birth to became the auxiliaries of the Saracens. Every one of these petty states, in a constant state of fear, eagerly purchased a few days of peace, or a few months of existence, by treaties with Bibars, treaties in which the common honour and interests of the Christians were almost always sacrificed. The sultan of Cairo did not disdain to conclude a treaty of alliance with a single city, or even with a town; and nothing is more curious than to see figuring in these acts of policy, on the one side the sovereign of Egypt, Syria, Mesopotamia, and twenty other provinces; and on the other a little city like Sidon* or Tortosa, with its fields, it orchards, and its mills: a deplorable contrast, which must have made the Christians feel the extent of their humiliation, and proved to them all they had to fear. In all these treaties it was the Mussulman policy to promote division among the Franks, and to hold them in a state of dependence, never considering them as allies, but as vassals, farmers or tributaries.

Such was the peace enjoyed by the Christian states in Syria; and a further matter to be deplored was, that there were then three pretenders to the kingdom of Jerusalem:—the king of Cyprus, the king of Sicily, and Mary of Antioch, who was descended from the fourth daughter of Isabella, the wife of Amaury. Parties disputed, and even fought for a kingdom half destroyed; or rather they contended for the disgrace of ruining it entirely, and giving it up, rent by discord, to the domination of the Saracens.

---

* The Arabian chroniclers have preserved several of these treaties: we find in the extracts from Oriental manuscripts, a treaty between the sultan of Cairo and the little city of Tortosa. When reading the titles and the dependencies of the masters and the inhabitants of Tortosa, we may fancy we read the lease of a bailiwick or a farm, made before a notary.

EDWARD III. OF ENGLAND KILLS HIS ATTEMPTED ASSASSIN.

The perfidious servant entered his chamber, poignard in hand, and immediately plunged at Edward, who was in bed. The blow was mis-directed, only wounding Edward in the arm. Edward, who was endowed with great strength, lifted himself up, overthrew the assassin, wrenched the poignard from his hand, and plunged it into the bosom of the Mussulman. It was thought that the poignard was poisoned, and Eleanor, the wife of the black prince, had the courage to suck the wound in the arm. Every effort was unavailing, and it was thought that Edward would die, when an Arab presented himself and offered to cure Edward if he would send away his wife and his mistress and follow his régime. The advice of this physician was followed and Edward recovered.—BOOK XV

Bibars, in the meanwhile, steadily pursued the course of his conquests; every day fame spread abroad an account of some fresh triumph; at one time he re-entered Cairo, dragging in his train a king of Nubia, whom he had just conquered; at another, he returned from Armenia, whence he brought thirty thousand horses and ten thousand children of both sexes. These accounts spread terror among the Christian cities, a terror that was very little mitigated by their treaties with the sultan of Egypt; no one could tell what might be the next conquest Bibars contemplated, and every city was trembling lest it should be the next object of his ambition or his fury, when the death of this fierce conqueror afforded the Christians a few moments of security and joy.

The end of Bibars is related after various manners; we will follow the account of the historian Ibn-Ferat, with whose expressions even we shall sometimes make free. Bibars was about to set out for Damascus, to fight the Tartars in the neighbourhood of the Euphrates; but before his departure he demanded an extraordinary impost. The imaun Mohyeddin Almoury addressed remonstrances to him on the subject; but the sultan replied: "Oh! my master, I will abolish this tax when I shall have conquered our enemies." When Bibars had triumphed over the Tartars, he wrote in the following terms to the chief of the divan at Damascus: "We will not dismount from our horse until thou hast levied an impost of two hundred thousand dirhems upon Damascus, one of three hundred thousand upon its territories, one of three hundred thousand upon its towns, and one of ten hundred thousand dirhems upon the southern provinces." Thus the joy created by the victory of Bibars was changed into sadness, and the people prayed for the death of the sultan. Complaints were carried to the cheick Mohyeddin, a pious and respected man;* and scarcely was the levy of the tribute begun when Bibars was razed from the roll of the living—he died poisoned.

The Arabian historians place Bibars among the great princes of the dynasty of the Baharite Mamelukes. He was originally sold as a slave, and although he only lived among soldiers, a penetrating sagacity of mind supplied the place of education. When afterwards, he had become familiar with war, and had been cast among the factions of the army, he had acquired all the knowledge that was necessary to enable him to reign over the Mamelukes. The quality which was of most service to him in the career of his ambition was his incredible activity; during the seventeen years of his reign, he did not allow himself one day of repose; he was present, almost at the same time, in Syria, in Egypt, and upon the banks of the Euphrates: the chronicles relate that he was frequently perambulating the streets of Damascus, whilst his courtiers were awaiting the moment of his waking at the gates of the palace of Cairo. As two sultans of Egypt had perished beneath his hands, and as he had arrived at empire by means of violent revolutions, that which he most dreaded was the influence of his own example; all those whose ambition he feared, or whose fidelity he doubted, were immediately sacrificed. The most simple communications between man and man were sufficient to alarm his fierce and suspicious temper; if oriental historians may be credited, during the reign of Bibars, friends shunned each other in the streets, and no man durst enter into the house of another. When it was important to him to conceal his designs, to cast a veil over his proceedings, or himself to avoid the public eye, woe to him who should divine his thought, pronounce his name, or salute him on his way. Severe with his soldiers, a flatterer with his emirs, entertaining no repugnance for artifice, preferring violence, sporting with treaties and oaths, practising a dissimulation that nobody could penetrate, possessed by an avarice that made him pitiless in the levying of tributes; having never retreated before an enemy, before an obstacle, or before a

---

* This account is much longer in Ibn-Ferat; whilst endeavouring to preserve the tone and the Oriental colouring of it, we have felt it necessary to abridge it. The chronicle of Ibn-Ferat, which is a collection of many other chronicles, contains several different versions; this appears to us the most probable, and, at the same time, the one best calculated to show what were the resources of the nations of Asia against the excesses of despotism.

crime, his genius and character seemed made for the government, which he had in some sort founded, a monstrous government, which sustained itself by vices and excesses, and which could not possibly have subsisted in conjunction with moderation and virtue.

His enemies and his subjects trembled equally before him; they trembled still around that litter which transported his remains from Damascus to Cairo. But so many excesses, so many violences, so many triumphs, which only ministered to his personal ambition, were not able to fix the crown in his family; his two sons only ascended the throne to descend from it again. Kelaoun, the bravest of the emirs, soon usurped the sovereign power; a uniform line of succession to the throne was not at all likely to be preserved in an army constantly exposed to sedition. Every Mameluke believed himself born for empire, and in this republic of slaves it appeared permissible for every one to dream of tyranny. A thing almost incredible,—that which appeared most calculated to ruin this band of turbulent soldiery, was precisely that which saved it; weakness or incapacity could never support itself long upon the throne, and amidst the tumult of factions, it almost always happened that the most brave and the most able was chosen to direct the government, and lead in war.

Bibars had commenced the ruin of the Christians; Kelaoun was destined to complete it. In the West, Gregory in vain prosecuted the preparations, or rather the preachings of the crusade; he several times renewed his entreaties to Rodolph of Hapsburg, but Rodolph had an empire to preserve; it was useless for the pope to threaten to deprive him of his crown; the new emperor saw much less danger for him in the anger of the sovereign pontiff than in an expedition which would lead him so far from his states. At length Gregory died, without having been able to fulfil the promises he had made to the Christians of the East. Palestine received, from time to time, some succours from Europe; but these succours, scarcely ever arriving seasonably, appeared less likely to increase than to compromise its safety. The king of Sicily, who had caused himself to be proclaimed king of Jerusalem, sent some soldiers and a governor to Ptolemaïs; he was preparing to make a formidable expedition into Syria, and his ambition, perhaps, might, in this circumstance, have been serviceable to the cause of the Christians, if a revolution had not suddenly put an end to his projects.

The discontent of the people in his states, particularly in Sicily, continually increased. The people had been burdened with a heavy tax for the last crusade, and the publication of a new one was received with many murmurs; the enemies of Charles saw nothing in the assumption of the cross but a signal for violence and brigandage: it is under this sacred banner, they said, that he is accustomed to shed innocent blood: they further remembered that the conquest of Naples had been made under the standard of the cross. At length the signal of revolt being given, eight thousand Frenchmen were immolated to the manes of Conradin, and the Sicilian vespers completed the destruction of all Charles's Eastern projects.

Kelaoun from that time had it in his power to attack the Christians; but busied in establishing his authority among the Mamelukes, and in repulsing the Tartars, who had advanced towards the Euphrates, he consented to conclude a truce with the Franks of Ptolemaïs. It may plainly be perceived by this treaty, which the Arabian authors have preserved, what were the designs of the sultans of Cairo, and the extent of the ascendancy they assumed over their feeble enemies. The Christians engaged, in the event of any prince of the Franks making an expedition into Asia, to warn the infidels of the coming of Christian armies from the West. This was at the same time signing a dishonourable condition, and renouncing all hopes of a crusade.

The armies of the West, besides, were fighting for other interests than those of the Holy Land, and there was no reason to believe they would be seen in Asia for a length of time. Most of the princes of Europe at that time never bestowed a thought upon the Mussulmans or their victories; such princes or states as had any interests to guard in the East,* not only allied themselves without scruple with the sultan of Egypt, but promised by treaties, and swore upon the Gospel, to declare themselves the enemies of all the Christian powers that should attack the states of their Mussulman ally.

Thus all these treaties, dictated sometimes by ambition and avarice, and sometimes by fear, raised every day a new barrier between the Christians of the East and those of the West. Besides, these treaties were no checks upon the sultan of Cairo, who always found some pretext for breaking them, when war presented more advantages than peace. It was thus with the fortress of Margat, situated upon the river Eleuctera, in the neighbourhood of Tripoli. The Hospitallers who guarded this castle were accused of making incursions upon the lands of the Mussulmans; and this accusation, which was not perhaps without foundation, was soon followed by the siege of the place. The towers and ramparts for a long time resisted the shock of the machines of war; the garrison repulsed every attack; but whilst they were fighting upon the walls, and at the foot of the walls, miners were digging away the earth from beneath them. At length the fortress, undermined on all sides, was ready to fall to pieces at the first signal. The Hospitallers made an honourable capitulation, and Margat opened its gates to the Mussulman army.

Upon the seacoast, between Margat and Tortosa, stood another castle, to which a Frank nobleman had retired, whom some of the Arabian chroniclers call the sieur de Telima, and others, the sieur Barthélemi. This Frank lord never ceased ravaging the lands of his neighbourhood, and every day returned home to his fortress loaded with the spoils of the Saracens. Kelaoun was desirous of attacking the castle of the sieur Barthélemi, but thinking it impregnable, he wrote to the count of Tripoli,—" It is thou who hast built, or hast allowed to be built, this castle; evil be to thee, evil be to thy capital, evil be to thy people, if it be not promptly demolished." The count of Tripoli was the more alarmed at these menaces, from the Mussulman troops being, at the moment he received the letter, in his territories: he offered the seigneur Barthélemi considerable lands in exchange for his castle; he made him the most brilliant promises and offers, but all in vain. At length the son of Barthélemi interfered in the negotiation, and set out to implore the compassion of the sultan of Cairo. The enraged old man flew after his son, overtook him in the city of Ptolemaïs, and poniarded him before the assembled people. This parricide disgusted all the Christians; and Barthélemi was at last abandoned by his own soldiers, who held his crime in great horror. The castle, which was left unprotected, was shortly after demolished. From that time the sieur Barthélemi became the most inveterate enemy of the Christians; and, retired among the infidels, was constantly employed in associating them with his vengeance, and in urging the destruction of the Christian cities.

His pitiless hatred had but too many opportunities of being satisfied. The sultan of Cairo pursued the war against the Christians, and everything seemed to favour his enterprizes. He had for a long time entertained the project of gaining possession of Laodicea, whose port rivalled that of Alexandria; but the citadel of that city, surrounded by the waters of the sea, was inaccessible; an

---

* M. de Sacy has translated a treaty concluded between the sultan of Egypt and the kings of Sicily and Arragon. The following is one of the clauses of this treaty:—" If the case should happen that the pope of Rome, the kings of the Franks, of the Greeks, of the Tartars, or others, should ask the king of Arragon or his brothers, or should cause to be asked in the states of their dominions, auxiliary troops or any succour, whether of cavalry, infantry, money, vessels, clothing, or arms, the said princes would give no consent to it, either openly or in secret; they would grant them no succour, and would consent to nothing of the kind. If the king of Arragon should learn that one of the above-named kings should have any intention of carrying war into the states of the sultan, or to cause him any prejudice, he will send and advise the sultan of it, and will inform him on what side his enemies propose to attack him, and that with the shortest delay possible, before they shall be put in motion, and he will conceal nothing concerning it from him." This treaty is very long, and provides against all difficulties. We may here make a general remark, which is, that most of the treaties made between the Orientals and the Christians surpass, in some sort, the sagacity of modern diplomacy; so much mistrust gave foresight to the negotiators and the contracting powers.

earthquake, which shook the towers of the forest, facilitated his conquest of it. The castle of Carac and some other forts, built on the coast of Phœnicia, fell into the hands of the Mussulmans. After having thus laid open all the avenues to Tripoli, the sultan turned the whole of his attention to the siege of that city. Neither the faith of treaties, nor the recent submissions of Bohemond, were able to retard for a moment the fall of a flourishing city: no Christian city, no prince of Palestine offered the least assistance to Tripoli. Such indeed was the spirit of division that always reigned among the Franks, that the Templars, in conjunction with the seigneur de Giblet, had entertained the project of introducing some Christian soldiers into Bohemond's city, and taking it by surprise. They were not able, it is true, to execute their design; but what evils must not these odious jealousies, these black treacheries, have brought upon the feeble remains of the Christian colonies!

A formidable army appeared before the walls of Tripoli, and a great number of machines were erected against the ramparts: after a siege of thirty-five days, the Mussulmans penetrated into the city, fire and sword in hand. Seven thousand Christians fell under the arms of the conqueror; the women and children were dragged away into slavery, and the terrified crowd vainly sought an asylum from the bloodthirsty Mamelukes in the island of St. Nicholas. Aboulfeda relates, that having occasion to go to that island, a few days after the taking of Tripoli, he found it covered with dead bodies. Some of the inhabitants having succeeded in getting on board ships, fled away from their desolate country; but the sea drove them back again upon the shore, where they were massacred by the Mussulmans. Not only the population of Tripoli was almost exterminated, but the sultan gave orders that the city should be burnt and demolished. The port of Tripoli attracted a great part of the commerce of the Mediterranean; the city contained more than four thousand silk-looms; its palaces were admired, its towers and its fortifications appeared impregnable. So many sources of prosperity, all that could cause peace to flourish or serve for defence in war, all perished under the flame, the axe, and the hammer! The principal aim of the Mussulman policy in this war, was to destroy all that the Christians had done; to leave no traces of their power upon the coasts of Syria; nothing which could afterwards attract thither the princes and warriors of the West, nothing that could yield them the means of maintaining themselves there if ever they should be tempted again to unfurl their standards in the East.

Ptolemaïs, which remained neuter in this cruel war, learnt the fall and destruction of a Christian city from some fugitives, who, having escaped the sword of the Mussulmans, came to entreat an asylum within its walls. From this sad intelligence, it might easily predict the misfortunes that awaited it. Ptolemaïs was then the capital of the Christian colonies, and the most considerable city of Syria. Most of the Franks, upon being driven from the other cities of Palestine, had taken refuge there, bringing with them all their portable wealth. In its port anchored all the warlike fleets that came from the West, with the richest trading vessels from most countries of the world. The city had not less increased in extent than population; it was constructed of square-cut stones; all the walls of the houses rose to an equal height, and a platform or terrace surmounted most of the buildings. The interior of the principal houses was ornamented with paintings, and they received light by the means of glass windows, which was at that time an extraordinary luxury. In the public places, coverings of silk or transparent stuffs screened the inhabitants from the ardours of the sun. Between the two ramparts which bounded the city on the east, were built castles and palaces, the residences of the great; the artizans and traders occupied the interior of the city. Among the princes and nobles who had mansions in Ptolemaïs, were the king of Jerusalem, his brothers and his family, the princes of Galilee and Antioch, the lieutenants of France and Sicily, the duke of Cæsarea, the counts of Tripoli and Jaffa, the lords of Barouth, Tyre, Tiberias, Ibelin, Arsaph, &c. We read in an old

THE DISHONORABLE TRUCE.

Kelaoun from that time had it in his power to attack the Christians; but busied in establishing his authority among the Mamelukes, and in repulsing the Tartars, who had advanced towards the Euphrates, he consented to conclude a truce with the Franks of Ptolemaïs. It may plainly be perceived by this treaty, which the Arabian authors have preserved, what were the designs of the sultans of Cairo, and the extent of the ascendancy they assumed over their feeble enemies. The Christians engaged, in the event of any prince of the Franks making an expedition into Asia, to warn the infidels of the coming of Christian armies from the West. This was at the same time signing a dishonorable condition, and renouncing all hopes of a crusade.—BOOK XV.

chronicle that all these magnates were accustomed to walk in the public places, wearing crowns of gold like kings, whilst the vestments of their numerous trains glittered with gold and precious stones. Every day was passed in festivity, spectacles or tournaments; whilst the port was a mart of exchange for the treasures of the East and the West, exhibiting at all times an animated picture of commerce and industry.

Contemporary history deplores with severity the corruption of morals that prevailed in Ptolemaïs, the crowds of strangers bringing with them the vices of all countries. Effeminacy and luxury pervaded every class, the clergy themselves being unable to escape the general contagion: the inhabitants of Ptolemaïs were esteemed the most voluptuous and dissolute of all the nations of Syria. Ptolemaïs was not only the richest city of Syria, it was further supposed to be the best fortified. St. Louis, during his abode in Palestine, had neglected nothing to repair and increase its fortifications. On the land side, a double wall surrounded the city, commanded at distances by lofty battlemented towers; and a wide and deep ditch prevented access to the ramparts. Towards the sea, the city was defended by a fortress built at the entrance of the port, by the castle of the temple on the south, and by the tower called the King's Tower, on the east.

Ptolemaïs appears then to have possessed much better means of defence than at the period at which it stood out for three years against all the forces of Europe. No power could have subdued it if it had been inhabited by true citizens, and not by foreigners, pilgrims, and traders, at all times ready to transport themselves and their wealth from one place to another. The persons who represented the king of Naples, the lieutenants of the king of Cyprus, the French, the English, the pope's legate, the patriarch of Jerusalem, the prince of Antioch, the three military orders, the Venetians, the Genoese, the Pisans, the Armenians, the Tartars, had all and each their separate quarter, their jurisdiction, their tribunals, their magistrates—all independent of each other, and all enjoying the right of sovereignty. All these quarters were as so many different cities, opposed to each other by customs, by language, by manners, and above all, by rivalries and jealousies. It was impossible to preserve order in a city in which so many sovereigns made laws, which had no uniform government, and in which the crime pursued in one part, was protected in another. Thus all the passions were without a check, and often gave birth to sanguinary and disgraceful scenes: in addition to the quarrels that took their rise in the country, there was not a feud in Europe, particularly in Italy, that was not felt in Ptolemaïs. The discords of the Guelphs and the Ghibelines were here carried on with warmth, and the rivalries of Venice and Genoa had caused torrents of blood to flow. Each nation had fortifications in the quarter it inhabited, against the others; and the churches even were fortified. At the entrance to each division was a fortress, with gates and iron chains; it was plainly to be perceived that all these means of defence had been employed less for the purpose of stopping the progress of an enemy, than as a barrier against neighbours and rivals.

The leaders of all the quarters and the principal inhabitants of the city sometimes assembled; but they seldom agreed, and were at all times mistrustful of each other: these assemblies never laid down any settled plan of conduct, never established any wholesome fixed rule, and, above all, never showed the least foresight.

The city at the same time demanded succours from the West, and solicited a truce with the Saracens. When a treaty was concluded, no one had sufficient power to secure its observance; on the contrary, every one had it in his power to violate it, and thus bring upon the city all the ills that this violation would produce.

After the taking of Tripoli, the sultan of Cairo menaced the city of Ptolemaïs; nevertheless, whether he dreaded the despair of the inhabitants, or thought that the favourable moment was not yet arrived, he yielded to their solicitations, and renewed a truce with them for two years, two months, two weeks, two days, and two hours. According to a chronicle, the pope's legate disapproved of the treaty, and caused some Mussulman traders, who came to Ptolemaïs, to be insulted: the Templars and the other military orders were desirous of making reparation to the sultan of Egypt; but the legate opposed them, and threatened to excommunicate all who should have the least intercourse with the infidels.

An Arabian author assigns another motive for the violences committed against the Mussulmans. He relates that the wife of a rich inhabitant of Ptolemaïs, being deeply enamoured of a young Mussulman, had appointed a meeting with him in one of the gardens that surround the city; the husband, warned of this outrage against conjugal fidelity, gathers together some friends, goes out from Ptolemaïs with them, surprises his wife and her seducer, and immolates them both to his injured honour. Some Mussulmans are drawn to the spot; the Christians come up in still greater numbers: the quarrel becomes angry and general; and every Mussulman is massacred.

These violences, which fame did not fail to exaggerate whilst narrating them, might give the sultan of Egypt a pretext for renewing the war; and the Christians, who plainly perceived their new perils, implored the assistance of the sovereign pontiff. The pope engaged Venice to furnish twenty-five galleys, and this fleet transported to Ptolemaïs a troop of sixteen hundred men, levied in haste in Italy. This reinforcement, which was sent to the inhabitants of Palestine for their defence, provoked their ruin; the soldiers of the Holy See, levied among adventurers and vagabonds, gave themselves up to all sorts of excesses. Having no regular pay, they plundered Christians and Mussulmans indiscriminately; at last, this undisciplined troop marched out of the city in arms, and made an incursion upon the lands of the Saracens. Everything was laid waste on their passage; towns and villages were pillaged, the inhabitants insulted, and many of them massacred. The sultan of Cairo sent ambassadors to the Christians to complain of these outrages, committed in a time of peace. On the arrival of the Mussulman envoys several councils were held in Ptolemaïs. Opinions were at first divided; some were willing to take the part of those who had broken the truce; others thought it more just and prudent to give satisfaction to the sultan, and solicit the continuation of the treaty. In the end, it was determined to send a deputation to Cairo, commissioned to make excuses and offer presents. Upon being admitted to an audience of Kelaoun, the deputation alleged that the offences had been committed by some soldiers who had come from the West, and in no case by the inhabitants of Ptolemaïs. The deputies, in the name of their city, offered to punish the authors of the disorders; but their submission and prayers produced no effect upon the sultan, who reproached them severely with making a jest of the faith of treaties, and with giving an asylum to disturbers of peace and foes to the laws of nations. He was the more inflexible, from thinking the opportunity a favourable one for carrying out his projects; he was aware that no crusade was in preparation in Europe, and he knew that all the succour from the West was reduced to this band of adventurers who had just broken the truce. Kelaoun sent back the ambassadors, threatening the city of Ptolemaïs with the whole weight of his anger: his orders were already given for preparations for war throughout all his provinces.

Immediately after the return of the ambassadors a grand council was called, at which were present the patriarch of Jerusalem, John de Gresli, who commanded for the king of France, Messire Oste de Granson for the king of England, the grand masters of the Temple and the Hospital, the principal persons of the city, and a great number of citizens and pilgrims. When the deputies had rendered an account of their mission, and repeated the threats of the sultan, the patriarch addressed the assembly; his virtues, his gray hairs, his zeal for the cause of the Christians, all inspired confidence and respect. This venerable prelate exhorted all who heard him to arm themselves for the defence of the city, to remember that they were Christians, and that it was their duty to die for the cause of Christ; he conjured them to forget their discords, to have no other enemies but the Mussulmans, and to show themselves worthy of the holy cause for which they were about to fight. His eloquence awakened the generous feelings of his audience, and all swore to obey the exhortations of the patriarch: happy would it have been for the city of Ptolemaïs if its inhabitants and its defenders had preserved the same dispositions and the same enthusiasm amidst the perils and mischances of war!

They asked for succour in all quarters; a few pilgrims arrived from the West, and a few warriors from the isles of the Mediterranean: the king of Cyprus landed with five hundred men. These new auxiliaries and all who were able to bear arms in the city, amounted to nine hundred horsemen and ten thousand foot soldiers. They were divided into four bodies, charged with the defence of the towers and the ramparts. The first of these divisions was under the command of Oste de Granson and John de Gresli, the one with the English and the Picards, the other with the French; the second division was commanded by the king of Cyprus, in conjunction with the grand master of the Teutonic order; the third by the grand master of St. John, and the grand master of the knights of Canterbury; the fourth by the grand masters of the Temple and of St. Lazarus: a council of eight leaders was to govern the city during the siege.

The Mussulmans were preparing for the war in all quarters; everything was in motion from the banks of the Nile to those of the Euphrates. The sultan Kelaoun, having fallen sick on leaving Cairo, sent before him seven principal emirs, each having four thousand horse and twenty thousand foot under his command. On their arrival upon the territories of Ptolemaïs, gardens, country-houses, the vines which covered the hills—everything was destroyed. The sight of the conflagration which arose on all sides, the distracted crowd of the inhabitants of the neighbourhood, who fled from their homes, with their goods, their flocks, and their families, warned Ptolemaïs of the execution of the threats and the sinister projects of the Saracens: there were several battles fought on the plain, but nothing remarkable or decisive; the Mussulmans waited the arrival of the sultan to commence the labours of the siege.

In the meanwhile, Kelaoun was still detained in Egypt by sickness, and feeling his end approach, the sultan sent for his son and his principal emirs; he recommended to the latter, to serve his son as they had served himself; and to the former, to follow up the war against the Christians without any intermission, conjuring him not to grant his remains the honour of sepulture before he had conquered the city of Ptolemaïs. Chalil swore to accomplish the last wishes of his father; and when Kelaoun had closed his eyes, the ulemas and the imauns assembled in the chapel in which his remains were deposited, and read during the whole night verses from the Koran, never ceasing to invoke their prophet against the disciples of Christ. Chalil did not delay setting forward on his march with his army. The Franks hoped that the death of Kelaoun would give birth to some disorders among the Mamelukes; but hatred for the Christians was a sufficient bond of union for the Mussulman soldiers; the siege even of Ptolemaïs, the hope of annihilating a Christian city, stifled all the germs of discord, and consolidated the power of Chalil, whom they proclaimed beforehand the conqueror of the Franks, and the *pacificator of the Mussulman religion.*

The sultan arrived before Ptolemaïs; his army covering a space of several leagues, from the sea to the mountains. More than three hundred machines of war were ready to batter the ramparts of the city. Aboulfeda, who was present at this siege, speaks of one of these machines which a hundred chariots were scarcely sufficient to transport.

This formidable preparation spread consternation among the inhabitants of Ptolemaïs. The grand master of the Templars, despairing of the defence or of the salvation of the city, assembled the leaders to consult if there were any means of renewing the truce, and thus escaping inevitable ruin. Repairing to the tent of the sultan, he demanded peace of him; and seeking to produce an effect upon his mind, he exaggerated the strength of Ptolemaïs; the sultan, dreading doubtless the difficulties of the siege, and hoping to find another opportunity of making himself master of the city, consented to a truce upon condition that every inhabitant should pay him a Venetian denier. The grand master on his return convoked an assembly of the people in the church of the Holy Cross, and laid before them the conditions the sultan placed upon the conclusion of a fresh truce. His advice was, that they should comply with these conditions, provided there were no other means of saving Ptolemaïs. Scarcely had he expressed his opinion, when the multitude rushed in in fury, uttering loud cries of *treachery!* and very nearly did the grand master expiate on the spot his foresight and zeal for the salvation of the city. From that time the only thought of this generous warrior was to die arms in hand for an ungrateful and frivolous people, incapable of repelling war by war, and not enduring to be saved by peace.

The presence of the sultan had redoubled the ardour of the Mussulman troops. From the day of his arrival the siege was prosecuted with incredible vigour. The army of the besiegers amounted to sixty thousand horse and a hundred and forty thousand foot, who constantly relieved each other, and left the besieged not a moment of repose. The machines hurled stones and enormous pieces of wood, the fall of which shook the palaces and houses of the city to their foundation. A shower of arrows, darts, fire-pots, and leaden balls was poured night and day upon the ramparts and towers. In the first assaults, the Christians killed a great number of the infidels who approached the walls with arrows and stones; they made many sorties, in one of which they penetrated to the tents of the Saracens. Being at length repulsed, some of them fell into the hands of the Mussulmans, and the Syrian horsemen, who had fastened the heads of the vanquished to the necks of their horses, went to display before the sultan of Cairo the barbarous trophies of a dearly-bought victory.

Danger at first united all the inhabitants of Ptolemaïs, and animated them with the same sentiments. In the early combats nothing could equal their ardour; they were sustained by the expectation of receiving succours from the West, and they hoped, also, that some advantages gained over the Saracens would force the besiegers to retreat; but in proportion as these hopes vanished, their zeal diminished; most of them were incapable of supporting lengthened fatigue; the sight of a peril which unceasingly returned exhausted their courage; the defenders of the ramparts perceived that their numbers were lessened daily; the port was covered with Christians departing from the city, and bearing their treasures with them. The example of those who thus fled completed the discouragement of those who remained; and in a city which numbered a hundred thousand inhabitants, and which, at the commencement of the siege, had furnished nearly twenty thousand warriors, only twelve thousand could at length be mustered under arms.

To desertion, another evil was soon added, which was dissension among the leaders; several of them disapproved of the measures that were adopted for the defence of the city, and because their opinions did not prevail in the council, they remained inactive, forgetful of the perils and evils which threatened both the city and themselves.

On the fourth day of May, after the siege had lasted nearly a month, the sultan of Cairo gave the signal for an assault. From daybreak, all the drums of the army, placed upon three hundred camels, spread a fearful and stunning noise. The most formidable of the machines of war were employed in battering the ramparts towards the gate and tower of St. Antony, on the east side of the city. This post was guarded by the soldiers of the king of Cyprus; the Mussulmans planted their ladders at the foot of the walls; the defence was not less spirited than the attack; the conflict lasted during the whole day, and night alone forced the Saracens to retreat. After this severe struggle, the king of Cyprus became more anxious for safety than glory, and determined to abandon a city which he had now no hopes of saving. He retired with his troop in the evening, under the pretence of taking some necessary repose, and, confiding the post of peril to the Teutonic knights, promised to return with daylight; but when the sun arose, the king of Cyprus had embarked with all his knights and three thousand soldiers. What were the surprise and indignation of the Christian warriors at the news of this dastardly desertion! "Would to heaven," says the author of an account that lies before us,—"would to heaven that a whirlwind had arisen, had submerged these base fugitives, and that they had sunk like lead to the bottom of the sea!"

On the morrow, the Mussulmans gave a fresh assault; covered by their long bucklers, they advanced in good order towards their machines, carrying a vast number of ladders. The Christians defended the approach to the walls for some time; but when the besiegers perceived that the towers, occupied on the preceding day by the Cypriots, were abandoned, their audacity increased, and they made incredible efforts to fill up the ditch, by casting into it stones, earth, and the carcases of their dead horses. Contemporary historians relate a circumstance of this part of the siege to which it is very difficult to give credit: a troop of sectaries, who were called *Chages,* followed the army of the Mamelukes; the devotion of these sectaries consisted in suffering all sorts of privations, and even in immolating themselves for the sake of Islamism: the sultan ordered them to fill up the ditch; they filled it up with their living bodies, and the Mussulman cavalry marched over them, to gain the foot of the walls!

The besiegers fought with fury; some planted their ladders and mounted in crowds to the ramparts; whilst others continued to batter the walls with the rams, and brought every available instrument into play to demolish them. At length a large breach opened a passage into the city, and this breach soon became the scene of a bloody and obstinate contest. Stones and arrows were abandoned, they now fought man to man, with lance, sword, and mace. The multitude of Saracens increased every instant, whilst no fresh succours were received by the Christians. After a long and brave resistance, the defenders of the rampart, worn out with fatigue and overwhelmed by numbers, were obliged to retreat into the city; the Saracens rushed forward in pursuit of them, and, what is scarcely to be believed, most of the inhabitants remained idle spectators, not because their courage was subdued by the sight of danger, but because the spirit of rivalry and jealousy was not stifled even by the feelings of a public and general calamity. "When the news of the entrance of the Saracens [we borrow the expressions of a contemporary historian] was spread through the city, many of the citizens, from malice towards each other, entertained not near so much pity for the common calamity as they ought to have done, and took no account of what might happen to them, thinking in their hearts that the sultan would do them no harm, because they had not consented to the violation of the truce." In their infatuation they preferred owing their safety to the clemency of the conqueror, rather than to the bravery of the Christian warriors; far from lending assistance to their neighbours, every one rejoiced in secret at their losses; the principal leaders of each quarter, or of each nation, were sparing of their soldiers, not in order to preserve their means of contending with the Saracens, but for the sake of having more empire in the city, and of husbanding their strength, so as to be on a future day the most powerful and formidable in the public dissensions.

True bravery, however, did not allow itself to be misled by such base passions; the troops of the Temple and the Hospital were found wherever danger called them. William de Clermont, marshal of the Hospitallers, hastened with his knights to the spot where peril was most imminent and the carnage the greatest. He met a crowd of Christians flying before their enemies; this brave warrior checked their flight and reanimated their courage, rushing among the Saracens, and cutting down all that came in his way; the Mussulmans, says an old chronicle, "fled away at his approach, like sheep before a wolf." Then most of those who had turned their backs on the enemy returned to the fight; the shock was terrible, the slaughter frightful: towards evening the trumpets of the Saracens sounded a retreat, and all who had escaped from the swords of the Christians retired in disorder through the breach they had made. This unexpected advantage had a wonderful effect upon the spirits of the besieged. Such as had taken no part in the contest, but remained quietly in their dwellings, began to fear that they should be accused of betraying the Christian cause. They set forward, with banners displayed, and directed their course towards the gate of St. Antony. The sight of the field of battle, still covered with traces of carnage, must have awakened in them some generous feelings, and if they had not exhibited their bravery, their brother warriors, stretched upon the earth, who implored them to help them and dress their wounds, at least offered them an opportunity of exercising their humanity. The wounded were attended to, the dead were buried, and they then set about repairing the walls and placing the machines: the whole of the night was employed in preparing means of defence for the day which was to follow.

Before sunrise the next morning, a general assembly was convoked in the house of the Hospitallers. Sadness was depicted on every countenance; they had lost two thousand Christian warriors in the battle of the preceding day; there now were only seven thousand combatants left in the city; these were not enough to defend the towers and the ramparts; they were no longer sustained by the hope of conquering their enemies; the future presented nothing but one terrible prospect of perils and calamities. When all were met, the patriarch of Jerusalem addressed the melancholy assembly. The venerable prelate directed no reproaches against them who had not assisted in the fight of the preceding day; the past must be forgotten; he did not praise them who had signalized their bravery, for fear of awakening jealousy; in his discourse he did not venture to speak of country, for Ptolemaïs was not the country of most of those who listened to him. The picture of the misfortunes which threatened the city and every one of its inhabitants, was presented in the darkest colours; there was no hope, no asylum for the vanquished; nothing was to be expected from the clemency of the Saracens, who always accomplished their threats, and never fulfilled their promises. It was but too certain that Europe would send them no succour; they had not vessels enough to enable them to think of flying by sea:—thus the patriarch took less pains to dissipate the alarms of his auditors than to animate them by despair. He terminated his speech by exhorting them to place all their confidence in God and their swords, to prepare for fight by penitence, to love each other, to help each other, and to endeavour to render their lives or their death glorious for themselves and serviceable to Christianity.

The speech of the patriarch made the deepest impression upon the assembly; nothing was heard but sobs and sighs; every person present was in tears; the religious sentiments which are generally awakened by the aspect of a great peril, filled all their hearts with an ardour and an enthusiasm they had never before experienced; most of them embraced each other, and exchanged reciprocal exhortations to brave every danger; they mutually confessed their sins, and even expressed a hope for the crown of martyrdom; those who had meditated desertion the day before, swore that they would never abandon the city, but would die on the ramparts with their brethren and companions.

The leaders and soldiers then went to the posts entrusted to their bravery. Such as were not employed in the defence of the ramparts and towers, made themselves ready to contend with their enemies, if they should gain access to the city; barriers were erected in all the streets, and heaps of stones were collected on the roofs, and at the doors of houses, to crush the Mussulmans, or impede them on their march.

Scarcely were these preparations finished, than the air resounded with the notes of trumpets and the beating of drums; a horrible noise, proceeding from the plain, announced the approach of the Saracens. After having discharged a multitude of arrows, they advanced confidently towards the wall they had broken through the day before. But they met with a resistance they did not expect; many were slain at the foot of the ramparts; but as their number momentarily increased, their constantly renewed attacks necessarily exhausted the strength of the Christians, at first in small numbers, and receiving no reinforcements. Towards the end of the day, the Christians had scarcely the power to hurl a javelin or handle a lance. The wall began again to give way beneath the strokes of the rams; then the patriarch, ever present at the point of danger, exclaimed in a supplicating tone,— "Oh, God! surround us with a rampart that men cannot destroy, and cover us with the ægis of Thy power!" At hearing this, the soldiers appeared to rally and make a last effort; they precipitated themselves upon the enemy, calling upon *the blessed Jesus, with a loud voice.* The Saracens, adds our chronicler, *called upon the name of their Mahomet,* and uttered the most fearful threats against the defenders of the Christian faith.

Whilst this conflict was going on upon the ramparts, the city awaited in great dread the issue of the battle; the agitation of men's minds gave birth to a thousand rumours, which were in turn adopted and rejected. It was reported in the most remote quarters, that the Christians were victorious, and the Mussulmans had fled; it was likewise added, that a fleet with an army on board had arrived from the West. To these news, which created a momentary joy, succeeded the most disheartening intelligence; and in all these reports there was nothing true but that which announced something inauspicious.

It was soon known that the Mussulmans had entered the city. The Christian warriors who defended the gate of St. Antony, had not been able to resist the shock of the enemy, and fled into the streets, imploring the assistance of the inhabitants. These latter then remembered the exhortations of the patriarch; reinforcements hasten from all quarters; the knights of the Hospital, with the valiant William at their head, reappear. A storm of stones falls from the tops of the houses; iron chains are stretched across the passage of the Mussulman cavalry; such as have been exhausted by fight recover their strength, and rush again into the *mêlée;* they who have come to their assistance follow their steps, break through the Mussulman battalions, disperse them and pursue them beyond the ramparts. In every one of these combats was exhibited all that valour can accomplish when united with despair. On contemplating, on one side the inevitable ruin of a great city, and on the other the efforts of a small number of defenders who put off, day after day, scenes of destruction and death, we cannot help feeling both compassion and surprise. The assaults were renewed without ceasing, and always with the same fury. At the end of every day's conflict, the unfortunate inhabitants of Ptolemaïs congratulated themselves upon having triumphed over their enemies; but on the morrow, when the sun appeared above the horizon, what were their thoughts when they beheld from the top of their ramparts the Mussulman army still the same, covering the plain from the sea to the foot of Karenba and Carmel!

The Saracens, on their part, became astonished at the resistance which all their attacks met with; so many combats, in which their innumerable multitude had not been able to obtain a decided advantage, began to give them discouragement. In the infidel army it was impossible to explain the invincible bravery of the Christian soldiers without assigning miraculous causes for it. A thousand extraordinary tales flew from mouth to mouth, and struck the imagination of the gross crowd of the

Mussulmans. They believed they saw two men in every one of those with whom they fought;[*] in the excess of their astonishment, they persuaded themselves that every warrior who fell beneath their stroke was reborn of himself, and returned stronger and more terrible than ever to the field of battle. The sultan of Cairo appeared to have lost all hope of taking the city by assault. It is asserted that the renegadoes, whose apostacy made them desirous of the ruin of the Christian name, sought every means to revive his courage; the sieur Barthélemi, who had sworn an eternal hatred to the Franks, followed the Mussulman army; this implacable deserter neglected nothing to encourage the leaders, to reanimate them for battle, and awaken in their hearts the furious passions that constantly devoured his own. In addition to these, the imauns and sheiks, who were numerous in the Mameluke camps, pervaded the ranks of the army to inflame the fanaticism of the soldiers: the sultan threatened all who flew before the enemy with punishment, and offered immense rewards for those who should plant the standard of the Prophet, not upon the walls of Ptolemaïs, but in the centre of the city.

On the 4th of May, a day fatal to the Christians, the signal for a fresh assault was given. At dawn the Mussulman army was under arms, the sultan animating the soldiers by his presence. Both the attack and the defence were much more animated and obstinate than they had been for some days before. Among those who fell on the field of battle, there were seven Mussulmans for one Christian; but the Mussulmans could repair their losses; those of the Christians were irreparable. The Saracens still directed all their efforts against the tower and the gate of St. Antony.

They were already upon the breach, when the knights of the Temple formed the rash resolution of making a sortie, and attacking the camp of the Mussulmans. They found the enemy's army drawn up in order of battle; after a bloody conflict, the Saracens repulsed the Christians, and pursued them to the foot of the ramparts. The grand-master of the Temple was struck by an arrow and fell in the midst of his knights. The grand-master of the Hospital, at the same time received a wound which disabled him. The rout then became general, and all hope of saving the city was lost. There were scarcely a thousand Christian warriors left to defend the gate of St. Antony against the whole Mussulman army.

The Christians were obliged to yield to the multitude of their enemies; they directed their course towards the house of the Templars, situated on the seacoast. It was then that a death-pall seemed stretched over the whole city of Ptolemaïs: the Saracens advanced full of fury; there was not a street that did not become the theatre of carnage; a battle was fought for every tower, for every palace, and at the entrance of every public building; and in all these combats, so many men were killed, that, according to the report of an historian, *they walked upon the dead as upon a bridge.*

As if angry heaven gave the signal for destruction, a violent storm, accompanied by hail and rain, burst over the city; the horizon was all at once covered with such impenetrable darkness, that the combatants could scarcely distinguish the colours they fought under, or see what standard floated over the towers; all the scourges contributed to the desolation of Ptolemaïs; the flames appeared in several quarters, without any one making an effort to extinguish them; the conquerors only thought of destroying the city, the only object of the conquered was to escape. A multitude of people fled away at hazard, without knowing where they could hope to find an asylum. Whole families took refuge in churches, where they were stifled by the flames, or cut to pieces at the foot of the altars; nuns and timid virgins mixed with the multitude which wandered through the city, or disfigured with wounds their faces and their bosoms,[†] to escape the brutality of the con-

---

[*] A German chronicle of Thomas Ebendorft relates the miraculous stories that were circulated among the Saracens. According to this chronicle, when a Christian expired, another issued from his mouth, *ex ore*. There were two souls in every body; *in uno corpore duo fuerunt hominis*.

[†] Wadin, the author of a chronicle entitled *Annales Minorum*, tom. ii., p. 585, quotes a circumstance which St. Antonine relates in the third part of his *Somme Historique*. After having said that the greater part of the French Cordeliers were killed by the Saracens, he adds these words: " But not one of

INVOCATION TO MAHOMET.

In the meanwhile, Kelaoun was still detained in Egypt by sickness, and feeling his end approach, the sultan sent for his son and his principal emirs; he recommended to the latter, to serve his son as they had served himself; and to the former, to follow up the war against the Christians without any intermission, conjuring him not to grant his remains the honor of sepulture before he had conquered the city of Ptolemaïs. Chalil swore to accomplish the last wishes of his father; and when Kelaoun had closed his eyes, the ulemas and the imauns assembled in the chapel in which his remains were deposited, and read during the whole night verses from the Koran, never ceasing to invoke their prophet against the disciples of Christ. Chalil did not delay setting forward on his march with his army. The Franks hoped that the death of Kelaoun would give birth to some disorders among the Mamelukes; but hatred for the Christians was a sufficient bond of union for the Mussulman soldiers; the siege even of Ptolemaïs, the hope of annihilating a Christian city, stifled all the germs of discord, and consolidated the power of Chalil, whom they proclaimed beforehand the conqueror of the Franks, and the PACIFICATOR OF THE MUSSULMAN RELIGION.—BOOK XV.

querors: what was most deplorable in the spectacle then presented in Ptolemaïs, was the desertion of the leaders, who abandoned a people in the height of its despair. John de Gresly and Oste de Granson, who had scarcely shown themselves upon the ramparts during the siege, fled away at the very commencement of the battle. Many others, who had taken the oath to die, at the aspect of this general destruction only thought of saving their lives, and threw away their arms to facilitate their flight. History, however, is able to contrast some acts of true heroism with these base desertions. Our readers cannot have forgotten the brilliant actions of William de Clermont. Amidst the ruins of Ptolemaïs, amidst the universal destruction, he still defied the enemy; attempting to rally some Christian warriors, he rode to the gate of St. Antony, which the Templars had just abandoned; though alone, he wished to renew the fight; he pierced through the ranks of the Saracens several times, and returned, still fighting; when he came back to the middle of the city, his war-horse (we copy a relation of the time) was much fatigued, as was he himself also; the war-horse no longer answered to the spur, and stopped in the street, as unable to do any more. The Saracens shot Brother William to the earth with arrows; and thus this loyal champion of Jesus Christ rendered up his soul to his Creator.

We cannot refuse our highest praise to the patriarch of Jerusalem, who, during the whole siege, shared all the dangers of the combatants; when he was dragged away towards the port by his friends, to evade the pursuit of the Mussulmans, the generous old man complained bitterly at being separated from his flock in the hour of peril. He was induced at last to embark, but as he insisted upon receiving on board his vessel all that presented themselves, the boat was sunk, and the faithful pastor died the victim of his charity.

The sea was tempestuous, the vessels could not approach close to land; the shore presented a heart-rending spectacle; here a mother called upon her son, there a son implored the assistance of his father; many precipitated themselves into the waves, in despair; the mass of people endeavoured to gain the vessels by swimming; some were drowned in the attempt, others were beaten off with oars. Several women of the noblest families flew in terror to the port, bringing with them their diamonds and their most valuable effects; they promised the mariners to become their wives, to give themselves and all their wealth up to them, if they would bear them away from this horrid scene; most of them were conveyed to the Isle of Cyprus: no pity was shown but to such as had treasures to bestow in return; thus, when tears had no effect upon hearts, avarice assumed the place of humanity, and saved some few victims. At length the Mussulman horsemen came down upon the port, and furiously pursued the Christians even into the waves: from that moment no one was able to escape the carnage.

Still, amidst the city given over to pillage, and a prey to the flames and the barbarity of the conquerors, several fortresses remained standing, and were defended by some Christian soldiers; these unfortunate warriors died sword in hand, without any other witnesses of their glorious end but their implacable enemies.

The castle of the Templars, in which all the knights who had escaped the steel of the Saracens

---

the virgins of St. Claire escaped." The abbess of this order, who possessed a masculine spirit, having learnt that the enemy had entered the city, called all her sisters together by the sound of the bell, and by the force of her words persuaded them to hold the promise they had made to Jesus Christ, their spouse, to preserve their chastity: "My dear daughters, my excellent sisters," said she, "we must, in this certain danger of life and modesty, show ourselves above our sex. The enemies are near to us; not so much to our bodies as to our souls; these barbarians, who, after having satisfied their brutal lusts upon all they meet, slay them with their swords. In this crisis we cannot hope to escape their fury by flight, but we can by a resolution, painful it is true, but sure. Most men are seduced by the beauty of women; let us deprive ourselves of this attraction, let us seek a preservative for our modesty in that which serves as a cause for its violation. Let us destroy our beauty to preserve our virginity pure. I will set you the example; let those who desire to meet their heavenly spouse imitate their mistress." At these words she cut her nose off with a razor; the others did the same, and boldly disfigured themselves, to present themselves more beautiful before Jesus Christ. By these means they preserved their purity, for the Saracens, on beholding their bleeding faces, conceived a disgust for them, and killed them all, without sparing one.

had taken refuge, was soon the only place in the city that held out. The sultan having granted them a capitulation, sent three hundred Mussulmans to execute the treaty. Scarcely had these entered one of the principal towers, the tower of the grand master, than they began to outrage the women who had taken refuge there. This violation of the rights of war irritated the Christian warriors to such a degree, that all the Saracens who had entered the tower were instantly immolated to their too just vengeance. The angry sultan ordered the siege to be prosecuted against the Christians in their last asylum, and that all should be put to the sword. The knights of the Temple and their companions defended themselves for several days: at length the tower of the grand master was undermined, and fell at the very moment the Mussulmans were mounting to an assault: they who attacked it and they who defended it were equally crushed by its fall; women, children, Christian warriors, all who had come to seek refuge in the house of the Templars, perished, buried beneath the ruins. Every church of Ptolemaïs was plundered, profaned, and then given up to the flames. The sultan ordered all the principal edifices, with the towers and ramparts, to be demolished.

The Mussulman soldiers expressed their joy by ferocious clamours; which joy formed a horrible contrast with the desolation of the conquered. Amidst the tumultuous scenes of victory were mingled the screams of women, upon whom the barbarians were committing violence in their camp, and the cries of little children, borne away into slavery. A distracted multitude of fugitives, driven from ruin to ruin, and finding no place of refuge, directed their course to the tent of the sultan, to implore his mercy; Chalil distributed these Christian supplicants among his emirs, who caused them all to be massacred. Macrisi makes the number of these unhappy victims amount to ten thousand.

After the taking and the destruction of Ptolemaïs, the sultan sent one of his emirs with a body of troops to take possession of the city of Tyre; this city, seized with terror, opened its gates without resistance. The conquerors likewise possessed themselves of Berytus, Sidon, and all the Christian cities along the coast. These cities, which had not afforded the least succour to Ptolemaïs, in the last great struggle, and which believed themselves protected by a truce, beheld their population massacred, dispersed, and led into slavery; the fury of the Mussulmans extended even to the stones, they seemed to wish to destroy the very earth which the Christians had trod upon; their houses, their temples, the monuments of their piety, their valour and their industry, everything was condemned to perish with them by the sword or by fire.

Most of the contemporary chronicles attribute such great disasters to the sins of the inhabitants of Palestine, and in the scenes of destruction only behold the effect of that divine anger which fell upon Nineveh and Babylon. History must not reject these easy explanations; but it is, doubtless, permitted to penetrate deeper into human affairs, and whilst recognising the intervention of Heaven in the political destinies of nations, it is bound at least to endeavour to discover the means which Providence has employed to raise, to maintain for a time, and at length, to destroy empires.

We have shown, in the course of our recital, to what point the ambition of the leaders, the want of discipline among the soldiers, the turbulent passions of the multitude, the corruption of morals, the spirit of discord and dissension, with egotism and selfishness, had urged on the kingdom of Jerusalem towards its decline and its destruction. We shall here offer but one general observation which belongs to our subject, and which ought not to be omitted in a history of the crusades.

This power of the Franks had been cast upon Asia, as by a tempest, and could not support itself there by its own strength. The true support of the kingdom of Jerusalem remained in the West, and the principle of its preservation, the source of its power was foreign to itself; its safety depended upon a crowd of circumstances which its leaders could not possibly foresee, upon a crowd of events which passed far from it; it depended above all upon feelings and opinions which prevailed among distant nations. Whilst the enthusiasm which had founded the Christian colonies was kept up in Europe, these colonies might hope to prolong their existence; the greatest of their calamities* was the indifference of the nations which dwelt beyond the seas; the kingdom of Jerusalem began with the crusades, it was destined to terminate with them.

A Mussulman chronicler, after having described the desolation of the coasts of Syria, and the expulsion of the citizens, terminates his account by this singular reflection: "Things, if it please God, will remain thus till the last judgment." The wishes of the Arabian historian have hitherto been but too completely fulfilled; the Mussulmans, for more than five centuries, have reigned over the countries occupied by the Christians, and with them has reigned the genius of destruction which presided over the wars we have described. The philosopher who contemplates these desolated regions, these fields uncultivated and deserted, these towns in ruins, these cities without industry, without laws, and almost without inhabitants, and who compares them with what they were in the times of the crusades, cannot avoid being deeply impressed by regret and compassion. Without dwelling upon the motives which governed the actions of the Crusaders, without approving all that a frequently blind enthusiasm inspired, he must at least acknowledge that these distant expeditions did some good, and that if they sometimes carried desolation to the coasts of Syria, they also carried thither the germs of prosperity and civilization.

---

* Among the marvellous accounts to which the destruction of the Christian colonies in Syria gave birth, history has preserved the following :—" In the year 1291, the house of the holy Virgin at Nazareth, in which she conceived the Son of God, was transported by angels to the top of a little mountain in Dalmatia, on the shore of the Adriatic Sea: three years afterwards it was transported to another shore of the same sea, in a wood which belonged to a widow named Loretto. There have been since built upon this spot a small city and a magnificent church, which still preserve the name of this widow."

BOOK XVI
Crusades Against the Turks
A.D. 1291 to 1396

SANUTI SHOWING MAPS OF THE EAST TO POPE JOHN XXII.

Sanuti thus describes the first audience he obtained with the sovereign pontiff: "I am not sent hither," said he, "by any king, any prince, or any republic; it is from the impulse of my own mind that I come to throw myself at the feet of your holiness, and to propose to you an easy means of crushing the enemies of the true faith, of extirpating the sect of Mohamet, and of recovering the Holy Land."

On finishing these words, Sanuti presented two books to the pope, one covered with red and the other with yellow, and four geographical charts, the first of the Mediterranean Sea, the second of the earth and of the sea, the third of the Holy Land, the fourth of Egypt. The books of the noble Venetian contained the history of the Christian establishments in the East, and wise counsels respecting the undertaking of another crusade.

The pope bestowed great praises upon Sanuti, and furnished him with introductions to several sovereigns of Europe. The Christian princes, particularly the king of France, received him with kindness, lauded his piety, and admired his talents, but took care not to follow his advice.—BOOK XVI.

BOOK XVI.

ATTEMPTED CRUSADES.

CRUSADES AGAINST THE TURKS.

A.D. 1291–1396.

Pope Nicholas IV. attempts to revive a fresh crusade against the East—Sends missionaries to the Tartars—Their contests with the Mussulmans revive the hopes of the Christians—Argun, the Tartar chief—Conquests of the Tartars—Cazan, the Mogul prince, sends ambassadors to the Pope—Clement IV. proclaims a crusade at the council of Vienna—Exploits of the Hospitallers—Conquests and wealth of the Templars—Accusations against them—Philip le Bel of France takes the cross—His death—Philip le Long—His death—Charles le Bel—His death—Raymond Lulli preaches a fresh crusade—Philip of Valois convokes an assembly at Paris for reviving a fresh crusade—Renewed persecutions of the Christians in Palestine—Brother Andrew of Antioch—Petrarch an apostle of the holy war—Humbert II., dauphin of Viennois, takes the cross—Hugh of Lusignan, king of Cyprus—Political troubles of France—King John taken prisoner at Poictiers—Engages in a fresh crusade—Urban V. convokes a meeting at Avignon—Peter de Lusignan, and Charles IV., emperor of Germany, engage in the crusade—Alexandria captured and burnt by the Crusaders—Barbary invaded by the Christian forces—Tripoli captured and burnt—Towns of Syria destroyed—Origin and history of the Turks and the Ottoman empire—Their conquests and invasion of Greece—Constantinople menaced by the Turks—Its tottering state—The emperors of Constantinople—Amurath, the Turkish sultan—Bajazet—Two popes at the same time—Crusade against the Turks determined on—Bajazet defeats the Christian forces with great slaughter—Defeats the Hungarians—Manuel, emperor of Constantinople, visits France—Distracted state of Europe—History and conquests of Tamerlane the Tartar—The Turks defeated, and Syria overrun by the Tartars—Bajazet raises the siege of Constantinople, and is defeated by Tamerlane—Smyrna captured and destroyed—The Ottomans reconquer the provinces overrun by Tamerlane—The Greek Church submits to papal authority—The barbarities of the Turks towards the Christians—Pope Eugenius exhorts the Christian states to another crusade—Cardinal Julian preaches in its favour—Amurath enters into a treaty of peace with the Crusaders, which being violated, they are defeated with great slaughter—Ladislaus, king of Poland, and Cardinal Julian, slain—Battle of Warna—Accession of Mahomet II. to the Ottoman throne—His extensive empire—Besieges Constantinople—Character of Constantine Palæologus, the Greek emperor—His great efforts in defence of his capital—Mahomet takes the city by storm—Death of the emperor and destruction of the Greek empire.

WE are now arrived at the end of the brilliant epoch of the crusades, but our task is not yet completed; for, as the curiosity of readers attaches a high value to the knowledge of the causes of events, in the same degree must it be desirous of knowing the influence that these events have had upon the laws, manners, and destinies of nations. After having witnessed the kindling of so many passions, which inflamed Europe and Asia during two centuries, who but must be curious to see in what manner these passions were progressively extinguished; what were the political combinations that weakened this universal enthusiasm; and what were the interests, the opinions, and the institutions which took place of the spirit of the holy wars. Here the philosophy of history comes at our wish to enlighten us with its lamp, and make clear to us the eternal course of human things. The end of a great revolution may be compared, in some sort, to the decline of the life of man, it is then that the fruits of long experience may be gathered, it is then that the past, with its remembrances and its lessons, is reflected as in a faithful mirror.

We will pursue, then, with confidence the work we have begun; if, in the career we have still to go through, we may have little to say that will awaken the curiosity of common minds, enlightened spirits will, doubtless, find some interest, in following with us all these long reverberations of a revolution which deeply agitated the world, and whose consequences will be felt by remotest posterity.

When the news of the taking of Ptolemaïs arrived in the West, Pope Nicholas IV. gave his whole attention to the preaching of a crusade. A bull addressed to all the faithful, deplored in pathetic terms the late disasters of the Christians; and the greater that these misfortunes were, the more fully did the pope offer the treasures of divine mercy and pontifical indulgences to new Crusaders. An indulgence of a hundred days was granted to those who would attend the sermons of the preachers of the crusade, or would come to the churches to listen to the groans of the city of God. The holy orators had permission to preach the war of the East in forbidden places; and, that great sinners might be induced to become soldiers of the cross, the preachers received the faculty of granting certain absolutions that had till that time been reserved for the supreme authority of the Holy See.

In many provinces, the clergy assembled in consequence of the directions of the pope, to deliberate upon the means of recovering Palestine. The prelates employed themselves in this pious mission with much zeal, and in order to secure the success of the enterprise, all united in conjuring the sovereign pontiff to labour without intermission in bringing about the reëstablishment of peace among Christian princes.

Several monarchs had already taken the cross; and Nicholas sent legates to press them to accomplish the vow they appeared to have forgotten. Edward, king of England, although he had levied the tenths upon the clergy for the expenses of the crusade, showed very little inclination to quit his states for the purpose of returning into Asia. The emperor Rodolph, who, in the conference of Lausanne, had promised the pope to make the voyage beyond the seas, died at this period, much more deeply engaged in the affairs of Germany, than in those of the Christians of the East. Nicholas IV. gave Philip to understand that the whole West had its eyes fixed upon him, and that his example might influence all Christendom; the sovereign pontiff at the same time exhorted the prelates of the Church of France to join with him in persuading the king, the nobles, and the people, to take arms against the infidels.

The father of the Christian world did not confine his endeavours to awakening the zeal of the princes and nations of the West; he sent apostolic messages to the Greek emperor, Andronicus Palæologus, the emperor of Trebizond, and the kings of Armenia, Georgia, and Cyprus, in which he announced to them the approaching deliverance of the holy places. As the Christians in their distress had sometimes turned their looks towards the Tartars, two missionaries were sent to the coast of Argun, with directions to offer the Mogul emperor the benedictions of the sovereign pontiff, and to solicit his powerful aid against the Mussulmans.

The exertions and exhortations of the pope did not succeed in arming Europe against the Saracens; contemporary chronicles say that Nicholas was not able to endure this indifference of the Christians, and that he died in despair. After his death, the conclave could not agree in the nomination of a head of the Church, and the Holy See remained vacant during twenty-seven months. In this long interval, the pulpits which had resounded with the complaints of the faithful of the East, remained mute, and Europe forgot the last calamities of the Holy Land.

In the East, the affairs of the Christians took a not more favourable turn. The discord that had arisen between the princes of the family of Hayton desolated Armenia, and gave it up to the invasion of the barbarians. The kingdom of Cyprus, the last asylum of the Franks established in Asia, only owed a transitory security to the sanguinary divisions of the Mamelukes of Egypt, and appeared to be fully engaged by its own dangers.

But whilst Christendom gave up all thoughts of the deliverance of Jerusalem, the Tartars of Persia, to whom the pope had sent missionaries, all at once revived the hopes of the Christians, by forming a project for wresting Syria and Palestine from the hands of the Mussulmans; an enterprise which only wanted to be a crusade, to have been proclaimed by the head of the Church.

The Tartars, for a long time, threatened the Mussulman powers, whom the Christians regarded as their most cruel enemies. Argun, when he died, was busied in preparations for a formidable war. These preparations had spread such serious alarm among his enemies, that the disciples of Mahomet considered his death as one of the number of miracles operated in favour of Islamism.

Among the successors of Argun, who were by turns the enemies and the friends of the Mussulmans, there was one able leader, who was warlike, and more animated by the thirst for conquests than the others. The Greek historian Pachymerus, and the Armenian Hayton, lavish the highest praises upon the bravery, the virtue, and even the piety of Cazan. This Mogul prince considered the Christians as his most faithful allies; and in his armies, in which the Georgians served, the standard of the cross floated by the side of the imperial standard. The conquest of the banks of the Nile and the Jordan engaged all his thoughts. When new cities were built in his states, he took a delight in bestowing upon them the names of Aleppo, Damascus, Alexandria, and of several other places in Egypt and Syria.

Cazan quitted Persia at the head of an army; and the king of Cyprus with the orders of St. John and the Temple, being made aware of his projects, joined his standards. A great battle was fought near Emessa, which was decided against the sultan of Egypt, who lost the greater part of his army, and was pursued by the Armenian cavalry to the verge of the desert. Aleppo and Damascus opened their gates to the conquerors; and if we may believe the historian Hayton, Christians once more entered Jerusalem, and the emperor of the Tartars visited in their company the tomb of Christ.

It was from that place Cazan sent ambassadors to the pope and the sovereigns of Europe, to solicit their alliance, and to offer them possession of the Holy Land. Among the singularities of this period, our readers will no doubt be astonished to find a Mogul emperor endeavouring to revive the spirit of the crusades among the princes of Christendom; and to see barbarians from the banks of the Irtis and the Jaxartes waiting upon Calvary and Mount Sion for the warriors of France, Germany, and Italy, in order to combat the enemies of Christ. The sovereign pontiff received the ambassadors of Cazan with distinction; but could only answer their demands and propositions by promises doomed to remain unexecuted. The haughtiness with which Boniface VIII., the successor of Nicholas, spoke to the Christian princes, together with his exhortations, which resembled commands more than entreaties, disgusted the sovereigns, particularly the king of France. Genoa, which then lay under an interdict, was the only city of Europe in which a crusade was seriously spoken of; and by a whimsical circumstance, it was the ladies who gave the signal and set the example.

We are still in possession of a brief of the pope's, in which the holy father felicitates the ladies who had taken the cross, upon their following the steps of Cazan, the emperor of the Tartars, *who, although a pagan, had conceived the generous resolution of delivering the Holy Land.* History has preserved two other letters of the pope, one addressed to Porchetto, archbishop of Genoa, and the other to four Genoese nobles, who had undertaken to direct the expedition. "Oh, prodigy! oh, miracle!" says he to Porchetto; "a weak and timid sex takes the advance of warriors in this great enterprise, in this war against the enemies of Christ, in this fight against the workers of iniquity. The kings and princes of the earth, regardless of all the solicitations that have been made to them, refuse to send succours to the Christians banished from the Holy Land, and here are women who come forward without being called! Whence can this magnanimous resolution come, if not from

God, the source of all strength and all virtue!!!" The pope terminated his letter by directing the archbishop to call together the clergy and the people, and proclaim the devotion of the noble Genoese ladies, in order that their example may cast seeds of good works into the hearts of the people.

This crusade, notwithstanding, never took place; it was doubtless only preached to rouse the emulation of the knights, and the pope only directed his attention to it to give a lesson to the princes of Christendom, by which they did not at all profit. The letters written upon this occasion by Boniface VIII. were preserved in the archives of the republic of Genoa for a long time. Even in the last century, the helmets and cuirasses which were to have been worn by the Genoese ladies in this expedition were exhibited in the arsenal of that city.

The Tartars, in spite of their victories, were not able to triumph over the constancy and discipline of the Mamelukes, who, like themselves, had issued from the deserts of Scythia. That which had so often happened to the Franks in the height of the crusades, now happened to the Moguls; they at first obtained great advantages, but events foreign to the Holy War recalled them into their own country, and forced them to abandon their conquests. Cazan was obliged to quit Syria and return into Persia; he attempted a second expedition, which he again abandoned; and he died in the third, amidst his triumphs, bearing with him to the tomb the last hopes of the Christians.

The Armenian and Cyprian warriors left the holy city, the ramparts of which they had begun to re-erect, and which was doomed never again to see the standard of the cross unfurled within its walls. This last reverse of the Christians of the East was scarcely known in Europe, where the name of Jerusalem was still pronounced in the congregations of the faithful, but had no longer the power to awaken the enthusiasm of knights and warriors. At the council of Vienna, Pope Clement V. proclaimed a crusade; but in this assembly, in which the abolition of the Templars was determined upon, Christians were exhorted very feebly to take up arms against the infidels.

The sovereign pontiff was then much more busy in levying tenths than in preparations for a holy war. One thing worthy of remark is, that Clement found himself obliged on this occasion to recommend moderation to the collectors of the tenths, and forbade them *to seize the chalices, the books, or the ornaments of the churches*. This prohibition of the pope's proves to us that violence had often been committed in collecting the tributes destined to the expenses of the holy wars; this violence must have assisted in relaxing the zeal and ardour of nations for distant enterprises, as the results of which, Christian cities were ruined, and the altars of Christ plundered.

Europe at that time awaited with great impatience the issue of an expedition undertaken by the knights of St. John of Jerusalem. A great number of warriors, excited by the relation of the adventures of chivalry, and by a passion for military glory, followed the Hospitallers in their enterprise; women even were desirous of taking a part in this expedition, and sold their diamonds and jewels to provide for the expenses of the war.

This army of new crusaders embarked at the port of Brendisi, and it soon became known in the West that the knights of the Hospital had taken possession of the Isle of Rhodes.

Renown published everywhere the exploits of the Hospitallers and their companions in arms; and these exploits, and the admiration they inspired throughout Christendom, naturally turned the attention and remembrances of the faithful to the Templars, who were reproached with the disgraceful repose in which they forgot both the Holy Land and the tomb of Christ.

The knights of the Temple, after having been received in the Isle of Cyprus, had returned to Sicily, where they were employed by the king in an expedition against Greece. United with the Catalans and some warriors from Italy, this warlike body took possession of Thessalonica, made themselves masters of Athens, advanced towards the Hellespont, and ravaged a part of Thrace. After this expedition the Templars disdained the possession of the cities which had fallen into their power, and leaving the conquered provinces to their companions in arms, they kept for themselves the riches of the people they had subdued. It was then that, loaded with the spoils of Greece, they came to establish themselves in the West, particularly in France, where their opulence, their luxury, and their idleness, scandalized the piety of the faithful, awakened envy, and provoked the hatred of both the people and the great.

It does not enter into the plan of this work to dilate upon the process instituted against the Templars; but if we have followed these noble knights in all their wars against the Mussulmans,—if we have been so long witnesses of their exploits, and, as it were, companions of their labours, we shall perhaps have acquired the right of expressing our opinion upon the accusations directed against them. We must at once declare that we have found nothing up to the period of the process, either in the chronicles of the East, or those of the West, which can give birth to or establish an idea, or even a suspicion, of the crimes imputed to them. How can it, in fact, be believed, that a warlike and religious order, which twenty years before had seen three hundred of its knights sacrifice themselves upon the ruins of Saphet, rather than embrace the Mussulman faith, that this order which had almost entirely buried itself under the ruins of Ptolemaïs, could possibly have contracted an alliance with infidels, outraged the Christian religion with horrible blasphemies, and given up to the Saracens that Holy Land filled with its military glory.

And at what period were all these odious reproaches addressed to the Templars? at a time when Christendom seemed to have forgotten Jerusalem, and in which the name of Christ was not sufficient to awaken the bravery of a Christian warrior. No doubt the order of the Templars had degenerated from the austerity of early times, and that it was no longer animated by that spirit of humility and religion of which St. Bernard so much boasted; no doubt some of the knights had brought with them that corruption which was then the reproach of all the Christians of the East, and of which Europe itself could offer them numerous examples; no doubt, in short, some among them might have wounded morality by their conduct, and offended the religion of Christ by their irregularities; but we do not hesitate to say that it was not the province of men to judge them, and that upon this occasion the merciful God of the Christians had not deputed his vengeance to human laws.

The real error of the Templars was having quitted the East, and renounced the spirit of their institution, which was to receive and protect pilgrims, and to combat with the enemies of the Christian faith. This order, richer than the most powerful monarchs, and whose knights were as a regular army, always ready for fight, became, naturally, dreaded by the princes who granted them an asylum. The Templars had not been free from all reproach during their abode in Cyprus; accustomed to rule in Palestine, they must have contracted a habit of obedience with difficulty. The example of the Teutonic knights, who, after quitting the East, founded a power in the north of Europe which was dreaded by the neighbouring states, was not likely to reassure princes who mistrusted the warlike spirit, and the active and enterprizing genius, of the knights of the Temple.

Such, probably, were the motives which armed the policy rather than the justice of sovereigns against them; nothing so clearly proves the fear they inspired as the rancour with which they were pursued, and the care that was taken to render them odious. As soon as their persecution began, they were only considered as enemies whom it was necessary to treat as criminals. As rigours without example preceded their abolition, it was necessary to justify that measure by fresh rigours. Vengeance and hatred finished that which the policy of princes had begun; a policy which had, perhaps, reasons for being suspicious, but which had none for proving itself barbarous. It is thus we must explain the tragical issue of this process, in which all the forms of justice were so violated, that even if the accusations be considered proved, we must still regard the Templars as victims and their judges as executioners.

Philip-le-Bel had promised the council of Vienna to go into the East to combat the infidels, without doubt to procure pardon for having pursued the knights of the Temple with so much inveteracy. Amidst the festivals that welcomed the arrival of Edward in Paris, the French monarch and the princes of his family took the cross. Most of the nobles of his court followed his example, and the ladies promised to accompany the knights to the holy war; but no one took any measures for setting out. Promises were then made to cross the seas by persons who had not any serious intention of leaving their homes. The vow to combat the Saracens appeared to be a vain ceremony, which engaged the swearer to nothing. It was taken with perfect indifference, and violated in the same manner; *considered as not more sacred than the vows the knights made to the ladies.*

Philip-le-Bel died without ever having thought of accomplishing his vow. Philip-le-Long, who succeeded him, entertained for a moment the project of going into the East. Edward, who had already several times sworn to fight the Saracens, at the same time renewed his promise. But the sovereign pontiff, whether that he doubted their sincerity, or whether that he stood in need of the concurrence of these two monarchs to reëstablish tranquillity in Europe, and to resist the emperor of Germany, against whom he had armed himself with the thunders of the Church, or whether, in short, he thought the moment an unfavourable one, did not approve of their expedition into Syria. "Before thinking of the voyage beyond the seas," wrote he to the king of England, "we would wish you to establish peace, first in your own conscience, then in your kingdom." The father of the faithful represented to the king of France that the peace, so necessary to be firm before a crusade should be undertaken, was almost banished from Christendom. England and Scotland were at war; the states of Germany were divided against each other; the king of Sicily and the king of Naples were only bound by a truce of short duration; reciprocal mistrust prevented the kings of Cyprus and Armenia from uniting their forces against the common enemy; the kings of Spain were quite sufficiently employed in defending their states against the Moors; the republics of Lombardy were all in arms against each other; all the cities of Italy were torn by factions, the provinces a prey to tyrants, the sea impracticable, the route by land thickly strewed with dangers. After having given this picture of the deplorable state of Christendom, the pope pressed Philip to inquire seriously how he could provide for the expenses of the war without ruining his people, *or without attempting*, he added, *to do that which is impossible, as has been done before.*

The paternal advice of the sovereign pontiff, and some troubles which arose in the bosom of his kingdom, determined Philip to postpone the execution of his project. A multitude of herdsmen and shepherds, of adventurers and vagabonds, setting up, as in the time of the captivity of St. Louis, the pilgrims' cross, assembled in many places, persecuted the Jews, and committed most culpable excesses. Force of arms and the full severity of the laws were obliged to be resorted to, in order to quell these disorders, of which the crusade was only a pretext. At the same time several provinces of France suffered greatly from an epidemic disease; the Jews were accused of having poisoned the wells, with the design of suspending the preparations for the holy war. They were accused of all sorts of plots against the Christians; and the general fermentation was the greater from the suspicions being vague, and from the impossibility of proving or contradicting the crimes alleged. Policy could discover no other means of dissipating the troubles than that of entering into the passions of the multitude, and driving all the Jews out of the kingdom. Amidst these unhappy circumstances, Philip fell ill, and died regretting his not having accomplished the vow he had made of warring against the Saracens.

In the state of abandonment in which the crusades had fallen, we are surprised at seeing the minds of the French still occasionally directed towards the delivery of the holy places. This last flickering of enthusiasm, which our ancestors kept alight amidst the general indifference, was not confined to religious sentiments, but extended to a feeling of patriotism and national glory. It was France which had given the first impulsion to the holy wars, as we have several times observed. The name of Palestine, the names of St. Jean d'Acre or Ptolemaïs, and that of Jerusalem appealed no less to patriotism than to piety. Although the two expeditions of Louis IX. had been unsuccessful, the example of the holy monarch was a great authority for the princes of his family, and often carried their thoughts to the places where he had suffered the glory of martyrdom. The memory of his exploits and even of his misfortunes, the memory of the heroes who had died on the banks of the Nile and the Jordan, interested all the families of the kingdom; and the city in which reposed the ashes of Godfrey and Baldwin of Bouillon, those distant regions in which so many glorious battles had been fought, could not be forgotten by French warriors.

After the death of Philip-le-Long, ambassadors arrived in Europe from the king of Armenia; this prince, abandoned by the Tartars, and threatened by the Mamelukes of Egypt, requested the assistance of the West. The pope wrote to Charles-le-Bel, the successor of Philip-le-Long, and conjured him to take up arms against the infidels. Charles received with respect the counsels and the exhortations of the sovereign pontiff, and was engaged in preparations for a crusade when the succession of the county of Flanders caused a war to break out in the Low Countries. From that time France became attentive only to the events that were passing before her eyes, and in which her own independence and safety were deeply interested. At the approach of death, and at a time when the kingdom had no longer anything to fear, Charles-le-Bel remembered his oath, and his last thoughts were directed towards the deliverance of Jerusalem. "I bequeath," says he in his will, "to the Holy Land fifty thousand livres, to be paid and delivered when the general passage shall be made; and it is my intention, if the passage be made in my lifetime, to go thither in person." It was thus that at this period the spirit of the crusades still occasionally showed itself; most of the testaments then made by princes and *rich men* (these words designated the nobility) contained some dispositions in favour of the Holy Land; but we must add, also, that the facility of purchasing the merit of pilgrimage for money must necessarily have greatly diminished the number of pilgrims and Crusaders.

Whilst dying people were thus prodigal of their treasure for the holy war, nobody took up arms. There still, however, remained some men endowed with a vivid imagination and an ardent temperament, who made incredible efforts to rekindle an enthusiasm on the point of being extinguished. The greater the indifference of nations, the greater were the ardour and zeal displayed by these men in their preachings. Among these latter apostles of the crusades, history cites the name of Raymond Lulli, one of the luminaries of the schools of the middle ages.

Lulli was possessed during his life but by one thought, and that was, to combat and convert the infidels. It was upon the proposition of this zealous missionary that the council of Vienna decided that chairs should be established in the universities of Rome, Bologna, Paris, and Salamanca, for instruction in the languages of the East. He presented to the pope several memorials upon the means of annihilating the worship of Mahomet and the domination of his disciples. Lulli, constantly occupied with his project, made a pilgrimage into Palestine, travelled through Syria, Armenia, and Egypt, and came back to Europe to describe the misfortunes, the captivity, and the disgraces of the

Christians beyond the seas. On his return, he visited all the courts of the West, seeking to communicate to sovereigns the sentiment by which he was animated. Finding his efforts were vain, his zeal carried him to the coast of Africa, where he endeavoured to convert by his eloquence those same Saracens against whom he had invoked the arms of Christian warriors. He returned to Europe, passed through Italy, France, and Spain, preaching everywhere the necessity for another crusade. He embarked again for Jerusalem, and brought back, as the fruit of his pilgrimage, some useful notions upon the best manner of attacking the countries of the infidels. All his labours, all his researches, all his prayers, produced no effect upon the indifference of kings and nations. Lulli, at length despairing of seeing his projects realised, and deploring the blindness of his contemporaries, retired to the island of Majorca, which was his native country. From the depth of his retreat he still issued memorials upon an expedition to the East; but solitude soon wearied his ardent and restless spirit, and he quitted Majorca, no more to waste his words upon the princes of Europe, who would not listen to him, but to return to the Mussulmans, whom he still hoped to lead to the Gospel by his eloquence. He repaired a second time to Africa, and at length suffered, as the reward of his preachings, the torments and the death of martyrs.

Whilst Lulli was striving to direct the efforts of the faithful to the deliverance of the holy places, a noble Venetian likewise consecrated his life and his talents to the revival of the spirit of the crusades. Sanuti thus describes the first audience he obtained of the sovereign pontiff: "I am not sent hither," said he, "by any king, any prince, or any republic; it is from the impulse of my own mind that I come to throw myself at the feet of your holiness, and to propose to you an easy means of crushing the enemies of the true faith, of extirpating the sect of Mahomet, and of recovering the Holy Land. My voyages in Cyprus, Armenia, and Egypt, together with a long sojourn in Romania, have furnished me with knowledge and information that may be turned to the profit of Christianity." On finishing these words, Sanuti presented two books to the pope, one covered with red and the other with yellow, and four geographical charts, the first of the Mediterranean Sea, the second of the earth and of the sea, the third of the Holy Land, the fourth, of Egypt. The two books of the noble Venetian contained the history of the Christian establishments in the East, and wise counsels respecting the undertaking of another crusade. His zeal, enlightened by experience, did not allow him to neglect the least detail upon the route that was to be followed, upon the point that it would be best to attack, upon the number of troops, and upon the fitting out and provisioning of the vessels. He advised that operations should commence by landing in Egypt, and weakening the power of the sultans of Cairo. The most certain means of effecting this latter purpose was to obtain directly from Bagdad the Indian merchandises which European commerce was accustomed to get by the cities of Alexandria and Damietta. Sanuti, at the same time, advised the sovereign pontiff to redouble the severity of his censures against those who carried into Egypt arms, metals, timber for building, or anything that could assist in equipping fleets or arming the Mameluke soldiery.

The pope bestowed great praises upon Sanuti, and furnished him with introductions to several sovereigns of Europe. The Christian princes, particularly the king of France, received him with kindness, lauded his piety, and admired his talents—but took care not to follow his advice. Sanuti addressed himself likewise to the emperor of Constantinople, to engage him in an expedition against the infidels; he sought everywhere, and by every means, to raise up enemies against the Mussulmans, and passed his life in preaching a crusade, without obtaining any more success than Raymond Lulli had done.

The zeal of the two men of whom we have just spoken can only be compared to that of Peter the Hermit; they were both much more enlightened than the cenobite Peter, but they could get no one to listen to them, and the fruitlessness of their efforts proves how much the times were changed. Peter preached in cities and in public places, and the multitude, inflamed by his discourses, led away and awakened the feelings of the great. In the times of Lulli and Sanuti, sovereigns alone could be addressed, and sovereigns, occupied by their own affairs, showed very little interest for projects which only concerned Christendom in general. In the early times of the crusades, the deliverance of the holy places was a matter of importance; simply to pronounce the name of Jerusalem was sufficient to appease differences among princes; later, the least interest of jealousy, ambition, or self-love had the power to arrest the progress of, or completely put an end to, a holy enterprise. Frequently, in the twelfth century, popes and simple preachers, arming themselves with the authority of Christ, commanded princes to take up the cross and set out for the East; in the thirteenth, but more particularly in the fourteenth century, it was necessary to pray and solicit; and, generally, the most humble prayers produced no effect.

Thus, the groans of Sion no longer melted hearts, and Christian eloquence was powerless against infidels. In order to awaken attention, it was necessary to mingle something of profane grandeur with the pathetic exhortations of religion; thus, Europe, which scarcely listened to the missionaries of the cross, appeared, all at once, to be aroused by the arrival of the king of Cyprus, soliciting, in person, the assistance of Christian princes. The pope, who was then at Avignon, eagerly announced to the faithful that an Eastern king was come to his court, and conjured the warriors of the West to take up arms against the Saracens. The king of Cyprus and Jerusalem described the invasions of the Mamelukes, the progress of the Turks, the dangers which surrounded his kingdom, that of Armenia, and the isle of Rhodes, and omitted no instance of the numerous persecutions endured by the Christians who remained in Syria and Egypt. These sad recitals, coming from a royal mouth, awakened some generous sentiments in men's minds; a league was formed between the sovereign pontiff, the king of France, and the republic of Venice; and the pope published a bull by which he ordered the bishops to cause a crusade to be preached.

Philip of Valois convoked an assembly at Paris, in the Holy Chapel, at which were present John, king of Bohemia, the king of Navarre, the dukes of Burgundy, Brittany, Lorraine, Brabant, and Bourbon, with most of the prelates and barons of the kingdom. Peter de la Palue, named patriarch of Jerusalem, and who had recently passed through Egypt and Palestine, harangued the auditory upon the necessity for attacking the infidels, and stopping the progress of their domination in the East. Philip, who had already taken the cross, renewed the vow he had made, and as he was preparing to quit his kingdom, the barons took the oath of obedience to his son Prince John, by raising their hands towards the crown of thorns of Christ. John of Bohemia, the king of Navarre, and a great number of princes and nobles, received the cross from the hands of the archbishop of Rouen. The crusade was preached throughout the kingdom, "and gave to all noble lords," says Froissart, "great delight, particularly to those who wished to pass their time in arms, and knew no means then of employing it otherwise more reasonably."

The king of France sent to the pope the archbishop of Rouen, who afterwards ascended the chair of St. Peter under the name of Clement VI. The archbishop, in full consistory, pronounced a discourse upon the crusade, and declared, in the presence of divine majesty, to the holy father, to the church of Rome and all Christendom, that Philip of Valois would set out for the East in the month of August, in the year 1336. The pope felicitated the French monarch upon his resolution, and granted him the tenths during six years. These circumstances are related by Philip Villani, who was at Avignon at the time, and who, after having spoken in his history of the promise made in the name of the king of France, exclaims:—"And I, the historian, I heard the oath pronounced which I have just related."

Philip gave orders that a fleet, assembled in the port of Marseilles, should be made ready to receive forty thousand Crusaders. Edward III., to whom the crusade offered an easy means of imposing taxes, promised to accompany the king of France with an army in the pilgrimage beyond the seas. Most of the republics of Italy, with the kings of Arragon, Majorca, and Hungary, engaged to supply money, troops, and vessels for the expedition. In the midst of their preparations, the Crusaders lost him who directed and was the soul of the enterprise. Everything was interrupted by the death of Pope John XXI., and in this place it becomes necessary to point out one of the causes which rendered abortive, in the thirteenth and fourteenth centuries, so many attempts to carry the war into the East. As the successors of St. Peter scarcely ever succeeded to the pontifical chair before they were of an advanced age, they were wanting in the energy and activity necessary for exciting the Christian world, directing distant wars, and kindling an enthusiasm, formerly so difficult to be restrained, now so difficult to be revived. Each crusade requiring long preparations, the life of one sovereign pontiff scarcely sufficed for the completion of such great enterprises. It most frequently happened, that he who had preached a holy war could not behold the departure of the Crusaders; and that he who saw the Christian armies set out, never lived long enough to follow them through their expeditions, conduct them in their triumphs, or succour them in their reverses. Thus we never find in the projects which circumstances had formed, that spirit of sequence and wholeness necessary to secure execution and success. Add to this, that since the popes had been established at Avignon, and their apostolic seat was no longer in the centre of Christendom, they did not exercise the same ascendancy over the distant provinces, and their authority every day lost something of that influence attached to the name only of Rome, considered, during so many centuries, the capital of the world.

The news of a fresh crusade having reached the East, the Christians who dwelt in Syria or Egypt, with pilgrims and European merchants, were exposed to all sorts of persecutions. The sultan of Cairo and several Mussulman princes assembled armies for the purpose of resisting the Crusaders, or to go and attack the Christians in the West. A descendant of the Abassides, who resided in Egypt, and assumed the title of caliph, sent letters and messages in every direction to engage all true believers to take up arms; promising the martyrs of the Mussulman faith that they should be present at delicious banquets, and that each of them should have seven virgins for wives.

The aim of this crusade, preached in the name of the prophet of Mecca, was to penetrate into Europe by the way of Gibraltar; the Mussulman warriors swore to annihilate Christianity, and to convert all the Christian temples into stables. In proportion as the Saracens were thus becoming inflamed for an expedition, which they also called a holy war, Europe beheld the zeal of the princes and warriors who had sworn to combat the enemies of Christ, grow fainter and fainter, and at length die away. When Benedict XI. succeeded John XXI., he found the minds of all changed; hatreds, mistrusts and jealousies had taken place of a transitory and insincere enthusiasm; it was in vain that Christians from the East described the persecutions they had undergone and the preparations of the infidels against the nations of the West; it was in vain that the pope continued his exhortations and his prayers; the greater that the reason was for undertaking a crusade, the more indifferent people became, and the more all ranks seemed to shun the idea of contending with the Saracens. It was at this period that Brother Andrew of Antioch came to Avignon with the design of imploring the aid of the pope and the princes of Christendom. Philip of Valois had come to the court of the sovereign pontiff, to inform him that he should defer his voyage into the East, and had mounted his horse to return to Paris, when Brother Andrew presented himself before him, and said: "Art thou Philip king of France, who promised God and his Church to deliver the Holy Land?" The king answered,

"Yes." Then the monk resumed: "If thy intention is to perform that which thou hast promised, I implore Jesus Christ to direct thy steps, and grant thee the victory; but if the enterprise thou hast commenced is only to turn to the shame and misfortunes of Christians, if thou art not, with the help of God, determined to finish it, if thou hast deceived the holy Catholic Church, divine justice will fall heavily on thy family and on thy kingdom, and the blood which the news of thy expedition has caused to flow will rise up against thee." The king, surprised at this strange appeal, answered: "Brother Andrew, come with us;" and Brother Andrew replied without being moved, and in an inspired tone: "If thou wast going into the East, I would go before thee, but as thou art going to the West, go on; I will return to perform penance for my sins in the land thou hast abandoned."

Such was even then the authority of the orators who spoke in the name of Jerusalem, that the last words of Brother Andrew left trouble and uneasiness in the mind of a powerful monarch; but fresh political storms had recently broken out. Edward III. had laid claim to the throne of the Capets, and his ambition was the signal for a war which lasted more than a century, and brought the greatest calamities upon France. Philip, attacked by a formidable enemy, was obliged to renounce his expedition beyond the seas, and employ, for the defence of his own kingdom, the troops and fleets that he had collected for the deliverance of the heritage of Christ.

The pope did not, however, abandon the project of the holy war. The poet Petrarch, who was then at Avignon, proved one of the most ardent apostles of the crusade; this illustrious poet, whom we are now accustomed to consider only as the ingenious singer of the praises of the fair Laura, and who was then deemed the most worthy interpreter of the wisdom of the ancients, and one of the great spirits of his age, addressed an eloquent letter to the Doge of Venice, to induce him to enter into a war against the Mussulmans. Some of the states of Italy united their forces to make an expedition into the East. A chronicle of the counts of Ason relates that a great number of Crusaders, clothed in white, with a red cross, marched out of Milan, and that a fleet, equipped by the sovereign pontiff, passed through the Archipelago, and surprised the city of Smyrna, in which the Crusaders were themselves quickly besieged by the Turks. The pope's legate and several knights perished in a sortie, which circumstance determined the sovereign pontiff to employ new efforts to revive a zeal for the crusade. It was at this period that the dauphin of Vienne, Humbert II., resolved to take the cross, and came to Avignon, to supplicate the pope to allow him to be the captain of the holy voyage against the Turks, and against the faithless vassals of the church of Rome. Humbert easily obtained all he asked, and returned to his states to make preparations for his expedition. He alienated his domains, he sold privileges to the nobility, and immunities to his cities; he levied considerable sums upon the Jews, and upon the Italian merchants established in the Dauphiny; he exacted a tribute from all his subjects who would not accompany him to the crusade, and having embarked, with a hundred men-at-arms, he went to seek in Asia either the fortune of a conqueror or the glory of a martyr. He found neither the one nor the other, and returned to Europe without renown and burdened with debts. History represents Humbert as a weak, inconstant and irresolute prince. He ruined himself, in the first place, by his dissipation, then by the expenses of the crusade; weary of the world and its affairs, he finished by abandoning to the crown of France his principality, which he had pledged to Philip of Valois, and retired to a monastery of Dominican Friars. In order to console him for not having conquered Egypt, or any other country, the pope bestowed upon him the title of patriarch of Alexandria· and the king of France, to make him forget Dauphiny, named him archbishop of Rheims.

Such were the events and the consequences of the crusade occasioned in Europe by the arrival of Hugh of Lusignan, king of Cyprus. Some years having glided away, this prince came again to solicit the aid of the sovereign pontiff; at this period most of the sovereigns were in a state of war, and the pope not being able to do anything for the king of Cyprus, conceived the singular idea of naming him tribune of Rome. Hugh of Lusignan accepted this function, and died in Italy, without having been able to send any succour to the East.

War was not then the only scourge that ravaged the world; the horrors of the plague were added to the destruction of arms; this contagion which was called the black plague, and which took its rise upon the great level plain of Tartary, extended its devastations over all the countries of the East and West, and in a few years carried off more than thirteen millions of men. Historians have remarked that this scourge in its funeral march followed the footsteps of the merchants who brought into Europe the productions of India, and of the pilgrims who returned from Palestine.

As soon as pestilence had ceased its ravages, war resumed all its fury. The deplorable state in which discord had plunged Europe at that time, and particularly France, must have made people regret the periods when the preaching of the crusade imposed silence upon all passions and suspended all hostilities. The pope had several times undertaken to reëstablish peace: he at first addressed supplications to the English monarch; he afterwards threatened him with the thunders of the Church, but the voice of the father of the faithful was lost in the din of arms.

Philip of Valois died amidst the terrible struggle he had to maintain against England. The loss of the battle of Poictiers and the captivity of King John became the signal for the greatest troubles that afflicted the kingdom of France in the middle ages. The plots of the king of Navarre, the intrigues of the great, the disorders of the people, the fury of factions, the sanguinary scenes of the Jacquerie, spread terror and desolation in the capital and through the provinces. When France had completed the exhaustion of her treasures by paying the ransom of King John, the presence of her monarch was not able to restore to her the repose she required to repair her misfortunes. The soldiers of both nations, who were disbanded without pay, and who found themselves without an asylum, formed themselves into armed bands, and under the name of *white companies*, pervaded the kingdom, braving the orders of the king and the excommunications of the pope, and carrying wherever they went license, murder and devastation. All that had escaped the sword of the English, and the avidity of the collectors of the imposts, became the prey of these brigands, whose numbers increased in proportion with their impunity and their excesses. The fields remained uncultivated; all commercial pursuits were interrupted; and terror and misery reigned in the cities. Thus the suspension of hostilities had brought no relief to the evils of nations, and the disorders which broke out during the peace were more insupportable than those which had been endured during the war.

It was in these unfortunate circumstances that Peter, the son of Hugh of Lusignan, came, after the example of his father, to solicit the assistance of the Christian princes against the infidels, and caused Urban V. to adopt the project of a new crusade. Perhaps he hoped that the state of confusion in which France was plunged offered him a means of raising troops, and that he might turn against his enemies of the East, all the furies of war which desolated the kingdom.

Peter of Lusignan proposed to attack the power of the sultans of Cairo, whose dominions extended to Jerusalem. Christendom had at that time more redoubtable enemies among the Mussulman nations than the Mamelukes of Egypt. The Turks, who had become masters of Asia Minor, had recently passed the Hellispont, pushed their conquests as far as Mount Hemus, and placed the seat of their empire at Adrianople. That was the enemy that doubtless ought to have been attacked, but the Turks did not as yet inspire serious alarm, except in the countries they had invaded or menaced. At the court of Avignon, at which were assembled the king of Cyprus, the king of France, and the king of Denmark, there was no mention made of the invasion of Romania, or of the dangers of Constantinople, but of the loss of the Christian colonies in Syria, and of the captivity in which the city of Christ was still held.

Peter of Lusignan spoke with enthusiasm of the war against the infidels, and of the deliverance of the holy places; King John did not listen to him without emotion, and finished by forgetting his own misfortunes, to interest himself about those of the Christians beyond the seas. Waldemar III., king of Denmark, was equally affected by the discourse and the accounts of the king of Cyprus. The pope preached the crusade before the three monarchs: it was holy week; the remembrance of the sufferings of Christ appeared to add authority to the words of the pontiff, and when he deplored the misfortunes of Jerusalem, the princes who listened to him could not refrain from shedding tears, and swore to go and fight the Saracens.

We may, doubtless, believe that the king of France was led to take the cross by a sentiment of piety, and by the eloquence of the pope; but we must likewise suppose that the counsels of policy were not entirely foreign to this determination. The spirit of the holy war, if once really awakened, would necessarily go far to appease, if not extinguish, the discords and passions kindled by revolution and civil war. King John might entertain the hope of uniting under the standard of the crusade, and seducing to follow him beyond the seas, the *white companies*, over whom he could exercise no authority; and the sovereign pontiff was no less anxious to get rid of these bands of brigands, who braved his spiritual power, and threatened to make him a prisoner in Avignon.

Several great nobles, John of Artois, the count of Eu, the count Dammartin, the count de Tancarville, and Marshal Boucicault, followed the example of King John. The Cardinal Talleyrand de Périgord was named legate of the pope in the crusade. The king of Denmark promised to unite his forces with those of the French. To encourage his zeal, the sovereign pontiff gave him a fragment of the true cross, and several other relics, the sight of which would constantly remind him of the holy cause he had sworn to defend. Waldemar III. had come to the court of Avignon to place his kingdom under the protection of the Holy See; he took all the oaths required of him; but the bulls he obtained from Urban, as the price of his submission, had no efficacy in restoring peace to his dominions, and the troubles which followed his return soon made him forget his promises regarding the holy war.

The king of Cyprus, with most pressing recommendations from the pope, visited all the courts of Europe; the zeal and the chivalric eloquence of the hero of the cross were universally admired; but he derived nothing but vague promises from his enterprise, and received nothing but vain felicitations for a devotion which found no imitators.

The king of France was the only one of all the Christian princes who appeared to engage himself earnestly in the crusade. Urban V., however, showed but little confidence in the firmness of his resolution, as he felt it necessary to threaten with excommunication all who should seek to divert him from the holy enterprise. But all these precautions of the pope, with the example of the king and the indulgences of the crusade, were powerless in inducing the nation to take arms, or in persuading the *white companies* to *leave the chamber*, as they called the kingdom they desolated with their brigandages. The time fixed for the expedition was very near at hand, and nothing was ready; there was neither an army nor a fleet. It was at this period King John died in London, whither he had returned to offer himself as an hostage for the duke of Anjou, who had escaped from prison; and perhaps also to get rid of the cares of an enterprise which he had no means of executing or directing with success.

The pope trembled in Avignon, and was compelled to use his utmost efforts to free himself from these formidable bands, whose leaders styled themselves *the friends of God and the enemies of*

THE VETERAN.

all the world. History says that he employed in his contests with them the small quantity of money which had been raised for the crusade, and that this excited violent murmurs. In this state of things, Charles IV., emperor of Germany, in concert with the king of Hungary, proposed to take the companies into their pay, and send them against the Turks. If this project had been executed, we should have been able to join the name of Bertrand Duguesclin to the glorious names that adorn the pages of this history; the Breton hero was to have been the leader of the troops destined to contend with the Mussulmans on the banks of the Danube. The sovereign pontiff himself wrote several letters to him to induce him to take part in this crusade; but the project of Charles IV. was in the end abandoned, and Duguesclin led the white companies into Spain.

The king of Cyprus, however, had succeeded in enrolling under his banners a great number of adventurers of all sorts and conditions, men who were accustomed to live amidst perils, and who were attracted by the hope of pillaging the richest countries of the east. The republic of Venice did not disdain to take part in an expedition from which her commerce was likely to derive great advantages. Peter of Lusignan likewise received succours from the brave knights of Rhodes, and, on his return to the isle of Cyprus, he embarked at the head of ten thousand men to realize his projects of conquests over the infidels. The Crusaders, to whom the pope sent a legate, went to attack Alexandria, which they found almost without defence. When the place had fallen into their power, the king of Cyprus wished that they should fortify themselves in it, and there await the armies of Cairo; but his soldiers and allies could not resist their inclination to plunder a flourishing city, and fearing to be surprised by the Mamelukes, they set fire to Alexandria, and abandoned it on the fourth day after the conquest. Without subduing the Mussulmans, they irritated them. After the precipitate departure of the Crusaders, the Egyptian people, listening to nothing but hatred and vengeance, indulged in all sorts of violence against the unfortunate Christians who dwelt in Egypt. By the orders of the sultan of Cairo, everything was seized that belonged to the Venetians; and the Mamelukes, having prepared a fleet, threatened, in their turn, to make descents upon the isles of Rhodes and Cyprus. Again the nations of the West were applied to; the pope entreated all Christian princes to take arms against the infidels; but not one of them would assume the cross, and the king of Cyprus was left alone, to fight out the war he had provoked.

To the ardour for crusades, in the minds of European warriors, had succeeded a passion for distinguishing and enriching themselves by chivalric enterprises and adventurous expeditions, in which, however, some remembrances of the holy wars were always mingled. The Genoese having formed the project of making war upon the coasts of Barbary, whose piratical inhabitants infested the Mediterranean, demanded a leader and troops of the king of France. On the report alone of such an enterprise, a crowd of warriors, eager to signalize their bravery, issued from all the provinces; the Count d'Auvergne, the sieur de Coucy, Guy de la Trimouille, and Messire Jean de Vienne, admiral of France, solicited the honour of combating the infidels in Africa; fourteen hundred knights and nobles, under the orders of the duke of Bourbon, repaired to Genoa, and embarked on board the fleet of that republic; the French and the Genoese, the first led by a desire for booty and the love of glory, the latter by the more positive interests of their commerce, went to this war beyond the sea as to a banquet. "Beautiful and pleasant," says Froissart, "was it to behold the order of their departure, and how those banners, pennons, and streamers, fairly and richly wrought with the arms of the noble knights, floated to the wind and glistened in the sun; and to hear those trumpets and clarions sound and resound, and other musicians performing their parts, with pipes, flutes, and macaires, as well as the sound and the voice which issued from them, reverberate over all the sea." After a few days' sailing, the Christian army arrived on the coast of Barbary, and laid siege to the city of *Africa*. The inhabitants offered some resistance, and not being able to conceive why they were thus attacked by an enemy they did not know, and of whom they had never heard, they sent deputies to the camp of the Christians to demand of them what motive had brought them beneath their walls. The Genoese, doubtless, reminded the deputies of the piracies carried on in the Mediterranean and upon the coasts of Italy; but the knights could not allege any grievance, and must have felt considerably embarrassed how to answer the questions of the besieged. Froissart, who gives an account of this expedition, informs us that the duke of Bourbon called a council of the principal leaders, and after they had deliberated upon the question proposed by the Saracens, he addressed this reply to them, which we shall report in the old language as near that of the times as we are able: "They who demand why war is made against them, must know that their lineage and race put to death and crucified the son of God named Jesus Christ, and that we wish to avenge upon them this fact and evil deed. Further, they do not believe in the holy baptism, nor in the Virgin Mary, the mother of Jesus Christ; and all these things being considered is why we hold the Saracens and all their sect as enemies." The besieged were not likely to be convinced by this explanation, "so," adds the good Froissart, "they only laughed at it, and said it was neither reasonable nor proved, for it was the Jews who put Christ to death, and not they."

The French knights had more bravery than knowledge, and were much more expert in fighting than in reasoning. They prosecuted the siege and made several assaults, but in all their attacks met with a determined resistance. They were, however, persuaded that Heaven declared in their favour, and performed miracles to assure them the victory. It was said in the camp, that a battalion of ladies in white had appeared amidst the combatants, and created great terror among the Saracens. They likewise told of a miraculous dog which God had sent to the Christian soldiers as a vigilant sentinel, and which had several times prevented their being surprised by the Mussulmans. We repeat these marvellous stories, in order to exhibit the spirit of the knights, who saw nothing but ladies under circumstances in which the early Crusaders would have seen saints and angels. The story of the miraculous dog serves to prove that the French warriors kept but a bad watch around their camp, and that they carried on the siege with more bravery than prudence. Several battles were fought, in which the most rash lost their lives. The heat of the climate and the season gave birth to contagious diseases. In proportion as obstacles multiplied around them, the ardour of the besiegers inclined daily towards depression. Discord, likewise, broke out in the Christian army, in which the French and the Genoese mutually reproached each other with their miseries: winter was drawing near, and they despaired of reducing the place; the duke of Bourbon resolved to raise the siege, and to return to Europe with his knights and soldiers.

During several months no news of this expedition had arrived in France; processions were made and public prayers were put up in all the provinces to ask of Heaven the safe return of the Crusaders. Old chronicles inform us,—"that the lady of Coucy, the lady of Sully, the dauphiness of Auvergne, and all the ladies of France whose lords and husbands were engaged in this voyage, were in great dismay for them whilst the voyage lasted; and when the news came to them that they had already passed the sea, they were all much rejoiced."

This expedition, which the Genoese had promoted with the intention of defending their commerce against the brigandages of pirates, only served to increase the evil they wished to remedy; vengeance, indignation, and fear armed the infidels against the Christians in every direction. Vessels issued from all the coasts of Africa, covered the Mediterranean, and intercepted the communications with Europe; the merchandises which had been accustomed to flow from Damascus, Cairo, and Alexandria, no longer appeared; and the historians of the times deplore, as a calamity, the impossibility of procuring spices in either France or Germany.

The war which had begun between Egypt and the kingdom of Cyprus was prosecuted with equal animosity on both sides. Whilst the sultan of Cairo threatened the poor remains of the Christian colonies of the East, the king of Cyprus and the knights of Rhodes spread terror along all the coasts of Syria; in one incursion they took possession of Tripoli, and gave the city up to the flames. Tortosa, Laodicea, and Belinas met with the same fate: this manner of making war in a country that they professed to wish to conquer for the sake of delivering it, excited everywhere the fury of the Mussulmans, without raising the hopes or the courage of the Christians who dwelt there. Pilgrimage to the Holy Land became impracticable, and, during several years, no European Christians were able to visit Jerusalem.

The sultan of Egypt, however, after many fruitless efforts to avenge the expedition against Alexandria, made peace with the king of Cyprus and the knights of Rhodes. It was agreed that the prisoners should be liberated on both sides, and that the king of Cyprus should receive half of the dues levied upon the merchandise which entered at Tyre, Berouth, Sidon, Alexandria, Jerusalem, and Damascus. The treaty regulated the tribute which pilgrims should pay in those places of the Holy Land to which their devotion called them. The sultan of Egypt restored to the knights of St. John the house they had formerly possessed in Jerusalem, and the knights had permission to cause the churches of the holy sepulchres of Bethlehem, of Nazareth, &c., to be repaired.

Europe at this period turned its eyes from countries which had so long excited its veneration and enthusiasm to direct them towards regions invaded or threatened by the Turks. We have seen, towards the end of the eleventh century, hordes from this nation spread themselves as conquerors over the whole of Asia. It may be remembered that it was their invasion of Palestine, and their violent domination over the holy city, which roused Christendom, and provoked the first crusade. Their power, which then extended as far as Nice, and which, even at that time, alarmed the Greeks, was checked by the victorious armies of the West. The Turks of whom we are now speaking, and of whom Christendom, towards the end of the fourteenth century, began to be very much in dread, like those who had preceded them, drew their origin from the Tartars. Their warlike tribes, formerly established in Carismia, had been driven thence by the successors of Gengiskan; and the remains of this conquering nation, after ravaging Syria and Mesopotamia, came, a few years before the first crusade of St. Louis, to seek an asylum in Asia Minor.

The weakness of the Greeks and the division of the Mussulman princes enabled them to conquer several provinces, and to found a new state among the ruins of several empires. The terror inspired by their fierce and brutal valour facilitated their progress, and opened for them the road to Greece. Countries which had been the cradle of civilization, of the arts, and of knowledge, soon succumbed beneath the laws of Ottoman despotism.

There can be no doubt that despotism, such as it was known then in Asia, and as it is seen in our days, is the most fragile of human institutions. The violent measures which it took to preserve itself, showed plainly that it itself felt a consciousness of its own fragility. When we see it immolate all the laws of nature to its own laws, hold the sword constantly suspended over all that approach it, and itself experience more fear than it inspires, we are tempted to believe that it has no veritable support. Whilst reading the oriental history of the middle ages, we are astonished to see all those empires which the genius of despotism raised in Asia, fall almost without resistance, and disappear from the scene of the world. But we must admit, when this monstrous government supports itself upon religious ideas, and upon the prejudices and passions of a great nation, its has also its popular ascendancy; it is also, to employ a mode of speaking very common at present, the expression of all its wills, and nothing can resist its action, or arrest the development of its power.

bility of procuring spices in either France or Germany.

Thus arose the Ottoman empire, which had for its springs of action a hatred of the Christians, and the conquest of the Greek empire, and which sustained itself by the double fanaticism of religion and victory. The Turks had but two ideas, or rather two ever-acting passions, which with them supplied the place of patriotism,—to extend their dominions and propagate the Mussulman faith. The ambition which led the sovereign to conquer Christian provinces, was found to be that of the whole nation, accustomed to enrich themselves by all the violences of war, and who believed they obeyed the most sacred precept of the Koran, by exterminating the race of infidels. If the prince was unceasingly obliged to animate the religious enthusiasm and the warlike ardour of his subjects, the subjects, in their turn, kept the prince as constantly in exercise. The absolute leader of the Ottomans might commit all sorts of crimes with impunity; but he could not live long in a state of peace with his neighbours, without risking his authority and his life. The Turks could not endure either a pacific prince, or a prince unfortunate in war; so thoroughly were they persuaded that they ought to be always fighting, and that they ought alway to conquer. The Ottoman people, to whom nothing was good or right but conquest, would obey none but a conqueror; and if they consented to be slaves, and tremble beneath the frown of a master, it was upon the sole condition that this all-powerful master should carry abroad the terror of his arms, and should give chains to other nations.

The Ottoman dynasty which began with the Turkish nation and gave its name to it, that dynasty, always the object of veneration, and respected by revolt itself, has presented by its stability a new spectacle in the East. It has exhibited to the world a succession of great princes, who have in history almost all the same physiognomy, and resemble each other in their pride, their ambition and their military genius: which proves that all these barbarian heroes were formed by their national manners, and that among the Turks, there is but one single road to greatness. We may judge what advantages this harmony between subjects and sovereign must have given to the Ottoman nation, in its wars against the Christians, or even against other Mussulman people.

Whilst the only defence of Europe consisted in feudal troops which were assembled at certain periods, and could not be held beneath their banners for any length of time together, the Ottomans were the only people who had a regular army always under arms. Their warriors, always animated by one same spirit, had moreover the advantage of discipline over the insubordinate chivalry of the Franks, who were constantly agitated by discord, and were put in action by a thousand different passions.

As the population of the Turks was not always sufficient for their armies, they forced each family of the countries they conquered to give up a fifth part of its male children for the military service. They thus levied a tribute upon the population of the Christians, and the sons of the effeminate Greeks became those invincible janissaries who were one day to besiege Byzantium, and destroy even the ruins of the empire of the Cæsars. Such were the new people who were about to place themselves between the East and the West, and engross all the attention of Christian Europe, until that time occupied with the deliverance of the holy places.

When we are acquainted with the power and the character of the Ottomans, we are astonished at seeing what remained of the Greek empire subsist a long time in their vicinity. We must here resume from a past period, the history of the feeble successors of Constantine, sometimes forming alliances with the Turks ready to plunder them, at others, imploring the assistance of the Latins, whom they hated, and seeking to awaken the spirit of the crusades whose consequences they dreaded.

At the period of the first invasion of Greece by the Turks, the emperor Andronicus sent an embassy to the Pope, to promise him to obey the Romish Church, and to request of him apostolic legates, with an army capable of driving away the infidels and opening the route to the Holy Sepulchre. Cantacuzenes, who followed the example of Andronicus, said to the envoys from the sovereign pontiff: "I shall consider it my glory to serve Christendom; my states shall afford the Crusaders a free and safe passage; my troops, my vessels, my treasures shall be devoted to the common defence, and my fate will be worthy of envy if I obtain the crown of martyrdom." Clement VI., to whom Cantacuzenes addressed himself, died without having been able to interest the Christian warriors in the fate of Constantinople. A short time afterwards, the emperor buried himself in a cloister; and the brother *Josaphat Christodulus*, confounded among the monks of Mount Athos, troubled himself no longer with a crusade among the Latins.

Under the reign of John Palæologus, the progress of the Turks became more alarming. The emperor himself went to solicit the aid of the sovereign pontiff. After having, in a public ceremony, kissed the hands and feet of the pope, he acknowledged the double *procession* of the Holy Ghost, and the supremacy of the Church of Rome. Touched by this humble submission, the pope protested he would come to the succour of the Greeks; but when he applied to the sovereigns of Europe, he could obtain nothing from them but vain promises. At the moment at which Palæologus was about to embark on his return to the East, he was arrested by his creditors, and remained thus during several months, without the pope or the princes he had come to solicit, and who had promised to assist him in the deliverance of his empire, making the least attempt to deliver him himself. Palæologus returned to Constantinople, to his divided family; and his subjects, who despised him, waited in vain for the performance of the promises of the pope and the European monarchs. In his despair, he at length formed the resolution of imploring the clemency of the sultan Amurath, and of purchasing by a tribute, permission to continue to reign over the wreck of his empire. He complained of this hard necessity to the pontiff of Rome, who caused a new crusade to be preached; but the Christian monarch beheld with indifference, a prince who had returned to the bosom of the Catholic Church, condemned to declare himself the vassal of infidels. The emperor of Byzantium and the head of the Church, by promising, the one, to arm the West in the cause of Greece, and the other, to subject the Greeks to the Roman Church, had formed engagements that they every day found it more difficult to fulfil. Whilst they were reciprocally upbraiding each other with not having kept their word, Amurath, who accomplished his threats better than the pope and the Christian princes did their promises, added new rigours to the fate of Palæologus, and interdicted even the repairing of the ramparts of his capital. Again the supplications to the sovereign were renewed, and again these supplications were passed on to the monarchs of Christendom; but they made no reply, or at most contented themselves with expressing pity for the emperor and people of Byzantium.

There is no doubt that the Greek emperors stood in great need of succour from the Latins, but this pusillanimous policy, which unceasingly invoked the assistance of other nations, only proclaimed the weakness of the empire, and necessarily deprived the Greeks, in the hour of peril, of all confidence in their own strength. On the other side, these cries of alarm, which constantly resounded throughout Europe, met with nothing but incredulous minds and indifferent hearts. It was in vain that the warriors of the West heard it for ever repeated that Constantinople was the barrier of Christendom; they could not consider a city which was unable to provide for its own defence, and was always in want of succour, as a barrier capable of arresting the course of a powerful enemy. When Gregory XI. solicited the emperor of Germany to assist Constantinople, that prince replied sharply that the Greeks had opened the gates of Europe to the Turks, and *let the wolf into the sheep-fold*.

At this time the miserable remains of the empire of the Cæsars was comprised within the extent of less than twenty leagues, and in this narrow space there was an empire of Byzantium, and an empire of Rodesto or Selivrea; the princes, whom ties of blood ought to have united, quarrelled with inveterate fury for the rags of the imperial purple. Brother was armed against brother, and father and son declared open war; all the crimes that had formerly been inspired by the ambition of obtaining the sceptre of the Roman world, were still committed for the advantage of reigning over a few miserable cities. Such was the empire of the East, upon which the Ottoman dominions continued on all sides to encroach.

At the period of which we are speaking, all the princes of the family of Palæologus having been commanded to repair to the court of Bajazet, obeyed his supreme order tremblingly; and if they came out safe and sound from the palace of the sultan, which was for them the den of the lion, it was because pity disarmed the executioner, and because the contempt they inspired among the Mussulmans was their safeguard. The Ottoman emperor contented himself with commanding Manuel, the son and successor of John Palæologus, not to deliver Constantinople up to him, but to remain shut up in it as in a prison, under the penalty of losing both his crown and his life.

Whilst the Greeks were thus trembling in the presence of the Turks, the janissaries passed through the straits of Thermopylæ without obstruction, and advanced into the Peloponnesus. On the other side, Bajazet, for whom the rapidity of his conquests procured the surname of *Iberim*, or *Lightning*, invaded the country of the Servians, afterwards that of the Bulgarians, and was preparing to carry the war into Hungary.

A deplorable schism then divided Christendom. Two popes shared the empire of the Church, and the European republic had no longer a head that could warn it of its dangers, an organ that could express its wishes and its fears, or a tie that could bind together its forces; religious opinions had no longer sufficient influence to bring about a crusade, and Christendom had nothing left to defend it but the spirit of chivalry, and the warlike character of some of the nations of Europe.

The ambassadors whom Manuel sent into the West, repeating the eternal lamentations of the Greeks over the barbarities of the Turks, solicited in vain the piety of the faithful. The envoys of Sigismund, king of Hungary, were more fortunate in their appeal to the bravery of the knights and barons of France. Charles VI. had not renounced, if the historians of the time may be believed, the idea of undertaking some great enterprise against the enemies of the true faith: "in order," says Froissart, "to free the souls of his predecessors, King Philip, of excellent memory, and King John, his grandfather." The Hungarian envoys took care to insinuate in their speeches, that the sultan of the Turks held Christian chivalry in contempt; nothing more was wanting to inflame the ardour of the French warriors; and when their monarch declared his intention of entering into the league against the infidels, every gallant knight in the kingdom flew to arms. This brave band was commanded by the duke de Nevers, son of the duke of Burgundy, a young prince whose rash courage afterwards procured for him the surname of Jean-sans-Peur (John the Fearless). Among other leaders were the count de la Marche, Henry and Philip de Bar, relations of the king of France, Philip of Artois, constable of the kingdom; John of Vienne, admiral; the sieur de Coucy, Guy de la Tremouille, and the marshal de Boucicault, whose name is mixed with the history of every war of his time.

All ideas of glory, all sentiments of religion and chivalry were bound up with this expedition. The leaders ruined themselves to make preparations for their voyage, and to astonish the East by their magnificence; the people implored the protection of Heaven for the success of their arms. The enterprise of the new Crusaders was already compared to that of Godfrey of Bouillon, and the poets of the times celebrated the near deliverance of the Holy Land.

The French army, in which were fourteen hundred knights and as many squires, traversed Germany, and was increased on its way by a crowd of warriors from Austria and Bavaria. When they arrived on the banks of the Danube, they found the entire nobility of Hungary and Bohemia under arms. Whilst reviewing the numerous soldiers thus assembled to oppose the Turks, Sigismund exclaimed with delight: "If heaven were to fall, the lances of the Christian army would stop it in its descent."

Never was a war begun under more happy auspices; not only had the spirit of chivalry drawn together a great number of warriors beneath the banners of the cross, but several maritime nations of Italy had taken up arms for the defence of their eastern commerce. A Venetian fleet, commanded by the noble Mocenigo, joined the vessels of the Greek emperor and of the knights of Rhodes near the mouth of the Danube, to procure the triumph of the standard of the Franks in the Hellespont, whilst the Christian army should march against Constantinople.

As soon as the signal for war was given, nothing could resist the impetuous valour of the Crusaders; they beat the Turks everywhere; they took several towns of Bulgaria and Servia, and laid siege to Nicopolis: happy had it been if these first advantages had not given them a blind confidence in victory!

The French knights, who were always found at the head of the Christian army, could not believe that Bajazet would dare to attack them; and when it was announced to them that the sultan, with his army, was drawing near, they chastised the bold scout who gave them the first intelligence of it. The Mussulman army, however, had crossed Mount Hemus, and was advancing towards Nicopolis. When the two armies were in presence of each other, Sigismund conjured his allies to moderate their warlike ardour, and to wait for a favourable opportunity of attacking an enemy with whom they were totally unacquainted. The duke de Nevers and the young nobles who accompanied him, listened with impatience to the advice of the Hungarians, and believed that they were desirous of disputing with them the honour of beginning the fight. Scarcely had the standard of the crescent met their eyes, than they rushed out of the camp and fell upon the enemy; the Turks retreated, and appeared to fly; the French pursued them in a disorderly manner, and soon became separated from the Hungarian army. All at once, clouds of spahis and janissaries poured down from the neighbouring forests, in which they had been placed in ambush. All about the country, pikes had been planted to impede the march of cavalry. The French warriors being unable either to advance or retreat, and surrounded by an innumerable army, no longer fought to conquer, but to die with glory, and sell their lives dearly. After having, during several hours, carried slaughter into the enemy's ranks, all the French engaged in the conflict either perished by the swords of the Mussulmans, or were made prisoners.

Bajazet, after this first victory, directed all his forces against the Hungarian army, which terror had already seized, and which was dispersed at the first shock. Sigismund, who, on the morning of that day, had counted a hundred thousand men beneath his banners, threw himself into a fishing-boat, and coasting along the shores of the Euxine, found refuge in Constantinople, where his mere presence announced his defeat, and spread consternation.

Such were the fruits of the presumption and want of discipline of the French warriors. History has lamented their reverses more than it has blamed their conduct; it has satisfied itself with saying, that in order to conquer the Turks, the Hungarians should have shown the valour of the French, or the French should have imitated the prudence of the Hungarians.

Bajazet, who was wounded in the battle, proved barbarous after victory. Some historians have said that the sultan had to avenge the death of many Mussulman captives, who had been massacred by the Christian army. He commanded all the prisoners, many of whom were wounded and plundered of their clothes, to be brought before him, and then gave orders to his janissaries to slaughter them before his eyes. Three thousand French warriors were immolated to his vengeance; but he spared the duke de Nevers, the count de la Marche, the sieur de Coucy, Philip of Artois, the count de Bar, Marshal Boucicault, and some other leaders, on account of the ransom he hoped to procure for them.

When fame carried the news of so great a disaster into France, the first who spoke of it were threatened with being thrown into the Seine: many were imprisoned in the châtelet of Paris by the king's orders. At length the most sinister reports were confirmed by the account of messire de Hély, whom Bajazet sent into France to announce the defeat of the Christians and the captivity of their leaders. This intelligence spread desolation through both the court of Charles VI. and the kingdom of France. Froissart adds, in his natural style, "that the high dames of France were much enraged, and had good cause, for this affected their hearts too closely."

In order to mitigate the wrath of the Turkish emperor, Charles VI. sent him magnificent presents. Messengers passing through Hungary and the territory of Constantinople, bore to the sultan white falcons from Norway, fine scarlet cloths, white and red linens from Rheims, *draps de hautes-lices*, or tapestries, worked at Arras, in Picardy, representing the history of Alexander, "which thing," add contemporary chronicles, "was very agreeable to all persons of worth and honour to look upon." At the court of France means could not be devised for sending into Turkey the money required for the liberation of the princes and nobles detained in the prisons of Bajazet. A banker of Paris performed that which no sovereign of Europe could then have done; in concert with some merchants of Genoa, he negotiated for the ransom of the prisoners, and undertook to pay for this ransom the sum agreed upon, of two hundred thousand ducats.

The noble captives, whom the sultan had dragged in his train as far as Brusa, at length were allowed to return to Europe. Of the number, all regained their native country, with the exception of two: Guy of Tremouille died in the isle of Rhodes. The lady de Coucy, who was incapable of consolation, sent a faithful knight among the Turks, to learn the fate of her husband, and the knight returned with the fatal intelligence that the sieur de Coucy had died in his prison.

When the duke de Nevers, with his companions in misfortune, quitted the camp of Bajazet, the sultan addressed the following words to him, as reported by Froissart:—"Count de Nevers, I know right well and am informed that thou art in thine own country a great lord, and the son of a great lord. Thou art young; thou mayest, perchance, take as an injury that requires vengeance that which has befallen thee in thy first chivalry, and wouldst willingly, to recover thy honour, assemble forces to come and give me battle; if I suspected this, and if it were my will, I would make thee swear upon thy faith and upon the law that thou shouldst never arm thyself against me, nor any of those that are in thy company; but no, I will neither require thee nor them to take this oath; but I wish to tell thee that if, when thou shalt have returned, it may please thee to assemble a power to come against me, thou wilt find me always ready and prepared for both thee and thy people."

This speech, which exhibited all the Ottoman pride, must, without doubt, have been a lesson for young warriors, whose mad presumption had brought on all the evils of the war. They despised Bajazet before their defeat; and his haughty disdain after victory could not appear in their eyes a vain bravado. "So," says Froissart, "they remembered it well as long as they lived."

On their return to France, the noble knights were received with the interest that unfortunate bravery inspires. The court of Charles VI. and that of Burgundy were never tired of hearing them recount their exploits, their tragical adventures, and the miseries of their captivity; they told wonders of the magnificence of Bajazet; and when they repeated the speeches of the sultan, who was accustomed to say *that he would be lord over all the world, that he would yet come to Rome, and make his horse eat his oats on the altar of St. Peter;* when they spoke of the armies which the emperor raised daily to accomplish his menaces, what fear must, doubtless, have been mixed in the minds of his auditors with feelings of curiosity and surprise.

The accounts of the duke de Nevers and his companions awakened, however, the emulation of the warriors, and their misfortunes in Asia inspired less compassion than a desire to avenge their defeat. A new expedition against the Turks was soon announced in France, and a crowd of young nobles and knights eagerly took up arms. The duke of Orleans, the brother of the king, was inconsolable at not being able to obtain permission to place himself at their head, and go with them to combat the infidels. It was the Marshal Boucicault, scarcely returned from captivity, who led these new Crusaders into the East. Their arrival on the shores of the Bosphorus delivered Byzantium, which was then besieged by Bajazet. Their exploits raised the courage of the Greeks, and redeemed the honour of the soldiers of the West among the Turks. When, after a year of labours and glorious combats, they returned to their own country, the Greek emperor Manuel believed he saw fresh evils ready to overwhelm him, and he resolved to follow Marshal Boucicault and solicit more assistance from Charles VI.; thus placing all the hopes of his empire in the French warriors. He was received with great honours on his passage through Italy; when he had crossed the Alps, brilliant festivities awaited him in all the great cities. At two leagues from Paris he found Charles VI., who, with all his nobles, had come out to meet him. He made his public entry into the capital, clothed in a robe of white silk, and mounted on a white horse, marks of supreme rank among the Franks. It was gratifying to see a successor of the Cæsars imploring the arms of chivalry; and the confidence which he placed in the bravery of the French, flattered the pride of the nation; but in the condition of France at that period, it was much more easy to offer Manuel the spectacle of tournaments, and the brilliant ceremonies of courts, than to furnish him with the treasures and armies of which he stood in need. Charles VI. began to feel the approach of that fatal malady which left the field open to factions, and threw the kingdom into the greatest misfortunes. England, whose assistance the emperor of Constantinople likewise solicited, was disturbed by the usurpation of Henry of Lancaster; and if the English monarch then took the cross, it was less with the intention of succouring the Greeks than to divert attention from his own injustice, and to have a pretext for levying imposts upon his people. At the same time, the deposition of Winceslaus set the whole German empire in motion; and the nascent heresy of John Huss already gave the signal for the disorders that were destined to trouble Bohemia during the fifteenth century. Amidst all these agitations in Christendom, the only power that could have reëstablished harmony was itself divided, and the Catholic Church, still a prey to the rival pretensions of two pontiffs, could neither give its attention to promote peace among the Christians, nor war against the Turks.

This state of France and Europe completely destroyed all the hopes of the Greek emperor. After passing two years in Paris, without obtaining anything, he determined to leave the West, and having embarked at Venice, he stopped in the Peloponnesus, where he waited patiently till Fortune should herself take charge of the entire ruin or the deliverance of his empire.

This deliverance, which could no longer be expected from the Christian powers, arrived all at once by means of a people still more barbarous than the Turks, whose conquests made the entire East tremble. Tamerlane, or Timour, from the bosom of civil wars, had been elevated to the throne of the Moguls, and revived in the north of Asia the formidable empire of Gengiskan. History is scarcely able to follow this new conqueror in his gigantic expeditions. The imagination is terrified at the rapidity with which, to make use of an expression of Timour himself, he carried "the destroying wind of desolation" from Zagathaï to the Indus, and from the Indus to the icy deserts of Siberia. Such was the scourge that Heaven sent to destroy the menacing pride of Bajazet. The historians of the times are not agreed as to the motives which armed the leader of the Moguls against the Ottoman emperor; some attribute Tamerlane's determination to the complaints of the Mussulman princes of Asia Minor, whom the sultan of the Turks had driven from their states; others, faithful to the spirit of their age, and seeking the causes of great events in celestial phenomena, explain the invasion of the Tartars by the appearance of a comet, which was visible during two months to affrighted Asia. Disdaining marvellous explanations, we will confine ourselves to saying that peace could not last between two men urged on by the same ambition, and who were not likely to pardon each other for having at the same time entertained the thought of conquering the world. Their character, as well as their policy, is plainly enough indicated in the violent threats they reciprocally addressed to each other before hostilities, and which became the signal for the most sanguinary catastrophes.

Tamerlane, having set out from Samarcand, first reduced Seborto, and as if he wished to give Bajazet, before he attacked him, the spectacle of the ravages which accompanied his arms everywhere, he all at once directed the course of his Tartar hordes towards Syria and the provinces governed by the Mamelukes of Egypt. The valour of his soldiers, the discords of his enemies, the treachery and perfidy which he never disdained to call in to the assistance of his power, opened for him the gates of Aleppo, Damascus, and Tripoli. Torrents of blood and pyramids of human heads marked the passage of the Mogul conqueror. His approach spread terror everywhere, as well among the Christians as among the Mussulmans; and although he boasted in his discourses of avenging the cause of the oppressed, Jerusalem might, on this occasion, be grateful that he did not think of delivering her.

At length the Tartars advanced towards Asia Minor. Timour traversed Anatolia with an army of eight hundred thousand men. Bajazet, who raised the siege of Constantinople to come to meet his redoubtable adversary, encountered him in the plains of Ancyra. At the end of a battle which lasted three days, the Ottoman emperor lost at once his empire and his liberty. The Greeks, to whom fame soon brought the news of this victory, tremblingly returned thanks to their fierce liberator; but the indifference with which he received their embassy, proved that he had had no intention of meriting their gratitude. Arrived on the shores of the Bosphorus, the conqueror of Bajazet directed his looks and his projects towards the West; but the master of the vast kingdoms of Asia had not a single barque in which to transport himself to the other side of the canal. Thus Constantinople, after having escaped the yoke of the Ottomans, had the good fortune to escape also the presence of the Tartars, and Europe saw this violent tempest dissipate itself at a distance from her.

The conqueror vented his anger upon the city of Smyrna, which was defended by the Knights of Rhodes. This city was carried by assault, delivered up to pillage, and reduced to ashes; the Mogul emperor returned to Samarcand in triumph, dragging the sultan Bajazet in his train, and meditating by turns the conquest of Africa, the invasion of the West, and a war against China.

After the battle of Ancyra, several princes of the family of Bajazet disputed the ravaged provinces of the Ottoman empire. If the Franks had then appeared in the Strait of Galliopoli and in Thrace, they might have profited by the defeat and discords of the Turks, and have driven them back beyond the Taurus; but the indifference of the Christian states, with the perfidy and cupidity of some of the maritime nations of Europe, allowed the Ottoman dynasty time and means to renovate its depressed power.

The Greeks derived no more advantage from the victory of Tamerlane than the Latins. Twenty years after the battle of Ancyra, the Ottomans had retaken all their provinces; their armies again environed Constantinople, and it is at this point we may apply to the power of the Turks the oriental comparison of that serpent of the desert which an elephant had crushed in its passage, which joins its dispersed rings together again, raises its head by degrees, reseizes the prey it had abandoned, and clasps it within its monstrous folds.

As long as the Greek emperors were in no fear for the safety of their capital, they kept up very little intercourse with the Christian princes of Europe; but upon the appearance of danger, the court of Byzantium renewed its supplications and its promises of obedience to the Church of Rome. A conversation of Manuel, reported by Phrantza, throws a light upon the situation of the Greeks, and upon the policy of the timid successors of Constantine. "The only resource we have left against the Turks," said this prince to his son, "is their fear of our union with the Latins, and the terror with which the warlike nations of the West inspire them. Whenever you are pressed by the infidels, send to the court of Rome, and prolong the negotiations, without ever taking a decisive part." Manuel added, that the vanity of the Latins and the obstinacy of the Greeks would always prevent any real or durable harmony; and that a union of any kind with the pope, by arousing the passions of both parties, would only give Byzantium up to the mercy of the barbarians.

Such counsels, which announce but little frankness in the policy of the Greeks, could not be long followed up with success. The dangers became more pressing, the circumstances more imperative; as Christendom only replied to vain negotiations by vain promises, the successor of Manuel found himself obliged to give pledges of his faith and sincerity. The idea of a council was at length adopted, in which the two churches should come to an understanding, and should approximate. The emperor John Palæologus and the doctors of the Greek Church repaired to Ferrara, and afterwards to Florence. After long debates, the union was sworn to on both sides, and solemnly proclaimed. In the West this event was celebrated as a victory; at Constantinople it raised cries of blasphemy, apostasy, and impiety. Thus was the prediction of Manuel accomplished; all the efforts employed to unite opinions, only served to raise a new barrier between the Greeks and the Latins.

At the councils of Ferrara and Florence, the deputies of the Armenians, the Maronites, the Jacobites of Syria and Egypt, the Nestorians, and the Ethiopians submitted, as well as the Greeks, to the pontifical authority, and without doubt also, in the same hope of being succoured by the Latins, and delivered from the tyranny of the Mussulmans. This solemn proceeding was less a submission to the Holy See than a homage rendered to the bravery of the Franks, in whom all the Christians of Asia and Africa beheld liberators.

Pope Eugenius, however, on receiving the submission of the Greeks, had promised to send succours to Constantinople and to the Christians of the East. The pontiff hoped that the union of the two churches and the preaching of a crusade would fix upon him the eyes of the Christian world, and restore to the pontifical authority the confidence and power of which the schisms of the West and the seditious decrees of the council of Bâle had deprived it. He wrote to all the princes of Christendom, exhorting them to unite to put a stop to the invasions of the Mussulmans. Eugenius, in his letter, described all the evils which the faithful suffered in the countries under the domination of the barbarians. "The Turks tied troops of men and women together, and dragged them along in their train. All the Christians whom they condemned to slavery, were confounded with the vilest booty, and sold like beasts of burden. In their barbarity they separated the son from the father, the brother from the sister, and the husband from the wife. Those whom age or infirmities prevented from walking were killed upon the high roads or in the middle of cities. Even infancy could not excite their pity; they put to death innocent victims that had scarcely begun to exist, and who, being yet ignorant of fear, smiled upon their executioners whilst receiving the mortal blow. Every Christian family was compelled to give up its own sons to the Ottoman empire, in the same manner as the people of Athens had been formerly forced to send as a tribute the flower of their youth to the monster of Crete. Wherever the Turks had penetrated, the fields were cursed with barrenness, and the cities were without laws or industry; the Christian religion had no longer either priests or altars; humanity no longer either support or asylum." In fact, the father of the faithful forgot none of the cruelties committed by the enemies of Christ; he could not restrain the sadness which so many painful images caused him, and conjured princes and nations to send assistance to the kingdom of Cyprus, the isle of Rhodes, and particularly to Constantinople, as these were the last bulwarks of the West.

The exhortations of the sovereign pontiff were addressed to none but indifferent hearts in the nations of England, France, and Spain. Neither the sentiment of humanity, nor that of patriotism, had power to revive the enthusiasm to which the spirit of religion and chivalry had in past times given birth. Distant crusades, whatever was their object, began to be considered as only the work of a jealous policy, the springs of which were set in motion, to banish the princes and nobles whose power and wealth were coveted. In the state in which Europe then was, such as loved war, had but too many opportunities for exercising their bravery, without quitting their homes. The Germans, who had set on foot forty thousand men to combat the heretics of Bohemia, remained motionless, when the Turks were represented to them as ready to carry the standard of Islamism to the extremities of the West.

The pope, however, was not satisfied with exhorting the faithful to take up arms, he was desirous of setting them the example; the pontiff levied soldiers and equipped vessels to make war against the Turks. The maritime cities of Flanders, and the republics of Genoa and Venice, which had great interests in the East, made some preparations; their fleets united under the standard of St. Peter, and directed their course towards the Hellespont. The fear of an approaching invasion awakened the zeal of the nations inhabiting the shores of the Dneister and the Danube. The crusade was preached in the diets of Poland and Hungary. Upon the frontiers threatened by the barbarians, the people, the clergy, and the nobility obeyed the voice of religion and patriotism.

The sovereign pontiff named, as legate with the Crusaders, Cardinal Julian, a prelate of an intrepid character and of an ardent genius, arming himself by turns with the sword of fight and with that of speech; as redoubtable in the field of battle as in the learned contests of the schools. After having obtained the confidence of the council of Bâle, Cardinal Julian distinguished himself in the council of Forence, by defending the dogmas of the Latin Church. His eloquence had roused up all Germany against the Hussites; now he burned to rouse up all Christendom against the Turks. The army collected under the banners of the cross had for leaders Hunniades and Ladislaus; the first, the waywode of Transylvania, was celebrated among Christian warriors, and the epithet of the *brigand*, which the Turks attached to his name, denoted the hatred and terror he inspired among the infidels. Upon the head of Ladislaus were united the two crowns of Poland and Hungary, and he merited, by the brilliant qualities of his youth, the love of both Poles and Hungarians. The Crusaders assembled on the Danube, and quickly received the signal for war. The fleets of the sovereign pontiff, of Venice, and Genoa cruised in the Hellespont. The inhabitants of Moldavia, Servia, and Greece promised to join the Christian army; the sultan of Caramania, the implacable enemy of the Ottomans, was to attack them in Asia. The Greek emperor, John Palæologus, announced great preparations, and got ready to march at the head of an army to meet his liberators.

Hunniades and Ladislaus advanced as far as Sophia, the capital of the Bulgarians. Two bat-

CONSTANTINE PALÆOLOGUS HARANGUING THE DEFENDERS OF CONSTANTINOPLE.

Amidst these deplorable disputes the voice of patriotism was never listened to, and indifference, selfishness, and cowardice were able to conceal themselves under the respectable appearance of religion and orthodoxy. A great part of the population of Constantinople had abandoned the city; among those that remained, the richest had buried their treasures, which they might have employed in the general defence, and which they soon lost, with their liberty and their lives. The imperial city only contained within its bosom four thousand nine hundred and seventy defenders, and the emperor was obliged to plunder the churches to support them. Thus, from eight to nine thousand combatants formed the entire garrison of Byzantium, and the last hope of the empire of the East.

Constantine called together the principal leaders of the garrison to deliberate upon the dangers which threatened the empire. In a pathetic discourse he endeavoured to revive the courage and the hopes of his companions in arms; speaking to the Greeks of patriotism, and to the Latin auxiliaries of religion and humanity, he exhorted them all to have patience, but above all to preserve concord. The warriors who were present at this last council listened to the emperor in melancholy silence; they did not dare to interrogate each other upon the means of defence, which all knew to be useless. They embraced each other with tears, and returned to the ramparts, filled with the most sinister forebodings.—BOOK XVI.

tles opened for them the passages of Mount Hemus and the road to Byzantium. The rigours of winter alone arrested the victorious march of the Christian warriors; and the army of the Crusaders returned into Hungary, to await the favourable season for renewing the war. They returned to Buda in triumph, amidst the acclamations of an immense population. The clergy celebrated, by hymns and thanksgivings, the first victories of the Christians, and Ladislaus repaired, barefooted, to the church of Notre Dame, in which he hung up the standards taken from the infidels.

Before the beginning of the war, the Mussulmans had been persuaded that the destruction of the Christians was written in the book of destiny. "When all the enemies of the prophet," said they among themselves, "shall be destroyed, each of us will have nothing to do but to guide his plough, and look at his war-horse in his stable." This opinion, the offspring of pride and victory, had proved sufficient to relax the zeal of the Ottoman warriors; and most of them remained in their homes, whilst the Christians marched towards Adrianopolis.

When fame informed them of the victories of the Franks upon the Danube, this blind security all at once gave place to fear. The sultan Amurath immediately sent ambassadors to sue for peace. History is silent as to the means of seduction employed by the Ottoman envoys to win the victorious Crusaders; but it is well known that they succeeded in obtaining a favourable hearing for their proposals. Peace was determined upon in the council of the leaders of the Christian army. The parties swore, the one upon the Koran, and the other upon the Gospel, to a truce of ten years. This unexpected resolution irritated the pride and zeal of Cardinal Julian, whose mission was to stimulate the Christians to war. When he saw the leaders of the crusade unite in a desire for peace, he preserved a haughty silence, and refused to sign a treaty he disapproved of. The inflexible legate waited for an opportunity in which he might give vent to his discontent, and force the Crusaders to resume their arms. This opportunity was not long in presenting itself.

Amurath, satisfied with having restored peace to his states, and fatigued with earthly grandeur, renounced the cares of empire, and buried himself in a retreat at Magnesia. The sultan of Caramania informed the Christians that their most redoubtable enemy *had lost his senses*, and had just exchanged the imperial crown for the cap of a cenobite. He added that Amurath had left the supreme authority in the hands of a child, and in his message compared this child *to a young plant which the slightest wind might tear up by the roots*.

The same sultan was so thoroughly persuaded that the Ottoman empire was in its decline, that he entered Anatolia at the head of an army. About the same time reports were spread that the emperor of Constantinople was advancing towards Thrace; that the Greeks of the Peloponnesus had taken up arms, and that the confederate fleets still awaited a fresh signal for war in the Hellespont. Another circumstance, not less important, seemed calculated to awaken the warlike ardour of the Crusaders; the victory gained near Sophia had given them a powerful ally in Greece. In this battle, the son of John Castuct, who commanded the van of the Ottoman army, suddenly abandoned the banners and the religion of the Turks, to defend the worship and the heritage of his ancestors in Albania. The messengers of Scanderberg announced to the leaders of the Christian army, that he was ready to join them at the head of twenty thousand Albanians, assembled under the standard of the cross.

All these news, arriving at once, had an immediate effect in changing men's minds as well as the face of affairs. A fresh council was called; Cardinal Julian arose among the leaders, and reproached them with having betrayed both their fortune and their glory; he reproached them in severe terms, with having signed a disgraceful peace, which was sacrilegious, fatal to Europe, and fatal to the Church. "You had sworn," said he, "to combat the eternal enemies of Christendom, and now you have sworn upon the Gospel, to lay down your arms. To which of these two oaths will you be faithful? You have just thought proper to conclude a treaty with the Mussulmans; but have you not also treaties with your allies? Will you abandon these generous allies at the moment that they are flying from all parts to your assistance, and are coming to share the perils of a war in which God has so visibly protected your first labours?

"But, what do I say? You not only abandon your allies, you leave, without support and without hope, that crowd of Christians whom you have promised to deliver from an insupportable yoke, and who must now remain a prey to all the outrages of the Mussulmans whom your victories have irritated. The groans of so many victims will pursue you into your retreat, and will accuse you before God and before men.

"You close for ever the gates of Asia against the Christian phalanxes, and you restore to the Mussulmans the hopes they had lost of invading the countries of Christendom. To what interests, answer me, have you sacrificed your own glory and the safety of the Christian world? Had not war already given you all that the sultan Amurath promises? Would he not have already given you still more; and do not the pledges obtained by victory inspire more confidence than the promises of infidels?

"What shall I say to the sovereign pontiff who has sent me to you, not to treat with Mussulmans, but to drive them beyond the seas? What shall I say to all the pastors of the Christian churches, and to all the faithful of the West, who are now offering up prayers to Heaven for the success of your arms?

"There is no doubt that the barbarians, whom we have twice conquered, would never have consented to a peace, if they had had the means of carrying on the war. Do you believe they will observe the truce, when fortune shall become more favourable to them? No; Christian warriors cannot remain bound by an impious compact which gives up the Church and Europe to the disciples of Mahomet. Learn that there is no peace between God and his enemies, between truth and falsehood, between Heaven and Hell. There is no necessity for me to absolve you from an oath evidently contrary to religion and morality, to all that which constitutes, among men, the sanctity and faith of promises. I exhort you then, in the name of God, in the name of the Gospel, to resume your arms and follow me in the road of salvation and glory."

The safety of Christendom may, no doubt, be pleaded in extenuation of the violence of this discourse; but impartial history, whatever may be the reasons alleged, cannot approve of this open violation of the faith of oaths. The leaders of the crusade might merit the reproaches of the apostolic legate, who accused them of having made a peace disgraceful in itself and dangerous to Christian Europe; but they certainly also deserve the contempt of posterity for violating treaties they had so recently concluded. When Cardinal Julian began to speak, the minds of his auditors were already wavering; when he had finished his discourse, the warlike ardour which animated him seized upon the whole assembly, and manifested itself by the loud acclamations of a general approbation. With one unanimous voice they all swore to recommence the war, on the same spot where they had just sworn to maintain peace.

The enthusiasm of most of the leaders was at its height; it scarcely allowed them to observe that they had lost half their army. A great number of the Crusaders had quitted their colours, some impatient to return to their homes, but by far the greater part dissatisfied with a treaty, which rendered their bravery and their exploits useless. The prince of Servia, a near neighbour of the Turks, and in dread of their vengeance, did not dare to run the risk of a new war, and sent no troops to the army of Hunniades and Ladislaus. They waited in vain for the reinforcements promised by

Scanderberg, who was obliged to defend Albania. There remained not more than twenty thousand men under the banners of the cross. A chief of the Wallachians, on joining the Crusaders with his cavalry, could not refrain from expressing his surprise to the king of Hungary, at the smallness of his numbers; and told him that the sultan they were going to contend with, was frequently followed to the chase by more slaves than the Christian warriors amounted to.

The principal leaders were advised to defer the commencement of the war till the arrival of fresh Crusaders, or the return of those that had left them; but Ladislaus, Hunniades, and particularly Julian, were persuaded that God protected the defenders of the cross, and that nothing could resist them. They set forward on their march, and crossing the deserts of Bulgaria, encamped at Warna, on the shores of the Black Sea.

It was there the Crusaders, instead of finding the fleet which was to second them, learned that Amurath had left his retreat at Magnesia, and was hastening to meet them at the head of sixty thousand combatants. At this intelligence all the extravagant confidence infused by the Cardinal Julian faded away, and in their despair they accused the Greeks of having betrayed or abandoned them; and the Genoese, with the nephew of the Pope, who commanded the Christian fleet, of having yielded the passage of Galliopoli to the Turks. This accusation is repeated in all the chronicles of the West; but the Turkish historians make no mention of it; they, on the contrary, say that Amurath crossed the Hellespont at a considerable distance from the places occupied by the Christian fleet; and that the grand vizier, who was upon the European shore, protected the passage of the Ottoman army by a battery of cannon. "As soon as the troops of Amurath," adds the Turkish historian Coggia Effendi, "gained the shore, they offered up prayers and thanks to the God of Mahomet, *and the zephyr of victory breathed upon the Mussulman banners.*" The sultan pursued his march, swearing by the prophets of Islamism, to punish its enemies for the violation of treaties. If some authors may be believed, the emperor of the Turks supplicated Jesus Christ himself to avenge the outrage committed upon his name by the perjured warriors. At the approach of the Ottomans, Hunniades and the legate advised retreat; but retreat became impossible, and Ladislaus determined to conquer or die. The battle began: and it was then, says the Ottoman historian, "that an infinite number of valiant men were borne to the valley of shadows by torrents of blood." At the commencement of the battle both the right and left wings of the Mussulman army were broken. Some authors say that Amurath thought of flying, and that he was stopped by a janissary, who retained him by the bridle of his horse; others celebrate the firm courage of the sultan, and compare him to a rock which resists all the blasts of the tempest. Coggia Effendi, whom we have already quoted, adds that the Ottoman emperor addressed, upon the field of battle, a prayer to the God of Mahomet, and conjured him with tears to remove from the Mussulmans the bitter cup of contempt and affliction.

Fortune appeared to favour the arms of the Crusaders. A great part of the Ottoman army fled before twenty-four thousand Christian soldiers, and nothing could resist the impetuous courage of the king of Hungary. A crowd of prelates and bishops, armed with cuirasses and swords, accompanied Ladislaus, and entreated him to direct his attacks towards the point at which Amurath still fought, defended by the bravest of his janissaries. He listened but too willingly to their imprudent advice, and having rushed among the enemy's battalions, he was instantly pierced by a thousand lances, and fell with all who had been able to follow him. His head, fixed upon the point of a lance, and shown to the Hungarians, spread consternation through their ranks. It was in vain Hunniades and the bishops endeavoured to revive the courage of the Crusaders, by telling them they were not fighting for an earthly king, but for Jesus Christ; the whole Christian army disbanded, and fled in the greatest disorder. Hunniades himself was carried away with the rest: ten thousand soldiers of the cross lost their lives, and the Turks made a great number of prisoners. Cardinal Julian perished either in the battle or the flight.

After his victory, Amurath traversed the field of battle; and as he observed he did not see among the Christian bodies one with a gray beard, his vizier replied that men arrived at the age of reason would never have attempted such a rash enterprise. These words were nothing more than a piece of flattery addressed to the sultan; but they might, nevertheless, serve to characterize a war in which the leaders of the Christian armies obeyed rather the impulses of the imprudent passions of youth, than the cooler dictates of experience and matured age.

The expeditions of the Christians against the Turks began almost all, like this, by brilliant successes, and finished by great disasters. Most frequently a crusade was terminated at the first or the second battle, because the Crusaders had only valour, and were totally deficient in qualities which could improve a victory or repair reverses. When conquerors, they quarrelled for the glory of the fight or the spoils of the enemy; when conquered, they were at once depressed and discouraged, and returned to their homes, accusing each other reciprocally of their defeats.

The battle of Warna secured to the Turks the European provinces they had invaded, and permitted them to make fresh conquests. Amurath, after having triumphed over his enemies, again renounced the imperial crown, and the solitude of Magnesia once more beheld the conqueror of the Hungarians clothed in the humble mantle of a hermit; but the janissaries, whom he had so often led to victory, would not permit him to renounce the world or enjoy the repose he was so anxious for. Forced to resume the command of armies and the reins of empire, he directed his views against Albania; and he afterwards returned to fight with Hunniades on the shores of the Danube. He passed the remainder of his days in making war against the Christians, and with his last breath recommended his successor to direct his arms against Constantinople.

Mahomet II., to whom Amurath bequeathed the conquest of Byzantium, did not succeed his father till six years after the battle of Warna. It was then that began the days of mourning and calamity for the Greeks; and it is at this period that hisory offers us, as a spectacle, a last and terrible conflict; on the one side, an old empire whose glory had filled the universe, and which had no defence or limits left but the ramparts of its capital; and on the other, a new empire, the name of which was scarcely known, and which already threatened the whole world with invasion.

Constantine and Mahomet, elevated almost at the same time,—the one to the throne of Otman, the other to that of the Cæsars, presented no less difference in their characters than in their destinies. The moderation and piety of Constantine were admired, and historians have celebrated his calm and prudent valour in the field of battle, with his heroic patience in reverses. Mahomet brought to the throne an active and enterprising spirit, an ardent and passionate policy, and an indomitable pride. It is asserted that he loved letters and the arts; but these peaceful pursuits were not able to soften his savage ferocity. In war, he neither spared the lives of his enemies nor of his soldiers; and the violences of his character often ensanguined even peace. Whilst in Constantine a monarch could be recognized brought up in the school of Christianity, in Mahomet was as easily known a prince formed by the warlike and intolerant maxims of the Koran. The last of the Cæsars had all the virtues that can honour and teach the endurance of a great misfortune. The son of Amurath exhibited the dark qualities of a conqueror, with all the passions which, in the day of victory, must leave nothing but despair to the vanquished.

When Mahomet succeeded to the empire, his first thought was the conquest of Byzantium. In the negotiations which preceded the rupture of the peace, Constantine did not conceal the weakness of the Greek empire, and displayed all the resignation of a Christian. "My confidence is in God," said he to the Ottoman prince; "if it should please him to soften your heart, I shall rejoice at that happy change; if it should please him to deliver up Constantinople to you, I shall submit to his will without a murmur."

The siege of Byzantium was fixed to begin in the spring of the year 1453; and the Greeks and the Turks passed the winter in preparation for the defence and the attack. Mahomet entered with ardour upon an enterprise to which, for a length of time, all the wishes of the Turkish nation and all the Ottoman policy has been directed. In the middle of a night, having sent for his vizier: "Thou seest," said Mahomet, "the disorder of my couch. I have carried to it the trouble which agitates and devours me; henceforth there will be neither repose nor sleep for me but in the capital of the Greeks."

Whilst Mahomet was getting together all his forces to commence the war, Constantine Palæologus implored assistance from the nations of Europe. Cries of alarm had so often been heard from Constantinople, that some regarded the dangers of the Greek empire as imaginary, and others, its ruin as inevitable. In vain Constantine promised, as all his predecessors had done, to unite the Greek Church with the Roman Church; the remembrance of so many promises, made in the hour of peril and forgotten in times of safety, added to the antipathy of the Latins for the people of Greece. The Pope exhorted feebly the warriors of the West to take arms, and satisfied himself with sending to the Greek emperor a legate and some ecclesiastics versed in the art of argumentation and in the study of theology. Although the Cardinal Isidore brought with him a considerable treasure, and had in his suite some Italian soldiers, his arrival at Constantinople must have spread discouragement among the Greeks, who expected other succours, and appeared to have attached a very high value to their submission to the Church of Rome.

The princes of the Morea and the Archipelago, with those of Hungary and Bulgaria, some, in dread of being themselves attacked, the others, restrained by indifference or the spirit of jealousy, refused to take any part in a war in which victory would decide their own fate. As Genoa and Venice had counting-houses and commercial establishments at Constantinople, two thousand Genoese soldiers and five or six hundred Venetians presented themselves to assist in defending the city. A troop of Catalans also arrived, an intrepid soldiery, by turns the scourge and hope of Greece, whom a love of war and peril brought to the imperial city. And this was all that was to represent warlike Europe at the siege of Byzantium.

At this period, several Christian powers were at war with each other: the continuator of Baronius remarks on this subject, that the soldiers who then perished in battles fought in the bosom of Christendom, would have been sufficient to disperse the Turks, and drive them back to the outward verge of Asia. But if history, on this occasion, accuses the nations of the West of indifference, what ought it to say of that of the Greeks for their own defence? The efforts of Constantine to unite the two Churches had weakened the confidence and zeal of his subjects, who prided themselves upon being orthodox. Among the Greeks, some, in order to owe nothing to the Latins, declared that God himself had undertaken to save his people, and upon the faith of some prophecies they had made, they awaited in inaction a miraculous deliverance. Others, more dark in their scholastic reveries, were not willing that Constantinople should be saved, because they had predicted that the empire must perish to expiate the crime of the union. Every hope of victory had in their eyes something impious and contrary to the will of Heaven. When the emperor spoke of the means of safety that still remained, and of the necessity for taking arms, these atrabilarious doctors drew back with a kind of horror, and the multitude they had misled ran after the monk Genadius, who, from the depth of his cell, cried out constantly to the people, that there was nothing to be done, and that all was lost.

When we study the whimsicalities of the human mind, that which most affects the enlightened observer is, to see there are men whose passion is words, whom self-love attaches to vain subtleties, and for whom the ruin of the world would be a less painful spectacle than the triumph of an opinion they have opposed. On the eve of the greatest perils, Constantinople was filled with people whom hatred for the Latins made forgetful of even the approach and menaces of the Turks. The grand duke Notares went so far as to say that he would like better to see in Byzantium the turban of Mahomet than the tiara of the pontiff of Rome.

It is not useless to remind our readers here, that in all these debates there was no question that affected the truths of Christianity,—nothing but some points of ecclesiastical discipline: celebrating the mass in the Latin tongue, consecrating unleavened bread, mixing some cold water in the chalice, communicating with azymites—these were things that were to be hated, things that were to be feared much more than Islamism. Such were the motives for which the Greeks repulsed the Franks, their natural allies, loaded them with anathemas, and invoked the maledictions of Heaven upon their own city.

Amidst these deplorable disputes the voice of patriotism was never listened to, and indifference, selfishness, and cowardice were able to conceal themselves under the respectable appearance of religion and orthodoxy. A great part of the population of Constantinople had abandoned the city; among those that remained, the richest had buried their treasures, which they might have employed in the general defence, and which they soon lost, with their liberty and their lives. The imperial city only contained within its bosom four thousand nine hundred and seventy defenders, and the emperor was obliged to plunder the churches to support them. Thus, from eight to nine thousand combatants formed the entire garrison of Byzantium, and the last hope of the empire of the East.

Mahomet had completed his immense preparations. As the conquest of Byzantium and the pillage of Constantinople were the richest recompence that could be offered to the valour of the Ottomans, all the soldiers were, in some sort, associated with the ambition of their leader. The warlike ardour and fanaticism which had distinguished the companions of Omar and the first champions of Islamism were now revived. From all the regions which extend from the chain of Taurus to the banks of the Ebro and the Danube came crowds of warriors, attracted to the army by the hopes of booty or the desire of distinguishing themselves in a religious and national war. In order at once to give a clear idea of the decay and weakness of the Greeks, and of the strength and power of the Ottomans, it will suffice to say, that Constantinople and all that remained of the territory of the empire contained a smaller number of inhabitants of all kinds than Mahomet mustered soldiers beneath his banners.

The Ottoman army set out from Adrianople at the beginning of March; and on the sixth of April Mahomet pitched his tent before the gate of St. Romanus. The signal for battle was speedily given on both sides. In the early days of the siege, the Greeks and the Turks displayed all that the art of war had invented or perfected among the ancients and moderns. Among his formidable preparations, Mahomet had not neglected artillery, the use of which was then spread through the West. One of his cannons, founded under his own eyes at Adrianople, was of such gigantic proportions, that three hundred oxen dragged it along with difficulty, and it launched a ball of seven hundred quintals (seven hundred pounds weight) to a distance of more than six hundred toises (six hundred fathoms). Almost all the historians of the time speak of this terrible instrument of war, but say very little of the effect it produced in the field of battle. On examining with care the accounts of contemporaries, and particularly the descriptions they have left us of these enormous machines of bronze, which they had so much trouble to move, we feel persuaded that at the siege of Byzantium the Ottoman artillery inspired more fright and surprise than it did execution. The Turks showed very little skill or zeal in seconding the Frank engineers and artillerymen whom Mahomet had taken into his service; and it was a great blessing for Christendom that so powerful a discovery was not perfected at once in the hands of barbarians, whom Europe could not have resisted if they had joined this new force to the advantages they already possessed in war.

The Turks employed other arms and other means of attack with much more success; such as mines dug under the ramparts, rolling towers, which were brought close up to the walls, rams which battered the walls, balistæ, which launched beams and stones, arrows, javelins, and even the Greek fire, which still rivalled gunpowder, although the latter was destined soon to make it neglected and forgotten. All these means of destruction were employed at the same time, and assaults were renewed unceasingly. The besieged could not avail themselves of all their machines, from the want of hands to work them; and when we reflect on the smallness of the number of the defenders of Constantinople, we are astonished that they were able to resist, for more than fifty days, the innumerable host of the Ottomans. This generous soldiery occupied a line of more than a league in length, repelling, night and day, the assaults of the enemy, repairing the breaches in the walls, and making sorties; they appeared to be everywhere at the same time, and to be equal to everything, animated by the presence of their leaders, and particularly by the example of Constantine. Several times fortune favoured the efforts of this heroic troop, and mingled a few gleams of hope with the sentiment of sadness and terror which prevailed in Constantinople. The besieged preserved one advantage, the city was inaccessible towards the Propontis and on the side of the port. Mahomet had assembled a numerous fleet in the canal of the Black Sea; but it only served for the transmission of provisions and warlike stores. The Ottoman marine could not contend with the marine of the Greeks, particularly with that of the Franks; and the Turks themselves acknowledged that they must yield the empire of the seas to the Christian nations.

About the middle of the siege, five vessels from the coasts of Italy and Greece arrived in the canal. The whole Ottoman fleet was immediately in motion, and advanced to meet them; from their numbers they surrounded them, and attacked them several times, with the view of getting possession of them, or of turning them from their course. Mahomet encouraged the combatants with voice and gesture from the shore. When the Ottomans appeared to be failing in their attempt, he could not restrain his anger; urging his horse into the sea, he seemed to threaten the elements, and, like a barbarian king of antiquity, to accuse the waves of being obstacles to his conquests. On the other side, the Greeks, collected on the ramparts of the city, awaited the issue of the combat in great anxiety. At length, after an obstinate and bloody conflict, all the Turkish ships were dispersed or cast upon the shore; and the Christian fleet, laden with provisions and soldiers, sailed in triumph into the port of Constantinople.

The sultan burned to avenge this disgrace to his arms, and resolved to make a last effort to render himself master of the port of Constantinople. As the entrance of it was guarded by several large vessels, and closed by a chain of iron that could neither be broken nor passed, the Ottoman monarch employed an extraordinary method, which the besieged had not foreseen, and the success of which displayed the force of his will and the extent of his power. In a single night, between seventy and eighty vessels, which were at anchor in the canal of the Black Sea, were transported by land to the gulf of Ceras. The road was covered with planks, plastered with grease, along which a multitude of soldiers and workmen made the vessels slide. The Turkish fleet, commanded by pilots, with sails unfurled, as if upon a maritime expedition, advanced over a hilly country, and traversed a space of two miles by the light of torches and flambeaux, to the sound of clarions and trumpets, without the Genoese, who inhabited Galata, daring to offer any opposition to its passage. The Greeks, fully occupied in guarding their ramparts, had no suspicion of the designs of the enemy. They could not comprehend what could be the cause or the object of all the tumult that was heard during the whole night from the sea-shore, until the dawn of day showed them the Mussulman standards floating in their port.

We naturally here inquire what resistance was made by the vessels which guarded the iron chain, and by those which had entered the port, after having dispersed the Ottoman fleet. We may suppose that every warrior who had fought in the Christian ships was then employed in defending the ramparts of the city; or, it is probable, that the part of the gulf in which the Turkish ships descended, was not deep enough to be accessible to large vessels. However this may have been, the Mussulmans lost no time in taking advantage of their success. Scarcely were the Turkish boats launched, when a multitude of workmen were busily engaged in constructing floating batteries on the same spot where the Venetians made their last assault in the fifth crusade.

This bold enterprise, carried out with such audacity and success, spread trouble and consternation among the besieged. They made several attempts to burn the fleet and destroy the works the enemy had begun; but they in vain had recourse to the Greek fire, which had so often saved Constantinople from the attacks of the barbarians. Forty of their most intrepid warriors, betrayed by their imprudent valour, and perhaps also by the Genoese, fell into the hands of the Turks, and a death amidst tortures was the reward of their generous devotion.

Constantine used reprisals, and exposed the heads of seventy of his captives upon the ramparts. This mode of making war announced that the combatants no longer listened to anything but the inspirations of despair or the furies of vengeance. The Mussulmans, who daily received supplies of all kinds, prosecuted the siege without intermission. The certainty of victory redoubled their ardour; Constantinople was assaulted on several sides at once, and the garrison, already weakened by the conflicts and labours of a long siege, were obliged to divide their forces to defend all the points attacked.

The repairs of the fortifications on the side of the port had been neglected. Towards the west, several of the towers, particularly that of St. Romanus, were falling into ruins. In this almost desperate situation, what was, if possible, still more deplorable, the garrison of Byzantium was possessed by the spirit of discord. Violent debates arose between the grand duke Notares and Justiniani, who commanded the Genoese troops. The Venetians and the Genoese were several times on the point of coming to blows; and yet history can scarcely point out the subjects of these unfortunate quarrels. Such was the blindness produced by the spirit of jealousy, or rather by despair, that in this chosen band of warriors, who were every day sacrificing their lives in the noble cause they had embraced, it was not uncommon to hear mutual accusations of cowardice and treachery.

Constantine endeavoured to appease them; and himself, always calm in the midst of discord, appeared to be actuated by no other feeling than a love of country and a thirst for glory. The character he exhibited when surrounded by dangers, ought to have procured him the confidence and the affection of the people; but the turbulent and seditious spirit of the Greeks, and the vanity of their disputes would not permit them to appreciate true greatness. They reproached Palæologus with misfortunes which were not his work, and which his virtue alone could have repaired. They accused him of completing the ruin of an empire which all the world abandoned, and which he alone was willing to defend. They not only no longer respected the authority or the intentions of the prince; but every one who was exalted either by rank or character, became an object of reprobation or mistrust. By a consequence of that restless spirit which, in public disorders, urges the multitude to seek obscure

MAHOMET II. BEFORE CONSTANTINOPLE.

Mahomet encouraged the combatants with voice and gesture from the shore. When the Ottomans appeared to be failing in their attempt, he could not restrain his anger; urging his horse into the sea, he seemed to threaten the elements, and, like a barbarian king of antiquity, to accuse the waves of being obstacles to his conquests. The sultan burned to avenge this disgrace to his arms, and resolved to make a last effort to render himself master of the port of Constantinople. As the entrance of it was guarded by several large vessels, and closed by a chain of iron that could neither be broken nor passed, the Ottoman monarch employed an extraordinary method, which the besieged had not foreseen, and the success of which displayed the force of his will and the extent of his power. In a single night, between seventy and eighty vessels, which were at anchor in the canal of the Black Sea, were transported by land to the gulf of Ceras. The road was covered with planks, plastered with grease, along which a multitude of soldiers and workmen made the vessels slide.—BOOK XVI.

supports, certain predictions, fully credited by the people, announced that the city of the Cæsars could only be saved by a miserable mendicant, in whose hand God would place the sword of his wrath.

As the day of their great calamities approached, the congregations of the churches proportionately increased. The image of the holy Virgin, the patroness of Constantinople, was solemnly exhibited, and carried in procession through the streets. These pious ceremonies, doubtless, presented something edifying, but they did not inspire the bravery necessary for the defence of a country and a religion in extreme danger; and Heaven, amidst the perils of war, did not listen to the prayers of an unarmed trembling people.

During the siege, capitulation had been several times spoken of. Mahomet required that the capital of an empire, of which he already possessed all the provinces, should be given up to him, and he would permit the Greeks to retire with their treasures. Palæologus was willing to consent to pay a tribute, but he would not give up Constantinople. At length, in a last message, the sultan threatened to immolate the Greek emperor with his family, and scatter his captive people throughout the earth, if he persisted in defending the city. Mahomet offered his enemy a principality in the Peloponnesus; Constantine rejected this proposition, and preferred a glorious death. From that moment peace was no more mentioned, and Byzantium was left to the chances of an implacable war.

The sultan announced to the army an approaching general assault: the wealth of Constantinople, the captives, the Greek women, were to be the rewards of the valour of the soldiers; he for himself, only reserved the city and the edifices. To add religious enthusiasm to that of war, dervises pervaded the ranks of the Ottoman army, exhorting the soldiers to purify their bodies by ablutions, and their souls by prayer; and promising the delights of paradise to the defenders of the Mussulman faith. At the end of the day, great fires, lighted by the orders of the sultan, spread a lurid splendour over all the shores of the sea, from the point of Galata to the Golden Gate. The Ottoman emperor then appeared in the midst of his army, promising again the plunder of Byzantium to his soldiers; and, to render his promise more solemn, he swore to it *by the soul of Amurath, by four thousand prophets, by his children, and lastly by his cimeter.* The whole army burst forth in exclamations of joy, and repeated several times: *God is God, and Mahomet is the messenger of God.* When this warlike ceremony was finished, the sultan ordered, under pain of death, that profound silence should be observed throughout the camp; and from that moment nothing was to be heard around Constantinople but the confused tumult of an army in which everything was in motion, preparing for a terrible and decisive combat.

In the city, the garrison kept watch upon the ramparts, and observed with anxiety the movements of the Ottoman army. They had heard with affright the noisy exclamations of the Turks; but the sudden silence which followed them redoubled their alarm. The light from the enemy's fires was reflected from the summits of the towers and from the domes of the churches, and rendered the darkness which covered the city more awful. Constantinople, in which the labours of industry and all the ordinary cares of life were suspended, was plunged in a profound calm, which, however, afforded neither sleep nor repose to any one; it was the dismal aspect of a city which some great scourge has rendered desolate. Only around the temples some few plaintive sounds were heard, imploring with the voice of prayer the mercy of heaven. Already might the words of the Persian poet be applied to that unfortunate city, which the conqueror repeated on the morrow in the pride of his triumph: *The spider silently spins his web beneath the roofs of the palaces, and the bird of darkness utters his mournful cries upon the towers of Efrasiab.*

Constantine called together the principal leaders of the garrison to deliberate upon the dangers which threatened the empire. In a pathetic discourse, he endeavoured to revive the courage and the hopes of his companions in arms; speaking to the Greeks of patriotism, and to the Latin auxiliaries of religion and humanity, he exhorted them all to have patience, but above all to preserve concord. The warriors who were present at this last council, listened to the emperor in melancholy silence; they did not dare to interrogate each other upon the means of defence, which all knew to be useless. They embraced each other with tears, and returned to the ramparts, filled with the most sinister forebodings.

The emperor entered the church of St. Sophia, where he received the sacrament of the communion; the sadness which was observable on his countenance, the pious humility with which he solicited forgetfulness of injuries, pardon for his faults, the touching words which he addressed to the people, which resembled eternal adieus, redoubled the general consternation. The sun of the last day of the Roman empire arose: it was the 29th of May; the signal for assault was given to the Turkish army before dawn: the multitude of Mussulman soldiers rushed towards the walls of the city. The attack was made at the same time on the side of the port, and near the gate of St. Romanus. In the first charge, the assailants everywhere met with a firm resistance; the Catalans and the Genoese did all that the courage of Franks could effect. Palæologus fought at the head of the Greeks, and the sight alone of the imperial banner filled the Ottoman soldiers with terror. Three hundred archers from the isle of Crete, sustained gloriously the ancient renown of the Cretans for their skill with the bow. Among this brave band it is but just to point out Cardinal Isidorus, who had caused the fortifications he was charged to protect to be repaired at his own expense, and who fought till the end of the siege, at the head of the soldiers he had brought from Italy. History likewise owes great praise to the monks of St. Basil, who had no doubt adopted the party of the union, and whose valour and glorious death expiated the blind and fatal obstinacy of the Byzantine clergy.

The historian Phrantza compares the close ranks of the Mussulmans to an extended tightened cord, which might have been placed round the city. The towers which defended the gate St. Romanus crumbled away beneath the blows of the rams and the discharges of the Ottoman artillery. The exterior walls were carried; the dead and the wounded, confounded with the ruins, filled up the ditches. And yet upon this horrible field of battle the defenders of Byzantium fought still; nothing could weary their constancy, nothing could shake their courage.

After two hours of frightful conflict, Mahomet advanced with his chosen troops and ten thousand janissaries. He appeared in the midst of them, with his mace in his hand, like the angel of destruction; his threatening looks animated the ardour of his soldiers, and he pointed out to them by his gestures the points that were to be attacked. Behind the battalions he led, a troop of those men whom despotism charges with the execution of its vengeance, punished or constrained all who wished to fly, and forced them forward to the carnage. The dust which arose from the steps of the combatants, with the smoke of the artillery, covered both the army and the city. The clang of the trumpets, the crash of the ruins, the explosion of the cannons, and the shock of arms completely drowned the voices of the leaders. The janissaries fought in disorder; and Constantine, who had remarked it, was exhorting his soldiers to make one last effort, when the aspect of the fight became all at once changed. Justinian having been struck by an arrow, the pain of the wound was so intense as to force him to quit the field of battle. The Genoese and most of the Latin auxiliaries followed his example. The Greeks, left alone, are soon overwhelmed by numbers; the Turks pass the ramparts, get possession of the towers, and break open the gates. Constantine fought still; but soon, covered with wounds, he fell among the heap of dead, and Constantinople was without a head and without defenders.

What a spectacle is that of an empire which has but one moment of existence left, and which is about to finish amidst the furies of war, and beneath the sword of barbarians! All at once every tie of society is broken; religion, patriotism, nature have no longer laws that can be invoked; even wisdom and experience can yield none but useless counsels. All the ascendancy and splendour of virtue, genius, or even valour, have no longer power to distinguish or protect the citizens. Those magnificent palaces which constituted the pride of princes, nobody possesses them now. Among all the numerous edifices of a great capital, no one can find an asylum or an abode. The city has no longer warriors or magistrates, nobles or plebeians, poor or rich; the whole population is but a troop of slaves, who await with terror the presence of an irritated master. Such was Constantinople at the moment the conquerors were preparing to enter it.

When some of those who had defended the ramparts retreated into the city, announcing the coming of the Turks, they could not obtain belief; when the Turkish battalions came pouring in, the people, says the Greek historian Ducas, "were half dead with fear, and could scarcely breathe." The multitude rushed about the streets, without knowing whither to go, and uttering piercing cries. Women, children, and old people flocked to the churches, as if the altars of Christ could prove an asylum against the savage disciples of Mahomet!

It is not our task to describe the disasters which followed the taking of Constantinople. The massacre of the unarmed inhabitants, the city given up to pillage, holy places profaned, virgins and matrons overwhelmed with outrages, an entire population loaded with chains; such are the horrible pictures that are to be found in the annals of the Turks, the Greeks, and the Latins. Such was the fate of that city which frequent revolutions had covered with ruins, and which became at length the ridicule and the prey of a nation it had long despised. If there be anything consolatory amidst so many distressing scenes, it is the virtue of Constantine, who would not survive his country, and whose death was the last glory of the empire of the East.*

When we consider the weakness of the Greek empire and the power of its enemies, we are astonished it was able to resist so long. The Ottomans were governed by all the passions which favour conquests; the Greeks had not one of the qualities which are useful in defence: to be convinced of this, we have but to see how the two nations acted. When Mahomet proclaimed his enterprise, the Ottomans flocked to his army from all parts of his empire; whilst at the first report of the siege, a great part of the population of Constantinople deserted the city. We have seen that the dervises encouraged the Mussulman soldiers, and held up to them the war against the Greeks as a holy war. The Greek priests, on the contrary, discouraged the defenders of Byzantium, and were not far from considering the resistance of Constantine as a sacrilegious action. During the assaults made upon the imperial city, the Turkish soldiers, to fill up the ditches, cast into them their tents and their baggage, preferring victory to all they possessed. It is well known that at the same time the richest Greeks were employed in burying their wealth, preferring treasures to patriotism. We could add other remarkable features, but these quite sufficiently show on which side the strength was. What most strongly foretold the ruin of Byzantium, was the small degree of confidence the Greeks had in the duration of their empire. Never did the ancient Romans more clearly show the power and ascendancy of their patriotism, than when they designated Rome, *the eternal city*. Constantinople saw the number of its defenders diminish, and their courage became weaker, in proportion with the facility with which the sinister predictions of its approaching ruin found credit among the people.

When Byzantium, at the beginning of the thirteenth century, fell into the hands of the Latins, the empire still possessed great means of defence, and yet twenty thousand Crusaders achieved the

---

* For the siege of Constantinople, the very detailed account of Gibbon, and the rapid but complete picture of M. Salabury, in his *History of the Turkish Empire*, may be consulted.

conquest of it; which places the valour of the Franks much above that of the Turks. This would perhaps be the best place to examine what was the influence of the crusades over the destiny of the empire of the East. In the first expedition of the Latins, Asia Minor was delivered from the Turks, who were already masters of Nice, and threatened Constantinople; but the Crusaders sold the services they had rendered at too high a price: on the one part, violence, on the other, perfidy, disturbed the harmony that ought to have subsisted between the Greeks and the Latins. At length the taking of Constantinople by the Franks was a mortal blow to the empire of Byzantium. Amidst the war, schism became enlarged by hatred; and schism, in its turn, doubled the reciprocal hatred. This division favoured the progress of the Turks, and opened the gates of Constantinople to them.

What is most unfortunate in the conquest of the Ottomans is, that they preserved nothing, not even the name of Byzantium. The barbarians who overthrew the empire of the West, adopted the religion and manners of the conquered nations; which, by degrees, caused the traces of invasion and conquest to disappear. The Turks, on the contrary, were resolved to make the Koran triumph wherever they carried their arms. As soon as they were masters of Constantinople, the altars of Christ were overturned, and everything changed with religion. The city of Constantine became more widely than ever separated from Christendom; and as it was for the infidels the gate of the West, Christian Europe, which during nearly three centuries had sent its fleets and its armies into Asia, had reason at last to tremble for itself. From that period crusades took a new character, and were nothing but defensive wars.

BOOK XVII

CRUSADES AGAINST THE TURKS

A.D. 1453 TO 1481

BOOK XVII.

CRUSADES AGAINST THE TURKS.

A.D. 1453–1481.

Consternation among the Christian states at the fall of Constantinople—Philip, duke of Burgundy, assembles his nobility at Lille—Curious festival held by—Enthusiasm in favour of a crusade against the Turks—Bishop Sylvius, John Capistran, Frederick III. of Germany, and Pope Calixtus III. endeavour to stir up the crusade—The Turks penetrate into Hungary—Valour of Hunniades—They are defeated at Belgrade—An alarming comet—Bishop Sylvius elected Pope—Extended conquests of Mahomet II.—He subdues Greece—The Pope convokes an assembly at Mantua to urge on the crusade—His negotiations with Mahomet—Bosnia conquered—Pius II. engages personally in the crusade, reaches Ancona, and dies—Scanderberg defeats the Turks—Mahomet II. swears to annihilate Christianity—The king of Persia marches against the Turks, and his army is destroyed—Cardinal Caraffa commands a fleet of Crusaders—Satalia and Smyrna pillaged by the Christian forces—Possessions of the Venetians and Genoese captured by the Turks—Jacques Cœur—Cyprus subjected to the Mussulmans—Taken possession of by the Turks—Rhodes bravely defended by the knights of St. John—The Turks invade Hungary and different parts of Europe simultaneously—Defeated by Corvinus, king of Hungary—Otranto captured by the Turks, and afterwards abandoned—Pope Sextus IV. implores the aid of Christian Europe against the Turks—Distracted state of Italy—Death of Mahomet II., and divisions in his family—Zizim disputes the Turkish empire with Bajazet, and visits Europe—Charles VIII. of Naples, engages in a crusade against the Turks—Alphonso II. of Arragon—Italy invaded, and Rome possessed by the French—Andrew Palæologus sells his claims to the empire of the East—Death of Zizim—Bajazet declares war against Venice—Negotiates a treaty—Undertakes an expedition against Portugal—Commercial ambition of Venice—Diet at Augsburgh—Helian's speech against the Venetians—Council of Lateran convoked by Julius II.—Bajazet II. dethroned, and succeeded by Selim—Disorders of Christendom—Selim conquers the king of Persia and the sultan of Egypt—Palestine and all the rival powers of the East under the domination of the Turks—Exertions of Leo X. for reviving a crusade against them—Vida, the Italian poet—Novagero's eulogies on Leo X.—Cultivation of Greek in Italy—Great preparations for the new crusade—Eloquence of Sadoletus, and letters of Francis I. in its favour—Sale of indulgences—Quarrels of the Augustines and the Dominicans—Preaching of Luther against indulgences—Soliman succeeds to the Ottoman empire—Belgrade and Rhodes captured by the Turks—The knights of St. John expelled from Rhodes, and transferred to Malta—Francis I. made prisoner at the battle of Pavia—The Hungarians defeated by the Turks, and Louis II. slain—Clement VII. imprisoned by Charles V.—Religious distractions of Europe—Vienna besieged by the Turks—Hungary enters into a treaty of peace—Policy of Henry VIII., of Francis I., and of Charles V.—The Barbary states taken under the protection of the Ottoman Porte—Preaching of Luther—Heroic defence of Malta—Death of Soliman, and accession of Selim—Capture of Cyprus—The Turks signally defeated at the naval battle of Lepanto—Universal rejoicings throughout Christendom—General spread of civilization in Europe—Brilliant age of Leo X.—The military power of the Turks begins to decline—Defeated by Sobieski before the walls of Vienna—Causes and history of their decline—The Moors driven from Spain—State of Christendom in Europe, and progress of the Reformation—Ignatius Loyola—Pilgrimages to the Holy Land—A spirit of resignation assumes the place of enthusiasm for the crusades.

THE West had heard of the dangers which threatened the Greek empire with indifference; but on learning the last triumph of the arms of Mahomet, all the Christian nations were seized with terror; and it was believed that the janissaries were already overturning the altars of the Gospel in the richest provinces of Germany. People trembled at the idea of one day hearing the Koran preached in the churches of Rome, changed into mosques. Murmurs arose on all sides against the Pope, Nicholas V., who was reproached with not having preached a crusade, to prevent the misfortune which all Christendom deplored. Assistance sent before the siege might, in fact, have saved Constantinople; but the city once in the power of the barbarians, the evil became irreparable. A union of all the Christian powers alone could wrest their conquests from the hands of the Turks, and against this union fresh obstacles arose daily.

In vain, to excite the West once more, the eloquence of Christian orators was addressed sometimes to the grief, and at others to the piety, of the faithful; in vain, by turns, the ascendancy of religious ideas and that of chivalry were employed: everybody deplored the progress of the Turks, but a blind resignation, or rather a cruel indifference, soon took place of the general consternation.

A short time after the taking of Constantinople, Philip the Good, duke of Burgundy, assembled

THE OTTOMANS PENETRATE HUNGARY.

Calixtus III. thanked the head of the empire for his advice, and pressed him to set the example. But the indolent Frederick contented himself with renewing his promises; and whilst the emperor was thus exhorting the pope to maintain a crusade, and the pope, on his side, was urging the emperor to take arms, the Ottomans penetrated into Hungary and advanced against Belgrade. On the 6th of August, 1456, the Turks were defeated under the walls of Belgrade, which they had besieged forty days, and which they had threatened to treat in the same manner as they had treated the Greek capital. The presence of Hunnriades and the ardent zeal of John Capistran had so excited the valour of the Hungarians that they destroyed the Ottoman fleet, which covered the Danube and the Save, and the army commanded by Mahomet himself. The festival of the Transfiguration, instituted by a bull of the pope, and marked to take place on the 6th of August, reminded the universal church, every year, of the defeat of the Turks before Belgrade.—BOOK XVII.

at Lille, in Flanders, all the nobility of his states; and in a festival of which history has preserved a faithful account, he endeavoured to awaken the zeal and valour of the knights, by the spectacle of everything that could at that period affect their chivalric imagination. In the first place, a great number of pictures and curious scenes were exhibited to the spectators, among which were the labours of Hercules, the adventures of Jason and Medea, and the enchantments of Melusina. After these, an elephant was led into the banquetting-hall by a Saracen giant; on the back of the elephant was a tower, from which issued a lady clothed in mourning, representing the Christian Church. The elephant having arrived in front of the table of the duke of Burgundy, the lady recited a long complaint, in verse, upon the evils with which she was afflicted; and addressing herself to the princes, dukes, and knights, she complained of their tardiness and their indifference in assisting her. Then appeared a herald-at-arms, who carried in his hand a pheasant, a bird which chivalry had adopted as the symbol and the prize of bravery. Two noble demoiselles, and several knights of the order of the Golden Fleece, approached the duke, and presented to him the bird of the brave, praying him *to hold them in remembrance*. Philip the Good, who knew, says Olivier de la Marche, with what intention he held this banquet, cast a look of compassion upon the Lady Holy Church, and drew from his bosom a writing, which the herald-at-arms read with a loud voice. In this writing the duke vowed *in the first place by God his Creator, and by the holy Virgin, and next by the ladies and the pheasant*, "that if it pleased the king of France to expose his body for the defence of the Christian faith, to resist the damnable enterprise of the Grand Turk, he would serve him with his person and his power in the said voyage, in the best manner that God would give him grace; if the said king committed this expedition to any prince of his blood, or other great lord, he swore to obey him; and if, on account of his great affairs, he was not disposed to go or to send, and other potent princes would take the cross, he offered to accompany them as soon as he possibly could. If, during the holy voyage, he could by any means or manner learn or know that the said Grand Turk would be willing to meet him body to body, he, Philip, for the sake of the said Christian faith, would willingly fight with him, with the help of the all-powerful God, and of his very sweet Virgin Mother, whom he always called upon to aid him."

The Lady Holy Church thanked the duke for the zeal he showed for her defence. All the lords and knights who were present, invoked, in their turns, the names of God and the Virgin, without forgetting the ladies and the pheasant, and swore to consecrate their wealth and their lives to the service of Jesus Christ, *and of their very redoubtable lord the duke of Burgundy*. All expressed the most ardent enthusiasm. Some distinguished themselves by the whimsicality and the singularity of their promises. The count d'Etampes, nephew to Philip the Good, engaged himself to offer a *challenge to any of the great princes and lords of the Grand Turk's company*, and promised to fight them *body to body, two to two, three to three, four to four, five to five, &c.* The bastard of Burgundy swore to fight with a Turk in any manner he might please, and engaged to have his challenge sent to *the hostel of the Turk*. The lord of Pons swore never to sojourn in any city till he had met with a Saracen with whom he might fight body to body, by the help of our Lady, for the love of whom *he would never sleep in a bed on a Saturday*, before the entire accomplishment of his vow.

Another knight undertook, from the day of his departure, never to eat anything on a Friday that had been killed, until he had exchanged blows with one or many enemies of the faith; if the banner of his lord and that of the Saracens were unfurled as the signal for fight, he made a vow to go straight to the banner of the Grand Turk, and *to strike it to the earth, or die in attempting to do so.*[*]

---

[*] Some modern historians who have spoken of these vows of the knights, have exaggerated the fantasticalness of them. I find, among others, in one of these historians, this sentence: "In short, what gives the best idea of the devotion of these new Crusaders is, that one vowed that *if, up to the moment of his departure, he could not obtain the favours of his mistress, he would marry the first demoiselle he should meet with having twenty thousand crowns.*" We have found nothing like this in either Montstrelet or Olivier de la Marche, who are the only authors of the times who speak of this festival.

The seigneur de Toulongeon, on his arrival in the country of the infidels, vowed to challenge one of the men-at-arms of the Grand Turk, and fight him in the presence of his lord, the duke of Burgundy; or if the Saracen were not willing to come, he proposed to go and fight him in the presence of the Grand Turk, *provided he might have good assurance of safety.*

'All these promises, which were never accomplished, serve at least to show us the spirit and the manners of chivalry. The simple confidence which the knights had in their arms, proves how little they were acquainted with the enemies against whom they declared war in this fashion.

When each one had pronounced his vows, a lady clothed in white, bearing upon her back this inscription in letters of gold,—*Grace-Dieu*, came and saluted the assembly, and presented twelve ladies with twelve knights. These ladies personated twelve virtues or qualities, the name of which each wore upon her shoulder:—Faith, Charity, Justice, Reason, Prudence, Temperance, Strength, Truth, Bounty (largesse), Diligence, Hope, Valour,—such were the chivalric virtues that were to preside over the crusade.

After this ceremony, says the chronicler we have quoted, the ladies *began to dance like mummers, and to give themselves up to gaiety, in order to carry on the festival more joyously.*

The details of this chivalric feast make us perceive a great change in the spirit and the manners of Europe. When we call to our minds the Council of Clermont, the preachings of Peter the Hermit and of St. Bernard, with the grave enthusiasm and the austere devotion which presided at the taking of the oaths of the Early Crusaders; and when we afterwards behold the brilliant solemnities of chivalry, the half-profane and half-religious promises of the knights, in short, all the worldly spectacles amidst which a holy war was proclaimed, we can fancy ourselves transported not only into another age, but amongst new nations. The religion which had precipitated the West upon Asia had no longer an empire, unless the ladies were its interpreters. It was less piety, or the desire of obtaining heavenly crowns, than the sentiment of gallantry with which they were animated in tournaments, that brought knights beneath the standard of the cross.

We likewise know that this kind of preaching produced only a transient effect upon the minds of the warriors; and that they had not any influence whatever upon the multitude. This observation must convince us of one truth, which is, that the most active and powerful motive among men will always be the spirit of religion, and that no other motive, emanating from human passions, could have excited the world like that which produced and kept up the crusades.

Some pious men, however, made incredible efforts to revive the spirit of the early times of the holy wars. John Capistran, a monk of St. Francis, and Æneas Sylvius, bishop of Sienna, neglected no means that they thought would inflame the minds of the people, and reanimate religious enthusiasm. The first, who passed for a saint, travelled through the cities of Germany and Hungary, describing to the assemblies of the people, the perils of the faith, and the threats of the wicked. The second, one of the most enlightened bishops of his age, versed in Greek and Latin literature, an orator and a poet, exhorted princes to take up arms to keep off invasion from their own states, and save the Christian republic from approaching destruction.

Æneas Sylvius wrote to the sovereign pontiff, and endeavoured to rouse his zeal by telling him, that the loss of Constantinople would weaken his credit and tarnish his name, if he did not use every effort to destroy the power of the Turks. The pious orator repaired to Rome, and preached the crusade in a consistory; and to show the necessity for a holy war, he quoted by turns, before the pope and cardinals, the authority of Greek philosophers, and that of fathers of the Church. He deplored the captivity of Jerusalem, the cradle of Christianity; and the slavery of Greece, the mother of the sciences and the arts. Æneas celebrated the heroic courage of the Germans, the noble devotion of the French, the generous pride of the Spaniards, and the love of glory which animated the nations of Italy. The king of Hungary, whose kingdom was threatened by Mahomet, was present at this assembly. The orator of the crusade, pointing out this monarch to the sovereign pontiff and the prelates, conjured them to have pity on his tears.

Frederick III., emperor of Germany, at the same time wrote to Pope Nicholas V., to implore him to save Christendom. "The words that issue from the mouth of man cannot give an idea of the calamity the Catholic Church has just experienced, or make known the ferocity of the people who are now desolating Greece, and who menace the West." The emperor pressed the pope to unite all the Christian powers against this formidable enemy; announcing that he himself was about to convoke the princes and states of Germany. The pope applauded the intentions of the emperor, and legates were sent to the diets of Ratisbon and Frankfort. Æneas Sylvius again preached the crusade against the Turks in these two assemblies. The duke of Burgundy, who was present at both, renewed, in the presence of the princes and states of the German empire, the vow he had made *to God, to the Blessed Virgin, to the ladies, and to the pheasant.* Hungarian deputies came to announce that the banks of the Danube and the frontiers of Germany were about to be invaded by the Turks, if Christians did not hasten, in all parts, to take up arms to repel them.

The diet decreed that ten thousand horse and thirty thousand foot should be sent against the Turks; but as nothing was decided as to the manner of levying this army, or as to how it should be maintained, the enthusiasm for the crusade soon declined, and nobody put himself forward to oppose the progress of the Ottomans. Æneas Sylvius explains to us, in one of his letters, the causes of this indifference and inaction of Christendom. "The Christian republic was nothing but a body without a head; they who ought to have been the leaders had nothing great about them but the name; Europe was divided into a crowd of inimical or rival states; discords that could not be appeased, diversity of interests, languages, and customs, left no hope of raising a common army, or of carrying on an active and regular war against the Turks."

Æneas Sylvius thus demonstrated the impossibility of a crusade, and yet, carried away by his zeal, he passed his whole life in preaching one. Whilst he was uselessly haranguing the princes of Germany, the pope was endeavouring to establish concord among the states of Italy. The ascendancy of the pontifical authority was not sufficient to calm angry spirits, and peace was the work of a poor hermit, whose words exercised a supreme authority over the hearts of the faithful. Brother Simon issued all at once from his retreat, perambulated the cities, and addressing both princes and people, exhorted them to unite against the enemies of Jesus Christ: at the voice of the holy orator, Venice, Florence, and the duke of Milan, laid down their arms, and a league was formed, into which most of the republics and principalities of Italy entered.

Advantage might have been taken of this union to declare war against the Turks. But the confederation had no leader capable of directing it. Two men were able to set both Germany and Italy in motion,—the Emperor Frederick and Pope Nicholas. They alone could have insured success to a crusade which they themselves had preached: but the one was restrained by the avarice and indolence of his character; the other, passionate in the pursuit of learned antiquity, always surrounded by scholars, employed himself much more earnestly in collecting the literary treasures of Greece and Rome, than in promoting attempts for the deliverance of the city of Constantine. When the Turks took Byzantium, he was causing translation to be made, at great expense, of the most celebrated Greek authors; and it would not be harsh to believe that the tenths levied for the crusade, were sometimes employed in the acquisition of the master-pieces of Plato, Herodotus, or Thucydides.

Nicholas confined himself to a few exhortations addressed to the faithful, and died without having removed any of the difficulties which opposed themselves to the undertaking of a holy war. Calixtus III., who succeeded him, showed more zeal, and at the very commencement of his pontificate he sent legates and preachers throughout Europe, to proclaim a crusade and levy tenths. An embassy from the pontiff went to solicit the kings of Persia and Armenia, and the khan of the Tartars, to unite with the Christians of the West, to make war against the Turks. Sixteen galleys, constructed with the produce of the tenths, put to sea under the command of the patriarch of Aquileia, and displayed the banner of St. Peter in the Archipelago, and on the coasts of Asia Minor; Æneas Sylvius harangued the pope in the name of the emperor of Germany, and promised him the concurrence of all the powers of Christendom, if his holiness opened the treasures of the Church, and, by his evangelical exhortations, called *all the workmen to the harvest*. Calixtus III. thanked the head of the empire for his advice, and pressed him to set the example. But the indolent Frederick contented himself with renewing his promises; and whilst the emperor was thus exhorting the pope to maintain a crusade, and the pope, on his side, was urging the emperor to take arms, the Ottomans penetrated into Hungary, and advanced against Belgrade.

This city, one of the bulwarks of the West, received no succour from Christendom. There remained no hope for it but in the valour of Hunniades, and in the apostolic zeal of John of Capistran. The one commanded the troops of the Hungarians, and excited them by his example; the other, who, by his preachings had got together a great number of German Crusaders, animated the Christian soldiers, and inspired them with an invincible ardour.

Contemporary chronicles inform us, that at this period a hairy comet appeared blazing in the east. The Christian nations believed they saw in this phenomenon a prophetic signal of the greatest evils; and as the evil then most to be dreaded was the invasion of the Turks, Calixtus was desirous of profiting by this feeling of the people, to revive the idea of a crusade. He exhorted the Christians to penitence; and pointed out the holy war as a means by which they might expiate their sins and appease the anger of heaven.

In no country, notwithstanding, did the people arm, except in those that were immediately menaced by the Turks. It was at this time that the pope ordered that every day at noon, the bells should be rung in all parishes, to call upon the faithful to pray for the Hungarians, and for those who were contending with the Turks. Calixtus granted indulgences to all Christians who, at this signal, would repeat the Dominical prayer and the angelic salutation three times. Such was the origin of the *Angelus*, which the customs of the Church have consecrated, and continued to modern times.

Heaven was doubtless touched by these fervent prayers, which arose at the same time and together, from all parts of Christian Europe. On the 6th of August, 1456, the Turks were defeated under the walls of Belgrade, which they had besieged forty days, and which they had threatened to treat in the same manner as they had treated the Greek capital. The presence of Hunniades and the ardent zeal of John Capistran had so excited the valour of the Hungarians, that they destroyed the Ottoman fleet, which covered the Danube and the Save, and the army commanded by Mahomet himself. More than twenty thousand Mussulmans lost their lives in the battle; the sultan was wounded amidst his janissaries, and escaped the pursuit of the victors with much difficulty. All Europe returned Heaven thanks for a victory, for the obtaining of which it had only concurred by its prayers, and which it must have considered a miracle. The tent and the arms of Mahomet were sent to the pope, as a trophy of the holy war, and as a homage rendered to the father of the faithful. Religion celebrated by its ceremonies, a day in which its most cruel enemies had been vanquished. The festival of the Transfiguration, instituted by a bull of the pope, and marked to take place on the 6th of August, reminded the universal Church, every year, of the defeat of the Turks before Belgrade.

Hunniades and Capistran did not long survive their triumphs; but both died whilst Christendom was still mixing their names with hymns of gratitude. The passion of jealousy empoisoned their last moments; and the scarcely evangelical warmth with which each of them claimed the honour of having saved Belgrade, left a stain upon their renown. Æneas Sylvius, when commending their memory to the esteem of posterity, celebrates the virtues of Capistran, and expresses astonishment that an humble cenobite, who had trampled under-foot all the riches of this world, should not have had sufficient strength to resist the charms of glory.

Whilst the Hungarians were beating the Turks before Belgrade, the pope's fleet gained some advantages in the Archipelago. Calixtus took care not to neglect to remind the faithful of the exploits and triumphs of the patriarch of Aquileia; persuaded that the news of victories gained over the Mussulmans would restore hope and courage to all those whom the reverses of the Christians had discouraged and terrified. A fresh crusade was preached in France, England, Germany, and even in the kingdoms of Castile, Arragon, and Portugal. The people everywhere listened with pious seriousness to the preachers of the crusade; but murmurs generally arose against the levying of the tenths. The clergy of Rouen, with the university and parliament of Paris, opposed the impost openly. In Germany complaints were more violent than elsewhere. In proportion as the spirit of the holy wars cooled, the means employed by the popes to renew these distant expeditions were judged with greater severity. It must likewise be admitted, that there were great abuses in the collection and the employment of the tenths. An open traffic of the indulgences of the court of Rome for the crusade was carried on, and the tribunal of penitence, on certain occasions, seemed to be nothing but a means of levying taxes upon the faithful. It was only by money that the favours of the Church and the mercies of Heaven could be obtained; the sins of Christians might be said, in some sort, to have a tariff; and we find in the history of Arragon, that disobedience to the decrees of the pope even had become the source of a new tribute. It may be remembered that the sovereign pontiffs had frequently forbidden Christians to convey munitions or arms to the infidels. The trade of the maritime cities often braved the menaces of the Holy See, and avarice led the merchants to transgress the severest orders on this point. A sum of money was then required, in the name of the pope, of all who were accused of this offence. They were condemned to pay the fourth or the fifth of the profits arising from their illicit commerce. Commissaries were appointed to levy this impost, and decrees regulated the collection of it, as in that of all other public revenues.

But that which most completely exposes the spirit of this age, and particularly that of the court of Rome, is, that in the preachings of the crusades, the faithful were much less earnestly exhorted to take arms than to pay a tribute in money. The levies raised in the name of the Holy See, were termed *succours for the Hungarians;* and as the Hungarians always stood in need of being succoured, the levying of the tenths became a permanent state of things, which the people and the clergy endured every day with less patience and resignation.

We ought likewise to add, that the Holy See did not always receive the produce of the tribute it imposed upon the Christians. Princes, under pretence of making war against the Turks, sometimes took possession of it; and the tenths destined for the holy war were too often employed in carrying out the quarrels of ambition.

At length the complaints of the Germans against the commissaries and agents of the court of Rome became so serious and so numerous, that the pope found himself obliged to reply to them. In his apology, drawn up by Æneas Sylvius, he declared that Scanderberg and the king of Hungary had received numerous succours; that fleets had been armed against the infidels, and that vessels and munitions of war had been sent to Rhodes, Cyprus, and Mytilene; that, in a word, the money levied for the defence of the faith and of Christendom upon the faithful, had never been otherwise employed. The apologist of the pope, after having thus justified him, felicitated him with having saved Europe.

This apology, which explains nothing, and which finishes with an eulogy, too strongly resembles that of the ancient Roman, who, upon being accused of having embezzled the public money, as his only reply, proposed that they should go to the Capitol, and give thanks to the gods for the victories he had gained over the enemies of the republic. It must, however, be admitted, that that which Æneas Sylvius said was not totally void of truth; and history can but applaud the zeal which the sovereign pontiff displayed, in order to arrest the progress of Mahomet, and save a crowd of victims from the tyranny of the Ottomans.

Calixtus never ceased soliciting the Christian princes to unite with him, and was particularly anxious to kindle the warlike enthusiasm of the French against the Turks. "If I were but seconded by the French," said he, "we would destroy the race of the infidels." He spared neither prayers nor promises to induce Charles VII. to succour Hungary, and defend the barriers of Europe. He sent him that golden rose which the popes were accustomed to bless on the fourth Sunday of Lent, and of which they made a present to Christian princes, as a particular mark of esteem and affection. These caresses and these civilities of the pontiff were a great change from the times in which the heads of the Church only spoke to monarchs in the name of irritated Heaven; and only exhorted them to take the cross whilst reproaching them with their sins, and recommending them to expiate them by the holy war. The popes, when preaching the crusades, were no longer the interpreters of dominant opinions; their wishes were no longer laws, and princes made ample use of the faculty they possessed of not obeying. Charles VII., who was in constant dread of the enterprises of the English, resisted the reiterated entreaties of Calixtus. It was in vain that the dauphin, who afterwards reigned under the title of Louis XI., and was then living at the court of Burgundy, openly declared himself favourable to the crusade, and wished to create a party for himself in the kingdom, by taking the cross; France remained uninterested in the war preached against the infidels, and Charles contented himself with permitting the levy of the tenths in his states, upon the express condition that he should superintend the employment of them.

Whilst the pope was imploring the assistance of Christendom for the Hungarians, Hungary was a prey to troubles created by the succession of Ladislaus, who was killed at the battle of Warna. The family of Hunniades was proscribed, and the ambition of the princes disputed the possession of the provinces threatened by the Turks. Calixtus employed the paternal authority of the Holy See to appease the furies of discord, and to reconcile the pretensions of the emperor of Germany with the rights of justice and with the rights of nations; and these generous efforts at length succeeded in reëstablishing peace. His conduct appeared less praiseworthy, and particularly less disinterested, when the succession of Alphonso, king of Naples, brought fresh wars upon Italy. History relates that the sovereign pontiff, on this occasion, forgot the perils of Christianity, and employed the treasures collected for the holy war in the defence of a cause which certainly was not that of religion.

But the indefatigable orator of the crusades, Æneas Sylvius, succeeded Calixtus III. in the chair of St. Peter. The tiara appeared to be the reward of his zeal for the war against the Turks, and everything gave reason for hope that he would neglect nothing to execute himself the projects he had conceived; and awaken among the nations of Christendom, that warlike enthusiasm, that religious patriotism, which breathed in his discourses.

Mahomet II. continued to follow up the course of his victories, and his power every day became more redoubtable. He was then employed in despoiling all the Greek princes who had escaped his first invasions, and whose weakness was concealed under the pompous titles of emperor of Trebizond, king of Iberia, and despot of the Morea. All these princes, to whom acts of submission cost nothing, provided they enabled them to reign a few days longer, had been eager, a short time after the taking of Constantinople, to send ambassadors to the victorious sultan, to congratulate him upon his triumphs; and the fierce conqueror saw nothing in them but a prey which it would be easy for him to devour,—enemies that he could subdue at leisure. Most of them dishonoured the last moments of their reign or their existence, by all that ambition, jealousy, and the spirit of discord could inspire that was perfidious, cruel, or treacherous. When the Mussulmans penetrated into the Greek provinces, stained with all the crimes of civil war, it might have been believed that they were sent to accomplish the menaces of heavenly anger.

Mahomet did not deign to put forth all his strength against the pusillanimous tyrants of Greece. Other enemies were worthy of employing his arms; he had but to speak a word, to pull the throne from under the prince of Synope or the emperor of Trebizond; and if all that remained of the family of the Comnenas were massacred by his orders, he, in this circumstance, was less obedient to the fears of a dark policy than to his natural ferocity. Seven years after the taking of Byzantium, he led his janissaries into the Peloponnesus: at his approach, all the princes of Achaia either took to flight, or became his slaves. Meeting with scarcely any resistance, he gathered with disdain the fruits of an easy conquest. He meditated projects more vast than such conquests; and when he unfurled the banner of the cross amidst the ruins of Sparta and Athens, he fixed his eyes earnestly upon the Sea of Sicily, and wished to find a route that might conduct him to the shores of Italy.

The first care of Pius II. was to proclaim the fresh dangers of Europe. He wrote to all the powers of Christendom, and convoked a general assembly at Mantua, to deliberate upon the means of arresting the progress of the Ottomans. The bull of the pontiff reminded the faithful, that the Church of Christ had often been beaten by the tempest, but that He who commands the winds was ever watchful over its safety. "My predecessors," added he, "have declared war against the Turks, both by land and by sea; it is for us now to carry it on; we will spare neither labour nor expense for a war so useful, so just, and so holy."

All the states of Christendom promised to send ambassadors to Mantua. Pius II. went thither himself; and in his opening discourse, he expatiated with strength against the indifference of princes and sovereigns. He pointed to the Turks then ravaging Bosnia and Greece, and ready to extend, like a rapid conflagration, their devastations over Italy, Germany, and all the countries of Europe. The pontiff declared he would not quit Mantua before the Christian princes and states had given him pledges of their devotion to the cause of Christendom; and at length protested, that if he were abandoned by the Christian powers, he would alone maintain this glorious struggle, and would die in defending the independence of Europe and of the Church.

The language of Pius II. was full of religion, and his religion was full of patriotism. When Demosthenes and the Greek orators mounted the tribune to press their fellow-citizens to defend the liberties of Greece against the enterprises of Philip, or the invasions of the great king, they spoke, without doubt, with more eloquence; but never were they inspired by greater interests or nobler motives.

Cardinal Bissarion, to whom Greece had given birth, and whom the Church of Rome had adopted, spoke after Pius II., and declared that the whole college of cardinals was animated by the same zeal as the father of the faithful. The deputies of Rhodes, Cyprus, Epirus; those of Illyria, Peloponnesus, and of several of the countries the Turks had invaded, made, before the council, a lamentable recital of all the evils the Christians were suffering under the domination of the Mussulmans;

but the ambassadors of the great powers of Europe were not yet arrived; and this delay announced but too plainly the indifference of the Christian monarchs for the crusades. The debates which afterwards arose relative to the pretensions of the families of Anjou and Arragon to the kingdom of Naples; and then the disputes upon etiquette and precedence, which occupied the council during several days, completely proved that the minds of the assembly were not sufficiently impressed by the dangers of Christian Europe, and that no generous resolution would be there taken to prevent them.

The pope proposed to levy for the crusade a tenth upon the revenues of the clergy, a twentieth upon the Jews, and a thirtieth upon princes and seculars. He proposed at the same time, to raise an army of a hundred thousand men in the different states of Europe, and to intrust the command of this army to the emperor of Germany. These propositions, in order to be executed, required the approbation of the sovereigns, and most of the ambassadors made only vague promises. A great number of conferences were held; the council lasted many months, and the pope quitted Mantua without having done anything decisive for the enterprise he meditated. He returned to Rome, whence he wrote again to the Christian princes, conjuring them to send ambassadors, to deliberate afresh upon the war against the Turks.

Constantly pursued by the thought of delivering the Christian world, and losing hope daily of being able to affect the West, he conceived the strange idea of addressing Mahomet II. himself, and of employing all the powers of reasoning and eloquence to convert the Mussulman prince to Christianity. His letter, which we still possess, presents a complete treatise of the philosophy and the theology of the time. The pontiff opposes to the apostles of Islamism, the authority of the prophets and the fathers of the Church, and the profane authority of Lycurgus and Solon. Aiming particularly at interesting the ambition of the Ottoman emperor, he proposes to him the example of the great Constantine, who obtained the empire of the world on receiving baptism, and investing himself with that sign by which it was given to him to conquer. The sultan had only to acknowledge the God from whom all authority comes, to have the Abyssinians, the Arabs, the Mamelukes, the Persians, with all the nations of Asia, submit to his domination; and if the intercession of the court of Rome were necessary for him to reign over the East, the head of the Church promised him the assistance of his prayers, and the support of the pontifical sovereignty.

In this singular negotiation with Mahomet II., the pope was not more fortunate than with the Christian princes. The latter, when he urged them to defend their own states, answered by vain protestations. Mahomet, to whom he offered the conquest of the world, contented himself with replying, that "he was innocent of the death of Jesus Christ, and that he thought with horror of those who had fastened him to the cross."

The Ottoman emperor had just obtained possession of Bosnia, and had caused the king of that unfortunate country, who had submitted to his arms, to perish in the midst of tortures. Ottoman troops ravaged the frontiers of Illyria, and threatened the city of Ragusa. The dangers of Italy became every day more pressing. The pope assembled his consistory, and represented to the members, that the time was come to stop the progress of the Turks, and to commence the holy war he had preached. "The duke of Burgundy and the Venetian republic were ready to second his enterprise. Whilst the Hungarians and the Poles were preparing to fight the Ottomans on the Dniester and the Danube, the Epirots and the Albanians were about to raise the standard of liberty among the Greeks: in Asia, the sultan of Caramania and the king of Persia would attack the Turks, and second the united efforts of the Christians. The pontiff declared that he was resolved to march himself against the infidels. When the Christian princes should behold the vicar of Jesus Christ setting out for the holy war, would they not be ashamed to remain inactive? Loaded with years and infirmities, he had but a few moments to live; it would be hastening to an almost certain death; but of what consequence was the hour or the place of his decease, provided he died for the cause of Christ, and for the safety of Christendom."

The cardinals gave a unanimous assent to the resolution of Pius II. From that time the pope employed himself in preparations for his departure, and addressed an exhortation to the faithful to engage them to second his designs. After having, in this apostolic exhortation, retraced, with lively eloquence, the misfortunes and the perils of the Christian Church, the pontiff expressed himself thus:—

"Our fathers lost Jerusalem and all Asia; we have lost Greece and a great part of Europe. Christendom is now nothing but a corner of the world. In this extreme peril, the common father of the faithful is himself going to meet the enemy. Doubtless, war is ill suited to the weakness of old age, or to the character of pontiff; but when religion is ready to succumb, who could restrain us? We will take our place during fight, either upon the poop of a vessel, or upon a lofty hill, pouring our benedictions upon the soldiers of Christ, and invoking for them the God of armies. Thus the patriarch Moses prayed upon the mountain, and raised his hands towards heaven, whilst Israel combated with the nations whom God had reproved. We shall be followed by our cardinals, and by a great number of bishops; we will march with the standard of the cross displayed, with the relics of saints, with Jesus Christ himself in his eucharist. What Christian will refuse to follow the vicar of God, going with his holy senate, and all the revered train of the Church, to the defence of religion and humanity?

"What war was ever more just or more necessary? The Turks attack all that we hold most dear, all that Christian society considers most holy. If you are men, can you be wanting in compassion for your fellow-men? If you are Christians, religion commands you to carry succour to your brethren. If the misfortunes of others touch you not, think of your own safety—have pity on yourselves. You imagine yourselves to be in safety, because you are as yet at a distance from peril: tomorrow the sword will be suspended over your heads. If you convey not assistance to those who are before you, those who are behind you will, in like manner, abandon you in the hour of danger.

"Do you feel yourselves strong enough to support the opprobrium and the humiliation of a barbarous domination? Remain in your dwellings, await your enemies there; await there those vile Asiatics, who are not even men, and yet have the insolent pretension to govern all the nations of Europe. But if you possess a noble heart, an elevated mind, a generous character, a Christian soul, you will follow the banners of the Church; you will send us succours; you will aid the army of the Lord.

"Such as will aid us, God will bless them; but such as remain indifferent shall have no part in the treasures of divine mercy. May the wicked and the impious, who shall trouble the public peace, be accursed of God! May Heaven pour upon them the scourges of its wrath! Let them live in unceasing fear, and may their life be as if suspended by a thread! Neither power nor riches shall defend them; the arrows of remorse shall reach them everywhere; the flames of the abyss shall consume their hearts."

The pontiff addressed this exhortation to the princes, the nobility, and the people of all nations. He fixed upon the city and port of Ancona as the place of meeting for the Crusaders. He promised the remission of their sins to all who would serve, during six months, at their own expense, or who would maintain one or two soldiers of the cross during the same space of time. He had nothing to bestow in this world upon the faithful who should take part in the crusade; but he conjured Heaven to direct all their steps, to multiply their days, to preserve and increase their kingdoms, their principalities, and their possessions. On terminating his apostolical discourse, he addressed the Omnipotent God: "Oh, thou who searchest reins and hearts, thou knowest if we have any other thought than that of combating for thy glory, and for the safety of the flock thou hast committed to our charge. Avenge the Christian blood which flows beneath the sword of the Turks, and which on all sides rises up towards thee. Turn a favourable eye upon thy people; guide us in the war undertaken for the triumph of thy faith. Do so, that Greece may be restored to thy worship, and that all Europe may bless thy name!"

This bull of the pope was sent throughout all the West, and read publicly in the churches. The assembled faithful shed tears at the recital of the misfortunes of Christendom. The cross and arms were taken in countries apparently most secure from the invasions of the Turks, even in the remotest north of Europe. Some repaired to Ancona; others directed their course towards Hungary, to join the army of Matthias Corvinus, ready to set out on its march against the Turks.

The pope wrote to the doge of Venice, to entreat him to assist in person in the war about to be made against the infidels. He told him that the presence of princes in armies inspired confidence in the soldiers and terror in their enemies. As the doge was advanced in years, Paul reminded him that his own hair was blanched by time, and that the duke of Burgundy, who promised to accompany the Crusaders to the East, had attained the days of old age. "We shall be," added the holy father, "three old men at the head of an army of Christians. God takes delight in the number three, and the Trinity which is in Heaven will not fail to protect this trinity upon earth."

These singular expressions of the pope belonged to the bad taste of the age. But in presenting old age as the only mover and the last hope of the crusade, they painted sufficiently clearly the spirit of the times with regard to holy wars, and might be believed to presage the little success of an enterprise, which, in order to succeed, stood in need of the ardour and activity that are only to be found in youth. The doge of Venice hesitated to embark; but as the republic was at war with Mahomet II., and as it was of importance to mix its interests with those of the crusade, it threatened to employ force, in order to compel the doge to follow the pontiff of Rome. The duke of Burgundy, who had been the first of all the Christian princes to swear to go and combat with the infidels, showed no inclination to join the Crusaders. The pope, in his letters, reminded him of his solemn promises, and reproached him with having deceived men,—with having deceived God himself. He added, that his breach of faith would throw the whole of Christendom into mourning, and might bring about the entire failure of the enterprise. Philip, in spite of the severe remonstrances of Pius II., could not make up his mind to leave his states, but contented himself with sending two thousand men-at-arms to the Christian army. He was at that time in dread of the crooked policy of Louis XI., who, when he was dauphin, was eager to fight the Turks; but having ascended the throne of France, had no other enemies but his neighbours.

Pius II., after having implored the protection of God, in the basilic of the holy Apostles, left Rome in the month of June, 1464. Being attacked by a slow fever, and fearing that the sight of his infirmities might discourage the soldiers of the cross, he concealed his sufferings, and desired his physician to be silent on the subject of his malady. All along his route the people put up prayers for the success of his enterprise. The city of Ancona received him in triumph, and saluted him as the liberator of the Christian world.

A great number of Crusaders had arrived in this city; but most of them were without arms or stores, and were almost naked. The earnest exhortations of the pope had had no effect upon the knights and barons of Christendom. The poor, and men of the lowest class of the people, appeared to have been more struck with the dangers of Europe than the rich and the great of the earth. The crowd of Crusaders collected at Ancona resembled a troop of vagabonds and mendicants much more than an army. Every day, want and disease made martyrs of them. Pius II. was touched with their misery; but as he could not provide for their maintenance, he retained such as were in a condition to go to the war at their own expense, and dismissed the others with the indulgences of the crusade.

The Christian army was to direct its course to the coasts of Greece, and join Scanderberg, who had recently beaten the Ottomans in the plains of Ocrida. Deputies were sent to the Hungarians, the king of Cyprus, and to all the enemies of the Turks in Asia, without forgetting the king of Persia, to warn them to hold themselves in readiness to commence the war against the followers of Mahomet.

The little city of Ancona attracted the attention of all Europe. In fact, what spectacle could be more interesting than that of the father of the faithful braving the perils of war and of the seas, to go into distant countries, for the purposes of avenging outraged humanity, breaking the chains of Christian captives, and visiting his children in their affliction? Unfortunately, the physical strength of Pius II. was not equal to his zeal, and would not permit him to perfect his sacrifice. The fleet was ready to set sail, when the fever which he had had on leaving Rome, aggravated by the fatigues of the voyage and his subsequent anxiety, became a mortal malady. Feeling his end approach, he called the cardinals around him, and made them swear to prosecute the war against the infidels. He died whilst commending the Christians of the East to their care; and the last looks he cast upon earth were directed towards Greece, then labouring under the oppression of the enemies of Christ.

Paul II., who was elected pope, promised, amidst the conclave, to follow the example of his predecessor. But the Crusaders assembled by Pius II. were already returned to their homes. The Venetians, left alone, carried the war into the Peloponnesus, without being able to obtain any great advantages over the Turks. They devastated the country they went to deliver; and the most remarkable of their trophies was the pillage of Athens. The Greeks of the canton of Lacedæmon and some other cities, who, in the hope of being succoured, had raised the standard of liberty, could not stand against the janissaries, and fell victims to their devotion to the cause of religion and patriotism. Scanderberg, whose capital the Turks besieged, came himself to solicit the assistance of the pope. Being received by Paul II. in presence of the cardinals, he declared before the sacred college, that there was no longer in the East any place but Epirus, and in Epirus only his little army, that still fought for the cause of the Christians. He added, that if he succumbed, nobody would be left to defend the routes to Italy. The pope bestowed the greatest praises upon Scanderberg, and made him a present of a sword which he had blessed. He at the same time wrote to the princes of Christendom, to persuade them to assist Albania. In a letter addressed to the duke of Burgundy, Paul II. lamented the fate of the nations of Greece, driven from their country by the barbarians; he deplored the exile and the misery of the Greek families coming to seek refuge in Italy, dying with hunger and in nakedness, crowded together upon the sea-shore, holding their hands up to Heaven, and supplicating their brothers the Christians to succour them or to avenge them. The head of the Church reminded them of all that his predecessors had done, and of all he himself had done, to avert such great misfortunes. He blamed the indifference of both monarchs and nations; and menaced Europe with the same calamities, if they did not speedily take up arms against the Turks. The exhortations of the pope remained without effect; Scanderberg, carrying nothing back with him but some sums of money which he had obtained from the Holy See, returned to his kingdom, then ravaged by the Ottomans, and a short time afterwards died at Lissa, covered with glory, but despairing of the noble cause for which he had fought all his life.

Such was the ascendancy of one great man, that under his banners the Greeks, for such a length of time degenerate, recalled the remembrance of the brightest days of the military glory of their country; the little province of Albania resisted during twenty years the whole power of the Ottoman empire. The death of Scanderberg threw his companions in arms into despair. "Hasten, brave Albanians," cried they in the public places, "redouble your courage; for the ramparts of the empire and of Macedon are now crumbled into dust." These words were at once the funeral oration of a hero and that of his people. Two years had scarcely passed away before most of the cities of Epirus fell into the power of the Turks; and, as Scanderberg himself had foretold to the pontiff of Rome, not a soldier of Christ remained east of the Adriatic Sea.

All enterprises against the infidels were from that time confined to a few maritime expeditions of the Venetians and the Knights of Rhodes. These expeditions were not sufficient to arrest the progress of the Ottomans. Mahomet II. never ceased to meditate an invasion of Germany and Italy. Resolved to aim one last blow at his enemies, he determined, after the example of the Roman pontiffs, to employ the ascendancy of religion, to excite the bravery and the enthusiasm of the Mussulmans. In the midst of a solemn ceremony, and in the presence of the divan and the mufti, he swore "to renounce all pleasures, and never to turn his countenance from the West to the East, until he had overthrown and trampled under the feet of his horses the gods of the nations,—those gods of wood, brass, silver, gold, and painting, that the disciples of Christ made with their hands." He swore "to exterminate the iniquity of the Christians from the face of the earth, and to proclaim, from the rising to the setting, the glory of the God of Sabaoth and of Mahomet." After this threatening declaration, the Turkish emperor pressed all the circumcised nations that followed his laws to join him, in order to obey the command of God and his prophet.

The oath of Mahomet II. was read in all the mosques of the empire, at the hour of prayer. The Ottoman warriors flocked to Constantinople from all parts. An army of the sultan's was already ravaging Croatia and Carniola; and soon a formidable fleet issued from the canal, and attacked the island of Euboea or Negropont, separated by the Euripus from the city of Athens, which the Turkish historians call the city or the country of the philosophers. At the first news of the danger, the pope ordered public prayers in the city of Rome. He himself walked barefooted in procession before the image of the Virgin; but Heaven, says one of the annalists of the Church, did not deign to listen to the prayers of the Christians; Negropont fell into the hands of the Turks, and the entire population of the island was either exterminated or dragged into slavery. A great number of those who had defended their country with courage expired in tortures. Fame soon carried to Europe an account of the excesses of Ottoman barbarity, and all Christian nations were filled with horror and fright.

After the last victories of the Turks, Germany had reason to dread a prompt invasion, and the coasts of Italy were at the same time threatened. Cardinal Bessarion addressed an eloquent exhortation to the Italians, and conjured them to unite against the common enemy. The pope did everything in his power to appease discord, and at length succeeded in forming a league among the Italian states, similar to that which was entered into after the taking of Constantinople. His legates solicited the assistance of the kings of France and England. Upon his pressing request, Frederick convoked a diet at Ratisbon, and afterwards at Nuremberg, in which appeared the deputies of Venice, Sienna, Naples, Hungary, and Carniola, who described the ravages of the Turks, and painted in the most striking colours the misfortunes which menaced Europe. In these two assemblies, several resolutions were formed for war against the Mussulmans; but not one of them was executed. Such was the general blindness, that neither the exhortations of the pope, nor the frightful progress of the

Turks, were able to awaken the zeal of princes or people. The chronicles of the times speak of several miracles by which God manifested his power in these unfortunate days; but there can be no doubt that the greatest miracle of Providence was, that Italy and Germany did not fall into the hands of the Ottomans, when not a human hand was raised to defend them.

After the death of Paul II., who had not time to achieve his work, and did not witness the effect of his preachings, his successor, Sextus IV., neglected nothing for the defence of Christendom. When scarcely seated on the pontifical throne, he deputed cardinals to several states of Europe, to preach peace among Christians and war against the Turks. The legates were specially intrusted to press the levying of the tenths for the crusade. They were authorized to launch the thunders of excommunication against those who should oppose this impost, or who misapplied the produce of it. This severity, which occasioned troubles in England, and still more in Germany, succeeded in other countries, and furnished the sovereign pontiff with means for preparing for war. But none of the princes of the West took up arms, and Christendom was still exposed to the greatest perils, when fortune sent succour it had no reason to look for from the depths of Asia.

Of all the powers that had promised to combat the Ottomans, the only one that did not fail, was the king of Persia, to whom Calixtus III. had sent a missionary, and who declared himself the faithful ally of the Christians. In his reply, the king of Persia bestowed the greatest praises on the pope, encouraged him in his resolution of attacking Mahomet, and announced to him that he himself would commence hostilities. At the time his letter was received at Rome, his troops were already crossing Armenia, and several Ottoman cities had fallen into the hands of the Persians. Mahomet was obliged to abandon or to suspend his projects of conquest on the side of Europe, to march against these new enemies, with the greater part of the strength of his empire.

Great advantage might have been taken of this powerful diversion of the Persians. But the Venetians, the king of Naples, and the pope, alone put themselves forward to make war against the Ottomans. The sovereign pontiff had caused twenty-four galleys to be built with the produce of the tenths levied for the crusade. This fleet, commanded by Cardinal Caraffa, and collected in the Tiber, after having been blessed by Sextus IV., went to join that of Venice and Naples, and cruised along the coasts of Ionia and Pamphylia, to the great terror of all the maritime Ottoman cities. The Venetians did not fail to direct the operations of the Christian fleet against the cities whose wealth and commerce gave them any cause for jealousy. Satalia and Smyrna were given up to the horrors of war; the first of these, situated on the coast of Pamphylia, was the *entrepôt* for the productions and the merchandise of India and Arabia. The second, situated in the Ionian Sea, possessed rich manufactures and a flourishing trade. The Christian soldiers committed in these two cities all the kinds of excess with which the Turks were then reproached. After this piratical expedition, the fleet regained the ports of Italy, and Cardinal Caraffa returned triumphant to Rome, followed by twenty-five captives mounted upon superb horses, and by twelve camels, loaded with the spoils of the enemy. The ensigns taken from the Mussulmans, and the chain of the port of Satalia, were solemnly suspended over the gate and in the vaulted roof of the Vatican.

Whilst these poor advantages over the Mussulmans were being celebrated at Rome, Mahomet was inflicting terrible blows upon his enemies; and when he returned to Constantinople, he had destroyed the armies of the king of Persia. That which gave the Turkish emperor an immense advantage over the powers which took up arms against him, was that they never acted in concert, either for defence or attack. Discord was not long in being revived among the Christian princes, and particularly among the states of Italy. The pope himself forgot the spirit of peace and union he had preached; he forgot the holy war; and Venice, left alone in the struggle against the Ottomans, was obliged to sue to Mahomet for peace.

The Ottomans took as much advantage of peace as of war to increase their power. There now remained nothing of the sad wreck of the Greek empire. Venice had lost all its possessions in the Archipelago and Greece; Genoa at length lost the rich colony of Caffa, in the Crimea. Of all the conquests of the Crusaders, the Christians had only preserved the kingdom of Cyprus and the isle of Rhodes.

During more than a century, the kings of Cyprus had implored the assistance of the West, and contended with some successes against the Saracens, particularly the Mamelukes of Egypt. The maritime cities of Italy protected a kingdom from which trade and navigation derived great advantage. Every day fresh warriors from Europe afforded it the support of their arms. A few years after the taking of Constantinople, history remarks Jacques Cœur, who had obtained the restitution of his wealth, establishing himself in the isle of Cyprus, and consecrating his fortune and his life to the defence of the Christians of the East. After his death, there was to be seen, in a church at Bourges which he had founded, this inscription:—"The Seigneur Jacques Cœur, Captain-general of the Church against the infidels."*

The kingdom of Cyprus, after having resisted the Mussulmans for a long time, became at last the theatre and the prey of revolutions. Abandoned, in some sort, by the Christian powers, and obliged to defend itself against the Turks, it placed itself under the protection of the Mamelukes of Egypt. In time of trouble, the malcontents retired to Cairo, and procured the protection of a power which had a great interest in keeping up discord. The family of Lusignan being nearly extinct, a daughter, the only scion of many kings, at first married a Portuguese prince, and afterwards Louis, count of Savoy. But the sultan of Cairo and Mahomet II. would not permit a Latin prince to wear the crown of Cyprus, and caused a natural son of the last king to be elected. James, whose illegitimate birth kept him from the throne, and who had disturbed the kingdom by his ambitious pretensions, was crowned king of Cyprus in the city of Cairo, under the auspices and in the presence of the Mamelukes. That which must have greatly added to the scandal of this coronation was, that the new king promised to be faithful to the sultan of Egypt, and to pay five thousand gold crowns for the support of the great mosques of Mecca and Jerusalem. It was upon the Gospel that he swore to keep this promise, and to omit nothing that the Mamelukes required. "If I break my word," added he, "I shall be an apostate and a forger; I shall deny the existence of Jesus Christ, and the virginity of his mother; I shall slay a camel upon the font of baptism, and I shall curse the priesthood." Such were the words which a desire of reigning placed in the mouth of a prince who was about to govern a kingdom founded by the soldiers of Jesus Christ. He died a short time after having taken possession of the supreme authority. His people thought the days of his life and his reign were shortened by divine justice.

The republic of Venice, which adopted Catherine Cornaro, the widow of James, then took possession of Cyprus, which it defended against the Mamelukes and against the Turks, and held it till the middle of the following century.

The eyes of the whole Christian world were fixed upon the isle of Rhodes. This isle, defended by the Knights of St. John, recalled to the faithful the remembrance of the Holy Land, and prevented the extinction of the hope of one day seeing the standard of Christ again floating over the walls of Jerusalem. The martial youth of all the countries of the West unceasingly flocked thither,

---

* Jacques Cœur was condemned to death, and his property was confiscated. Charles VII. contented himself with banishing Jacques Cœur; but his property was not restored for a long time. Sixty of the clerks of Jacques Cœur subscribed together, and made up a sum of 60,000 crowns, with which he retired to the isle of Cyprus, and reëstablished his trade. He founded an hospital for pilgrims there, and a Carmelite convent, in which he was buried. Jacques Cœur built many houses at Marseilles, Montpellier, and Bourges: among others, the beautiful house which is now the municipality. It was Louis XI. who reinstated the memory of Jacques Cœur. The inscription which is here mentioned must have been also in the hospital for pilgrims at Cyprus.

THE SINEWS OF WAR.

After the death of Paul II., who had not time to achieve his work, and did not witness the effect of his preachings, his successor, Sextus IV., neglected nothing for the defence of Christendom. When scarcely seated on the pontifical throne, he deputed cardinals to several states of Europe, to preach peace among Christians and war against the Turks. The legates were specially intrusted to press the levying of the tenths for the crusade. They were authorized to launch the thunders of excommunication against those who should oppose this impost, or who misapplied the produce of it. This severity, which occasioned troubles in England, and still more in Germany, succeeded in other countries, and furnished the sovereign pontiff with means for preparing for war.

Great advantage might have been taken of a powerful diversion of the Persians. But the Venetians, the king of Naples, and the pope, alone put themselves forward to make war against the Ottomans. The sovereign pontiff had caused twenty-four galleys to be built with the produce of the tenths levied for the crusade. This fleet, commanded by Cardinal Caraffa, and collected in the Tiber, after having been blessed by Sextus IV., went to join that of Venice and Naples, and cruised along the coasts of Ionia and Pamphylia, to the great terror of all the maritime Ottoman cities. The Venetians did not fail to direct the operations of the Christian fleet against the cities whose wealth and commerce gave them any cause for jealousy. Satalia and Smyrna were given up to the horrors of war; the first of these, situated on the coast of Pamphylia, was the ENTREPÔT *for the productions and the merchandise of India and Arabia. The second, situated in the Ionian Sea, possessed rich manufactures and a flourishing trade. The Christian soldiers committed in these two cities all the kinds of excess with which the Turks were then reproached. After this piratical expedition, the fleet regained the ports of Italy, and Cardinal Caraffa returned triumphant to Rome, followed by twenty-five captives mounted upon superb horses, and by twelve camels, loaded with the spoils of the enemy. The ensigns taken from the Mussulmans, and the chain of the port of Satalia, were solemnly suspended over the gate and in the vaulted roof of the Vatican.*—BOOK XVII.

and, in some sort, revived the ardour, the zeal, and the exploits of the first crusades. The order of the Hospitallers, faithful to its first institution, always protected pilgrims repairing to Palestine, and defended Christian vessels against the attacks of Turks, Mamelukes, and pirates. At the commencement of his reign, Mahomet II. summoned the grand-master to pay him a tribute, as to his sovereign. The latter contented himself with answering: "We only owe the sovereignty of Rhodes to God and our swords. It is our duty to be the enemies, and not the tributaries, of the Ottomans!" This reply wounded the pride of the sultan; but he dissembled his anger, persuaded that victory would soon give that which was refused, and at the same time avenge him for the noble disdain of the Knights of St. John.

The Ottoman emperor, after having triumphed over the Persians, returned to Constantinople with fresh projects for conquests in Europe, and with increased animosity against the Christians; and the whole of his empire prepared to minister to his ambition and his anger. If the Turks had not till that period carried their invasions into the West, it was because the difference of religion and manners kept them from all communication with the Christian nations; and because they were entirely ignorant of the state and dispositions of Christendom, of the forces that might be opposed to them, and even of the best routes for them to pursue. They became gradually acquainted with the frontiers of Europe, and with the sea-coasts; and, like the lion of Holy Writ, which prowls constantly about in search of its prey, were ever on the watch for favourable opportunities. They secured advanced posts, and marched with precaution towards the country they wished to conquer, as an army draws round a place it is about to besiege. By frequently-repeated incursions, they spread terror among the nations they intended to attack; and by the ravages they exercised, they weakened the means of resistance of their enemies. Mahomet at first made himself master of Scutari and Negropont, in order to dominate, in a manner, over the coasts of the Adriatic and the Sea of Naples; on the other side, several of his armies directed their course towards the Danube, to lay open the routes to Germany; and Ottoman troops had penetrated, with fire and sword, as far as Friuli, to terrify the republic of Venice, and reconnoitre the avenues that lead to Italy.

When everything was ready for the execution of his terrible designs, the leader of the Ottoman empire resolved to attack Christendom at several points at once. A numerous army set out on its march to invade Hungary, and all the countries in the vicinity of the Danube. Two numerous fleets, with a vast number of troops on board, were despatched, one against the Knights of Rhodes, whose bravery Mahomet dreaded; and the other against the coast of Naples, the conquest of which would open the way towards Rome and southern Italy. In such a pressing danger, the hopes of the Germans, and even of a portion of the Italian states, reposed entirely upon the Hungarians. The king of Hungary was then considered as the guardian of the frontiers of Europe; and to be always in a condition to meet the Turks, he received every year succours in money from the republic of Venice and the emperor of Germany. The pope added to these succours a part of the tenths levied for the crusade, and his legates and missionaries were always present to excite the valour of the Hungarian soldiers.

At the approach of the Ottoman army, all Hungary, governed by Matthias Corvinus, son of Hunniades, flew to arms. The Hungarian army met the Turks in the plains of Transylvania, and gave them battle. Victory was obtained by the Christians, who, in a single battle, destroyed the enemy's army. Contemporary chronicles take less pains to describe this terrible conflict, than to exhibit the joy of the conquerors after their triumph. The entire victorious army assisted at a banquet prepared upon the field of battle, still covered with dead, and all smoking with carnage. The leaders and the soldiers mingled their songs of joy with the cries of the wounded and the dying, and in the intoxication of victory and festivity performed barbarous dances upon the bloody carcasses of their enemies.

The war between the Christians and the Turks became every day more cruel, and presented nothing but scenes of barbarity and destruction. The menaces of Mahomet; the constant violation by the Turks, in peace as well as in war, of the rights of nations and the faith of oaths; many thousands of Christians condemned to die in tortures for having defended their country and their religion, with twenty years of combats and misfortunes, had altogether excited the hatred of the soldiers of the cross; the thirst of vengeance rendered them sometimes as ferocious as their enemies; and in their triumphs they too frequently forgot that they were fighting in the cause of the Gospel.

Whilst the Turkish army experienced a sanguinary defeat upon the Danube, the fleet of Mahomet, which was directed against the isle of Rhodes, was destined to find, in the Knights of St. John, enemies not less intrepid or less to be dreaded than the Hungarians. The pacha who commanded this expedition, belonged to the imperial family of Palæologus, whose humble prayers had so frequently solicited the aid of Christian Europe. After the taking of Constantinople, he embraced the Mussulman religion, and from that time only sought to second Mahomet in his project of exterminating the race of the Christians in the East.

Several historians have related at great length the events of the siege of Rhodes; and this is, perhaps, a fitting opportunity to repair a great injustice committed upon one of the writers who have preceded us. An expression, escaped from the Abbé de Vertot, and with which criticism has armed itself, has proved sufficient to deprive him of the noblest reward of the labours of an historian,—the reputation for veracity.* After having examined with much care the historical monuments we possess, and according to which the author of the *History of the Knights of Malta* has described the siege of Rhodes, we feel great pleasure in rendering homage to the fidelity of his account, and we do not hesitate to refer our readers to it. In this elegant historian will be found the heroic constancy of Aubusson, grand-master of the order of St. John, and the indefatigable intrepidity of his knights, defending themselves amidst ruins, against a hundred thousand Mussulmans, armed with all that the art of sieges and the genius of war had invented. At the approach of the Turks, the grand-master of Rhodes implored the arms and aid of the Christian princes; but all the succours that were sent them consisted of two Neapolitan vessels, which did not arrive till after the siege was raised, and some sums of money which were the produce of a jubilee ordered by the pope at the request of Louis XI.

The third expedition of Mahomet, and the most important for his projects of conquest, was that which was to have been directed against the kingdom of Naples. The Ottoman fleet stopped before Otranto. After a siege of a few days, this city was taken by assault, given up to pillage, and its population massacred or dragged away into slavery. This invasion of the Turks, which was quite unexpected, spread terror throughout Italy. Boufinius informs us that the pope entertained for a moment the thought of quitting the city of the Apostles, and of going beyond the Alps, to seek an asylum in the kingdom of France.

It is probable that if Mahomet II. had united all his forces in an invasion of the kingdom of Naples, he might have pushed his conquests as far as Rome. But the loss of his army in Hungary, and the check experienced by his best troops before the city of Rhodes, must have suspended or

---

* The saying of the Abbé de Vertot was but an expression of politeness addressed to somebody who offered him documents, not in the interests of truth, but in the interest of some families, who wished that their names should be mentioned. In fact, if the documents they offered him concerned the truth, they had nothing to do but to publish them; now, we see nothing that has been published upon the siege of Rhodes that proves that the Abbé de Vertot was mistaken, or forgot anything of importance. It has not even been attempted to attack the authenticity of the facts he relates by any criticism that has survived to our times. There only remains the famous expression, *my siege is completed*, without any one having sought to explain in what sense and upon what subject this expression was made.

stopped the execution of his projects. Sextus IV., when recovered from his first terrors, implored the assistance of Christendom. The sovereign pontiff addressed all the ecclesiastical and secular powers, as well as the Christians of all conditions; he conjured them, by the mercy and sufferings of Christ; by the last judgment, in which every one would be placed according to his works; by the promises of baptism; by the obedience due to the Church,—he supplicated them to preserve among themselves, at least during three years, charity, peace, and concord. He sent legates in all directions, charged to appease the troubles and wars which divided the Christian world. These legates were instructed to act with moderation and prudence; to lead nations and kings, by means of persuasion, to the true spirit of the Gospel, and to resemble, in their pious courses, the dove which came back to the ark, bearing the pacific olive-branch. In order to encourage princes by his example, the pontiff ordered the galleys he had destined to succour Rhodes, to set sail for the coast of Naples. At the same time he commanded public prayers to be put up; and, to draw down the blessings of Heaven upon the arms of the Christians, and excite the piety of the faithful, he directed that the octave of All Saints should be celebrated in the universal Church, to begin with the year 1480, which he called in his bull the "Octave of the age."

Previously to the taking of Otranto, Italy had been more divided than ever. The heat of factions and the animosities which were created by jealousy had so perverted men's minds, that several states and many citizens only contemplated in an invasion of the Turks the ruin of a neighbouring state or of a rival faction. Venice was accused of having drawn the Ottoman troops into the kingdom of Naples. We must, however, in justice, say that the presence of danger, and particularly the account of the cruelties practised by the fierce conquerors of Otranto, awakened generous sentiments in all hearts; and when the sovereign pontiff, addressing the Italians, said that the moment was come to rise in arms, if they wished to defend their lands, their families, their faith, their liberty, all Italy listened to his exhortations, and united as one man against the common enemy.

The discourses and the prayers of the head of the Church did not produce the same effect in England, Germany, or France. The legates were everywhere received with respect, but they could not put an end to the war between England and Scotland, or stifle the germs of a quarrel always ready to break out between Louis XI. and the emperor Maximilian. In a Germanic diet which was convoked, as usual, pathetic speeches were made upon the calamities which threatened Christian Europe; but no one took up arms.

The Ottomans, shut up in Otranto, had not, it is true, strength enough to advance into Italy; but they might every day expect reinforcements. After having raised three armies, the Turkish emperor levied a fourth in Bithynia, to be employed, according to circumstances, against the Mamelukes of Egypt, or against the Christians of the West. But even these preparations, or the fresh invasions which they had reason to fear, were not able to remove the general indifference. The nations and the princes who did not believe themselves threatened with approximate danger, returned to their divisions and their quarrels. They had abandoned the safety of Christendom to the care of Providence, when they learnt the death of Mahomet II.: this news appeared to be spread everywhere at once, and was received like the announcement of a great victory, particularly in the countries which were in dread of the Ottoman invasions. At Rome, where the dread had been most lively, the pope ordered prayers, festivals, and processions, which lasted three days; and during those three days, the pacific artillery of the castle of St. Angelo never ceased to thunder forth the intelligence of the deliverance of Italy.

This joy of the Christians paints better than the long recitals of history the ambition, the genius, the fortune, and the policy of the barbarous hero of Islamism. During the course of this reign,* five pontiffs had succeeded to the chair of St. Peter; all had employed the ascendancy of their spiritual and temporal power in endeavouring to check the progress of his arms, and all died with the grief of seeing the growth and extension of that empire, before which all the East trembled, and of whose invasions the West was in constant dread.

A. D. 1481–1571.

The Turks abandoned Otranto, and the divisions which arose in the family of Mahomet suspended for a time the projects of Ottoman policy. Jem-Jem, whom the Latin chronicles called Zizim, disputed the empire with Bajazet, and being conquered, came into the West to await a favourable opportunity for recommencing the war. The Knights of Rhodes received him with great honours. He was afterwards sent into France, and, by one of the whimsical sports of fortune, an obscure commandery in the province of Auvergne became for a moment the asylum of a prince who pretended to the vast empire of the Crescent. His presence among the Christian powers gave serious uneasiness to Bajazet. The king of Hungary and the king of Naples had already promised to give the fugitive prince the support of their armies. The Ottoman emperor sent ambassadors to Charles VIII.; he informed the French monarch that his design was to conquer Egypt, and that he would voluntarily cede Jerusalem to him if he would place Zizim in his hands. At the same time, the sultan of Cairo sent one of the Latin fathers of the Holy Sepulchre to the pope, and requested also that the brother of Bajazet should be delivered up to him, as he wished to show him at the head of his army in a war against the Turks. He offered the sovereign pontiff, in exchange for such a great service, a hundred thousand gold ducats, the possession of the holy city, and even of the city of Constantinople, if they succeeded in driving the Turks from it. Charles VIII. had not arrived at the age for reigning, and the queen regent, engaged in reëstablishing peace in the kingdom, did not listen to the proposition of Bajazet. Neither did the pope accept the splendid offers of the sultan of Egypt; but the importance that appeared to be attached to the person of Zizim gave him the idea that he could himself derive some advantage from him. He demanded and obtained that the brother of Bajazet should be given up to him, and then he exhorted the Christian princes to unite with him, and promised to go in person to the conquest of Greece and Syria. The enterprise of Innocent VIII. reminds us of that of Pius II., and was destined to be equally unfortunate. The pontiff was employed in his scheme, with more zeal than success, when he died. Alexander VI., who succeeded him, had created for himself a name which repelled the confidence of the faithful, and left no hope that the preparations for a holy war would ever be able to divert him from the cares of his personal ambition, or tear him away from his profane affections.

The kingdom of Naples, however, which had occasioned so many wars, begun and carried on under the banners of the cross, gave rise, under these circumstances, to the idea of an enterprise which resembled a crusade. The duke of Milan, and several other small states, constantly occupied in disturbing Italy, and in calling thither foreign arms, for the purpose of increasing or preserving their own power, persuaded Charles VIII., then seated on the throne, to endeavour to establish the rights of the house of Anjou. Their solicitations and their brilliant promises awakened the ambition of the young king, who resolved to conquer the kingdom of Naples, and proclaimed the design of extending his views to the territories of the infidels.

The passion for arms, the spirit of chivalry, and the little that remained in men's hearts of the ancient ardour for crusades and distant expeditions, seconded the enterprise of the French monarch.

---

* Mahomet II. took Constantinople in 1453, and died in 1481.

Public prayers were offered up, and processions were formed throughout the kingdom, for the success of an expedition against the Turks. The preachings, or rather the poetical inspirations of some writers of the time, announced to all Europe the deliverance of the East.

When Charles VIII. had passed the Alps with his army, all the nations of Italy received him with the most lively demonstrations of joy; the love of liberty, the spirit of devotion, the sentiment of gallantry, all the passions which then prevailed, appeared to attach some hope to the issue of this expedition. The nations looked to the king of France and his knights for their independence. Amidst the brilliant festivities of chivalry, the French warriors were received as the *champions of the honour of ladies*. They gave Charles VIII. the titles of *envoy of God*, of *liberator of the Romish Church*, and of *defender of the faith*. All the acts of the king gave reason to believe that his expedition had for its object the glory and safety of Christendom. He wrote to the bishops of France to demand of them the tenths of a crusade. "Our intention," said he to them in his letters, "is not only to recover our kingdom of Naples, but to secure the welfare of Italy, and to effect the deliverance of the Holy Land."

Whilst the nations on both sides of the Alps gave themselves up to hope and joy, terror reigned in the kingdom of Naples. Alphonso addressed himself to all his allies; he, in particular, implored the succour of the Holy See, and, by a singular contrast, whilst he placed his greatest hopes in the court of Rome, he sent ambassadors to Constantinople, to warn Bajazet of the projects of Charles VIII. respecting Greece, and to conjure the Mussulman emperor to assist him in defending his kingdom against the invasion of the French. Alexander VI., who had embraced the cause of the princes of Arragon, beheld with the most lively inquietude the triumphant march of the king of France, who was advancing towards Rome without encountering any obstacles. In vain he called to his aid both the states of Italy and the Mussulman masters of Greece; in vain he employed the ascendancy of his spiritual power; he soon found himself obliged to submit, and to open the gates of his capital to a prince whom he regarded as his enemy, and whom he had by turns threatened with the anger of Heaven and with that of Bajazet.

Thus the war which the king of France had sworn to make against the infidels began by a victory obtained over the pope. According to one of the conditions imposed upon the sovereign pontiff, the brother of Bajazet was placed in the hands of Charles VIII. The unfortunate *Jem-Jem*, who knew nothing of the policy of which he was soon to become the victim, thanked the pope for having restored him to liberty. He congratulated himself upon being *protected by the great king of the West*, and entertained no doubt that the victorious arms of the Christians would replace him on the Ottoman throne. Charles VIII., however, appeared but very little disposed to restore to him the empire of Constantinople, which he had just purchased for himself. In the course of the last century, an act was found in the chancery of Rome, by which Andrew Palæologus, the despot of Achaia, and nephew of Constantine, sold to the king of France all his claims to the empire of the East, for the sum of four thousand three hundred gold ducats! This act, by which an empire was sold in the presence of a notary, and which could only be ratified by victory, appears to us a very curious historical monument; and serves to enlighten us upon the spirit and policy of these remote times. We must admit, however, that the French monarch seemed even then to attach very little value to this kind of treaty, and fulfilled none of the conditions of it. His attention was principally directed towards the kingdom of Naples, which fortune was about to place in his hands, without requiring him to fight a single battle.

Whilst Charles prolonged his sojourn at Rome, Alphonso II., abandoned to his own resources, a prey to terror and remorse, and pursued by the complaints of the Neapolitans, descended from his throne, and went to bury himself in a monastery of Sicily. His son Ferdinand, who succeeded him, although he had driven the Turks out of the city of Otranto, and had been proclaimed liberator of Italy, could neither revive the courage of his army nor the fidelity of his subjects. From the moment the arrival of the French was announced, the yoke of the house of Arragon appeared to become every day more insupportable. When Charles quitted the Roman states, instead of encountering the armies of an enemy, he only met on his road with deputations which came to offer him the crown of Naples. The capital soon received him in triumph, and the whole kingdom placed itself under his subjection.

Fame was not long in carrying into Greece the news of the marvellous conquests of Charles VIII. The Turks of Epirus, struck with terror, dreaded every instant to see the French arrive. Nicolas Vignier adds, that Bajazet was possessed by such fear, that he caused all his navy to come to the Straits of St. George, to enable him to escape into Asia.

The presence of Zizim in the Christian army particularly excited the alarms of the Mussulmans; but fortune had exhausted all her prodigies in favour of the French. *Jem-Jem*, whom the king of France hoped to exhibit to the enemies of the faith, died almost suddenly on arriving in the kingdom of Naples. Alexander VI. was accused of bringing about this death; Bajazet having promised him three hundred thousand gold ducats, *if he would aid his brother in escaping from the miseries of this life*. Turkish historians relate this event after a different manner: they say that a barber of Constantinople, named Mustapha, was sent to poison Zizim; and, what paints with a single stroke the spirit and the character of the Ottoman despotism, when the barber returned to announce that the brother of the sultan was dead, Bajazet raised him to the post of vizier; so important did the service appear, and so worthy of reward was the crime.

The conquests of Charles VIII., which gave the Turks so much alarm, began to create lively inquietudes in several Christian states. A league was formed against the French, into which entered the pope, the emperor Maximilian, the king of Spain, and the principal states of Italy. After the example of Charles VIII., this league assumed as a pretext a war against the Turks; but its real design did not remain long concealed; for it solicited the approbation and the assistance of Bajazet. Policy, on this occasion, did not hesitate to sacrifice Christian victims, to cement an alliance with the disciples of the Koran. As the Greeks of Epirus and the Peloponnesus were eager to profit by the enterprise of the king of France to shake off the yoke of the Ottomans, they sent deputies into Italy. The senate of Venice caused these deputies to be arrested, and gave up their papers to the envoys of the sultan. Fifty thousand of the inhabitants of Greece perished victims to this base act of treachery.

On another side, the inconstancy of the people, who had at first been favourable to the arms of the king of France, and the discontent which is always inspired by the presence of a victorious army, all at once changed the state of things in the kingdom of Naples. The French, who had been received with so much enthusiasm, became odious, and the hopes of all were directed towards the family of Arragon, so recently abandoned. Charles, instead of directing his looks towards Greece, turned them towards France. Whilst he was in the act of causing himself to be crowned emperor of Byzantium and king of Sicily, his thoughts were fixed upon the abandonment of his conquests. It was a singular contrast which the spectacle presented, of preparations for a retreat, and a triumphal ceremony, going on at the same time. Whilst the nobility, the clergy, and all the public bodies of the state, came to congratulate the victorious prince, the people were invoking the protection of Heaven against him, and the French awaited in silence the order and signal for its departure. On the day following his coronation, and as if he had only come to Naples for the sake of this vain ceremony, Charles VIII. set out, accompanied by the most distinguished of his knights, and resumed sorrowfully the road to his own kingdom. On his arrival in Italy, he had heard nothing in his march but benedictions and songs of triumph. On his return, he heard only the maledictions of the people and the threats of his enemies. In the first place he had crossed Italy without opposition; in order to leave it, he was forced to give battle; and considered as a victory the liberty which was left to him to drag back the wreck of his army over the Alps.

Thus terminated this enterprise of Charles VIII., which at first was pretended to be a holy war, which was directed by a short-sighted policy, and the consequences of which became so fatal to France and Italy. Whilst the preparations for this war were going on, there appeared, as we have said above, several writings in prose and verse, in which great victories were predicted. The aim of these predictions was not only to excite the enthusiasm of the people, but to strengthen a weak and irresolute prince in his undertaking. When we read the prophetic songs and hymns of the poets, we may fancy we see the French setting out for the conquest of the holy places. But the scene changes when we turn our eyes to the pages of history. Everything leads us to conclude, that on this occasion religious opinions and sentiments of chivalry were but the auxiliaries of unfortunate ambition. It is particularly to this expedition that we may apply what J. J. Rousseau somewhere says of the crusades: "The intrigues of cabinets embroiled affairs, and religion was the pretext."

The policy of Venice did not preserve her from the anger of Bajazet, who declared war against her. Alexander VI. published a jubilate, and demanded tenths of the clergy of Europe for the preparations for a crusade against the Turks. The emperor Maximilian, Louis XII., and the kings of Castile, Portugal, and Hungary, appeared to listen for a moment to the propositions of the pope. But reciprocal mistrust speedily dissolved this Christian league: in vain the preachers of the crusade repeated in their discourses the menaces of Bajazet; they could not overcome the indifference of the people; and the sovereign pontiff found everywhere equal obstacles to the levying of the tenths and the distribution of indulgences. The French clergy on this occasion braved ecclesiastical censures; and what shows the decline of the pontifical power, at least as far as regards the crusades, a simple decision of the Faculty of Theology of Paris was at that time sufficient to stand against all the terrible array of the menaces and thunders of Rome.

We have shown how and by what causes the spirit of the crusades had become enfeebled. Towards the end of the fifteenth century and the commencement of the sixteenth, two great events completed the diversion of attention from the East. America had recently been revealed to the ancient world, and the Portuguese had doubled the Cape of Good Hope. There is no doubt that the progress of navigation during the holy wars had contributed to the discoveries of Vasco de Gama and Christopher Columbus. But these discoveries, when they once became known in Europe, entirely occupied that active, enterprising, and adventurous spirit which had so long kept up the ardour for expeditions against the infidels. The direction of men's minds, views of policy, speculations of commerce, all were changed; and the great revolution of the crusades on its decline, was seen, in some sort, to clash with the new revolution which was born of the discovery and conquest of a new world.

The Venetians, masters of the ancient routes and commerce of India, were the first to be aware of the changes that were in operation, the consequences of which must prove so injurious to them. They secretly sent deputies to the sultan of Cairo, as much interested as themselves in opposing the interests of the Portuguese. The deputation from Venice advised the sultan of Egypt to ally himself with the king of Calcutta and other Indian powers, to attack the fleets and troops of Portugal. The republic undertook to send into Egypt and to the coasts of Arabia artisans to found cannon, and carpenters to construct vessels of war. The Egyptian monarch, whose interests were the same as those of Venice, readily entered into the plan proposed to him; and in order to arrest the progress of the Portuguese in India, he endeavoured to inspire a fear with regard to the holy places, which had so long been, and still were, objects of veneration for the faithful of the West. He threatened to raze to the ground the church of the Holy Sepulchre, to cast the ashes and monuments of the martyrs to the winds, and to force all the Christians of his states to abjure the faith of Christ. A Cordelier of Jerusalem came to Rome to express the alarms of the Christians of Palestine, and of the guardians of the holy tomb. The pope was seized with terror, and hastened to send the Cordelier to the king of Portugal, whom he conjured to make the sacrifice of his new conquests to God and Christendom. The Portuguese monarch received the envoy of the pope and the Oriental Christians with kindness, gave him considerable sums for the support of the holy places, and replied to the sovereign pontiff, that he did not at all fear seeing the threats of the sultan carried out, but, on the contrary, he hoped to burn both Mecca and Medina, and bring vast regions under the law of the Gospel, if the princes of Christendom were willing to coöperate with him.

The sultan of Egypt, who received tribute from all pilgrims, did not destroy the churches of Jerusalem, but he attempted an expedition against the Portuguese, in concert with the king of Cambay and Calcutta. They equipped at Suez a fleet composed of six galleys, a galleon, and four storeships, in which were embarked eight hundred Mamelukes. The Egyptian fleet descended along the shores of the Red Sea, coasted Arabia, doubled the Gulf of Persia, and cast anchor at the island and in the port of Diu, one of the most important points for the commerce of India. It is of this expedition the author of the Lusiad speaks in his ninth book: "With the help of the fleets from the port of Arsinoë, the Calicutians hoped to reduce those of Emanuel to ashes; but the arbiter of heaven and earth always finds means to execute the decrees of his profound wisdom."

The expedition of the Mamelukes, notwithstanding the success it at first obtained, produced not the results that the sultan of Cairo and the republic of Venice expected. The Portuguese, in their despair, endeavoured to persuade the king of Ethiopia to divert the course of the Nile. A project for shutting up the new routes of commerce and the passage of the Cape of Good Hope was scarcely more reasonable. Instead of having recourse to arms, the sultans of the Mamelukes would have much better served the interests of Venice, and those of their own power, if they had multiplied canals in their provinces, and opened a commodious, quick, and safe passage for the commerce of India: by that means they would have preserved for the navigation of the Mediterranean the advantage it had enjoyed for ages over the navigation of the ocean; and the maritime cities of Egypt and Italy would not have seen the sources of their prosperity suddenly dried up.

Whilst the republic of Venice contemplated with terror the causes of her future decline, she still inspired considerable jealousy by the splendour of her wealth and magnificence. Many complaints arose against the Venetians, who were universally accused of sacrificing everything to the interests of their commerce, and of betraying or serving the cause of the Christians, as fidelity or treachery became most profitable to them. In a diet which Maximilian convoked at Augsburg, Hélian, the ambassador of Louis XII., pronounced a vehement discourse against the Venetian nation. He reproached them, in the first place, with having thwarted, by their hostility and their intrigues, a league formed by the pope, the emperor of Germany, the king of France, and the king of Arragon, against the Turks. The orator then reproached the Venetians with having refused to succour Constantinople when besieged by Mahomet II. "Their fleet was in the Hellespont during the siege; they could hear the groans of a Christian people, sinking under the sword of the barbarians. Nothing could excite their pity. They remained unaffected and motionless, and when the city was taken,

THE CRUSADERS CROSSING MOUNT TAURUS.

Terror opened to the pilgrims all the passages of Mount Taurus. Throughout their triumphant march the Christians had nothing to dread but famine, the heat of the climate, and the badness of the roads. They had, particularly, much to suffer in crossing a mountain situated between Coxon and Marash, which their historians denominate "THE MOUNTAIN OF THE DEVIL." This mountain was very steep, and offered only one narrow path, in which the foot soldiers marched with difficulty; the horses, which could not keep their footing, dragged each other down the abysses; and the army lost a great part of its baggage. In the course of this disastrous march, says an historian who was an eye-witness, the soldiers gave themselves up to despair, and refused to proceed. Being encumbered with their arms, they either sold them at a low price or cast them down the precipices. On all sides were to be seen warriors wounded by their frequent falls, and pilgrims exhausted with fatigue, who could not continue their route, and filled the air and mountains with their cries and groans.—BOOK II.

they purchased the spoils of the vanquished, and sold to the Mussulmans the unfortunate inhabitants of Greece, who had taken refuge beneath their banners. At a later period, when the Ottomans were besieging Otranto, not only cities and princes, but the mendicant orders, sent assistance to the besieged. The Venetians, whose fleet was then at anchor before Corfu, beheld with indifference, perhaps with joy, the dangers and the misfortunes of a Christian city. No, God cannot pardon a nation, which, by its avarice, its jealousy, and its ambition, has betrayed the cause of Christendom, and appears to maintain an understanding with the Turks, in order to reign with them over the East and over the West." Hélian, on terminating his discourse, pressed the states and the princes to combine their efforts, to execute the decrees of divine justice, and complete the ruin of the republic of Venice.

This discourse, in which the name of Christianity was invoked, but which breathed nothing but vengeance and hatred, made a lively impression upon the assembly. The passions which inflamed the diet of Augsburg, and which left no room for a thought of a war against the Turks, but too plainly showed the state of agitation and discord in which Christendom was then plunged. It is not consistent with our purpose to speak of the league formed, in the first place, against Venice, or of the league afterwards formed against Louis XII., or of the events which brought trouble into Italy, and even into the bosom of the Church, then threatened with a schism.

At the council of the Lateran, convoked by Julius II., the disorders of Christendom were deplored, without the least remedy being proposed for them. They touched upon the war with the Turks, without bestowing any attention upon the means for carrying it on. The exhortations of the pope, which were supposed to be animated by an ambitious policy, inspired no confidence. The pontiff, whom Voltaire represents as a bad priest but a good prince, entered in an active manner into the wars between Christian powers. Since war was carried on in his name, he could not fill the honourable part of a conciliator, and enjoyed no longer the consideration attached to the title of Father of the Faithful. He was not able to reëstablish the peace he had himself broken, and found it impossible to direct an enterprise against the infidels.

The preaching for a crusade, so often repeated, no longer made any impression on men's minds; misfortunes which never arrived had been so often announced to nations, that they ceased to awaken any alarm. After the death of Mahomet, the Turks seemed to have renounced all idea of conquering Europe. Bajazet at first attacked the Mamelukes of Egypt without success; he afterwards sunk into voluptuousness and the pleasures of the seraglio, which gave the Christians a few years of repose and safety. But as an indolent and effeminate prince did not fulfil the first condition of Ottoman despotism, which was war, he irritated the army, and his pacific tastes brought about his fall from the throne. Selim, who succeeded him, more ambitious and more cruel than Mahomet, accused of poisoning his father, and covered with the blood of his family, had scarcely attained empire before he promised to the janissaries the conquest of the world, and threatened, at the same time, Italy, Germany, Persia, and Egypt.

In the twelfth and last sitting of the fifth council of the Lateran, Leo X. took upon him to preach a crusade against the redoubtable emperor of the Ottomans. He ordered to be read before the fathers of the council a letter from the emperor Maximilian, who expressed great grief at seeing Christendom always exposed to the invasions of a barbarous nation.

At the same time the emperor of Germany, writing to his counsellor at the diet of Nuremberg, expressed the desire he had always felt of reëstablishing the empire of Constantine, and delivering Greece from the domination of the Turks. "We would willingly," said he, "have employed our power and even our person in this enterprise, if the other leaders of Christendom had assisted,"

When reading these letters of Maximilian, we might be led to believe that this prince was touched more than others by the misfortunes of the Greeks and the perils of Christendom. But the inconstancy and levity of his character would not allow him to carry on with ardour an enterprise to which he appeared to attach so much importance. He passed his life in forming projects against the Turks, and in making war against Christian powers; and in his old age consoled himself by thinking that the glory of saving Europe might perhaps one day belong to a prince of his family.

Whilst the Christian princes were thus reciprocally exhorting each other to take arms, without any one of them renouncing the interests of his own ambition, or offering an example of a generous devotion, Selim, after having conquered the king of Persia, attacked the army of the Mamelukes, dethroned the sultan of Cairo, and united to his vast dominions all the countries that the Franks had inhabited or possessed in Asia. Jerusalem then beheld the standard of the crescent floating over its walls, and the son of Bajazet, after the example of Omar, profaned by his presence the church of the Holy Sepulchre. Palestine only fell under a fresh domination, and no change took place in the fate of the Christians. But as Europe dreaded the Turks more than the Mamelukes, against whom war had ceased to be carried on, the news of the conquests of Selim spread consternation and grief everywhere. It appeared to Christendom as if the holy city passed for the first time under the yoke of the infidels; and the sentiments of grief and mourning that the Christians then experienced, necessarily revived the idea of delivering the tomb of Christ.

We must add that the late victories of Selim completed the overthrow of all the powers in the East that had rivalled the Turks, and that whilst increasing in a fearful manner the strength of the Ottoman empire, they left it no other enemies to contend with but the nations of the West.

Leo X. contemplated seriously the dangers which threatened Christendom, and resolved to arm the principal powers of Europe against the Turks. The sovereign pontiff announced his project to the college of cardinals. The prelates most distinguished for their learning and their skill in negotiations, were sent into England, Spain, and Germany, with the mission of appeasing all quarrels that divided princes, and forming a powerful league against the enemies of the Christian republic. Leo X., who declared himself beforehand the head of this holy league, proclaimed a truce of five years among all the states of Europe, and threatened those who disturbed the peace with excommunication.

Whilst the pope was thus giving all his attention to preparations for a crusade, the poets and orators, whose labours he encouraged, represented him as already the liberator of the Christian world. The celebrated Vida, in a Sapphic ode addressed to Leo X., sang the future labours and conquests of the pontiff. Carried away by his poetical enthusiasm, he swore to go, clad in shining steel, to the extremities of the world, and to drink from a brazen helmet the waters of the Xanthus and the Indus. He boasts of cutting down with his sword the barbarous heroes of Asia, and fancies that he already sees posterity placing his name among those of warriors who had never known fear. Vida, in his ode, speaks of neither Christ nor the cross, but of Bellona and Apollo. His verses appear to be much less an inspiration of the Gospel than an imitation of Horace; and the praises he addresses to the head of the Christian Church resemble, both in tone and form, those which the bard of the Tiber addressed to Augustus. Whilst Vida, in profane verses, thus felicitated Leo X. upon the laurels he was about to gather amidst the labours and perils of the holy war, another writer not less celebrated, in a prose epistle printed at the head of the Orations of Cicero, addressed the sovereign pontiff with the same congratulations and the same eulogies. Novagero took delight in celebrating beforehand those days of glory in which the pope would return in triumph to the eternal city, after having extended the limits of the Christian world,—those happy days in which all Italy, in which all nations, should revere him as a divinity descended from heaven for their deliverance.

Italy was then filled with fugitive Greeks, amongst whom were some illustrious scholars, who exercised a great influence over men's minds, and never ceased to represent the Turks as a barbarous and ferocious people. The Greek tongue was taught with success in the most celebrated schools, and the new direction of studies, with the admiration which the masterpieces of Greece inspired, added greatly to the hatred of the people for the fierce dominators of Byzantium, Athens, and Jerusalem. Thus all the disciples of Homer and Plato associated themselves, in some sort, by their wishes and their discourses, with the enterprise of the sovereign pontiff. It may have been remarked, that the manner of preaching the crusades, and the motives alleged to excite the ardour of the Christians, differed according to circumstances, and were almost always analogous to the prevailing ideas of each period. In the times of which we now speak, everything naturally bears the character and stamp of the great age of Leo X.; and if the crusade had been able to contribute to the restoration of letters, it was just that letters in their turn should do something in a war undertaken against the enemies of civilization and intelligence.

The envoys of the court of Rome were received with distinction in all the states of Europe, and neglected neither evangelical exhortations, nor seductions, nor promises, nor any of the resources of profane policy, to induce Christian princes to join the crusade proclaimed by the pope. The sacred college rejoiced at the success of their mission, and the pope, to prove his gratitude to Heaven, and to draw down divine blessings upon his enterprise, ordered that processions should be made and prayers put up, during three days, in the capital of the Christian world. He himself celebrated the divine office, distributed alms, and walked barefooted and with his head uncovered to the church of the Holy Apostles.

Sadoletus, secretary to the Holy See, one of the most distinguished favourites of the Muses, and who, in the judgment of Erasmus, possessed in his writings the copiousness and the manner of Cicero, pronounced, in the presence of the clergy and the Roman people, a discourse, in which he celebrated the zeal and the activity of the sovereign pontiff, the eagerness of the Christian princes to make peace with each other, and the desire they evinced to unite their powers against the Turks: the orator reminded his auditory of the emperor of Germany and the king of France, glorious pillars of Christendom; of the army of Charles, king of Castile, whose youth exhibited all the virtues of ripened age; of the king of England, the invincible defender of the faith; of Emanuel, king of Portugal, always ready to sacrifice his own interests to those of the Church; of Louis II., king of Hungary; and Sigismund, king of Poland; the first, a young prince, the hope of Christians; the second, worthy to be their leader; of the king of Denmark, with whose devotion to religion Europe was well acquainted; and of James, king of Scotland, the examples of whose family must keep him in the road of virtue and glory. Among the Christian states, upon which humanity and religion must build their hopes, Sadoletus did not forget the Helvetians, a powerful and warlike nation, which burned with such zeal for the war against the Turks, that its numerous bands of soldiers were already prepared to march, and only waited for the signal of the head of the Church. The holy orator finished by a vehement apostrophe against the race of the Ottomans, whom he threatened with the united forces of Europe, and by an invocation to God, whom he conjured to bless the arms of so many princes, of so many Christian nations, in order that the empire of the world might be wrested from Mahomet, and that the praises of Jesus Christ might at length resound from the south to the north, and from the west to the east.

Leo X. was constantly engaged with the crusade he had preached. He consulted with able captains, and acquired information concerning the strength of the Turks, and upon the means of attacking them with advantage: the most certain means was to raise numerous armies. In his let ters to the princes and the faithful, he exhorted Christians not to neglect prayers and the austerities of penitence; but he recommended them above all things to prepare their arms, and to oppose their redoubtable enemies with strength and valour. In concert with the principal states of Christendom, he laid down the plan of the holy war. The emperor of Germany was to furnish an army to which the Hungarian and Polish cavalry should be united. The king of France, with all his forces, all those of the Venetians, and several states of Italy, and sixteen thousand Swiss, was to embark at Brindisi, and make a descent upon the coast of Greece; whilst the fleets of Spain, Portugal, and England, should set sail from Carthagena and the neighbouring ports, to transport Spanish troops to the shores of the Hellespont. The pope proposed to embark himself at the port of Ancona, to repair to Constantinople, under the walls of which city all the forces of the Christian powers were to meet.

This plan was gigantic, and never would the Ottoman empire have been in greater danger, if such vast designs could have been carried into execution. But the Christian monarchs were only able to observe the truce proclaimed by the pope, and which they had accepted for a very few months; each of them had engaged to furnish for the crusade troops which every day became more necessary to them in their own states, and which they wished to aggrandize or defend. The old age of Maximilian, and the approaching vacancy of the imperial throne, at that time held all the ambitious in a state of expectation: very shortly the rivalry of Charles V. and Francis I. rekindled war in Europe, and Christendom, disturbed by the quarrels of princes, no longer thought it probable they should be invaded by the Turks.

But these political dissensions were not the only obstacles to the execution of the projects of Leo X. Another difficulty arose from the levy of the tenths. The clergy everywhere appeared to have the same indifference for the wars which ruined them. The people dreaded to see their alms employed in enterprises which had not for object the triumph of religion. The legate of the pope in Spain addressed himself first to the Arragonese, who replied by a formal refusal, expressed in a national synod. Cardinal Ximenes declared, in the name of the king of Castile, that the Spaniards did not believe in the threats of the Turks, and that they would not give their money until the pope had positively announced how he would employ it. If the dispositions and the will of the court of Rome found less resistance and occasioned no troubles in England or France, it was because Cardinal Wolsey, minister of Henry VIII., was associated in the mission of the apostolic legate, and that Leo X. abandoned the tenths of his kingdom to Francis I.

We have before us several historical documents which have never been printed, and which throw a great light upon the circumstances of which we are speaking. The first is a letter from Francis I., dated from Amboise, the 16th of December, 1516, by which *Master Josse de Lagarde, doctor in theology, vicar-general of the cathedral church of Thoulouse*, is named commissary, *touching the fact of the crusade in the diocese*. The king of France exposes in another letter the aim of the jubilate that is about to be opened: *it was to implore means to make war against the infidels, and conquer the Holy Land and the empire of Greece, detained and usurped by the said infidels*. To these letters patent are joined instructions given by the king, in concert with the legate of the pope, for the execution of the bull which orders the preaching of the crusade in the kingdom of France during the two years 1517 and 1518. These instructions, in the first place, recommend the choice of good preachers, charged *to make good and devout sermons to the people, and to explain the faculties and dispensations which are contained in the bull*, as well as why *the just and holy causes for which it is ordered, that during two years all other indulgences, all other general and particular pardons, are suspended and revoked*.

After having spoken of the choice of preachers, and of the manner in which they ought to preach, the letters patent of the king give some instructions upon the choice of confessors. The commissary-general of the crusade could appoint as many as seemed necessary to him for every church in which were *troncs et questes* (poor-boxes and gatherings) for the jubilee. He was commanded to name six for the cathedral of the diocese, *gens de bonne conscience, hors de suspicion* (worthy people, above suspicion). The ecclesiastics thus chosen by the commissary had the mission to confess all such as were desirous of indulgences; and to avoid the disorders that might arise from the spirit of rivalry, they had, to the exclusion of all others, the power to make compositions and restitutions, and give absolutions, &c., &c.

In short, the royal ordinance omitted none of the circumstances which accompanied the preaching of a crusade, or of the forms which ought to be adopted in the distribution of indulgences. It goes so far as to regulate the shape of the *troncs* placed in the churches to receive the offerings of the faithful, and the religious ceremonies that were to be observed during the jubilee.* Among other orders, one commanded that a great number of confessionals, or bills of absolution and indulgence, should be made; that these bills, signed by a notary, should be sent to the commissary-general, who would seal them WITH HIS SEAL sent by the king, and that there should be left upon them a blank space for the name of him or her who wished to procure them. The royal instruction added, that the commissary should cause his *tronc* to be properly and handsomely set up, and that there should be in the centre of it a large handsome cross, upon which should be written, in great, fair letters, IN HOC SIGNO VINCES. In order that nothing might be wanting to excite the people to devotion, it was besides ordered, that solemn processions should be made, and that in them a handsome banner should be carried, upon which should be, on one side, the portraits of the pope and the king of France, and on the other, *paintings full of Turks and other infidels*.

In this ordinance, of which it gives us great pleasure to recall the spirit and the expressions, that which history particularly observes, is the numerous precautions against infidelity and fraud. The distributors of the indulgences were obliged to consult an assessment for their government in all expenses and reinstatements. The *troncs*, in which the money of the faithful was deposited, had three locks and three keys, and were only to be opened in the presence of witnesses; among the documents we have quoted, is one which is the legal order for the opening of the *troncs*, with an account rendered of the receipts and expenditure, in which the most minute details are not neglected, and which shows to what a degree exactitude and watchfulness were carried. These rigorous precautions were the more necessary, from the people being led to be suspicious by the examples of past times; it was pretty well known that many of the collectors of the money for the crusades were not *people of worth, and above suspicion*. The more sacred the motive for levying this tribute was said to be, the more promptly was suspicion awakened; and the more anxious did charity itself appear as to the manner in which its offerings might be expended. Upon this point, as upon others, authority had so much the more necessity for keeping a severe watch, from there always being among the orators of the crusades some who showed more zeal than wisdom, and whose preachings were really a subject of scandal. As most of them received a salary proportionate with the amount of money dropped into the *troncs* of the churches, many did not hesitate to exaggerate the promises of the sovereign pontiff and the privileges attached to gifts of charity. History gives us the example of a preacher who put forth from the evangelical pulpit the following culpable maxim: *When a piece of money shall be placed in the tronc of the crusade for the deliverance of a soul from purgatory, immedi-*

---

* This is the passage of the ordinance that relates to the banners that were to be carried in procession:—"There shall be made, at the same time, a handsome banner, upon which shall be painted our holy father the pope, in his full pontificals, accompanied by several cardinals and other prelates, being in pontificals, and mitred with white mitres; the pope shall be on the dexter, the king on the sinister, armed completely in white except his armour of state, which shall be borne by his squire, accompanied by several princes and other lords, all armed; on the other side of the said banner, histories and other pictures, full of Turks and other infidels."

ately that soul will be delivered, and will fly away towards heaven. The Faculty of Theology of Paris censured this proposition as contrary to the dogmas of the Church. The prudence of the heads of the Gallican Church, and the wise measures adopted by the king of France, thus prevented great disorders. It was not so in Germany, where the greatest excitement and dissatisfaction prevailed, and where seeds of heresy and trouble began to spring up even in the bosom of the clergy.

It may have been observed, how much more easy the court of Rome had hitherto daily made the opening of the treasury of pontifical indulgences. In the early expeditions to the East, these indulgences were only granted to the pilgrims of the Holy Land. They were afterwards granted to all who contributed to the support of the Crusaders. Still later, they were granted to the faithful who listened to the sermons of the preachers of the crusades; sometimes even to those who were present at the mass of the pope's legates. As the distribution or sale of indulgences was an inexhaustible source of wealth, Leo X. took upon him to grant them not only to those who, by their alms, were willing to aid in defraying the expenses of the war against the Turks, but to all the faithful whose pious liberality should contribute to the amount necessary for the completion of the building of the church of St. Peter, which had been begun by his predecessor Julius II. Although this destination might have something noble and truly useful in it; although it might be worthy, in some sort, of an age in which the arts burst forth with great splendour, many Christians, particularly in Germany, saw nothing in it but an actual profanation, and a new means by which the court of Rome sought to enrich itself at the expense of the faithful.

Albert, archbishop of Mayence, charged with appointing the preachers of the jubilee and the distributors of papal indulgences, named for Saxony, Dominicans, to the exclusion of Cordeliers or Augustines, who had sometimes filled these kinds of missions. The latter showed themselves jealous of this preference; and as no precaution had been taken either to avert the effects of this species of rivalry, or put a stop to the abuses which might be committed, it happened that the Augustines censured severely the conduct, manners, and opinions of the Dominicans, and that the latter but too well justified the complaints of their adversaries.

Luther, an Augustine monk, put himself forward in these violent quarrels, and distinguished himself by his fervid eloquence;[*] he spoke strongly against the preachers that had been selected to receive the contributions of the faithful; and among the propositions he put forth from the pulpit, history has preserved the following, which was censured by Leo X.: "It is a sin to resist the Turks, seeing that Providence makes use of this faithless nation, to visit the iniquities of his people." This strange maxim obtained faith amongst the partisans of Luther; and when the pope's legate demanded, at the diet of Ratisbon, the levy of the tenths destined for the crusade, he met with a warm opposition. Murmurs and complaints arose in all parts of Germany. The court of Rome was reproached with putting holy things up for sale: it was compared to the unfaithful shepherd, who shears the sheep confided to his care; it was accused of despoiling credulous people; of ruining nations and kings; and of accumulating upon Christians more miseries than the domination of the Turks could cause them.

For more than a century, these kinds of accusations resounded throughout Germany, every time that money was raised for crusades; or that any tribute whatever was imposed upon the Christians by the sovereign pontiff. The reformers took advantage of this disposition of men's minds to circulate new ideas, and to attempt a revolution in the Church. Among a nation led by its genius and

---

[*] Some writers have pretended, against the opinion of Bossuet and David Hume, that Luther was not drawn into his opposition by a motive of jealousy, and by a sentiment of self-love. In spite of their objections, the fact is demonstrated. The learned Mosheim, in his history, has not thought proper to justify Luther on this head; which is besides of very little importance.

character to speculative ideas, philosophic and religious novelties were sure to find more warm partisans and ardent apostles than elsewhere. It must likewise be added, that Germany was one of the countries of Christendom that Rome had, in its omnipotence, spared the least; and that the spirit of opposition had *there* taken rise, amidst long quarrels between the priesthood and the empire. When once the tie that united the minds of people was broken, and the yoke of an authority consecrated by time was shaken off, opposition knew no bounds; there was no longer a limit to opinions: the Church was attacked on all sides at once, and by a thousand different sects, all opposed to the court of Rome, and most of them opposed to each other. From that period burst forth that revolution which was destined to separate forever many nations of Christendom from the Romish communion.

It is not our task to describe the events which accompanied the schism of Luther; but it is curious to observe, that the origin of the Reformation should be connected, not directly with the crusades, but with the abuse of the indulgences promulgated for the crusades.

Like all who begin revolutions, Luther was not at all aware of the extent to which his opposition to the court of Rome might be carried: he at first began by attacking some abuses of the pontifical authority, and soon finished by attacking the authority itself. The opinions he had kindled by his eloquence, the passions he had given birth to among his disciples, led him himself much further than he could possibly have foreseen: those who had the greatest reason to combat the doctrines of the reformers saw, no more than he did, what those doctrines were to bring with them. Germany, divided into a thousand different states, and given up to all kinds of disorders, had no authority sufficiently strong and sufficiently prescient to anticipate the effects of a schism. At the court of Rome nobody could have believed that a simple monk could ever shake the pillars of the Church. Amidst the pomp and the splendour of the arts which he patronized, and diverted by the cares of an ambitious policy, Leo X. perhaps was too neglectful of the progress of Luther. Above all, he was wrong in entirely abandoning the expedition against the Turks, which he had announced to the Christian world, and which might, at least at the first, have offered a useful distraction to minds agitated by ideas of reformation. The undertaking of a holy war which he had followed up with so much warmth at the beginning of his pontificate, and for which the poets promised him eternal glory,—this enterprise, at his death, no longer engaged his thoughts, or those of his contemporaries.

In the mean time Soliman, the successor of Selim, had recently taken possession of Belgrade, and threatened the isle of Rhodes. This isle was then the last colony of the Christians in Asia. As long as the Knights of St. John remained masters of it, the sultan of the Turks had reason to fear that some great expedition might be formed in the West for the recovery of Palestine and Syria, or even for the conquest of Egypt, which had lately been united to the Ottoman empire.

The grand master of the Hospitallers sent to solicit the assistance of Christian Europe. Charles V. had just united, in his own person, the imperial crown with that of the Spains. Entirely occupied with opposing the power of France, and anxious to draw Pope Adrian VI. into a war against the most Christian king, the emperor was very little affected by the danger which threatened the Knights of Rhodes. The sovereign pontiff did not dare to succour them, or solicit for them the support of Christendom. Francis I. exhibited more generous sentiments; but in the situation in which his kingdom was then placed, he was unable to send them the assistance he had promised.

The Knights of Rhodes were left to their own resources. History has celebrated the labours and the prodigies of heroism by which the order of the Hospitallers illustrated its defence. After many months of combats, Rhodes fell into the hands of Soliman. It was a sad spectacle to behold the grand master L'Isle-Adam, the father of his knights and of his subjects, dragging with him the sad remains of the order, and all the people of Rhodes, who had determined to follow him. He landed at first upon the coast of Naples, not far from the spot where Virgil makes the pious Æneas land, with the glorious wreck of Troy. If the spirit of the crusades could have revived, what heart could have remained unmoved, at seeing this venerable old man, followed by his faithful companions in misfortune, seeking an asylum, imploring compassion, and soliciting, as a reward of their past services, a little corner of earth upon which he and his warriors might still unfurl the standard of religion, and combat the infidels.

When the grand master set forward on his march towards Rome, Adrian VI. had declared war against the king of France; a league was formed by the sovereign pontiff, the emperor, the king of England, and the duke of Milan. In this state of affairs, the Christians of the East could not hope for any succour. After the death of Adrian, Pope Clement VII. showed himself more favourable to the order of the Hospitallers. He received the grand master with all the demonstrations of a paternal tenderness. When the chancellor of the order related, in the consistory, the exploits and the reverses of the knights, the sovereign pontiff and the Romish prelates shed tears, and promised to interest all the powers of the Christian world for such noble sufferers. Unfortunately for the order of St. John, the powers of Europe were more than ever divided among themselves. Francis I. was made prisoner at the battle of Pavia. The pope, who had wished to resume the old papal title of the conciliator, only drew down upon himself the hatred and the anger of Charles V. Amidst these divisions, the Knights of Rhodes were forgotten; and it was not till ten years after the conquest of Soliman, that these noble warriors were able to obtain from the emperor, the rock of Malta, where they became again the terror of the Mussulmans

Whilst Europe was thus troubled, the conqueror of Rhodes and Belgrade reappeared in a threatening attitude upon the banks of the Danube. Louis II. endeavoured to reanimate the patriotism of the Hungarians, and caused the old custom of exposing in public a bloody sabre to be revived, as a signal of war and of danger for the country. But neither the exhortations of the monarch, nor those of the clergy, nor even the approach of the enemy, were able to appease the discords, born of feudal anarchy and the lengthened misfortunes of Hungary. The Hungarian monarch was only able to get together an army of twenty-two thousand men, to oppose to that of Soliman. Louis, a young prince without experience, who allowed himself to be led, even in war, by ecclesiastics, named, as general of his army, Paul Temory, lately issued from a convent of Cordeliers, to become archbishop of Colotza. We are unable to ascertain whether, in this circumstance, the king of Hungary was obliged to put himself in the hands of the clergy, because he was abandoned by the nobility; or, if the nobility abandoned him, because he had put himself in the hands of the clergy. As the pope constantly excited the Hungarians to defend their own country, the ecclesiastics of Hungary, who were his interpreters to the faithful, and even to the king, must naturally have exercised a great influence in all that concerned the crusade.

In this war twenty-two thousand Christians had to contend with an army of a hundred thousand Ottomans; and this was the Hungarian army which, according to the advice of the bishops, offered battle to the infidels. What is very remarkable in holy wars is, that the clergy may almost always be recognised by the rashness of the enterprises. The persuasion of the ecclesiastics, that they were fighting for the cause of God, with their ignorance of the art of war, prevented them from seeing perils, did not allow them to doubt of victory, and made them often neglect the means of human prudence. It was then, in the confidence of a miraculous success, that the archbishop of Colotza did not hesitate to venture upon a decisive battle. The clergy who accompanied him animated the combatants by their discourses, and set an example of bravery; but religious and warlike enthusiasm cannot tri-

AN ENEMY OF THE CRUSADERS.

The fountain of Siloe, which only flowed at intervals, could not suffice for such a multitude. A skinful of fetid water, brought from a distance of three leagues, cost as much as three silver deniers. Overcome by thirst and heat, the soldiers turned up the soil with their swords, and burying themselves in the freshly-moved earth, eagerly carried to their lips every moist clod that presented itself. During the day they looked anxiously for the night, and at night longed for the break of day, in the constantly disappointed hope that the return of either the one or the other would bring some little freshness, or a few drops of rain. Every morning they were seen to glue their parched lips to the marbles covered with dew. During the heat of the day the most robust languished beneath their tents, seeming not to have even strength left to implore the assistance of heaven.

When some fortunate pilgrims discovered a spring or a cistern, in a remote or obscure place, they concealed it from their companions, and prevented their approach to it. Quarrels of a violent nature broke out on this account daily; and not unfrequently the Crusaders drew their swords for the sake of a little muddy water; in short, the want of water was so insupportable an evil, that they hardly noticed the scarcity of food. The intensity of thirst and the heat of the climate made them forget the horrors of the famine which seemed to pursue the Christians everywhere.

[BOOK IV.

umph over numbers, and most of the prelates received the palm of martyrdom in the *mêlée*. Eighteen thousand Christians were left upon the field of battle; and what added greatly to the misfortune, Louis II. disappeared, and perished in the general rout, leaving his kingdom torn by factions and ravaged by the Turks.

The defeat of the Hungarians brought despair to the mind of Clement VII. The pontiff wrote to all the sovereigns of Europe; he even formed the project of visiting them in person, and to engage them by his prayers and his tears to defend Christendom. Neither the touching exhortations of the pope, nor his suppliant attitude, were able to move the princes; and it is here that we can plainly perceive the rapid decline of the pontifical power, which we have so lately seen armed with all the terrors of the Church, and whose decisions were considered as the decrees of Heaven. War was about to be rekindled in Italy, and the pope was not long in becoming himself the victim of the disorders he would willingly have prevented. The imperial troops entered Rome as into an enemy's city. The emperor, who assumed the title of temporal head of the Church, did not fear to offer to Europe the scandal of the captivity of a pontiff.

Although the authority of the head of the Church no longer inspired the same veneration, or exercised the same ascendancy over men's minds, nevertheless the violences of Charles V. excited general indignation. England and France flew to arms. All Europe was troubled: some wished to avenge the pope, others to take advantage of the disorder; but none thought of defending Christendom against the invasion of the Turks.

Clement VII., however, from the depths of the prison in which the emperor detained him, still watched over the defence of Christian Europe: his legates went to exhort the Hungarians to fight for their God and their country. As the pontiff had been ruined by the calamities of war, he implored the charity of the faithful; he ordered that the plate should be sold in all the churches of Italy; he solicited the assistance of several Italian states; and he ordered that indulgences might be distributed and the tenths collected to support the expenses of the holy war.

The active solicitude of the pope went so far as to seek enemies against the Turks even in the East and among the infidels. Acomath, who had in Egypt shaken off the yoke of the Porte, received encouragement from the court of Rome. A legate of the pope went to promise him the support of the Christians of the West. The sovereign pontiff kept up continual relations on all the frontiers and in all the provinces of the Turkish empire, in order to be made aware of the designs and preparations of the sultans of Constantinople. It is not out of place to say here, that most of the predecessors of Clement had taken, as he did, the greatest care in watching the projects of the infidels. Thus the heads of the Church did not confine themselves to exciting the Christians to defend themselves upon their own territories; but, like vigilant sentinels, they constantly kept their eyes fixed upon the enemies of Christendom, to warn Europe of the perils which threatened it.

When the emperor broke the chains of Clement VII., the holy pontiff forgot the outrages he had received, to give all his cares to the danger of the German empire, which was about to be attacked by the Turks. The capital of Austria was soon besieged, and only owed its safety to the bravery of its garrison. In the diets of Augsburg and Spire, the pope's legate endeavoured, in the name of religion, to rouse the ardour of the people of Germany for their own defence. A physician, named Riccius, spoke in the name of the emperor, and added his exhortations to those of the apostolic legate; he made an appeal to the ancient virtue of the Germans, and reminded his auditors of the example of their ancestors, who had never endured a foreign domination. He pressed princes, magistrates, and people, to fight for their own independence and safety. Ferdinand, king of Bohemia and Hungary, urged the princes and states of the empire to adopt prompt and effective measures against the Turks. These exhortations and counsels met with but little success, but had to encounter a strong opposition from the still too active spirit of the new doctrines. All the cities, all the provinces, were occupied by questions agitated by the Reformation. We may at this time compare the nations of Germany, menaced by the Turks, to the Greeks of the lower empire, whom history represents as given up to vain disputes, when the barbarians were at their gates. As among the Greeks, there was a crowd of men among the Germans, who entertained less dread of seeing in their cities the turban of Mahomet than the tiara of the pontiff of Rome; some, governed by a spirit of fatalism scarcely to be equalled in the Koran, asserted that God had judged Hungary, and that the safety of that kingdom was not in the power of men; others (the Millenarians) announced with a fanatical joy the approach of the last judgment; and whilst the preachers of the crusades were exhorting the Germans to defend their country, the jealous pride of an impious sect called for the days of universal desolation.

The paternal proceedings and counsels of the pope were neither able to calm men's minds, nor to rekindle an enthusiasm for the holy war, in Germany, or even among the Hungarians. Ferdinand, brother of Charles V., whom the imperial power had caused to be declared king of Hungary; and the vaiwode of Transylvania, who, with permission of the Turks, reigned over the ruins of his country, were contending for this unfortunate kingdom, oppressed at the same time by its enemies and its allies. When Soliman returned, for the third time, to the banks of the Danube, called thither by a party of the Hungarian nobility, he found no army to oppose his march. The Ottomans advanced towards the capital of Austria, and prepared to invade the richest provinces of Germany. So pressing a danger determined the head and the princes of the empire to unite their forces against the common enemy. But when the Turks retired in disorder, no one thought of either fighting with them, or pursuing them in their precipitate retreat. The king of Hungary, abandoned all at once by the Germans, and fearing fresh attacks, had no resource but to sue to his enemies for peace. It is a circumstance worthy of remark, that the pope was comprised in the treaty: Soliman gave the title of father to the Roman pontiff, and that of brother to the king of Hungary. Clement VII., after so many useless attempts to interest the princes of Christendom, appeared to entertain no hope but in Providence; and exclaimed with bitterness, when approving the issue of the pacific negotiations, "We have nothing left but to supplicate Heaven to watch itself over the Christian world."

It might be believed that the holy wars were drawing towards an end, when the head of the Church had laid down his arms, and made peace with the infidels. But this treaty of peace, like others that had preceded it, could only be considered as a truce, and war would most likely break out again when either the Christians or the Mussulmans saw any hopes of carrying it on with advantage. Such was the policy of the times; particularly that which governed the Christian and Mussulman powers in their mutual relations. Soliman had abandoned his projects upon Germany and Hungary, less out of respect for treaties, than because he was employing his forces against the Persians, or that he required his army to quell some revolts which had broken out in Asia against his authority. On the other side, Christendom left the Ottomans in peace, because it was a prey to discord; and because most Christian princes, occupied by their own interests, listened to nothing but the counsels of their ambition.

Europe had at that time three great monarchs, whose united strength would have been quite sufficient to crush the power of the Turks; but these three princes were as much opposed to each other by their policy as by their character and their genius. Henry VIII. of England, who had refuted Luther, and leagued himself with the king of France, to deliver the captive pope, had just separated himself from the Romish Church. Sometimes allied with France, sometimes allied with the emperor, occupied in bringing about the triumph of the schism of which he was the apostle and the head, he had no time to bestow upon war with the infidels. Francis I. had, in the first place, made pretensions to the imperial crown, and afterwards to the duchy of Milan and the kingdom of Naples. These pretensions, which were a source of misfortunes to himself and France, disturbed the whole of his reign, and never allowed him an opportunity for seriously undertaking a crusade against the Turks, a crusade which he himself had preached in his states. The feeling of vengeance and jealousy which animated him against a fortunate and powerful rival, inspired him twice with the idea of seeking an alliance with Soliman. To the great scandal of Christendom, an Ottoman fleet was received in the port of Marseilles, and the standard of the lilies was mingled with the crescent under the walls of Nice. Charles V., master of all the Spains, head of the German empire, sovereign of the Low Countries, and possessor of several empires in the new world, was much more anxious to humble the French monarchy, and establish his domination in Europe, than to defend Christendom against the invasion of the Turks. During the greater part of his reign, this monarch conciliated the Protestants of Germany, on account of the Ottomans; and avoided collision with the Ottomans, on account of his enemies in the Christian republic. He satisfied himself with protecting, by his arms, the capital of Austria, when threatened by the Turks; but when the pope conjured him to employ his forces for the deliverance of Hungary, he preferred attempting an expedition to the coast of Africa. A war against the Moors of Africa was more popular in Spain than an expedition upon the Danube; and Charles was more desirous of acquiring popularity among the Spaniards, than of meriting the gratitude of Christendom. The Barbary powers were recently formed, under the protection of the Ottoman Porte, and began to render themselves formidable in the Mediterranean. Charles carried his arms twice to the coast of Africa: in the first expedition, he got possession of Tunis, planted his standards upon the ruins of Carthage, and delivered twenty thousand captives, who went to publish his victories in every part of the Christian world; in his second expedition, he would have annihilated the Barbary powers, so destructive to the navigation of the Franks; but a hurricane, which destroyed his fleet and his army, dispersed the hopes of commerce and navigators.

At the time Charles experienced so great a disaster whilst combating the Mussulmans of Africa, the Ottomans, invited by Francis I., were ravaging the coasts of Italy, and had recently entered Hungary, from whence they threatened Germany.

Then fresh cries of alarm resounded all over Europe, and among those who exhorted the nations to oppose the Turks, the voice of Martin Luther was heard. In a book entitled *Prayer against the Turk*, the reformer condemned the indifference of people and kings, and advised the Christians to resist the Mussulmans, if they did not wish to be led into captivity, as the children of Israel had formerly been. In a formula of prayer which he had composed, he expressed himself thus: "Arise, Lord, great God, and sanctify thy name, which thy enemies outrage; strengthen thy reign, which they wish to destroy, and suffer us not to be trampled under-foot by those who are not willing that thou shouldst be our God."

Murmurs had several times arisen against Luther, who was accused of having, by his doctrines, weakened the courage of the Germans. Some time before the period of which we are speaking, he published an apology, in which, without disavowing the famous proposition censured by the pope, he gave to his words a different sense from that which the court of Rome gave them, and which he himself, no doubt, had given them in the first instance. All his explanations, which it is not very easy to analyze, were reduced to this idea:—" That it was allowable to fight with the Turks, but that it was not allowable to fight with them under the banners of Christianity." Although the leader of the reformation required all the qualities of a perfect Christian in the warriors called upon to fight the Mussulmans, and although he drew all the principles of his preaching from the religion of Christ, the standard of the cross in a Christian army, caused him, he said, more horror than the sight of the demon. The true motive for his repugnance for a crusade may be easily guessed; a crusade appeared necessarily to require the concurrence of the pope; and the concurrence of the pope, in a war which interested Christendom, was the thing in the world most dreaded by Luther. He had so strong an aversion to the court of Rome, that in his writings he asks himself if war ought not to be made against the pope as well as the Turk; and in the excess of his hatred, does not hesitate to answer, *against the one as against the other.*

We will not repeat here the declamations and the sophisms of Luther. Through the puerile subtleties and the contrary reasonings which he employs for his justification, we must, however, remark the distinction he has made between civil authority and ecclesiastical authority: it is to the first, says the reformer, that it belongs to combat the Turks; the duty of the second is to wait, to submit, to pray, and to groan. He adds, that war was not the business of bishops, but of magistrates; that the emperor, in this circumstance, ought to be considered as the head of the German confederation, and not as the protector of the Church, nor as the support of the Christian faith; a title which can only properly be given to Jesus Christ. All these arguments, doubtless, had something reasonable in them; and the opinion of Luther upon the civil authority, although he might have adopted it only out of opposition to the papal power, would have obtained the approbation of enlightened minds, if he had not employed, in supporting it, all the passion of irritated pride; and if his apology, in particular, had not been stained by abuse which decency will not allow history to repeat.

Not content with this apology, which had for title, *Of the War against the Turks,* Luther, two years after the siege of Vienna, published another work, entitled, *A Military Discourse,* in which he also urges the Germans to take arms. This second discourse begins, as the first had done, by theological distinctions and subtleties; by declamations against the pope and the bishops; by predictions upon the approaching end of the world; and upon the power of the Turks; which the author finds clearly announced in Daniel. Although he endeavours to prove, as in his first writing, that the war against the Mussulmans is not at all a religious war, but an enterprise entirely political; he promises, not the less, the palms of martyrdom to those who shall die with arms in their hands. He represents this war as agreeable to the Divinity, and as the duty of a true disciple of the Gospel. "Thy arm and thy lance," says he to every Christian soldier who shall take arms against the infidels, "shall be the arm and the lance of God. In immolating Turks, thou wilt not shed innocent blood, and the world will consider thee as the executioner of the decrees of divine justice; for thou wilt but kill those whom God has himself condemned. The Turk," adds he, "ravishes terrestrial life from Christians, and procures them eternal life; he at the same time kills himself, and precipitates himself into hell." Luther appears to be so penetrated with this idea, that he is on the point of deploring the fate of the Mussulmans; and to chastise indifferent Christians, and pusillanimous Germans, he has no punishment to wish them, unless it be that they should become Turks, and thus be the property of the devil.

A short extract is not sufficient to show what whimsical and singular ideas are contained in Luther's discourse; it may, however, be easily perceived how much this kind of preaching differs from that of the orators who preached the crusade in preceding ages. In the second part of his discourse, the leader of the Reformation addressed himself to the various classes of society; to the nobility, who are immersed in luxury and pleasures, but for whom the hour of fight is at length come; to the citizens and merchants, for too long a time addicted to usury and cupidity; to the labourers and peasants, whom he accuses of deceiving and robbing their neighbours. The tone of the preacher is full of an excessive severity; he speaks like a man who feels no sorrow at the misfortunes which are about to happen, because he has foretold them, and his warnings and prophecies have been despised. He says, with a sort of satisfaction, that after days of joy and debauchery, after seasons of festivity and pleasures, comes the time of tears, miseries, and alarms. He finishes by a vehement apostrophe, addressed to all who shall remain deaf to his voice, and whom the enemy shall find without defence: " Listen now, then, to the devil in the Turk, you who are not willing to listen to God in Jesus Christ; the Turk will burn your dwellings; he will bear away your cattle and your harvests; he will outrage and slaughter your wives and your daughters before your eyes; he will impale your little children upon the very stakes of the hedge which serves as an inclosure to your heritage; he will immolate you yourselves, or will carry you away into Turkey, to expose you in the market, like unclean animals; it is he who will teach you what you will have lost, and what you ought to have done. It is to the Turk belongs the task to humble the haughty nobility, to render citizens docile, and to chastise and tame the gross multitude."

Luther then gives his advice upon the manner of making war against the Turks; he is desirous that all should defend themselves even to death, and that all the countries through which the enemy was about to pass should be laid waste; he terminates his discourse by addressing consolations to them who shall fall into the hands of the Turks, and traces out for them a plan of conduct for the time of their captivity among the infidels.

This language, of which we are far from exaggerating the singularity, was not at all calculated to warm and rally men's minds for a struggle against the enemies of Germany and Christendom. At this period, the princes and the states of the empire frequently met to deliberate on their own dangers. It was more easy to convoke diets than to get together armies. The Protestants were not willing to take arms against the Turks, for fear of strengthening their adversaries; and the Catholics were restrained by their fear of the Protestants: amidst the violent debates that agitated Germany, the Church, and even the civil authority which Luther had proclaimed, lost all that unity of action, without which it is impossible to combat a formidable enemy with advantage. Among the Germans, the spirit of sect weakened by degrees the spirit of patriotism; among Christians, the hatred they conceived for one another caused them to lose that pious ardour which had animated them against the Mussulmans. In proportion as the Reformation proceeded, Germany became divided into two parties, which were like two enemies face to face. Both parties soon had recourse to arms, and, in the fury of civil wars, the invasions of the Turks were forgotten. It was thus that the Reformation, which took its birth at the end of the crusades, completely extinguished the enthusiasm for holy wars, and no longer permitted the nations of Christendom to unite against the infidels.

The name of the Turks was still pronounced in the diets of Germany, and even in the council of Trent; but no measures were adopted for making war against them. From that time there passed nothing in either Hungary or the East which was able to fix the attention of the Christian world. The only event upon which Europe seemed interested was the defence of Malta against all the forces of Soliman. This defence increased the reputation of the military order of St. John. The port of Malta became the only place of shelter for Christian vessels on the route to Egypt, Syria, or Greece. The corsairs of Tunis and Algiers, and all the pirates who infested the Mediterranean, trembled at the sight of the rock, and of the galleys over which floated the standard of the cross. This military colony, always armed against the infidels, and constantly recruited from the warlike nobility of Europe, offered, up to the end of the eighteenth century, a living image of ancient chivalry, and of the heroic epoch of the crusades. We have described the origin of this illustrious order,—we have followed it in its days of triumph, and in its reverses, still more glorious than its victories. We will not say by what revolution it is fallen, nor how it has lost that isle which was given to it as the reward of its bravery, and which it defended, during more than two hundred years, against the Ottoman forces and the barbarians of Africa.

Whilst the Turks miscarried in their expedition against Malta, Soliman was pursuing the war in Hungary, and still threatening Germany. He died on the banks of the Danube, in the midst of victories obtained over the Christians. Christendom must have rejoiced at his death, as it had rejoiced at the death of Mahomet II. Under the reign of Soliman, who was the greatest prince of the Ottoman dynasty, the Turks not only invaded a part of the German empire, but their marine, seconded by the genius of Barberossa and Dragut, made a progress that must have alarmed all the maritime powers of Europe. Selim II., who succeeded him, had neither his qualities nor the genius of most of his predecessors; but he followed not the less their projects of aggrandizement, or the views of their ambitious policy. The Ottomans, masters of the coasts of Greece, Syria, and Africa, were desirous of adding to their conquests the kingdom of Cyprus, which was then possessed by the Venetians.

After a siege of several months, the Ottoman army obtained possession of the cities of Famagousta and Nicosia. The Turks stained their victory by cruelties without example. The bravest of the defenders of Cyprus expiated in tortures the glory of an obstinate resistance; and it may be said, it was the executioners that finished the war. The barbarity of the Turks disgusted the Christian nations afresh; and the maritime countries of the West beheld with terror an invasion which threatened to exclude Europeans from every road to the East.

At the approach of the danger, Pope Pius V. exhorted the Christian powers to take up arms against the Ottomans. A confederation was formed, consisting of the republic of Venice, Philip II., king of Spain, and the pope himself, always ready to add the authority of his example to his preaching. A numerous fleet, equipped for the defence of the isle of Cyprus, arrived too late in the Eastern seas, and was only able to repair the disgrace of the Christian arms. This fleet, commanded by Don John of Austria, met that of the Ottomans in the Gulf of Lepanto. It was in this sea Antony and Augustus disputed the mastership of the Roman world. The battle which took place between the Christians and the Turks reminds us in some degree of the spirit and enthusiasm of the crusades. Before the commencement of the conflict, Don John hoisted on board his ship the standard of St. Peter, which he had received from the pope, and the army saluted with cries of joy this religious signal of victory. The leaders of the Christians passed along the line of barques, exhorting the soldiers to fight for the cause of Christ. All the warriors, falling upon their knees, implored divine protection, and arose full of confidence in their own bravery and the miracles of heaven.

No naval battle of antiquity can be compared to this of Lepanto, in which the Turks fought for the empire of the world, and the Christians for the defence of Europe. The courage and skill of Don John and the other leaders, the intrepidity and ardour of the soldiers, and the superiority of the Franks in manœuvring their vessels, and in their artillery, procured for the Christian fleet a decisive victory. Two hundred of the enemy's ships were taken, burnt, or sunk. The wreck of the Turkish fleet, whilst announcing the victory of the Christians, carried consternation to the coasts of Greece and to the capital of the Ottoman empire.

Terrified by the results of this battle, Selim caused the famous castle of the Dardanelles to be built, which to the present day defends the entrance to the canal of Constantinople. At the time of the battle, the roof of the temple of Mecca fell in, and the Turks believed they saw in this accident a sign of the anger of Heaven. The roof was of wood; and that it might become, says Cantemir, a more solid emblem of the empire, the son of Soliman ordered it to be reconstructed of brick.

Whilst the Turks deplored the first reverse their arms had met with, the whole of Christendom learnt the news of the victory of Lepanto with the greatest joy. The Venetians, who had awaited in terror the issue of the battle, celebrated the triumph of the Christian fleet by extraordinary festivities. In order that no feeling of sadness should be mingled with the universal joy, the senate set all prisoners at liberty, and forbade the subjects of the republic to wear mourning for their relations or friends who had been killed fighting against the Turks. The battle of Lepanto was inscribed upon coins, and as the infidels were defeated on the day of St. Justin, the seigneury ordered that this happy day should be every year a festival for the whole population of Venice.

At Toledo, and in all the churches of Spain, the people and the clergy offered up hymns of gratitude to Heaven for the victory it had granted to the valour of the Christian soldiers. No nation, no prince of Europe, was indifferent to the defeat of the Turks; and, if one historian may be believed, the king of England, James I., celebrated in a poem the glorious day of Lepanto.

As the pope had effectively contributed to the success of the Christian arms, it was at Rome that the strongest symptoms of delight were exhibited. Mark Antony Colonna, who had commanded the vessels of the sovereign pontiff, was received in triumph, and conducted to the Capitol, preceded by a great number of prisoners of war. The ensigns taken from the enemy were suspended in the church of Ara-Cœli. After a solemn mass, Mark Antony Mureti pronounced the panegyric of the triumphant general. Thus the ceremonies of ancient Rome were mingled with those of the modern, to celebrate the valour and exploits of the defenders of Christendom. The Church itself was desirous of consecrating a victory gained over its enemies among its festivals; Pius V. instituted one in honour of the Virgin, by whose intercession it was believed the Mussulmans had been conquered. This festival was celebrated on the 7th October, the day of the battle of Lepanto, under the denomination of "Our Lady of Victories."

Thus a unanimous concert of prayers and thanksgivings arose towards heaven, and all Christians at the same time showed their gratitude to the God of armies for having delivered Europe from the invasion of the Mussulmans. But it was not long before this happy harmony was disturbed: ambition, reciprocal mistrusts, diversity of interests, all that had till that time favoured the progress of the Turks, prevented the Christians from deriving the proper advantages from their victory. The Venetians were anxious to pursue the war, in order to recover the isle of Cyprus; but Philip II., dreading any increase in the power of Venice, withdrew from the confederation. The Venetian republic, abandoned by its allies, hastened to make peace. It obtained it by sacrificing all the possessions it had lost during the war,—a strange result of victory; by which the vanquished dictated laws to the conqueror, and which plainly shows us to what extent the pretensions of the Turks would have been carried if fortune had favoured their arms.

The war which was terminated by the battle of Lepanto, was the last in which the standard of the cross animated or rallied Christian warriors.

The spirit of the holy wars at first arose from popular opinions. When these opinions became weakened and great powers were formed, all that relates to war or peace became concentrated in the councils of monarchs. No more projects for distant expeditions were formed in public councils; no more warlike enterprises were recommended from the pulpits of the churches, or before assemblies of the faithful. States and princes, placed at the head of human affairs, even when they made war against the Mussulmans, obeyed much less the influence of religious ideas than interests purely political. From that period the enthusiasm of the multitude, and all the passions that had given birth to the crusades, were reckoned as nothing.

The alliance of Francis I. with Soliman was at first a great scandal for all Christendom. The king of France justified himself by accusing the ambition and the perfidy of Charles V. His example was quickly followed by Charles himself, and by other Christian states. Policy, disengaging itself more and more from that which was religious in it, came at last to consider the Ottoman Porte, no longer an enemy against whom it was a duty always to be fighting, but as a great power, whom it was sometimes necessary to conciliate, and whose support might be sought without outraging the Deity, or affecting the interests of the Church.

As the voice of the sovereign pontiff was always the instrument to summon Christians to take arms against the infidels, the spirit of the crusades necessarily grew weaker as the authority of the popes declined. It may be added, that the political system of Europe was making its development, and the ties and springs which were to found the equilibrium of the Christian republic had an increasing tendency to their establishment. Each state had its plan of defence and aggrandisement, which it followed with a constant activity; all were employed in endeavouring to attain the degree of power, force, and influence to which their position and the fortune of their arms entitled them. Hence those restless ambitions, those mutual mistrusts, that ever active spirit of rivalry, which scarcely ever permitted sovereigns to turn their attention towards distant wars.

Whilst ambition and the desire of increasing and defending their power detained princes in their own states, the people became attached to their homes by the blessings and the enjoyments of a rapidly-rising civilization. In the eleventh century, the Franks, the Normans, and other barbarians from the north, had not quite lost the character and habits of nomadic races, which favoured the rise and the progress of that warlike enthusiasm which had precipitated the Crusaders upon the East. In the sixteenth century, institutions consecrated by time, the precepts of Christianity better understood, respect for ancestry, love of settled property, the constantly increasing wealth of cities, with the progress of industry and of agriculture, had changed the character of the Franks, destroyed their partiality for a wandering life, and had become so many ties to attach them to their country.

In the preceding century the genius of navigation had discovered America and the passage of the Cape of Good Hope. The results of this discovery effected a great revolution in commerce, attracted the attention of all nations, and gave a new direction to the human mind. All the speculations of industry, for so long a time founded upon the crusades, were directed towards America or the East Indies. Great empires, rich climates, offered themselves all at once to the ambition or the cupidity of all who sought for glory, fortune, or adventures—the wonders of a new world made men forgetful of those of the East.

At this so memorable epoch, a general emulation arose in Europe for the cultivation of arts and of letters. The age of Leo X. produced masterpieces of all kinds.* France, Spain, and still more Italy, turned the newly-discovered art of printing greatly to the advantage of knowledge. The splendid geniuses of Greece and Rome were everywhere revived. In proportion as men's minds became enlightened, the new career opened before them expanded. Another enthusiasm succeeded to that of religious enterprises; and the exploits of the heroic times of our history excited much more admiration in our romances and poets, than they created desire in people of the world to imitate them. Then the Epic Muse, whose voice only celebrates distant events, sang the heroes of the holy wars; and the crusades, for the same reason that Tasso became at liberty to adorn the recital of them with all the wealth of his imagination,—the crusades, we say, were no longer anything for Europe but a poetical remembrance.

---

* The fruit became ripe in the age of Leo, and therefore he generally has the merit of the cultivation. Nicholas V. promoted the growth of intelligence and the arts quite as earnestly as Leo, and with more prudence and less pretension. But this is a common error: no age was ever more forgetful that all knowledge is progressive, than the present; we enjoy much, and claim all the merit of it; but very unjustly.—TRANS.

THE BATTLE OF LEPANTO.

This fleet, commanded by Don John of Austria, met that of the Ottomans in the Gulf of Lepanto. It was in this sea Antony and Augustus disputed the mastership of the Roman world. The battle which took place between the Christians and the Turks reminds us in some degree of the spirit and enthusiasm of the Crusades. No naval battle of antiquity can be compared to this of Lepanto, in which the Turks fought for the empire of the world, and the Christians for the defence of Europe. The courage and skill of Don John and the other leaders, the intrepidity and ardour of the soldiers, and the superiority of the Franks in manœuvring their vessels, and in their artillery, procured for the Christian fleet a decisive victory. Two hundred of the enemy's ships were taken, burnt or sunk. The wreck of the Turkish fleet, whilst announcing the victory to the Christians, carried consternation to the coasts of Greece and to the capital of the Ottoman empire.—BOOK XVII.

One fortunate circumstance for Christendom is, that at the period when the crusades, which had for their object the defence of Europe, drew near to their end, the Turks began to lose some part of that military power which they had displayed in their contests with the Christian nations. The Ottomans had at first been, as we have already said, the only nation that kept on foot a regular standing army, which gave it a vast superiority over powers that it was desirous of subduing. In the sixteenth century, most of the great states of Europe had likewise armies which they could at any time bring against their enemies. Discipline and military tactics had made great progress in Christendom; artillery and marine became more perfect in the West every day, whilst the Turks, in all that concerns the art of war, or that of navigation, gathered no advantage from either the lessons of experience, or from the knowledge to which time and circumstances had given birth among their neighbours. We ought to add, that the spirit of superstition and intolerance which the Turks associated with their wars, was very injurious to the preservation and extent of their conquests. When they took possession of a province, they insisted upon making their laws, their customs, and their worship paramount. They must change everything, they must destroy everything, in the country in which they wished to establish themselves; they must either exterminate the population, or reduce it to the impossibility of disturbing a foreign domination. Thus it may be remarked, that, although several times masters of Hungary, they retired from it after every campaign, and were never able, amidst all their victories, to found a colony or make any durable establishment there. The Ottoman population which had sufficed for occupying and enslaving the Greek empire, could not people and preserve more distant countries. It was this, above everything, which saved Germany and Italy from the invasion of the Turks. The Ottomans might, perhaps, have conquered the world if they had been able to impose their manners upon it, or furnish it with inhabitants.

After the battle of Lepanto, although they had preserved the isle of Cyprus, and dictated laws to the republic of Venice, the Turks not the less lost the idea of their being invincible, or that all the world must submit to their arms. It was observed that from that time most of the leaders of Turkish armies or fleets became more timid, and felt less assured of victory, when in the presence of an enemy. Astrologers, who had till then beheld in the phenomena of the heavens the increase and the glory of the Ottoman empire, saw nothing during the reign of Soliman and following reigns but sinister auguries in the aspects of the celestial bodies. We mention astrologers, because their predictions have considerable influence upon the policy of the Turks. It is not improbable that these pretended conjurers did not confine their observations to the celestial bodies, but that they watched the manners and the opinions of the people, and the march of events and affairs. It is for this reason that their prophecies were found true, and that they belong, in some sort, to history.

The spirit of conquest, however, which had so long animated the nation, still subsisted, and sometimes fortune favoured the Ottoman banner with victory.

Towards the end of the sixteenth century, the Turks carried war to both the banks of the Danube and to the frontiers of Persia. Among the Christian warriors who flew to the aid of Germany, the duke of Mercœur, brother of the duke of Mayenne, must not be forgotten; he was followed by a crowd of French soldiers, who had fought against Henry IV., and who went to expiate the crimes of civil war by fighting the infidels. The duke of Mercœur, to whom the emperor Rodolph II. gave the command of the imperial army, gained several advantages over the Ottomans.

Whilst the war was being carried on in Hungary, the king of Persia sent an embassy to the emperor of Germany and the princes of the West, to persuade them to form an alliance with him against the Turks. The Persian ambassadors repaired to the court of the sovereign pontiff, and to those of several Christian powers, conjuring them to declare war against the Ottomans. This embassy of the king of Persia, and the exploits of the French on the Danube, created great uneasiness in the Divan, and an ambassador was sent to the king of France, as the most to be feared of the Christian princes. The letters of credit of the Turkish envoy bore this title: "To the most glorious, magnanimous, and greatest lord of the faith of Jesus, pacificator of the differences which arise among Christian princes, lord of greatness, majesty, and riches, and glorious guide of the greatest, Henry IV., emperor of France." The sultan of the Turks conjured the French monarch, in his letter, to bring about a truce between the Porte and the emperor of Germany, and to recall from Hungary the duke of Mercœur, whose valour and skill brought victory to the banners of the Germans. Henry IV. interrogated the Ottoman ambassador, and asked him why the Turks dreaded the duke of Mercœur so much. The ambassador replied, that a prophecy, credited by the Turks, declared that the sword of the French would drive them from Europe, and overthrow their empire. Henry IV. did not recall the duke of Mercœur: this able captain continued to beat the Ottomans, and having covered himself with glory in the war against the infidels, he was seized, whilst on his return to France, by a purple fever, "which," says Mezerai, "sent him to triumph in heaven."

In their wars against the Christians, the Turks often found themselves on the defensive, which was for them a sign of decline. History remarks that at no period did their reverses cause them more alarm, or their victories more surprise and joy. Their defeats were almost always a signal for sedition and revolt, which the decline of power rendered bold.

And yet the Ottoman empire still carried on war, and advanced like a storm ready to burst. In the middle of the seventeenth century, the isle of Chio, which had belonged to the Genoese, was added to its maritime possessions, and the Turks directed their victorious arms towards Candia, an important colony of the Venetians. At the same time an Ottoman army entered Transylvania, and greatly alarmed Austria.

Pope Alexander VII., pressed by the emperor Leopold I. and by the Venetian senate, endeavoured to form a league among the princes and states of Christendom, and addressed the king of Poland, the king of Spain, and more particularly the king of France, to implore their succour against the Turks.

Louis XIV. yielded to the prayers of the sovereign pontiff, and sent to Rome an ambassador charged to announce to his holiness, that he entered into the confederation of the Christian princes. On the other side, the states of the Germanic empire, which were the allies of France, assembled at Frankfort, and engaged to raise money and troops, promising to unite their efforts with those of the French monarch, for the defence of Christendom.

This generous forwardness on the part of the king of France and his allies merited, no doubt, the gratitude of Leopold; but, what is difficult to be believed, the zeal they showed for the common cause, and which exceeded what was first hoped for, only awakened the jealous uneasiness of the emperor. We have even reason to think that this uneasiness extended to the sovereign pontiff; for his holiness welcomed the propositions of Louis XIV. very coldly; and when the resolutions of the Germanic body reached Rome, Alexander received with indifference news for which any other pope, say the memoirs of the time, would not have failed to go and return solemn thanks in the church of St. Peter or of St. John of the Lateran. The king of France could not dissemble his surprise; and in a letter, which he caused to be written to his ambassador, are these remarkable words: "For the rest, it is more an affair of his holiness than ours; it will suffice for his majesty, for his own satisfaction and his duty towards God, to have made all the advances with respect to this league, that a king, the eldest son of the Church, and the principal defender of religion, could do 'n a danger imminent for Christendom."

It was soon known that the Turks were making progress, and had penetrated into Moravia. The emperor Leopold, at their approach, quitted his capital. The pope then consented to resume the suspended negotiations. But they were resumed with a sentiment of jealousy and reciprocal mistrust, that left no hope of a happy result. Louis XIV., nevertheless, omitted nothing to prove the frankness of his intentions, or to forward the formation of a league. It was then believed that an enterprise against the Turks was the business of all Christendom, and that, in this case, one Christian power alone ought not to decide for peace or war.

We enter into some details here, because these details have not been hitherto generally known, and that present circumstances may give them additional interest. We know, likewise, in the days in which we live, we must search for examples in old remembrances, and often for our true titles to glory likewise.

The emperor could not be reassured by the demonstrations of the French monarch; and the rancour which he retained on account of the treaty of Westphalia, made him forgetful of his own dangers and those of the Germanic body. Louis XIV. engaged to set on foot an army of twenty thousand men, and the confederates of Germany offered as many. Leopold feared this army on his own account. In the end, Louis satisfied himself with furnishing six thousand soldiers, under the command of the count de Coligny and the marquis de la Feuillade. The pope, not to remain neuter in the war against the Mussulmans, granted the emperor a subsidy of 70,000 florins, and the faculty of levying tenths upon all the ecclesiastical property in the Austrian states. All the united succours of Germany, the king of France, and the other confederate states, formed an army of thirty thousand men. This army marched to Hungary. When united to the troops of the emperor, they gained many advantages over the Turks, and defeated them completely at the battle of St. Gothard. The Ottomans solicited a suspension of arms, and the jealous passions which had at first prevented the war being carried on with vigour, allowed the Divan to conclude an advantageous peace.

The Ottomans, thus delivered from a formidable war, were able to direct all their strength against Candia, which Venice, now left alone, was not strong enough to defend. A great number of French warriors then flew to the succour of a Christian city besieged by the infidels: among the knights whom the love of glory led to this perilous and distant war, history takes pleasure in naming the marquis de Fénelon, whose care had brought up the archbishop of Cambrai, and whom his age considered as the model of gallant gentlemen. His young son, whom he took with him, was wounded in an affair against the Turks, and died of his wounds. France, in the same expedition, had to lament another hero, the young duke of Beaufort; Mascaron, who pronounced the funeral oration of this new Maccabeus, thus describes his death: "After the flight of all the others, yielding rather to number than to strength, he fell upon his own trophies, and died the most glorious death that a Christian hero could wish, sword in hand against the enemies of his God and his king, in the sight of Europe, Asia, and Africa; and more than all that, in the sight of God and his angels." Louis XIV., always considering it consistent with his glory to protect the Christian states, sent fresh succours to Candia; four French vessels appeared before the isle; but they arrived too late; the city of Candia, after a siege of two years and four months, had just capitulated.

This conquest revived the courage of the Turks, and their power, sustained by the genius of Kiouprouli, whom the Mussulmans called *the great destroyer of the bells of impiety*, might have still rendered themselves formidable to the Christian nations, if their policy had not been governed by a foolish pride. Intoxicated with some trifling successes, the Turks resumed their project of invading Germany. Towards the end of the seventeenth century, they made a last attempt, and the capital of Austria beheld beneath its walls an army of two hundred thousand infidels.

Germany was exhausted by the thirty years' war. The king of Poland, urged by the pope to come to the succour of the Germanic empire, hastened with his Polish cavalry to the scene of action, and revived the courage of the Germans and the garrison of Vienna. The Turks, upon being attacked with impetuosity, abandoned their camp, their artillery, and their baggage. The wreck of the Ottoman army did not rally till they reached the banks of the Raab, where they encamped around the tent of the grand vizier, the only one that had not fallen into the hands of the conquerors. John Sobieski entered in triumph into the city he had saved by his courage. This happy event was celebrated throughout Germany by public rejoicings; and, as had been done after the victory gained by Don John of Austria, amidst the ceremonies of the Church, these words from Scripture were repeated: "There was a man sent from God, named John."

The defeat of Vienna was for the Turks a signal for the greatest reverses. The vengeance of the people and the army pursued the grand vizier, who had conducted the war; and the sultan, Mahomet IV., fell from the throne at the report of these sanguinary disasters, the effects of which were felt to the very heart of the empire. The famous treaty of Carlowitz testifies the losses that the Ottoman nation had undergone, and the incontestable superiority of its enemies. The decline of Turkey, as a maritime power, had commenced at the battle of Lepanto; its decline as a military or conquering power, dates from the defeat of Vienna. History has two things to remark in the negotiations of Carlowitz. Hungary, which had for so long a time resisted the Turks, weakened at length by civil discords and foreign wars, and given up at the same time to the emperors of Germany and the sultans of Constantinople, then lost its national independence, and became united to the possessions of the house of Austria. Among the states and princes who signed the treaty, the czars of Muscovy, who were destined, at a later period, to inflict such terrible blows upon the Ottoman empire, appeared for the first time as a power interested in the Christian struggle against the infidels.

We have described the origin and progress of the Turks; it only remains for us now to speak of the causes of their decline.

The Turks were only constituted to contend with a barbarous people, like themselves, or with a degenerate people, like the Greeks. When they met with nations that were not corrupted, and were not deficient in bravery or patriotism, their career was checked. It is a circumstance worthy of remark, that they were never able to make an impression upon any of the nations of the Latin Church; the only nation that was separated from Christendom by the conquests of the Turks was one that had separated itself from it. When the Ottomans were no longer able to prosecute their scheme of general invasion, all the passions which had stimulated them to conquest only served to disturb their own empire; which is the ordinary destiny of mere conquering nations.

The wars they prosecuted at the same time against Christian Europe and Persia, were the principal causes of the decay of the military power of the Turks. The efforts they made against the Persians diverted their forces from their expeditions against the Christians; and their expeditions against the Christians crippled their means for the wars in Asia. In these two kinds of war they had a very different manner of fighting. After having for any length of time contended with the warriors of the Oxus or Caucasus, they were incapacitated for making war in Europe. They were never able to triumph completely over either Persia or the Christian nations; and remained at last pressed between two enemies, equally interested in their ruin, and equally animated by religious passions.

The Turks, like all the hordes from the north of Asia, brought with them the feudal government. The first thing to be done by all nomadic nations, who established themselves in conquered countries, was the division of the lands, with certain conditions of protection and obedience. From this division naturally emanated feudalism. The difference, however, which existed between the

Turks and the other barbarians who conquered the West, was, that the jealous despotism of the sultans never allowed fiefs to become hereditary, or that an aristocracy should grow up round it, as in the monarchies of Christendom. Thus in the Turkish empire nothing was to be seen on one side, but the authority of an absolute master; and on the other, nothing but a military democracy. The Ottoman monarchy was thus built upon that which is weakest in political societies—the will of a single man, or that of the multitude.

The Turks have been compared to the Romans. Both nations began in the same manner; for both were nothing but bands of brigands. What distinguishes them in history is, that the Turks have remained the same as they were in their origin; whilst the Romans, in their conquests, never rejected the knowledge, the customs, or even the gods of the people they conquered. The Turks, on the contrary, took nothing from other nations, and made it their pride to continue barbarians.

We have said above, that hereditary aristocracy has never been established by the side of despotism; and this is, perhaps, the reason why the Ottoman nation has remained in a state of barbarism. They who have studied the march of human societies know that it is by the aristocracy that the manners and morals of a people are formed, and that it is in the middle classes that knowledge has its birth, and civilization begins.* The absence of an aristocracy in oriental governments, not only explains to us the fragility of those governments, but it assists us also in explaining why progress has not been made in a country where nothing distinguished the men from each other, where no one had sufficient influence to guide the crowd, or was sufficiently elevated to serve as an example or model.

In consequence of the indifference of the Turks for the arts and sciences, the labours of industry, agriculture, and navigation, were confided to their slaves, who were their enemies. As they held in horror everything new, or that they had not brought from Asia with them, they were obliged to have recourse to foreigners for everything that was invented or perfected in Europe. Thus the sources of prosperity and power, the strength of their armies and their fleets, were not at all in their own hands. Every one knows what the Turks have lost by neglecting to learn or to follow the progress of the military tactics of the Europeans. At the battle of Lepanto, disorder was introduced into their fleet entirely from their having promised liberty to their sailors, who were all Christians.

Some modern writers, seeking everywhere for similitudes, have compared the janissaries to the pretorian cohorts. This comparison has nothing exact in it: among the Romans, the empire was elective, and the pretorians got possession of it for the purpose of putting it up to sale. Among the Turks, the idea of choosing their prince never suggested itself to the minds of either the people or the soldiery. The janissaries contented themselves with disturbing the government, and keeping it in such a state of disorder, that they could never be dismissed, and might always remain masters. All their opposition consisted in preventing any amelioration whatever in discipline or military usages. The abuses and prejudices the most difficult to be destroyed in a nation, are those which adhere to a body or a class in which power happens to be placed. All-powerful despotism was never able to overcome the opposition of the janissaries and spahis; and these redoubtable corps, which had so effectively contributed to ancient conquests, became the greatest obstacle to the making of new ones.

The Turks established in Greece had more respect for old usages and old prejudices, than they had of love for the country they inhabited. Masters of Stamboul, they had their eyes constantly fixed upon the places of their origin, and appeared to be but travellers, or passing conquerors of

---

* This question, we think, will admit of another decision. M. Michaud confounds the aristocracy with the middle class. When a class becomes raised, by any means, to an hereditary superiority, not purchased by individual merit of any other kind, manners are too frequently set at defiance, and morals become corrupt. What he says of the middle class is quite correct. The whole history of the world cannot furnish such an instance of stability and prosperity, as is now offered by the influence of an intelligent, prudent, moral middle class.—TRANS.

Europe. They preserved the manners of Asia, the laws of Asia, the remembrances of Asia; and the West was, in their estimation, less a country than a theatre for their exploits.

Amidst their decline, nothing was more fatal to the Turks than the memory of their past glory; nothing was more injurious to them than that national pride which was no longer in harmony with their fortune, or in proportion with their strength. The illusions of a power that no longer existed prevented them from foreseeing the obstacles they were likely to meet with in their enterprises, or the dangers with which they were threatened. When the Ottomans made an unsuccessful war, or an unfavourable treaty, they never failed to lay the blame on their leaders, whom popular vengeance devoted to death or exile; and whilst they thus immolated victims to their vanity, their reverses became the more irreparable, from their persisting in mistaking the true causes of them.

Tacitus somewhere expresses the joy he felt in seeing barbarians making war upon one another; and we experience something of this joy when we see despotism threatened by its own institutions, and tormented by the very instruments of its power. Another spectacle, no less consoling to all who love humanity and justice, is to behold this family of fierce despots, before whom the entire East trembled, devouring itself. It is well known what victims each sultan, on ascending the throne, was compelled to offer to the suspicious genius of despotism. But Heaven does not permit the most sacred laws of nature to be constantly violated with impunity; and the Ottoman dynasty, in expiation of so many crimes against family ties, sunk at last into a species of degradation. The Ottoman princes, brought up in subjection and fear, lost the energy and the faculties necessary for conducting the government of a great empire. Soliman II. only increased the evil by decreeing a constitutional law, that no son of the sultan's should command armies or govern provinces. From that time none but effeminate princes, timid and senseless men, occupied the Ottoman throne.

If the will of the prince became corrupt, it was quite sufficient to render the corruption general. In proportion as the character of the sultans degenerated, everything degenerated around them. A universal apathy displaced the noisy activity of war and victory. To the passion for conquests succeeded cupidity, ambition, selfishness, and all the vices that signalize and complete the decline of empires. When states rise and march on towards prosperity, there is an emulation to increase their powers; when they decline, there is also an emulation to urge on their destruction, and take advantage of their ruin.

The empire had always a numerous army; but that army, in which discipline every day degenerated, was only formidable in time of peace. A crowd of *Thimariots*, or possessors of fiefs for life, having nothing to leave to their families, passed over the lands that were given to them like locusts, which, in the plains where the winds have wafted them, destroy even to the germs of the harvests. The pachas governed the provinces as conquerors. The wealth of the people was for them like the booty which conquerors distributed among themselves on the day of victory. Such as could amass treasures were able to purchase impunity. Such as had armies proclaimed their independence. Subalterns everywhere followed the example of the leaders. In the government, as well as in the army, everything was put up to sale, everything was subject to pillage. Thus this empire, which had displayed such energy, fell like a prey into the hands of all those whom fortune or the favour of the prince called to authority; and if we may be permitted to employ a not very elevated comparison to express the degree of abasement of a nation, the Ottoman power no longer presented any aspect but that of those lifeless bodies in which we can perceive no motion but in the insects that are devouring them.

The sultans of Constantinople, while slumbering in their seraglios, were often awakened by the thunder of popular revolts. Violences of the army or the people were the only justice able to reach despotism. But this justice itself was one calamity the more, and only assisted in precipitating the general decline.

Although the successors of Othman, after the reign of Selim, were the pontiffs of the national faith, this important dignity added nothing to their power. The Mussulman faith, which commanded with severity the observance of many minute practices, did not at all repress the passions of the multitude. A religious belief which permitted a prince to commit fratricide could be no safeguard for either the authority or the life of the prince. A religion always ready to consecrate the triumph of force, could find no motives in its moral code for the condemnation of revolt, particularly when the revolt happened to be crowned with success.

But what is remarkably singular, the Turks, when they rose against a prince of the Ottoman dynasty, preserved a profound veneration for that dynasty. They immolated the tyrant to their vengeance, and were ready to immolate themselves for the tyranny. Thus license, in its greatest excesses, always respected despotism; and what carried disorder to its highest pitch was, that despotism in its turn respected license.

The Turks lived in this state of decline as in their natural condition. Nothing is more remarkable in history than the carelessness of a nation in the midst of a revolution that is dragging it down to its ruin; and this revolution with the Turks was not brought about by new ideas, but by old ideas; not by love of liberty, but by habits of slavery. They respected the causes of their ruin, because these causes were connected with the history of barbarous times; and religion, by constantly repeating to them that "he who is in the fire ought to be resigned," prevented them from seeking a remedy for the ills they suffered.

Among nations which incline towards destruction, in the very bosom of corruption a certain politeness, a certain polish or elegance of manners, may be observed. The Turks, on the contrary, had a brutal and savage corruption, and their empire grew old without the nation's losing anything of that fierceness of character, of that proud roughness, which belong to the infancy of society.

We shall be asked why Christendom did not take advantage of this decline of the Turks to drive them back again into Asia. We have seen in this history, that the nations of Christian Europe were never able to combine and agree for the defence of Constantinople, when it was attacked by the Turks; and they showed no more inclination to combine to deliver it after it was taken. We may add that the less redoubtable the Turks became, the fewer were the efforts made to conquer them. They inspired, besides, no jealousy in the commercial nations of Christendom. It was in vain that fortune placed them between the East and the West; that she rendered them masters of the Archipelago, of the coasts of Africa, of the ports of the Black Sea and the Red Sea: their finest provinces were deserts, their cities were abandoned. Everything perished in the hands of an indolent and unpolished people. The Turks were spared, because they made no use of their advantages; and because they were, to employ an expression of Montesquieu's, the men the most fit to hold great empires carelessly.

Before we terminate this rapid sketch of the Turkish empire in the seventeenth century, we beg to be allowed to add some reflections which circumstances may cause to be appreciated. Nothing was more monstrous than the presence upon the same territory, of two nations and two religions that hated and cursed each other reciprocally. Spain had presented a similar spectacle; but the energy and the magnanimous constancy of the Spaniards triumphed over an adverse people and an adverse religion; and at the very time at which the Turks established themselves in Greece, the Moors, carrying with them their foreign worship, abandoned their conquests and returned to Africa, from whence they came. The Greeks, after the invasion of the Ottomans, neither showed the same energy nor the same courage; although their patriotism ought to have been constantly animated by the soil they trod on, and by their very name, of which the conqueror had not been able to deprive them.

Nevertheless, amidst their abasement and their misery, they were still able to place their hope in the ascendancy of religious ideas, and in the wish for civilization, which acted as a tie between all Christian societies. Whilst the manners and the worship of Islamism rendered the Turks foreign and even odious to Christendom, the religion of Christ and the remembrances of history placed the Greeks in relation with the other nations of Europe.

In proportion as the knowledge derived from antiquity made progress among the Franks, Greece became for them a sacred country. The language of Plato and Demosthenes, in which the charms of liberty had been celebrated with so much eloquence, became more dear to them than their own maternal tongue. The poetical sites of Greece, which the love of letters rendered so familiar to the studious class, were for us like places in which we had passed our infancy. Europe had not a scholar in whom the city of Aristotle, that of Lycurgus, or that of Epaminondas, did not inspire something resembling the sentiments we feel for our own country. If the Greeks were degenerated; if they viewed with indifference the ruins of their country, ancient Greece still lived for every enlightened man, and was ever present, wherever a taste for the arts or a love of learning existed.

The warmer that the interest for the Greeks became, the more barbarous the Turks appeared. The Ottoman nation came and established itself in the richest countries of Europe, and remained in sight of all European people, without becoming acquainted with their languages, their laws, or their policy; like those troops of wild animals which sometimes stop in the neighbourhood of the dwellings of man, ignorant of that which is going on in these places, and having no means to seize their prey or defend themselves, but their activity, their natural strength, and the means which a gross instinct gives them. This state of things was opposed both to the laws of society and the laws of nature, which do not permit men or nations to live together and in the same place, except when they possess similar qualities, and are able to employ their faculties in common. The Turks may have been protected, at first by the fortune of their own arms, and afterwards by the policy of certain cabinets; but what real support could they have in the West, when they were repulsed by the manners, feelings, and opinions of the European nations, to whom they became every day more foreign?

On one side, the antipathy entertained for a barbarous people; on the other, the relations which united nations civilized by Christianity, were likely, sooner or later, to revive that spirit of fraternity which produced the crusades; and God has willed that this spirit, from which the holy wars were born, should manifest itself in the same century which had for a long time refused to acknowledge the effects or to admire the prodigies of them.

At the moment in which we are finishing this history, the Greeks have thrown forth a cry of alarm and this cry has resounded throughout the Christian world. Is the moment of their deliverance arrived? When we examine the present state of Europe, we find a much greater force than would be necessary to conquer Byzantium; but on the other side, the diversity of interests and opinions will not permit the Christian republic to unite for this great enterprise. We have seen that the Turks really possess nothing but the soil of their vast empire; the riches that are there produced belong to the nations of Christendom, and these nations are for the Turkish provinces, which they cultivate to their profit, that which an active and industrious farmer is for the fields he ploughs and reaps. Add to this, that most of the Christian powers appear to fear that the displacing of a great empire may break the ties of the European confederation; they do not, as formerly, dread the strength of the Ottomans, but the difficulties and divisions that the conquest would produce. That which may add to their fears is that impatience for change, that ardent passion for novelty, which is spread

THE DEPARTURE.

all at once among the nations like a contagious fever; whilst the Greeks are imploring Europe for their liberty, restless and dissatisfied spirits look to the East for I do not know what signal for a revolution in Europe. Thus Christendom, divided by its various interests, tormented by a thousand different passions, and fearing for its own repose, awaits with anxiety the events that are preparing, and appears to recoil from victories which the superiority of her intelligence and her armies hold out to her.

What will be the issue of all the warlike demonstrations and all the pacific negotiations of which fame informs us every day? There is no doubt the cross will again arise in the East, and the fate of Christians residing there will receive some amelioration; but are we arrived at the moment which is to render Europe entirely Christian? Will the Ottoman empire, whose weakness now appears so great, yield to the power of its enemies, or will it hasten its own ruin? Will Greece, so long enslaved, resume that rank among nations from which she formerly descended so ingloriously, or will she fall into the hands of her liberators? A thousand other questions present themselves to the mind; but we will not forestall events; above all, we will avoid multiplying conjectures and hypotheses, or producing here the brilliant reveries of philosophers and poets, which the severity of history rejects. When we set a high value upon truth, and have sought it for a length of time in all that the remembrances of the past contain that is most positive, we learn to speak of the future with much circumspection and reserve.

It may be thought that we have dwelt too long upon the Ottoman empire; but the origin of that empire, its progress and its decline, are connected with all the events we have had to describe. The sketch we have traced of it may have been sometimes serviceable in making our readers acquainted with the spirit and the character of the wars against the infidels; and in this view our labour has not been useless.

At the period we have now gained, the passions which had given birth to the prodigies of the crusades had become speculative opinions, which occupied the attention of writers rather than that of kings or nations. Thus the holy wars, with their causes and effects, became the objects of the discussions of doctors and philosophers. We may remember the opinion of Luther; and although he had partly disavowed or retracted his first opinion upon the war against the Turks, most of his partisans continued to evince a great aversion for the crusades.

The minister Jurieu goes much further than Luther. That ardent apostle of the Reformation, far from thinking that war ought to be made against the Mussulmans, did not hesitate to consider the Turks as auxiliaries of the Protestants, and said that the fierce sectaries of Mahomet were sent to "labour with the Reformers in the great work of God," which was the ruin of the papal empire. After the raising of the last siege of Vienna, in 1683, and the revocation of the edict of Nantes, the same Jurieu was afflicted at the disgrace of the Reformers and the defeat of the Turks; adding, at the same time, "that God had only abased them, in order to raise them together again, and make them the instruments of his vengeance against the popes." Such is the excess of blindness to which the spirit of party or sect has power to carry us, when misled by hatred, and irritated by persecution.

Other writers, however, celebrated for their genius, and who also were connected with the Reformation, maintained that wars against the infidels ought to be carried on: they deplored the indifference of Christendom, and the wars that were breaking out daily among Christian nations, whilst they left in peace a people, a foe to all other peoples. Chancellor Bacon, in his dialogue *de bello sacro*, employs all his logic to prove that the Turks are excluded from the law of nations. He invokes, by turns, natural right, the rights of nations, and divine right, against the barbarians, to whom he refuses the name of a people, and maintains that war should be carried on against them as against pirates, anthropophagi, or wild animals. The illustrious chancellor quotes, in support of his opinion, maxims from Aristotle, maxims from the Bible, with examples from history, and even from fable. His manner of reasoning savours a little of the policy and philosophy of the sixteenth century, and we do not feel ourselves called upon to repeat arguments, of which many would not be of a nature to convince minds of the present century.

We prefer developing some of the ideas of Leibnitz, who, in order to revive the spirit of distant expeditions, addressed himself to the ambition of princes, and whose political views have received a memorable application in modern times. At the moment in which Louis XIV. was preparing to carry his arms into the Low Countries, the German philosopher sent him a long memorial, to persuade him to renew the expedition of St. Louis into Egypt. The conquest of that rich country, which Leibnitz calls the Holland of the East, would favour the triumph and the propagation of the faith; it would procure for the Most Christian king the renown of Alexander, and for the French monarchy vast means of power and prosperity. After the occupation of Alexandria and Cairo, fortune would offer the conquerors some happy opportunity for restoring the empire of the East; the Ottoman power, attacked by the Poles and the Germans, and troubled by internal divisions, was ready to sink into ruin; Muscovy and Persia were already preparing to take advantage of its fall; if France put forth her strength, nothing would be more easy than to gather together again the immense heritage of Constantine, to dominate over the Mediterranean, to extend her empire over the Red Sea, over the Sea of Ethiopia, over the Persian Gulf, and obtain possession of the commerce of India; everything the most brilliant in the glory and grandeur of empires then presented itself to the imagination of Leibnitz; and this exalted genius, dazzled by his own idea, and allying his policy with the prejudices of his age, could see nothing greater than the conquest of Egypt, *but the discovery of the philosopher's stone:* he beheld already, in a shortly distant futurity, the Christian religion flourishing again in Asia, the empire and the commerce of the East and the West divided between the king of France and the house of Austria and Spain, the world rendered peaceful, and governed by these two conquering powers!

After having developed the advantages of the vast enterprise he proposed, Leibnitz neglected none of the means that would be likely to secure the success or facilitate the execution of it. It was in this part of his memorial that he showed all the superiority of his genius; and when we read the account of the last war of the French in Egypt, we cannot but feel persuaded that Buonaparte was well acquainted with the plan of campaign addressed by Leibnitz to Louis XIV. But certainly this gigantic enterprise, whose result was likely to be more brilliant than either solid or durable, was less suited to a monarch guided in his policy by the sentiments of real greatness, than to the modern hero, always enamoured of an adventurous and romantic glory. Nevertheless, the ideas of Leibnitz, although not favourably received by the cabinet of Versailles, did not fail to produce a lively impression upon the statesmen of the seventeenth century. It is known likewise, that the king of France had already thought seriously of a war against the Turks; and we have reason to believe that Boileau alluded to all these projects of distant conquests, when he said in his epistle to the king:

Je t'attends dans six mois aux bords de l'Hellespont.*

The eloquence, or even the flattery of authors, could not induce princes to take up arms against the infidels; and the Crusaders finished, as they began, with pilgrimages. Among the celebrated pilgrims who repaired to the East after the holy wars, one of the most remarkable was Ignatius Loyola. He visited the holy places twice, and, like St. Jerome, would have ended his days in Palestine, if the Latin priests had not advised him to return into Europe, where he established the order of the Jesuits. As was the case before the crusades, princes mixed with the crowd of Christians who

---

* I look for you six months hence on the shores of the Hellespont.

went to the Holy Land. Frederick III., before he ascended the imperial throne, went on a pilgrimage to the holy city. We still possess an account of the voyages which were made successively into Palestine by a prince of Radziwil, a duke of Bavaria, a duke of Austria, and three electors of Saxony, among whom was he who was the protector of Luther.

Pilgrims from the West were no longer received at Jerusalem, as in the early times, by the Knights of St. John, but by the Latin fathers of the order of St. Francis of Assisi, who devoted themselves to the guardianship of the holy sepulchre. Preserving the hospitable manners of ancient times, the guardian father himself washed the feet of travellers, and furnished them with the necessary assistance for their pilgrimage. Pilgrims embarked at Venice, where vessels were always ready to transport them to the coast of Syria. People could obtain all the benefits attached to the pilgrimage of the Holy Land, without quitting their homes; either by commissioning pious men who were sent beyond the seas, or cenobites who resided on the spot.

The greater part of the sovereigns of Christendom, after the example of Charlemagne, thought it consistent with their glory, not only to deliver, but to protect the city of Jesus Christ from the outrages of the Mussulmans. The capitulations of Francis I., renewed by most of his successors, contain* several conditions which contribute to secure peace to the Christians, with the free exercise of their religion in the East. In the reign of Henry IV., Deshayes, the ambassador from France to Constantinople, went to visit the faithful at Jerusalem, and conveyed to them the consolations of a charity worthy of royalty. The count of Nointel, who represented Louis XIV. at the court of the sultan of Turkey, also went into the Holy Land; and Jerusalem received in triumph the envoy of the powerful monarch, whose credit and renown were employed to protect the Christians beyond the seas.

Most of the princes of Christendom every year sent their tributes to the holy city; and in solemn ceremonies, the church of the Resurrection displayed the treasures offered by the kings of the West. The guardians of the holy places, who entertained and took charge of pilgrims, possessed nothing on earth; but the gifts of the faithful were for them like the manna of the desert, sent every day from heaven. By a species of miracle constantly renewed, the holy monuments of the Christian religion, for a long time defended by the armies of the West, having no longer any defence but religious remembrances, preserved themselves amidst the barbarous sectaries of Islamism: the security enjoyed by the city of Jerusalem made its deliverance less thought of. That which produced the spirit of the crusades in the eleventh century was, above all other causes, the persecution directed against pilgrims, and the state of misery in which the Christians of the East existed. When they ceased to be persecuted, and had fewer miseries to endure, lamentable accounts no longer awakened the pity and indignation of the western nations; and Christendom satisfied itself with addressing prayers to God for the preservation of peace in the places he had sanctified by his miracles. There was then a spirit of resignation† which took place of the enthusiasm of the crusades; the city of David and of Godfrey became confounded in the minds of Christians with the heavenly Jerusalem, and as sacred orators said, "it was necessary to pass through Heaven to arrive at the Holy Land," it was of no use appealing to the bravery of warriors, but to the devotion and charity of the faithful.

---

* The last capitulations are of the reign of Louis XV.

† This resignation is expressed in a very singular manner in an extract from the manuscript of the library of Berne,—" Upon the cause why the Saracens possess the Holy Land."

Brother Vincent, in a sermon which he made, and which had for its text, " Ecce ascendimus Hierosoleman," gives three reasons for it :—" The first," said he, "is to excuse the Christians ; the second is for the confusion of the Saracens ; and the third is for the conversion of the Jews. As to the first reason, we ought all to know that there is no Christian, however holy, who does not sin, and has not sinned, except Jesus and his mother, the glorious Virgin Mary ; and God is not willing that Christians should sin in the land in which Jesus Christ, his son, suffered the passion for the sins of men ; and would account it a great offence. But He is not thus offended by the Saracens ; for they are dogs. It would displease the king if his children or his knights should make water in his chamber; but when a dog makes water there, he takes no account of it." See *Catalogus Codicum MSS., Bibliothecæ Bernensis*, &c., tom. i., p. 79.

THE ORDER OF CHIVALRY.

This institution, so ingeniously called "Fountain of courtesy, which comes from God," is still much more admirable when considered under the all-powerful influence of religious ideas. Christian charity claimed all the affections of the knight, and demanded of him a perpetual devotion for the defence of pilgrims and the care of the sick. It was thus that were established the orders of St. John, of the Temple, of the Teutonic Knights, and several others, all instituted to combat the Saracens and solace human miseries. The infidels admired their virtues as much as they dreaded their bravery.—BOOK XVIII.

BOOK XVIII

Upon the State of Europe

A.D. 1571 to 1685

BOOK XVIII.
UPON THE STATE OF EUROPE.
A.D. 1571–1685.

Reflections on the state of Europe, on the various classes of society, and on the progress of navigation, industry, arts, and general knowledge during and after the crusades.

WE have made known the origin, the spirit, and the character of the crusades; it is now our task to show their influence on the state of society. Before giving our opinion upon the results of the holy wars, it has appeared to us desirable to lay before our readers, in a few words, the judgments that others have passed upon them. In the seventeenth century, so abounding in men of genius, the heroic bravery of the Crusaders was admired, their reverses were deplored, and, without a question as to the good or evil which these distant expeditions had brought about, the pious motives which had made the warriors of the West take arms were respected. The eighteenth century, which had adopted all the opinions of the Reformation, and exaggerated them,—the eighteenth century did not spare the crusades, and did not fail to accuse the ignorance, barbarity, and fanaticism of our ancestors as the causes of them. *Voltaire published a history of the crusades, in 1753; the subject he had chosen was at that time so low in public opinion, and he himself cast so much ridicule upon the events he described, that his book created no curiosity, and found no readers. Nothing can equal the violence with which the authors of the *Encyclopédie*, a short time afterwards, surpassed even the acerbity of Voltaire. This manner of judging the crusades became so general, that the panegyrists of St. Louis allowed themselves to be drawn into it, and several among them, in their discourses, were scarcely inclined to pardon the pious monarch for his exploits and his misfortunes in Egypt and before Tunis.

A philosophy, however, enlightened by the spirit of research and analysis, traced events to their causes, studied their effects, and, from holding truth as the only object worthy of inquiry, neglected declamation and despised satire. The judicious Robertson, in his introduction to the History of Charles V., gave it as his opinion, that the crusades had favoured the progress of liberty and the development of the human mind. Whether this perception flattered some of the opinions of the time, or whether it exercised over the public the natural ascendancy of truth, it met with a sufficient number of partisans; and from that time the expeditions of the Crusaders into the East have been judged with less severity.

---

* This account of the crusades at first appeared in the *Mercury*, and was afterwards printed in a little volume. It is now merged in Voltaire's *Histoire Générale*.

A few years ago the Institute of France proposed a question, by which they invited the learned to point out all the advantages society had derived from the crusades; and if we may judge by the memorials which obtained the prize in this learned contest,* the holy wars brought more benefits for posterity in their train, than they produced calamities for the generations contemporary with them. Thus, opinions upon the crusades had changed several times in less than two centuries; a great lesson for those who pronounce with so much assurance upon the revolutions which we have seen begin, but which we shall not see end; when there is so much difficulty in judging of revolutions long ago accomplished, and whose results are all before our eyes!

Perhaps we are arrived at the favourable moment for appreciating with some truth the influence of the crusades, and the opinions of those who have reflected upon them before us: we may say, that the revolutions of the present age are for us a torch which enlightens the history of past times; none of the lessons which are afforded by great political concussions have been wanting for the present generation, and on that account, no doubt, our age will some day merit the title of the age of enlightenment.

We may safely say, that that which the crusades were deficient in, in order to have found more indulgent judges, was success; let us suppose for a moment that the crusades had succeeded, as they who undertook them hoped they would, and let us see, in that case, what would have been their results. Egypt, Syria, and Greece would have become Christian colonies; the nations of the East and the West would have pursued together the great march of civilization; the languages of the Franks would have penetrated to the extremes of Asia; the Barbary coast, now inhabited by pirates, would have received the morals and the laws of Europe; and the interior of Africa would not have been for a long time a land impenetrable to the relations of commerce and the researches of learned men and travellers. In order to judge what nations under the same laws and the same religion would have gained by this union, we have but to remember the state of the Roman world under the successors of Augustus, forming, as it were, one people, living under the same law, speaking the same language. All the seas were free, and the most distant provinces communicated with each other by easy and commodious routes; cities exchanged the objects of their arts and their industry, climates their various productions, nations their knowledge. If the crusades had subdued the East to Christianity, it is fair to believe that this grand spectacle, which the human race had only once beheld, would have been repeated in modern times, and opinions would not now be divided as to the advantages of the holy wars. Unfortunately, the Crusaders were unable to extend or preserve their conquests. The results of the crusades are thus more difficult to seize, and the good attributed to them does not strike all minds with equal force.

Among the results of the crusades, impartial history cannot pass over the evils they caused humanity to undergo; but these evils were felt in the time itself of the holy wars; and the faithful picture of that period has been quite sufficient to make us acquainted with them. As to the good the crusades produced, it has been like the germ, which remains a long time concealed in the earth, and develops itself slowly. After the account of each crusade, our readers will remember that, in a short summary, we have pointed out the immediate results of it. Now we will embrace all the epochs of the Eastern expeditions in a general review. When the ages to which the events of which we have spoken belonged become better known, the spirit of these events and their consequences will be better understood and better judged of: we are about to exhibit societies such as they were in the middle ages, and the progress they have made towards civilization; leaving to enlightened readers the care of appreciating that which belongs to the crusades.

---

* Two memorials obtained prizes; one was by M. Hercen, the other by M. Choisseul d'Aullecourt. Both are remarkable for erudition and spirit of criticism; they marked out the way we have followed, and we take pleasure in acknowledging all we owe them.

We will in the first place examine the state of the different powers of Europe, and will begin with France.

When we remember the state of weakness and decay in which the commencement of the twelfth century found the French monarchy, we are astonished at the degree of prosperity and splendour it attained in subsequent ages. Skilful negotiations, successful wars, useful alliances, the decay of the feudal system, and the progressive enfranchisement of the commons, favoured the dynasty of the Capets, in the aggrandizement of their states, and in the increase of their authority. Several centuries were employed in consummating this great work of fortune and policy; and the more slowly that this revolution was operated, the more durable proved its effects. One plan of conduct, followed up by all the princes of one same family, and the success it obtained in the prosperity and aggrandizement of the kingdom, and the glory and independence of the nation, at the present day, merit all the attention of history. Frenchmen cannot help feeling both gratitude and admiration when they reflect that the union of so many rich provinces—that this French monarchy, which has grown from age to age, and which finished by extending from the Rhine to the Pyrenees; that this beautiful France, in a word, such as we see it, is the work of the august family which governs it at the present day.

The policy of our kings was no doubt seconded by the great events of the crusades; it was natural that the nation which took the greatest share in these events should profit more than others by it, in the increase of its power and the amelioration of its social condition. The glory which the French arms acquired beyond the seas gave a new lustre to the monarchy; royal authority profited equally by the exploits and the reverses of the numerous warriors whom the holy wars attracted into Asia; the absence, the death, or the ruin of the great vassals permitted royalty to rise from the bosom of feudal anarchy, and establish order in the kingdom.

More than a century before the first crusade, the barons and prelates had ceased to meet in general assembly to regulate the forms of justice, and lend to the acts of royal authority the support of their political influence. At the second crusade, there were several assemblies of the great men of the kingdom, in which preparations for the expedition, and measures for the maintenance of public order and the execution of the laws during the absence of Louis VII., were deliberated upon. In these meetings, which were very numerous, the French might trace at least a faint image of those assemblies, so celebrated under the first races, in which the kings and their subjects deliberated together upon the means of securing the independence of the nation and the safety of the throne.

Thus the crusades aided the kings of France in resuming their legislative power, and the most enlightened part of the nation, in recovering those ancient prerogatives which they had exercised under the children of Clovis and Charlemagne.

It may be remembered, that after the accession of Hugh Capet, the great vassals not only did no longer assemble around their prince, but had entirely separated their cause from that of the crown; several even scarcely acknowledged a king of France, and covering their opposition with a pious pretext, they, in their public acts, designated the year of the reign of Jesus Christ, instead of that of the king. This opposition, which lasted more than a century, at last gave way to other feelings, when they saw the French monarchs at the head of those expeditions which attracted the attention of all Christendom, and in which the cause of Jesus Christ himself, as well as of all Christian nations, seemed interested. In order to perceive clearly what the kings of France owed to the holy wars, and what in particular they gained by taking part in them, it would suffice to compare Philip I., shut up in his palace, in a melancholy manner, during the Council of Clermont, excommunicated by Urban, condemned by the bishops, and abandoned by his nobles, with Philip Augustus, in the first place conqueror of Saladin in Syria, and afterwards triumphant at Beauvines, over the enemies of his kingdom; or with Louis IX., surrounded in his reverses by a faithful nobility, ever respected by the clergy and the people, revered as the firmest support of the Church, and proclaimed by his own age the arbiter of Europe.

We will speak hereafter of the changes which were then effected in the different classes of society; we will confine ourselves here to saying that the crusades were the signal for a new order of things in France, and that this new order of things cast solid foundations during the holy wars.

If royalty in France was weak at the period of the first crusade, in England it was strong and powerful; royalty and feudalism oppressed England with all the weight of the conquests of William; but an authority founded upon victory, and sustained by violence, created at an early period in men's minds a feeling of opposition, which time and circumstances were destined to develop. Military despotism had been able to impose silence upon opinions; but it had not entirely changed the manners of the English, or destroyed their attachment to old customs. Passions suppressed by the sword broke out with greater violence in the end.

An all-powerful monarchy exhibited a tendency to decline, and in England was seen the contrary of that which had been seen in France. Liberty made advances at the expense of royal authority. It does not enter into our plan to explain in detail the causes of this revolution. Several English monarchs allowed themselves to be led away by an imprudent and passionate policy, which threw them into fatal extravagances; their excesses, their violences, and particularly the crimes of John Lack-land, alienated the minds of their subjects, and united the whole nation in one feeling of resistance to absolute power. Another cause of decline not less remarkable, and to which history has not sufficiently drawn attention, was the ambition of the English princes, which inspired them with the senseless project of conquering the kingdom of France. The ruinous wars which they maintained against an enemy they could not subdue, placed them at the discretion of the barons and the English people, who furnished them with subsidies and fought under their banners.

The crusades had, perhaps, less influence upon the civilization of England than upon that of several other states of Europe. They might, however, concur with many circumstances of that period in effecting the changes which the English monarchy underwent.

Richard Cœur de Lion was more anxious to acquire the renown of a great captain than the reputation of a great king; the glory of arms made him forget the cares of his kingdom. It may be remembered that before his departure he sold the charges, the prerogatives, and the domains of the crown; he would have sold, as he himself said, the city of London, if he could have found a purchaser; his reverses and his captivity ruined his people, and his long absence kept up the spirit of faction among his nobles, and more especially in his own family.

The English barons were several times desirous of going into the East, against the will of the king; and the idea of opposing a monarch they did not love, often added to their impatience to embark for Palestine. Kings likewise took advantage of the opinions of their times, and engaged themselves to set out for the crusades, with the sole view of obtaining subsidies, which they employed in other enterprises. These means, too often employed, drew contempt upon the policy of princes, and only served to increase the public mistrust.

But that which completed the overthrow of the foundations of an absolute monarchy in England, was the violent enterprises of the popes against the English kings; enterprises which the spirit of religious wars favoured. In the league of the barons against Henry III., the rebels wore a cross, as in the wars beyond the seas; and the priests promised the palms of martyrdom to those who should die in the cause of liberty. One very curious circumstance is, that the head of the league formed for the independence of the English nation, was a French gentleman, the son of that count de Montfort so renowned in the crusade against the Albigeois.

But the long efforts of England to obtain liberty deserve so much the more to fix the attention of history, from their having, in the end, attained a positive and durable result. So many other nations, after having contended for a long time, sometimes against license, sometimes against tyranny, have only met with misery, shame, and slavery. If the English revolution produced in the end salutary effects, it was because all classes of society concurred together in it; because it was made in the interests of all, according to the character and the manners of the nation, and according to the spirit of Christianity, which then presided over all which ought to last among men. Unanimity of opinions and sentiments, the accordance of manners and laws, of policy and religion, founded from that time that public spirit of which England still offers us the model; and this public spirit became in the end the most firm support and the most sure safeguard of liberty.

Whilst England was wresting liberty from its kings, and France was requiring hers back again of royalty, Germany presented another spectacle; the German empire, which had thrown out great splendour up to the eleventh century, declined rapidly during the crusades.

The emperors, in order to resist the great vassals, granted several advantages to the clergy, and bestowed privileges upon the cities. The clergy employed these advantages in favour of the popes, who attacked the imperial power; the cities profited by the concessions which were made to found their independence. All the efforts of the emperors had proved unable to prevent the crown continuing elective, whilst the great fiefs became hereditary. Thus the heads of the empire depended for their election upon the princes and nobles whom they themselves had freed from all dependence. In the competition of the pretenders to the throne, in a competition which was almost always decided by fortune, intrigue, or victory, it may easily be supposed that ambition was often more successful than moderation and virtue. Among the princes who ascended the imperial throne, many were men of great character; but their active and restless genius led them into adventurous and gigantic enterprises, which exhausted their strength and hastened the decline of the empire.

The memories of ancient Rome and of the power of the Cæsars were always present to their imagination. One of the greatest errors of their policy was turning their views towards Italy; they encountered on their way thither the popes, who declared a war of extermination against them; two families of emperors succumbed beneath the thunders of Rome; they were never able to reign over Italy, and whilst they exhausted themselves in vain efforts to establish their domination there, they completed the loss of their influence in Germany.

It is a consoling remark for humanity, that most of the conquerors of the middle ages weakened themselves by their undertakings, victory itself only serving to bring about the ruin of their power. The kings of France of this period evinced, perhaps, less talent and genius than the emperors of Germany; but their policy was wiser and more fortunate; they confined themselves to conquering their own kingdom; their conquests only tended to unite the scattered members of a large family; and their authority became more popular in proportion with their being considered as a natural tie between the French of all the provinces.

The glory which the emperors of Germany acquired by their conquests was but a personal glory, and did not at all interest the German people. This manifestation of their power had nothing in common with the nations of which they were the head. As soon as this power was no longer a bond or a support for the people, they separated themselves from it, and every one sought his safety or his aggrandizement in his own strength.

A state of things arose from this which was, perhaps, more fatal to Germany than the absolute authority of the emperors; upon the ruins of the imperial grandeur arose a crowd of states, opposed to each other by diversity of laws and the spirit of rivalry. All those ecclesiastical and secular principalities in which the spirit of monarchy prevailed; those cities in which the spirit of liberty fermented; that nobility animated by the pretensions of aristocracy, could not possibly have the same interests or the same policy to direct their efforts towards one common and salutary aim.

The popes, after having weakened the power of the emperors, wished to dispose of the broken sceptre of Charlemagne, and offered it to all who appeared likely to promote their scheme of vengeance. A crowd of princes then started up as pretenders to the empire thus held out by the popes, and the greater the number of these, the more rapidly the empire declined. Amidst civil discords, Germany completed the loss of its political unity, and at last its religious unity.

In order to judge to what a degree it was difficult to put in motion that enormous mass called the German confederation, it is only necessary to contemplate, in the history of the fourteenth and fifteenth centuries, those numerous diets which assembled to deliberate upon the war against the Turks, in which the presence of imminent peril even was never able to produce one energetic decision for the safety of Germany.

The popes sometimes made use of the pretext of the crusades to drive the emperors to a distance, and to precipitate them into disastrous expeditions; thus the enthusiasm for the holy wars, which had a tendency to establish union among Christian nations, had no power to bring together the members of the German nation, and only served to keep up trouble and disorder in the bosom of the empire. We must, however, repeat here what has been read in this history; it was under the auspices and by the influence of the court of Rome, when occupied seriously by a crusade, that the family of Rodolph of Hapsburg arose, a family whose power restored the empire to something of its ancient splendour, and saved Europe from the invasion of the Turks.

We have likewise to add that, at the period of the crusades, Germany augmented its territories and its population. The expeditions against the infidels of the East gave birth to the idea of attacking the pagans and idolaters, whose hordes inhabited the banks of the Vistula and the coasts of the Baltic. These races, when subdued by the Crusaders, entered into the Christian republic, and formed part of the German confederation. At the aspect of the cross, such cities as Dantzic, Thorn, Elbing, Kœnigsberg, &c., sprang up from the bosom of forests and deserts. Finland, Lithuania, Pomerania, and Silesia became flourishing provinces; new nations arose, new states were formed, and, to complete these prodigies, the arms of the Crusaders marked the spot in which a monarchy was to appear that did not exist in the middle ages, but which the present age has seen all at once take its place in the rank of the great powers of Europe. At the end of the thirteenth century, the provinces from which the Prussian monarchy derives both its name and its origin, were separated from Christendom by idolatry and savage manners; the conquest and the civilization of these provinces were the work of the holy wars.

If from Germany we pass into Italy, we there meet with other forms of government, and other revolutions.

When the last columns of the Roman empire crumbled away, Italy was covered with ruins. The Huns, the Franks, the Vandals, the Goths, the Germans, and the Lombards, held over this beautiful country, in turns, the scourge of their domination, and all left behind them traces of their manners, their legislation, and their character.

In the tenth century the emperors of Constantinople being unable any longer to retain Italy, other powers arose, some from conquests, others by good fortune, and others from circumstances which history has much difficulty in indicating. The influence of the popes sometimes defended the independence of Italy against the invasions and the yoke of the German emperors; but the struggle was so long, and the war between the two powers exhibited so many vicissitudes, that it only served to perpetuate trouble and discord; during several centuries, the Guelphs and the Ghibellines desolated Italy without defending it.

In every nation of Europe there was then a power, or rather a preponderating authority, which was as a rallying-point, or centre, around which society formed and united its forces to defend its political existence.

Italy had not, like France and other countries, this precious means of conservation. Nothing proves better the dissolution in which this rich country was plunged, than the manner by which it endeavoured to establish its independence in the middle ages. That division into many states, that parcelling out of territory, that numerous population split into a thousand fractions, all announced the absence of any tie, or any common centre. Italy comprised many nations; twenty republics had each their own laws, their own interests, and their own history. Those perpetual wars between the citizens of the same cities; those animosities between republic and republic; that necessity of the inhabitants for calling in strangers in their internal quarrels; those mistrusts which bore harder upon the citizens than upon the stipendiary adventurers, tended to efface the true sentiment of patriotism, and at length caused even the name of the Italian nation to be forgotten.

The feudal system was abolished earlier in Italy than elsewhere; but with feudalism departed the ancient honour of brave knights, and the virtues of chivalry. In republics defended by mercenaries, bravery, and all the generous sentiments that accompany it, ceased to be esteemed. Violent passions had no longer any check, either in the laws or in the opinions of men; it was at this unhappy period that those hatreds and vengeances displayed themselves which appear so improbable to us in our tragedies; no spectacle can be more afflicting than that of Italy in the fourteenth century; and we may safely say that Dante had but to look around him to find the model for his Hell.

Society, always ready to split to pieces, appeared to have no other motive but the fury of parties, no other principle of life but discord and civil war; there was no other guarantee against license but tyranny; or against tyranny, but the despair of factions, and the poniard of conspirators. As the strength of most of the little states which covered Italy was seldom equal to their ambition; and as princes and citizens, by the same reason that they were weak, wanted both moderation and courage; they sought their elevation or their safety in all the means that treachery and perfidy could suggest. Plots, political stratagems, odious crimes, everything appeared right to them; everything seemed properly available that could sustain their quarrels, and satisfy their ambition or their jealousy. At length, all morality disappeared; and it was then that school of policy was formed, which is to be found in the lessons, or rather in the satire, of Machiavel's book.

It is said that the Italians were the first to form the idea of what publicists call the balance of power. We do not think that Italy merits such a glory; that which is understood by the balance of power is not an invention: it is nothing but the natural resource of the weakness which seeks a support. If we follow the progress of events, we shall find that this system, so long boasted, became fatal to Italy, by calling thither conquerors, who made it, even up to our own days, the theatre of most sanguinary wars.

At the period of the crusades, the cities of Lombardy, and the republics of Genoa, Pisa, and Venice, had attained great prosperity; and that which gave them this prosperity was the commerce of the East, which Italy carried on before the crusades, and persevered in, with all the advantages accruing from the expeditions beyond the seas.

But these republics, which contended for the empire of the sea, and only occupied a little corner of land upon the Mediterranean,—which had their eyes constantly fixed upon Syria, Egypt, and Greece,—which left to strangers the care of defending their territories, and only armed their citizens for the defence of their commerce,—these mercantile republics were much better calculated to enrich Italy than to keep up the sentiment of a true independence among the Italian nations.

We cannot, however, refrain from admiring that republic of Venice, whose power everywhere preceded the arms of the Crusaders, and which the nations of the middle ages looked upon as the queen of the East. The decline of this great republic did not begin before the period at which the progress of navigation, that it had so much contributed to, at length opened the route to India, and led to the discovery of a new world. Most of the other republics of Italy neither displayed the same splendour nor enjoyed the same duration; many among them—particularly those in which democracy prevailed—had disappeared at the end of the crusades, in the chaos and tumult of discords and civil wars. In their place arose dukes and princes, who substituted the intrigues of policy for popular passions, and sometimes made it their ambition to favour the revival of arts and letters, the true glory of Italy.

The kingdom of Naples and Sicily, situated at the extremity of Italy, was for the Crusaders the road to Greece and the East. The riches of this country, which appeared never to have any guardians,—a territory which its inhabitants were never able to defend,—must have often tempted the cupidity and the ambition of the princes and even of the knights who went to seek their fortunes in Asia. The history of this fine country is mixed up during two centuries with that of the holy wars, the crusades often furnishing a pretext or an opportunity for the conquest of it. The wars undertaken for the kingdom of Naples,—those wars which produced more monstrous crimes than glorious exploits, more revolts than battles,—completed the corruption of the Neapolitan character, in which has always been remarked, on the one part, an inclination to shake off the yoke of present domination, and, on the other, an extreme resignation in submitting to the yoke of victory.

Whilst glancing thus at the principal states of Europe, we are particularly struck with the great diversity that exists in the manners, the institutions, and the destinies of nations. How is it possible to follow the march of civilization amidst so many republics and monarchies, some bursting with splendour from the bosom of barbarism, others sinking into ruins? And how is it possible to point out the influence of the crusades through so many revolutions, which have often the same causes, but whose effects are so different, and sometimes so opposite? Spain, to which we are now about to turn our attention, will present us with other pictures, and must furnish fresh subjects for meditation.

During the course of the crusades, we see Spain occupied in its own boundaries with defending itself against those same Saracens whom the other nations of Europe went to contend with in the East; in the north of the Peninsula, some Christian sovereignties had maintained themselves, which began to be formidable under Sancho the Great, king of Castile and Arragon. The valour of the Castilians, sustained by the example of the Cid, and by the influence of chivalric manners, and seconded by warriors from all the provinces of France, took Toledo, before the end of the eleventh century. But the conquests of the Spaniards did not afterwards correspond with the splendour of their early triumphs; as fast as they retook provinces from the Moors, they made separate kingdoms of them; and the Spanish power, thus divided, became, in some sort, weakened by its own victories.

The invasion of the Moors in Spain bore some resemblance to that of the Franks in Asia. It was the religion of Mahomet that animated the Saracen warriors to the fight, as the Christian religion inflamed the zeal and ardour of the soldiers of the cross. Africa and Asia often answered to the appeal of the Mussulman colonies in Spain, as Europe did to the cries of alarm of the Christian colonies in Syria. Enthusiasm gave birth on both sides to prodigies of heroism, and held fortune for a long time suspended between the two inimical nations and the two inimical religions.

A spirit of independence naturally grew up among the Spaniards, during a war in which the state had need of all its citizens, and in which every citizen, by that means, acquired a great degree of importance. It has been remarked, with reason, that a people that has done great things, that an entire people called to the defence of its country, experiences an exaggerated sentiment of its rights, shows itself more exacting, sometimes more unjust towards those who govern, and often feels tempted to employ against its sovereigns the strength it had employed against its enemies. Thus we may see in the Spanish annals, that the nobility and the people were more turbulent than in other countries, and that monarchy was there at first more limited than among the other nations of Europe.

The institution of the Cortes, the enfranchisement of the commons, and a crowd of privileges granted to cities, signalized very early, among the Spaniards, the decay of the feudal system and of the absolute authority of the monarchs. If we may judge by public acts of legislation, we might believe that the Spanish people enjoyed liberty before all the other nations of Europe. But, in times of trouble, we must be guarded in judging of the liberty of a nation by that which is said on political rostrums, or in charters and institutions, by turns obtained by violence and destroyed by power, always placed between two rocks,—anarchy and despotism. The history of Spain, at this period, is full of crimes and monstrous deeds, that stain the cause of princes as well as that of the people: which proves at least that morals did not keep pace with laws, and that institutions, created among public discords, did not soften the national character.

Amidst the revolutions which agitated Spain, political passions sometimes caused even the domination of the Moors to be forgotten. When at the end of the thirteenth century, the Mussulmans, conquered by James of Arragon, abandoned the Balearic isles and the kingdom of Valencia and Murcia, the Spaniards all at once suspended the progress of their arms. Whilst in the East, the victorious Mamelukes redoubled their efforts to completely drive the Franks from the coast of Syria; in the West, the Moors remained, during two centuries, in possession of a part of Spain, without the Spaniards ever seriously attempting to complete the conquest of their own country. The standard of Mahomet floated over the cities of Granada, up to the reign of Ferdinand and Isabella. It was only at this period that the Spanish monarchy issued all-powerful from the chaos of revolutions, and revived in the people the warlike and religious enthusiasm which completed the expulsion of the Moors. Then terminated the struggle which had lasted during eight centuries, and in which, according to Spanish authors, three thousand seven hundred battles were fought. So many combats, which were nothing but one long crusade, must have been a school of bravery and heroism; thus the Spaniards, in the sixteenth and seventeenth centuries, were considered the most brave and warlike nation of Europe. Philosophers have sought to explain by the influence of climate that spirit of haughtiness and pride, that grave and austere character which to this day distinguish the Spanish nation. It appears to us that a much more natural explanation of this national character is to be found in a war at once patriotic and religious, in which twenty successive generations were engaged, the perils of which must have inspired serious thoughts as well as noble sentiments.

The aversion for the yoke and the religion of the Moors, redoubled the attachment of the people for their religion and their ancient customs. The remembrance of that glorious struggle has not failed to animate the ardour and courage of the Spaniards at a recent period;—fortunate had it been for Spain if, at the moment at which I am speaking, she had not forgotten her own examples!

THE RETURN.

Towards the end of the war against the Moors, Spain adopted the Inquisition with more warmth than the other Christian nations. I will not attempt to repel the reproaches which modern philosophers have addressed to her; but it appears to me that sufficient account has not been taken of the motives which would render more excusable in Spain than elsewhere, those suspicions and those dark jealousies for all which was not the national religion. How could they forget that the standard of a foreign worship had so long floated over the Peninsula, and that during many ages, Christian warriors had fought, not only for the faith of their fathers, but for the very soil of their country against the infidels? According to my opinion, may it not be believed, that among the Spaniards, religious intolerance, or rather a hatred for all foreign religion, had something in itself which was less a jealous devotion than an ardent, restless patriotism?

Spain took no part in the crusades, till the spirit of these wars began to die away in the rest of Europe. We must, however, remark, that this kingdom derived some advantages from the Eastern expeditions. In almost all the enterprises of Christendom against the Mussulmans of Asia, a great number of the Crusaders stopped on the coast of Spain to combat the Moors. Many crusades were published in the West against the infidels who were masters of the Peninsula. The celebrated victory of Tolosa over the Moors was the fruit of a crusade preached in Europe, and particularly in France, by order of the sovereign pontiff. Expeditions beyond the sea were likewise favourable to the Spaniards, by retaining in their own country the Saracens of Egypt and Syria, who might have joined those on the coast of Africa. It has been shown in this history that the kingdom of Portugal was conquered and founded by Crusaders. The crusades gave the idea of those orders of chivalry, which, in imitation of those of Palestine, were formed in Spain, and without the succour of which the Spanish nation would not perhaps have triumphed over the Moors.

We may add, that Spain is the country in which the memory of the crusades was preserved the longest. In the last century, the bull called *Crusada* was there published every year in all the provinces. This solemn publication reminded the Spaniards of the triumphs they had formerly obtained over the Mussulmans.

We have shown the state of the principal powers of Europe during the crusades; it now remains for us to speak of a power which dominated over all the others, and which was as a tie or centre to all the powers;—we mean the authority of the heads of the Church.

The popes, as a temporal power and as a spiritual power, presented a singular contrast in the middle ages. As sovereigns of Rome, they had almost no authority, and were often banished from their own states: as heads of Christendom, they exercised an absolute empire to the extremities of the world, and their name was revered wherever the Gospel was preached.

It has been said that the popes made the crusades; they who maintain this opinion are far from being acquainted with the general movement which then affected the Christian world; no power on earth could have been able to produce such a great revolution; it only belonged to Him whose will gives birth to and disperses tempests, to throw all at once into human hearts that enthusiasm which silenced all other passions, and drew on the multitude as if by an invisible power. In this volume we have shown how the enthusiasm for the holy wars developed itself by degrees, and how it broke forth towards the end of the eleventh century, without any other influence but that of the dominant ideas: it led away the whole of society, and the popes were led away as nations of people were; one proof that the sovereign pontiffs did not produce this extraordinary revolution is, that they were never able to revive the spirit of the crusades, when that spirit became extinct among Christian nations.

It has likewise been said that the crusades very much increased the authority of the popes; we shall soon see what truth there is in that assertion. Among the causes which contributed to the growth of the pontifical authority, we may name the invasion of the barbarians of the North, who overthrew the empire of the West, and the progress of the Saracens, who would not allow the emperors of the East leisure to turn their attention towards Italy, or even to preserve any domination over that country. The popes thus found themselves freed from two powers upon which they depended; and remained in possession of the city of Rome, which appeared to have no other master. Other circumstances added from that time to the authority of the successors of St. Peter. However it may be, everybody knows that this authority had already made immense progress before the crusades; the head of the most powerful monarchs had already bowed before the thunders of the Vatican; and Christendom seemed to have already adopted the maxim of Gregory VII., that "the pope, in quality of Vicar of Jesus Christ, ought to be superior to every human power."

It cannot be doubted that a religious war was calculated to favour the development of the pontifical authority. But this war itself produced events, and gave rise to circumstances which were less a means of aggrandizement for the power of the popes, than a rock against which that power was dashed and injured. But it is positive, that the end of the crusades left the sovereign pontiffs less powerful than they had been at the commencement of the holy wars.

Let us, in the first place, say a few words of the advantages which the heads of the Church derived from the expeditions against the infidels. Recourse was always had to the sovereign pontiffs when the question of a crusade was agitated; the holy war was preached in their name, and carried on under their auspices. Warriors enrolled under the banners of the cross, received from the pope privileges which freed them from all other dependence but that of the Church; the popes were the protectors of the Crusaders, the support of their families, the guardians of their properties; it was to the popes the Crusaders submitted all their differences, and confided all their interests.

The sovereign pontiffs were not at first aware of the advantages they might derive from the crusades. In the first crusade, Urban, who had enemies to contend with, did not think of asking the assistance of the warriors he had persuaded to take the cross; it was not till the second crusade that the popes perceived the ascendancy the holy wars must give them. At this period a king of France and an emperor of Germany were, in a manner, lieutenants of the Holy See; in the third crusade, the pope compelled Henry II. to take the cross, to expiate the murder of Thomas à Becket. After the death of Henry, his son Richard set out for the East, at the signal of the sovereign pontiff. In consequence of this crusade, great disorders, as we have related, disturbed the kingdom of England; the popes took advantage of them to give laws to the English people, and a few years after the death of Richard, his brother and successor acknowledged himself the vassal of the court of Rome.

The crusades were for the popes a pretext to usurp, in all the states of Europe, the principal attributes of sovereignty; they became possessed, in the name of the holy war, of the right of levying everywhere both armies and imposts; the legates they employed in all the countries of Christendom exercised supreme authority in their name; the presence of these legates inspired respect and fear; their wills were laws. Armed with the cross, they commanded all the clergy as masters; and as the clergy, among all Christian nations, had the greatest ascendancy, the empire of the popes had no longer any opposition or limits.

It may be perceived that we have forgotten none of the advantages the heads of the Church found in the crusades: here are the obstacles and the rocks they met with in the exercise of their power.

It must be allowed that the empire of the popes received but very little increase in Asia during the holy wars; the quarrels and disputes which constantly disturbed the Christian colonies in the

East, and in which they were obliged to interfere, multiplied their embarrassments, without adding to their power.

Their voice was not always listened to by the multitude of the Crusaders; sometimes even the soldiers of the cross resisted the will and despised the counsels of the pontiffs. The legates of the Holy See were frequently in opposition to the leaders of the army, and their character was not always respected in camps. As the popes were supposed to direct the crusades, they were, in some sort, responsible for the misfortunes and disorders they had no power to prevent: this moral responsibility exposed them sometimes to be judged with rigour, and was injurious to their reputation for wisdom and ability.

By an abuse of the spirit of the crusades, the popes were dragged into wars in which their ambition was often more interested than religion; they then thought of their temporal power, and that was their weakest point; they were never strong but when they depended upon a higher support; the crusades became for them as a lever, which they employed to elevate themselves; but it must be allowed that they depended upon it too much, and when this lever failed them, their authority trembled. Seeking to regain what they had lost, the popes made, in the fourteenth and fifteenth centuries, incredible efforts to revive the spirit of the crusades; the question then being no longer to go and fight the Saracens in Asia, but to defend Europe against the invasion of the Turks. Amidst the perils of Christendom, the conduct of the popes merited the greatest praise, and the zeal they displayed has not been sufficiently appreciated by historians. But the time of the fervour for crusades was past. The success obtained by the sovereign pontiffs was never proportionate with their efforts, and the uselessness of their attempts necessarily weakened the idea entertained of their ascendancy and their power.

The crusade against the Albigeois procured them very little advantage; the intolerance which gave birth to that war proceeded from the crusades; the Inquisition, which arose from it, awakened more passions than it suppressed. By the Inquisition, the Church assumed in this world a jurisdiction which partook too strongly of humanity; her decrees were much more respected when they were referred to heaven or to a future life.

Nothing can equal the enormity of the tributes that were imposed upon the clergy for carrying on the holy wars. The tenths were not only levied for the crusades, but for every attempt at a crusade; not only for expeditions to the East, but for every enterprise against the enemies of the court of Rome. They were at length levied under the most vain pretexts; all Europe addressed warm remonstrances to the popes; at first the rigour with which the agents collected the tributes was complained of; and afterwards their infidelity in the application of the treasures extorted from the faithful became equally a subject of scandal. Nothing could be more injurious to the pontifical authority than these complaints, which arose from all quarters, and which, in the end, furnished weapons for the formidable heresy of Luther.

The history of the popes in the middle ages completes the proof of that which we have said. Their domination went on constantly increasing during a century up to Innocent III.; it after that period declined during another century, down to Boniface VIII., at which time crusades beyond the seas ended.

In latter days, publicists have said a great deal about the power of the heads of the Church; but they have judged rather according to systems than according to facts,—more after the spirit of our own age than that of the middle ages. The genius of the sovereign pontiffs has been much lauded, particularly for the purpose of placing their ambition in a stronger light. But if the popes really had the genius and the ambition attributed to them, we must believe they would have been principally employed in aggrandizing their states, and increasing their authority as sovereigns. Nevertheless, they did not succeed in this, or else they never attempted it. In fact, what could men do, who were mostly arrived at the age of decrepitude?—what could princes do, who merely passed over the throne, to strengthen their authority, and master the passions belonging to the infancy and the youth of societies? Among the crowd of popes who succeeded each other, many were endowed with a superior genius, whilst others only possessed a moderate capacity; men of all characters and all turns of mind occupied, in succession, the chair of St. Peter; nevertheless, these men, so different by their tastes, their passions, and their talents, all aimed at and all did the same thing; they had, therefore, an impulsion which was not in themselves, the motive of which must be sought elsewhere than in the vulgar policy of princes.

That would be a curious history which would trace, in the same picture, the spiritual empire and the temporal empire of the popes. Who would not be surprised at seeing in it, on one side, a force which nothing could resist, which moves the very world,—a will always the same, which is transmitted from pontiff to pontiff, like a deposit, or like a sacred heritage; on the other, a policy weak and changeable, like man,—a power which can scarcely defend itself against the lowest of its enemies, and which at every moment the breath of revolutions has power to shake? In this parallel, the imagination would be dazzled when such an empire should be presented to it as has never been seen upon earth, and which would lead to the belief that the popes did not belong to this fragile and transitory world,—a power which hell cannot pull down,—which the world cannot corrupt,—which, without the help of any army, and by the simple ascendancy of a few words, subdues things sooner, and proves itself more formidable, than ancient Rome, with all her victories. What more magnificent spectacle can the history of empires present to us? But, in the other part of the picture, who would not be moved to pity at beholding a government without vigour, an administration without foresight,—that people, descended from *the king people*, led by an indolent, timid old man, the eternal city falling into ruins, and as hidden beneath the grass? When we see—so near to a power almost supernatural—weakness, uncertainty, the fragility common to things below, and humanity with all its miseries, why may we not be permitted to compare the double power of the popes to Jesus Christ himself, of whom they were the vicars and images upon earth,—to Jesus Christ, whose double nature presents us, on one side, a God beaming with splendour, and on the other a simple mortal, loaded with the cross, and crowned with thorns?

If the principal features of this picture are not wanting in truthfulness, how can we believe in the policy of the popes as it is represented to us?—is it not more natural to think that the sovereign pontiffs, in all they did that was great, followed the spirit of Christianity? In the middle ages, which was the period of their power, they were much more directed by this spirit than they directed it themselves; later, and when popes entertained projects like those that are attributed to their genius and ambition, their power declined. We have but to compare Gregory VII., giving himself up to the spirit of his age, and supporting himself by the ascendancy of the Church, with Julius II., whom Voltaire calls a great prince, and who only employed the known combinations of policy.

The pontifical authority was the only one that had its bases and roots in opinions and beliefs. This power gave the world, or, rather, the world asked of it, laws, knowledge, and a support. The popes were right in the famous comparison of the two great luminaries. The authority of the heads of the Church was much more in advance towards civilization than the authority of princes. In order that the world might be civilized, it was important for the popes to have great power; and the need that was felt for their power favoured the progress of it.

As long as the world was governed by opinions and beliefs, rather than by civil laws and political authorities, the popes exercised the greatest influence; when the interests and rights of princes and nations became better regulated; when the world passed from the empire of opinions to that of laws; when, in a word, temporal power was well established in Europe, and prevailed over the spiritual of society, the pontiffs necessarily lost their ascendancy. Such is the history of the origin, of the progress, and of the decay of the pontifical power in the ages which have preceded us.

That which we have said of the popes clearly shows what influence the Church exercised over the society of Europe in the middle ages; but gross minds were not yet prepared to receive all the benefits of Christianity. The alliance of barbarism with superstition retarded the progress of true knowledge. The passions and customs of barbarians were still mingled with some salutary institutions.

The Franks, the Germans, and Goths, when obtaining possession of the richest countries of Europe, had employed all the rights of conquest, and these rights had become the laws of European society. We may form an idea of the government of the middle ages by representing to ourselves a victorious army, which disperses itself throughout the conquered country, shares the territory and those who inhabit it, and is always ready to march at the signal of its officers and its supreme general, to combat the common enemy, and defend its possessions.

As long as discipline and subordination subsisted in this military colony, public order was not entirely disturbed; and this kind of government might supply the place of wiser institutions. But as soon as the relations of assistance and fidelity, obedience and protection, became weakened, society —or rather the feudal government—no longer presented anything but the aspect of an army given up to license,—of an army whose officers and soldiers no longer acknowledged a head, were no longer subject to direction, and fought at hazard under a thousand different standards.

The vassals depended, in the first place, on the prince, because they held their lands and their offices of him. These lands and these offices becoming hereditary, their holders soon desired to render themselves independent, and to arrogate to themselves privileges which only belonged to the sovereign; such as coining money, holding a jurisdiction, and making war in their own name. From that time there remained scarcely any trace of subordination.

This decline of society, or, rather, this corruption of the feudal system, is referrible to the end of the second race. Charlemagne, in his endeavours to reëstablish the empire of the Cæsars, committed violence upon the social compact, and his extraordinary efforts exhausted the powers of royalty. The bow which he had too strongly bent, broke in the hands of his successors, and his empire crumbled away, when no longer sustained by the ascendancy of a great character. Charlemagne wished to emancipate himself from the laws of feudalism; under his feeble successors, feudalism, in its turn, was desirous of emancipating itself from the crown. The greatest evil of the feudal system was that it destroyed all protective power, all tutelary legislation, which could watch over the order and safety of society.

The monarch, despoiled of all authority, could neither be the support of innocence nor the avenger of crime; nor the mediator in war, nor the arbitrator in disputes that disturbed peace. Sovereignty, exercised by every man who wore a sword, was spread everywhere, without any one acknowledging its power anywhere; such was the disorder and confusion among those who disputed, sword in hand, for the wreck of sovereign power.

Nothing is more afflicting than this picture; the excesses which accompanied feudal anarchy no one is ignorant of. It does not form part of our plan to speak of it to any extent; the task we have to perform is a less painful one: if we turn our looks towards old times, it is only in order to discover the origin of our institutions; and among the revolutions of a barbarous age, we have only to make known what they produced that is salutary and durable. Before we proceed further, and in order to mix a few consolatory ideas with sad and painful images, we will show, by the side of the abuses of feudalism, the advantages contemporary society received from the feudal system, and the happy germs of civilization which grew from it for the benefit of following ages.

If the feudal government contained sources of disorder, it prevented disorder being carried to its height, and the evil from remaining without remedy. If it favoured anarchy and civil wars, it preserved Europe from the fury of conquerors, and from that of despotism. Vassals did not willingly consent to leave their lands; they were only bound to follow their sovereign to war for a stipulated time. This condition of the feudal compact, which was general in Europe, was found favourable for the defence of territory, and placed obstacles in the way of every project of invasion. Forces, spread about in all parts, served to protect every country against a foreign enemy, and could not be collected anywhere to assist the designs of an ambitious leader.

At a time in which passions did everything and laws were nothing, in which no political interest bound people together, what could have prevented a prince from assembling armies and ravaging Europe? What could have prevented a conqueror from subduing several kingdoms, and subjecting the people to all the excesses of tyranny, supported by the force of arms alone? It was then to the spirit of resistance of the feudal nobility that European society owed, in the midst of barbarism, the advantage of not becoming a prey to Eastern despotism, and security from wars of invasion.

Feudalism had rights and privileges to defend; the defence of these rights and privileges naturally led to ideas of independence, and these ideas of independence spread in the end through all classes of society. It must not be forgotten that the English barons established liberty in their country, whilst defending the privileges and rights of the feudal compact.

The reciprocity of obedience and protection, of services and duties, kept alive some generous sentiments. From feudal relations was born that spirit of devotion and respect for the sovereign which is neither the blind submission of the slave, nor the reasonable submission of the republican. This sentiment, which was considered, up to modern times, as the conservative principle of society in monarchies, became particularly the distinctive character of the French nobility.

The history of the crusades presents us with several examples of this devotion of the barons and knights to their monarch. When the kings of France who took the cross, were in any dangers in the East, what proofs of respect and love did they not receive from the gallant knights who accompanied them? What spectacle can be more touching than that of the imprisoned army in Egypt, forgetting its own captivity to deplore that of Louis IX! Who is not affected at seeing, upon the coast of Africa, the French warriors overwhelmed with evils, but finding no tears in their miseries but to weep for the death of a king of France?

These ties of fidelity, which arose from feudal relations, were so powerful over men's minds, that the preachers of the crusades sometimes invoked them in their exhortations. They preached the duties of feudalism concurrently with the precepts of the Gospel, and in order to excite Christian warriors to take the cross, they called them "the vassals of Jesus Christ."

It is to the times of the feudal government we must go back, to find in all its purity, that susceptibility upon the point of honour, that inviolable fidelity to the word, which then supplied the absence of laws, and which in polished societies often render men better than laws themselves. All our ideas of military glory, that boundless esteem which we accord to bravery, that profound contempt which, amongst us, is attached to falsehood or felony, are to be traced to this remote period. Feudalism was so completely mixed up with the spirit and character of nations, that modern societies have no institutions that have not some relation with it; and we have everywhere traces of it in our habits, our manners, and even in our speech

Let me be allowed to add here one single observation. It is in vain we protest against our origin by our words; we are incessantly reminded of it by our tastes, by our sentiments, and sometimes by our pleasures. In fact, if, on one side, our reason, formed in the school of new ideas, finds nothing that is not revolting in the middle ages, why, on the other, does our imagination, moved by the spectacle of generous passions, delight in representing to itself olden times, and mingling with gallant knights and paladins? Whilst a severe philosophy heaps measureless blame upon the barbarous customs of feudalism, and the Gothic manners of our ancestors, how is it that the remembrances which these manners and these customs have left us inspire still our poets with pictures which appear to us so full of charms? Why are these remembrances revived every day with the same success, in our poems, in our romances, and upon our stage? Would it be true to say that there is more patriotism in our imagination than in our reason, since the one would make us forget the history of our country, and the other unceasingly reminds us of it?

The crusades assisted in destroying the abuses of the feudal system; they served to preserve all that the system inspired of generous sentiments, and concurred at the same time in developing that which it contained that was favourable to civilization. We will finish our sketch of the manners of feudalism and the salutary effects of the crusades, by describing the revolution which operated at this time upon the different classes of society. The nobility will fix our attention in the first place.

Nobles are found in every nation where the memory of ancestors is reckoned for anything. There can be no doubt that nobility was common among the Franks and other barbarous people who invaded Europe. But in what point of view was this nobility looked upon before the eleventh and twelfth centuries? How was it at first constituted? How was the illustration of races transmitted? We are in possession of very few monuments to assist in deciding these questions; and when we have thoroughly studied the history of the middle ages, we have nothing better to do than to imitate the genealogists, who, when embarrassed in explaining the origin of the most ancient families, content themselves with assigning it to the night-time of the past.

When we reflect upon the rapidity with which generations pass away, and how difficult it is, even in civilized times, for most families to make out their own history during a single century, can we be astonished that, in times of ignorance and barbarism there have been so few means of preserving the memory of the most illustrious families? In addition to the almost entire absence of written documents, the idea of true grandeur, the idea of that which constitutes heroic illustration, did not yet strike men's minds sufficiently forcibly to make them preserve a long remembrance of it.* In those barbarous times, men, and even princes, were most frequently only distinguished by their physical qualities or their bodily defects. To be convinced of this truth we have but to glance at the list of kings of the middle ages, in which we find the names of Pepin-le-Bref (Pepin the Short), Charles-le-Chauve (Charles the Bald), William-le-Roux (William Rufus, or the Red), Louis-le-Gros (Louis the Fat), Frederick-Barbereusse (Frederick Barbarossa, or Red Beard), and many others, whom their age only designated by that which struck their eyes and was obvious to the grossest perception. There are few things more curious for an observer, than to see how old chronicles make us acquainted with the personages whose actions they give an account of. They never omit in their pictures, either the colour of the hair, or the stature, or the countenance of the princes and heroes; and their historical portraits (may I be allowed the comparison?) bear much less resemblance to a passage of history, than to those descriptions which are now-a-days written upon the passports of travellers.

---

* The chronicle of Tours tells us, with the greatest simplicity, that Charlemagne was called the *Great* on account of his *great good luck*; thus historians confounded, as the vulgar do, glory with fortune.

If, as a writer has said, entire man was not yet understood, it cannot be said that virtue was not known, as at any other period; but the idea of virtue was then lost in that of duty, and with the single sentiment of duty, which was but the voice of conscience or the modest instinct of habit, they dreamt not of living in the memory of men. The desire for illustrating a name belongs to a nascent civilization. When civilization threw forth its first rays, moral ideas of greatness were attached to the names of ancient families; and it may be safely said that nobility was not truly instituted before the value of glory began to be felt. But what is very certain is, that in the crusades nobility acquired an eminence that it had never before enjoyed. The exploits of nobles in the cause of Christianity, were very different affairs from those wars of castle against castle, with which they employed themselves in Europe. Nobility from that time found its archives in history, and the opinion the world entertained of its valour became its loftiest title.

If we consult the most authentic facts and the most probable opinions, we have reason to believe that the distinctions of nobility were at first founded upon great offices, but principally upon property. It was for the land or estate that, in the feudal system, the oath of fealty or homage was taken, and the protection of the sovereign claimed. For the man who was not a proprietor there was no contract, no privilege; he had nothing to give, nothing to receive; in the times of Joinville, nobles were called *rich men*. In France, a great proprietor was, by right, noble; if he was ruined or despoiled, his descendants sank into the crowd again: thus had the customs of a barbarous age established it. A strange thing it is, that there are times in which extreme civilization can make a nation revert to the same estate as extreme barbarism. When political illusions shall be dispersed, and there shall remain nothing but the mere substance of society, it is still property, it is the estate which will establish pre-eminence and denote ranks. Lands will no longer furnish soldiers, but they will pay taxes for the support of them; they will no longer be held by the tenure of complying with the duty of feudal aid; but they will still owe the sovereign the support of their influence, in exchange for the protection they shall receive from the sovereign authority.

If, in the middle ages, aristocracy was founded upon land, society derived a great advantage from the circumstance; for territorial property, which does not change, which is always the same, preserves the institutions and manners of a people better than industrial property, which most frequently belongs no more to one country than another, and which, on that account, bears within itself the germs of corruption. If it was for this reason that formerly nobility was degraded by giving itself up to the speculations of commerce and industry, it must be agreed that the usage thus established, had at least a respectable aim, and arose from a salutary principle.

Territorial property had then such an influence over the social state, that it is quite enough to be acquainted with the changes it experienced, to judge of the changes to which society was subjected. "As soon as the state of the property of a certain period is discovered," says Robertson, "we may determine with precision what was at the same time the degree of power then enjoyed by the king or the nobility." During the crusades, ecclesiastical and civil laws permitted nobles to alienate their domains. A great number of them availed themselves of this fatal privilege, and did not hesitate to sell their lands; which displaced property, and consequently power. The nobility thus lost its power, and the crown gained that which the aristocracy lost.

The crusades, however, were not unproductive of good fruit for the nobility; gentlemen acquired principalities in the East; most of the cities of Greece and Syria became so many lordships, which recognised as masters counts and barons enrolled under the banners of the holy wars; some, still more fortunate, ascended the throne of David, or that of Constantine, and took place among the greatest monarchs of Christendom.

The military orders likewise presented the nobility with amends for the losses they experienced in ruinous wars. These orders had immense possessions in both the West and the East; they were for the European nobility, an asylum in peace, and a school of heroism in war.

It was at this period that the use of surnames was introduced, and coats of arms were assumed. Every gentleman added to his own name the name of his estate, or the title of the lordship he possessed; he placed in his coat of arms a sign which distinguished his family and marked his nobility; genealogy became a science, and consecrated, by its researches, the illustration of races. Whatever value may be now-a-days attached to this science, it must be admitted that it often threw a great light upon the history of illustrious families, and sometimes upon the general history of a country to which these families belonged.

Everything leads us to believe that the origin of surnames, but more particularly of coats of arms, is due to the Crusaders. The lord stood in no need of a mark of distinction when he did not go off his own manor; but he became aware of the necessity for distinguishing himself from others when he found himself at a distance from home, and confounded in the crowd of the Crusaders: a great number of families ruined themselves, or became extinct, in the holy wars. Such as were ruined attached themselves more strongly to the remembrance of their nobility, the only wealth that was left them; after the extinction of families, the necessity for replacing them was felt; it was under Philip-le-Hardi that the practice of creating nobles was introduced. As soon as there were new nobles, it became of more consequence to be considered ancient ones. Property did not appear sufficient to preserve and transmit a name which itself became a property, consecrated by history and acknowledged by society. It was then that nobility attached more value to marks of distinction.

At the end of the feudal government, the nobility, it is true, still constituted, in a great degree, the strength of the army; but it served the state in a new character; it conformed more with the spirit of chivalry than with that of feudalism. A gentleman no longer paid homage to his sovereign for his estate, but he swore upon his sword to be faithful to him.

As soon as feudal services ceased to be required, the nobility increased in zeal for personal service. Kings eagerly welcomed them when they were no longer formidable; thus they recovered in the favour of courts a great portion of the advantages they had lost. As they still held the first rank in society, and preserved a great ascendancy over the other classes, they continued, by their example, to polish the spirit and the manners of the nation; and it is by their means particularly, that those elegant manners were formed which have so long distinguished the French among all the nations of Europe.

It is difficult, however, to say with precision what the nobility gained and what they lost by the changes that were effected. Their existence, doubtless, had something more brilliant in it, but also something less solid. The honorary prerogatives which they retained, without giving them any real strength, armed more jealous passions against them than territorial power had done; for it may be remarked, that man's self-love endures riches and power in others, with a better grace than it endures distinctions.

We must add, likewise, that as society progressed, new means of illustration, new kinds of notability arose; the moral power of opinion, which had been attached exclusively to nobility, communicated itself by degrees to those who contributed to the prosperity of society by their talents, their knowledge, or their industry.

We have seen the brilliant side of feudalism; we have now to speak of the state in which the inhabitants of the cities and the country groaned. Most of the villages and cities depended upon some baron, whose protection they purchased, and who exercised an arbitrary jurisdiction over them.

Man, reduced to servitude, or rather slavery, had no law which guarded him against oppression; the produce of his labour, the wages of his sweat, did not belong to him; he was himself a property which could be claimed anywhere, if he fled away from his home. Chained to the glebe, he must often have envied the animal who helped him to trace the furrow, or the palfrey, the noble companion of his master. The serf had no other hope but that which religion afforded him, and left nothing to his children but the example of his patience in suffering. He could neither make a contract during his lifetime, nor a testament at the hour of death. His last will was not recognised by law; it died with him. To excuse the barbarity of this gross age, we must remember the still more frightful fate of slaves among the Greeks and Romans. We have no need to point out the obstacles this state of things must have opposed to the development of the industry and the social faculties of man. Thus the country was covered with forests, and most of the cities presented nothing but an aspect of poverty and misery.

The cities of Lombardy, and a great part of Italy, were the first places that shook off the yoke of feudalism. The emperors of Germany, as we have seen, were almost always at variance with the popes. The cities took advantage of these quarrels, to arrogate rights which no one disputed. Others purchased them of the emperors, who believed they made a good bargain when they sold that which they had not the power to refuse. Towards the middle of the eleventh century, the clergy and nobility had already no more influence in the cities of Italy. According to the evidence of Otho of Freisengen, a contemporary author, Italy was full of free cities, all of which had obliged their bishops to reside within their walls; there was scarcely a noble who was not subject to the laws and government of a city. In Germany the cities obtained their freedom at a later period. These Germans, who, according to Tacitus, considered dwelling in cities as a mark of servitude, not only in the end built cities, but sought liberty in them. The cities of the Rhine appear to have been made free by the emperors in the eleventh century. But most of these cities were poor, they contained but few inhabitants, and were not able to defend themselves against the German oligarchy. At the commencement of the fourteenth century, several free cities, enriched by the commerce of the East, and by the communications opened by the crusades, formed a confederation, and by that means made their independence respected.

In England, the spirit of liberty did not take its spring before the holy wars; the cities, with the exception of that of London, which had obtained several privileges, scarcely dreamt of independence; the Britons, as in the times of Virgil, appeared still separated from the rest of the world. It may be said that liberty in the English nation was not an affair of locality, but a general affair, which was to be decided at a later period.

In Spain, the war against the Moors, as we have already said, favoured the independence of the commons. We are in possession of historical documents of the eleventh century, which prove that several Spanish cities enjoyed certain immunities at this period. But the first of these cities which were summoned to the Cortes, urged by a spirit of jealousy, refused to admit the others, which was very injurious to the development and progress of liberty in Spain.

In the south of France, the archives of the communes present us with some traces of liberty, a long time before the period of the crusades. The influence of a fine climate, the vivacity which animated the inhabitants, with some traditions of the Roman law, preserved, in the provinces which border on Spain and Italy, habits of independence which might serve as models or examples. When the kings of France thought of enfranchising some communes, it was from the south of the kingdom they must have taken the idea.

These enfranchisements of the southern cities, however, were rather consecrated by custom than by positive laws. According to the best opinions, the formal and legal enfranchisement of communes in France dates from Louis-le-Gros, who granted privileges to some cities situated within the domains of the crown. The example of Louis-le-Gros was followed by Louis VII. and Philip Augustus. A great number of cities saw all sorts of slavery excluded from their walls, chose their own magistrates, levied their own taxes, kept up a military force, and had a jurisdiction entirely their own. Such was the first blow given in France to the feudal government.

Before this period it was customary to implore the aid of the barons against violence and robbery. This support was abandoned as soon as another tutelary power arose. The serfs, and even the freemen, who had at first sought safety in castles, soon sought it in cities, against their former protectors, the castellans; the first engagements of the inhabitants of cities were mutual defence and reciprocal protection.

The liberty of cities began by the corporations; men could only be strong when united. This necessity for union in moments of crisis or peril is so natural, that when society is disturbed, factions and parties are formed which are like corporations. The spirit of a public body, or the spirit of party, in whatever way it may be considered, holds essentially with the social character. Liberty was much more considered in relation with the community than in relation with individual man; it was considered a benefit that could only be enjoyed in common. Thus society did not find itself subordinate to the individual, but the individual to society. Isolated man could do nothing; strength lay with the association, which effectually protected the rights of all, and watched over the conservation of individual liberty and public liberty.

When cities situated within the royal domains had obtained their franchises, the spirit of independence soon possessed the other cities of the kingdom. The communes which succeeded in gaining their enfranchisement, did not all obtain the same advantages; they were, more or less, favoured by circumstances. Here, liberty was purchased of the lord; there, the yoke was shaken off by force; in other places, treaties were effected, in which the spirit of liberty and feudal power made mutual concessions.

During the crusades, the long absence of the barons must have multiplied, for the communes, opportunities of enfranchising themselves. Most of the lords who ruined themselves for the holy wars, exchanged, for the money of which they stood in need, all their rights over the cities which depended upon them—rights which they yielded the more willingly from hoping to win principalities in Asia.

This enfranchisement of communes produced a very different effect for the great vassals and the crown. It weakened the authority of the lords, because the spirit of liberty was against them; it increased the royal authority, because the cities which we fre or had a desire to be so, looked to the king. Cities, when their independence was threatened, implored the king's protection. We find in old chronicles, that Philip Augustus granted letters of protection to cities dependent upon barons. Thus kings became the hope of all the communes of the kingdom, and liberty supported itself by royalty. This is why the cities of France, to defend their franchises, formed no league, as they did in other countries; for they found a natural defence in royal power.

The revolution which was destined to destroy feudalism, appeared to act as of itself. There is, in the possession of a newly-acquired good, a restlessness, an anxiety, a fear of losing it, which kept the communes always on the alert; there is, on the contrary, in the possession of an anciently-acquired good, an indolent security, which did not permit the barons to see the true state of things. The lords only opposed new ideas by a short-sighted disdain, and believed they had lost nothing as long as they retained their swords by their sides.

If, however, we may judge by the complaints of Guibert, abbot of Nogent, a contemporary historian, the enfranchisement of the communes met with some opposition. There was no want of sour spirits, who considered it a dangerous and destructive innovation. But we may believe that these complaints were only inspired by that natural repugnance which the greater part of men entertain for seeing anything change which is consecrated by time, and by that vague mistrust which novelty produces, under whatever form it may appear. The truth is, that nobody knew, or could possibly judge, of the extent of the changes that were then in operation. Revolutions, whatever may be their object or their character, are never thoroughly understood before they have finished their course, and never reveal their secret at their commencement.

A century after Louis-le-Gros, Louis VIII. pretended to have the right of immediate sovereignty over all the communes. This was a signal for all the cities to complete their emancipation from the barons; this was the mortal blow to the feudal aristocracy. This great revolution of the social state went on so rapidly, that history can with difficulty follow its progress, and cannot assign the part which the crusades bore in it.

Happy had it been for society if that spirit of liberty which then set it in motion, and which advanced without ceasing, sowing blessings and evils on its route, had produced none but wise institutions; if, always confined within just bounds, it had not frequently kindled bloody discords, and had not at last mingled itself with the blind passions of the multitude! What a picture were that which should exhibit the consequences of this revolution up to modern times, which should represent monarchy rising from the ruins of feudalism, and then itself succumbing in a new revolution! What a subject for serious thoughts in the historian, when, embracing with a rapid glance ancient and modern times, he sees the two most active forces of society, at the revival of civilization,—royalty and liberty, marching constantly one towards the other, demanding of each other reciprocal support, overthrowing all the barriers that separated them, destroying all they found in their passage; at last, after several ages of endeavours, meeting face to face upon the ruins accumulated around them, taking each other at first sight for enemies, declaring war against each other, and falling together on the same field of battle!

God forbid that I should here be thought to present discouraging images! I have only wished to show the fragility of human affairs, and the want of foresight in those who direct societies. The revolution we have beheld is, perhaps, less the work of liberty than of the equality which is seen to figure, for the first time, in the political world.

This equality, such as the moderns have constituted it, was scarcely known in the ancient republics, of which the language had no word to express it. The first book that spoke of equality was the Gospel. Christianity constantly represents all men as equal before God. The object of the Gospel was to lower the pride of the great; which was salutary. I know not what false philosophy made use of equality to raise the pride of the low;—and then society was shaken to its very foundations.

The great revolution which has been effected in the manners and laws of Europe, and which began at the times of the crusades, may be divided into two principal epochs. At first it was desirable to wrest from the feudal lords a power which they abused: that was the first epoch,—that was the revolution of liberty. When the feudal lords had nothing left but distinctions, these distinctions irritated pride and jealousy, which, in the end, persuaded themselves that every political superiority was a tyranny, which must be brought low. This was the second epoch,—the revolution of equality; much more terrible than the first, because it had for motive, passions much more difficult to satisfy than the love of liberty.

But the peasants and serfs of the country, whilst the cities were in the enjoyment of liberty, still

THE CHRISTIAN ARMY IN THE MOUNTAINS OF JUDEA.

In going from Lydda the Crusaders approached the mountains of Judea. These mountains on which Jerusalem is situated, do not resemble those of Taurus or Lybia: the bluish summits of the Judean range have neither verdure nor shade, and its solitudes have no other inhabitant than the bear and the gazelle, the eagle and the vulture. Their physiognomy has something of the sadness of Israel, and recalls the austere and melancholy poetry of the prophets. The Christian army advanced through a narrow valley, between two mountains burning with the rays of the sun. The route which it followed had been cut into gullies by torrents of rain, which had also loosened large masses of rock, and these descending into the valley, choked the narrow passages. In such difficult situations a few Mussulmans would attack and kill many of the Crusaders.—BOOK IV.

groaned in slavery. Up to the fourteenth century, this numerous class found no abatement in the rigours of their servitude. The greatest advantage the crusades could have bestowed upon the peasants, was the momentary cessation of brigandage, and the peace which reigned in the country, all the time the wars against the Saracens were being carried on.

It is probable that serfs in Europe were not better treated, according to the legislation and customs of the West, than they were in the Holy Land, according to the *Assizes of Jerusalem*. There is no doubt that peasants taken from the glebe for the crusade became free men; but most of them perished by misery or by the swords of the Mussulmans. What became of the few who revisited their homes cannot be ascertained.

A population dispersed and scattered about a country did not present, as in cities, a formidable mass, capable of resistance. Peasants rarely communicated with each other, and could not support any demand, or establish any common right. Man requires some intelligence to make him sensible of the advantages of liberty, and the peasant class was then brutified by ignorance. We must likewise add, that the love of independence came with riches; and this is why it arose earlier in cities than in the country, and earlier in flourishing cities than in poorer ones. The serfs of the country were poor; they would not have known what use to make of liberty. Liberty is of little value to him who is in want of the first necessaries of life. Among warlike and barbarous hordes, who entertained a repugnance for labour, it was natural that they should be despised who gave themselves up to the painful toil of cultivating the earth. This repugnance was necessarily more strong among nomad nations, like those that conquered Europe. The contempt felt in the middle ages for the peasantry was injurious to their liberty; and this contempt even survived their servitude. People felt, in some sort, forced to treat as slaves men who performed a task which was considered necessary, but which every free man disdained.

The inhabitant of the country, abandoned to his own resources, did not aspire to independence; the only good he could pretend to was the choice of slavery. As the Church inspired more confidence than the nobles, a crowd of unfortunate beings took refuge, in a manner, at the foot of the altars, and devoted their liberty and that of their children to this church or that monastery, to which they looked for protection. Nothing is more curious than the formulæ by which the clergy received this sacrifice of individual liberty. They congratulated the new serfs with having preferred "the domination of Jesus Christ to the liberty of the age; they added, that "to serve God was to reign," and that "a holy servitude was true independence." These words must have been in harmony with the manners and ideas of the times, since a multitude of men and women were seen every day flocking to the monasteries, and conjuring the Church to admit them among "the serfs of Jesus Christ." That they should believe themselves, on that account, much more free than other men, we may at the present day be astonished; but was there not a sort of liberty in wearing chains they had chosen, and with which they had fettered themselves?

Some free cities of Germany contributed to the enfranchisement of the peasants of their territory. The same thing happened in Italy and in Spain, where the territory of cities was considerable; in England, the peasantry waited a long time for any amelioration of their fate. But nothing is more difficult than to ascertain with certainty the destiny which, during many ages, this multitude of men who covered the plains of Europe underwent; in the darkness of the middle ages, numberless generations of serfs passed over the earth, without leaving any traces in history. We can with difficulty catch, in old chronicles and acts of administration, here and there a few scattered gleams to throw a light upon our researches.

In France, it is not till the commencement of the fourteenth century that any ordinances of the kings upon the enfranchisement of the serfs are to be found. In an ordinance of 1315, Louis X. made use of these remarkable words: "Many persons among our common people are enchained in the bonds of servitude, which displeases us greatly. . . . . Our kingdom," he added, "is called and named the kingdom of the Franks; we are desirous that the thing should in truth be in accordance with its name," &c. In this ordinance, made only for the royal domains, the king of France pressed the nobles to follow his example. We are in possession of a letter-patent of the same king, by which commissaries were commanded to transport themselves to the bailiwick of Senlis, and "to give freedom to all who required it," on condition, nevertheless, of paying a sum for the rights of servitude, which reverted to the crown.

All the historical documents of this period prove, more and more, that the kings had placed themselves at the head of the general movement of society. In all they then did, their motive, doubtless, was to reëstablish order in the kingdom, and to found their authority upon the protection granted to those who suffered from the violences and excesses of feudal anarchy. If, however, we may judge by the ordinance just quoted, and by many other similar ones, their policy was not always disinterested, and, like most of the barons, they sometimes sold rather than granted the freedom of the serfs and the communes.

Many peasants showed themselves but little disposed to receive a liberty which was to be sold to them. Some from poverty, others from mistrust, a great number from unwillingness to change their condition, refused the benefit that was offered to them. Such is the spirit of man, that they resolved to remain serfs, because they were condemned to be such no longer. In several provinces, even disorders were created by their resistance. This was slaves fighting, with their chains, against Liberty herself. At a later period, the *jaquerie* proved that it was more easy to kindle the passions of a gross people, than to make them free; and that it was far, as regarded the serfs, from impatience under the yoke and hatred for their masters, to the true love of liberty.

When we are desirous of breaking the chains of the multitude, it is never to the multitude that we must address ourselves; in order that the fate of the lower classes should be ameliorated, the amelioration must come from the superior classes, by whom knowledge is spread and institutions are established. This is what happened at the period of which we are speaking. The servitude of the country was much softened by the maxims of the clergy, but more particularly by the influence of that French magistracy which had arisen contemporaneously with civilization.

In the middle of the fifteenth century, some serfs of Cataloina, who had taken refuge in France, being claimed by their lords, the parliament of Thoulouse declared that every man who entered into the kingdom crying *France!* became free. Mezerai, who relates this fact, adds: "Such is the kingdom of France, that its air communicates liberty to those who breathe it, and our kings are so august that they only reign over free men."

At the beginning of the sixteenth century, scarcely a trace of servitude could be found in the cities or the country. History could but applaud this revolution, if the fall even of feudalism, whilst destroying ancient abuses, had not placed governments in antagonism with difficulties which had not been foreseen, and whose consequences were destined to be deplorable. When the feudal government, which cost the people nothing, was quite overthrown, it became necessary to provide for the expenses of a new administration; when the state had lost the defenders which the feudal laws provided for it, others were to be sought, and their services to be remunerated. Thence came the necessity for stipendiary armies and regular and permanent taxes. To provide the money wanted, the coinage was debased, the Jews were persecuted, violence was had recourse to, and justice was sold,—all of which tended to corrupt both the government and the nation. The embarrassment of the finances, and the disorders it produced, have only increased up to the present day. To remedy this, the moral strength and life of society have often been neglected, and means of raising money have constituted the whole policy of states. To have credit, or not to have it, that is, now-a-days, life or death for governments. *Credit, deficit, bankruptcy,* are three words, of which the ancients and the middle ages were quite ignorant; but which are now constantly present to the restless, uneasy minds of kings and ministers. These three words will perhaps one day be sufficient to explain the decline and fall of empires.

Whatever was the weight of the public impositions, it must be allowed that the taxes gave rise to more frequent relations between governments and the people, which proved advantageous to liberty. People gave more attention to the administration which they paid for with the fruit of their industry and labour. Sovereigns had more consideration for the different classes of citizens of whom they demanded tribute; and were constrained to consult them in certain circumstances, in order that the people, says Pasquier, might not have occasion to be dissatisfied or murmur. The origin of representative government, as it exists in many European nations in our days, has been sought for in remote times; but everything leads us to believe that it owed its birth to the relations which the wants of states and the necessity for taxes naturally established between peoples and governments.

That which most increased the embarrassments of the majority of European monarchies, after the fall of feudalism, was the excessive enlargement of their military establishments. At the moment I am writing, there is no necessity to point out this fearful rock of modern societies. It is not a century since Montesquieu predicted that Europe would perish by its armies. God grant that this prophecy be not about to be accomplished! The military force of Europe has given us reason to dread all the evils it was intended to prevent. It was to defend every kingdom from foreign invasions; and yet there is not a kingdom in Europe that has not been invaded, or threatened with invasion. It was deemed necessary to restrain the multitude by means of armies; and armies have been raised to such numbers of men, that they have become the multitude itself under arms. Can it be true, as has been said, that there is no remedy for this evil? Deplorable state of things, without which society cannot last, with which it cannot exist!

The crusades have been reproached with having given birth to the idea of imposts; this idea is too simple not to have arisen without the help of the crusades. It is probable that the manner in which the tenths were collected for the holy war, might serve as a model for those who afterwards established regular contributions. As to regular armies, the expeditions to the East might furnish the first idea of them. It is certain that these distant expeditions changed the conditions of the feudal service, and accustomed people to see permanent armies maintained and commanded by princes.

Among the institutions which contended with the barbarism of the middle ages, we will, in the first place, consider chivalry, the exploits of which are much better known than its origin. At a time when everything was decided by force, and everything was determined by the sword;—in which, as Montesquieu says, to judge was to fight—women, children, and orphans were not able to defend their rights, and were abandoned a prey to iniquity. Generous warriors came forward to defend them; their devotion was applauded,—their example was followed. Shortly the order of Paladins was formed, who perambulated the world, seeking for wrongs to redress, and felons to combat with. Such was, doubtless, the origin of chivalry, which is so uselessly sought for in the forests of Germany. This institution sprang from the extreme disorder of society, and arose like a bulwark, which human generosity opposed to the irruptions of license, and the passions of a barbarous age.

Chivalry was known in the West before the crusades. These wars, which appeared to have the same aim as chivalry,—that of defending the oppressed, serving the cause of God, and combating with infidels,—gave this institution more splendour and consistency,—a direction more extended and salutary.

Religion, which mingled itself with all the institutions and all the passions of the middle ages, purified the sentiments of the knights, and elevated them to the enthusiasm of virtue. Christianity lent chivalry its ceremonies and its emblems, and tempered, by the mildness of its maxims, the asperities of warlike manners.

Piety, bravery, and modesty were the distinctive qualities of chivalry: " Serve God, and he will help you; be mild and courteous to every gentleman, by divesting yourself of all pride; be neither a flatterer nor a slanderer, for such people seldom come to great excellence. Be loyal in words and deeds; keep your word; be helpful to the poor and to orphans, and God will reward you." Thus said the mother of Bayard to her son; and these instructions of a virtuous mother comprised the whole code of chivalry.

The most admirable part of this institution was the entire abnegation of self,—that loyalty which made it the duty of every knight to forget his own glory, and only publish the lofty deeds of his companions in arms. The deeds of valour of a knight were his fortune, his means of living; *and he who was silent upon them was a robber of the property of others.* Nothing appeared more reprehensible than for a knight to praise himself. " If the squire," says le Code des Preux, "be vain-glorious of what he has done, he is not worthy to become a knight." An historian of the crusades offers us a singular example of this virtue, which is not entirely humility, and might be called the false modesty of glory, when he describes Tancred checking his career in the field of battle, to make his squire swear to be for ever silent upon his exploits.

The most cruel insult that could be offered to a knight, was to accuse him of falsehood. Want of truth, and perjury, were considered the most shameful of all crimes. If oppressed innocence implored the succour of a knight, woe to him who did not respond to the appeal! Shame followed every offence towards the weak, and every aggression towards an unarmed man.

The spirit of chivalry kept up and strengthened among warriors the generous sentiments which the military spirit of feudalism had given birth to: devotion to his sovereign was the first virtue, or rather the first duty, of a knight. Thus in every state of Europe grew up a young military power, always ready for fight, and always ready to sacrifice itself for prince or for country, as for the cause of justice and innocence.

One of the most remarkable characteristics of chivalry, and that which at the present day most strongly excites our surprise and curiosity, was the alliance of religious sentiments with gallantry. *Devotion and love,*—such was the principle of action of a knight: *God and the ladies,*—such was his device.

To form an idea of the manners of chivalry, we have but to glance at the tournaments, which owed their origin to it, and which were as schools of courtesy and festivals of bravery. At this period, the nobility were dispersed, and lived isolated in their castles. Tournaments furnished them with opportunities for assembling; and it was at these brilliant meetings that the memory of ancient gallant knights was revived,—that youth took them for models, and imbibed chivalric virtues by receiving rewards from the hands of beauty. We have seen in one of the truces between the Crusaders and the Saracens, that it was celebrated by a tournament.

As the ladies were the judges of the actions and the bravery of the knights, they exercised an absolute empire over the minds of the warriors; and I have no occasion to say that this ascendancy of the softer sex threw a charm over the heroism of the *preux* and the *paladins.* Europe began to escape from barbarism from the moment the most weak commanded the most strong,—from the moment when the love of glory, when the noblest feelings of the heart, the tenderest affections of the soul, everything that constitutes the moral force of society, was able to triumph over every other force.

Louis IX., a prisoner in Egypt, replies to the Saracens, that he will do nothing without Queen Marguerite, "who is his lady." The orientals could not comprehend such deference; and it is because they did not comprehend this deference, that they have remained so far in the rear of the nations of Europe, in nobleness of sentiment, purity of morals, and elegance of manners.

Heroes of antiquity wandered over the world to deliver it from scourges and monsters; but these heroes were not actuated by religion, which elevates the soul, nor by that courtesy which softens the manners. They were acquainted with friendship, as in the cases of Theseus and Pirithous, and Hercules and Lycas; but they knew nothing of the delicacy of love. The ancient poets take delight in representing the misfortunes of certain heroines abandoned by their lovers; but, in their touching pictures, there never escapes from their plaintive muse the least expression of blame against the hero, who thus caused the tears of beauty to flow. In the middle ages, or according to the manners of chivalry, a warrior who should have imitated the conduct of Theseus to Ariadne, or that of the son of Anchises towards Dido, would not have failed to incur the reproach of treachery.

Another difference between the spirit of antiquity and the sentiments of the moderns is, that among the ancients love was supposed to enervate the courage of heroes; and that in the days of chivalry, the women, who were the judges of valour, constantly kept alive the love of glory and an enthusiasm for virtue, in the hearts of the warriors. We find in Alain Chartier, a conversation of several ladies, who express their opinions upon the conduct of their knights, who had been present at the battle of Agincourt. One of these knights had sought safety in flight, and the lady of his thoughts exclaims: "According to the law of love, I should have loved him better dead than alive." In the first crusade, Adela, countess of Blois, wrote to her husband, who was gone to the East with Godfrey of Bouillon: "Beware of meriting the reproaches of the brave." As the count of Blois returned to Europe before the taking of Jerusalem, his wife made him blush at his desertion, and forced him to return to Palestine, where he fought bravely, and found a glorious death. Thus the spirit and the sentiments of chivalry gave birth to prodigies equally with the most ardent patriotism of ancient Lacedæmon; and these prodigies appeared so simple, so natural, that the chroniclers only repeat them in passing, and without testifying the least surprise at them.

This institution, so ingeniously called "Fountain of courtesy, which comes from God," is still much more admirable when considered under the all-powerful influence of religious ideas. Christian charity claimed all the affections of the knight, and demanded of him a perpetual devotion for the defence of pilgrims and the care of the sick. It was thus that were established the orders of St. John, of the Temple, of the Teutonic Knights, and several others, all instituted to combat the Saracens and solace human miseries. The infidels admired their virtues, as much as they dreaded their bravery. Nothing is more touching than the spectacle of these noble warriors, who were seen by turns in the field of battle and in the asylum of pain; sometimes the terror of the enemy, and as frequently the consolers of all who suffered. That which the paladins of the West did for beauty, the knights of Palestine did for poverty and misfortune. The former devoted their lives to the ladies of their thoughts; the latter devoted theirs to the poor and the infirm. The grand-master of the military order of St. John took the title of "Guardian of the poor of Jesus Christ," and the knights called the sick and the poor "Our lords." It appears almost an incredible thing, but the grand-master of the order of St. Lazarus, instituted for the cure and the relief of leprosy, was obliged to be chosen from among the lepers. Thus the charity of the knights, in order to be the better acquainted with human miseries, in a manner ennobled that which is most disgusting in the diseases of man. Did not this grand-master of St. Lazarus, who was obliged himself to be afflicted with the infirmities he was called upon to alleviate in others, imitate, as much as is possible on earth, the example of the Son of God, who assumed a human form in order to deliver humanity?

It may be thought that there was ostentation in so great a charity; but Christianity, as we have said, had subdued the pride of the warriors, and that was, without doubt, one of the noblest miracles of the religion of the middle ages. All who then visited the Holy Land could but admire in the knights of St. John, the Temple, and St. Lazarus, their resignation in suffering all the pains of life, their submission to all the rigours of discipline, and their docility to the least wish of their leader. During the sojourn of St. Louis in Palestine, the Hospitallers having had a quarrel with some Crusaders who were hunting on Mount Carmel, the latter brought their complaint before the grand-master. The head of the Hospital ordered before him the brothers who had outraged the Crusaders, and to punish them, condemned them to eat their food on the ground upon their mantles. "It happened," says the sieur de Joinville, "that I was present with the knights who had complained, and we requested the master to allow the brothers to arise from their mantles, which he refused." Thus the rigour of the cloisters and the austere humility of cenobites had nothing repulsive for these warriors. Such were the heroes that religion and the spirit of the crusades had formed. I know that this submission and humility in men accustomed to arms may be turned into ridicule; but an enlightened philosophy takes pleasure in recognising the happy influence of religious ideas upon the manners of a society given up to barbarous passions. In an age when all power was derived from the sword, in which passion and anger might have carried warriors to all kinds of excesses, what more agreeable spectacle for humanity could there be than that of valour humbling itself, and strength forgetting itself?

We are aware that the spirit of chivalry was sometimes abused, and that its noble maxims did not govern the conduct of all knights. We have described in the history of the crusades, the lengthened discords which jealousy created between the two orders of St. John and the Temple. We have spoken of the vices with which the Templars were reproached towards the end of the holy wars. We could speak still more of the absurdities of knight-errantry; but our task is here to write the history of institutions, and not that of human passions. Whatever may be thought of the corruption of men, it will always be true that chivalry, allied with the spirit of courtesy and the spirit of Christianity, awakened in human hearts virtues and sentiments of which the ancients were ignorant.

That which proves that everything was not barbarous in the middle ages is, that the institution of chivalry obtained, from its birth, the esteem and admiration of all Christendom. There was no gentleman who was not desirous of being a knight. Princes and kings took honour to themselves for belonging to chivalry. In it warriors came to take lessons of politeness, bravery, and humanity. Admirable school, in which victory laid aside its pride, and grandeur its haughty disdain; to which those who had riches and power came to learn only to make use of them with moderation and generosity.

As the education of the people was formed upon the example of the higher classes of society, the generous sentiments of chivalry spread themselves by degrees through all ranks, and mingled with the character of the European nations; gradually, there arose against those who were wanting in their duties of knighthood, a general opinion, more severe than the laws themselves, which was as the code of honour, as the cry of the public conscience. What might not be hoped from a state of society, in which all the discourses held in camps, in tournaments, in meetings of warriors, was reduced to these words: "Evil be to him who forgets the promises he has made to religion, to patriotism, to virtuous love; evil be to him who betrays his God, his king, or his lady?"

When the institution of chivalry fell by the abuse that was made of it, or rather in consequence of the changes in the military system of Europe; there remained still in European society some of the sentiments it had inspired, in the same manner as there remains with those who have forgotten the religion in which they were born, something of its precepts, and particularly of the profound impressions which they received from it in their infancy. In the times of chivalry, the reward of good actions was glory and honour. This coin, which is so useful to nations, and which costs them nothing, did not fail to have some currency in following ages. Such is the effect of a glorious remembrance, that the marks and distinctions of chivalry serve still in our days to recompense merit and bravery.

Since it can with truth be said that the crusades added some lustre and gave some ascendancy to chivalry, it must be agreed that they rendered essential service to humanity.

If the institution of chivalry was a barrier against license and barbarism, the institution of the clergy, founded upon more fixed and durable principles, ought to have rendered still greater services to civilization.

The ascendancy and wealth of the clergy placed them on an equality with the nobility, in the feudal system; but it must be allowed that the rank assigned them in this order of things was repugnant to their character and to the state of society. We do not hesitate to say that the feudal system had a tendency to corrupt the institution of the clergy, as the clergy corrupted the feudal system. The clergy, instructed in principles of peace, were not fit to carry out the conditions of the military régime; on the other side, the military régime was sure to change the pacific manners of the clergy. It was not at all uncommon to see prelates clad in cuirass and helmet. Sometimes country priests led to battle the flock which a religion of peace had confided to them. This military spirit in ecclesiastics was much increased by the crusades, in which their arms were sanctified by the object of the war. The clergy, however, never became sufficiently warlike to fulfil all the feudal engagements; and we may add likewise, that they were not always sufficiently pacific to fulfil all their religious duties.

It may be concluded, from what we have just said, that the ecclesiastical order and the feudal government would, in the long run, repel each other. If we consult the history of the middle ages, we shall see that the barons and nobles often showed themselves jealous of the power of the clergy, and that the clergy, in the end, contributed to the ruin of the foundations of feudalism.

The existence of the clergy underwent many modifications, according to times, places, and circumstances. In Italy, they enjoyed but very little credit, and took part in most popular factions. In Germany, the high clergy shared with the nobility the wrecks of imperial power. In Spain, they contributed greatly to the expulsion of the Moors, and the spoils of the vanquished added to their wealth. In England, the clergy associated themselves with the barons, and contended with the crown. In France, they attached themselves to royalty, and favoured the constantly increasing power of the monarchs.

If we may judge by the councils which were held during the crusades, most of which were occupied with reforming ecclesiastical discipline, we have reason to believe that the morals of the clergy had then a strong tendency to corruption. Old chronicles are particularly severe against the Crusaders and the clergy of the East, whom they unceasingly accuse of outraging morality and religion by their excesses. Some of the chroniclers even, like James of Vitry, draw such hideous pictures, that they are suspected of injustice, or at least of exaggeration. It is not useless, for the sake of historical truth, to remark here, that most of the historians of whom we now speak, belonged to the class of preachers charged with the task of censuring their age, and who were often obliged to dark en their colours in order to move the multitude. In all times, sacred orators have been seen exaggerating the vices it was their object to combat; and if we were not aware of the charity which animates them, we might sometimes mistake their discourses for violent satires. This is an observation of which we ought not to lose sight whilst reading the chronicles of the middle ages, which are almost all drawn up by ecclesiastics, accustomed by their profession to judge their contemporaries with severity. Another observation proved by history is, that corruption is spoken of with more bitterness in times in which it is scarcely known, than in times in which it has become general. In ages in which some ideas of virtue still prevail, people accuse themselves; and in ages quite corrupt, they praise themselves.

A chronicle of the time of the first crusades tells us, that the iniquities of men had then reached their height; and, what at once characterizes the spirit of the chronicler and that of his age, he adds that these iniquities would have shortened the duration of the world, "if it had not been that some new monastic congregations were formed." In fact, during the twelfth and thirteenth centuries, more monasteries were founded than in all the other centuries of the middle ages. The enthusiasm for the holy wars, by exalting the imaginations of nations, had produced a mental revolution; prodigies were everywhere seen that had never been observed till that time; devotion itself believed that it could no longer attain salvation by ordinary ways: whilst a crowd of warriors precipitated themselves upon the East, many pious souls, to perform penance, sought for private mortifications, and devoted themselves to the rigours of a voluntary exile, or buried themselves in deserts.

At the head of the monastic congregations which were formed at this period, we must place that of the Brothers of Mercy, which had its birth in the third crusade, and was instituted for the purpose of delivering captives. These venerable cenobites, after the example of the heroes of chivalry, sought for victims to console, and for the miserable to succour. Like knights, they exposed themselves to a thousand dangers, and braved death in the exercise of beneficence and charity. It was during the sixth crusade that the two orders of St. Dominic and St. Francis arose, orders which, according to the expression of the abbot of Usberg, renewed the youth of the Church. From the thirteenth century these two orders sent missions into the East, and into the north of Asia. Whilst the Tartar hordes were overturning empires, ravaging Europe, and threatening all Christendom, poor priests traversed the solitudes of Tartary, penetrated even into China; and, peaceful conquerors, armed with the Gospel, extended the empire of Christianity, and planted the standard of the cross at the extremities of the known world. The religious colonies which they then founded in Asia lasted much longer than the colonies founded by the Crusaders.

We will not attempt to enumerate all the services which religious communities rendered society. They had regulations which might serve for models in the infancy of political legislation. They were in all respects like the corporations of cities. Whilst anarchy disturbed cities, the woods had their legislation; and the germs of civilization developed themselves in silence and in solitude.

It was in monasteries that were found the only schools in which letters were taught, and that the Latin language, and the wonders it produced, were preserved. It was in them that studious men kept a faithful register of events, and employed themselves in transmitting to us those historical documents without which the glory and the manners of our ancestors would be unknown to us.

Besides that the clergy contributed greatly to the fertilizing of uncultivated lands, they protected the labourers with the whole power of the Church. The Truce of God, which was the work of the clergy, placed under the safeguard of Heaven, the inhabitants of the fields, the oxen, the companions of their labours, and even the instruments of their tillage. The Church went still further; it multiplied the festivals of the calendar, for the sake of the people. By augmenting the number of

CONFESSION.

religious solemnities, the Church had two motives: the first, to bring more frequently to the foot of the altar an ignorant and gross multitude, who there found the instruction necessary for the amelioration of their morals and the consolation of their evils; the second, to procure some days of repose for that crowd of serfs, condemned by the avarice of their masters to labours which had no end, and of which they did not gather the fruit.*

Amidst wars which revived without ceasing, the peasantry often found an asylum near a monastery inhabited by peaceful men, and protected by the opinions of the times. Nothing can prove better the ascendancy of the Church, than seeing, on one side, the nobility shut up in their strong castles, and on the other, cenobites dwelling in cloisters scarcely closed, and defended only by faith and confidence. As might be expected, the peace which reigned in the neighbourhood of monasteries attracted a numerous population around them. Many towns, and even cities, owed their origin to the vicinity of a monastery, whose name they still preserve.

The maxims of the clergy, more perhaps than their example, contributed to the enfranchisement of serfs. Gregory the Great, when giving liberty to some slaves, said that the Redeemer came upon earth to release men from slavery, and to substitute the rights of the people for the code of servitude. In the middle ages, many charters of liberty were granted for "the love of God,—for the salvation of the soul,—for the remission of sins." It was at the hour of death, and by testamentary dispositions, that most enfranchisements were granted; from which we may conclude that it was the work of the priests who assisted the dying. The clergy represented the enfranchisement of slaves as a thing agreeable to God; the ceremony of manumission was performed in the church as a solemn religious act. It was at the foot of the altars that the holy words were pronounced which broke the bonds of slavery. Thus everything announced that the spirit of the Gospel was everywhere mingled with the progress of civilization, and that the liberty of modern nations was to be one of the blessings of Christianity.

There was another mode of gaining liberty, which was by entering into holy orders, or to take vows in a monastery. So great a number of slaves escaped by that means from the yoke of their masters, that this custom was obliged to be restrained, and at last entirely abolished, in almost all the states of Europe. The crusades often bestowed upon the serfs the same privileges that the clergy did. Beneath the banners of the cross, serfs found the enfranchisement they had before found in monasteries. This facility which peasants possessed, of breaking their chains by going to the Holy Land, would have depopulated the plains, if new regulations had not placed restrictions and limits to it.

It has been said that the clergy became enriched by the crusades. This assertion, which has been so often repeated by the writers of the last century, requires to be examined by the impartiality of history. The clergy were rich at the period of the first crusade. Their enemies accused them for a long time of having usurped immense properties. In France, under the two first races, their wealth had given umbrage to the barons, who had several times despoiled them, under the pretext

---

* For serfs this might be a blessing, but for free labour it was complained of as an evil. La Fontaine's Cobbler, when describing his state to the Financier, says:—

" Chaque jour amène son pain,
Tantôt plus, tantôt moins: le mal est que toujours
(Et sans cela nos gains seraient assez honnêtes),
Le mal est que dans l'an s' entremêlent des jours
Qu'il faut chômer; on nous ruine en fêtes;
L'une fait tort à l'autre; et monsieur le curé
De quelque nouveau saint charge toujours son prône."

[Every day brings its bread; sometimes more, sometimes less: the worst is that always (and without that our gains would be very tolerable), the evil is, that in the year so many days creep in in which we must be idle—we are ruined in festivals; one treads upon the heels of another; and master curate is always introducing some new saint into his sermon.]

that they did not defend the state, and that the property they held belonged to them whose bravery watched over the safety of the kingdom.

If the crusades enriched the clergy, it might be supposed that the clergy would be most rich in countries which took the greatest part in the crusades. Now, the clergy of Germany, and several other states of Europe, surpassed in wealth the clergy of the kingdom of France, where the crusades excited so much enthusiasm, and caused so many warriors to take arms. The clergy, it is true, found new possessions in the East; but, after the crusades, nothing of them was left but vain titles.

The first crusade must have been, as we have said, very profitable to the clergy; they were not obliged to pay the expenses of it; the zeal of the faithful furnished them. Nevertheless they did take part in this crusade; and the priests who set out, with the other Crusaders, certainly did not enrich themselves in their pilgrimage. Many, no doubt, shared the fate of Robert, abbot of St. Remi, the historian of the first crusade, who, on his return from Jerusalem, was expelled by his monks for having ruined his convent.

At the second crusade, contributions were levied upon the churches, without any regard to the warm remonstrances of the ecclesiastics. From that time an opinion, which became very injurious to the clergy, was established throughout the Christian world, which was, that wars undertaken for the glory of Jesus Christ and the deliverance of the holy places, ought to be paid for by the Church. Tributes were at once levied upon the clergy, without consulting any other authority, or following any other regulations than those of necessity and circumstances. To reckon from the third crusade, after the publication of the *Saladin tenth*, more regular imposts were established, which were fixed by the popes or councils, and which were collected with such rigour, that churches were despoiled of their ornaments, and sometimes the sacred vases were put up to sale. It is true that the clergy sometimes received offerings and bequests from those who went to the Holy Land, or had made a vow to go; but what did such tributes of piety amount to when compared to the tributes they themselves were compelled to pay? We do not hesitate to affirm that, in the space of two hundred years, the clergy paid towards the holy wars more money than would have been required to purchase all their property: and thus the zeal of ecclesiastics for the deliverance of the holy places was observed perceptibly to cool; and it may be said that the indifference which followed among Christian nations the ardour for the crusades, began by the clergy. In Germany, and many other countries, their discontent was carried so far, that at last the popes did not dare to trust the preaching of crusades to the bishops, and only gave this mission to the mendicant orders, who possessed nothing, and had nothing to pay for the expeditions against the infidels.

It has been said that the clergy took advantage of the crusades to buy at low prices the property of the nobility, as, in our days, we have seen many people take advantage of a revolution, to purchase at a moderate price the property of the clergy themselves. We find, in fact, examples of such acquisitions in the first crusades; but these examples must have been more rare in the holy wars, of which the clergy were obliged to pay the expenses. The great advantage that the clergy had over the nobility was, that the nobles were able to pawn or alienate their possessions, and that ecclesiastics were never allowed to pledge or alienate their property. Another advantage the clergy possessed was, that they formed a body always animated by the same spirit, and always governed by the same laws. Whilst everything changed around them, they never changed. It was thus they resisted the revolution which was effected in property.

We have seen, that in the twelfth and thirteenth centuries a great number of monasteries were established. By that means wild, uncultivated places became fertile lands; and these conquests made over the desert added to the domains of the clergy. We must likewise add, that the jurisdiction of the clergy, which every day made fresh progress, was for them a source of wealth. It was in the nature of things, as we have already remarked, that the most enlightened class should become the richest. The clergy had therefore no need of profiting by the ruin of the Crusaders in order to become rich; their knowledge, their spirit of order and economy, *with the ascendancy they possessed over the people*, offered them ample means for increasing or preserving their possessions.

Everybody, besides, had reason to rejoice at seeing the clergy acquire wealth; for this wealth belonged to everybody. In fact, every man could enter into the clergy, and the clergy belonged to all families. This order, so powerful in the middle ages, was as a natural link, as an intermediate point, which drew together and united all the classes of society. In the quarrels which jealousy sometimes raised between the clergy and the nobility, the great vassals reproached the ecclesiastics with being *the children of serfs*. It was not uncommon to see men who had issued from the lowest class of the people, in the highest functions of the Church; a certain proof that the clergy offered every one a way by which he might elevate himself, and that they thus assisted in reëstablishing the harmony destroyed by feudal inequality.

The clergy—such as our fathers saw it—only now exists in the memory of men. In proportion as this institution, with all the advantages we have spoken of, shall be further removed from us, we shall perhaps become the more aware of its value. There are things of which we judge more favourably when memory recalls them to us, than when they are present.

After a revolution which has ruined so many families, in which so many hopes have been deceived,—at a time in which a numerous youth is crowded in the confined circle of public employments,—in which the divers professions, among the enlightened class, by no means suffice for the vast number of the candidates,—let me ask whether the Church, with its riches and its consolatory morality, would not be as a port in the storm,—as a refuge always open for those to whom the world has nothing to give? At a time in which everything is uncertain, moving, and transitory,—in which no man is sure of his destiny, who but must envy those men whose fate never changed,—who lived always in the same manner,—who saw the present without cmplaining,—to whom the future gave no uneasiness, and who might justly be compared to the young ones of the birds, of which Scripture speaks? If I durst utter all my thought—and I speak less in the name of religion than in the names of philosophy and humanity—I should even regret those austere retreats, open to piety, and consecrated by peace and prayer. There, at least, a shelter was found from the passions which disturb society, as they trouble the heart of man. Why, in fact, should there not be hospitals for the miseries of the soul, as there are for other human infirmities? Why are not they who have suffered from the storms of life, and whose heart is torn by deep wounds, to find a refuge against their ills, as well as those whom indigence overtakes, or as well as the war-mutilated soldier? Who does not know that great revolutions, like great griefs, inspire a desire for concealing existence, and seeking repose in solitude? "When the storm growls," says Pythagoras, "worship echo." Let us look back to the times which preceded the middle ages,—to those times in which the world was ready to fall to pieces with the Roman empire: it was at this deplorable epoch that the deserts of the Thebais were peopled with pious cenobites, who were no longer able to support the spectacle of human passions. It was not only simple and vulgar men who flocked to the solitudes of Cetteus and Memphis, but learned men, warriors,—men who had been seen in the courts of emperors. Whilst society was shaken to its foundations,—whilst disorder and corruption spread their baneful influence everywhere, elevated minds, whom this state of things drove to despair, went to bury themselves in retirement, embracing the altars of that Christian religion which was the only support left to unfortunate virtue, and was the last hope of civilization.

The swords of knights and the maxims of the clergy, as we have seen, contended with advantage against the excesses of barbarism; but no institution had yet attained sufficient consistence to guarantee the security of European societies. In spite of all efforts for the reëstablishment of order, anarchy still subsisted. In order to know what, either in an age or a people, is the spirit of civilization, it is sufficient to be acquainted with the progress that has been made in that same age, or among that same people, in the administration of justice. Of all the monuments the human mind can raise, a civil and criminal code is that which requires the most extensive knowledge, and the profoundest acquaintance with the passions of man.

In the middle ages, society, immersed in darkness, had lost the lessons and examples of antiquity in all which concerned judicial order; and found itself, in a manner, reduced to the experience of the barbarians.

When the barons usurped from the crown the right of administering justice, there were as many jurisdictions in France as there were lordships. Judicial administration then lost that spirit of *wholeness*, that uniformity, which gives weight and rectitude to its decisions. Judgment was no longer given but according to local customs, or uncertain traditions. When, in the seventeenth century, the judicial customs and traditions which had been found in preceding ages were collected, there were found two hundred and eighty-five of them; a certain proof that in the times of which we speak, there could be no fixed rule, and that anarchy had invaded the sanctuary of justice.

Royalty could not watch over seignorial jurisdictions, and the ordinances of the kings were powerless out of the domains of the crown. The great vassals had no mutual understanding that might modify or regulate legislation. It is a remarkable thing that France, after the decline of the empire of Charlemagne, remained more than two centuries without recognising any authority to which it could carry its griefs and its complaints,—without having, either in the person of the monarch or the assemblies of the great, a power which could establish regulations, repair injustices, correct abuses, and consecrate the maxims of experience. If the kingdom was able to subsist for so long a time in this state, have we not reason to believe that there is in every society an unknown force, which defends that society against its own excesses, and saves the people in spite of their passions,—in spite of all which seems calculated to bring on their ruin?

To decide in civil and criminal causes, there was no other guide, no other intelligence, but the instincts and the conscience of the judges. These feeble means were not competent, in complicated cases, to assign to actions their true intention, or to appreciate the language of innocence or the denegations of crime. All matters were then treated according to verbal conventions, and judged according to unwritten testimonies. Words, often ill-interpreted, sometimes partially effaced from the memory, frequently contradicted or falsified, could not enlighten justice. Good faith was implored; the consciences of witnesses and parties were appealed to; but it was too frequently perjury that answered, and which commanded the decisions of the judges. At length, it was believed that an infallible means was discovered for detecting falsehood and fraud; an appeal was made from the consciences of men to the justice of Heaven. He who was accused, he whose evidence was contradicted, submitted to the ordeals of fire, boiling water, or red-hot iron. It was believed that Heaven would not permit injustice, and that it would rather suspend the laws of nature than the laws of society.

These proofs, however, were abandoned to the vulgar; judicial combat was the ordeal of nobles or of freemen. This species of justice, in which every warrior had only his own valour as the arbiter of his destiny, conformed exceedingly well with the military spirit of the age.

So barbarous a custom was generally adopted: not satisfied with having recourse to judicial combat in criminal cases, civil questions were subject to its decisions. A gentleman had not only a right to defy his adversary, he might also challenge the witnesses themselves, and force sometimes even the judges to descend with him into the arena. Justice was then only seen in victory, or rather victory became the sole justice. Thus the Franks, in the crusades, often expressed their astonishment that God should sometimes allow the Mussulmans to conquer the Christians.

The sword decided everything; the places where justice pronounced her decrees resounded with the cries of fury and hatred. They were stained, by turns, with the blood of the innocent or with the blood of the guilty, as skill, strength, or fortune favoured the arms of the combatants. In the face of such combats, how was it possible to preserve the idea of justice or injustice? Must not ferocity of manners have increased, and education become unnatural?

We ought, however, to remember the circumstances which brought about this custom, and which may render it excusable in the eyes of enlightened philosophy. In the impossibility in which the judges often found themselves of ascertaining the truth or pronouncing with certainty, fraud, perjury, and falsehood triumphed over the laws, and threatened to invade the whole of society. No better means could be discovered to prevent this misfortune than to terrify imposture and perfidy, by the preparations, "pomp, and circumstance," of a judicial combat. Justice, being unable to reveal herself amidst the darkness of barbarism, surrounded herself with terrible images, and would only allow her sanctuary to be approached with mistrust and fear. The terror which the idea even of a judicial combat inspired, the uncertainty of such a judgment, must have prevented many contests, and that was a great advantage. No other more certain means, besides, were to be found to appease quarrels, which could not be prolonged without perilling the whole of society. In an age in which the passions were mixed with everything, it was doubtless important for society that justice should terminate debates in an equitable manner; but it was likewise important that these debates should terminate promptly.

At the first aspect, we only see in this custom a privilege and a monstrous employment of physical force. But without this employment of physical force, the world was perhaps likely to become the prey of perjured, faithless men. We ought then to sigh less over this revolting abuse than over the state of society in which it appeared necessary, in order to prevent abuses still more revolting. It required much trouble afterwards to reform the judicial combat. The prejudices most difficult to be destroyed are those in which bravery and the point of honour believe themselves interested. Neither the power of kings, nor religion, nor philosophy, have been able to abolish duels among modern nations; and duels, in some respects, are nothing but the justice which was rendered by the sword in the middle ages.

We have not yet made known all the obstacles which the triumph of justice met with in the manners and customs of these remote times. The absence of laws caused great disorders; but the yoke of the laws was more insupportable to the barons than anarchy itself. The confidence which the barons felt in their arms, rendered them at least indifferent to all kinds of legislation. In any society whatever, the men who have power or force in their hands are seldom the first to appeal to laws; because nobody can be unjust towards them with impunity, and they have always the means of doing themselves justice.

Judicial order, as we understand it now-a-days, could be nothing, in the twelfth century, but an abstraction which did not enter into men's minds. The warlike nobility of Europe would have had nothing to do with any kind of justice which did not present an image of war. The barons could not form an idea that legislation might be a safeguard for themselves as well as society. They only felt an injustice as they felt a wound in the field of battle; and personal resentment was the only motive which animated them to the pursuit of the guilty. Equity then scarcely passed for a virtue, but revenge was a duty. There were no laws against those who were unjust, but there were laws against those who did not avenge themselves.

With these manners and this character, the barons were not able to renounce the practice of private wars, which the Franks and other barbarians had brought with them into Europe. Every noble who fancied himself attacked in either his honour or his property, took arms to defend his rights or avenge his quarrel. All the relations and vassals of the belligerent parties were obliged to take part in the quarrel. Fields were ravaged, towns and villages were burnt, and it was thus they demanded or rendered justice. During many centuries Europe was desolated by these intestine wars. Sanguinary discords, which were transmitted from generation to generation, became an habitual state, for which customs and regulations were invoked; and whilst society was without laws, civil war had its jurisprudence.

It was not easy to remedy such vast disorders. How could force be disarmed, and despoiled of a prerogative it seemed to prefer to all other privileges? Society, such as it then was, had but one single power capable of counterbalancing that of the warlike passions which desolated Europe; this was the force of religious ideas and the ascendancy of Christianity. The authority of councils was invoked against private wars; the saints were made to speak; superstition itself was called in; visions, revelations, and prodigies were had recourse to. The Church put forth all its threats and launched all its thunders. These means sometimes suspended the progress of the evil, but the principle of discord always subsisted. It was not possible to put an end to private wars, but they were at length suppressed during certain days of the week; and all the good that such a powerful religion could do was to bring about the adoption of the Truce of God. It was here the crusades wonderfully seconded the zeal of the clergy. Whenever war was declared against the Saracens, discords were all at once appeased, as if by miracle, and Europe remained in profound silence before the standard of the cross.

The efforts of the clergy, however, in conjunction with some other favourable circumstances, were destined in the end to bring about the triumph of justice and humanity. Before civil justice was established, the Church possessed a holy jurisdiction which judged the faithful. This justice stood in no need of pursuing the guilty; the guilty came to give themselves up to its judgments: it was not blind, like human justice; the most secret folds of the conscience developed themselves before it: it met with no resistance, it excited no murmurs; those whom it condemned, condemned themselves. To cause its laws to be executed, and to sanction its decisions, it had the power of remorse, the fear of an avenging God, the promises of heaven, the menaces of hell. Such was the tribunal of penitence, which, in the absence of civil laws, held the place sometimes of other tribunals, and watched over public order, as a triumph of religion. A tribunal so formidable necessarily increased the influence of the clergy, and contributed, no doubt, to extend their jurisdiction even to affairs in which evangelical morality was not at all interested. People, persuaded that all justice comes from God, were likely to be led to believe that God pronounced his least judgments by the organs of his ministers upon earth. When the popes were reproached with interfering in the policy of princes, they answered that the acts of that policy might be sins, and thence these acts came under the pontifical jurisdiction. The clergy usurped judicial authority in civil affairs, as the sovereign pontiffs had usurped temporal authority.* In the middle ages the clergy declared themselves arbi-

---

* Nothing has been better said upon the influence of the clergy and religion, in the middle ages, than that which we read in a work entitled *Des Intérêts et des Opinions*, by M. Fievée :—" At a time in which the Church imposed public penitences, whilst the tribunals only ordered judgments by arms, we cannot see how the high police could not have fallen into the hands of the ecclesiastics; and it was because they alone exercised it, that, in the civil wars, fortunate princes confided to the monks the guarding of princes, from whom the fate of battle or treachery took the rights they possessed to share the king-

ters of the just and the unjust; and as their jurisdiction was much more favourable to humanity, more conformable to reason than that of the barons, it made rapid progress. Among the privileges which the popes granted to the Crusaders, that of being judged by the ecclesiastical laws was placed in the first rank. The clergy took advantage of the absence, the death, or the ruin of the nobles who were gone to the crusades, to extend their jurisdiction, as the commons availed themselves of this circumstance to obtain their liberty, and kings to increase their power. At last this jurisdiction became so powerful that it awakened the jealousy of the feudal nobility. Towards the middle of the thirteenth century, the nobles formed a league against the clergy, and in a manifesto, which we still possess, they demanded that "they should render to Cæsar that which belonged to Cæsar." They forbade their vassals to appeal to the ecclesiastical tribunals, except in cases of heresy, marriage, and usury, and threatened delinquents with the loss of their property and the mutilation of a member. "The clerks," added they, "enriched at our expense, shall be brought back to the state of the primitive church and to a contemplative life, leaving to us the action which becomes us, and presenting to us the miracles which we have not seen for a long time."

As the influence of the clergy arose from Christianity, the nobles, in their manifesto, wished to claim the advantage of having alone converted the Gauls by their arms. All that they said in support of this assertion gave reason to predict that they would not triumph in a contest in which Victory would range herself on the side of knowledge and intelligence.

This was not an ordinary war, but a veritable war of opinions; and as the lords had, to sustain it, nothing but their swords, they were at last obliged to renounce their pretensions.

The society of Europe, however, arrived at that period so fatal to nations, at that crisis, almost always a sanguinary one, in which new opinions and old opinions declare an obstinate war against each other; in which all that is new ferments, and is agitated violently; in which all that is ancient resists, and falls to pieces with a crash. For a length of time old laws were powerless; and the laws which were endeavoured to be established, had, in their execution, neither the force that is acquired by habit, nor that which is conferred by experience. A universal crisis was experienced throughout Europe; and the West, troubled by revolutions and civil wars, was, for a moment, upon the point of falling back into the darkness and chaos of the tenth century.

It was at this period that was established in Germany the imperial chamber, instituted for the purpose of appeasing discords and repressing brigandage. In Arragon the tutelary authority of the *justiza* was created, who was armed against license with all the power of a dictator. In all countries brotherhoods and associations were formed against the excesses of anarchy. It was in France, above all, that the necessity was felt to call in justice to the support of shaken social order, and to place it under the safeguard of royalty. Royal power was born, in some sort, amongst the perils and fears of society. There is an instinct which, in moments of crisis, guides people towards the authority which is to protect them; and this authority becomes all-powerful, from the reason that its assistance is implored, and that it is the object of all hopes.

Ecclesiastical jurisdiction had already dealt a mortal blow to feudal justice. The study of the Roman law caused something of the experience of the ancients to revive among nations scarcely escaped from barbarism. A new judicial order sprang up in Europe, particularly in France.* This

---

dom. It was necessary that the void left by the laws should be filled up, or the state would perish; and the priests alone enjoyed a moral authority sufficiently great to supply the weakness of legislation;—exalted passions, more powerful virtues, great crimes, great remorse; a proud independence, salutary fears; an excess of force, and no regulations; courage in everything and everywhere: such was, at this period, the state of society;—it is easy to perceive that religion alone contended with barbarism." We regret not to be able to quote more than a fragment of a work filled with ingenious perceptions and profound views, upon the march of civilization in the middle ages.

* The author of *A Memoir to serve as a New History of Louis XII.* carries the first appearance of judicial reform in France to the reign of that monarch. He has prosecuted on this subject learned researches, and his work has given us much information upon the spirit and the march of our legisla-

judicial order was at first very complicated, in consequence of that natural disposition of men of the pen and of the robe to multiply forms in all affairs. To follow the clue through the labyrinth of the new laws, the barons were deficient in knowledge, and more particularly in patience. If it be true that lawyers complicated legislation in order to remain the sole interpreters of it, their hopes were not deceived; for they in the end took the places of the feudal nobles in judicial functions.

It is true that seignorial justices were not abolished; but an appeal was permitted from their decisions to the judgment of the crown. There were, besides, cases in which the justice of the barons was found incompetent, and as this incompetence was almost always judged of by the jurisdiction of the king, the latter finished by attracting to itself most of the causes of any weight or importance. As it is otherwise important that justice should be protected by a force that can make it respected, as the power of the barons declined, and as that of the king increased daily, the royal jurisdiction prevailed, and custom sanctioned the maxim that all justice emanates from the king. When once this maxim was recognised and proclaimed in all the provinces, Beaumanier was right in saying, "that the king was sovereign over everything, and that he had by right the general guardianship of the kingdom."

It was at this period arose that French magistracy which afterwards became so eminent. The parliaments exhibited the frankness and loyalty of old times, united with the intelligence of modern times. They sometimes defended the rights of the people against the crown, and were often a buckler for the crown against factions. Perhaps their roots did not strike deeply enough into the society whose rights they defended. The fundamental laws of the kingdom had neither regulated their rights, nor fixed with precision the limits of their power. Their authority was due less to written constitutions than to that want of justice which is felt among civilized people, than to that supreme ascendancy which they almost always obtain whose function it is to be exponents of the law. We have seen parliaments perish amidst public disorders, for which they themselves gave the imprudent signal. They saw the faults of administration, but they were deficient in positive knowledge to point out the proper remedy: they appealed to the people, and factions answered; they invoked liberty, and the revolution burst forth. Now, when this magistracy no longer exists among us, and that it can have no place in the order of things which events have given birth to, it appears to us the moment is come for everybody to be just towards it, and to praise that noble disinterestedness, that enlightened firmness, that inflexible probity, which formed its principal character. "It is for the observer of the present period," says an English writer, "and not for the historian of past times, to decide if those virtues which distinguished the ancient French magistracy are sufficiently common now-a-days, not to be remembered with great praise, and exhibited to our contemporaries as useful examples."

In the revolution which was effected, we are astonished that the barons showed so little foresight; they opposed the privileges of an order of things which no longer existed, when, without their intervention and without their concurrence, a new order of things was established; the greater that was their need of union to defend themselves, the more obstinacy they showed for maintaining the too fatal privilege of making war upon each other. The habit of warlike and feudal manners made them prefer to all other functions the occupation of arms, which they considered, with reason, as the most glorious career; but which ruined them, kept them in their ignorance, and drove them from affairs, whilst others enriched themselves in peaceful employments, exercised their faculties usefully, and employed themselves exclusively with power. In the end, the nobility, after the most generous

---

tion in the middle ages. Although we do not always agree as to the consequences of the principles he develops, particularly as to their application to that which is passing at present, we take pleasure in rendering justice to the rare sagacity with which he has cleared up questions which have been scarcely perceived by our best historians.

MIRACLES.

The ancient chroniclers were simple and pious men; they considered the least falsehood as a mortal sin; they were scrupulous in telling the truth when they were acquainted with it. Most of them would have thought themselves deficient in the duties of an historian, if they had not gone back to the creation of the world, or at least to the deluge. Among the events which they relate, they never forgot such as would strike the vulgar, and which struck themselves; as the revolutions of nature, famines, prodigies, &c.—BOOK XVIII.

sacrifices, became nothing but an aristocracy without action in the government, whilst those who lent a hand to the administration became really the masters.

The revolutions we have just described have made us for a moment forget the crusades; the holy wars, however, may be reckoned among the causes which ameliorated legislation. The departure of the Crusaders gave occasion for a number of actions; precautions against fraud were multiplied; public notaries were called in; the use of charters,—called *chartres chirographaires,* or *chartres parties,*—was adopted, or rather revived. We have already said that many regulations were made to limit the numbers of the Crusaders, and these regulations were so many laws added to those which existed. The Crusaders, whilst passing through distant countries, might remark many wise customs, which they brought back into their own country. Villehardouin informs us with what astonishment the French nobles, on their arrival at Venice, beheld the senate, the doge, and the people deliberating in their presence. This spectacle could not fail to enlighten them. When the Latins were masters of Constantinople, they there became acquainted with the legislation of Greece; in Palestine, the Assizes of Jerusalem gave them an idea of a legislation less imperfect than their own; the code which for a long time governed the Christian colonies led Louis IX. to think of making a collection of laws, which he did not, it is true, put in practice, but which no doubt spread much useful information. The example of St. Louis, and the encouragement that jurisconsults received on his return from Egypt, contributed to create among the people the love of justice; and this love of justice, which began to be felt among all classes, was the best guarantee of a nascent civilization.

Skilful writers have gone over before us this epoch, so abundant in great events and in lessons of policy. They have shown how royalty rose from the bosom of disorder; how legislation progressively prevailed over anarchy; and how several states of Europe—particularly France—attained that degree of strength and splendour in which we have seen them during the eighteenth century. There would remain but very little for us to say, after the great publicists who have preceded us, if recent revolutions had not broken forth to enlighten us. The experience of the present times has thrown a new light over past ages; and we are better acquainted with the nature and origin of old institutions, since we have seen them sink into ruins. The tree of our ancient monarchy has not been able to resist the concussions which have shaken society; its branches have strewed the earth, and its roots have been laid bare. It then became easy for us to see by what secret conduits strength and life had been circulated; how had grown, and how had fallen,—

> "That tree whose head approached to heaven,
> And whose feet touched the empire of the dead."*

After having gone through the different classes of society, and shown the origins of our institutions during the crusades, we are about to see what was, at the same period, the progress of navigation, commerce, industry, the sciences, letters, the arts, and general knowledge.

Before the twelfth century, the seas of Europe and Asia, with the exception of the Mediterranean, were scarcely frequented even by the nations who dwelt upon their shores. At the period of the first crusades, that which formed the kingdom of France had but two or three ports upon the coast of Normandy, and had not a single one upon the ocean, or the Mediterranean, when, in the seventh crusade, Louis IX. caused that of Aigues-Mortes to be dug. England was scarcely more advanced; that kingdom abandoned the navigation of the seas which surrounded it to pirates. It appeared that the world was not yet large enough for the ambition and genius of the English nation, which at the present day dominates over all the known seas. Some cities on the shores of the Baltic, of Holland, Flanders, and Spain, made maritime expeditions, but which scarcely deserve to be described in the

---

* La Fontaine.

history of the crusades. When the crusades began, the spirit of devotion, united with that of commerce, gave a new and more extended direction to the voyages and labours of navigators. The inhabitants of Denmark appeared in the seas of Syria; and Norwegians, who came by sea, assisted at the taking of Sidon. Citizens of Lubeck aud Bremen were present at the siege of Ptolemaïs. From all the coasts of the West, vessels and fleets transported pilgrims, provisions, and arms into the kingdom of Jerusalem and the other Christian principalities established in Asia by the victories of the Crusaders.

Thus navigators from all countries met in the seas of the East. It was, in some sort, under the auspices of the cross, that advantageous relations began to be established among the maritime nations of Europe. At the commencement of the twelfth century, a fleet of Pisans, joined with some other Italians, came to assist the Arragonese in conquering the Balearic Isles. The navigators of Italy were so little acquainted with the seas of Spain, that they took the coasts of Arragon for the country of the Moors. This first alliance between distant nations was the work of a crusade preached by Pope Pascal III., and seconded by a great number of knights of Provence and Languedoc.

The navigators of Lubeck, Bremen, and Denmark, after having tried their strength in long voyages, took advantage of the experience they had gained, to visit the unknown seas of the Baltic. These new enterprises presented to their pious zeal and their ambition a nearer sea, and savage peoples which they might bring under their faith, and make subservient to their commercial views. Maritime expeditions were mixed with the crusades preached against nations still living in a state of paganism. At the aspect of the cross and the flag of navigators, rich cities sprang up, and barbarous regions began to be acquainted with the blessings of civilization.

It was at this period that navigation opened for itself a new career, and saw the theatre of its useful labours expand. Nothing could have favoured its progress like the communication that was then established between the Baltic, the Mediterranean, the Spanish Ocean, and the seas of the north. By uniting nations in pursuit of the same advantages, it multiplied their relations, their ties, and their interests, and redoubled their emulation. In this career thus opened to all the nations of Europe, practical knowledge became rectified, was much increased, and spread everywhere; the configuration of coasts, the position of capes, ports, bays, isles, &c., &c., were all ascertained; the depth of the ocean was fathomed; the direction of winds, currents, and tides was observed; much information was gained upon all the points of hydrography, and very soon that ignorance of the eleventh and twelfth centuries was dispersed, which had occasioned so many shipwrecks, that the chroniclers of the times of the first crusades, as they tremblingly recount them, can only ascribe them to the anger of Heaven.

We would here speak of the mariner's compass, if the period of its invention could be ascertained clearly. A passage of James of Vitry, which we have elsewhere given, does not permit us to doubt that the properties of the loadstone were known in the time of the crusades, and that navigators derived great assistance from it in their long voyages; but, on the other hand, there is nothing to prove that the use of the mariner's compass was then general. We may believe that so valuable a discovery was still a secret from the vulgar, and that those who were in possession of this secret, only sought to profit by it for their own interest, without thinking of the advantages that might be drawn from it for the progress of navigation. We will add that that which has happened to the mariner's compass, has happened also to most of the inventions of industry, of which history can rarely assign the epochs, because their authors, from a spirit of cupidity or jealousy, have not only not promulgated them, but have concealed them carefully from the knowledge of their contemporaries.

Naval architecture was much improved during the crusades. The vessels were greatly enlarged, to enable them to contain the multitudes of pilgrims to be transported. The dangers incidental to long voyages, caused the ships destined for the East to be constructed in a more solid manner. The art of setting up several masts in the same vessel, the art of multiplying the sails, and of disposing them so as to enable the ship to sail against the wind, were the happy fruit of the emulation which then animated navigators.

Thus the activity and the genius of man triumphed over all obstacles, commanded the elements, and took possession of the empire of the sea. But this empire, like that of the land, was, in the middle ages, a prey to brigandage and violence; tempests, contrary winds, shipwrecks, were not the only evils to be apprehended in long voyages. On every sea no right was known but the right of the strongest, and the absence of a maritime code added greatly to the perils of distant navigation.

The necessity for a legislation that might assure the interests and the freedom of navigators was strongly felt. It was Spain that furnished the first model of one. At the commencement of the twelfth century a code of maritime rights was drawn up by the ancient *prudhommes* of the Sea of Barcelona. The Venetians adopted it in an assembly held at St. Sophia, in 1255. This code was afterwards adopted by the Pisans and Genoese, and, under the name of the Consulat of the Sea, became the common law or right of the eastern seas. Another code, published at first by Eleanor of Guienne, and afterwards by Richard Cœur-de-Lion, under the title of "Rolls of Oleron," obtained the assent of several maritime nations, and was at last accepted in all the seas of the West.

Protected by this code, navigators were enabled to gather the fruit of their long labours, and soon disputed advantageously the empire of the Mediterranean with the infidels. If Italy and several other countries of the West escaped the yoke of the Saracens, they owed their safety more to the superiority of their fleets than to that of their armies.

I have spoken in the preceding book of the discovery of America, and of the passage to India by the Cape of Good Hope. It is probable that, without the crusades, the genius of navigators would, although later, have surmounted the immense space and numberless dangers that separated the Baltic and the Mediterranean from the Indian Ocean, and the Old World from the New. We may at least say that the distant expeditions and the perilous enterprises undertaken beneath the banners of the cross, prepared the way for the last prodigies of navigation, by opening everywhere new routes for industry, and, above all, by favouring the progress of commerce, the natural and necessary link between the divers nations and the different countries of the globe.

Each climate has its productions; and this diversity of riches creates for men an obligation for exchanges. This obligation for exchanges produces communication among all nations, so that in time the most widely-separated regions cannot remain unknown to each other. It may truly be said, that Providence has thus placed various productions in different climates, that it has denied to some countries what it has granted to others, to create for men dispersed over the face of the earth, the necessity for reciprocally seeking each other, for trading to supply their mutual wants, for communicating their knowledge, and for marching together towards civilization.

In the middle ages, the indolent and effeminate Greeks neglected to bring into the West the merchandises of Asia. The Saracens only anchored on the coasts of Europe, to bring thither the scourges of war. The commerce of the West went to seek that which was not brought to it; and frequent voyages to the East were all for the profit of the West.

A long time before the crusades, the merchandises of India and Asia had arrived in Europe, sometimes by land, crossing the Greek empire, Hungary, and the country of the Bulgarians; but more frequently by the Mediterranean, in which were all the ports of Italy. These routes were both made more familiar by the holy wars, and from that time nothing could stop the rapid progress of commerce, protected in its march by the standard of the cross.

Most of the maritime cities of the West not only got rich by furnishing Europe with the productions of the East, but they found further a considerable advantage in the transport of pilgrims and Christian armies. Fleets followed along the coasts of the countries in which the Crusaders were fighting, and sold them the munitions of war, and the provisions of which they always stood in need. Thus commerce brought back into Europe a part of the treasures which the princes and barons, who ruined themselves to go and fight the infidels, carried into Asia.

All the wealth of the maritime cities of Syria, and even of Greece, belonged to the merchants of the West. They were the masters of a great part of the Christian cities of Asia; we know what was the share of the Venetians after the taking of Constantinople. They possessed all the isles of the Archipelago, and half of Byzantium. The Greek empire was as another Venice, with its laws, its fleets, and its armies.

The Latins soon lost Constantinople, Jerusalem, and most of the countries which submitted to their arms. Commerce, more fortunate, preserved its conquests after the crusades. The city of Tana, built at the mouth of the Tanais, became for Venice a colony, which opened for her useful relations with Persia and Tartary, and which dominated in the markets of Tauris, Trebizond, Bagdad, and Bassora. Some Genoese, assembled in a little city of the Crimea,—Caffa, at the time even when the Turks were threatening Europe, employed themselves in working the mines of the Caucasus, and receiving the treasures of India by way of Astracan. European commerce established stores even among nations that made cruel war against the Christians. The terror which the Mamelukes inspired did not prevent colonies of merchants establishing themselves in Egypt. Africa, particularly the coast of the Mediterranean, was all subservient to their mercantile ambition, and the places which St. Louis had not been able to conquer, became tributaries to their industry.

Whilst the commerce of all parts of the world was thus placed in the hands of a few maritime cities, many of the great kingdoms of Europe were still strangers to it. England, which had no other wealth but its wools, gladly received in its capital the merchandises of Asia, brought thither by Italian and Spanish merchants. The cities of France took but little part in the commerce of the East. The crusades were the work of the French; others gathered the fruits of them. Marseilles was, in the middle ages, the only French city which kept up any relation with distant nations. This city, founded by the Phocians, for the sake of the commerce with the Gauls, had never ceased to turn its eyes towards the places of its origin, and have commercial relations with Syria and Greece. Spain, whose industry developed itself early, took more advantage from the crusades, and, towards the end of the holy wars, the Spaniards had warehouses upon all the coasts of Asia.

No country, however, derived more advantage from the trade of the East than Italy. This country, which dominated over the Mediterranean, and which lay open to all parts of the known world, was placed in the most favourable position. This position, which had formerly facilitated the conquests of the Romans, assisted the nations of Italy in their new enterprises, and subdued the world to their speculations, as it had subdued it to their arms. Whilst their fleets set out for the East, they sent into Europe, not legions and pro-consuls, as Rome had done, but caravans of merchants, who subdued the provinces they passed through to the calculations and the wants of commerce. These merchants disposed of, by their industrious traffic, all the money which then circulated in the West. In all countries they had numerous colonies and considerable establishments. Europe has no great cities in which the name of the Lombards, given to a street, to a quarter, does not, even at the present day, attest the long sojourn of the Italian merchants.

We cannot help admiring this power of commerce; but it had likewise its principle of destruction. What rivalries, what jealous passions, did it not give birth to daily! Pacific conquests were contended for without ceasing, swords in hand. In this struggle many cities succumbed; Pisa was destroyed by Genoa; Genoa, in her turn, could not maintain its rivalry against Venice. Another rock for these commercial powers, was the mobility of the commerce which had elevated them, and which carried unceasingly its favours and its gifts from one place to another. If commerce changed its route or its direction, that was quite enough to make a city prosper, or to precipitate its fall. In the middle ages a crowd of cities disappeared, without discord or war having at all contributed to their ruin. It appeared as if fortune took a pleasure in destroying her own work, and as if she disdained on that account to associate herself with human passions.

It is not possible to separate the progress of industry and even of agriculture from that of commerce. To ascertain what industry and agriculture could gain by relations with the East, it would perhaps be sufficient to ascertain in what state these two sources of prosperity then were among the Orientals. Among so many travellers, there were, doubtless, some who had an interest in observing the usages and practices of the distant countries they visited. We know that in the expeditions of the Crusaders, such as were masters of a trade, or were skilful in a mechanical art, were enrolled in preference to others. These industrious pilgrims did not always make a voyage barren of advantages for their country; and in those holy wars, in which the knights of the cross only sought victory and renown, industry, if I may venture to say so, had also its crusade, whose peaceful trophies consisted in precious discoveries, stolen from the Greeks or the Saracens, and in the happy imitation of that which they had admired in the arts of the East.

The Saracens had manufactures of stuffs before the crusades. At Damascus, and in the cities of Egypt, metals were worked with greater perfection than in the West. Old chronicles inform us that the Christians of Palestine went sometimes to Damascus to purchase arms. Joinville relates that, being on a pilgrimage to our lady of Tortosa, he bought at Tripoli some camlets, fabricated in that city. He sent some pieces of them to Queen Marguerite, who, he tells us, at first took them for relics, and fell on her knees to receive them; but upon discovering her mistake arose, saying, "Mischief upon the seneschal! who has made me kneel to his camlets."* Joinville was directed by Louis IX. to purchase a quantity of this stuff, which proves that the manufactory in which it was fabricated had some reputation.

There were at this period, in the same city of Tripoli, and in several cities of Greece, a great number of silk-looms, the produce of which must have excited great attention in the merchants and pilgrims who visited the East. About the middle of the twelfth century, Roger II., king of Sicily, caused several of these looms to be transported to Palermo; this was the fruit of an expedition to the coasts of Greece. The mulberry-tree flourished and multiplied under the beautiful sky of Italy, as well as under that of the Morea, and this useful conquest gave the Sicilians the means of soon surpassing the industry of the Greeks. The principal workshop was placed in the palace of the kings, as if to display the richness and magnificence of this new art.

Many useful inventions came to us at this period from the countries of the East. Some writers affirm that windmills were known in Europe before the crusades; but we should remember that they might have been due to the early pilgrimages into Asia, which it is so difficult to separate, upon such matters, from the holy wars.†

---

* Hotspur says to his lady— "Swear me, Kate, like a lady, as thou art,
 A good mouth-filling oath!"

The queen's anathema upon Joinville is, in the original, something of this character.—TRANS.

† M. de Choiseul d'Aillecourt gives in his *Mémoire* a very extended nomenclature of the inventions brought from the East into Europe by the Crusaders.

Tyre was at this time famous for its glass. The sand found in its vicinity gave to the fabrication of glass a perfection unknown in other countries. The use of glass was much more common in Palestine than in the West. The Venetians obtained from Tyre the idea of their beautiful works in glass, so celebrated in the middle ages.

The Crusaders, as has been seen in this history, always evinced great surprise at witnessing the explosion of the Greek fire. But what appears very strange, they never seemed to envy the Saracens this great advantage. The Frank warriors, in the field of battle, preferred the sword and lance to a means of fighting which, in their minds, took away something from personal bravery. It is not at all improbable, however, that the Greek fire, in the end, furnished the idea of gunpowder; an invention fatal to humanity, but which placed a formidable weapon in the hands of European society, when threatened by the Turks and Tartars.

We have already spoken of the maize, or Turkish wheat, sent into Italy by Boniface of Montferrat, in the fourth crusade. The Damascus plum was brought at the same time into Europe by a duke of Anjou, who visited Jerusalem. Our gardens owe to the holy wars the ranunculus, so prized by Orientals, and shalots, which take their name from Ascalon; the knowledge, or rather the use of saffron, alum, and indigo, in Europe, may be traced to the times of the crusades.

We may remember with what delight the Crusaders saw for the first time the sugar-canes of the territory of Tripoli. The plant was transported to Sicily, about the middle of the twelfth century. It is not correct, however, to say that it passed from thence into the new world. If the Spaniards afterwards transported the sugar-cane to the island of Madeira, we may believe they found it in the kingdom of Granada, whither the Moors had brought it from Africa. But it is also probable that notice was only taken of this plant because the taste for sugar was widely spread, and that the substance, which was brought from Egypt, became an important branch of commerce. It is thus we may render honour to the crusades.

Natural history, which is connected with the progress of industry and agriculture, was enriched likewise by some useful notions. Distant climates not only exchanged their vegetable productions, but the crusades procured for Europe an acquaintance with several animals of Africa and Asia. We have mentioned that the Mamelukes of Egypt sent Louis IX. an elephant, of which the French monarch made a present to the king of England. A short time after the first expedition of Louis IX., Bibars sent to Mainfrey, son of Frederick II., several Mogul prisoners, with their horses, which were of Tartar breed. Among the Oriental productions which the Egyptian ambassadors were directed to present to the king of Sicily, was a giraffe, an animal that had never till that time been seen in the West.

The curious circumstances which we could further produce, would add nothing to the opinion that must be already entertained of the happy influence of the crusades upon the progress of agriculture and industry. The riches of Asia, when brought into Europe, soon gave birth to a desire for the cultivation of the arts which embellish life, and of the sciences which double the faculties of man.

In the tenth century, architecture consisted in the construction of towers, ramparts, and fortresses. In the habitations of the great, everything was sacrificed to the necessity of providing defences against an enemy; nothing could be afforded to comfort or magnificence. The dwellings of the people, even in cities, scarcely protected them from the injuries of weather or the intemperance of seasons. The only architectural monuments were those which devotion raised to ancestors. Before magnificent palaces for princes, or convenient houses for the rich were thought of, edifices consecrated to religion were constructed. It is scarcely possible to enumerate the churches and monasteries built in the eleventh and twelfth centuries. According to the opinion of the time, the most certain mode of expiating sins, was to build a church or a monastery. Thus architectural monuments arose at the voice of repentance, and religious inspirations revived, in some sort, the prodigies which fabulous antiquity attributed to the lyre of Amphion.

In every city, in every town, the inhabitants made it their pride to ornament their cathedral, and the altars at which they invoked the saint whom the parish had chosen for its patron. It may be said that there was something like patriotism in this pious zeal; for the basilic, or paternal church, was then the most noble and the most sensible image of the country.

At the commencement of the crusades, there existed a religious confraternity composed of men practised in the labours of building; they travelled about the world, offering their services to the faithful to build or repair churches. Another confraternity was formed with the useful design of constructing bridges for pilgrims and travellers. A chapel or an oratory reminded passengers that the bridge they were crossing was the work of charity.

The clergy, who were rich, and could only display their opulence in buildings, made it their glory to erect churches. To complete their work, they called in the aid of painting and sculpture, which, like architecture, owed their first encouragement to piety, and whose earliest masterpieces were consecrated to the ornamenting of the altars of the Christian religion. Nothing was more common than to see noble Crusaders, on their departure for Palestine, or on their return to the West, found a monastery or a church. Several pilgrims are named, who, on coming back from Jerusalem, employed their treasures in constructing churches, the form of which might offer them an image of the holy sepulchre they had visited. The treasures conquered from the infidels were often appropriated to such buildings. Before the first crusade, some cities of Italy undertook an expedition into Africa, and the spoils were reserved for the ornamenting of churches. We read in an Italian chronicle, that the Pisans ceded to the Greek emperor Calo-John, several cities which belonged to them in Asia Minor, upon the condition that this emperor would defray the expenses necessary for the building of the archbishop's palace at Pisa, and ornamenting the cathedral of Palermo.

During the crusades, the sight of the monuments of architecture which were admired in the East, must have awakened the emulation of the western pilgrims. Nothing could exceed the surprise of the Crusaders at beholding the city of Constantine. Foucher de Chartres exclaimed in his enthusiasm: "Oh, what a vast and beautiful city is Constantinople!" The German historian Gunther likewise expresses his admiration, and says that such magnificence could not be believed if it were not seen. The marshal of Champagne relates that the French knights, on seeing the beautiful towers and the superb palaces of Byzantium, could not persuade themselves *that there could be such a rich city in all the world!*

Italy, which derived such advantages from its relations with the East, profited greatly by the masterpieces of Greece. The inhabitants of Rome, and of several other cities founded and embellished by the Romans, had before them remains of antiquity that might serve them as models. The riches which their commerce brought them furnished them with the means of encouraging industry and the arts, which assist in the embellishment of cities. The cities of Italy,—Venice in particular.—had palaces and sumptuous edifices before the crusades. In the thirteenth and fourteenth centuries, the taste for beautiful architecture changed the face of Italy, and spread by degrees throughout the rest of Europe.

We must add, however, that the fine arts, with the exception of architecture, owed very little to the frequent communications with the East. Painting was despised among the Mussulmans, to whom the Koran forbade the reproduction of the images of man or of animated beings. The Latins likewise, as our readers may remember, after the taking of Constantinople, destroyed most of the monuments raised by the genius of sculpture, and converted the masterpieces of Phidias and Praxiteles into pieces of coin.

The indolent and silent character of the orientals was not calculated to carry music to perfection, as this art bespeaks a lively and warm imagination in a people; and the Greeks had for a long time lost the secret of those melodious songs which, in the times of Linus and Orpheus, charmed the heights of Rhodope and the woods of Mænalus. The history of music, then, has very little to do with that of the holy wars. When Italy saw the fine arts revive, they sprang up as a natural production of the soil, as plants indigenous to the climate; they owed their splendour to the prosperous state of society, and followed, as a consequence of the opulence and luxury which commerce and industry had produced.

The revival of the fine arts announced that of letters. But if it be true that letters owed a part of their progress to the influence of the crusades, it must be confessed that the Crusaders did not always show themselves disposed to profit by them for themselves: nothing can exceed the ignorance of the Crusaders who then set out for the East. History informs us that after the taking of Jerusalem, they burnt at Tripoli a library which contained the most precious monuments of oriental literature; at the taking of Constantinople, a conflagration devoured the literary treasures of ancient Greece. The Crusaders beheld this misfortune with so much indifference, that not one of their chronicles makes mention of it, and posterity would have been ignorant of it but for the eloquent complaints of Nicetas.

The science which gained most by these distant expeditions was doubtless geography. Before the crusades, this science was quite unknown. Countries, the least distant from each other, had no intercommunication. Burgundy was scarcely known at Paris; in Burgundy Paris was considered as a very remote place. The Crusaders who followed Peter the Hermit were not acquainted with the names of the cities of Germany and Hungary which they passed through. They experienced a defeat at Mersbourg, and the contemporary chronicles that speak of it content themselves with calling the Hungarian city *Malleville*, or the city of misfortune.

If the Franks scarcely knew their own country, what must have been their ignorance of the countries of the East? We may judge by the necessity they felt for taking their guides from among the Greeks, whom they mistrusted, and by their extreme embarrassment whenever these guides abandoned them. Several armies perished from want of knowing the places to which victory conducted them. Most of the chroniclers knew no more about the matter than the Crusaders; and this it is that renders it so difficult to follow them in Asia Minor and Syria.

One most remarkable circumstance is, that out of more than two hundred chronicles that speak of Egypt, we have not been able to find more than one that makes mention of the Pyramids. James of Vitry, who sojourned for a long time in Syria, and who appears to have possessed as much knowledge as was then common to the learned, repeats, in his descriptions of the East, the fables of Herodotus; such as the history of the Amazons and that of the phœnix. We can scarcely forbear laughing at the simple credulity of Joinville, who tells us gravely, in his memoirs, that the trees of the terrestrial paradise produce cinnamon, ginger, and cloves, and that these spices are fished out of the waters of the Nile, whither they have been carried by the winds.

The Crusaders, constantly engaged in fighting, never entertained the idea of making themselves acquainted with the countries subdued by their arms. Nevertheless, in consequence of them, religion and commerce,—the one led by the desire of spreading the Gospel, the other by the hopes of gaining wealth, opened some new routes, and gained useful notions concerning the East during the crusades. The missionaries sent by the court of Rome and by St. Louis travelled over the vast regions

THE BATTLE OF ARSUR.

King Philip had returned to Europe; Richard remained at the head of one hundred thousand Crusaders. He left Ptolemaïs and marched towards Cæsarea, a distance of twelve leagues, requiring six days; a fleet from Ptolemaïs kept close to the shore, and transported the war machines, baggage, and provisions of the Crusaders. Saladin, compared to a lioness which has lost her young, set out in pursuit, harassing the flanks, at times attacking the van, and destroying the country through which the Crusaders were going to march. Across the plain of Arsur flowed a torrent; at this point Saladin awaited the Crusaders to offer them a decisive battle. . . . . The battle lasted almost during the whole day. Towards evening the Mussulmans were broken on all sides, and the wreck of Saladin's army retreated into the forest of Saron, and Richard was not wise enough to pursue and destroy it.—BOOK VIII.

of Asia, and commerce either followed or went before them in these distant journeys. The accounts of Rubruquis, Asselin, John Plan Carpin, and Marco Paolo, contain observations of which the truth and correctness are recognized at the present day.

We may add that the Crusaders, who went from all the countries of Europe, became acquainted with each other beneath the standard of the cross. Nations were no longer foreign to each other; which dissipated the ignorance in which they had been regarding the names of the cities and provinces of the West.

The geographical charts of this period neither give the configuration of the globe, nor the extent of countries, nor the position or limits of emperors; they merely trace, by vague designations, that which struck travellers most forcibly,—such as the curiosities of each country, the animals, the buildings, and the various dresses of men. We have seen a map of the world, which is attached to the chronicle of St. Denis, and which appears to have been made in the thirteenth century: we do not find, as in modern maps, the names of the four cardinal points set down, but on the four sides are written the names of the principal winds, to the number of twelve. Jerusalem, according to the opinion of the time, is placed in the centre of the three parts of the known world; a large edifice surmounted by a cross represents the holy city. Around this queen of cities, the author of the map has figured, by other edifices, the cities of Palestine, Syria, Egypt, &c.: the distances are marked without any attention to exactness; all appears thrown at random on the paper: this confused mass of edifices or houses, seems to be less a representation of the universe than the shapeless picture of a great city, built without plan or regularity.

We may judge by this how completely geography was then in its infancy; but, at the same time, it renders it evident that it was not quite neglected, as till that time it had been. Thus, we have a right to believe they would not stand still there, and that geographical knowledge would soon advance. In the fourteenth century, the countries of the East were already much better known, if we may judge by the chart which Sanuti presented to the pope, and which may be seen in the collection of the historians of the crusades by Bengars.

The sciences most useful to man, such as medicine, might have made some progress during the crusades, if the Crusaders had profited by the knowledge of the Orientals. In medicine particularly, the Arabians had more positive knowledge than the Latins. At the siege of Ptolemaïs, we have seen that Saladin sent his physicians to Richard; but we do not learn that the king of England sent his to Saladin, when he fell ill. In the first crusade of St. Louis, the physicians who accompanied the army of the Crusaders understood nothing of the scurvy and other epidemic diseases, which exercised such ravages in the camp of the Christians. Their ignorance was not less fatal than the contagion: when Louis IX. and his warriors became the prisoners of the Mussulmans, the diseases which desolated them ceased all at once, because they were no longer attended by their own physicians, but were placed under the care of the Arabians.

The East then furnished Europe with several processes and remedies from which modern medicine, for a length of time, derived great advantage. Cassia and senna came from Asia, and became known in the West at the period of the crusades. Theriaca, which played so great a part in the medicine of the middle ages, was brought from Antioch to Venice. Robert of Normandy, on his return from the Holy Land, after the taking of Jerusalem, obtained from the school of Salerno a collection of Hygeian precepts, which became proverbs among all the nations of Europe.

And yet these discoveries, and this knowledge of the Orientals, did not much enlighten the West in the art of curing. Properly to receive lessons of experience of this kind, preliminary studies were necessary, and the physicians of Europe were then too ignorant to profit by the learning of the

Arabians. At this period, religious charity raised a great number of open asylums for suffering humanity. But this charity, however admirable, when its object was to attend the sick, and comfort them in their sufferings, knew but very little of the symptoms or the character of the numberless diseases which attack the life of man. It may be safely said, that during the crusades, we received from the East many more serious diseases than true instruction in medicine. We know that there were numerous lazar-houses established in Europe in the time of the crusades; but we know nothing of the remedies employed for the cure of leprosy. Isolation appears to have been the only curative or preservative means known for this malady, which many learned physicians now look upon as mere prejudice. The spirit of devotion richly endowed lepers, without doing anything for their cure. Leprosy, in the end, disappeared without the assistance of medicine, and the property bestowed upon lazar-houses was transferred to the hospitals; which was advantageous to humanity, and may be set down as one of the benefits of the crusades.

We will say nothing of the other sciences, which owed still less than geography and medicine to the holy wars.

The Saracens of Syria were very little enlightened in the middle ages. In the East, the state of knowledge, like everything else, depended upon the reign of a great prince; whilst this prince reigned, knowledge flourished by his influence; at his death, everything returned to darkness, as the natural state of countries governed by Islamism.*

The Franks gained more by their commerce with the Greeks than by that with the Saracens. The Crusaders established continual relations between the cities of Italy and the empire of Byzantium. Some sparks of the genius of the Greeks were glimmering in Italy before the taking of Constantinople by the Turks.

A college for young Greeks was established at Paris in the reign of Philip Augustus. In the thirteenth century universities flourished at Bologna, Paris, and Salamanca, in which the Greek language was taught; and later, the Oriental languages were added, by a decree of the council of Vienna.

We find in a chronicle of St. Denis these remarkable words:—"This year, 1257, William, a physician, brought some Greek books from Constantinople." Thus, the arrival of some volumes from Greece was an event worthy of being recorded, and the importance attached to it, already announced the disposition of men's minds.

When the Turks became masters of Constantinople, the learned, exiled from their country, came to establish themselves in Italy, where the Greek muses formed an alliance with the Latin muses. The venerable interpreters of antiquity were hailed everywhere with eagerness, and the communication of their knowledge was repaid by generous hospitality. Among the distinguished men to whom the muses of ancient Greece owed an honourable protection, we must not forget Nicholas V., who, as the head of the Christians of the West, excommunicated the Greek Church, and, as a scholar, seemed to have vowed a worship to the genius of Homer and Plato. Printing, which had then recently been invented, was employed to preserve the literary treasures brought from the East, and made them for ever safe from the scythe of Time, the furies of war, or the hands of barbarians. The Iliad and the Odyssey found readers in places which had inspired the Æneid; the orations of Demosthenes were again read amid the wrecks of the forum, where the learned might believe they still listened to the voice of Cicero. The genius of the Italians, kindled by the masterpieces of ancient Rome and of old Athens, produced fresh masterpieces; and Italy presented a phenomenon which

---

* The Moors of Spain may be adduced as an example against this opinion. It is true that the Moors of Granada cultivated the arts and sciences for a long time, and with much success; but what became of them when they returned to the coast of Africa?

the world will, perhaps, never see again,—that of a nation which, in the space of a few centuries, obtained twice the palm of literature in two different languages.

It was from Constantinople we received the philosophy of Aristotle. We can scarcely say to what extent the true friends of intelligence ought to congratulate themselves on this head. Aristotle had disciples, partisans, and martyrs; the philosopher of Stagyra was very near being preferred to the Bible; the contemners of Aristotle were called *Biblici*. At that period a mania for subtleties was introduced into the schools, which dishonoured the teaching of philosophy. Reason was no longer studied in the mind of man, but in a book; nature was no longer studied in the universe, but in Aristotle. The schools became like fencing-matches. In an age in which everything was decided by violence, the human mind wished to have its species of warfare; so that victory in most affairs was considered justice; and became, in the schools, the only reason. We may believe that this philosophy did not much assist the march of true wisdom; but we must admit, that if it did, for a moment, lead the human mind astray, it did not quite arrest its progress. It exercised the faculties of man, and by that means assisted in their development. At the commencement of societies, it is less the errors of the mind than its inaction that retains nations in the darkness of barbarism.

Universities had never been so attended as at this period. The number of students in the schools of Paris, Bologna, and Oxford were said to amount to ten thousand. The great privileges granted to universities, prove the esteem in which learning was then held. The doctors disputed for precedency with knighthood itself. If Bartholo is to be believed, ten years' teaching of the Roman law conferred the title of *knight*. This dignity was called *the knighthood of learning*, and they who attained it were called *knights-clerks*.

Among all the productions of mind, those which ought to be ranked first, were such as had for object the preservation of the memory of events. At all periods of the middle ages, chronicles appeared, to which were consigned the important facts of history. In many monasteries were kept registers or journals, in which was inserted everything remarkable that happened in the various parts of the world. Monks, in the general assemblies, sometimes communicated these registers to each other, and this communication assisted them in rendering their chronicles more complete. In ages less remote from us, other cenobites have collected, with laborious care, these same chronicles, concealed in the solitude of cloisters, and have transmitted them to posterity as the most precious monuments of old times.

The ancient chroniclers were simple and pious men; they considered the least falsehood as a mortal sin; they were scrupulous in telling the truth, when they were acquainted with it. Most of them would have thought themselves deficient in the duties of an historian, if they had not gone back to the creation of the world, or at least to the deluge. Among the events which they relate, they never forgot such as would strike the vulgar, and which struck themselves; as the revolutions of nature, famines, prodigies, &c. According to the spirit of their age, the foundation of a monastery holds a more conspicuous place in their recitals than that of a kingdom or of a republic. Politics are quite unknown to them; and everything which astonishes them, everything they do not easily comprehend, they rarely fail to account for by a miracle.

Such is the character of our old chroniclers; and even when they do not inform us of that which we desire to know, their simplicity touches us, and their ingenuousness interests us. When they tell us of wonderful things which were believed in their times, and of which they appear fully persuaded, they do nothing but paint themselves and their age.

But we must beware of fancying the Oriental chronicles of the same period more perfect than our own. We find in them the same spirit of superstition and credulity, united to that spirit of fatalism which characterizes the Mussulman faith.

It is quite in vain for us to seek in Arabian historians any of those thoughts that instruct us in the knowledge of human passions or political revolutions. They almost always neglect the most important circumstances of events, in order to describe whimsical particularities, or to enter into insignificant details; thus, obeying the spirit of Oriental despotism, which wills that man should be always occupied with little things. When they relate the fall of an empire, if asked why it has fallen, they reply: "God knows, God has willed it so." In all their chronicles which we have consulted, whenever the Mussulmans triumph over the Christians, we never find any other reflection but this: "God is God, and Mahomet is his prophet." When the Christians gain a victory, the Mussulman chronicles preserve a perfect silence, contenting themselves with saying: "May God curse them!"

Oriental historical productions are very far from redeeming this absence of remark by another merit, such as order, clearness, or elegance; most of their accounts are nothing but a nomenclature of facts confusedly arranged. Quotations from the Koran, verses made upon the occurrence of an event, some comparisons which belong rather to poetry than history,—such are the only ornaments of their narrations.

We see by this that our chronicles of the middle ages have nothing to envy in those of the East. Most of them, it is true, are of an extreme dryness, and have neither precision nor method. But still some few of them do not appear unworthy of attracting the attention of scholars and men of taste. As their authors wrote in Latin, we have reason to believe that the great works of antiquity were not unknown to them, and in many of their recitals, we may easily perceive they have had models.

History must have made some progress during the crusades. These long wars between the Christians and the Mussulmans were like a great spectacle at which Europe and Asia were present. The importance of the events, and the lively interest which Christendom took in them, inspired several writers with the desire of retracing the history of them. A crowd of chroniclers arose in the West, among whom some were not unworthy of the name of historians. Everybody is acquainted with William of Tyre, who may be called the Livy of the crusades, Albert d'Aix, Baudry, archbishop of Dol, Odo of Deuil, and particularly James of Vitry, in whom we meet with vivid and animated descriptions, a rapid and flowing style, and a narration almost always elegant:—and, though last, not least, Villehardouin and Joinville, who wrote in the French language, and whose memoirs are the earliest monuments of French literature.

But all these events which presented to historians such rich pictures, the wonders of nascent institutions, the prodigies of the social world issuing from the chaos of barbarism, must not only have awakened the curiosity, they must have struck vividly the minds of new generations. This grand spectacle, without doubt, contributed to the development of the faculties connected with the imagination. After having seen the simple and faithful relations of events, the genius of poets was called upon to add something to the truthful pictures of the chroniclers. The troubadours who flourished during the crusades were not likely to neglect the exploits of so many gallant knights. We hear their voices constantly mingling with those of the preachers of the holy wars, and find their poetical fictions everywhere confounded with the narrations of history.

Among the warriors who went into the East to combat the infidels, a great number of troubadours and trouvères distinguished themselves. We have seen the romance of Raoul de Couci, and the verses of Thibault, count of Champagne. We may add to these names known in the *fasti* of the French muses, those of the count of Poictiers, the count of Anjou, the duke of Brittany, Frederick II., and Richard Cœur-de-Lion. Often would these princely and lordly Crusaders charm the tediousness of a long pilgrimage by poetical relaxations and remembrances. The count of Soissons, when a prisoner with St. Louis, sang the praises of the dames of France, in the presence and beneath the very swords of the Saracens. One chronicle relates that at the end of the third crusade, the duke of Burgundy made a satire against Richard, and that Richard replied by a poem. The example of these princes was enough to arouse the emulation of the poets; and as they composed their verses in the French language, this language, which was then spoken at Jerusalem, Constantinople, and many other places in the East, must have prevailed over all contemporary idioms.

The muse of the troubadours celebrated chivalry, love, and beauty; that of the trouvères, who dwelt on the banks of the Loire, and in the provinces situated beyond that river, delighted in songs of a more serious kind. The trouvères had rivals in England and Germany. These poets had created for themselves an heroic and new world, which inspired them with noble actions. They celebrated the lofty deeds of Arthur and Rinaldo, the knights of the Round Table, Charlemagne, Roland, and the twelve peers of France. They added to these names those of Godfrey, Tancred, Richard, and Saladin, the remembrance of whom vividly interested all the Christian nations of the middle ages.

The marvellous, among a people, belongs to their habits, to the effects of climate, and to the great revolutions of society. In consequence of the mixture and confusion of divers nations in the middle ages, the wonderful traditions of the North became confounded with those of the South, and produced a semi-barbarous mythology, which differed widely from the laughing mythology of the Greeks. But the labours, the perils, the exploits of a religious war, of a distant war, like those of the crusades, must have given a more noble direction to the imagination of poets, and preserved it from that which was common and whimsical in the romantic conceptions of a gross age. That which was then passing upon the real theatre of events, was more extraordinary than the inventions of poetry; and the marvellous of that period was the more easy to be seized, from being all to be found in actual history.

A new literature then was born, conforming with the genius of a new state of society. If this literature, which, to employ the expression of the learned Heren, bore a character of national and contemporary originality, had produced great works like the Iliad and the Odyssey, the muses would have opened for themselves a career unknown to the ancients; language would have been, from that time enriched, perfected, fixed by the masterpieces themselves; and history would have spoken of the age of the crusades, as it speaks to us of the age of Augustus or Pericles.

Unfortunately, our literature of the middle ages only produced indifferent poems, which were not able to make us forget the great works of antiquity. There were none but romantic productions, in which the interest of the subject was not at all raised by talent, and poems whose authors, though witty and ingenious, had none of that authority of genius which carries away the opinions of an age, and even of posterity.

We have more than one reason for regretting that the human mind did not open for itself a new career at the period of the crusades. There is no doubt that the ancients offer us the more perfect models of taste; but in proportion as people, in the end, became impassioned for the Greeks and the Latins, modern nations disdained their own antiquities for those of Athens and Rome. With the study of masterpieces which had nothing to do with our own glory, the remembrance of our own ancestors was not at all mixed; and the knowledge they have given us has added nothing to our patriotism. What an interest and what a value would the remembrances of our country have had for us, if they had been traced by a literature, formed according to the manners of the nation, and which would, in some sort, have commenced with the nation itself!

Most of the romancers, and even the poets of these times, who had no models and wanted taste, found no other means of interesting their readers, than by exaggerating the sentiments of chivalry.

Imitation, pushed to the extreme, was taken for reality, and there were found knights who wished to do that which they saw in romances and poems. Thence came knight-errantry. Thus, in all times, the state of society has acted upon literature, and literature, in its turn, has reacted upon the state of society.

The romances which were consecrated to chivalry and the crusades, underwent the modifications that manners and customs received; and this species of composition has come down to our days, expressing, by turns, the tastes, sentiments, and opinions of each age. This was quite unknown to antiquity. It was born with the Romance language, whose name it took; and they who now derive pleasure from it ought to be thankful for it to the age of the crusades.

These kinds of productions, which attracted the curiosity and attention of the vulgar, contributed to form the national language, which then appeared to be scorned by the learned. The Latin language still remained the language of the sciences and of learning. But it lost its correctness and its purity. The Latin of the fifteenth century was more corrupt than that of the twelfth. The Romance language and the Latin language had a tendency to corrupt each other, by their mixture and their reciprocal borrowings.

Knowledge, however, continued to increase and spread, and assisted greatly in polishing the manners of the nations of Europe. One proof that the crusades were not unconnected with these first steps of civilization is, that knowledge and letters first flourished among the peoples enriched by the commerce which the holy wars favoured, as in Italy; and with the peoples who had most communication with the Orientals, as the Spaniards. Two inventions were destined to complete this happy revolution, and mark the commencement and the end of the period of the crusades. The first was the invention of paper, which became known in Europe just before the first expedition into the East; the second, the invention of printing, which took place towards the end of the holy wars.

There remains but little for us to say upon the results of the crusades. Several distinguished writers have spoken of them before us, and the information they have given upon this important subject, whilst it facilitates our labour, only leaves us the advantage of expressing an opinion which their authority has consecrated, and which has no longer any need of being defended.

The better to explain and make clear all the good that the holy wars brought with them, we have elsewhere examined what would have happened if they had had all the success they might have had. Let us now attempt another hypothesis, and let our minds dwell for a moment upon the state in which Europe would have been, without the expeditions which the West so many times repeated against the nations of Asia and Africa. In the eleventh century, several European countries were invaded, and others were threatened by the Saracens. What means of defence had the Christian republic then, when most of the states were given up to license, troubled by discords, and plunged in barbarism? If Christendom, as M. De Bonald remarks, had not then gone out by all its gates, and at repeated times, to attack a formidable enemy, have we not a right to believe that this enemy would have profited by the inaction of the Christian nations, and that he would have surprised them amidst their divisions, and subdued them one after another? Which of us does not tremble with horror at thinking that France, Germany, England, and Italy might have experienced the fate of Greece and Palestine?

We have said, when commencing our history, that the crusades offered the spectacle of a sanguinary and terrible struggle between two religions which contended for the empire of the world; the victory to belong to that one of these two religions which would inspire its disciples and defenders with the most generous sentiments, and which, favouring among them the progress of civilization, would give them the greater force and power to defend their territories and assure their conquests.

In this formidable struggle, the true means of defence consisted in superiority of knowledge and of social qualities. As long as the ignorance of barbarism reigned over the nations of the West as well as over those of Asia, victory continued uncertain; perhaps even the greater strength was then on the side of the more barbarous people, for they were already possessed of all the conditions of their political existence. But when the dawn of civilization rose over Europe, she became aware of her own security, and her enemies began to be sensible of fear.

The Mussulman religion, by its doctrine of fatalism, appeared to interdict all foresight to its disciples, and in days of mischance contained nothing to revive the courage of its warriors. The Christians, on the contrary, lost none of their faculties in reverses: reverses often even redoubled their energy and activity. What is most astonishing in the history of the crusades, is to observe that the defeats of the Christians in Asia excited, among the warlike populations of Europe, much more enthusiasm than their victories. The preachers of the holy wars, to persuade Christian warriors to take up arms against the infidels, said nothing of the glory and the power of Jerusalem; but endeavoured, in their pathetic lamentations, to exaggerate the perils, the misfortunes, and the decline of the Christian colonies.

We see by this what advantage Christianity had over the worship of Mahomet, in the war between the East and the West.

Another vice of the Koran is, that it has a tendency to isolate men; which is injurious to the development of their social qualities. Under the empire of Islamism, there is nothing strong but despotism; but the strength of despotism is, almost always, nothing but the weakness of the nation it rules over. The Christian religion has another aim, when it says to its disciples, *Love one another as brothers*. One of its most admirable characteristics is the spirit of sociability with which it inspires men. By all its maxims, it orders them to unite, to help one another, to enlighten one another. It thus doubles their strength, by placing them constantly in community of labours and dangers, fears and hopes, opinions and feelings. It was this spirit of sociability which gave birth to the crusades, and sustained them during two centuries. If this spirit was unable to assure success, it at least prepared the Christian republic, at a later period, to defend itself with advantage. It made the nations of Europe like fasces that cannot be broken. It created, in the midst of disorders even, a moral force which nothing could conquer; and Christianity, defended by this moral force, was at length able to say to the barbarians, masters of Constantinople, that which God said to the waves of the sea: *You shall go no further*.

Thus Christianity, and the heroic virtues with which it inspired its disciples, were, in the middle ages, an invincible buckler for Christian Europe. When the enthusiasm for crusades beyond the seas began to die away, the heads of the Church still invoked the spirit of the Gospel, to animate the nations against the Mussulmans, on the point of invading Germany and Italy; and, still holding up to Christian warriors the cross of Christ, sometimes succeeded in awakening in hearts sentiments of a religious and patriotic heroism. It cannot then be denied that the crusades contributed to save European societies from the invasion of the barbarians; and this was, without doubt, the first and greatest of the advantages which humanity derived from them.

Here I am, then, arrived at the termination of my labour. To resume my opinions and render a last homage to truth, I must say, that, among the results of the crusades, there are some which appear incontestable, others which cannot be determined with precision. I ought to add, that many circumstances concurred with the civil wars in assisting the progress of knowledge and civilization,

Nothing can be more complicated than the springs which set modern societies in motion; and he who would desire to explain the march of things by one single cause, must fall into great error. The same events do not produce always or everywhere similar effects; as may be seen by the picture we have traced of Europe in the middle ages. The holy wars assisted, in France, in abasing the great vassals, whilst feudal power received scarcely any injury from it in Germany and other countries. During this period some states were enlarged, others marched rapidly towards their fall. Among some nations, liberty took deep root, and presided over young institutions; among others, the power of princes was elevated, at times freeing itself from all restraints, at others, being limited by wise laws. Here flourished commerce, the arts and sciences; elsewhere industry made no progress, and the human mind remained immersed in darkness. The germs of civilization, in the times of the crusades, were like those seeds which the storm carries with it, and scatters, some in barren places, where they remain unknown and unproductive; others, upon propitious land, where the action of the sun, a happy temperature, and the fecundity of the soil, favour their development, and cause them to bear good fruits.

Every age has its dominant opinions; and when these opinions are connected with great events, they leave their impress upon the institutions of societies. Other events, other opinions come, in their turn, to give a new direction to human affairs, and to modify, ameliorate, or corrupt the morals and the laws of nations. Thus, the political world is unceasingly renewed; by turns, disturbed by violent shocks, and ruled by generally-spread truths or errors. If, in the future, societies assume still another new face, there is no doubt their institutions will, one day, be explained by the influence of the revolutions we have seen, as we now explain the institutions of times past, by the influence of the crusades. May posterity gather and preserve the fruit of our misfortunes, better than we ourselves have gathered and preserved the fruit of the experience and of the misfortunes of our fathers!

THE END.

TROUBADOURS SINGING THE GLORIES OF THE CRUSADES.

The muse of the troubadours celebrated chivalry, love, and beauty. They celebrated the lofty deeds of Arthur and Rinaldo, the Knights of the Round Table. . . . They added to these names those of Godfrey, Tancred, Richard and Saladin. The troubadours who flourished during the Crusades were not likely to neglect the exploits of so many gallant knights. We hear their voices constantly mingling with those of the preachers of the holy wars, and find their poetical fictions confounded with the narrations of history.—BOOK XVIII.

TABLE OF CONTENTS, VOL II.

BOOK XII.

THE SIXTH CRUSADE.
A. D. 1200–1215.

Famine in Egypt, and its frightful consequences—Saadi, the Persian poet—Death of Bohémond III.—John of Brienne accepts the young queen of Jerusalem in marriage—Malek-Adel renews hostilities against the Christians—John of Brienne takes possession of Ptolemaïs—First dawnings of the Reformation—Philip Augustus king of France, and John king of England, engage in the crusade—Battle of Bouvines—The pope assembles the council of Lateran, and stimulates all Europe to the holy war—His death and character—Censius Savelli chosen pope, under the title of Honorius III.—He urges the crusade—Andrew II., king of Hungary, engages in it—Paganism of Prussia in the thirteenth century—Political state of Hungary—Her king returns from Palestine—The tower of Damietta captured by the Crusaders—Death and character of Malek-Adel—Cardinal Pelagius instigates the prosecution of the crusade, and proceeds to Egypt—Conspiracy to dethrone the sultan of Cairo—Battle before the walls of Damietta—The Mohammedans propose conditions of peace—Damietta captured, and the inhabitants destroyed by famine—The Mohammedans burn the fleet of the Crusaders on the Nile, and compel them to capitulate—Melik-Kamel enters into a treaty of peace, by which Damietta is surrendered to the Mussulmans—The Georgians—Invasions of the Tartars—Marriage of Frederick II., emperor of Germany, with the heiress of the king of Jerusalem—Acknowledged to be king—Persecutions of the Albigeois—The Guelphs and Ghibellines—Frederick of Germany engages in the holy war, sets sail, and returns to Otranto—Gregory IX. succeeds Pope Honorius—His rage against Frederick of Germany—Death of Conraddin, sultan of Damascus—Frederick acknowledged king of Jerusalem—He quits Palestine for Europe—Excommunicated by Gregory IX.—The pope determines on renewing the holy war—Thibault V., king of Navarre, and Pierre de Dreux, engage in it—Council of Tours for promoting the cause of the Crusaders—Decline of the Latin empire in Constantinople—John of Brienne called to the throne—His death—Baldwin, his son-in-law, driven from the throne—Battle of Gaza—Death of Gregory IX.—Richard, duke of Cornwall, joins the Crusaders at Ptolemaïs—Pope Celestine IV.—Pilgrims buy off their vows—Songs of the Troubadours—Leprosy in the West—The sanguinary wars in the name of religion...page 6

BOOK XIII.

THE SEVENTH CRUSADE.
A. D. 1242–1245.

The Tartars of the middle ages—Their history and conquests—Gengiskhan, the Tartar Chief—Temugin—Prester John—Khan of the Karaites—Conquest of China, Carismia, and other extensive countries in Asia and Europe, by Gengiskhan—His death—Victorious career of Octaï, khan of the Tartars—Hungary conquered—The warriors of Carismia join the sultan of Cairo, and capture Jerusalem—The Mohammedans of Syria defeated by the Carismians, and Damascus captured—The Carismians rebel against the sultan of Cairo—They are defeated and dispersed—Barbarous hordes of the Comans—Distress of the Christians—Valeran, bishop of Berytus—Innocent IV., at the council of Lyons, determines on the seventh crusade, and excommunicates Frederick, emperor of Germany—Cardinals first clothed in scarlet—Louis IX., king of France, recovers from a dangerous malady, and determines on prosecuting the seventh crusade against the infidels—The illustrious names engaged in it—Blanche, the queen-mother—Agitated state of Germany and Italy—Frederick of Germany deposed by the pope—Civil contests thence arising—The nobles of France form a league to resist the exactions of the pope—Louis makes extensive preparations for the holy war—The earl of Salisbury, and Haco, king of Norway, engage in it—Ameliorated state of society resulting from the crusades—Louis embarks and arrives at Cyprus—Pope Innocent IV. takes charge of his kingdom—Marguerite, wife of Louis—Archambault de Bourbon—Sieur de Joinville—Antioch ravaged by the Turcomans—Louis receives an embassy from the Tartar prince, Ecalthai—Political discord among the Mohammedans—Family of the Ayoubites—Malek-Salek Negmeddin, sultan of Egypt—Military and political state of Egypt at the time of the crusade—Louis IX. and the Christian forces arrive before Damietta—His address to the Crusaders—He besieges Damietta—Fakreddin, the Egyptian leader—Louis attacks and defeats the infidel troops—Damietta captured—Negotiations with Negmeddin—Livre Tournois—Bravery of the Bedouin Arabs—Sidon captured by the Mohammedans..page 87

TABLE OF CONTENTS.

BOOK XIV.

DAMIETTA AND LOUIS IX.

A. D. 1248–1255.

Alphonse, count of Poictiers, and Hugh Lebrun, count of Angoulême, engage in the holy war—Opposition of Henry III. of England to his barons and the pope—Raymond, count of Thoulouse—Count d'Artois—Death of Negmeddin—Beauty and genius of Chegger-Eddour, sultana of Egypt—Scharmesah captured by the Crusaders—Fakreddin takes the command of the Egyptian forces—Treachery of the Mamelukes—Military operations on the canal of Aschmoum—Terrific effects of the Greek fire—Fakreddin slain and the Saracens defeated—Rashness of count d'Artois, and his death—Battle of Mansourah—The Crusaders defeated by the Mamelukes—The earl of Salisbury, Robert de Vair, and other illustrious warriors slain—Continued contests with the Egyptians, and severe losses of the Crusaders—Instances of devoted heroism and individual bravery—The Crusaders exposed to famine and pestilence, and the Saracens victorious—The canal of Mehallah fatal to the Crusaders—Sufferings and losses of the Christian army—Guy du Chatel, Gaucher de Chatillon, and other distinguished crusaders slain—Louis attempts to regain Damietta—Is defeated, and surrenders as a prisoner of war—His entire army annihilated by the Saracens—Sieur de Joinville taken prisoner—Agonizing situation of Marguerite, consort of Louis—30,000 Crusaders massacred, or taken into slavery—Religious resignation of Louis—He enters into an abject treaty for his ransom—Revolt of the Mamelukes—Death of Almoadan—Octaï, chief of the Mamelukes—The emirs of Egypt—Chegger-Eddour elected sultana of Egypt, and Ezz-Eddin Aybek the governor—Extinction of the Ayoubite dynasty—Damietta delivered up to the Mussulmans—Ransom paid for Louis—Consternation in France on hearing of his capture—He arrives at Ptolemaïs—Deliberates with his knights as to their future operations—The Syrians refuse to acknowledge the authority of the Mamelukes—Civil commotions in Egypt—Chegger-Eddour marries Ezz-Eddin, and yields her regal authority—Death of Frederick II. of Germany—Conrad, his successor, excommunicated—Jacob of Hungary—"Pastors"—Pope Innocent IV. urges the preaching of a fresh crusade—Singular message of the "Old Man of the Mountain" to Louis—A visit to his court—Cities of Palestine fortified by Louis—War between the sultans of Cairo and Damascus—Treaty between them, and hostilities resumed against the Christians—The Turcomans surprise Sidon, and slaughter the inhabitants—Belinas pillaged by the Crusaders—Pious devotedness of Louis—He fortifies Sidon—Death of Blanche, queen-regent of France—Louis quits Palestine, and arrives at Paris—Excellence of Joinville's history—On the character and misfortunes of Louis—Damietta destroyed by the Mussulmans, and the mouth of the Nile filled with stones—Rise and fall of the Mamelukes—Hospital of Quinze-Vingts—The Tartars and Moguls—"Assizes of Jerusalem"—Characters of Frederick II. of Germany and Pope Innocent IV.—Papal crusade against Eccelino de Romano..page 143

BOOK XV.

EIGHTH CRUSADE.

A. D. 1255–1270.

Christian cities of Palestine fortified by Louis IX.—Quarrels among the Crusaders—Divisions among the Saracens—Aibek, sultan of Egypt, assassinated—Chegger-Adour, the sultana, assassinated—The Moguls, or Tartars, capture Bagdad—Koutouz elected sultan of Egypt—The Moguls capture the principal cities of Syria—The general terror inspired among the Mussulmans and Christians—Apprehensions of Bela IV., king of Hungary—Assassination of Koutouz—The Mamelukes of Egypt—Bibars proclaimed sultan of Egypt—Declares war against the Christians of Palestine—The Mamelukes defeat and expel the Tartars from Palestine—Constantinople recaptured by the Greeks, and the Latins expelled—The Christians defeated by the Mamelukes, and Palestine laid waste—Cæsarea, Arsouf, and Sefed besieged and captured—Slaughter of the Christians—Mohammedanism not a religion of the sword—Charlemagne's career—Capture of Jaffa by the sultan of Egypt—Bohemond forms a treaty with Bibars—Antioch captured and destroyed, and the inhabitants slaughtered—Quarrels of the popes with the sovereigns of Europe—Royal family of Swabia—Charles, count of Anjou, crowned by the pope as king of Sicily—Mainfroy—Conraddin disputes the crown of Sicily—Louis IX. determines upon a fresh crusade to the Holy Land—The illustrious personages who take the cross in his support—Joinville declines to accompany him—Abaga, khan of the Tartars, sends ambassadors to Rome—Pope Clement IV. supports the new crusade—The clergy oppose the levying of contributions—A council held at Northampton for aiding the crusade—James king of Arragon, and Edward prince of England, engage in the crusade—Death of Clement IV.—The Crusaders arrive at Tunis—Historical notice of Tunis—The Mohammedans resist the Crusaders—Sickness and mortality among the Crusaders—Death of the duke de Nevers—Illness and fervent devotion of Louis—His death—Charles of Anjou lands at Tunis, and takes the command of the Crusaders—Returns to France with the bodies of his father, wife, and brother—The virtues and piety of Louis IX.—Prince Edward of England arrives in Palestine—Nazareth captured by the Crusaders—Prince Edward returns to England—Thibault elected pope, under the title of Gregory X.—He convokes the council of Lyons for reviving a new crusade—Curious document issued by Humbert de Romanis—Three pretenders to the throne of Jerusalem—The continued victories of Bibars—His death and character—Death of Gregory X.—Revolt in Sicily—The Sicilian vespers—Kealaoun, the sultan of Egypt, concludes a treaty with the Christians of Ptolemaïs, and enters into treaties with European princes—Fort of Margat captured by the Mussulmans—Sieur Barthélemi becomes a Mohammedan renegade—Tripoli captured and destroyed, and the Christians slaughtered—Description of Ptolemaïs—Chalil elected sultan of Egypt—The Mussulman sect of Chages—Ptolemaïs captured and destroyed by Chalil—Virgins of St. Clair self-mutilated and destroyed—Death of William de Clermont—Devoted heroism of the Templars—Capture and destruction of Tyre, Berytus, Sidon, and all the Christian cities along the coast of Palestine.................page 213

BOOK XVI.

ATTEMPTED CRUSADES—CRUSADES AGAINST THE TURKS.

A. D. 1291–1396.

Pope Nicholas IV. attempts to revive a fresh crusade against the East—Sends missionaries to the Tartars—Their contests with the Mussulmans revive the hopes of the Christians—Argun, the Tartar chief—Conquests of the Tartars—Cazan, the Mogul prince, sends ambassadors to the Pope—Clement IV. proclaims a crusade at the council of Vienna—Exploits of the Hospitallers—Conquests and wealth of the Templars—Accusations against them—Philip le Bel of France takes the cross—His death—Philip le Long—His death—Charles le Bel—His death—Raymond Lulli preaches a fresh crusade—Philip of Valois convokes an assembly at Paris for reviving a fresh crusade—Renewed persecutions of the Christians in Palestine—Brother Andrew of Antioch—Petrarch an apostle of the holy war—Humbert II., dauphin of Viennois, takes the cross—Hugh of Lusignan, king of Cyprus—Political troubles of France—King John taken prisoner at Poictiers—Engages in a fresh crusade—Urban V. convokes a meeting at Avignon—Peter de Lusignan, and Charles IV., emperor of Germany, engage in the crusade—Alexandria captured and burnt by the Crusaders—Barbary invaded by the Christian forces—Tripoli captured and burnt—Towns of Syria destroyed—Origin and history of the Turks and the Ottoman empire—Their conquests and invasion of Greece—Constantinople menaced by the Turks—Its tottering state—The emperors of Constantinople—Amurath, the Turkish sultan—Bajazet—Two popes at the same time—Crusade against the Turks determined on—Bajazet defeats the Christian forces with great slaughter—Defeats the Hungarians—Manuel, emperor of Constantinople, visits France—Distracted state of Europe—History and conquests of Tamerlane the Tartar—The Turks defeated, and Syria overrun by the Tartars—Bajazet raises the siege of Constantinople, and is defeated by Tamerlane—Smyrna captured and destroyed—The Ottomans reconquer the provinces overrun by Tamerlane—The Greek Church submits to papal authority—The barbarities of the Turks towards the Christians—Pope Eugenius exhorts the Christian states to another crusade—Cardinal Julian preaches in its favour—Amurath enters into a treaty of peace with the Crusaders, which being violated, they are defeated with great slaughter—Ladislaus, king of Poland, and Cardinal Julian, slain—Battle of Warna—Accession of Mahomet II. to the Ottoman throne—His extensive empire—Besieges Constantinople—Character of Constantine Palæologus, the Greek emperor—His great efforts in defence of his capital—Mahomet takes the city by storm—Death of the emperor and destruction of the Greek empire.......................................page 285

BOOK XVII.

CRUSADES AGAINST THE TURKS.

A. D. 1453–1481.

Consternation among the Christian states at the fall of Constantinople—Philip, duke of Burgundy, assembles his nobility at Lille—Curious festival held by—Enthusiasm in favour of a crusade against the Turks—Bishop Sylvius, John Capistran, Frederick III. of Germany, and Pope Calixtus III. endeavour to stir up the crusade—The Turks penetrate into Hungary—Valour of Hunniades—They are defeated at Belgrade—An alarming comet—Bishop Sylvius elected Pope—Extended conquests of Mahomet II.—He subdues Greece—The Pope convokes an assembly at Mantua to urge on the crusade—His negotiations with Mahomet—Bosnia conquered—Pius II. engages personally in the crusade, reaches Ancona, and dies—Scanderberg defeats the Turks—Mahomet II. swears to annihilate Christianity—The king of Persia marches against the Turks, and his army is destroyed—Cardinal Caraffa commands a fleet of Crusaders—Satalia and Smyrna pillaged by the Christian forces—Possessions of the Venetians and Genoese captured by the Turks—Jacques Cœur—Cyprus subjected to the Mussulmans—Taken possession of by the Turks—Rhodes bravely defended by the Knights of St. John—The Turks invade Hungary and different parts of Europe simultaneously—Defeated by Corvinus, king of Hungary—Otranto captured by the Turks, and afterwards abandoned—Pope Sextus IV. implores the aid of Christian Europe against the Turks—Distracted state of Italy—Death of Mahomet II., and divisions in his family—Zizim disputes the Turkish empire with Bajazet, and visits Europe—Charles VIII. of Naples engages in a crusade against the Turks—Alphonso II. of Arragon—Italy invaded, and Rome possessed by the

TABLE OF CONTENTS.

French—Andrew Palæologus sells his claims to the empire of the East—Death of Zizim—Bajazet declares war against Venice—Negotiates a treaty—Undertakes an expedition against Portugal—Commercial ambition of Venice—Diet at Augsburgh—Helian's speech against the Venetians—Council of Lateran convoked by Julius II.—Bajazet II. dethroned, and succeeded by Selim—Disorders of Christendom—Selim conquers the king of Persia and the sultan of Egypt—Palestine and all the rival powers of the East under the domination of the Turks—Exertions of Leo X. for reviving a crusade against them—Vida, the Italian poet—Novagero's eulogies on Leo X.—Cultivation of Greek in Italy—Great preparations for the new crusade—Eloquence of Sadoletus, and letters of Francis I. in its favour—Sale of indulgences—Quarrels of the Augustines and the Dominicans—Preaching of Luther against indulgences—Soliman succeeds to the Ottoman empire—Belgrade and Rhodes captured by the Turks—The knights of St. John expelled from Rhodes, and transferred to Malta—Francis I. made prisoner at the battle of Pavia—The Hungarians defeated by the Turks, and Louis II. slain—Clement VII. imprisoned by Charles V.—Religious distractions of Europe—Vienna besieged by the Turks—Hungary enters into a treaty of peace—Policy of Henry VIII., of Francis I., and of Charles V.—The Barbary states taken under the protection of the Ottoman Porte—Preaching of Luther—Heroic defence of Malta—Death of Soliman, and accession of Selim—Capture of Cyprus—The Turks signally defeated at the naval battle of Lepanto—Universal rejoicings throughout Christendom—General spread of civilization in Europe—Brilliant age of Leo X.—The military power of the Turks begins to decline—Defeated by Sobieski before the walls of Vienna—Causes and history of their decline—The Moors driven from Spain—State of Christendom in Europe, and progress of the Reformation—Ignatius Loyola—Pilgrimages to the Holy Land—A spirit of resignation assumes the place of enthusiasm for the crusades..page 332

BOOK XVIII.

UPON THE STATE OF EUROPE.

A. D. 1571—1685.

Reflections on the state of Europe, on the various classes of society, and on the progress of navigation, industry, arts, and general knowledge during and after the crusades...page 398

Started in Volume 1
Restored Special Edition

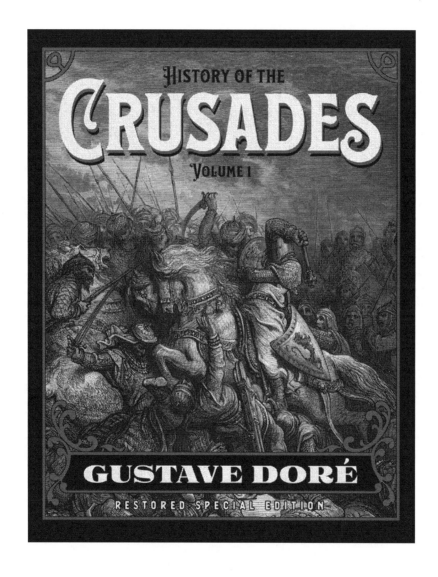

More Doré from CGR Publishing at www.CGRpublishing.com

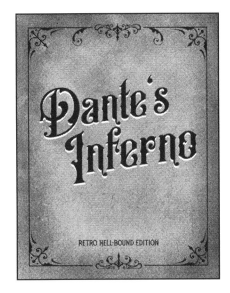
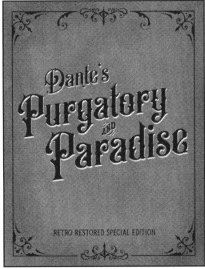
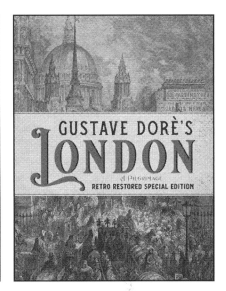

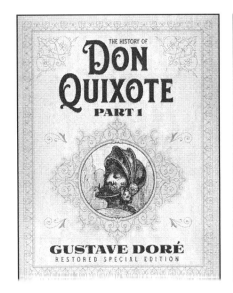
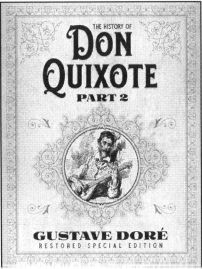
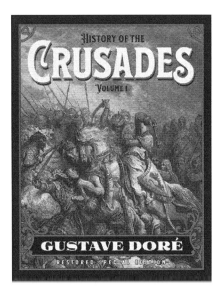

OTHER BOOKS FROM CGR PUBLISHING AT CGRPUBLISHING.COM

1939 New York World's Fair: The World of Tomorrow in Photographs

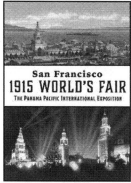
San Francisco 1915 World's Fair: The Panama-Pacific International Expo.

1904 St. Louis World's Fair: The Louisiana Purchase Exposition in Photographs

Chicago 1933 World's Fair: A Century of Progress in Photographs

19th Century New York: A Dramatic Collection of Images

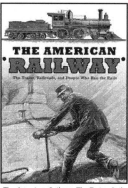
The American Railway: The Trains, Railroads, and People Who Ran the Rails

The Aeroplane Speaks: Illustrated Historical Guide to Airplanes

The World's Fair of 1893 Ultra Massive Photographic Adventure Vol. 1

The World's Fair of 1893 Ultra Massive Photographic Adventure Vol. 2

The World's Fair of 1893 Ultra Massive Photographic Adventure Vol. 3

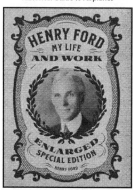
Henry Ford: My Life and Work - Enlarged Special Edition

Magnum Skywolf #1

Ethel the Cyborg Ninja Book 1

The Complete Ford Model T Guide: Enlarged Illustrated Special Edition

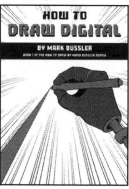
How To Draw Digital by Mark Bussler

Best of Gustave Doré Volume 1: Illustrations from History's Most Versatile...

OTHER BOOKS FROM CGR PUBLISHING AT CGRPUBLISHING.COM

Ultra Massive Video Game Console Guide Volume 1

Ultra Massive Video Game Console Guide Volume 2

Ultra Massive Video Game Console Guide Volume 3

Ultra Massive Sega Genesis Guide

Antique Cars and Motor Vehicles: Illustrated Guide to Operation...

Chicago's White City Cookbook

The Clock Book: A Detailed Illustrated Collection of Classic Clocks

The Complete Book of Birds: Illustrated Enlarged Special Edition

1901 Buffalo World's Fair: The Pan-American Exposition in Photographs

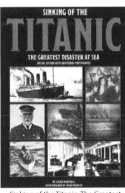
Sinking of the Titanic: The Greatest Disaster at Sea

Gustave Doré's London: A Pilgrimage: Retro Restored Special Edition

Milton's Paradise Lost: Gustave Doré Retro Restored Edition

The Art of World War 1

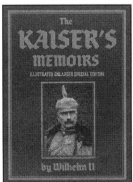
The Kaiser's Memoirs: Illustrated Enlarged Special Edition

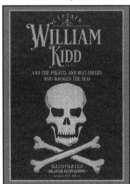
Captain William Kidd and the Pirates and Buccaneers Who Ravaged the Seas

The Complete Butterfly Book: Enlarged Illustrated Special Edition

- MAILING LIST -
JOIN FOR EXCLUSIVE OFFERS

www.CGRpublishing.com/subscribe

Made in the USA
Monee, IL
03 November 2024

1b1332d5-8ce8-43dc-aafa-549edf2ac519R01